ALEXANDER
SOLZHENITSYN

ALEXANDER
SOLZHENITSYN

A CENTURY IN HIS LIFE

D.M. THOMAS

ST. MARTIN'S PRESS
NEW YORK

The author is grateful for permission to reprint excerpts from copyrighted
material. These permissions appear on page viii, which constitutes a continuation of this copyright page.

*The lettering on the dust jacket spells out "Alexander Solzhenitsyn" in the
Cyrillic alphabet.*

MAP BY ANITA KARL AND JIM KEMP

DESIGN BY MAUREEN TROY

Library of Congress Cataloging-in-Publication Data

Thomas, D. M.
    Alexander Solzhenitsyn : a century in his life / D.M. Thomas —
1st ed.
        p.   cm.
    Includes bibliographical references and index.
    ISBN 0-312-18036-5
    1. Solzhenitsyn, Aleksandr Isaevich, 1918-   —Biography.
2. Authors, Russian—20th century—Biography.   I. Title.
PG3488.O4Z8887   1998
891.73'44—dc21
    [B]   97-35457
                                                            CIP

First Edition: February 1998

    10 9 8 7 6 5 4 3 2 1

In memory of Zofia Ilinska,
poet, friend, lover of Poland and Cornwall,
who encouraged me to write this book

2889

CONTENTS

PART I

OCTOBER'S TWIN   1918–1941

PART II

BARBAROSSA   1941–1953

PART III

NEW WORLDS   1953–1965

PART IV

HOSTILITIES   1965–1974

PART V

IRON CURTAINS   1974–

PROLOGUE

I ASKED A RETIRED KGB COLONEL, NOW GIVEN THE JOB OF IM-
proving Russia's *image* abroad, what image he would choose to represent
the beginning of the Bolshevik era. We were at a Helsinki hotel, overlooking
the frozen sea. Some mutual friends had said he knew something about
KGB attempts on Solzhenitsyn's life; he was disappointingly vague on that
subject, but enjoyed talking with me about Russian history and art over a
bottle of vodka.

"What image?" he mused, gazing out through the icy window at the Gulf
of Finland. A few weeks before, a car ferry, the *Estonia*, had sunk in heavy
seas, with a thousand deaths. It had seemed, we had agreed, an apt image
for the end of Communism: a tiny crack, widening swiftly through a weight
of water, capsizing the unbalanced boat. "I would choose," he replied at
last, "a moment described in Nathan Milstein's autobiography. As a *symbolic*
beginning, you understand. Milstein was a music student in Petersburg during the First World War. And he writes that, in 1916, in the winter, he was
walking along the Moika Canal. In front of the Yousoupov Palace he heard
agitated voices, and saw people craning to look over the parapet into the
frozen river. So Milstein looked down too, and saw some of the ice was
broken, and there, the water had pink swirls in it. People around him were
shouting, 'Rasputin! Bastard! Serve him right!' Milstein realized the pinkish
swirls were the blood of Rasputin—one of the most powerful men in the
empire. Imagine it: hurrying along a frozen canal—a day in December like
this one, perhaps late for a violin lesson—and you see Rasputin's blood! . . .
Well, I've seen lots of blood, even shed quite a lot of it. . . . But anyway, if
I were a writer, or maybe a filmmaker, that's how I'd start: looking down
at broken ice and seeing swirls of blood. Like a dream . . ."

Beginning this biography, I see the old KGB man and the swirl of Rasputin's blood. The single most important aspect of Solzhenitsyn's life is that
he was born a year after the Bolshevik Revolution. He is "October's twin."
Other great Russian writers who suffered intensely under Communism, but
who spent their childhood and youth in normal bourgeois circumstances
under tsarism, can refer to the beginning of their lives with a lucid defi-
niteness. Anna Akhmatova: "I was born in the same year [1889] as Charlie

Chaplin, Tolstoy's *Kreuzer Sonata*, the Eiffel Tower, and, it seems, T. S. Eliot."[1] Boris Pasternak: "I was born in 1890 in Moscow, on the 29th of January according to the Old Calendar, in Lyzhin's house opposite the Seminary in Oruzheiny Street. Surprisingly, something has remained in my memory of my walks in autumn with my wet-nurse in the Seminary park—sodden paths heaped with fallen leaves, ponds and artificial hills, the painted Seminary railings, the noisy games and fights of the seminarists during their recreation."[2]

The lighthearted juxtaposition of Chaplin and Eliot in the former, and the rich sensuous detail in the latter, have no counterpart in Solzhenitsyn's brief references to his childhood. No other writer has used his adult life as material to the degree Solzhenitsyn has done, yet from the very beginnings one finds a kind of Dickensian fog and murk. Perhaps one consequence of this was that, while he seemed to develop a very sure sense of identity, he continually explored different fictional self-portrayals—Nerzhin in *The First Circle*, Kostoglotov in *Cancer Ward*, Vorotyntsev in *August 1914*—as if the misty beginnings make him need to keep looking for himself.

His self-representations are of the fully grown man—soldier, writer, *zek*;* not, however, husband or lover, with rare exceptions; and for any "portrait of the artist as a young man" or as a child we look in vain. Instead of any clear statement of where and when he was born, there is a sense of confused, almost mythic, birth. It could not have been other, for a child born in the turbulence of 1918, and already fatherless.

It was, after all, the time of facelessness. In Akhmatova's horrifying image of the Revolution:

> As though, in night's terrible mirror
>   Man, raving, denied his image
>   And tried to disappear. . . .[3]

The human face disappeared, and also its divine image. In the classical world a slave was called *aprosopos*, "faceless"; literally, one who cannot be seen. The Bolsheviks gloried in facelessness.

It is inconceivable that Solzhenitsyn could have written, "I was born in the same year as Nicolae Ceauşescu, Kurt Waldheim, and Ella Fitzgerald, on 11 December 1918, in Kislovodsk. . . ."

Out of that violent beginning, he became the last in a great line of poets and novelists that began with Pushkin. They were more than writers; they were, since they all lived under authoritarian or tyrannical regimes, "another government," in Solzhenitsyn's phrase: cherished by their fellow Russians because they felt a special responsibility to be truthful.

Solzhenitsyn's long life is unique and extraordinary. He has embraced

---

*Term for an inmate of Stalin's labor camps.

almost the totality of his country's terrible century. Born amid chaos; caught up, as a schoolboy, in the heavily propagandized excitement of the first Bolshevik years; then a front-line Red Army soldier; the shock of arrest, for writing imprudent letters criticizing Stalin; the horror of a Lubyanka interrogation, followed by the camps and "perpetual exile"; release from it in the milder years of Khrushchev; sudden fame as the author of *One Day in the Life of Ivan Denisovich*, which devastatingly brought what had only been whispered about into the open; then, losing favor, becoming a dissident of incredible fearlessness and enterprise; publication of *The Gulag Archipelago*, his exposure of the whole Soviet tyranny from Lenin on; rearrest and enforced exile from his country—the first Russian to suffer this fate since Trotsky; quarrels with his hosts in the West; eventual return to a Russia where, for very different reasons, he found it necessary to be a kind of dissident still. . . .

Solzhenitsyn helped to bring down the greatest tyranny the world has seen, besides educating the West as to its full horror. No other writer of the twentieth century has had such an influence on history.

But his story is not of one century alone. When Alexander Tvardovsky, editor of the journal *Novy Mir*, sent for the unknown writer to discuss the manuscript of *Ivan Denisovich*, Solzhenitsyn paused beneath Pushkin's statue in Strastnaya Square, "partly to beg for his support, and partly to promise that I knew the path I must follow and would not stray from it. It was a sort of prayer."[4] This is much more than the respectful homage an English or American novelist might pay to a bust of Shakespeare: Solzhenitsyn saw Pushkin as his contemporary.

When I was thinking hard and long about whether to accept an invitation to write this biography, I had a dream in which I was in the small Cornish town of my childhood. Suddenly floodwaters rose, and I found myself swept along by them. At first it was quite exhilarating—even though I can't swim; I expected to round a corner and see my old school; I could cling on to a wall. But when the billows swept me round the corner, I saw, in place of the expected road and school, a flat sea of turbulent water. Fear gripped me.

Along with many other personal associations, the dream was obviously warning me I might drown if I entered this unfamiliar territory: I am a novelist and poet, not a biographer. I might drown under the horrifying weight of a densely packed life like Solzhenitsyn's; or under his wrath, since he hates unapproved biographers as much as he hated the Soviet censors. But I chose to see the dream in a more positive light. I could see the flood as pointing in the direction of one of the great seminal works of Russian literature, Pushkin's *The Bronze Horseman* (1833). In that great narrative poem, a flood sweeps over St. Petersburg and devastates the life of "my poor, poor Yevgeni," a humble clerk. Driven mad, Yevgeni shakes his fist at the famous equestrian statue of Peter the Great, crying "All right, you wonder-worker, just you wait!" Peter was the egoistical monster who had ordered the creation of a capital city on marshy Finnish ground. He thought nothing of the thousands of lives his dream would cost in the construction of it.

But the Russians still have an admiration for Peter—just as too many of them still admire Stalin and would like to see him back. Any reference in a literary work of the Bolshevik era to *The Bronze Horseman* can immediately be interpreted as a comment on Stalinism. Russian life and literature is a country, with limitless intercommunications—not a history. "Russian literature," wrote the scholar and translator Max Hayward, is "a single enterprise in which no one writer can be separated from another. Each one of them is best viewed through the many-sided prism constituted by all of them taken together. A later generation consciously takes up the motifs of its predecessors, responds to them, echoes them, and sometimes consummates them in the light of the intervening historical experience."[5]

This seems to me the only worthwhile kind of "writers' union"; and to write a life of Solzhenitsyn is inevitably to write about a century—or perhaps two. I have felt myself to be a visitor in the "country of Russian literature" since I first inadequately learned Russian during two years of military service in the 1950s. Being reminded by the dream of that great fellowship of Russian writers, for whom two centuries are but a single moment, helped to persuade me to yield to the flood, for good or ill. Another persuasion was that Solzhenitsyn's life has been a fantastic and inspiring story; but one so complicated by politics that it is difficult to see the wood for the plethora of trees. It challenged me to use my fictive experience to tell a story that is truly stranger than fiction.

ACKNOWLEDGMENTS

ANY BIOGRAPHER WHO FOLLOWS IN THE WAKE OF MICHAEL SCAM-
mell's monumental *Solzhenitsyn* (New York and London, 1984) must
be greatly indebted to it. It would have been impossible to attempt to rival
that work's scope, the fruit of ten year's research and writing. Modestly he
describes his biography as a chronicle, since its one thousand dense pages
teem with facts. My biography, I freely confess, carries less information—
but perhaps enough. Since that biography appeared, the Soviet Union has
become extinct. It is possible to see Solzhenitsyn's life and work "freed"
from the ongoing struggle against tyranny; and so from a different perspec-
tive. He is now, more distinctly, a writer rather than a fighter for rights;
though that superhuman struggle will always be an essential factor in any
assessment of him.

Two requests for an interview with him were not acknowledged; however,
he has better things to do with his time than to cooperate with a biographer;
nor do I feel that in a few hours—the most time I could have expected to
have been granted—I could have formed a substantially different impression of him or of his work.

I thank him for having stood up to tyranny: a rather more important
matter than whether he was polite to a biographer. This is not an authorized
biography; but I console myself that much of his greatness has consisted in
courageously opposing the very concept of "authorized" books. The writer
must answer to his own conscience alone.

I particularly wish to thank Victoria Field, who organized my research
brilliantly, and was ever ready to draw on her knowledge of, and love for,
Russia and Russians on my behalf; and Denise Brown, in the United States,
who brought enthusiasm, skill, initiative, and patience to the task of researching Solzhenitsyn's American years, and devoted countless hours to it.
Jo Durden-Smith and Elena Zagrevskaya helped me constantly, with important contacts, information, and suggestions: their friendship and encouragement were all-important. Sasha Kozhin provided valuable assistance and
hospitality during a two-day visit to Rostov-on-Don.

Professor Alexis Klimoff was generous with his assistance in the United
States. Natalya Reshetovskaya, though in poor health, was always prepared
to respond to questions, and generously allowed me to draw on her

collection of photographs. Philip Marsden and Charlotte Hobson made valuable contacts for me in Rostov, the Kuban, and the Caucasus. Michael Jacobs assisted me greatly by reading the biography in manuscript, with assiduous care, literary perception, and psychological insight. Susan Roberts combed the archives of the Library of Congress to find articles and news items. Louise Ross never failed to find me an out-of-print book when I approached her with a request. My editor at St. Martin's Press, Robert Weil, has brought an unflagging energy, enthusiasm, and dedication to this project.

I would like to acknowledge also the help of Joseph Brodsky, Olga Carlisle, Victor Chalmayev, Lena Khryshtov, Prof. Dr. W. W. Krysko, Professor Lev Loseff, Anna Makarova, Gerard Mansell, Emil Mazin, Denis Molchanov, David Morton, Natalya Perova, Roberta Reeder, Vladimir Retsepter, M. A. Schliafirner, Laura Shatkina, Y. Shklavresky, Susan Smallheer, Jonathan Steele, Veronica Stein, Sean Thomas, Rainer Voight, and Mike Wallace. Denise and Ross Thomas helped enormously through their unobtrusive support and long-suffering patience, and, in Ross's case, constantly rescuing me from computer disasters.

There were many people in Russia who talked to me on condition of confidentiality, including some who gave most generously of their time and hospitality. I thank them all.

All errors and wrong interpretations are, of course, my responsibility alone. It has been my decision also not to seek a pedantic consistency in the transliteration of Russian names. I have been cavalier with patronymics, so troublesome to Western readers, and with feminine endings, where I use them or not according to euphony and common usage: thus, Orlova, but not Solzhenitsyna. May the spirit of the great Russian language forgive me. And may the spirits of Stalin's lawyers and judges, those sticklers for the literal truth, forgive me for having occasionally let imagination make an event more vivid—though I hope never against the grain of the known reality.

D. M. THOMAS
Cornwall, England
August 1997

CHRONOLOGY

1918 Alexander (Sanya) Isayevich Solzhenitsyn born in Kislovodsk, southern Russia, 11 December, the son of Taissia (Shcherbak) Solzhenitsyn and Isaaki Solzhenitsyn, a soldier, who had died in June, in a hunting accident. Taissia and Sanya live with her sister Maria in Kislovodsk.

1919 Solzhenitsyn's grandparents Zakhar and Yevdokia Shcherbak, driven from their Armavir estate by the Bolsheviks' advance in the Civil War upheaval, move to Maria's villa in Kislovodsk.

1921 Taissia moves to Rostov, three hundred miles to the north, to find work, leaving Sanya behind in Kislovodsk with his aunt Maria and his grandmother Yevdokia.

1924 Sanya reunited with his mother in Rostov.

1926 Sanya begins school in Rostov.

1930–37 Solzhenitsyn in senior high school in Rostov. Meets Natalya (Natasha) Reshetovskaya.

1940 27 April: Solzhenitsyn marries Natasha. He plans his contribution to Russian literature, an epic novel of the Revolution.

1941 Solzhenitsyn graduates from Department of Physics and Mathematics, Rostov University. 22 June: Germany invades Soviet Union. After serving as a village schoolteacher, he enlists as a private in the Red Army.

1942 Attends the Third Leningrad Artillery School at Kostroma, 180 miles northeast of Moscow. Promoted to lieutenant.

1943 Promoted to first lieutenant and awarded Order of the Patriotic War after entering Orel on 5 August, following Red Army counterattack.

1944   January: His mother, Taissia, dies in Georgievsk. June: Solzhenitsyn promoted to captain.

1945   January: Red Army launches its final offensive in the West, advancing toward Berlin, an experience Solzhenitsyn will re-create in his narrative poem, *Prussian Nights*. February: Solzhenitsyn arrested for expressing anti-Stalinist views and removed from his battery command in a village east of Königsberg. Transferred to Lubyanka prison in Moscow; Solzhenitsyn's reception and interrogation there are described in his novel *The First Circle*. Moved to Butyrki prison. July: Sentenced to eight years' imprisonment. Transferred to New Jerusalem, where he works in the clay pit of a brick factory; then to Kaluga Gate prison.

1946   Solzhenitsyn transferred back to Butyrki; then to *sharashka* (prison scientific research institute) in Rybinsk, upper Volga; then to Zagorsk, outside Moscow.

1947   Solzhenitsyn transferred to Marfino *sharashka*, near Ostankino Park, Moscow. Solzhenitsyn and Natasha reunited at Marfino.

1950   Solzhenitsyn is sent to the Ekibastuz labor camp in Kazakhstan.

1951   Works as a bricklayer in Ekibastuz. Natasha, in Ryazan, files for divorce.

1953   Solzhenitsyn released, exiled to Kok Terek in southern Kazakhstan. Begins teaching Berlik High School.

1954   January–March: Solzhenitsyn is hospitalized in Tashkent for radiation treatment of cancer.

1956   April: His sentence is annulled. June: Returns from exile to Moscow. Takes teaching post at Torfoprodukt, 130 miles east of Moscow.

1957   February: Natasha and Solzhenitsyn's divorce is annulled. September: Solzhenitsyn begins teaching at Ryazan High School No. 2.

1959   Composes *Shch-854* (later to be retitled *One Day in the Life of Ivan Denisovich*).

1961   *Novy Mir* editor Alexander Tvardovsky reads *Shch-854*, by "A. Ryazanksy," aka Alexander Solzhenitsyn, and moves quickly to lobby for publication of his discovery.

1962   October: Khrushchev approves publication. 17 November: *Ivan Denisovich* published in *Novy Mir*.

1963   Two more stories, "Matryona's House" and "An Incident at Krech-etovka Station," are published in *Novy Mir*.

1964   Khrushchev is deposed.

1965   *The First Circle* manuscript, seized from friends of Solzhenitsyn's, is "arrested" by KGB. The plays *The Love-Girl and the Innocent* and *A Feast of Conquerors* are also confiscated, as are early drafts of *Ivan Denisovich*. Natasha hides notes for and drafts of *The Gulag Archipelago*.

1967   Solzhenitsyn returns to Moscow from Estonia to discuss publication of *Cancer Ward* with Tvardovsky.

1968   In the spring, Solzhenitsyn and his "assistants" convene in Rozh-destvo to complete and edit the manuscript of *The Gulag Archipel-ago*. August: Solzhenitsyn meets Natalya (Alya) Svetlova in Moscow. Fall: *Cancer Ward* and *The First Circle* are published in English.

1969   November: Solzhenitsyn is expelled from the Ryazan Writers' Union. His letter in reply is published in the *New York Times*.

1970   Solzhenitsyn is awarded the Nobel Prize for literature. December: Yermolai Solzhenitsyn born, first of three sons of Solzhenitsyn and Natalya Svetlova.

1971   June: YMCA Press, Paris, publishes Russian-language edition of *August 1914*. August: Solzhenitsyn travels by car to the South, returns ill or poisoned. October: Submits formal petition for divorce.

1972   September: Ignat Solzhenitsyn born.

1973   March: Natasha and Solzhenitsyn's divorce finalized. April: Solzhe-nitsyn and Alya married. *Gulag* seized by KGB. December: YMCA Press brings out the Russian-language *Gulag*. Stepan Solzhenitsyn born.

1974   February: Solzhenitsyn, arrested and expelled from the Soviet Union, exiled to West Germany. March: YMCA publishes *Letter to the Leaders*. Solzhenitsyn joined in exile by his family. June: *The Gulag Archipelago* is published in English and French. December: Solzhenitsyn collects Nobel Prize in Stockholm.

1975   Speaks to AFL-CIO in Washington, D.C.

1976   Solzhenitsyn and family move to property near Cavendish, Vermont.

1978   Solzhenitsyn delivers Harvard commencement lecture, "A World Split Apart."

1989   First long extract from *Gulag* published in *Novy Mir*.

1991   After failed coup and rise of democratic forces supporting Boris Yeltsin, Soviet Communist Party is dissolved. Legal obstacles to Solzhenitsyn's return to Russia are removed.

1994   Solzhenitsyn leaves United States and returns to Russia.

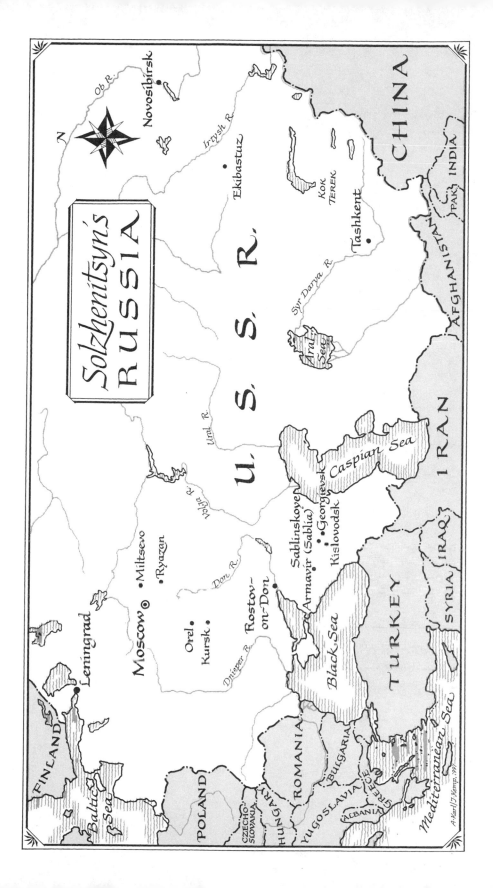

Solzhenitsyn's RUSSIA

N

Ob R.

Novosibirsk

Irtysh R.

Ekibastuz

KOK
TEREK

Tashkent

Syr Darya R.

CHINA

AFGHANISTAN

PAK.

INDIA

Aral
Sea

U. S. S. R.

Ural R.

Caspian Sea

IRAN

Volga R.

Sablinskoye

Georgievsk

Armavir (Sablia)

Kislovodsk

Miltsevo

Ryazan

Moscow

Don R.

Rostov-
on-Don

Orel

Kursk

Dnieper R.

Leningrad

Black Sea

TURKEY

IRAQ

SYRIA

Mediterranean Sea

FINLAND

Baltic
Sea

POLAND

CZECHO-
SLOVAKIA

HUNGARY

ROMANIA

YUGOSLAVIA

BULGARIA

GREECE

ALBANIA

A.Karl/J.Kemp, 1997

PART I

Ростовъ н/Д. — Общій видъ города.

October's Twin

1918 – 1941

VIEW OF ROSTOV ON DON, around 1900, from a postcard.

1

Ancestral Voices

I saw it fifty years ago
Before the thunderbolt had riven it,
Green leaves, ripe leaves, leaves thick as butter,
Fat, greasy life. . . .
— W. B. YEATS, *Purgatory*

HAPPY IS THE WRITER WHO REMEMBERS DRAWING IN THE DEVOTED love of a woman and, through her, the riches of his native traditions. For Pushkin, at the start of the nineteenth century, that woman was his nurse, Arina Rodionovna, whose simple peasant love consoled him for the coldness of his mother. The fairy tales and folk stories she told him in Russian broke through the genteel French of polite society. He paid tribute to her in a tender poem that imagines her sighing like a sentry on guard, at an upstairs window, her gnarled hands knitting more slowly now, as she gazes at the forgotten gate, the distant blackened road; he is late, and she fearfully imagines . . .

The lyrical fragment breaks off at that point. But their two imaginings have touched for a moment again in his adulthood and his adulteries.

Solzhenitsyn's Arina was *Irina*, an aunt. She had married into his maternal grandfather's family, the Shcherbaks, and she conjured up almost a biblical story of a patriarch coming dressed in rags out of a foreign land. . . .

Zakhar Shcherbak was his name.

Zakhar had been born to a peasant family in 1858 in the Taurla, in southern Ukraine. This was a year when Tsar Alexander II was receiving universal homage for setting in motion the emancipation of the serfs. The great, though inevitably flawed, liberation was enacted in 1861, by which time the chorus of praise had become shouts for the complete liberalization of society. Nothing of this would presumably have touched the lives of Zakhar's family. They lived, or they subsisted, in peace; it cost the United States a bloody civil war to achieve a similar emancipation.

After a year of schooling, Zakhar became a shepherd boy. When he was twelve, his father moved his family southeastward to the North Caucasus region in search of work as hired labor. Somehow Zakhar impressed their employer with his intelligence and resourcefulness, and the unusually thoughtful farmer gave the youth a dozen sheep, some piglets, and a cow, urging him to make an independent life for himself.

Slowly he began to prosper, and took a wife, a village blacksmith's daughter, Yevdokia Ilyinichna. In photographs she is stately, stout, square-faced, her hair pulled primly back. She was pious and obedient, and eventually bore Zakhar nine children. Doubtless by the time the first babies arrived, her husband was able to provide a somewhat more comfortable home than that of most peasants, who lived in extreme squalor. In a log-built *izba*, measuring about twenty-foot square of dirt floor, a whole family would be crowded, with a stove in one corner and icons in another. Few *izbas* had chimneys. In winter, the humans shared their smoke-filled hovel with pigs, lambs, and calves. Beetles and cockroaches swarmed. Human and animal excrement was piled in the yard, for sometimes a whole village did not have a single privy.

Zakhar Shcherbak dragged himself and Yevdokia out of that. Both pious believers, they must have thanked God and his Mother constantly for the way their lives throve. And if the blacksmith's daughter was thrashed sometimes by her lively, virile, irascible husband—that too, she felt, was what providence had ordained. She admired his cleverness: he could read the Lives of the Saints, and write after a fashion. As for his eye for business, no one could match him. He invested shrewdly, built up capital. Sometime in the 1880s he moved his family 150 miles northwest to the Armavir region in the Kuban and bought the land, between river and new railroad, built in 1875, where he founded his estate. Around him were many fellow Ukrainians, and also German settlers from whom he learned good economy. The soil was rich: "In the steppe there was a splendid black soil, so heavy and firm that the herd left no traces where they passed over it. On it grew a strong-scented grass standing as high as a horse's belly," as Mikhail Sholokhov* observes in *And Quiet Flows the Don*.

The former shepherd boy was now the owner of a grand two-story house, with a wrought-iron balcony running all round it at second-floor level. The ample rooms had imitation-walnut paneling, and were furnished in the best, dark-polished Victorian way. There was electricity from a generator, piped water from four sources. The surrounding park had avenues of balsam and pyramid poplars, a pond for swimming, orchard, Moorish garden, herb and rose gardens, vineyard. Lawn mowers cut the lawn of fresh green English ryegrass alongside the driveway.

The vast steppe land of more than five thousand acres held twenty thousand sheep. The cultivated land was split up into rectangular sectors by windbreaks of acacia plantations; the six-field crop rotation system was in use: wheat and maize alternating with horsebeans, sunflowers, lucerne,

---

*Though his authorship is disputed.

and esparto grass, yielding heavier, lusher crops year by year. The whole great "economy" bristled with scores of servants, cooks, butlers, chauffeur, coachman, bailiff, accountant, clerks, grooms, gardeners, mechanics . . . all working with Germanic industriousness and efficiency. A marriage of work and beauty.

The swift and vast increase in Zakhar's wealth, from herdsboy to millionaire in a generation, seems a miracle. He must have been as remarkable a man as his famous grandson was to be. For Yevdokia, the transformation from poverty to unbelievable wealth must have been bewildering. But her feet were firmly on the fertile black earth; her religious faith was not weakened when, in the space of a week, scarlet fever scythed through six of their children.

I imagine Zakhar, that terrible week, continuing to order his estate, poring over accounts, discussing with his chief clerk whether he could afford a Mercedes, or should he stick to the phaeton? Holding firm against the cry of women. Deaths of children were commonplace; and not only in Russia, of course. Did the burials echo one that Pushkin observed at his family's run-down estate? . . .

> Oh, here comes a peasant, with two women behind him:
> Bareheaded, a child's coffin under his arm;
> From afar he shouts out to the priest's lazy son
> To call his father and open up the church.
> "Hurry up! We haven't got all day!"[1]

Very likely; for Zakhar never stopped being a peasant at heart. What the great Lev Tolstoy at his Yasnaya Polyana estate dreamed of turning into—yet never could, however slovenly his smock, however hard he scythed at harvest—Zakhar Shcherbak would never cease to be. For all the feather-beds available, Zakhar always preferred to sleep on the warm stove, in the traditional peasant way. His grandson, Alexander Solzhenitsyn, would also, metaphorically, sleep on the stove, preferring a spartan way of life. (Though it was quite nice to be spartan within a substantial property that you owned. . . . Here too Solzhenitsyn would show he was Zakhar Shcherbak's grandson.)

In the pre–First World War epoch, when the distant Tsar Nicholas II was vacillating between holding the line against change and yielding to constitutional reform, the three surviving offspring of Zakhar and Yevdokia were living a cosseted existence on the Kuban estate. By far the oldest of the three was Roman Shcherbak. Something of a liberal in politics, an admirer of the proletarian writer Maxim Gorky's socialism, Roman nevertheless enjoyed playing the English-style young country gent, wearing tweeds, knee breeches, and patent-leather boots. Mustached and sometimes donning a raffish naval-style peaked cap, he lorded it, with a cool English haughtiness, in a white Rolls-Royce—one of only nine in Russia.

Much of his wealth he owed to his wife, Solzhenitsyn's aunt Irina. Irina's father had a ruthless streak that probably appealed to Zakhar Shcherbak. When already old and ailing, this extremely rich ex-soldier bribed his bishop with forty thousand rubles to let him divorce his elderly childless wife and marry a girl with whom he had fallen in love. Irina became their only child. She had only just left school when her father, knowing he was dying, betrothed her to thirty-year-old Roman Shcherbak.

In Solzhenitsyn's novel *August 1914*, Roman and Irina appear under their real names. Solzhenitsyn has made it clear, in interviews, that the "family saga" episodes, interwoven with the far more extensive war scenes, are not merely "based on" his own family but depict them as they were; or rather, as he imagined them to have been, before his lifetime. Solzhenitsyn never strays far from real life. So we can be sure that Roman did, in fact, take Irina home from parties, before the drunken landowners tossed their women into the air, indiscriminately, so that several male hands could grab their naked thighs under their flying-up skirts.[2] Where such a custom was observed openly, one can be sure manners could be even coarser on the quiet.

Irina brought great wealth to the already well-off Shcherbaks. Roman wasn't educated, but he enjoyed taking her to Petersburg and Moscow for two months every year, and to Europe for another two months. In the Louvre, in the purple room of the Venus de Milo, where no one was supposed to sit down, he would bribe the attendant with a ten-franc note to fetch *"la chaise,"* so he could rest and have a smoke while Irina admired bits of broken crockery. Then, moving to the next room: "Now put the chair there, please, my good man: right there!" He became an early jet-setter. In the Moscow–St. Petersburg rally, he burned up the miles in the Daimler sports car he had bought in Stuttgart.

It doesn't seem to have been a happy marriage, judging by Irina's comment, in old age, that the Shcherbak men did nothing but drink, play cards, and fornicate. She remained childless, and Roman—apparently—coldhearted. Her frustrated emotions were poured into religion—Orthodoxy, tinged with an exotic belief in reincarnation. She loved literature, was very traditional and conservative, though with a theatrical streak, since, loving the hunt, she carried a Browning revolver in her purse and hung a shotgun on her bedroom wall. Perhaps she would have liked to shoot her husband. The revolver in her purse reminds one of Hedda Gabler; there was a similar secret rage in her, beneath her piety.

Roman had two much younger sisters, Maria and Taissia. Taissia, the youngest child, was eleven when she found herself with a seventeen-year-old sister-in-law, who became attached to her. Taissia, the darling of her father, was headstrong, lively and intelligent. Much later, photographs show her as grim-faced—life was hard on her; yet in *August 1914*, where Taissia is called Ksenia, her son tells us she "shook with laughter" when recalling the women being thrown up into the air at parties. She was clearly no puritan.

Solzhenitsyn evokes the great house and thriving, humming estate as a lost paradise, dominated by two girls, his mother and his aunt. Successive chapters open with delicious and, for Solzhenitsyn, rare scenes of feminine "leisure" and languor. First Irina awakes. She is not quite happy since she remembers she has quarreled with Roman, and he is not with her. There is a distinct echo of the opening of *Anna Karenina*, where Oblonsky has the same recollection of a quarrel with his spouse over his infidelity. Just as Oblonsky can't help smiling despite his marital troubles, so the marvelous morning and her overbrimming nature counteract Irina's sadness: "She threw open the shutters giving on to the park. It was a wonderful morning, with just a touch of coolness in the air from the shade of the Himalayan silver firs, whose branches spread to the window ledges of the first-floor rooms."[3]

Next, Ksenia (Taissia) awakes in another room, to luxuriate in the comfort of her bed, her "sweet little blue room, still dark although the sunlight was already beating against the shutters. And all the time in the world to laze about—a day, a week, even a month!" She gives a "delicious yawn, a stretch, then another stretch," her fists clenched above her head.[4]

She hears her brother, Roman, knock and ask her if she is awake, he needs to fetch something from the safe. Shouting out "All right!" Ksenia "jumped out of bed without using her hands, with one bound of her strong legs." The opening of the novel, so redolent of old Russia, of the great estates, is infused with an innocent eroticism, in a mélange of girlish self-indulgence and the ordered, beautiful life of a grand house. The close association of the two sisters-in-law is significant; they were the erotic archetypes in Solzhenitsyn's imagination. Ksenia's laughter, when relating the bawdy party "game," evokes a free spirit that tragically had to be suppressed later in life: just as her son suppressed the same element in himself.

Irina "gave" him the great house in early, Leninist childhood, telling him—in a suitably selective form—stories that the little boy, later to be a great author, stored behind his wide-open blue eyes. She did not tell him that she thought the Shcherbaks were boors, living like pigs; that old Zakhar whipped his wife and threatened to knife Roman. These impressions she left for her embittered old age, with the KGB as prompters. She told little Sanya (Alexander) about the spacious rooms, whose furnishings she helped to plan, and the tree-lined avenues; the orchard, the rose garden, the herb garden.

He would see it for himself one day, she told him; even get to own it. . . . He did get to see it, but only by pressing his face between wrought-iron railings. It was *The Cherry Orchard* after Lopakhin had had the trees cut down; commissars strutted about.

But the dream of it never left him; he was to do his best to re-create it, more than once.

That was one side of his family. And at the end of the brief—too brief—scenes involving Irina and Ksenia in *August 1914,* there is a glimpse of the other side. For he describes how a young man by the name of Isaaki (Sanya) Lazhenitsyn was traveling in a train alongside a rich estate. He is about to enlist and go to war. Through the trees he sees "clearly on a wrought-iron corner balcony the figure of a woman wearing a white dress—the gay white dress of a woman of leisure."[5]

The poplars hide her from view.

The name of the author's father was Isaaki (Sanya) Solzhenitsyn.

The name Solzhenitsyn, unusual in Russia, may derive from *solod,* malt. There may indeed have been a headstrong, intemperate element in the blood, for there were family legends of early rebelliousness. A Fillip Solzhenitsyn from Voronezh province was said to have displeased Peter the Great for having illegally changed his place of abode. Peter burned down the entire village in his wrath. A century later, Alexander Solzhenitsyn's great-great-grandfather joined in an act of rebellion, and the rebels suffered banishment to the virgin lands of the Caucasus. Such punishments were a traditional way of opening up new territory; like the pioneers moving west across America, the migrants could take what land they wanted. According to Solzhenitsyn, the banished rebels were not fettered in irons, nor sent to a remote garrison or gulag, but let loose in the wild steppe country beyond the Kuma River. Here they lived in harmony, with land in such abundance that they didn't have to divide it up in strips. They sowed where they plowed, sheared sheep with no one to hinder them, and put down roots.

Poised between the Cossack tribes of the Kuban and Terek rivers, the settlers were known contemptuously to the Cossacks as *inogorodniye,* outsiders. They wore the title with pride: Russians within Russia, yet alien. The rebellious writer, in his time, would not be too bothered about conforming or "belonging."

The Solzhenitsyn farm was six miles east of Sablia (now commonly marked on maps as Sablinskoye), a posting stage on the road between Stavropol, the provincial capital, and Georgievsk, in the foothills of the Caucasus. Only the mountains glimpsed in the distance distinguished the village, which by the 1880s had a church and a parish school. A shallow many-forked stream flowed through the village in winter. A single street of adobe houses yielded at the back to kitchen gardens and sheds. The Solzhenitsyn farm, out in the country, consisted of a low clay farmhouse and some outbuildings in the midst of open steppe. Alexander's great-grandfather Yefim gazes into the lens of an early camera, tall and erect in a field of corn, a bearded and mustached Victorian yeoman farmer. Family legend has it that two brothers came, in soldiers' uniforms; one brother wasted his money, the other—Yefim—was careful, and throve.

Yefim begat Semyon, Alexander's grandfather. His wife Pelageya gave him the ideal progeny of two sturdy sons first, Konstantin and Vasili, then two daughters, Yevdokia and Anastasia. During her fifth pregnancy, she probably felt it was time for another son; and God was good: on 6 June 1891 (Old Style)—more than twenty years after the first—a third son was born, and named Isaaki.

The aged Irina would please the KGB by claiming the Solzhenitsyns were rich, like the Shcherbaks ("Money found money"), but Solzhenitsyn denies this. Semyon Solzhenitsyn owned, his grandson has claimed, a dozen or so cows, a few pairs of oxen and horses for plowing, a couple of hundred sheep. There were, it appears, no hired hands, suggesting the farm was not extensive in size. Semyon ran it with the help of his older sons. It is helpful again to think of the American pioneers. The Solzhenitsyns were isolated and no doubt quite self-sufficient; the villagers would see them when they drove the wagon in to load up provisions or for churchgoing.

The truth may lie much closer to Irina's version. According to Vasili's daughter, Ksenia Kulikova, who still lives in Sablia, Semyon also owned the main, substantial house in the village, which is now its hospital. His eldest sons owned the houses on either side. Before the Revolution, Semyon was very rich, owning two thousand sheep, and did have workers. The family was so important that some people called the village Solzhenitsyn. Everyone loved Semyon; he was helpful and clever, always a source of good advice.[6]

When Isaaki was still only a child, his mother, Pelageya, died. Semyon, well into middle life, might have considered settling into comfortable widowerhood; one of the girls could stay unmarried, cook and clean without protest; but presumably his eye could still rove. He remarried. His second wife, Marfa, gave him another son and daughter, Ilya and Maria.

And brought division into the home. According to Solzhenitsyn in *August 1914*, this second wife was a "bold, domineering, greedy woman who kept the whole household on a short rein, making sure that no one stood in the way of her own children."[7] The older sons could not get on with her, no doubt resented their father for remarrying; having enough money to buy farms of their own, they left. The two older girls married and moved away to nearby villages. Anastasia, in the village of Nagutskoye, would have a neighbor who gave birth in 1914 to Yuri Andropov: KGB chief and persecutor of Anastasia's nephew, Alexander Solzhenitsyn.

In both the Shcherbak and the Solzhenitsyn families, it was the younger children who were given the advantages of education. For a short time, indeed, Taissia Shcherbak and Isaaki Solzhenitsyn were being educated at lycées in the same Caucasian spa town of Pyatigorsk; though the two didn't meet and, even had they, Isaaki would not have noticed the immature timid schoolgirl. When Taissia reached thirteen, in 1908, Irina and Roman persuaded old Zakhar to send his daughter to Rostov. Alexandra Andreyeva, principal of the private Andreyeva Gymnasium, found herself stormed in her office by a knobbly-nosed, beetle-browed, bewhiskered old man in a rustic woolen suit who shouted his request that her school admit his daughter. Madame Andreyeva, recently widowed, was genteel in manner, gray haired and pince-nezed. Despite appearances, she was actually a thoroughgoing modern liberal and feminist; she readily admitted Jews, and paid scant respect to God or the Tsar. Stern but kindly, she rather took to the uncouth, loudly laughing farmer for whom money was clearly no object. Since her own eldest daughter was going to Moscow to be educated, she even let herself be persuaded to rent out her room to the new pupil.

Taissia Shcherbak was very happy in Madame Andreyeva's school and family, and flourished academically. She learned to speak fluently three languages; browsed at will among shelves well stocked with enlightened books; learned to dance better than any schoolgirl in Rostov—with a passion for the free-flowing style of Isadora Duncan. Taissia began to feel that her home, to which she returned on vacations, was very backward, with its boring icons and morning and evening prayers. She loved school so much she even turned down an offer from Roman and Irina to take her on a grand tour abroad. She graduated with the gold medal, as the school's star pupil.

But how—her "fictional" self wonders in *August 1914*—can she persuade people she is well educated and intelligent when she looks so countrified with her round, swarthy, healthy face! She must cultivate pallor; is too much the steppe-girl, the Ukrainian. All she wants to do is dance, dance, dance, like Isadora!

Her father had other ideas; he needed an agronomist, and in 1912 Taissia entered the Princess Golitsyn School of Agriculture, in Moscow. The yearning of so many provincial Chekhovian girls had become realized for her; even though she had had to compromise over her future career, at the point when the Great War started, life was good.

Isaaki Solzhenitsyn had a harder task to persuade his father to give him a good education; perhaps Semyon thought it would be unfair if any of his younger children were given opportunities that the older ones had not had. Sanya—as he was familiarly known—could work on the farm as his brothers had done. But the boy was stubborn and determined; after a year of argument he got his way, and entered the Gymnasium at Pyatigorsk, an excellent school. Four years later, he had to spend another wearisome year persuading his father to let him go on to university. At first he went to the University of Kharkov, to study literature and history. There may have been difficulty in gaining entry because of his name; Solzhenitsyn reports in the original *August 1914*, though he later doubted the story's truth and removed the reference, that the authorities thought Isaaki a Jewish name rather than an old-fashioned Orthodox one, and since their Jewish quota was filled they turned him away.

Certainly the Jewish-sounding name encouraged the KGB, in the Brezhnev era, to claim that the troublesome author's surname was Solzhenitser.

Isaaki did not feel comfortable in Kharkov, and the teaching was mediocre. After one year, in 1912, he transferred to Moscow University. He began to feel an emotional tie with the heart of Russia, which he was now seeing for the first time, that heartland from which his family had originally sprung. Also he was determined that his education would not separate him from the people. It was for them, for the *narod*, that he wished to be educated. In the 1870s, idealistic people, some twenty-five hundred of them, chose to go out into the villages to educate and care for the peasants; they believed they would stir up a desire for rebellion in them; but they returned to the cities sadly disillusioned. Isaaki, rather late in the day, took those young people as his inspiration. He would use his education to go back to the people with the book, the word, and with love.

In keeping with this idealism, he idolized Tolstoy, and tried to put the master's beliefs into effect. So, even though he craved meat, he tried to be vegetarian; even though he liked writing verses he tried not to, recalling that poetry led away from the simplicity of truth; and even though he loved sensual waltzes, he stopped himself indulging in such dancing, because Tolstoy said they evoked emotions that were false and dangerous.

In this respect he differed from Roman Shcherbak, who admired Tolstoy so much that he filled the Shcherbak house with portraits of him, but lived an idle, pampered life totally at odds with Tolstoyan asceticism and his own belief that society must change. But Roman was neither the first nor the last to combine a pampered life with egalitarian ideals.

Isaaki Solzhenitsyn loved coming home from Moscow on his university vacations to work on the farm; even though the villagers teased him for his city ways and clothes. Traveling home that summer of 1914 just before the war, seeing the insubstantial Caucasus range shimmer on the flat horizon, he may have remembered how Tolstoy had taken this road south, at the same age, twenty-three, on his way to the Terek Cossacks. He may not have known how muddled Tolstoy's mind had been, and would always be: full of tortured idealism, wishing his mind were not filled with thoughts of lust, gambling, and vanity.

Moscow gave way in Isaaki's mind to the country tracks, turning from forgotten memory into reality before his eyes. "Every recollection of the place where one grew up brings a twinge of nostalgia. Others may be indifferent to it or think it a very ordinary place, but to each one of us it is the best on earth—the unique sadness evoked by the memory of a country cart-track as it twists and turns to avoid the boundary posts; the rickety, lopsided coach-shed; the sundial in the middle of the yard; the bumpy, neglected, unfenced tennis-court; the roofless summer-house made of birch shingles."[8]

It was August 1914. At the onset of "the real twentieth century," in Akhmatova's phrase, as distinct from its meaningless calendar beginning, when the world still lived in an illusion.

As a believer in Tolstoyanism, Sanya should not have enlisted in the military; but something called him to do so. Maybe he felt sorry for Russia, as *August 1914* would suggest. Maybe it seemed cowardly and uninteresting to accept his right as a student not to serve. So he boarded the familiar train, determined to enlist, and took what might be his last look at beloved Kuban meadows, vast fields ripe for harvest. And saw the upper story of a brick house, and the figure of a girl in a white dress on a wrought-iron corner balcony. . . .

The peasant-student took an officer training course at the Sergiev School of Heavy Artillery, in Moscow, then was sent to the front to serve with an artillery Guards brigade. He fought bravely throughout the war, once being mentioned in dispatches for having rescued several boxes of ammunition from a fire started by enemy shells. He won the George and Anna crosses.

In February 1917 the Tsar was forced to abdicate. Isaaki was elected to the Brigade Soviet of Soldiers' Deputies—indicating that his men knew he sympathized with their cause. The following month the Soviet enacted a decree designed to liberalize the harsh discipline of the tsarist army and reduce the privileges of the career officer caste. In the same month Isaaki went to Moscow for a short leave; at some kind of student celebration or reunion, he met a student of agronomy from his own home region called Taissia Shcherbak, and for both of them it was love at first sight.

2

Demons

The dictatorship means—learn this once and for all —
unrestrained power based on force, not on law.
—V. I. LENIN[1]

FOR ALEXANDER SOLZHENITSYN, THE CHILD OF THAT WARTIME RO-
mance, the house and estate of his maternal grandfather had a symbolic
value similar to that of the ruined manor house in W. B Yeats's one-act
drama *Purgatory* (1938). Once a year, a window of the ruin is lit up, revealing the degradation of a cultured girl by her husband, a drunken groom.
Yeats was thinking, among many other things, of the richly cultured life of
the Anglo-Irish aristocratic house, before the First World War, the Irish
Civil War, and a leveling tide swept that life away. Alexander Solzhenitsyn,
too, came to believe—though not until he had suffered under Stalinism—
that the "Russia House" had been brutally, pointlessly destroyed.

But for the first twenty-five years of his life he was an ardent supporter
of Lenin's Revolution. Two facing pages of a 1994 anthology of Russian
photography present the case for revolutionary upheaval in Nicholas II's
Russia: a case strengthened further by the miseries of war.[2] Both of the
facing photographs are from St. Petersburg—but they might be from different universes. One shows a glittering social occasion, the Ball of the
Colored Wigs, held at a countess's palace. Seated around circular tables
adorned with gazebos of flowers and even songbirds in cages are such fab-
ulously rich families as the Tolstoys, Gorchakovs, Orlovs, and Dolgorukovs.
Twenty or so smart waiters stand at the back of the chandeliered and col-
umned dining room, ready to move swiftly between the tables. The ladies
are wigged and powdered as if at Versailles, the men in military uniform.
They gaze with trim-mustached smiles toward the camera lens. We know,
looking in, that nemesis awaits, that within months (the photo is from early
1914) many of these officers will have been mown down by German machine guns in the forests of Tannenberg; but the living figures did not know
this, and their complacent world did not include, did not even acknowledge

the existence of, the soup kitchen on Vasilevsky Island of the facing photograph, which comes from the same period.

Ranks of former peasants, from those who have streamed into the capital seeking work in the factories, crowd at long plank tables smeared with slops. The dark, windowless, claustrophobic brick building, perhaps a derelict factory, provides a fitting backdrop to gray despair. Apart from a couple of faces that stare angrily at this intrusion upon their hunger, these are men who have no awareness of each other or of anyone: they don't even stare into the distance, but at some nothingness a few inches from their lowered eyes. The sadness of the picture, the sense of tragic waste, is emphasized by the air of thoughtfulness, of intelligence, in some of the deep-sunken eyes, in contrast to the fleshly vapidity of many of the faces at the countess's ball.

Pictures don't tell the whole story. Similar contrasts could easily be found in any city in the world today. Here was not—as there often was in Russia, and would be much more terribly in the USSR—absolute starvation; the photo was probably taken to draw attention to Christian charity rather than to the poverty. Russia was already the fourth greatest industrial nation, and conditions for the workers were not noticeably worse than in the West. With ninety days of religious holiday a year, they actually spent less time in the dark factories than their Western counterparts. Some of the power of this particular contrast comes from subjective factors, notably our knowledge of the coming catastrophe. But enough intrinsic potency remains to make it explicable why certain men—Lenin, Trotsky, Kamenev, Zinoviev, and so on—men who had never done a day's paid work in their lives, and who had no connection with the working class—thought the only answer was for the proletariat to take power. The slaves of the Petersburg soup kitchen could only have decent lives if the bewigged ladies and their sleek, pampered escorts were wiped out. Law could never achieve that, only dictatorship, harsh duress, and terror.

The fact of intolerable social injustice, and the fact that the privileged inside and outside Russia would stop at nothing to defend their position, made the most extreme action, "unrestrained, lawless power," seem rational to a dedicated minority. If some revolutionary seer had predicted in a memo to Lenin that sixty million people,[3] most of them poor, would perish in bringing about and sustaining Bolshevism, he would probably have shrugged and scrawled "To be filed" on the memo. And the lawless dictatorship seemed rational—more, worth living and dying for—to many thousands of highly intelligent, idealistic, and *decent* people until long after Stalin's death. To Lev Kopelev, for instance, who became one of Solzhenitsyn's closest friends in imprisonment; a black-bearded giant, brilliant linguist, and convinced Stalinist. Born to a wealthy Jewish family in the Ukraine, he suffered the memory of his mother sending a valet to his school each day, bearing his dinner on a silver platter. Therefore, when he became a Komsomol member of the grain-collecting brigades in the thirties, he could think the famine killing the Ukrainian peasantry was justifiable, a necessary evil.

Kopelev and his wife, the late Raisa Orlova, are two of the most idealistic ex-Communists whose troubled memoirs try to make sense of the "rational" evil they condoned and even took part in. Orlova, an editor of the journal *Foreign Literature*, was at one time a trusted Communist functionary; she listened to Khrushchev's revelations about Stalin in the hall where Natasha Rostov, the fictional heroine of *War and Peace*, had once danced. Orlova looks back in her *Memoirs* at when she joined in expelling some innocent comrade, or denounced someone, as at a night full of bad dreams. She senses that there is ultimately no reasonable explanation for what she did, and what Communism did. . . .

> All the time I keep seeking rational explanations, I keep seeking a comparatively simple, in any event basic, connection among the facts. Yet there is always something more important out of the realm of the irrational that does not submit to any "computation." There are some kinds of profound abysses in a person that Dostoyevsky knew about and that contemporary writers and artists know about.
>
> In our falsely rational world we have denied this and continue to do so. I know that this world abyss does exist. I know it in my mind. And I don't know how to live with the knowledge that it does exist.[4]

One of the signs of the "profound abyss" that opened up in Russia was the rational justification for illegality and savagery. This had first occurred among Russia's intelligentsia almost half a century before the October Revolution of 1917. Some of the idealistic young men and women who had donned peasant clothes and gone into the villages to help stir up the peasants, but who had found themselves jeered at and stoned, seethed with anger at Tsar and peasants alike; they formed a secret society called the People's Will, a terrorist organization. A symbolically crucial event was the trial of Vera Zasulich in 1878. Zasulich, a plain, rather confused woman, already a seasoned revolutionary at twenty-six, fired point-blank into the face of General Trepov, the brutal police chief of St. Petersburg, wounding but not killing him. There was absolutely no doubt of her guilt, but at her trial the jury calmly found her not guilty. And the educated classes burst into frenzied applause.

The police tried to rearrest her, but she was spirited away to Geneva, where she became a leading revolutionary figure. In Russia, the sincere Kopelevs and Orlovas of their age began to understand and excuse the terrorism being practiced by others. That attitude was to become a hallmark of the intelligentsia in many countries for the next century and more.

With a "logic" that came partly from the evidence of their eyes, but also from their own unreasoning "abysses," the terrorists and revolutionaries seemed to choose moments of hope in which to wreak destruction. It was so in 1881, when Alexander II, the "Tsar-Liberator" of the serfs, was returning to the Winter Palace in Petersburg after signing a limited form of constitutional government. A member of the People's Will hurled a grenade at the racing carriage. About twenty bystanders were killed or maimed, but the Tsar escaped. He made the mistake, however, of ordering his carriage to stop so that he could comfort the dying. A nationalist Pole lobbed a grenade between his legs, blasting them off. "I'm cold, so cold," he whispered to his guards. "Take me to the Palace . . . to die." His son, Alexander III, immediately canceled the inadequate but promising constitution.

After the Revolution of 1905, Alexander III's successor, Nicholas II, was compelled to introduce a parliamentary assembly, or Duma. He chose as his First Minister Pyotr Stolypin, a man who was ardently patriotic, severe but just, honest, and with brilliant organizational ability. Having controlled terrorism by stern measures (exceedingly light by later standards), he set about agrarian reform. The new laws freed peasants from all legal restraints, and encouraged the brighter, more go-ahead peasants to buy land for themselves, then cooperate with their neighbors to form their own communes. Productivity greatly increased; indeed, the Soviet system of agriculture only caught up with pre-1914 productivity in the 1960s, with the aid of modern machinery and with a vastly increased population to feed.

In *August 1914* Solzhenitsyn would depict Stolypin, not quite realistically, as very nearly a saint; but he is far from alone in valuing him highly. The British ambassador of the time, Sir Arthur Nicolson, thought him the most outstanding man in Europe. He would have succeeded in saving Russia, Solzhenitsyn is convinced—had not a Socialist Revolutionary and police informer called Bogrov stalked him into a Kiev theater and shot him at point-blank range. Stolypin—a tall, stiff man, with chalk white face and dead black beard—turned to face the Emperor in his box, made the sign of the cross, and fell mortally wounded.

Still, if the Emperor had not plunged his nation into war, revolution almost certainly would have been avoided. Rasputin, half charlatan, half seer, sent this terrible prophecy to the Tsar from a Siberian hospital in July 1914: "Dear Friend again I say to thee there is storm cloud over Russia disaster much grief darkness and no break in the cloud. A sea of tears and is there no end to bloodshed? What shall I say? There are no words the horror is indescribable. I know that all want war from thee they know not that it is for ruin. God's punishment is heavy when he takes away reason. That is the beginning of war. Thou Tsar and father of thy people do not let the madmen triumph and destroy thee and thy people. Germany will be beaten but what of Russia? If you think there has truly been no worse martyr through the ages always drowning in blood. Great destruction grief without end. Grigori."[5]

The Tsar on this occasion unwisely did not heed the advice of the wild and filthy peasant whom the Empress adored, convinced he was preserving her hemophiliac son's life. And yet the apocalyptic imagery of Russia's writers makes one believe that Russia was fated to explore the profound abyss—to go to its very depths. Pushkin's lyric "Demons"—written in 1830, one hundred years before Stalin's wrath fell on the peasants—portrays a coach that is wildly out of control in a blizzard; the horses are being tormented by swarms of demons, and led to their doom. By the time of Dostoyevsky's *Demons* (usually translated as *The Possessed*), the devils have become accepted as saviors by the liberal intelligentsia. If God was no longer believed in, Dostoyevsky warned, then everything was permitted. By the turn of the century, to the Symbolist poets, more concerned with aesthetics than morality, Dostoyevsky's warning had become transformed to a triumphant battle cry. "You are free, Godhead!" shouted Viacheslav Ivanov in a lecture attended by the greatest Symbolist poet Alexander Blok. "Everything is permitted, only dare!" Ivanov, who held famous salon evenings in his high-rise Petersburg apartment, the "Tower," believed in mixing Christ and Dionysus. He would never have shot anyone, but he was willing to encourage murder.

Akhmatova, for whom art and morality were one, saw the "real" century, in which "Man, raving, denied his image / And tried to disappear," as a shadow that moved quietly, inexorably, along the Neva's historic embankment.[6] Almost alone among the poets, she predicted the horror, and became known as a modern Cassandra. After writing *Requiem* in the 1930s while standing in prison queues, hoping in vain for news of her son, who had been sentenced to death, she wrote an obsessional work of repentance for the amorality of artists before the Revolution—*Poem Without a Hero*.

Even the aristocracy seemed to have the abyss within them. How else to explain the reaction of court ladies to Rasputin? He would tell them temptations of the flesh should be yielded to, in order to gain God's forgiveness. "The first word of the Saviour was repent," he told them. "How can we repent if we have not first sinned?" He gathered his female disciples, eager to repent. "These women found it titillating to be ravished by a smelly peasant, who ate with his hands, tore at his food with blackened teeth, used the foulest language in their presence, described in coarse detail the sexual acts of the horses on his father's farm in Siberia, and violated them quickly and brutally, with the vaguely muttered assurance that 'now, Mother, everything is in order.' "[7]

The precise moment when the demons conquered is different, of course, for every person who witnessed it. Sometimes it takes the form of an image, an event frozen as in a film. So, for the young virtuoso violinist Nathan Milstein, Rasputin's blood streaking the Neva water; or perhaps, another time, in the winter of 1917, seeing a procession of women in black, carrying a large white sheet on which was handwritten in huge letters, BREAD! The women moved slowly, silently, with dignity. And the police opened fire on them. Then the Cossacks, the Tsar's most loyal troops, reacted in an entirely unexpected way: "I saw one of the Cossacks bare his sabre and, bending over slightly, cut off the head of a policeman who was shooting. One blow—and the head flew off! All this was too much for me. Terrified, I ran home."[8]

That, Milstein adds, is how the revolution to overthrow the Russian Tsar began.

The February Revolution of 1917, which brought to power a moderate left government under a young lawyer, Alexander Kerensky, bred initially a freedom-loving, tolerant spirit. It would long be remembered how Kerensky marched through angry crowds of soldiers, pale and with arm upraised, to save the lives of fallen tsarist ministers. He begged the vengeful mob to keep the Revolution undefiled by bloodshed, and the people acquiesced. Prisoners were released from Siberia. Capital punishment was abolished.

It was at this hopeful time that Isaaki Solzhenitsyn and Taissia Shcherbak met in Moscow and fell in love. Isaaki had to go back to the front, where, increasingly, Russian battalions were refusing to fight.

In the city that had been St. Petersburg but was now Russianized into Petrograd, the city "tormented and dostoievsky,"[9] the atmosphere became violent and ugly as the year went on. Gangs of armed soldiers, defecting from the front, roamed the streets. Someone saw a former colonel of the elite Imperial Guards begging a bowl of soup from the head waiter who had once served him at the Evropeiskaya Hotel.

The Revolution was "designed" by supremely rational men, Marx and Engels among them, yet when it came it was no more rational than the symbolic blizzard raging through Pushkin's "Demons," Blok's "The Twelve," and Akhmatova's *Poem Without a Hero*.

A French diplomat saw two soldiers shoot dead an old woman street vendor, close to the American embassy, rather than pay for two tiny green apples. In "The Twelve," a villainous gang of Red Guards stumble through black night and driving snow, ready to destroy everything in their path. (It may be among them is someone from the Vasilevsky soup kitchen.) They lust to drink, have pleasure, and uphold the Revolution. Nothing is sacred. "Now with my knife / I will slash, I will slash!" Behind them limps a starving dog—the old world. They think of sticking a bayonet in it, but turn their attention back to what goes always before them, barely visible in the thick snow, a red flag. Bearing that flag, leading the cutthroats, walking lightly above the storm—is Jesus Christ.

Christ and the Devil have changed places.

Throughout 1917 Isaaki Solzhenitsyn kept to his post. Two months before Kerensky's government was overthrown by the Bolsheviks, small in numbers but "full of passionate intensity,"* Isaaki arranged for Taissia to come to the front in Belorussia, where they were married by the brigade chaplain. They spent their first night together in the shadow of an artillery gun. Then she returned to Moscow and he went on serving.

---

*W. B. Yeats, "The Second Coming."

3

The Shot

Was it for this the clay grew tall?
—WILFRED OWEN

IN THE SUMMER OF 1917, RUSSIA'S SOLDIERS WERE DESERTING IN droves. They swarmed onto troop trains whose doors swung loose, whose windows were broken; they died under the wheels, or had their heads smashed against bridges as they clung on outside. No danger or hardship mattered compared with their exhausted craving to get home.[1] Isaaki Solzhenitsyn did not desert. His bride, after the Bolsheviks had seized power in October, decided to go south to wait for him. Taissia would have done her best, in a train packed with soldiers and peasants, to look poor and dowdy. There were men in plenty—officers and officials—who were disguising their ranks, or pretending to be wounded. A former president of the Duma, Mikhail Rodzianko, a loyal and sensible monarchist, traveled south in one such train as an "invalid," his 280-pound bulk squeezed into a wheelchair.[2]

These men were heading for Novocherkassk, capital of the Don Cossacks, upriver from the great commercial port of Rostov-on-Don.

The Cossacks of the Don had a contradictory reputation for being mighty battlers for freedom and the Tsars' staunchest defenders. Serfs and slaves, from as early as the fifteenth century, had run away south from Muscovy's tyranny, to become lost in the hundred thousand square miles of the Don Basin, the vast and virgin steppe where the grass grew taller than a man on horseback. Rebel Cossacks, notably the freebooter Stenka Razin (in 1660–61) and the peasant Emelian Pugachev (in 1773–74), had turned mobs of the oppressed into great armies of liberation from serfdom, heading up the great rivers, killing landowners and officials as they went. Peasants of the nineteenth century still dated events from the Pugachev revolts rather than from the birth of Christ. Pugachev was captured, brought to Moscow in a cage, and executed. The wily Empress, Catherine the Great, appeased the

Cossacks with generous gifts of land and a measure of autonomy; they became thereafter the Tsars' main bulwark against rebellion.

They fought with savage efficiency. Against all enemies—Napoleon, the
English, the Turks, the Japanese. The German armies of 1914 quailed on
hearing the cry of "*Kosaken kommen!*" Even in the Second World War,
they were feared enemies. Practically living in the saddle, masters of con-
cealment and diversion, a Cossack cavalry division, supposedly outmoded,
could move seventy miles over bad ground in a night, their sturdy horses
towing light artillery.[3]

It was natural in the chaos of 1917 for those who detested Bolshevism
to try to make their way to the Don capital. Viewed either as the defenders
of Tsar, faith, and country or as defenders of freedom, the Cossacks would
surely stand fast and defeat the godless Bolsheviks.

The disorganized fugitives, who formed the nucleus of the volunteer
White Army, did not reckon with the effect of an exhausting war. As the
young Milstein had witnessed to his astonishment, Cossacks were no longer
totally reliable defenders of the old order. Many felt Russia was no longer
their affair. Also the Whites had not taken account of the non-Cossacks, the
inogorodniye, who made up almost half of the Don population but owned
only a tenth of the land. Few had prospered like the Solzhenitsyns—let
alone the Shcherbaks—but owned less than four acres, or had been forced
by rising rents to seek work in mines and factories. Many thought they had
little to lose from supporting the Bolsheviks. And the non-Cossack proletariat of Rostov, Taganrog, on the Sea of Azov, and the Donbass coal-mining
region came out at once for the Bolsheviks. A month after the revolution
in Moscow and Petrograd, these workers proclaimed the Soviet Republic
of the Don in Rostov. The Cossack general Kaledin ordered his men to
retake Rostov, but his younger "men from the front" refused.[4] Kaledin then
turned to the few hundred Whites for their help, and the Bolsheviks were
driven out. "My heart is heavy," Kaledin told the citizens of Rostov. "Blood
was shed and we have nothing to be glad about."[5]

Soon no general would have conceived of uttering such humane sentiments. In Ireland, Yeats was writing, in "The Second Coming," "Mere an-
archy is loosed upon the world, / The blood-dimmed tide is loosed . . ." and
this accurately portrayed Russia in the winter of 1917–18. Especially in the
great cities the mobs were looting, smashing, slashing, killing. "I saw clearly
unbounded hatred everywhere," the White general Denikin remembered.
"Only one desire reigned supreme—to seize or destroy."[6] The palaces of
St. Petersburg were turned over to slum dwellers; peasants who had stinking
rags round their feet found themselves for the first time in first-class rail
compartments; and so they tore off the velvet upholstery. The chaos was
compounded by famine, as fierce snowstorms in December buried under
drifts the trains bringing grain.

Meanwhile the war with Germany drifted on, though St. Petersburg was choked with mobs of soldiers who had given up and who were looting the wine cellars. In January the Bolsheviks tried to dominate the elected Constituent Assembly, but when they found they could not, dissolved it by posting armed guards outside. The slightly more moderate Left SRs (Socialist Revolutionaries)—later to become victims themselves—supported Lenin's belief in "a higher form of democracy." In March the Bolsheviks, to save their revolution, signed away to the Germans sixty million Russians (two-fifths of the total population) and a million and a half square miles of Russia's territory. One-third of its agricultural land, and three-quarters of its coal mines, iron foundries, and steel mills were lost.

Now the soldiers, monarchists and democrats alike, whose courage and devotion had led only to that devastating political surrender, were moving south in droves to join Denikin's volunteers. The lines of the Civil War (1918–21) were already drawn. The great poet Marina Tsvetayeva, whose husband was already in the South, wrote in a notebook, "For men who believe in duty, valor, and honor, the place to be at the beginning of 1918 must be: 'On the Don!' "[7]

Tsvetayeva could not join her husband but had to remain in Moscow, the new capital; travel was already too difficult as Reds and Whites began the fighting. The toll of death from famine mounted; the workers' daily ration was 306 calories—a tenth of that required for normal sustenance. With some justification, Lenin blamed the *kulaks*, the more enterprising peasants, for hoarding. "Kill the rich *kulaks* to the last man!" he commanded. Typhus became epidemic. Even one louse could kill a man, and lice uniquely flourished and grew fat in the new Russia. When the uniforms of Red Army soldiers were taken off for disinfection, dead lice were so thick on the floor, reported *Pravda,* that they looked like a two-inch layer of gray sand.

The Germans took possession of the Ukraine and the Crimea. The Ukrainians anticipated a civilized economic union, but instead found they faced concentration camps, food requisition, and mass executions. Some twenty years later they would welcome the Germans again with flowers and cheers, as their liberators, and again would find a different reality. The twentieth century is an illustration of the Freudian doctrine of "the compulsion to repeat."

Two hundred miles to the southeast of Novocherkassk, at Sablia, the Solzhenitsyn family went on doggedly tending their sheep and pigs, and trying not to take too much notice of the disturbances occurring in nearby Cossack settlements. Semyon, kneeling before the icons, hoped piously that his youngest son, Isaaki, had survived.

Taissia, the daughter-in-law he had never met, was at Kislovodsk in the Caucasus with the rest of the Shcherbaks. She was staying with Roman and Irina, who owned a summer villa in the famous spa resort. Maria

Karpushina, Taissia's older sister, and her landowner husband also had a villa in the town. They had taken in her elderly parents, who had been driven out of their Kuban estate by local Red Guards.

If one had to flee in the night—and old Zakhar would not have liked it one bit—it was good to be able to flee to the Caucasus. Kislovodsk, "Bitter Water," was the most select of the Caucasian resorts. It lay in a richly vegetated glen twenty-six hundred feet above sea level, surrounded by mountains that warded off all winds. Its plentiful warm springs, good for heart and respiratory conditions, included the famous Narzan, the richest carbonic spring in the world. The summer villas of the rich were the tsarist equivalent of estates at Malibu. Fyodor Chaliapin, the famous operatic bass, and the last Tsar's mistress, the ballerina Kshesinskaya, were among those who had homes there.[8]

Notable among its many attractive features were the Narzan Gallery, built in English Gothic in the mid-nineteenth century; the Narzan Bathhouse, in the form of an Indian temple; the casino; the avenue of poplars, along which the fashionable paraded. Winters were warm, rain fell on only sixty or seventy days of the year. Romantic legends were told of the two rivers, Elkusha and Olkhovka, which flowed through the glen. Like the Caucasus as a whole, celebrated by Pushkin, Lermontov, and Tolstoy, it was a place suitable for romantic legends.

Though there were numerous short pathways with frequent benches for those with heart conditions, more hearts were probably broken by unhappy love affairs, in this leisured and luxurious world, than were cured. Not even the Soviet era, which would attempt to proletarianize the spa through such names as Lenin and Dzerzhinsky Prospekts, and October, Kirov, Victory, Commune, and Gagarin streets, could completely remove the aura of magic.

The ladies and gentlemen still paraded under the poplars in their finery; but the atmosphere was heavy with the threat of storm. How long could this protected world survive? For almost a year, since just after the February Revolution in Petrograd, Kislovodsk had been administered locally by a soviet, but the commissars were moderate—perhaps overawed by all the luxury. They talked big about destroying privilege, but so far nothing much had happened.[9]

In early spring of 1918, Isaaki made his way to Kislovodsk to join his wife.

When the past offers nothing but silence about an event, the fictive imagination starts to itch to make its own scenarios. I can imagine—

Taissia is in the garden of her sister Maria's villa, strolling under the trees, enjoying the first scent of spring. A few white wispy clouds hang motionless in the dazzling sky. Her fingers still tingle from, and her mind holds the melody of, a Chopin Prelude she has been practicing. The hem of her lilac skirt swishes over the long grass under the magnolia tree. She wonders if she should take up Irina's suggestion, yesterday, that they ride up to Seriye Kamni, Gray Stones, from where they can get a glimpse of the peak of distant Elbrus. Taissia believes her sister-in-law wants to air her complaints against Roman. She is jealous, Taissia thinks, that she has married for love.

She hears the snap of a twig just behind her, and turns to see, not six feet away, a man wearing an officer's cap and open greatcoat, and with a rifle slung over his shoulder. At first he seems to be a stranger, this man with the exhausted, stubbled, grimy face, and she is alarmed; then—"Sanya!" and she flings herself into his arms. After the long kiss has made her gasp for breath, she scolds him with a smile: "Why didn't you warn me you were coming, darling? Roman could have driven me to Rostov, and—"

In reality, we know only that he arrived, he got Taissia pregnant, and they soon left for the rougher, bleaker surroundings of Sablia, sixty miles to the east.

Trying to analyze why he did not stay longer in Kislovodsk, or later events in that tragic year, is almost as much an exercise of the fictive imagination. One may imagine, as Michael Scammell has done, that Isaaki got bored with the comforts, and perhaps was irritated by the loud laments over lost estates by Zakhar and Maria's husband. They survived; unlike so many of his army comrades. Isaaki may have found Roman not to his taste: liberal ideas, and portraits of Tolstoy, but languid upper-class habits. The Rolls-Royce and the Havanas. The luxury could have struck a soldier, returning from the hell of the front line, as nauseous.

In any case, he took Taissia off to stay with his own family—including the scheming, disliked stepmother, Marfa. He may have wanted to show his cultivated bride off to them. He may have thought it his duty to join the Volunteers, after short stays with both sets of parents. If so, he changed his mind, lingering in Sablia.

It was natural, when all is said and imagined, for a young soldier to want to go home, to see again that "unique sadness" of the home landscape. It would be good, after the carnage, to swing the scythe again, helping his aged father. The wide Russian sky, the hum of insects, a chance to reflect, after the devilry of screaming shells.

One final *imagining*: he may have feared, with good reason, that Taissia's life might be in danger if she stayed in Kislovodsk. He had seen the hatred elsewhere; there was an urge for vengeance. "Kill the rich *kulaks* to the last man!" Or woman. It was only a matter of time before a terrible wrath overwhelmed the opulent villas of Kislovodsk. She and the baby in her womb would be much safer on the modest, isolated Sablia farm.

This much is certain: to any objective onlooker at the time, Isaaki and Taissia must have seemed among the flower of Russia's future destiny: both idealistic, highly intelligent, well educated, and determined. Isaaki had shown patriotism and courage; Taissia had been the brightest pupil of the best school in Rostov. And she would become a graduate in agronomy, a skill of which Russia was desperately in need.

It must have been rather strange at the Solzhenitsyn farm. One wonders how Taissia got on with her stepmother-in-law, whether she did much helping out, or played the needing-to-be-cosseted mother-to-be. It must have been strangely quiet. Quiet in the midst of a savage war. The Bolsheviks were in control of most of the South, but alienated the Cossacks and many others by their terror. The war had become one of the most monstrously inhuman in history, an ideological struggle to the death. General Denikin recalled how a diver found the bodies of White officers drowned by the Reds in the harbor at Novorossisk, their "living, greenish, swollen, mangled corpses kept upright owing to the weights tied to their legs [so that they] stood in serried ranks, swaying to and fro, as if talking to one another."[10] He recalled his troops finding the body of a man who had been buried alive after having his hands and feet cut off and his stomach ripped open: all simply because his son had joined the Whites. The Civil War, Denikin confessed, "deformed the soul."

The Whites could hold their own in savagery. Once, three freight cars were filled with obscenely exposed Red corpses, and sent off with the marking "Fresh meat, destination Petrograd." But the Reds alone possessed an absolute policy of revolutionary terror. Lenin spoke of terror and death sentences with an air of satisfaction, and found an equal enthusiast in the head of the *Cheka* (secret police), "Iron Felix" Dzerzhinsky, bureaucrat of torture, thin-faced, goatee-bearded El Greco of terror, death's Stakhanovite. Only saints and scoundrels were fit to be members of the security forces, he said (there were never many saints). Scarcely sleeping or eating, consumed by class hatred, he had mused to friends before the Revolution that "class-genocide" might solve Russia's problems. The first question to ask a prisoner—which would decide his guilt or innocence—was what was his class origin. After just a year of Cheka work, on 1 January 1919, he told his comrades he had spilled so much blood they should shoot him there and then.[11]

They did not, unfortunately. And he toughened up his somewhat sentimental organization. The Cheka executed an estimated one hundred thousand "class aliens" between the Revolution and Lenin's death: seven times as many as were killed under the Tsars in the previous century. And the forms of execution often were of a barbarity that Genghis Khan would have admired: dismemberment with axes, slow boiling or burning, crucifixion, skinning alive, twisting off heads.

Soon after Isaaki and Taissia had left Kislovodsk, the neighboring town of Essentuki found itself taken over by a drunken gang of Bolsheviks who proceeded to go on rampages, demanding gold and valuables and looking for food. They imposed levies, and took off the leading citizens to Pyatigorsk as hostages. Their families were not too worried, assuming they would be released when the money was paid. But suddenly rough posters appeared in the town declaring that the hostages had been "liquidated" as "enemies of the people." The effect on the populace was devastating. Suddenly—as

Jews or Gypsies would be, under the Nazis, because of race—you were a criminal, subject to summary execution, because of class.

Now there were Bolsheviks, extortions, and executions in Kislovodsk also. The Shcherbaks went in fear of their lives. Isaaki seemed to have made a wise choice. In the Sablia region, a few Cossack villages rose up against the Reds, but the mainly non-Cossack peasants of Sablia stayed quiet and uncommitted.

With the strange unpredictability of memory, a daughter of Anastasia, Isaaki's sister, can remember the very moment when Isaaki came home. She was five years old. What impressed itself on her memory was his uniform, his highly lacquered boots, his sword. He was handsome and upright. Taissia followed him in. He walked slowly around the large room, and Taissia did likewise. The old woman remembers Isaaki gave her a green poplin dress, a thick coat, and a beautiful doll.[12] It is touching to think that he spent some of his short time in Kislovodsk shopping for his little niece.

On 8 June 1918, something happened that would have a profound effect on the life of the unborn author. Basing his account mainly on his interview with Solzhenitsyn in 1977, Michael Scammell first of all writes that "the exact circumstances of the accident are shrouded in obscurity," then gives what seems a very detailed account of the "shrouded" events.[13]

Isaaki and a friend* went out hunting for small game in the forests of the surrounding hills. They were in a horse-drawn cart. When they were stationary Isaaki stood up in the cart to gut a hare they had caught, and "in a moment of carelessness leaned his cocked shotgun against the cart's side. The horse started, as if bitten by a fly. The cart gave a jerk, and the shotgun fell and exploded, peppering Isaaki's chest and abdomen with shot."

They returned at once to the farm; then, with Taissia accompanying him, the injured man was driven by way of Sablia to Georgievsk, forty miles to the southwest. It was a long and immensely painful journey, by horse and cart along a rough road. The unsprung cart had to go very slowly to spare Isaaki unbearable suffering. It took them twenty-four hours to cover the distance. At Georgievsk, the wounded man was admitted straightaway to the hospital and operated on. However, in the Civil War situation the care was not of a good standard; the operation was hasty and some of the shot (and the wad, which had also entered his chest) was not removed. The wounds turned septic. Taissia sent a telegram to Kislovodsk, "Isai in mortal danger," and Roman and Irina traveled the hundred or so miles to be with the distraught woman. In old age Irina claimed she heard Isaaki say to her, "Take care of my son. I'm sure I'm going to have a son." On 15 June, four days before his twenty-eighth birthday, Isaaki died.

After the funeral in the Georgievsk town cemetery, Taissia went back

---

*Anastasia's daughter thinks his eldest brother, Konstantin, was his companion.

with Roman and Irina to Kislovodsk. She and Sanya had enjoyed just three months of marriage; they were still in the honeymoon period, and had too the excitement of approaching parenthood. Suddenly a tragic curtain had descended.

A school friend of Alexander Solzhenitsyn in Rostov, by the name of Kirill Simonyan, published in 1976 a pamphlet entitled *Who Is Solzhenitsyn?* in an obscure left-wing Danish newspaper.[14] Among several slanderous and absurd accusations against the by-then exiled writer—such as that he had got himself arrested in the war to avoid further fighting—Simonyan alleged that Solzhenitsyn's mother had once told him that her husband had committed suicide.

He had been terrified, she allegedly told the youngster, because of the Bolshevik takeover.

Simonyan had fallen out with Solzhenitsyn many years before, was uncomfortable with his dissident stance, and was under pressure from the KGB. It may almost have been a blessing that Simonyan died of a heart attack before his work appeared in print. If there was an intention to publish the original in the Soviet Union, the idea was dropped.

Nevertheless, even granting that Simonyan was prepared to speak ill of the living, it is a little harder to think he would lightly speak ill of the dead; or ascribe words to them that they never uttered. Simonyan was Armenian, and Armenians have a certain tradition of moral decorum, which might make all but the most villainous hesitate before a lie of such seriousness. Simonyan might have thought no sensible person could believe Solzhenitsyn was a coward, so to lie about his arrest wouldn't matter; but if he lied in saying he heard his mother say Isaaki had committed suicide—that could be credible, and a really dreadful lie.

Dieter Steiner, a *Stern* reporter who, with a few KGB helpers, interviewed Irina in 1971, also surmises, without adducing any evidence, that the death was probably suicide.

Isaaki had everything to live for. You do not commit suicide when your new wife is pregnant. . . .

But we do not know his mental and emotional state after four years of warfare; and now a civil war of unimaginable brutality. The heart, as Turgenev wrote, is a dark forest. Which is like the Russian proverb, We are born in a clear field and we die in a dark wood. Perhaps he had entered the dark wood early.

It was to say the least ironic that this man who had fought bravely, and preserved his life, for four years, now died from a carelessly placed shotgun and a bolting horse. . . . And yet this is the kind of thing that happens. If he had tried to shoot himself would he have made such a mess of it?

The fictive imagination, that KGB of a thousand lying plots, starts up its interrogations again, and then its plausible or bizarre narrative twists. Why are Isaaki's family seemingly out of the picture? Here was the clever son, an officer no less, the returning hero; now to be taken from them by the most atrocious accident. . . . Why that drab burial in the town cemetery?

What more natural and touching than that Taissia, in harassed and sick middle age, should confess to a gentle, sensitive Armenian boy—who she may have sensed had a tormenting secret himself: he was homosexual—the dread secret she has been nursing all these years?

That might have been natural, and yet—it might also have been natural for the adult Simonyan, with a KGB man's heavy arm on his shoulder, to have yielded to extreme pressure. Probably Isaaki's death was accidental, as Alexander Solzhenitsyn himself firmly believes.

I suspect, however, that he has been haunted by the last hours and minutes of his father's life. While he was still in the womb, his life had one of its most crucial experiences. Not only was he deprived of a father, he was also cut off from his father's family. Fate continued to be cruel to the Solzhenitsyns: in 1919 typhus killed Semyon and three of his diminished family—his wife Marfa and two of his children, Vasili and Anastasia.

Only once did Taissia take her son to visit Sablia, but she regularly took him to Georgievsk to visit his father's grave. Then in 1931 the Soviets built a sports stadium where the cemetery had been: just as twenty years later, in Kiev, they would cover over Babi Yar with a television center. The Soviets were not sentimental about the dead, except in Lenin's case.

Isaaki became buried alive in his son's imagination. Taissia had given him the same familiar form of his name, Sanya. Fate aided at times by choice seemed to be ensuring that he repeated his father's life. Both at the same age went to Moscow to study. In 1914, when Isaaki was twenty-three, the First World War started, and he enlisted in the artillery, serving in Belorussia and East Prussia. At twenty-three, in 1941, when Germany launched Barbarossa, Alexander enlisted and became an artillery officer, fighting on the same front. Already married, he could not have a wedding at the front, but he persuaded his wife to come for a romantic visit. *This* rather Tolstoyan Sanya did not die at twenty-seven, but entered another sort of grave thanks to the carelessly cocked gun of some rude jokes about Stalin. And because of it, paradoxically, began a new spiritual life.

Since Taissia would not remarry, saying it might disturb her son, Sanya had to live two lives for her. I believe an important motive for his epic fiction of the years 1914–17, *The Red Wheel*, begun when he was still at school and completed or abandoned almost sixty years later, was to bring his father to life. He would re-create that world so intensely, so exhaustively, so accurately, that his father could not fail to live. During the decades of writing the work in Vermont, it was his father's portrait that stood on his desk.

In his play *A Feast of Conquerors*, conceived in the Gulag, Solzhenitsyn shows his hero Nerzhin (a run-in for the famous Nerzhin of *The First Circle*) answering questions about his origins. Most of his answers link him precisely to the author: his mother had been a clerk; his father, killed six months before his birth, had been a student, the son of a peasant. Then: "Who killed him? Whose bullet? Whose shrapnel?"

"German."

Solzhenitsyn may have wished that this had been the case. Or is it just conceivable that this too is accurate; that Isaaki shot himself with a German Army revolver? It may be significant that Nerzhin does not say that the Germans killed his father.

There is another passage in Solzhenitsyn's writings that may have an emotional connection with his father's death. It is the wonderfully moving passage in *August 1914*, the first volume of *The Red Wheel*, in which General Samsonov resolves to die, following the catastrophic first campaign of the war, the Battle of Tannenberg. He must bear responsibility for the stupidity and incompetence of others. . . .

It was completely quiet. The whole world was silent, as though the clash of armies had never been; only the breath of a gentle night breeze sighed in the tops of the pine-trees. There was nothing hostile about this forest: it was not a German or a Russian forest, but simply God's forest which gave refuge to all manner of creatures.

Leaning against a trunk, Samsonov stood and listened to the sound of the forest. From nearby came the rustle of a piece of torn pine-bark, and from above the faint, soothing hum of wind-blown tree-tops.

He felt increasingly tranquil. He had lived out a long life of army service in which the risks of danger and death were inevitable; now that he had reached the moment of death and was ready for it, he realised for the first time how easy, how great a relief it would be.

The only problem was that suicide was accounted a sin.

With a faint click, the hammer of his revolver slipped readily into the cocked position. Samsonov put it into his upturned cap, which he had laid on the ground. He took off his curved sword and kissed it, then felt for his wife's medallion and kissed it too.

He walked a few paces to a small clearing open to the sky.

It was cloudy now, and only one small star could be seen. It vanished, then appeared again. He knelt down on the warm pine-needles, and because he did not know where the east lay he prayed to the star.

He began with the set prayers, then none at all, simply breathing on his knees and looking up into the sky. Then, casting aside restraint, he groaned aloud, like any dying creature of the forest:

"O Lord, if Thou canst, forgive me and receive me. Thou seest— I could do no other, and can do no other now."[15]

The reference to Samsonov's wife is probably one of the author's brilliantly truthful imaginative touches, but just possibly might have a link with that prenatal event at Sablia. The emphasis upon the sounds of the forest reminds us that the settings were similar for Samsonov's and Isaaki's deaths.

There is a marvelous empathy with the feelings of a soldier, who knows he has done his duty and now wants to rest. Probably he sensed his father's exhaustion, and hopes that he achieved serenity. Isaaki was, by his son's own account, "a soft, lyrical, philosophical man, very soft," in contrast to tough, energetic Grandfather Zakhar.[16]

Not all accidental deaths occur by accident. They can happen out of exhaustion, a willed carelessness, a calm indifference, or a despair over the future.

4

The Child on Tolstoy Street

The children of Russia's terrible years . . .
—BLOK

A MONTH AFTER THE SHOT THAT KILLED ISAAKI SOLZHENITSYN, armed guards entered a basement in the Ipatiev House, Ekaterinburg, and their leader rapped out a sentence to a man who sat on a wooden chair amid his family and a few servants: "Nicholas Alexandrovich, by order of the Regional Soviet of the Urals, you are to be shot, along with all your family." The moment is frozen in time, as in a frozen video recording: the deposed Tsar with Alexei, the Tsarevich, seated beside him—deathly pale, because he has recently suffered a severe hemorrhage; Alexandra seated to the side; standing behind, the four young Grand Duchesses, Anastasia with her pet dog in her arms; doctor, valet, cook, and housemaid, also standing. It is night. They were wakened and told they must dress quickly, they were being moved elsewhere: the White Army in the East was moving close.

But the paused video moved on: Nicholas scarcely had time to leap to his feet and utter "*Chto?*"—"What?"—before Yakoff Yurovsky shot him in the head, then turned and fired two shots at Alexei. The other Chekists opened fire. The Empress and one of her daughters managed to cross themselves before bullets shattered jewels hidden in heavily padded brassieres. Another volley finished the servants. Silence fell; the Tsarevich moaned, whereupon Yurovsky fired two more shots into him. Anastasia moaned too, though she had scarcely been wounded; one of the guards drove his bayonet into her several times, then smashed her pet dog's head with his rifle butt.[1] The dark room was awash with blood.

All Russia was running in blood; though for a while Kislovodsk, far away in the South, remained quiet. The grieving Taissia lived in Maria's villa on Tolstoy Street, in a well-known quarter of the town, Rebrova Balka, near the railroad station.[2] In the later stages of Taissia's pregnancy, the atmosphere became more threatening. An armored train, headquarters of the

Revolutionary Army of the North Caucasus, stood in the railroad terminus. The relatively moderate commander in chief, Avtonomov, was recalled to Moscow on charges of counterrevolutionary activity; he was replaced by two new commissars, Axelrode and Gay. The latter's beautiful and flamboyant wife, Ksenia, bedecked herself in jewels extorted from hostages. Those who refused to, or could not, comply with the extortions, were shot—following the Ekaterinburg example—in a cellar.[3]

The Shcherbaks in their two villas that announced wealth and class enemies closed their shutters and stayed in, hardly daring to breathe, waiting for the crash of a rifle butt against the door, obscene shouts. Before going to bed they made the sign of the cross at the door, hoping it would guard them in the night. Maria's husband, Afanasy Karpushin, fell a victim to a silent intruder no walls could keep out: typhus. So both sisters had lost their husbands in the same year. Fortunately the Shcherbaks, unlike the Solzhenitsyn family in 1919, escaped with just the one death. Taissia must have trembled for her unborn child.

There were not only Reds *versus* Whites, there were bands of Ukrainian bandits. The most fearsome was under the command of an anarchist and anti-Semite called Makhno. Makhno's men delighted in "drying the herrings," as they called the process of hanging Jews. They would suspend several between posts on a loose rope; as the rope tightened the victims tried to cling on to each other in their death-agonies, the *Makhnovtsi* sitting around laughing, drinking, and betting on who would survive the longest.

Towns changed hands with such rapidity that the only sure way for the inhabitants to know who was in charge was for children to hang around the streets listening to the way the armed men greeted each other. *"Tovarisch"* (comrade) indicated Bolsheviks; *"rebyata"* (mate) indicated Whites; while *"patsani"* (boys) revealed Ukrainian bandits.[4]

Fighting raged over the North Caucasus through the summer of 1918. The Whites recaptured Rostov and Stavropol; the Reds abandoned Armavir in the Kuban, where Zakhar's estate was situated. With Axelrode and Gay in control, and drunken gangs on the loose, Kislovodsk was in the grip of terror; and the Shcherbaks were fortunate to survive with just one bad scare. Perhaps Roman's somewhat hypocritical liberalism was known about and respected by the Bolshevik leaders. But one night a gang of armed men burst into his villa, seized him, and took him to Pyatigorsk. There he was interrogated, and Dzerzhinsky's one essential question did not even need a verbal answer—he was so obviously a class enemy. When Irina heard he had been sentenced to death, she forgot it was a poor marriage, did not waste time weeping and praying before an icon, swiftly collected jewelry and money, and traveled to the Bolshevik headquarters in Pyatigorsk. Risking life and honor, passionately arguing Roman's hatred of the old regime and placing jewels and money on the table, she won her husband's release.[5] Some Chekist had clearly gone soft; she was not even raped.

Throughout the South, each short-lived occupation was marked with revenge killings. In September 1918 a retired Cossack officer, Colonel A. G. Shkuro, a supporter of democratic reform, led a White force into Kislovodsk and took three thousand Bolshevik prisoners. He executed their leaders, including Commissar Gay and his flamboyant, greedy, murderous wife. Ksenia Gay demanded a last cigarette, then coolly ascended the gallows, saying, "We today, you tomorrow."[6] That same night, in Pyatigorsk, a Polish Bolshevik, Andziewski, beheaded 155 White hostages in the glow of specially lit fires.

Ksenia Gay's prediction was soon borne out, as Shkuro's men were driven out by the Reds and revenge executions took place. Again the Shcherbaks were unharmed. And it seemed a miracle, a sign of grace, when Taissia gave birth, on 11 December, to a son. At the church of St. Panteleimon, high on the hill, he was christened Alexander: a name of rich assertiveness in both military glory and poetry. His godmother was Jewish, a woman by the name of Maria Kremer.[7] Instead of the slightly clumsy true patronymic, Isaakievich, Taissia chose the softer "Isayevich." And she called him "Sanya," like his father.

The priest of St. Panteleimon, Father Alexei, was known far and wide for his spiritual fervor. Just three weeks after he had blessed the newborn child, he was called upon to lead the town's rejoicing at being freed again from the Bolshevik yoke: Shkuro had invaded a second time, and overcome. He recalled in his *Memoirs of a White Partisan:* "On 6 January I arrived in Kislovodsk and was given a tumultuous welcome by the populace, which had suffered grievously under the Bolshevik regime. The town had also suffered. Many houses had been pillaged, and the celebrated poplar avenue had been cut down. The Red butchers had slaughtered hundreds of the townsfolk with sword and bullet. Since it was Epiphany there was the blessing of the Waters and a thanksgiving mass, after which I held a parade of my troops."[8]

Alexander Solzhenitsyn's first few months of life coincided with a surge forward in the White cause, with General Denikin advancing on Moscow from the south and Admiral Kolchak from Siberia. Now that the Central Powers had surrendered, the Allies could at last send aid and reinforcements. Zakhar and Yevdokia rejoiced at being able to return to his estate. Maria, a simple, kindhearted soul who had left school at seventeen to marry Karpushin, was probably thankful in her bereavement and childlessness to have Taissia and her new baby sharing her house.

Perhaps soon, once the Whites had taken back the country, they could all go to that wonderful house in the Kuban, with the old couple; and Taissia could combine motherhood with agronomy. . . . The nightmare would be over. Yet in reality the year 1919 marked the decisive upturn in the fortunes of the Reds. As their territory shrank to the area of old Muscovy, their strength became more concentrated, their objective more unified—a Communist Russia; whereas the Whites became overextended, and their leaders fatally at odds as to whether they sought the old imperial Russia, a democratic republic, or various independent states. They lost support through mirroring the atrocities of the Reds. Trotsky's Red Army was becoming a mighty and disciplined force. Even as they were defeated, Lenin and Trotsky felt their future triumph was assured, while with every victory the Whites became gloomier. By the end of the summer, General Budenny's Red Cossack cavalry was driving the White forces back.

In the North Caucasus, Armavir became a site of Bolshevik reprisals. The Ukrainian herdsboy who had become a landowner "able to feed all of Russia," was forced to leave his estate for the last time. He and Yevdokia escaped with a few bits and pieces of furniture. They headed for Kislovodsk again—a sad, bitter arrival of carts and carriages, at Maria's villa in Tolstoy Street.

The South was drowning in horror. An English governess in Rostov, Rhoda Power, has given a vivid portrait of the violence of that seaport, in which Solzhenitsyn would spend his later childhood and youth. She writes of young White officers, sentenced to death, who couldn't endure waiting for a Bolshevik official to arrive, so themselves gave the shooting party the order to fire. She writes of a little boy who sees his White officer father killed; the Red Guards rush up to him and seize him. "You can follow your damned daddy!" they shout at him; and he says, "Will you let me lie down? I am so weak." They shoot him as he lies on the ground.

Once, Miss Power and a companion, out walking with peasant scarves tied round their heads, heard shouts of mirth. They turned a corner and a crowd of small boys rushed at them. "They've cut off a White officer's head, ladies," the merry lads announced; "it's lying on the ground and we're trying to hit the nose with snowballs." A friend was strolling on Pushkin Street behind a Red Guard one day. On the other side of the road a student was walking. The revolutionary shouted across the street, "Ha! Another of the intelligentsia. So you will educate yourself above the people, will you? There!" And shot him through the head. The youth gave a little cry and fell; and before he was quite dead his clothes were off him and being sold to a passing peasant.[9]

A maid went out and came across the body of a fair-haired youth lying naked in the snow. She crossed herself and covered the youth with her apron, but soldiers who stood beside it laughed. They had sold the victim's clothes in the market and were counting the notes.

Red Guards searched the railroad station, checking for escaping White officers. "Peasants" with fine white fingers were bayoneted.

The remarkably cool young Englishwoman not only witnessed the horrors of the Civil War in the South, she had also seen the vast gulf between the classes that the miseries of world war had brought to crisis point. "While we ate cakes and chocolates at twenty roubles a pound, caviare, and good fresh meat, peasants stood shivering hour after hour outside the bakery, their tickets clutched between blue fingers, waiting for a loaf of bread. If there were not enough to go round they went away empty handed. Some of them lined up at midnight and waited till the shops opened in the morning. . . . I used to watch their patient, tired faces, and the pale little children, sitting in the snow on overturned baskets, and wonder how long it would be before they would rebel."[10]

Meanwhile "we lived on the fat of the land. The war scarcely seemed to touch us. Life consisted in seeking amusement to pass the time." The frivolous empty-headed girl in her charge couldn't wait to get married, so that she could take a lover.

When the Whites briefly recaptured Rostov, early in the Civil War, all the bourgeoisie, furred and jeweled, rushed into the main boulevard, Sadovaya, to greet the victorious army. But an old peasant woman—not some Bolshevik agitator but a simple peasant—standing behind Miss Power and her companions spat at them, "You can wear your new hats again now." Another old toothless woman swayed in a kind of trance, chanting, "O Lord God! O my Lord God! Let the rich be slain. God, God, God!"

As machine guns rattled nearby, Miss Power observed a queue of people standing before a brightly illuminated building, and she realized that the hour for the opening of the cinemas was at hand and the youth of Rostov were waiting to be amused.

Throughout Russia during the first four years of Solzhenitsyn's life, between ten million and twenty-five million people died unnaturally, including deaths from the terrible famine of 1921–22. Roughly speaking, one Russian in every ten perished. It would have been strange if the Shcherbak family, who were comparatively fortunate in losing only property and possessions, did not consider joining the diaspora. Perhaps old Zakhar still had hopes of somehow regaining his estate; perhaps Roman's desire for a more just society was staunch enough to persuade the family to stay and bite the bullet.

Through the winter of 1920 the Shcherbaks were virtually starving, forced to barter their elegant furniture for bread. One of Solzhenitsyn's earliest memories is of a commotion in church. His mother held him up so that he could see armed Bolshevik horsemen advancing arrogantly through the worshipers with their candles. It was a time when church property was being confiscated. The event must have had a powerful, frightening effect on the little boy, to have stayed in his memory from such an early age: not much more than two at most. We can be fairly certain of this since, early in 1921, Taissia moved to Rostov to find work, leaving her son behind with Aunt Maria and his grandmother.

Maria, "simple and uneducated" in her famous nephew's memory of her, found another husband quickly. Evidently she appealed to men seeking quiet, efficient domesticity in a second wife: her first husband had been a widower when he married her; her second husband, a good-natured giant of an ex-guardsman called Fyodor Garin, brought with him two girls and a boy from a previous marriage. Maria's house was becoming crowded, since Zakhar and Yevdokia were living there too. There was good reason, therefore, for Taissia and her baby to move out. But leaving her two-year-old son behind, and moving to Rostov, three hundred miles to the north, was a surprising and drastic move. Irina and Roman were moving too, but only as far as a quiet nearby hamlet called Minutka, where they felt they would be less conspicuous to the Bolshevik witch-hunters. It would have been natural for Taissia to have moved in with them.

Instead she went to Rostov, without her son, and with no security. Despite having some friends in Rostov—notably the family of Madame Andreyeva, her former headmistress—she had to struggle to pay for a shack to live in, and to find employment in face of the policy of giving the bourgeois only menial jobs. She took a secretarial course, and an influential contact managed to get her a shorthand-typist post with a building combine. However, someone informed on her as a class alien, and she was dismissed. Some half a dozen times, over the next few years, this pattern repeated itself. Life was very hard for her. Yet she evidently preferred being uncomfortable in Rostov to being taken care of by members of her family, and being with Sanya.

It seems likely that Taissia left her family and her son in a desperate effort to gain freedom. Once her mourning had subsided, she probably felt stifled in Kislovodsk. For one thing, Maria, Irina, her mother and father were so pious. Taissia had absorbed much more liberal attitudes in Madame Andreyeva's lycée and in Moscow. Later in life, she would strike her daughter-in-law as "very religious";[11] but that was perhaps by comparison with the prevailing militant atheism. There may have been other bones of contention; when she was living with Maria at a later stage of her life, she complained in letters that her sister was mean with money, and kept them short of food. Irina struck her as sly, and eventually she and her sister-in-law ceased to have anything to do with each other.[12]

Taissia, educated, her father's darling, was a free spirit, a young woman who wished she could be a dancer like Isadora Duncan—that Isadora who around this time was dancing half naked in Boston, then denouncing the scandalized puritans. Nudity was truth, she told them; no bodily part was more evil than any other; her art was symbolic of the freedom of woman and emancipation from hidebound conventions.[13] Taissia need not have shared all the bohemian beliefs of her heroine to have wanted to make a break for freedom.

She had experienced love and passion briefly; and here was her more homely sister, less intelligent, less educated, already proving that she needed a man to love—and finding one. The example of Maria's remarriage might have been the spur to Taissia's departure. Though according to her son she decided not to remarry for his sake, that decision may not have come straightaway; possibly not before some unsuccessful relationships in Rostov.

Her brother-in-law, Konstantin Solzhenitsyn, visited her on occasions and helped her. And sometimes she visited Sablia. She and the widow of Vasili

Solzhenitsyn shared each other's sorrow. Konstantin had five sons and a daughter. When Vasili's widow died, in or around 1923, the kindly Konstantin also took her three orphaned children into his care.[14]

Possibly it occurred to Taissia to fetch Sanya and bring him to be looked after by Konstantin and his wife. However, the child stayed in Kislovodsk, looked after by Aunt Maria (affectionately, Marusha) and his grandmother; though he spent his summers with Irina and Roman (Auntie Ira and Uncle Romasha) in Minutka. He loved his auntie Ira, who had a much more powerful and long-lasting influence on him than either Marusia or Yevdokia, but did not take to Uncle Romasha.

Then in 1924 the familiar house, room, corner icon were withdrawn from the child. Maria's villa was ordered to be confiscated. She and Garin used the last of their money to buy a small adobe house in Georgievsk, and were going to divide it so that her parents could have one large room. Zakhar and Yevdokia, however, found it hard to settle in this strange place, and moved back near their Armavir estate. They lived with a cousin in the village of Gulkevichi, and were given food by some of their former workers who felt sorry for them.

The family was splitting up; Irina and Roman also moved again that year—north to Novocherkassk. The Cossack stronghold might provide a safer environment. In the fall of 1924, just before Sanya's sixth birthday, Irina and Roman came to take him on a long train journey. He recalls that journey, then a drive along a snowbound boulevard in Novocherkassk. A few days later he was taken to be reunited with his mother.

I imagine . . .

Who is this strange lady, crying all over me? . . .

Must I stay in this hole with her? Why can't I go and stay with Aunt Ira?

I mustn't cry. My papa was a soldier. . . .

It is always perilous to ascribe adult characteristics to childhood events and circumstances; and especially in Russia of this epoch, when the state played a hugely formative role. Solzhenitsyn himself has played down the importance of family—but that is all the more reason to believe his earliest years *were* of great importance in helping to mold his character and personality.

The first period of his life coincided with the violent beginnings of the Bolshevik state. He was born into two houses full of grief and anger—the Russia house and the Shcherbak house. Born to a huge loss. The violence in the child's response, mostly locked in the fragile skull, can only be guessed at.

For much of the first year of his life the war situation had eased, but his mother and aunt Maria were newly bereaved, and his grandparents had lost their estate and home—they hoped only temporarily. Then the tide turned decisively in favor of the Reds. The great Shcherbak estate was gone forever; to loss and bereavement was added fear; a mortal terror, indeed, as the adults crouched in silence in the shuttered houses of Sheremetyev and Tolstoy Streets, waiting to be dragged out and killed. Each evening, as they made the sign of the cross at the door, they could not be sure they would be alive the next morning. In this, the situation was exactly comparable to that of the Terror of 1937–38. Hundreds of "class enemies" in Kislovodsk were killed. They also feared that other common form of death—which in 1919 was killing whole trainloads of people—typhus.

Later the fear of Bolshevik atrocity and reprisal gradually lessened, but now there was semi-starvation; the frantic selling off of possessions in order to survive; the threat of total ruin. There was still fierce fighting by partisan bands in the Caucasus, until the Soviets put an end to it in 1924. Michael Scammell believes that "the infant Solzhenitsyn was presumably secure and oblivious of these hardships."[15] Yet could a sensitive child have been unaware of fear, fear that can be smelled? He would see a womanly figure freeze at a noise outside, hear held breaths being released. No doubt there was care to ensure he never wanted for food and warmth and above all love; indeed, the danger must have sharpened acutely the expression of love toward this child who represented the family's future. His mother, Maria, Yevdokia, and Irina all bent over his crib with a desperate love: creating a pattern in his life, the certainty that he could demand and expect adoring love and sacrifice from a circle of women. He would make full use of this in his struggles against his Communist oppressors.

When he was two years old, his mother went away. She effectively "died." We cannot know how this child reacted to such a death; but characteristically in such circumstances "at first he protests vigorously and tries by all the means available to him to recover his mother. Later he seems to despair of recovering her but none the less remains preoccupied with her and vigilant for her return. Later still he seems to lose his interest in his mother and to become emotionally detached from her." The three common stages are linked successively to separation anxiety, grief and mourning, and defense.[16] "After great pain, a formal feeling comes" (Emily Dickinson).

During the Second World War, in Hampstead, London, Anna Freud and Dorothy Burlingham established a nursery for young children deprived of their mothers. They discovered, to their surprise, that the reaction of children aged between one and three was particularly violent, full of frustrated longing and despair.[17] Slightly older children felt they were being punished for some misdeed. Children who endured the blitz with their mother were more secure than those who had the peace of evacuation to the country, without their mothers.

Sanya was cherished by three women for whom his life was a comfort and consolation for *their* losses. Nevertheless, it is inconceivable that the infant sailed happily through the sudden and total loss of his mother. Far from it; it would have been a desolation worse than the Gulag; and time for an infant is endless.

Then, after the stage of despair—detachment; the detachment he was able to cultivate so well in the camps, and later. There is a revealing moment in a television interview of April 1994, just a few days before his return to Russia from American exile, when he gleefully points out to the interviewer the different-colored pencils on his desk, which he uses for different types of writing.[18] One sees in his seventy-five-year-old eyes the pleased self-absorption of a child: a child, we might infer, whose mother has betrayed him by "dying," and who—in spite of other caring hands—is forced back upon himself for narcissistic satisfaction.

Apart from his memory of the violated church service, Solzhenitsyn does not admit to any negative early memories. But there is a memory he claims as pleasant, which may strike us as ambiguous. He recalls an icon that hung in a corner of his bedroom. From near the ceiling it "tilted downwards so that its holy face seemed to be gazing directly at him. At night the candle in front of it would flicker and shudder. And at that magic moment between waking and sleeping, the radiant visage seemed to detach itself and float out over his bed, like a true guardian angel. In the mornings, instructed by his grandmother Yevdokia, he would kneel before the icon and recite his prayers."[19]

It would not be surprising if the venerated image, the divine figure flickering and shuddering, aroused fear in him at times, as he lay in the gloom. The icon may have hovered, in his embryonic imagination, between threat and comfort. In its latter guise, it is reminiscent of what an English psychoanalyst has called a "transitional object," standing for the maternal breast that has been lost. "It becomes vitally important to the infant for use at the time of going to sleep, and is a defence against anxiety, especially anxiety of depressive type. . . . It must seem to give warmth, or to move, or to have texture, or to do something that seems to show it has vitality or reality of its own."[20]

The icon—what it stands for—would come to have more trustworthy, more eternal value for Solzhenitsyn than any mortal person.

For millions of children in Russia at this time, there were no comforting icons or soft toys. Prof. Dr. W. W. Krysko recalls—toward the end of the twentieth century—a terrifying scene that greeted his ten-year-old self in the spring of 1920. As the snows melted in the field outside his father's factory in Rostov, mounds of corpses and skeletons appeared. Thousands of bodies had been dumped there for eventual burial. There were horses' carcasses too, whose rib cages became shelters for hundreds of wild dogs, wolves, jackals, and hyenas. And among them lived bands of equally wild children, orphaned or abandoned.[21]

The whole of Russia was full of such children: the *bezprizornye*, the uncared-for. Lenin's wife, Krupskaya, estimated their number in 1923 as some eight million. A British journalist, Malcolm Muggeridge, describes them "going about in packs, barely articulate or recognisably human, with pinched animal faces, tangled hair and empty eyes. I saw them in Moscow and Leningrad, clustered under bridges, lurking in railway stations, suddenly emerging like a pack of wild monkeys, then scattering and disappearing."[22] Some were as young as three years old. All survived by thieving and scrounging; most, both boys and girls, were prostitutes. Eventually the state placed as many as could be caught in colonies, "children's republics." Socially and psychologically beyond rescue, these teeming victims of the Civil War became later a superb source of amoral manpower to run the camps of the Gulag Archipelago.

Compared with those millions of poor children, Solzhenitsyn had a blessed, privileged childhood. He had a close family who loved him dearly, and focused their hopes and prayers on him. Undoubtedly this was largely responsible for his firm ego and self-assurance, his strength of character. Yet it is certain he was indelibly affected by the sorrow and fear in those looking after him; while the prolonged loss of his mother must have been devastating. I think there is evidence of the "formal feeling" and defensiveness that followed his "great pain." Although *August 1914* begins with a magical evocation of the Caucasus Mountains, they are seen from a distance and the novelist was emulating a Tolstoyan opening image; apart from one visit in his sixteenth year, when he professed himself delighted with his birthplace, he showed no interest in it.

He felt respect and admiration for his mother, but in a rather detached way; and with other women in his writing, respect, admiration, desire—but at a distance. He insisted to Natalya Reshetovskaya, his first wife, that he did not want children, and there are no significant parent-children relationships in his fiction. He has, however, a close bond with the three sons of his second marriage.

He built a high wall of silence around his childhood, like the wall around his farm in Vermont, during exile, and his later dacha outside Moscow: redoubts. More important, there are psychological walls: his work schedule, in which not a minute must be unaccounted for; the vast work that *must* be finished; the intensive safeguards and stratagems to ward off unpleasant surprises; the need for secrecy and control; the stern ruling out of pleasure in favor of work.

I am reminded of Freud's description of the "anal" temperament: the repression and repudiation of the possibilities for pleasure.[23] Yet we can be thankful for Solzhenitsyn's "anal" temperament in that another of its characteristics is stubbornness. Only a superhuman stubbornness could have permitted him to go on fighting Communism, against all reason. And if, still in Freudian terms, he has sublimated Eros: sublimation be praised for giving the world *The Gulag Archipelago*.

Not long after Sanya joined his mother in Rostov, she had his portrait taken in a studio. The photograph shows him holding a toy gun, at present arms. There is a bold intelligence about the bright wide-open eyes, but the mouth, slightly downturned, gives him a vulnerable, anxious look. Undoubt-edly this is a face that says "Watch out: I'm going to do great things!" Giving a print of it many years later to his first wife, he inscribed on the back the words, "From a little robber." Maybe he had the Civil War period uncon-sciously in mind: the ever-present fear of intruders. But more fittingly he could have written "On guard."

5

R o s t o v

To this very day I love its stones.[1]
—SOLZHENITSYN

SANYA HAD ALSO, WITH TAISSIA'S ENTIRE COMPLICITY, "ROBBED"
her of a second husband and more children. The landowner's daughter was
living in miserable conditions: a leaky, one-room shack, No. 16 Soglasia
Lane, off Khalturinsky Street. Six tumbledown shacks clustered around a
rubble-strewn yard, tucked away behind the grand Cheka headquarters.
Mother and son ate, studied, slept in one small room, and shared an outside
privy with other families. Water had to be fetched from a long way away.
Even at night the stranger-mother often was out working, and when she
came home she had to do the laundry and the cleaning. No wonder she
was always getting sick.

It seems highly unlikely a child could have dealt with such a dramatic
change of environment, the loss of familiar caregivers, the resurrection of
a mother he had buried a long time ago, without disturbed behavior of
some kind. Whether through tantrums and bed-wetting or a sullen silence,
did "His Majesty the child" (Sigmund Freud) make her feel so guilty that
she took a vow to sacrifice herself for him? If she remarried, she said, she
was afraid the stepfather would treat Alexander harshly: which may suggest
he had become a "difficult" child. He later came to feel that her decision
had been bad for both of them; a husband could have spared her some of
her burdens, and given him some much needed discipline.

Then, just when he was settling down with her a little, she was telling
him he had to go to school. . . . It was so scary, for a time, that even their
awful little shack began to seem desirable.

But school, once he had settled, brought him a much grander house—
or so he was enthusiastically drilled to believe—than Aunt Marusha's house
in Kislovodsk: the house that Lenin built.

By 1926, when Taissia led her son to school for the first time, Lenin had become a saintly relic, his mummified corpse displayed in a temporary wooden mausoleum on Red Square. His stern image was everywhere, and multiplying like fetal cells. In portraits his eyes looked large, clear, visionary; but a photographer, A. I. Kuprin, had observed them as slanting, often screwed up, with pupils so small they were little more than pinpricks; and they were the color, he reported, of a lemur. A writer, Ariadna Tyrkova, who had met him often, invoked a different animal: "Lenin was an evil man. And he had the evil eyes of a wolf."[2] Lemur or wolf, he had in him the mixed blood of Slav, Kalmyk (Asian), German, and Jew: so, in a way, embodying the Russian experience.

Lenin's brother, Alexander Ulyanov, had been executed in 1887 for plotting to kill Alexander III. The revolutionary could have saved his life by asking for clemency, but bravely chose not to. The Tsar asked Madame Ulyanova to forgive him for taking the life of her son not long after she had been widowed. Vladimir Ulyanov, aka Lenin, would not waste too much time offering clemency on request, or asking his victims' mothers to forgive him. Indeed, thousands of mothers were his victims too. And the city of Ulyanovsk (formerly Simbrisk) spent millions of rubles in 1921 erecting a giant statue of Marx—the First Person in the new Trinity of Marx, Engels, Lenin—when famine was laying waste to the country, and demented mothers were eating their own children.

Against enormous odds, Lenin achieved his vision: persuading a nation occupying a seventh of the earth's surface that any moral law could be broken in the interest of one class. Within a few years he had prefigured all the evils that Stalinism would consolidate: unlimited power of the Party and the bureaucracy; total regimentation of public life and thought as a substitute for religion; the liquidation of "alien elements"; an all-embracing organ of state terror, with a vast system of slave laborcamps throughout Siberia and the North.

If the people threatened this happiness he planned for them, they would have to be punished. Scores of peasant revolts were extinguished. The vast unpopularity of the Bolsheviks shook Lenin, and forced him to reintroduce private enterprise on a small scale, under the NEP (New Economic Plan). But he had no intention, had he lived, of letting this compromise continue indefinitely. As he wrote to Kamenev: "It is the biggest mistake to think that NEP will put an end to the terror. We shall return to the terror, and to economic terror."[3]

Taissia, born to luxury, did not easily flourish in the dynamic new order; she was hesitant, could not make up her mind. She talked to Sanya about the father he had never known, and showed him his photograph. That was all well enough, but he looked quite soft, and his mama confirmed that he was. Lenin was strong and decisive. Sanya's teachers assured the children over and over that Vladimir Ilyich was their kindly, caring friend; yet he could be a scourge to those who would harm these little ones: you only had to look at his picture, boys and girls—those burning eyes, that outthrust chin and flung-out arm, defending you! . . .

"A huge country, basically Christian, had been made over into a nursery for rearing a new breed of men under conditions of widescale terror and atheism. A new society, governed by primitives, began taking shape. Without asking the consent of the peasants or anyone else, the party heads, to achieve their own ends, unleashed their thugs over our vast land and fettered it in slavery. The young Communist state proceeded to mutilate and crush whatever opposed it, secular or sacred, to bury human life under atrocities."[4]

And they were not even granted the dignity, the sole dignity that slaves have, of knowing they were being oppressed. Rather they were being assured they had entered paradise (though of course it would take time and great effort to realize it fully) and must constantly praise it. Not even the ancient Egyptians, as they whipped their Israelite slaves, had the nerve to pretend that those being whipped were the new rulers.

Rostov was known as "The Gateway to the Caucasus." Situated high on the right bank of the Don, it has a long open seaway, through the Gulf of Taganrog, the Sea of Azov, and the Black Sea, to the distant Mediterranean, and takes on some of its warmth, color, and vibrancy. Founded by the Empress Elizaveta in 1749, it grew steadily to a population of ten thousand a century later; then it surged to over a quarter of a million by 1914, exceeding by far that of any other North Caucasian city. It had a flourishing export trade in grain and other agricultural produce, and imported a vast array of industrial products. An English company, Sidney, James and Co., had been established in the town as early as 1778. The first steamer used for regular navigational use along the Don was the *Donetz*, built in England. The French laid down water mains, Belgians dredged the waterways. Before the Great War, in Rostov's multilingual markets one could find Tottenham Court Road furniture, Sheffield cutlery, Persian rugs, Caucasian silks, Turkish sweetmeats, and the most modern farm machines. Most of the machinery for Zakhar Shcherbak's efficient estate would have come through Rostov. Around the beginning of the twentieth century, a crude frontier town, with fuel lamps lighting the corners of dirty streets, became transformed into a city of broad avenues and electric street lighting.

The adventurous Rhoda Power, traveling from Newcastle in the north of England to Rostov in the middle of a major war, was surprised to find that "there were more Greeks, Armenians, and Southern Jews than Russians and Cossacks, and that society was divided into numberless cliques."[5] Catherine the Great had allowed thousands of Armenians and many Greeks to resettle from the Crimea after the Russo-Turkish War of 1768–74; the Armenians had founded an independent township, Nakhichevan, which by the twentieth century had become an elegant suburb to the more shabby, ill-planned

Rostov. Like some Slavic Marseilles, Rostov had its problems; at the turn of the century it had the world's third highest cholera death rate after Calcutta and Shanghai.

Rostov was notorious also for its thievery and brigandage. A favorite target was the splendid Caucasian wine being moved by train northward for the imperial wine cellars in St. Petersburg. While the trains halted in Rostov station for the paperwork to be done, handing the cargo on from one private railroad company to another, thieves skillfully drilled holes through the floorboards and then into the barrels. It was beneath the imperial dignity to lodge a complaint. The wine was sold in Rostov at cut-rate, and it became a joke to ask one's host, "From which bore hole did this exceptionally good drop of wine originate?" Street "muggings" were common, but it was an honor among the thieves not to harm old people or children.[6]

While the native Rostovian Professor Wladimir Krysko recalls little anti-Semitism, owing to the city's multi-ethnic population, the English Miss Power was amazed to find how much the Jews were hated. This suggests the hatred may have been covert, and more apparent to the English outsider than to someone who was part Jewish himself. Peasants would spit on the ground, the governess observed, if anyone mentioned a Jew by name; and the educated classes also kept them at arm's length. She once asked her pupil who had played tennis with her that afternoon, and the girl replied, "Oh, Pyotr Petrovich, Marie Vassilyevna, and a Jew."[7] The Jews were faceless ones. After the Revolution, one of the first changes she noticed was that there were more, and more self-confident, Jews on the streets.

These Russian Jews were coming into their own. "It was not a matter of any great note," writes Professor Krysko, "that Jews were playing a large role in the remaking of Russia because Jews represented the only group of people destined by their own history to lead a New Order which was going to do away with interference in government by national and religious groups and promote international brotherhood."[8] It *was* of note, of course, to those bitterly opposed to Jews, or the Bolshevik form of "international brotherhood," or both.

Rostov, its terraces falling away to the broad harbor, struck Rhoda Power as like a Cubist painting, "all higgledy-piggledy, a jumble of vivid colours, domes, and oddly shaped houses." Next to a large and ornate mansion with statues at the door there might be a tiny wooden hut thatched with straw and built half underground, so that the windows were on a level with the road. Some poor workman lived there who refused to be bought up. Inside there was hardly any light; children, poultry, and dogs crawled about indiscriminately. Always there were color prints of the Tsar, icons, a samovar in pride of place in the corner, and a stove on which the old folk slept. In similarly democratic contrast, rich emporiums stood beside tiny stalls where peasants chattered like rooks, pressing bargains on the passersby.

She felt sorry for the servants, who on the whole were badly treated. They rarely undressed to sleep, went about mostly barefoot, not being able to afford shoes. Hardly a servant in the city could read or write; one of the few genuine achievements of the Revolution was a campaign to make the people literate. The maids played cards, did a little sewing, believed in fortune-tellers totally, and survived by cheating their employers. And the male servants drank themselves regularly into a stupor. Some were so ignorant they did not know what the word "republic" meant; "Who's this Republic who's taken over from the Tsar, then?" "Maybe she's a woman." "Well, that's okay, as long as she's got good tits. Hooray!"

The warm breath of Asia touched the busy city. Wladimir Krysko remembers "camel caravans laden with tea from China and Mongolia . . . winding their way wearily along the streets after the long journey across the steppes." They would halt at a water cistern, and the local children would rush up to be given *makavki* (crushed nuts and poppyseed in honey) and *kumis* (fermented mare's milk) by the friendly Kalmyk and Kirgiz camel drivers. Professor Krysko also recalls hearing, at night, a sudden clanking sound, silencing everyone. It was the sound of chains being dragged along Pushkinskaya Street by prisoners as they were marched to the railroad station. A detachment of Don Cossacks surrounded them, each carrying a burning torch in one hand and his naked sword, resting on his shoulder, in the other, "its tip moving in time to the marching feet. The prisoners would be singing one of their deeply moving songs which made the scene more like an act from an opera than the stark reality it actually was of a gang of political prisoners and petty criminals beginning a journey to exile in Siberia." Onlookers would give the prisoners money, food, and small comforts—even bottles of vodka.[9]

Prisoners of the Bolsheviks were not given food and vodka, nor did their departure to Siberia or Hades resemble an opera.

Asked to define the spirit of Rostov, Solzhenitsyn has called it "commercial." But in reality that spirit was hard to pin down. It could be revolutionary— thirty thousand workers went on strike in 1902; yet the port became a center for White resistance, and was nicknamed White Guard City. It could be, to different observers, anti-Semitic or tolerant. For a time, during the Brest-Litovsk negotiations of 1917, the German army had illegally occupied Rostov, and most of its inhabitants—like most Parisians in 1940 –greeted the conquerors with equanimity, happy to have order imposed. Rostov was raffish, independent, moneymaking, competitive, relatively democratic, and with a touch of hedonism—before the Revolution and Civil War brought economic and human disaster.

By the time Sanya started to live there, the city had begun to recover some of its old buoyancy. There were Greek and Italian ships in the harbor, horse cabbies vied with motor cars on the road, church bells continued to ring, and the ancient place names had not yet yielded to the *Prospekt Lenina* and its Marxist comrades. The NEP, and the natural moneymaking energies of the natives, seemed to promise a buoyant future.[10]

Sanya was to spend most of his childhood and youth in the city; yet he never fully gave himself to it. His imagination would be drawn further north, to the more understated Russian landscape, temperament, and speech. The rich southern form of Russian does not appeal to him, and the people are too boisterous and cosmopolitan for his taste. Yet he could say of Rostov, "To this very day I love its stones."

In *August 1914* he describes how Ksenia Tomchak / Taissia Shcherbak's heart always beat faster on returning to it. Especially in early morning, "when Sadovaya Street was fresh and clean in the deep shade of trees as it climbed the hill towards Dolomanovsky, and the cab-driver furiously put on speed so as not to be overtaken by the tram. . . ." She loved the special latticework bridges, which were put across flooded streets in the rainstorms, and were kept on the sidewalks when the weather was dry. And along Taganrogsky, there are the fish stalls with "their eternal reek from the huge bream, carp and *suly* which were abundantly displayed right on the pavement, and it was at this time, in the morning, that the whole of the night's catch, as yet unsold, was lying still alive, silvery, twitching and splashing across the counters."[11]

Rostov is evoked in only a few pages of this very long novel: so, evidently, it hardly filled Solzhenitsyn's imagination as Dublin filled Joyce's. The pre-revolutionary city is offered to us in a bravura cameo, fresh and affectionate; yet toward a place in which he had so many powerful first experiences—of books, friendship, music, theater, love and passion, academic achievement and literary creation—one might have expected him to feel a stronger pull. Again there is a suspicion of a defense at work.

Solzhenitsyn has said scornfully of his early schooling that it was mostly play, and consequently he learned as little as do modern American children. Despite their success with adult literacy, the Bolsheviks abandoned by 1923 their declared policy of free and universal education. In the relatively prosperous years of 1925–26, per capita allocations for education were a third lower than those of 1913. In 1928, the government was spending only a quarter of the sums that had been spent by the tsarist government on secondary education.[12] Teachers—downgraded to "school workers"—were miserably paid; they were not allowed to discipline pupils, assign them homework, or set examinations and grades. Students' progress was to be judged by a collective. Anatoli Lunacharsky, the Commissar for "Narkompros" (Enlightenment), sought to introduce on a mass scale the principles of progressive Western education, such as Dewey's "activity school," and the Montessori method. More radical voices called for the abolition of schools and the shift of education to collective farms and factories.[13]

As the failures of this experimentation became apparent, more traditional methods were introduced, together with a greater stress on indoctrination. Solzhenitsyn recalls how stirred he was by the parades, the drums, the tales of the heroic revolutionaries and Red Army.[14]

The little boy helped his mother to bury his father's medals. That was an imperial war, and his father was an officer. If only he had fought in the Red Army! Then he could have taken those medals to school. . . . He felt torn in the way radical Americans might be, contemplating a dead father's Vietnam medals.

But toward Lenin—thanks to teachers, Komsomol leaders, banners, and statues—Sanya felt nothing but reverence. What a man! That flung-up fist and outthrust jaw! Such energy! Sanya knew only one man who had a similar energy: his grandfather—who sometimes said very unpleasant things about Lenin.

He went, in 1926–27, to stay with his grandparents in Gulkevichi, the village near the lost estate, the first two summer holidays of his schooling. He was happy there, playing with the village boys; but even more he enjoyed wandering away on his own, into the countryside, communing with nature. His imagination was expanding; and he felt compelled to that urge which never left him—to be alone, to reflect.

His grandfather was burning with energy and rage still; and surely took Sanya to gaze through wrought-iron railings at the manor house stolen from him. Zakhar resembled the murderous old man in Yeats's *Purgatory* who brings his plebeian son to look at the ruined ghostly house of his parents. The old man's drunken, brutal father had degraded his cultured wife and burned the house down. Here, in Russia, there were fifteen or twenty million ghosts, just from the Civil War and the famine alone. Zakhar might have said to God, "Mankind can do no more. Appease / The misery of the living and the remorse of the dead." But probably he was too aware of his own misery to worry overmuch about Russia's.

In any case, mankind—as represented by the Communists and their Nazi opponents in Germany—was about to show it could do *much* more.

Stooping old peasants who had once trembled before the master's stern voice and the crack of his whip now shuffled in with a gift of goat's cheese for Zakhar and Yevdokia's dinner. Gnarled hands stroked and blessed the young boy's head; and how like the master he was! So quick and energetic and determined.

Sanya learned a lot more from later holiday visits to Aunt Ira and Uncle Romasha. They were constantly on the move in these years; after Novocherkassk they moved to Yeisk, a small fishing town seventy miles down the Gulf of Taganrog from Rostov. Roman was cool and distant, but Irina could see that her nephew's intelligence was flowering as she had hoped and expected; she loved having him with her. She had been the first woman to take him to church; now that antireligious fervor was abating somewhat she took him again, and showed him how the history and culture of Russia was bound up with Orthodoxy.

At least as valuable to him was her splendid library. Through all her travels and trials she had managed to keep her books together. In the sleepy seaside town there was little to occupy a boy but to swim in the harbor, talk to Aunt Ira, listen to her stories of the great estate, and read. He read the Russian classics: Pushkin, Gogol, Tolstoy, Dostoyevsky, Turgenev. Although he would later lament that he did not have a wide knowledge of foreign literature, he read and was impressed by Shakespeare, Schiller, Dickens, and Jack London—that oddly perennial favorite with Russians. He first read *War and Peace*, he says, when he was ten, and reread it several times in successive summers.[15]

Tolstoy became a central figure in his imagination, and he may not have been much older when he started to dream of writing an epic novel that would make sense of his Leninist century. An ambition to become a writer—an important writer at that—interwove with dreams of becoming a priest (Aunt Ira's influence) or a general. He could have echoed the self-belief of Sigmund Freud: "I seem to remember that through the whole of this time [adolescence] there ran a premonition of a task ahead."[16] Freud too sometimes dreamed of military prowess, and later called himself a *conquistador;* he had writing ambitions, but settled for being a secular priest, a psychoanalyst. Freud ascribed this sense of destiny and self-worth to the assurance of a mother's absolute love; the ceaseless toil and sacrifice of Taissia, and summertime spoiling by Aunt Ira, must have given Sanya a similar confidence—though tempered by the early fears and losses that Freud escaped.

Sanya seems to have become so assured in himself that he "felt sorry" for his class at school if an illness prevented him from attending. He had the grandiose feeling that if he wasn't there they somehow ceased to exist. It was a form of narcissism that Tolstoy had experienced in his youth, when often he would whirl around to see if he could catch sight of the nothingness. Once, Sanya's classmates *proved* they still existed by visiting the sick boy at his home. One of them, Laura Shatkin, remembers that, while everyone was undergoing hardship, Sanya lived in worse conditions than others. "He lived in a small room, with poor furniture, though there were lots of books. He lived poorer than other people. He didn't appear embarrassed, but pleased to see us."[17]

Solzhenitsyn would become a very effective army officer; and it is clear, from his mastery of strategy and large-scale movement of forces in *August 1914*, that he could easily have become a general. His books serve a spiritual, priestly function. He would achieve every one of his childhood ambitions.

Taissia's closest friends were the daughter and son-in-law of her old headmistress, Madame Andreyeva. Despite her liberal ideals, which she had combined with stern discipline, Madame Andreyeva had seen her excellent school closed down for ideological reasons. Now an old lady, she sat at home playing endless games of patience. Her two sons, White Guard officers, had vanished in the Civil War.

There remained her daughter, Zhenia, whose bedroom Taissia had used while a schoolgirl. They had become great friends later, when they were both studying in Moscow. Zhenia had fallen in love and got herself pregnant. This had taxed her mother's liberalism exceedingly—she had been horrified. However, the young couple had married, and Madame Andreyeva had cause to be grateful. Vladimir Fedorovsky was a warmhearted, cultured, hardworking man, and his profession as a mining engineer attracted high esteem and reward in the new state. Madame Andreyeva had lost her school apartment, but her daughter's, to which she moved, was just as comfortable and spacious. The family was privileged; Michael Scammell's comment that "apart from the loss of the school and the disappearance of Zhenia's two brothers during the Civil War, the Andreyevs and Fedorovskys had come through the Revolution quite well"[18] is true in terms of living conditions; yet lost sons weigh heavily on the spirit. A nice apartment on broad Sredni Prospekt hardly compensated.

But for Sanya Solzhenitsyn this apartment, with a balcony overlooking a secluded yard, became home away from home. He would come here after school to wait for his mother; with the Fedorovskys' children, Misha and Lyalya, he would design illustrated newspapers and journals. Since his mother often had to work in the evenings too, he spent a lot of time here. After dinner, Vladimir Fedorovsky would normally withdraw to his study to work late into the night; but on Saturdays and holidays he would throw a party, "let his hair down." There would be cards and charades, and dancing to the piano; plenty to eat and drink. He was thin and dapper, carrying one shoulder higher than another; had pince-nez and a habitual stoop and a slightly melancholy smile. A very Chekhovian figure; salt of the Russian earth.

It was because of Fedorovsky, and also a kindly Jewish engineer called Alexander Arkhangorodsky, father of another schoolfriend of his mother, that Solzhenitsyn developed an idealization. "It so happens," he wrote in The Gulag Archipelago, "that I was brought up in an engineering milieu, and I can remember the engineers of the twenties perfectly—that candidly luminous intellect, that unrestrained and inoffensive humour, that freedom and breadth of thought, the ease with which they moved from one field of engineering to another, or in general from technical subjects to current affairs and art. And they were so well-educated, with such good taste. Their Russian was excellent, rhythmical and correct, and devoid of popular slang. Some played an instrument, others painted, and one and all had the stamp of spiritual nobility on their faces."[19] So profound was his admiration that when he read in Izvestia (he became very early a compulsive newspaper reader) of engineers found guilty of sabotage, he knew it was not true.

The children also listened in to the adults, at the Fedorovskys, as they discussed serious issues. Yevgeny Shklavresky, several years older than Solzhenitsyn, recalls being present at some of these evenings with his mother, who worked with Fedorovsky:

We drank tea; there were several people—a dermatologist, a

mathematics professor, an actor from the musical comedy theater, and close friends and relatives of the Fedorovskys, including an aunt from Novocherkassk. This aunt thought she knew a lot about music, and we used to tease her. There was a grand piano; she'd say to me, "Play some Beethoven"; I'd play Prokofiev, or something, and she'd say, "Wonderful! Oh, how I love Beethoven!" I remember Solzhenitsyn's mother being there; she was very simple, modest—sat quietly. She always brought her son: a fair-haired boy; I'm afraid I didn't pay much attention to him. I remember a scarf around his head, because he had struck his head. He was too young to participate in the conversation. He smiled, he didn't interrupt. Everyone discussed literature, art, music, religion. . . . They were very warm, friendly people, the Fedorovskys. . . . [20]

Shklavresky, ill, paper-thin, and trembling in 1995, could not remember seeing the old lady, Madame Andreyeva. Probably she preferred sitting somewhere quietly, playing patience; grieving for her sons, wondering what had happened to them.

In the Fedorovsky milieu, there was a sense of quiet optimism about the future, but everyone was anti-Bolshevik, and did not try to hide it from Sanya. He felt an enormous tension between home and school. He now says this tension was all-important in his life and work.

Taissia's one precious possession, out of all the possessions and dreams of her youth, was a grand piano of her own. It had to be stored elsewhere; there was no room in the shack for anything but a table in the middle, a bed, a divan, a stove, a study table for Sanya, and a dressing table with a mirror. Now she was being told her shack was going to be demolished. If she sold her grand, however, she might be able to afford one of the apartments that the City Cooperative was building. It was a terrible decision to have to make. She was tormented by it.

Finally, her heart weighing like a stone, she let the grand go, and put the money down for one of the apartments. Over thirty, she felt old, pinched and lined; she found it hard to smile. But she would sacrifice everything for her clever son.

The first apartments, hers among them, were to be ready in two years. But then, when they had been built, someone bribed an official to let him have the one assigned for Taissia. She was told there was a further delay, but more were being constructed. Five years passed; still nothing; Taissia requested her money back. Another year passed. By the time her money had been repaid its value had been reduced to less than half because of inflation. Buying a flat with it was now out of the question.

The only tiny comfort was that they didn't, after all, demolish the shack.°

°It was still there, indeed, in 1995; and a neighbor of theirs in the 1930s was still trying to be rehoused. . . . The building where the Fedorovskys had lived had fallen, by 1995, into as ruinous a

She was as haunted by her piano as Akaky Akakievich by his stolen overcoat in Gogol's short story. The loss gnawed at her.

Solzhenitsyn related the infinitely sad and very Soviet story of the piano and the flat to an interviewer,[21] yet his former wife, Natalya Reshetovskaya, who was very fond of his mother, denies that Taissia ever sold her piano.[22] She blames a mistranslation. "We live lives based on selected fictions." I believe the story. Even were it not literally true, it carries essential truth. Taissia's life was desperately deprived. Her photographic portrait in maturity tells the tale.

It is puzzling why Roman and Irina didn't help more, at least during the twenties. They were having to struggle, like almost everyone of their class who wasn't an engineer; but their house in Yeisk was still comfortable. In 1930, however, they had to sell the house and move into an apartment. What, for them, was a decline, would have been for Roman's sister and her son a wonderful improvement. Roman, at fifty-two, took his first job, driving for a local firm, and later drove a bus. Long gone, the days of the white Rolls, the Daimler sports car, the Moscow–Petersburg rally, and the purple room at the Louvre.

In the summer of 1930, Sanya went with his mother to Georgievsk to visit Aunt Maria and her family, and Zakhar and Yevdokia, who were again living with them. The old man was in a terrible state, depressed at having nothing—no money, no work, no home. He was worse off than that herdsboy in the Tauria, who at least had youth and strength. He was sunk in silent gloom most of the time, though with occasional bursts of violent rage against the Bolsheviks for their theft of his property.

During their holiday, Taissia took Sanya on what would prove to be their last visit to his father's grave. The next time Solzhenitsyn came, he would see not gravestones and grass but a sports stadium.

As if she knew an era was ending in this visit to Georgievsk, Taissia made a detour to let him see, for the first and only time, his father's birthplace, Sablia. Time and typhus had taken away most of the boy's relatives, but he met two of his uncles: Konstantin, now a gray-haired sixty-year-old, and Isaaki's half brother, Ilya. The farm seemed desolate. Sheep wandered over the open steppe. The visit made little overt impression on the boy.[23]

A few months later, Konstantin and Ilya vanished into the Siberian permafrost.

---

state as the Solzhenitsyns' slum quarters. It housed communal "apartments," dirty and rotting, slum housing for people who seemed without hope.

6

A Wolf to Man

The idiocy of village life . . .
—KARL MARX

KONSTANTIN AND ILYA SOLZHENITSYN WERE VICTIMS OF ONE OF
the great wars of the twentieth century, a war in which only one side was
armed. Robert Conquest begins his powerful and passionate book *The Harvest of Sorrow* with this devastating summary:

"Fifty years ago as I write these words, the Ukraine and the Ukrainian,
Cossack and other areas to its east—a great stretch of territory with some
forty million inhabitants—was like one vast Belsen. A quarter of the rural
population, men, women and children, lay dead or dying, the rest in various
stages of debilitation with no strength to bury their families or neighbours.
At the same time (as at Belsen), well-fed squads of police or party officials
supervised the victims."[1]

The evidence for what happened is as cumulative and overwhelming as
the evidence for the Jewish Holocaust; yet for decades the facts were as
distorted and suppressed as the holocaust would have been had Nazi Germany
won the Second World War. "One thing is striking," wrote a Soviet
author in 1972: "in not a single textbook on contemporary history will you
find the merest reference to 1933, the year marked by a terrible tragedy."[2]
In the West, liberal educated opinion did not want to hear anything bad
about the brave Soviet experiment; and, like the Auschwitz gas chambers,
the tales brought back by a few honest journalists and writers were vastly
beyond a good liberal's imagination, so were not believed.

Lenin had warned that terror, and economic terror, must and would
return. Possibly he would have been more temperate than Stalin, yet he
too would have known that the peasants had to be crushed. The Russian
intelligentsia, from which the liberal and socialist movements of the nineteenth
century sprang, had contradictory ideas about the peasants. In one
sense they saw them as the soul of Russia, patient, enduring, and sincere,

free of the falsities brought by wealth. "He does not try to seem what he is not," wrote Alexander Herzen. The *narodniki* (from *narod*, people) went into the villages in the 1870s, hoping to stir revolutionary thoughts in these good, simple souls; but found no response. Mostly, in fact, the result was mutual antagonism. The *narodniki* movement had largely died out by the time the idealistic Isaaki Solzhenitsyn felt its appeal. But Isaaki came from the peasants himself, and understood them; the urban intellectuals concluded merely that the peasants were backward and mulish, the "dark people." The founder of Russian Marxism, Georgi Plekhanov, described them as "barbarian tillers of the soil, cruel and merciless, beasts of burden whose life provided no opportunity for the luxury of thought," and Lenin saw them as "fiercely and meanly individualistic." For Stalin, so Khrushchev tells us, peasants were scum.

A scum comprising 90 percent of the Russian people.

The poorer ones could be herded into collective farms; but those with a little more enterprise, the so-called *kulaks*,° were a class enemy that had to be destroyed, either by deportation or death. Most of them had only a few cows and horses. Only one in a hundred farms had more than one hired worker. The average kulak's income was lower than that of the average rural official persecuting him. In reality the term was a mere convenience, as vague as "Fascist" would become. Any peasant whatever was liable to de-kulakization.

The humane Maxim Gorky, in 1922, had expressed the hope that "the uncivilized, stupid, turgid people in the Russian villages will die out, all those almost terrifying people . . . and a new race of literate, rational, energetic people will take their place." Now Stalin was intent on granting his wish.

Stalin could kill two birds with one stone. The second bird was the Ukraine. Ukrainians stubbornly went on struggling to assert their linguistic and cultural separation from Russia. One of the central tenets of Marxism-Leninism was that the proletariat has no country. Nationhood was a characteristic of capitalism, said Lenin, and the aim of socialism was to merge nations. Classless, urban, international, without private conscience or private values, without property, without a spiritual dimension—this was to be the new *Homo sovieticus*.

On 29 December 1929 Stalin announced laconically in *Pravda*: "We have gone over from a policy of limiting the exploiting tendencies of the kulak to a policy of liquidating the kulak as a class." On 30 January 1942, ten days after the Wannsee Conference had reaffirmed the "final solution," Hitler proclaimed in a broadcast speech: "The result of this war will be the complete annihilation of the Jews." The latter, a genocide of race, the former, of class, though also with a nationalist (anti-Ukrainian) element.

°Literally, *kulak* means "fist"—i.e., "tightfist."

The victims, those who were not summarily dealt with, were ordered to leave their villages, where they had lived all their lives, and were sent off to the taiga and the tundra. Women gave birth on the way, and the guards threw the dead babies out of the train. Up to 20 percent of the deportees died en route. If there was no established settlement at the end of the journey, they were set down in the frozen wilderness. The weakest and youngest died. By 1935 it is estimated that out of eleven million deportees a third, mostly children, had perished; three or four million more survived a few years longer before succumbing.

Vasily Grossman, a Jew who also wrote powerfully about the Holocaust, has described a typical departure scene:

> From our village . . . the "kulaks" were driven out on foot. They took what they could carry on their backs: bedding, clothing. The mud was so deep it pulled the boots off their feet. It was terrible to watch them. They marched along in a column and looked back at their huts, and their bodies still held the warmth from their own stoves. What pain they must have suffered! After all, they had been born in those houses; they had given their daughters in marriage in those cabins. They had heated up their stoves, and the cabbage soup they had cooked was left there behind them. The milk had not been drunk, and smoke was still rising from their chimneys. The women were sobbing—but were afraid to scream. The Party activists didn't give a damn about them. We drove them off like geese. And behind came the cart, and on it were Pelageya the blind, and old Dmitri Ivanovich, who had not left his hut for ten whole years, and Marusya the Idiot, a paralytic, a kulak's daughter who had been kicked by a horse in childhood and had never been normal since.[3]

Some, taken to the far Siberian North, were shipped down the great rivers by raft, and were mostly lost in the rapids. Imagine a man, woman, and two or three children, plucked from the mild Kuban, hurtling down the icy, wild Yenisei.

But we should steel ourselves against bourgeois compassion. Or so argued Ilya Ehrenburg, writing as Robert Conquest says with "exceptional frankness" in a novel of 1934. "Not one of them was guilty of anything; but they belonged to a class that was guilty of everything."[4]

What is it about the twentieth-century mind that it so readily dealt with masses, categories, rather than considering people as individuals?

In July 1932, decisions were taken which ensured that millions from the Ukraine, Kuban, Don, and Lower Volga would die of starvation in the next year. Collectivization and dekulakization had wrought havoc with the harvest, and poorish weather had further damaged it; nevertheless, the famine was deliberate; in those regions—and those regions only—that the regime wanted to lay waste, impossibly large requisitions of grain for the towns were ordered. Bands of activists were sent into the villages to make sure every last ear of wheat was collected. Watchtowers were erected in the fields. The peasants toiled, and starved. They had witnessed the deportations; fools that we were, wrote Grossman, we thought there could be no worse fate than that.

Women and children whose limbs were swelling up, and who did not have the strength to rise, were threatened with shooting unless they gave up hoarded grain. "In the terrible spring of 1933," writes Kopelev, Solzhenitsyn's prisoner-friend at the Marfino *sharashka*, "I saw people dying from hunger. I saw women and children with distended bellies, turning blue, still breathing but with vacant, lifeless eyes. And corpses—corpses in ragged sheepskin coats and cheap felt boots; corpses in peasant huts, in the melting snow of the old Vologda, under the bridges of Kharkov . . . I saw all of this and did not go out of my mind or commit suicide. Nor did I curse those who had sent me out to take away the peasants' grain in the winter, and in the spring to persuade the barely walking, skeleton-thin or sickly-swollen people to go into the fields in order to 'fulfil the bolshevik sowing plan in shock-worker style.'

"Nor did I lose my faith. As before, I believed because I wanted to believe."[5]

He "reasoned"—that potent twentieth-century word!—that the ends justified the means; that for the sake of the triumph of Communism everything was permissible, even to destroy millions of people. "All is permitted, if God does not exist."

Kopelev was unmistakably a noble individual. He suffered imprisonment for the "crime" of trying to save POWs and German women and children from Red Army atrocities. Solzhenitsyn and numerous others have borne witness to his human decency. Yet even he was caught up during his student years in an evil that, as he confessed, could never be expiated, only lived with.

During the collectivization and famine, idealistic Communists, as well as intellectuals from other countries, fell prey to the same disease that consumed the Nazis. Indeed, there were doubtless a few—a very few—SS officers who sincerely believed that humanity would ultimately gain from the liquidation of the Jewish race; SS men who suffered while doing their duty, but believed "the ends justified the means." Himmler congratulated the SS, and himself, for having "stuck it out" and remained "decent fellows." We could say—he told the weary soldiers—"that we have fulfilled this most difficult duty for the love of our people. And our spirit, our soul, our character has not suffered injury from it."[6] It was indeed a remarkable achievement on the part of the SS if their souls suffered no injury. Likewise the Communist activists. Two leading lights of the Labour movement in Britain, Sidney and Beatrice Webb, in fact, congratulated the Soviet *Einsatzgruppen* in similar terms: "Strong must have been the faith and resolute the will of the men who, in the interest of what seemed to them the public good, could take so momentous a decision." This from a book called *Soviet Communism: A New Civilization.*

The village schools were closed, as the famine took hold, and the teachers withdrew to the cities. What was the point of teaching those doomed to die? The starved victims ate everything: all the worms, leather, glue. Some mothers cradled their aged, birdlike children and went on telling them stories even when they could hardly speak themselves; others started to hate the children who were making them suffer so much; they ran away from their endless crying. At first they went to the railway line and held up their ghastly, swollen-bellied children, pleading with the travelers for help. A few crusts were sometimes thrown out. But then the order came that the train guards should pull down the blinds while traveling through the country. But the final stage, Vasily Grossman observed, was when they just lay in their huts and did not even wish to eat.

Conscience, where it exists, can be eased by the argument that those being killed are not really human. The Nazis were masters of this; whether the victims were "life unworthy of life," the severely handicapped, or simply a Jewish bacillus. Again a "bacillus" himself, Grossman relates how small children became "kulak bastards," "bloodsuckers," "swine." A woman activist explained, "I told myself they weren't human beings, they were kulaks." The military personnel guarding them on their monthlong journey "were not vicious. They merely treated them like cattle, and that was that." Conveniently, people in extremis often behave in a way which supports the idea that they are subhuman. Those who became cannibals, for instance; women who went mad and cooked and ate their own children. Hundreds of Ukrainian cannibals were reportedly serving life sentences in Baltic–White Sea Canal prison camps in the late thirties.

The vigilantes staring down from their watchtowers to make sure some woman wasn't stealing a few grains of corn for a dying child did not need to become cannibals. They had plenty of food. A Party restaurant in Pohrebyshcha . . . "Day and night it was guarded by militia keeping the starving peasants and their children away. . . . At very low prices, white bread, meat, poultry, canned fruit and delicacies, wines and sweets were served to the district bosses. At the same time, the employees of the dining hall were issued the special Party-worker ration, which contained twenty different articles of food.

"Around these oases famine and death were raging."[7]

As in the Holocaust, living people were sometimes thrown into mass graves, to save an extra lorry trip. The Kuban and the Don suffered extremely. Every day two mysterious, empty trains would leave Kavkaz, moving in the direction of Rostov. A few hours later they returned, full of corpses of famine victims collected from various villages; the dead were secretly buried near some quarries. Even some of the North Caucasian cities (though not, it would seem, Rostov) experienced famine; 50,000 of a population of 140,000 died in Stavropol, and similar numbers in Krasnodar. The Cossacks had been largely wiped out, from death and deportation. A Party official reported desolation in the countryside; the fertile land overgrown with weeds; hedges, fences, and gates had gone, used for fuel; houses falling to pieces. No work, no grain, no cattle.

Inevitably the former Shcherbak estate, in Stavropol province—what was left of it after the destruction of the Civil War period—would have shared in the devastation.

Total deaths, from deportation and famine, 1930–34, are estimated to have been at least fourteen million. Around seven million died in the famine, including five million in the Ukraine and a million in the North Caucasus. Three million of the famine victims were children.

However, George Bernard Shaw "did not see a single under-nourished person in Russia, young or old. Were they padded? Were their hollow cheeks distended by pieces of india rubber inside?"[8] Friends had loaded him up with canned food, but he had thrown it all out of the window on crossing the border, he told a Russian audience. There were gasps; but they failed to discourage the jovial speaker. He knew the tales of shortages were "poppycock"—hadn't he just had a marvelous meal? Before leaving for home, he told his hosts: "When you carry your experiment to its final triumph, and I know that you will, we in the West, we who are still playing at socialism, will have to follow in your footsteps whether we like it or no."[9] They should have asked the keen-eyed Irishman to man one of the watchtowers. The British embassy lamented that it was impossible to persuade educated opinion in the democracies that anything terrible was taking place. In the USA, "it was a bad time for a writer to become known as an anti-Communist or even as a member of a dissenting radical faction. . . . To have one's name on a Communist-sponsored appeal or protest considerably enhanced one's standing in the cultural community."[10] Artists, by repute so independent-minded, love to huddle together under a left-leaning shelter. Diana Trilling, who learned quickly recalls with shame the raised armed, fist-clenched oath of allegiance to the Revolution, the singing of "Arise, ye prisoners of starvation. / Arise, ye wretched of the earth! . . ." The idiocy of *urban* life, perhaps.

Arthur Koestler, who visited Russia in 1932–33, saw for himself the prisoners of Soviet starvation; saw dead children who "looked like embryos from alcohol bottles." In Kharkov, he felt how unreal it was to be reading the local papers, full of young people smiling under banners, giant combines in the Urals, rewards to Stakhanovite workers—and not one word about the famine, the epidemics, the dying out of whole villages. A blanket of silence covered the whole enormous land.[11]

Starting in 1928 there had been a renewed assault on religion. Priests were deported, and sometimes shot; churches were closed, and turned into workers' clubs, cultural institutes, granaries. Bells were sent for scrap. By the end of 1930 four-fifths of the country's village churches were closed.

Ironically, Nadezhda Alliluyeva, Stalin's wife, became a devout churchgoer in these years; her religious feelings consoling her—or perhaps adding to her torment—for her sense that she was married to a monster, and (it was not unconnected) the belief that she was a sister to her own children. At a banquet, the night before she committed suicide or was murdered, she shouted at the revelers: "I hate you all! Look at this table, and the people are starving!"

Stalin wept over her death; and we know what happens when dictators weep. Auden has told us: "the little children die in the street."

There were other ways besides the attack on religion—rather droll, dramatic ways—of destroying "the idiocy of village life." One such is related by Shostakovich. In the Ukraine, blind bards, called Kobzars, wandered from village to village, reminding people of the heroic past with their songs. During collectivization, the First All-Ukrainian Congress of Folksingers was announced. The Homeric figures "came to the Congress from all over the Ukraine, from tiny, forgotten villages. There were several hundred of them at the Congress, they say. It was a living museum, the country's living history; all its songs, all its music and poetry. And they were almost all shot, almost all those pathetic blind men killed."[12]

At intervals Stalin would complain that officials had been overzealous, and should be punished for their excesses. For a while there would be a slight easing. Then the "excesses" would begin again. Finally Stalin had what he wanted, a docile peasantry in collectives. Almost half the USSR's people were again serfs, since they could not change their place of abode without permission. Serfs without any escape into the realm of the spirit.

To engage with what happened to the Jews, we have to assist us the familiar searing images of the Nazi death camps and ghettos, from the Allied advances of 1945. But there were no liberations of the camps and settlements in the incomprehensible wastes of Siberia; so, added to the deliberate suppression of the truth, we have nothing visual to help us imagine the unimaginable. One can say "At least fourteen million died" in a split second, and the words have little meaning. The dead, too, are not the only, or often the main, victims. A single image, and a still alive victim, to focus on. One poor Ukrainian peasant refused to join the kolkhoz. He was arrested, beaten up, and deported. "His wife then hanged herself in their barn and a childless family took in their little boy. He spent his time haunting his deserted home, coming back to them only to sleep on the oven, never speaking."[13]

Try to imagine the little boy, coming day after day to the empty house. Try to imagine his feelings, his suffering. Multiply by fourteen million. Impossible examination questions.

7

Crosses

I know thee not, old man!
—HENRY IV, *Part Two*

I would gladly give my life for Lenin.
—SOLZHENITSYN, wartime letter
to his wife

AT JUST THIS TIME, FIRED WITH THE SUCCESSES AND IDEALS OF
Communism, Sanya became its ardent follower. When Auschwitz-style cattle trucks were rumbling through the Kuban and Don regions, and in large
and quite nearby towns—not to mention the countryside—multitudes were
dying from a man-made famine, this intelligent, idealistic schoolboy, scorn-
ing the views of family and the Fedorovskys, chose the Communist way.
When the adult population of Russia's cities and towns were fooled too, no
possible criticism can attach to a boy. But can those adults be completely
exonerated?

True, the newspapers of the early 1930s were full of happy shock-workers
and vibrantly fulfilled proletarian gymnasts. Likewise, German newspapers
in 1941–44 were not informative about the "final solution," and for German
civilians there was the general chaos and destruction of war, yet we are
rightly incredulous that they could have been totally ignorant of events in
the East. Krasnodar and Stavropol, where a third are estimated to have died
of starvation, were not in a foreign country. The peasants in the villages
were fellow Russians, fellow Cossacks: brothers and sisters. Was there absolutely no contact? True, people traveled little; but the activists in the field
had to come home, they would surely whisper to their wives, and the wives
would whisper to their neighbors. Was nothing known?

Something, it seems; but not enough. It was known that the kulaks, faced
with collectivization, were being awkward and hoarding grain; it was known
that there was an inexplicable famine. More than that—better not to inquire. The part-deliberate ignorance argues a national schizophrenia. The
peasants were a different breed. "Man, raving, denied his image / And tried
to disappear. . . ." The city looked at the country, saw nothing, and glanced

away again. "How everything turns away / Quite leisurely from the disaster," as W. H. Auden observes in "Musée des Beaux Arts."

Solzhenitsyn's personal world was changing too; in fact, seemed to be collapsing. A few months after the summer visit to Zakhar and Yevdokia and Aunt Maria in Georgievsk in 1930, Grandfather Zakhar turned up in Rostov; later in winter he burst into their shack, like an eruption from that unequal, grossly unjust prerevolutionary world: riding boots and old-fashioned hip-length waisted coat. With shaven head, bulbous purple nose, and Daliesque mustaches, he was clearly out of his period; Alexander loved him very much, but really! He seemed almost crazy, crouching down in the corner, leafing through the Bible he had brought with him, and loudly bewailing his useless life and the wickedness of the thieving Bolsheviks.[1] "It was for you, Sanya! Roman would have been useless, I knew that; but you— you would have looked after the estate so well! Now, it's all gone, all gone!" He wept, and blew his purple nose.

The boy tried to console him in a priggish way: "Don't worry about it, Grandpa. I wouldn't have wanted your estate. I'd have refused it on principle."

Zakhar is unlikely to have been comforted. It may have seemed like the last straw, to see Sanya turn into a cold young Communist ideologue. In any case, the tragic old man curled up to sleep on the floor—there was nowhere else for him in the tiny shack. First thing in the morning he went off to church before Taissia and Sanya were awake. They were woken by a thunder of kicks on the door. Two OGPU agents (the former Cheka) in sheepskin coats burst in, expecting to find Zakhar. They had followed him from Georgievsk, and were astonished by his disappearance. They wanted the gold he must be hoarding. Temporarily denied their target, they turned on his daughter, another class enemy. Give us your money, gold, jewels, they demanded. She told them she had nothing, whereupon they cursed her and insisted she sign a document to declare she had no valuables. If they searched and found she had lied, she would be thrown into jail. Taissia then asked if valuables included her wedding ring, and they said yes. So she took off her wedding ring and gave it to them; she also brought her dead husband's wedding ring.

Zakhar came back from church; as the agents demanded his gold he went to kneel and pray before the icon, but they hauled him to his feet and started to body-search him. Finding nothing, they cursed him, said they'd get him one day, and left.

The old man returned to Georgievsk. This melancholy and dramatic visit was the last time Sanya would see either of his grandparents; for two months later, in February 1931—when Stalin was ordering "agricultural specialists" into the collective farms, and stripped Leon Trotsky of his Soviet citizenship—Yevdokia died. Taissia and her son could not go to the funeral, but with great bravery, given the prevailing antireligious campaign, Taissia arranged a funeral mass for her in Rostov Cathedral. She might well have lost her job. Sanya was reported to his headmaster, and reprimanded for conduct unbecoming a Pioneer.

He may have felt a certain injustice in this, as probably his attendance at the mass was out of respect for his mother and grandmother, rather than religious conviction. Already when he was ten he had had his crucifix, worn around his neck from infancy, ripped off by some Pioneers. A yearlong campaign by his orthodox—that is, non-Orthodox—schoolfellows seems to have been effective in persuading him away from religious belief and into the Pioneers. It would be the last time in his life that he would be pressurized into conformity, and suggests that Alexander may have been more conscious of *non*conformity, of a rebellion against his mother and the rest of his family.

For her part, Taissia seems to have become more religious as she got older. Natalya Reshetovskaya remembers her as a devout woman.[2] A year after the funeral mass for her mother, Taissia was called upon to arrange another, for her father. The end of Zakhar's amazing life is mysterious and theatrically sad. Crazed with grief after Yevdokia's death, harried still by OGPU agents, he wandered back to the region of his lost estate. One day the officers at the Armavir OGPU headquarters were confronted by a crazy old man bowed under a heavy wooden cross.[3] "You've taken everything I have," he said. "You've driven my poor wife into the grave. Now you might as well finish the job by crucifying me."

Did he collapse with a heart attack under the weight of the cross? Nobody knows. The news of his death took a long time to reach Taissia and Sanya. The boy must have grieved deeply. "Grandfather Zakhar," he said, "was in effect the only man in the family. . . ." So much for Uncle Roman! "I had no father so grandfather somehow took his place. I loved them dearly, Zakhar and Yevdokia. I didn't visit them all that often, but they weren't remote from me at all. Grandma was a woman of rare goodness and kindness. But granddad was a man of exceptional energy, and had a drastic temper. In certain respects, I take after him in my character. I got all my energy from him, for example, because papa was a completely different sort of person. Papa was a soft, lyrical, philosophical man, very soft. So my energy comes from my grandfather."[4]

As he stood in the cathedral for the second time in twelve months, beside his thin, black-veiled mother, Sanya gazed at the guttering candles of the iconostasis and reflected that this was very beautiful—Aunt Irina was right—but its time had passed. The church in Russia had been tied to the Tsar, and once the latter had proved mortal it was not difficult for the people to let go of the church. Tolstoy would have approved of its shrinking. But this service was necessary for Mama, and he gave her gloved hand a squeeze. With her right hand she went through the ritual of crossing herself, and with the tip of a white handkerchief touched her moist eyes.

The great building was almost empty. Apart from a few friends of his mother, there were just two or three babushkas, kneeling toward the back;

having no connection with the dead man, they were praying for their own sorrows.

Then mother and son went back to the shack, at the end of a cul-de-sac; past the rubble heap and the maze of washing lines, in through the tiny entry with its box for coal, its bucket of water; into the one room they had to share for everything. It was cramped and cluttered. He probably headed straight for his desk, with its pile of books, between the stove and the narrow divan on which he slept. Asked by a French interviewer what sensations were rekindled in his mind when thinking of his childhood, Solzhenitsyn replied:

Hardships. I'm afraid the word won't mean much to you for all your experience of the war and the Nazis, especially as it doesn't apply to my childhood alone. Things were no better when I became an adult. Up to the age of forty I knew nothing but a kind of dignified destitution. From the end of 1918, the year I was born, until 1941, I didn't know what a house was. We lived in huts which were constantly assailed by the cold. Never enough fuel to keep us warm. No water in the room where we lived—we had to go out and fetch it from some distance away. A pair of shoes or a suit of clothes had to last for several years. As for the food, don't talk about it. After the starvation of the 1930s, ordinary shortages were a minor evil. In some mysterious way, all these things struck me as more or less normal.[5]

He exaggerates in saying he didn't know what a house was. He is forgetting Kislovodsk, the houses of Irina and Roman; and the Fedorovskys' comfortable flat, which was "almost a second home." But clearly he and his mother were living in conditions of poverty and hardship beyond almost any Western writer's experience. True, these were normal conditions for most Rostov people, and therefore more tolerable. It was common to have to queue up continually for six months in order to get a pair of shoes, for example. Many of the people in the queues for shoes—or for news of possible shoes—were those very servants whom Rhoda Power, before the Revolution, had observed going barefoot. Similarly the endless queues for bread had not diminished. And there were still the privileged people who were eating Swiss chocolates and caviar. The difference was that now they were the *nomenklatura*, those who shopped at special stores; and their privileges, which rose in a pyramid of luxury, were secret.

Also, since nothing was owned, but only lent by the state, those who so vulnerably enjoyed benefits were kept docile. Stalin had created the perfect slave state.

Sanya helped his mother, fetching water and coal; and in return she loved to help him with his studies. He followed in her footsteps in that he was usually at the top of his class. At first he found drawing a problem; but he worked hard and conquered it. His privilege—and it made up for all the hardships—was that his school, which he had entered at the age of seven, was considered the best in Rostov. The former Pokrovsky College, it was renamed for Zinoviev after the Civil War, but for many years was popularly known as the Malevich Gymnasium, after its excellent headmaster. In 1930, however, Vladimir Malevich was forced out of the school, and in thirty-seven or thirty-eight was arrested and sent to a labor camp. In the same year the school lost a brilliant teacher of mathematics, Nikolai Chefranov. His teaching awoke in Solzhenitsyn the fascination for mathematics that would complement his literary interests—and allow him an entry into the "first circle."

Among his other favorite teachers was his junior school teacher, Elena Belgorodtseva, who was strict yet kind—and had an icon in her home. Their affection was mutual, and she, no less than the Fedorovskys, must have played an important part in enabling him to settle down with his mother in Rostov.

But the burden Taissia placed on him—of increasingly living for him alone, rejecting all suitors—was a heavy one, especially as puberty brought the normal urge to break free. And brought other anxious delights. For an adolescent boy and his widowed mother to be living and sleeping in the same room, undressing and dressing before each other, was commonplace; and so it is possible to claim that it was no problem.[6] Yet like every youth, entering his most intensely erotic period, his sexual dream time, he must have been disturbed if only unconsciously. And perhaps she, who had sacrificed everything, by his presence.

Among the first girls to make him tremble with innocent desire was Lyalya Fedorovsky, sister of his best friend, Misha. "The long-legged blonde with the tousled hair"[7] was sixteen in 1931 to Alexander's twelve—nudging womanhood, while to her he had become rather a nuisance. He hung around the desk where she painted watercolors, his head swimming with her cheap scent, her rustling dress as she stretched for a brush. Perfume and the rustle of a skirt would be erotic icons in his fiction.

One way in which he rebelled was to assert that the private life fell far below public life in importance. He prided himself in reading about politics, not knowing how corrupt the reports in *Izvestia* and *Pravda* were. But he would check sources, and sometimes found that words from Lenin were misleading when quoted out of their context. As we have seen, he instinctively felt that the trials of "wrecker-engineers," in 1928 and 1930, were rigged.

Stalin had made good use of the engineers trained before the Revolution, those outstanding men of culture and breeding that Solzhenitsyn singled out for praise; but they were unreliable for that very reason. It was time to get rid of them and bring in the new postrevolutionary breed of engineers. They were poorly educated, but loyal to Communism. It was not good to make them wait too long before entering into their kingdom. The show trials were an excellent way of finding room for them. And the "saboteurs," if they weren't shot, could be usefully employed in slave labor camps working on grandiose schemes for changing nature.

It is likely that Sanya's skepticism was partly fed by conversations overheard at the Fedorovskys. Vladimir, that kindly, hardworking man, almost a father to Sanya, must have been deeply disturbed and frightened by the show trials. The first, in 1928, involved a "criminal network" of engineers in the town of Shakhty, not far to the north of Rostov. Five people were executed after confessions extracted by torture. The 1930 trial was in Kuibyshev. Forty-eight "conspirators" are said to have been shot *before* the trial. Professor Leonid Ramzin, an associate of Lenin, entrusted by him with planning the "Electrification of the Country" campaign, confessed to setting up a capitalist-inspired party among the engineers, with a membership of over two thousand. The "treachery" of such a man truly electrified the country. He was sentenced to a long term of imprisonment but was quite quickly released. Only seven of his fellow conspirators had been arrested and sentenced: where on earth were all the others? The "organs" would be tireless in seeking them out. Here was work, and an atmosphere of suspicion, for years ahead.

While Sanya smelled a rat, and was suspicious of Stalin, his admiration for Lenin only deepened.

He tried his young hand at fiction; wrote a novel title in a notebook: "The Twentieth Century." Then the subtitle: "The Meaning of the Twentieth Century." Material for this modest enterprise was not slow in coming. Heading for the Fedorovsky apartment building one slushy evening in March 1932, he saw Fedorovsky being frog-marched by two strangers to a car. In his hand Vladimir held a small parcel tied up with string. He did not see Sanya; hunched, dazed, he saw nothing. Solzhenitsyn rushed into the apartment and found the engineer's family, distraught, weeping, amid a scene of total chaos: drawers emptied, carpets ripped up, books and ornaments everywhere. The OGPU agents had searched for a whole twenty-four hours. All they had managed to find was a photograph from an engineering congress in which both Vladimir and the "guilty" Professor Ramzin appeared.

This was only the opening of an overwhelming family tragedy. Within a few days of her son-in-law's arrest, Madame Andreyeva suffered a stroke in the midst of a game of patience, leading to paralysis and death. Her daughter, Zhenia, had the double shock and grief of a husband's arrest and a mother's passing; but these were as nothing: by a particularly malign fate, her son, Misha, Sanya's great friend, banged his head in a skating accident. It seems he was afraid to tell anyone his head hurt. Meningitis set in, and within a short time he was dead.

Taissia and Sanya felt bowed down by this sorrow too. And the multiple tragedy brought an end to the closeness between the families. For when

Taissia and her son called on Zhenia and Lyalya, they could see the pain and resentment in Zhenia's eyes—much as she fought against it—that Sanya lived while her precious boy was in the grave.

Vladimir Fedorovsky was interrogated for a year and then released. But he was broken in health and unnerved by Misha's death, the news of which was spat at him by an interrogator. He never returned to his work, but existed for another ten years, dying in Tashkent in 1943. Solzhenitsyn would always honor this cultured, gentle man, who worked at his desk late into the night, yet once a week and on holidays burst into song and dance, the life and soul of the party.

There were no traitorous engineers, of course. Stalin knew it. He didn't care whom he destroyed.

It is impossible to compute and compare suffering. Impossible to weigh Zhenia and Vladimir Fedorovsky's suffering against the voiceless millions dying of famine or watching their children die. One can only say that at the start of the 1930s the Soviet Union was a hellish country. Unsuspecting the class genocide all around, the young Pioneer Alexander Solzhenitsyn nevertheless suspected massive illegality, witnessed the harassment of his mother and grandfather, and the brutal detainment of a much liked and respected father figure. He saw and felt the hardship and drabness of Rostov life. Yet, with the willful self-blindness that so many mature adults suffered from, he became an enthusiastic young Communist.

As an only child in what would now be termed a single-parent family, he was sensitive to the pressures, crude or subtle, applied by his school, which, as he was deprived of other influences and began to feel resentful of his mother's emotional demands, increasingly filled up his life. The school drew from the elite of Rostov, the children of Party officials, and from the old White classes who had managed to survive intact—like, earlier, the Fedorovskys. Solzhenitsyn was in neither of those categories, and he suffered guilt. His school was the south Russian equivalent of an English public (that is, private) school, where the pressures to conform are well-known—and which therefore occasionally produces mavericks and rebels, a Philby or a Blunt. Solzhenitsyn would become a kind of "internal" Philby, but not yet. For the moment he shared the view of himself, and his kind, that the Party elite in the school had: his family used to be rich, so he must atone.

Yet to judge by one rather strange incident, versions of which have cropped up, with distortions, throughout his life, he refused to submit to the politically correct opinions of his day. The overtly minor incident is first described fictionally in *The First Circle*.[8] Adam Roitman, a "decent" MVD major at a prison research institute in the late 1940s, is awake in the night, troubled. There are hints of growing official anti-Semitism; even the word "cosmopolitan," hitherto innocent or even noble, is being used in a pejorative sense. Roitman reflects that for a long time after the Revolution, Jews were considered more reliable than Russians, since "they had all been on the side of the Revolution which delivered them from pogroms and the Pale of Settlement." How threatening it was, now, that something you couldn't change, your race, could be used to persecute you.

Solzhenitsyn uses a rather strained device to allow the Jewish major to think of his school days. Half the boys in his class in that "southern town" had been Jewish. "Although they were the sons of lawyers, dentists or even small shopkeepers, they all fervently believed themselves to be proletarians." He recalls ardently denouncing one of the non-Jews, called Oleg Rozhdestvensky, for anti-Semitism. "Oleg, a pale thin boy who was top of the class, never talked about politics and had joined the Pioneers with obvious reluctance." The others, the Jews, had tried to catch him out. At last he had played into their hands by saying, "Everybody has the right to say anything he thinks." A boy called Shtitelman had retorted: "When someone calls me a dirty Yid, is that all right too?" And Oleg had said, "Everybody should be able to *say* what he likes."

Organized persecution had got under way. Two of Oleg's friends testified that "they had seen him go to church with his mother, and that he had once come to school with a little cross round his neck. At one meeting after another twelve-year-old Robespierres got up and in front of the whole school denounced this accomplice of the anti-Semites." Oleg was too frightened to tell his parents he had been thrown out of the Pioneers and would soon be expelled from the school.

Roitman now burns with shame. He had joined in the persecution. And if he, Roitman, couldn't change his race, Oleg hadn't been able to change his class and family background either. "If you wanted to put the world to rights, who should you begin with: yourself, or others? . . ."

The reality on which this was based had less serious consequences. Sanya's classmates Dmitri Shtitelman (the name retained in the novel) and Valeri Nikolsky were scuffling, when the latter muttered an abusive phrase usually applied by Ukrainians to Russians. Shtitelman accused Nikolsky of anti-Semitism. Sanya refused to support the former, saying "Everybody has the right to say what he likes." He too was accused of anti-Semitism and had to answer the charge before a special meeting of the Pioneers. He was not, however, expelled from either the school or the Pioneers.[9]

He was forced to set the record straight, after a former close school friend, Kirill Simonyan, related a scurrilous version in his highly suspect memoir.[10] According to Simonyan, Solzhenitsyn called a Jewish classmate by the name of Kagan a Yid, and Kagan punched him, causing his forehead to hit a doorpost: hence the scar that is visible to this day. The scar is so deeply entrenched that Kagan must have been a Samson or a Goliath to have indirectly inflicted it. The version bears the imprint of the KGB fiction department.

According to Natalya Reshetovskaya,[11] in a version which probably was also "fed" to her to help undermine Solzhenitsyn, he had been vain and ultrasensitive.° The scar was caused by his falling against his desk in a faint, after being criticized by the history teacher, Alexander Bershadsky.

What actually caused the scar, Solzhenitsyn declared in an interview, did involve Kagan but not anti-Semitism. The painful incident occurred on 9 September 1930, six months before his politically incorrect defense of free speech. He and Kagan were scuffling over a sheath knife. Kagan accidentally pricked a nerve in Sanya's hand; he became dizzy, started to walk toward the lavatory in order to put his hand under a tap, but then fainted and fell, striking his brow on the stone doorpost. His classmates picked him up, copiously bleeding, and carried him to the lavatory. He was taken to the outpatient department of the local hospital to have the gash stitched. However, this was crudely done (an odd echo of the fatal mishandling of his father in a the Georgievsk hospital), and his wound turned septic. He had to spend over a month in bed.[12] Ever afterward he had an embarrassing tendency to faint when experiencing physical pain.

Finally, in this maze of truth and deception, he *was* once threatened with expulsion, about two years later, and both Kagan and Bershadsky were involved. Solzhenitsyn and Kagan (apparently no worse friends for their dramatic and traumatic fight) and another boy skipped classes to play soccer. Sanya hid the class register behind a cupboard as part of the cover-up. His crime exposed, he was threatened by Bershadsky with expulsion, but pleas for mercy from the class, especially from the girls, brought a reprieve.[13] It is rather strange to hear of such a Tolstoyan figure having a scuffle over a sheath knife, and truanting to play soccer; he also longed to skate and play tennis, but poverty prevented it.

Though the KGB, using vulnerable people as pawns, produced gross distortions, it is clear that one aspect of the social tension in Solzhenitsyn's childhood and youth involved the Jews. What was happening, under the Jewish-Gentile scuffles in his classroom, and outside it?

As Rhoda Power observed, the Jews were hated by many in imperial Rostov—though perhaps less fanatically than in the Ukraine. Confined to the Pale of Settlement, and subject to pogroms, Jews emigrated in mass numbers to the United States or, if they stayed, were often drawn to revolutionary action. The urban, sophisticated, international nature of assimilated Jews responded to, where it did not create, the antinationalist outlook of socialism. ("The proletariat has no country.")

There was a common saying that the Revolution had been made by "Jewish tongues and Latvian bayonets." Most of the Red Commissars in the Civil War were Jewish. This naturally inflamed still further the anti-Semitism of many Whites. The White forces, and occasionally the Reds, carried out pogroms. In a savage prevision of Nazi atrocities, White soldiers sang obscene songs as they forced Jewish survivors to bury their own

---

°But at least not anti-Semitic; she may have been trying to be helpful with this milder criticism.

mothers, wives, children. An agent in Denikin's intelligence service spoke of killing the "Jewish microbe." In Kiev, the city later infamous for the Babi Yar atrocities, "gigantic five- and six-storey buildings [began] to shriek from top to bottom as Denikin's men threw defenceless Jews from upper storeys."[14]

In the wake of Bolshevism's victory, it was hardly surprising if Jews were among the most enthusiastic and vigilant in looking for backsliders. Even the young children, among them most of the Pioneers who ripped the crucifix from Solzhenitsyn's neck, and later put him on trial for anti-Semitism.

At a personal level, there is not a trace of evidence that Solzhenitsyn was anti-Semitic. His mother had been steeped in tolerance by Madame Andreyeva's school, and her "best friend," Liuba Arkhangorodsky, was Jewish. Sanya too, later in his school career, would have a close Jewish friend. But human feelings are ambivalent. When his classmate Nikolsky was accused of anti-Semitism, he may have leapt to his defense partly to defend free speech, partly to support a member of his own Russian tribe. And vestiges of his White and Orthodox Christian sympathies, which he believed to have been cast out, were still alive, below the surface. To have brought the "Yid" episode into *The First Circle* in a less than natural way implies that something rankled.

Education had become more formal, and also more political; in the crucial senior high school years, Solzhenitsyn received, by his own admission, a very good education. Also important to him was the strong friendship that developed among four of the brightest pupils in his bright class. In background and circumstances, the friends were quite a representative sample of Rostov life.

Nikolai (Koka) Vitkevich was Alexander's closest and oldest friend. His father, a tsarist civil servant, had died during the Civil War; Nikolai was being brought up alone by his mother, Antonina, who became a shorthand typist. The boys therefore had a lot in common. A significant difference was that Nikolai's mother was tougher than Taissia; she had joined the Party and could therefore work in official departments. She had nursed no foolish ideas about sacrificing her own happiness for her son, but remarried. Her husband, a Muslim from Dagestan, had taken her and Nikolai off to that mountainous, primitive, oriental "autonomous republic" on the western shores of the Caspian. Then, in 1934, he had died, and mother and son returned to Rostov. With pleasure, "Koka" and Sanya resumed their broken relationship, one that would have a huge impact on both their lives and on modern history.

Kirill Simonyan (Kira: though teasingly also Kirilla or Kirochka, from his rather feminine, theatrical nature) was an Armenian whose father, a wealthy businessman, had fled to Persia when the indulgent NEP era ended. His mother, with two children to support, had emphysema and was too ill to work. The close-knit Armenian community supported the abandoned family, but Kirill and his mother and sister lived in a hovel even poorer and bleaker than the Solzhenitsyns'. The family's inner life was rich, though; Kirill, despite a hearing defect, played the piano well, and his sister, Nadezhda, became a celebrated composer. Kirill took Alexander to free concerts at the May First Gardens and expanded his musical knowledge. He organized séances, was interested in dream interpretations, and generally stimulated Sanya's imagination beyond the norm in drab Stalinist Rostov. In a photograph taken in someone's flat, Kirill so obviously enjoys wearing a gaudy shawl, arching his thick black brows and coquettishly tilting his head toward a mock-scowling Sanya. Soulful, darkly attractive, fond of extravagant hand movements, he contrasted with the stocky, self-contained, masculine type of Nikolai Vitkevich.

The soulful Armenian boy became, unromantically, "Ostrich" to his friends when he suddenly shot up in height in his early teens; Sanya was "Walrus" because he loved cold weather. And all three fatherless boys knew themselves as the "Three Musketeers." "We looked up to them and admired them," says Sanya's classmate Laura Shatkin, who was to become a doctor; "they were the leaders of our class, its best students. They were honorable, read a lot, were honest. They were kind and helpful to those who had problems with their studies."[15]

Kirill Simonyan became romantically attached to the only girl in a quartet of friends, Lydia (Lida) Ezherets. She was Jewish, sweet natured, generous, kind, intelligent, and pretty. A photograph with her classmates and their literature teacher Anastasia Grünau (looking almost as young as her charges, who adored her) shows Lida open-faced, plaited, winsome—every teacher's dream pupil. Her background was secure and comfortable, her well-liked father, Dr. Alexander Ezherets, head of the main Rostov polyclinic and director of the Black Sea Regional Health Board. Lydia had as deep a love of literature as did Kirill and Sanya (Nikolai was more interested in philosophy and politics). She would marry Kirill in 1944, but then unfortunately found he was homosexual.

Anastasia Grünau, one of two sisters teaching at the school, was "more than a teacher, she was a mother to us too. We could speak to her on any topic, she was humane; but for all her kindness she was a strong teacher. She gave us a love of literature. We could discuss and argue—the whole class was involved in the discussions"[16]—one of those marvelous teachers (and Sanya, her pupil, became another) who can change and light up people's lives.

Anastasia encouraged her star pupils, the "Three Musketeers," to write. She actually thought Nikolai a more talented writer than Sanya. One of Sanya's early stories, "The Money Box," has a heroine called Alya Svetlova, which is the name, and even affectionate nickname, of the woman who became his second wife, Natalya Svetlova. The three friends would usually meet at Lydia Ezherets's home, a luxurious apartment, to read and discuss their writings.[17]

If Sanya was envious of the luxury, he was sure there was far greater inequality in the West. If, in 1934, he suspected Stalin was responsible for the murder of Kirov, the popular head of the Party in Leningrad, the crime did not match what was happening in Spain. If he started to see queues of silent, unhappy women in Nikolsky Lane, between his home and his school, where the forbidding back of the OGPU prison was; and if he saw approaching columns of prisoners, and heard a guard shout, "Move out of line and you'll be shot!"; and if he once heard of someone who'd jumped out of a high window and within ten minutes all sign of him had been scrubbed from the sidewalk . . . and if someone told him, in a whisper, that there were dungeons actually underneath the lane . . . Well, in the southern states of America innocent black men were lynched practically every day, and chain gangs of starved convicts were being whipped and worked to death. . . . There was no comparison.

And if he knew that a favorite torture technique in Rostov prison was to thump the prisoner in the stomach with a sandbag . . . It often caused death, and a doctor (but probably not the good Dr. Ezherets) would ascribe it to a malign tumor:[18] but Sanya of course did not know it.

He was hungry for learning and culture, and his hunger was being fed. As the 1930s moved on, he felt that broadening out of intellectual horizons which for an intelligent youth is as exciting as the erotic flood. He had an intense need to do well, better than anyone else; he did not faint if a teacher criticized him, but he certainly didn't enjoy it.

It was honorable to want to be first, to want to star. Here was Pushkin predicting fame for himself. . . . Anastasia was quoting to them in her beautiful voice, her eyes closed, the famous *Exegi Monumentum*. Hearing the immortal lines, Sanya burned with emulative fire. . . .

> I have erected a monument to myself
> Not built by hands; the track of it, though trodden
> By the people, shall not become overgrown,
> And it stands higher than Alexander's column. . . .

Later, perhaps, a rehearsal for the star role in *Cyrano*. He loved acting. He had been attending Yury Zavadsky's youth workshop at the Rostov Bolshoi, and had got through the first round of selection for drama school. He was seriously considering acting as a career. The charismatic director had burst out laughing as Sanya auditioned with one of the Cyrano speeches, and congratulated him on his sense of comedy. A famous Moscow director, Zavadsky had unaccountably been banished to the provinces; but it was great for Rostov.

Home now, to the empty shack, to do some chores so mother could rest when she came in; then a couple more hours at the library.

The slim, fair-haired, blue-eyed youth felt as if there were some explosive material inside him. He couldn't, and didn't want to, get back grandfather's estate, but he would create something at least as imposing. He would see what would happen in the third round at the theater, but probably writing would win out. Hadn't Uncle Roman sent one of his nephew's richly descriptive letters, from the Black Sea Pioneer trip, to Maxim Gorky himself? And hadn't Gorky's secretary responded that the great man thought the boy had it in him to be a writer? Yes, indeed! His father would be proud of him. Beyond the grave.

8

Days of Wine and Roses

Life has become better. Life has become more joyful. . . .
—1930s SLOGAN

HE HAD BECOME THE PERFECT STUDENT, BOTH INTELLECTUALLY
and socially. In his last school year, 1936, he was nominated by his headmaster for a civics prize. However, when the list of winners was published,
his name did not appear. His nomination had been blocked because of his
background. Usually, at the small price of describing his father's occupation
as "office worker" rather than "officer," he avoided discrimination. This
time, his headmaster was so angry with the authorities that they hastily
backpedaled—by awarding Solzhenitsyn a bicycle. For Sanya this was far
better than the normal prize would have been. Bicycles were an unafford-
able luxury.

Armed with the headmaster's letter, he arrived at the sports shop to be
told, Sorry, sold out; but the manager promised to tip him off when the
next shipment was expected. Eventually the tip-off came; Sanya, Nikolai,
and Kirill started an all-night queue—by morning there were about 150
queueing outside the shop. The three boys had the pick of the new stock,
and thereafter cycling was a favorite hobby. Their first long trip was into
the Caucasus Mountains. They went by train to Ordzhonikidze, and cycled
from there. The town was named in honor of Stalin's Old Bolshevik colleague, who was about to be invited to shoot himself.[1] Sanya kept a journal
of his cycling holiday, "My Travels, Volume IV, Books 1, 2 and 3." He
expressed indignation at how Georgian men treated women, either as slaves
or as easy conquests (if the women were Russian). The sight of a TB sanatorium also aroused indignation: "Two things cause tuberculosis—poverty
and the impotence of medicine. The Revolution has liquidated poverty.
Medicine, why are you lagging behind? Tear these unfortunates from
death's grasping paws!"

Despite the banal expression, the concern was genuine; his own mother, worn down by overwork, the cold, damp shack, and the general poverty which had been "liquidated," had contracted TB. Sometimes with a temperature of over a hundred and a doctor's sick note, she would still drag herself out of bed to go and look for extra work. It is not surprising that she is described, by a work colleague called Anna Voloshina, as a woman who rarely smiled. Taissia was reserved in the extreme, and spoke only when spoken to. Apart from work, Voloshina only recalled her talking about music, which Taissia said was a consolation.

At forty, she was tall and thin, always dressed in a black or dark gray skirt and a severe high-necked blouse. Her brown hair was streaked with gray. She never wore jewelry. She was a workhorse and the best at her job of anyone. She never complained.[2]

This is the girl who wanted to dance like Isadora Duncan, and whom Alexander's aunt Irina, in old age, described as "arrogant and silly."[3]

It is amazing that Sanya could write that the Revolution had liquidated poverty, in view of his home circumstances, and the patches on his clothes. For a short time he and his mother lived at Maly Lane, No. 5, a former stables, then moved to another shack in Voroshilov Street, where they lived from 1936 to 1940. They were an improvement on their first home, but not by much.

Tensions in the close mother-son relationship appeared as he became increasingly confident in himself and independent. She would weep, and complain that he was moving away from her, did not share as much with her anymore. She must have felt that his close school friendships meant more to him than she. He also started to see a girl with gypsyish dark good looks; Taissia had the terror of many mothers in her lonely situation, that she had sacrificed her whole life to him, and soon he would be gone. She was ill, poorly dressed, and had lost her looks; it was too late to attract a man. Soon she would be alone.

So she took out her grief on her son. Of course she was proud of his brilliance; but it hurt that she had had to let her mind stultify, and so could no longer keep up with him. She also didn't like it that he had joined the Komsomol. An "October child"—one born after the Revolution, therefore with none of the bourgeois notions of "virtue" and "morality"—he had thrown off the world to which she, in her innermost being, was still loyal. The more she complained to him, and wept, the more irritated with her he got, and the more he longed to break away.

But he remained a faithful son. Rarely did he finish a meal without kissing her in appreciation. He dreamed of going to Moscow to study literature; but he couldn't possibly leave her, and she was too ill to make such a move with him. He would have to resign himself to attending the University of Rostov: which meant also studying mathematics, rather than literature. Rostov University specialized in engineering and the sciences, as befitted an industrial seaport; literature was only offered at the teachers' institute, as part of a training for high school teaching. He had no interest in regurgitating gobbets of criticism for bored pupils, year after year.

There was one rich compensation for staying in Rostov, and that was that the Three Musketeers and Lydia would still be together. In the fall of 1936, all four started their undergraduate studies. Lydia was at the teachers' college, and would become a teacher of German literature. Nikolai and Kirill both entered the chemistry faculty, though the latter transferred to medicine after a year.

Nikolai Vitkevich found himself sitting in lectures beside a serious-minded and charming chestnut-haired girl called Natalya. They became friends, and were teased for being great gossips, whispering away during the lectures. "Koka" was drawn to her, but too shy or too immersed in his studies to make his feelings known. Kirill Simonyan was impressed too. "She's just like us!" he said to Lydia. Besides chemistry, she liked working out mathemetical problems as a hobby, was a talented pianist studying at the conservatory, and loved literature too. With her musical and literary talents, she would have seemed a fitting match for Kirill, had he and Lydia not been seeing each other. And had he liked girls. . . . But perhaps Kirill himself didn't realize yet that he was—different.

Natalya Reshetovskaya was three-quarters Cossack, one-quarter Polish. Her half-Polish mother, Maria, had been educated at Novocherkassk Girls' High School, then for six months at a women's college in Moscow. Her mother's death interrupting her studies, she had gone back to Novocherkassk, found a position as a governess, and married a lawyer from a prominent Cossack family. Alexei Reshetovsky fought in the tsarist army, then for the Whites in the Civil War. His and Maria's first offspring, prematurely born twins, died in infancy. The only surviving child, Natalya, was ten months old when her father fled abroad with the remnants of the White Army in December 1919.[4] Maria would have gone with him, but stayed for the sake of her baby.

Maria had moved to Rostov, first getting a job as a teacher, then retraining as a bookkeeper. She had been joined by her former husband's two spinster sisters, and all three women doted on Natalya (Natasha), yet without spoiling her. Natasha was capable, sensible, and hardworking; yet also stood out by being always well-groomed and well-dressed. One of her aunts made pretty, rather un-Soviet dresses for her.

One lunchtime, soon after the beginning of his first university semester, Sanya decided to pay a visit to the other two Musketeers. They happened to be at the top of the stairs in the chemistry department, chatting with Natasha. Looking down, seeing a familiar crown of thick sandy hair, the lanky frame bounding up, they cried, "Ah, the Walrus!" They introduced him to Natasha. He told her later that he hadn't seen the bottom half of her face at first because she was biting into an enormous apple. He noticed her light gray eyes, however. For her part she was conscious of how mobile his features were, and how rapid-fire his speech. Everything about Sanya, she would find, was done at top speed and with intensity.

Natasha's conversation at home was so full of her new friends that her mother said she had better bring them home. She did so, along with three girl students, on 7 November 1936. She would not forget the date. Her mother liked them all, but especially Simonyan, with his sad, expressive eyes. The young people, with the innocence of their era, played games with forfeits; Natasha had to play the piano, performing Chopin's Fourteenth Etude. Solzhenitsyn's response—this early in their relationship—was unequivocal: "I must tell you, Natasha," he murmured, pouring water over her hands from a pitcher, "that you play the piano beautifully!"[5]

Two weeks later they met at a birthday party organized for another of Sanya's former classmates. In 1956, Natasha would receive a letter from her estranged husband and read, with amazement, "Today is exactly twenty years from the day when I considered myself utterly and irrevocably in love with you: the party at Liulya's; you in a white silk dress and I (playing games, joking, but taking it all quite seriously) on my knees before you. The next day was a holiday—I wandered along Pushkin boulevard and was out of my mind with love for you."[6]

Yet he did not tell her his feelings at the time. That year she was more often with Vitkevich, who taught her to play chess and ride a bike. Koka even wrote her a romantic letter during the grand Caucasian tour, but it failed to arrive.

Solzhenitsyn poured out his feelings to his notebooks, in poetry. He was in love with love. And with life. He was getting A's just as he had at school, and was a leading light of the Komsomol. He felt a Tolstoyan sense of animal healthiness as he pedaled his bicycle energetically. There were dancing classes that only Sanya, of the Three Musketeers, signed up for, along with Natasha; and it was natural they should become partners. It felt wonderful to take her soft warm hand in his, and smell her freshly washed hair.

It was as the familiar slogan proclaimed: "Life has become better. Life has become more joyful."

The year 1938 saw Solzhenitsyn's enthusiasm for Communism grow to a point of obsession. It may be the main reason why, for so long, he did not tell Natasha he loved her. He was deeply in love also with Communism, and this love was far more important than a mere private emotion. He studied dialectical materialism with passionate intensity, and was joined in that by Nikolai Vitkevich.

True, there were a few students and a few tutors who disappeared from view; but it did not trouble him. It doesn't seem to have occurred to him to wonder where they had gone. People hid their fear and sometimes grief. One fellow student called Tanya, with whom he studied side by side for five years, never revealed that her unchanging expression had masked tragic events in her family. Only fifty years later did she reveal it to Solzhenitsyn, when he visited Rostov and she made herself known to him. He asked her if she recalled a particular class photograph being taken, and the old woman replied, "How could I not remember? Just twenty days later, my father was arrested; and three days after that, my uncle. . . ." Solzhenitsyn related this, fittingly, in a talk to students at the university.*

Kirill Simonyan had a better sense, Solzhenitsyn has admitted, of what was occurring.

Gradually, Sanya and Natasha were seeing more of each other. At parties now they danced only with each other. He would pick her up at home, and before they left she would usually play something for him on the piano.

He was going to be cycling with his friends through the Ukraine and Crimea. On July 2, 1938, without any warning, in Rostov's Theatrical Park, he declared his love. He visualized her being with him always, he said; he wished for an answer.

Full of ideals of love culled from books, wondering if Sanya was everything to her, suspecting he was not the whole world, yet knowing she cared for him a lot, Natasha laid her head on the back of the park bench and began to cry.

A few days later she broke through her intense reserve and wrote him a note saying she loved him. Now a tenderness crept into their relationship; it became harder to say good night without giving way to desire, and this upset her. She wrote a note suggesting they part; but he countered with a letter that had been prepared for such an eventuality. He would always take pride in being ready for the worst; yet to write such a letter, knowing it might not be needed, seems highly bizarre. He simply could not see her life separated from his, he wrote. And yet—he too had been suffering— the "myriad and inevitable trivia of married life" might ruin them before they had a chance to "spread their wings." And children . . . Well, that too would be a "pleasant-unpleasant consequence."[7]

She would almost become jealous of Lenin, he was such an idol to Sanya. Natasha had little interest in politics, and was the only member of what was now a pentagon of friends not to be in the Komsomol. When they listened to the radio, and some leader or announcer was saying, as usual, that everything was so nice in their country, everyone was happy, she would say to Sanya it's so boring. And he would reply, curtly, "Nado"—it's necessary.[8]

While waiting for a play to start—say, Ostrovsky's *Wolves and Sheep* or Leonid Andreyev's *Days of Our Life*—Sanya would get her to test him with some cards with historical dates and other information written on them. Not a moment was to be lost. He always had these cards in his pocket to flip over: waiting for a tram, for a lecture to start, the lights to go down in the cinema, everywhere. Make the most of your talents—that was the way to serve Communism.

---

*20 September 1994.

Life was indeed pretty wonderful! To have spent a fulfilling evening helping the Komsomol, then working in the library, devouring Hegel, Marx,
Engels, Lenin . . . and *still* to have awaiting you the warm kisses of Natasha!
He got things done by compartmentalizing life. While he was in the library,
sitting opposite Vitkevich, Natasha hardly existed. There is an almost erotic
tenderness in lines from an unpublished autobiographical poem, "The
Way" . . . "A book, a desk, you opposite me— / And nobody else in the
world exists! / And no regrets for this curious / Wineless, girl-less, bachelor
youth of ours."[9] Sometimes Nikolai would say, "It's almost ten—aren't you
meeting Natasha?" Sanya, glancing up at the clock, would murmur, "No,
there's still five minutes' working time."

It appears that Vitkevich still had an interest in Natasha, and didn't know
how serious her relationship with Sanya was. The as-if-casual exchange in
the library sounds like some feeling-out by Nikolai, with Sanya parrying; yet
the determination to work on until the exact second of closing time is utterly
characteristic. The Three Musketeers enrolled for English classes at the
evening institute, and were joined by Sanya's mother: perhaps an effort by
her to find an activity she could still share with him. He felt that he lacked
"world-culture," and next persuaded Koka and Kira to enroll with him as
external students at the Moscow Institute of Philosophy, Literature and
History (MIFLI). It was the most prestigious humanities institute in the
Soviet Union, and even maintained a degree of intellectual freedom under
Stalin.[10] The program for the Rostov students would involve correspondence
tuition, and twice a year, summer and winter, a welcome trip to Moscow
to attend lectures and be examined. Sanya enrolled for literature, Vitkevich
for philosophy, and Simonyan, comparative literature.

Early in 1939 Natasha and Sanya agreed to get married in the spring of
1940, near the end of their four-year degree course. But it was Koka with
whom he spent much of the summer holiday of 1939. They traveled to
Moscow to register for the MIFLI course, then went to Kazan on the Volga
and bought a spacious rowboat, in which they intended to spend three
weeks exploring the great river Volga, in the very heart of Russia. They slept
in the bottom of the boat, and by day rowed or drifted downstream, stopping
when they pleased to light a campfire or visit some place of interest. "The
Way" describes them waking in the chilly dawn, dusted with hoarfrost; they
would leap naked into the Volga to swim, then race and wrestle on the
shore to get dry and warm. It is a very Lawrentian scene of male intimacy,
a deeper intimacy, almost certainly, than Sanya had yet experienced with
any female; and perhaps at a psychic level he would never attain such intimacy with a woman. He had experienced all too much of close contact
with woman—his mother; it was the male, the father, that was a yawning
gap in his life.

Or is that too Western an interpretation? Russian students of that era—
and especially in the Komsomol—were brought up to regard sexual difference as unimportant; they were all workers together.

He had not told Vitkevich that he and Natasha were engaged. He may have feared that the very mention of Natasha would disturb the perfect harmony of this slow drift through meadows and marshes, virgin forests and grassy steppe. This heartland, he decided, was *his* Russia.

The young travelers were disappointed only by the air of neglect and torpor in the villages. When they tried to supplement their supply of dry biscuits and potatoes, they could find nothing but apples. The shelves at the village cooperative stores were always empty. At a "tea shop" they found only fumes of hand-rolled tobacco and a rough offer of vodka: there was no tea. Trite propaganda jingles blared from loudspeakers. Houses were dilapidated. This wasn't how the Russian village was in Turgenev or Chekhov! The life seemed to have been drained away, and they couldn't understand why.

Moored at a place called Krasnaya Glinka, they found themselves suddenly surrounded by armed guards with snarling search dogs. The guards were looking for two escapees. When they realized these were just two students, they snarled at them to move on, and dashed away. Near Zhiguli they saw crowds of ragged men digging foundations for a power station, and once a launch passed them containing shaven-headed prisoners handcuffed together who gave them sad, shy smiles.

They thought little of these episodes. They were excited about the lectures they had attended at MIFLI; they read and read, interspersed their studies with serious discussions of the war brewing in the West, imperialist England and France fighting it out with Fascism. Sanya felt that one day the USSR would have to defend itself in battle. He had no disagreement with the belief, so ardently expressed at Komsomol meetings, that a strong NKVD was vital, to guard against internal enemies, though he did not regret turning down the chance of a well-rewarded career in it. He just didn't see himself in that role.

This summer would never be forgotten. It was a huge relief to escape for a while from the pain to which his mother's suffering was exposing him; to be involved in literature again, after the drier stimulation of math; to get his first taste of Moscow and the expansiveness, the *prostranstvo,* of Russia's heartland.

How serene this homeland, this *rodina,* was! Right now, drifting down the Volga—life, Nikolai and he agreed, could hardly be better. Summer nights on the water. The low sun striking red through the forest, sparkling on the river; the blue sky fading to gray; the first exhilarating chill.

Everything to live for in a country of unlimited potential. That miraculous Moscow metro! And the Moscow people, the professors and students they'd met—so full of confidence and optimism!

Following the enchanted summer, he became once again the driven student and activist. The flash cards, recording Latin expressions or historical dates, were invariably with him, ready to be whipped out of his pocket. Natasha was kept strictly for after the reading-room closing time, which may have contributed to Nikolai's being lulled into thinking she and Sanya were not really dating. Natasha would occasionally bump into her secret fiancé while she was on her way to the *banya,* the bathhouse, and she would blush—imagining he was mentally seeing her undressed for bathing. She need not have worried; he had his head down, frowning, rushing to a Komsomol meeting or a lecture; he hardly saw her—sometimes not at all.

Yet, after ten at night, he was charming to her, attentive, and made it clear he appreciated her dress sense, her elegance, her deportment. One of her aunts, with whom she lived, Aunt Nina, had been a headmistress, and she had made the girl put a ruler down her back, and still kept her social graces up to the mark. Consequently Natasha was a real young lady, as well as beautiful and talented, and Sanya felt proud of her.

Among all his other activities, he had begun working on a novel. Most young novelists begin with a theme within their experience, and Sanya had good material: the life of a great southern seaport, recovering from the Civil War, and the self-sacrificial devotion of a young widow to her son. A touch of conflict, as the son finds romance with a striking Cossack girl. . . . But neither Rostov, nor his mother, nor romance, appealed to him as a major subject. The cult of the grandiose led him from "The Meaning of the Twentieth Century" to the slightly more specific "a big novel about the Revolution." It was to explore, according to Natalya Reshetovskaya, "the complete triumph of the Revolution on a global scale."[11] He had quickly decided he would have to start with the war. He couldn't hope to deal with all of it, but the Battle of Tannenberg, of August 1914, and the noble, badly let-down General Samsonov, started to grip his imagination. He plunged into research and wrote some scenes. Sometimes he grimaced when ten o'clock came and he had to blot his notebook, gather his notes together, and rush out to greet Natasha.

Was it self-absorption and egotism—the gesture of someone used to a mother's unconditional love—that made him give Natasha a photograph of himself on their wedding day, 27 April 1940? And with an inscription not saying, as one might expect, "I love you," but "Will you, under all circumstances, love the man with whom you have joined your life?" Or was it a genuine need to be reassured? Superstitiously attached to the number nine, Sanya chose one of its multiples for the fateful day of registration. It was a warm and windy day, Reshetovskaya recollects; there was nothing exotic or particularly memorable. For Solzhenitsyn, recalling the day thirty years on, the chief memory is that the pen flew out of her hand, somersaulted, and landed on his forehead, leaving a large blot. "It was an omen," he considered.[12] They told no one about the wedding, and returned to their own homes that night as though nothing had happened.

Soon after the low-key wedding, Natasha had to go to Moscow to do some practical work. Her husband joined her on 18 June, when he arrived for his half-yearly program at MIFLI. Fourteen-year-old Veronica Turkin,

Natasha's cousin, found her newly met relative sparkling with vitality and happiness and astonishingly well dressed, thanks to her industrious aunts. Sanya she found too full of himself, impatient and brusque. Tall and thin, with a mop of fair hair flying in the wind, his shirttails hanging out, he had little time for a pigtailed schoolgirl.[13] But Sanya, and Natasha too, were charmed and impressed by Veronica's father, who had divorced her mother and remarried. Valentin Turkin was a film historian and critic. Sanya was in awe of the cultured cosmopolitan who seemed to know everything and everybody.

The young couple wrote home to announce at last that they were married. Sweet-sour replies came. Sanya's aunts Irina and Maria in Georgievsk, informed by Taissia, were outraged there hadn't been a church wedding. They considered them to be living in sin. Nikolai Vitkevich congratulated them, but it was clear he felt wounded; and Simonyan's congratulations were restrained; he told Natasha much later he had feared Sanya's despotism would overwhelm her.

Natasha developed suddenly an alarming infection of the neck glands. Another of her distinguished relatives, a neuropathologist, saved a dangerous situation by persuading a surgeon to operate in a private house. The glands were gone and Natasha well again. And then they were shown another example of the special treatment available to some: Uncle Valentin spent his summers, with other intellectuals and artists, at the village of Tarusa, seventy miles south of Moscow. He suggested that as they still hadn't had a honeymoon (Sanya had been staying in a MIFLI hostel) they might find Tarusa a suitable place. They accepted with alacrity and were driven to the charming village. There, they found for themselves a modest hut at the edge of a forest, slightly apart from the colony of artists' dachas. They gaped at the celebrities from the film and theater world, enjoying the best of food and drink: bacon, sugar, coffee beans, cases of wine and vodka, basement iceboxes filled with imported fresh meat, fruit, and vegetables.[14]

In contrast to this luxury, the flyblown village cooperative and market, used by the locals, were almost empty; almost as forlorn as the village stores glimpsed on the Volga holiday. Did Sanya not wonder at the difference? And did he not suspect some other emotions churning beneath the surface as the intellectuals lightheartedly swam, sunbathed, and played tennis?

It seems not. Of course, blindness to others is forgivable when one is consumed by passion. There was excitement and rapture in Natasha's arms; and then—no sooner had the early dawn glimmered between the curtains than he was jumping out of bed, leaving her asleep, and rushing out to the veranda, to plunge into the enthralling logic of Lenin's *Materialism and Empirio-Criticism*.

"I believe to the marrow of my bones . . . I harbour no doubts, no hesitations—life is crystal clear to me."[15]

He worked on the MIFLI course; read aloud some exquisite rural lyrics of Yesenin to his wife. They stayed on in Tarusa until early fall; he loved this central Russian landscape, birchwood and melancholy winding river; felt, as he had the previous summer, that he had found his rightful place.

At a stop on the journey back to Rostov another train, not quite passenger and not quite freight, halted alongside for a couple of minutes. Solzhenitsyn saw gaunt, shaven heads, sunken eyes, staring insolently. They didn't seem human. Natasha said, "Who are they, Sanya?" He shook his head, not knowing; the trains moved apart, and the strange faces, vanishing, ceased to exist.

At the age of twenty-one, Sanya had had only one disappointment in his climb toward success; and that had merely served to confirm him in his choice of literature as his destiny. The arrival in Rostov of director Yury Zavadsky had swayed him toward the theater. Zavadsky had started with the Vakhtangov Theatre in 1915, at the age of twenty, and from that point had held high positions as an actor-director. He was also exceedingly beautiful; the great poet Marina Tsvetayeva had become besotted with him in 1919, when forcibly separated from her White Guard husband, and had written passionate poems to him.[16] Under Stalin's regime he had been sent to take over the Bolshoi Theater, Rostov, as an extremely mild punishment for being too aesthetic in his art, or perhaps for having made someone jealous. His productions thrilled the provincial city—and young Sanya.

He had joined Zavadsky's youth theater, and passed stage one of the entrance examination leading to professional training. Zavadsky admired his talent for comedy. But one day the director asked him to call Simonyan back, saying he wanted a word with him; Sanya shouted, or tried to; and Zavadsky, with a regretful smile, said, "Sorry, Sanya—voice too weak."

9

To Be or Not to Be...

... And take away the lanterns. Night.
—AKHMATOVA, *Requiem*

WHILE SANYA AND HIS FRIENDS WERE ENJOYING THEIR SWEET UNI-
versity years between 1937 and 1940, the country was suffering a mortal
convulsion. Millions were dying or being consigned to a living death. It is
as if there were no connection.

Stalin, who trained to become an Orthodox priest, had no need of exam
certificates to be a consummate actor-director. All Russia was his stage.

Take his brilliant entrance during one of the show trials: in the dark
Kremlin courtroom, a spotlight suddenly picked out from the darkness a
secret observer, sitting as in a theatrical box. The already condemned accused could see it was Stalin, and the sight sent a shudder through him,
almost killed him there and then. "The play's the thing / Wherewith I'll
catch the conscience of the king. . . ." This time the king was the trickster,
not his victim. Yet Stalin was observing the death of the last shreds of his
own humanity, symbolized by the broken figure in the dock.

Hamlet was a banned play. Well, it wasn't officially banned, but it was
known that Stalin didn't wish it to be performed. It was in rehearsal at
Stalin's favorite theater, the Moscow Art, and Stalin stopped it by asking
jocularly, "Why is this necessary—playing *Hamlet* in the Art Theater, eh?"
So the play was removed; the actor who found the cup passing him by—to
borrow an image from Pasternak's Zhivago poem "Hamlet"—drank himself
to death. Vsevolod Meyerhold, most original and dictatorial of directors
apart from Stalin himself, commissioned Pasternak to translate the tragedy,
but his version was never produced; it was not to be.

Meyerhold—obsessional, chain-smoking as he paced around the stage—
was obsessed with *Hamlet*. He said if all the plays ever written suddenly
disappeared and only *Hamlet* miraculously survived, all the theaters in the
world would be saved. They could all put on *Hamlet* and be successful and

draw audiences.[1] Yet in all his teeming productive life he never could get it on the stage.

But he kept imagining how he might produce this or that scene. He had it in mind to have two Hamlets; one of them would read the tragic soliloquies and the other would be a comic version. The former would be played by a woman: his wife, Zinaida Raikh. Raikh was a notably beautiful actress, with dark hair, a white, round face, and a fondness for clothes and jewels. Meyerhold adored her as much as he adored *Hamlet*. She had been married before, to the poet Yesenin, to whom she bore two children. Despite Yesenin's famous relationship with Isadora Duncan, it was said he had never got over Zinaida, that she was the woman he hated and adored. And that Zinaida, too, would have walked through snow or hail if Yesenin had snapped his fingers.

Too late for that now, since he had committed suicide. Or—as is increasingly believed in post-Communist Russia—had been murdered by OGPU (KGB), who had then staged a suicide.[*]

Hamlet had always fascinated the Russians, because it asked that unanswerable question, What is to be done? The first serf theaters had performed it. Every Soviet director or actor in the 1930s brooded about *Hamlet*, if not with the passionate commitment of Meyerhold. Because the country was Elsinore to the nth degree. Airlessness, corruption, murder. Things rank and gross in nature possessed it merely. Observe the two portraits—Lenin, Stalin. Stalin knew how audiences would interpret *Hamlet*, which is why he *wished* it not to be performed. In one of the few Communist-era productions of the play, in 1924, Chekhov's nephew Mikhail had played it as though Elsinore were a purely abstract, spiritual concept, and all the characters dead.

And indeed, vast numbers of the victims of the Terror of 1937–40 were already spiritual corpses, before the deaths of their bodies. For now Stalin attacked the faithful, the Party high-ups, as well as senior officers, intellectuals, and ordinary people. Thousands of those purged had helped in the holocaust of collectivization and famine, giving the verminous kulaks, their precursors in the Gulag, not a thought. The young revolutionaries, by the late thirties, "had turned into graying forty-year-olds, sitting in offices equipped with telephones and secretaries, wearing jackets and ties instead of field shirts, going about in autos. They had acquired a taste for good wines, for spas like Kislovodsk, for famous doctors. . . . They were all inhuman—including those who loved nature, poetry, music, or good times. They clearly understood that the new world was being built for the sake of the people." Yet the people themselves had stood in the way, and they'd had no qualms about wiping them out.[2] Now it was their turn; now Stalin was killing *them*—important people!

---

[*]There is even uncertainty, according to T. Krasavchenko, that the poet Mayakovsky, a Soviet icon who had, like Yesenin, begun to have doubts, shot himself in 1930.

It was always for nothing. Yevgenia Ginzburg, receiving a prison sentence, complained, "But I'm innocent!" "Of course you're innocent," she was told; "do you think you'd only have got ten years if you were guilty?"

Most often arrests were made at night, by officers of the NKVD (the name new, the terror old) who drove black sedans that were called "ravens." Pushkin's lyric "Insomnia" was prophetic; Russia was full of insomniacs. Most people kept a small bag packed. Perhaps something in the lining of your coat. The poet Mandelstam, who died in Kolyma in 1938, had kept a book hidden there, Dante's *Inferno*. As you got older, he said, you needed fewer and fewer books. He did not possess the idea of the best-seller.

One girl who had been to a party arrived home in the early morning hours and rang the bell. Her father came to the door; he was fully dressed and had a bag in hand. He slapped her face when he saw who it was. But it did not have to be at night; you could be taken quietly from lecture rooms, at the fancy food counter of the Gastronom store, between acts of *Swan Lake* at the Bolshoi. Akhmatova said she and all her friends lived in a constant state of "holy terror." In her city, Leningrad, one person in four was at some point arrested.

Stalin liked theater as he pondered the "lists," night after night. He would hesitate over a name, teasing; then he might say to his henchman, Yezhov, head of the NKVD (who would be a victim too), "No, we won't touch the wife of Mayakovsky," and lift his pen nib. And with Pasternak too: the theatrical hesitation, the poised nib; then, "Let this cloud-dweller be." He assured a historian, Yuri Steklov, that he was safe, patting him affectionately on the back, only a few hours before the "raven" came for him in the night. Sheer theatrical brilliance! A gift for black comedy!

He didn't need to be present to create a comedy. Once he called up the head of the music bureaucracy and said, "I greatly enjoyed the broadcast of Yudina playing the Mozart Concerto No. 23; was it recorded?" "Of course." "Then send it to my dacha." But there was no recording; the concert had been live. The terrified producer got Marya Yudina and the orchestra and conductor into a recording studio straightaway, to record through the night. Everyone except Yudina was shaking with fright; they were already dead men. The first conductor collapsed; a replacement was trembling so badly he confused the players; only a third conductor was in any shape to finish the concerto, and the recording was completed by morning. A single copy. It was rushed to Stalin.

Soon after, Yudina received an envelope with twenty thousand rubles. She was told it came by order of Stalin. She wrote to him: "I thank you, Josif Vissarionovich, for your aid. I will pray for you day and night and ask the Lord to forgive your great sins before the people and the country. The Lord is merciful and He'll forgive you. I gave the money to the church that I attend."[3]

She was a good woman; at the opposite pole from a woman in Kiev who denounced around eight thousand people, most of whom died. Nikita Khrushchev recalled that the sidewalks emptied as she walked through the city. People sought to avoid her gaze.[4]

Surprisingly, nothing bad happened to Yudina. Stalin may have thought she had acted so crazily she must be a holy fool, and therefore to be left well alone. He was also capable of admiring courage. Let her go on playing for him, praying for him.

There was no such charity for Vsevolod Meyerhold. Stalin hated Meyerhold. Shostakovich says it was because the brooding, obsessed director would never lower himself to become a toady. Or it may be because the great leader learned he was obsessed with Hamlet, the regicide. Meyerhold's theater was closed down in 1938, but its director Stalin kept dangling for another year or two. Then, in January 1940, he had him arrested. A few days later a gang of "thieves"—unquestionably from the NKVD—broke into the Meyerhold apartment and brutally murdered his wife, Zinaida. They stabbed her body through her elegant dress seventeen times, and then knifed her in the eyes. She screamed for a long time, but none of the neighbors dared investigate.

This was the wife Meyerhold loved madly—Shostakovich said he had never witnessed such obsessive love. Someone would surely have shown photographs of the murdered woman to the imprisoned director. If not a movie documentary with soundtrack. Probably there was sexual violence done to her also. That is conjecture; but we know that the NKVD's most brutal interrogator forced Meyerhold to drink his own urine, then broke his left arm while forcing him to sign a "confession" with his right.[5]

Lavrenti Beria, head of the NKVD, moved his sixteen-year-old mistress into the empty Meyerhold flat.

Meyerhold hadn't suffered enough. "We have the testimony of witnesses present at [his] interrogation. One of the twentieth century's greatest theatrical producers lay on the floor with a fractured hip and blood streaming down his battered face while an interrogator urinated on him."[6]

The rest is silence.

10

A Room on Chekhov Lane

Ah, Moscow! Moscow!

THE NEWSPAPERS THAT SANYA DEVOURED ON 6 MARCH 1940, AS HE
waited impatiently for the end of virginity, had spoken of Soviet advances
against the barbaric Finns, but not of the Politburo meeting which had
minuted (5 March) the murder of twenty thousand Poles at a place called
Katyn.[1] Brazenness could scarcely go further than that.

The artists and intellectuals vacationing at Tarusa did not know that more
people were killed, in one camp, Serpantinka, in the year 1938, than were
executed in the last century of Romanov rule. But they knew how many of
their Tarusa neighbors and Moscow friends were no longer swimming, sunbathing, and partnering them at tennis.

Sanya remained, in his mind, a virgin. It was not that he trusted Stalin;
he had understood the falsity of the show trials of engineers; he sensed
Stalin's guilt in Kirov's murder. Yet "we had no sense of living in the midst
of a plague, that people were dropping all around us."[2] He blamed "the
astonishing swinishness of egotistical youth."

Like the honorable Lev Kopelev, who took part in grain extortions while
seeing children die of famine before his eyes, he believed because he
wanted to believe. Though *I* can't believe that Solzhenitsyn would have
taken such a "rational" line, faced with the evidence of his own eyes.

Since he was not faced with it—he believed. Absolutely. He had a tendency towards absolutism. His planned great novel, "Love the Revolution!,"
had to have a grandiose scale; it was to be a literary Magnitogorsk. In fact,
it would have turned out to be a White Sea Canal—a white elephant*—

---

*Magnitogorsk, an industrial city in the Urals, and the White Sea Canal were built under in-
tolerable conditions; the latter cost a hundred thousand lives, and proved practically useless because
it was too shallow.

since there can be no good fiction without inner tension. Whether as student or Komsomol activist, he needed to be the best. And he was. Those tendencies, toward absolutism and toward supremacy, went together.

He has said, in part explanation of his early espousal of Communism, that the thirties were totally different in spirit from the twenties. Then, life had still seemed in touch with the prerevolutionary world; but by the time Stalinism had begun to make its mark, it was as if the tsarist world had never been. And so he, and other young idealists, had felt they should make the most of the only reality they had.

Returning to Rostov to "face the music" of having deceived everybody, Natasha probably felt that Kirill's fears of Sanya's despotism were unnecessary; a touch of husbandly authority could be a not unpleasant experience for a fatherless girl; though she was not one to be trodden on. What was less congenial was to be ignored. She had had a taste of that already in Tarusa, when they were at leisure, and it became even more noticeable when they went back to their studies. No longer, she recalls, did he fear marriage might ruin his future plans. "He realised that by marrying he had not only lost nothing in the way of precious time, but actually had gained more. No longer did he have to make appointments with her; take her frequently to concerts, theatres, films; or stroll with her at night along streets and boulevards. When he was particularly desirous of her, she was always right there, at his side. True, sometimes the wife whined and deplored the fact that there were fewer amusements in their life, that the notions of 'being guests' and 'entertaining guests' had almost ceased to exist."[3] In referring to herself in the third person, Natalya suggests that she felt depersonalized. He was treating her like a knapsack, to use an image from Tolstoy: by marrying, you can sling the erotic attachment over your shoulder, and forget it. Yet there was sexual passion: rather coyly in her memoir she says he was more willing to give up sleep than his evenings of study.

His hard work brought rewards. Starting his last year, he was given one of the newly instituted Stalin scholarships for outstanding achievement. Only seven of these were awarded in the entire university. His grant was two and a half times higher than the norm, and more than the average doctor or teacher was earning. He was on the ladder to high privilege in Stalin's state. The university also found for the married couple, and partly paid for, a room in a red-brick house in Chekhov Lane. It was conveniently close to their mothers' homes, and to Sanya's two favorite reading rooms. The only minor drawback was a cantankerous landlady, whose kitchen they had to share. Their room was on an upper floor, sparsely furnished and gloomy.

However, during this hectic academic year, 1940–41, they were rarely in it except at night. Both had to dash out first thing in the morning to go to lectures or library. Precisely at three they would turn up at his mother-in-law's for the day's main meal. If it was served even five minutes late, Sanya would grow restive, and pull out the flash cards for Natasha to test him. He worked even more frenziedly this year. Apart from two degree courses and "Love the Revolution!" he transformed a moribund Komsomol tabloid, that hardly changed from one year to another, into a stimulating, highly acclaimed magazine, changed every week.

After the lunch he would dash off for more work, and Natasha would settle to the piano, practicing toward her conservatory examinations. At ten o'clock in the evening she would walk to meet him at the reading room. She would bring a dish cooked by her mother; once in Chekhov Lane she would warm it up and serve it.

And then—he might study until two. . . . Or call it a night.

Only—no children. Sanya was adamant about that. He wanted to travel and have no burdens. Natasha would have liked to settle down into a conventional marriage, with children. Yet, after all, there was plenty of time for him to change his mind.

Sex, Natasha claims, was not of prime importance in their lives; or in hers, anyway. In fact, she would enrage Sanya some thirty years later by telling him—admittedly when angry—she hadn't loved him for the first four years of their marriage. The frenetic schedule was hardly conducive to her feeling romantic.

On Sundays they allowed themselves to stay in bed later. This was their day for visiting Sanya's mother. Relations between Taissia and Natasha were warm; Taissia could even joke that she knew Sanya had a girlfriend when he no longer kissed her after a meal![4] As soon as Taissia had received her son's letter relating the surprise news, she had hurried around to the home of Natasha's mother and aunts. They had talked together for four hours, and formed a bond. The two mothers had, after all, a lot in common. They became good friends, and continued to visit each other.

Taissia was therefore prepared to welcome her daughter-in-law, and must have felt that her son had chosen well. Natasha, for her part, became very fond of Taissia; and the picture she paints of her has nothing in common either with Aunt Irina's "silly and arrogant" or her colleague's picture of an uncomplaining, unsmiling, unspeaking workhorse. The Sunday visits, Reshetovskaya recalls, were always festive occasions for Taissia. "She put all her talents, all her love into serving us the most delicious meals possible. The energy, the deftness, the speed with which she did everything, despite her illness (she had active tuberculosis), were amazing. Her speech was rapid-fire, just like her son's, only interrupted by brief coughing spells; and she had the same mobile features."[5]

It may be that this was Taissia's normal personality, and the efficient but mouselike creature at work was a mask to stave off curiosity. More probably, she was grateful to have a daughter-in-law to talk to, someone who—though clever and talented—wasn't so awesomely brilliant and absorbed in work as Sanya. A wedding brings new life. She was glad, with her own life uncertain, to see him settled. She could imagine, if the good Lord spared her, dandling grandchildren. . . .

Of course the young people didn't exactly hang around after lunch. Sanya would start to shuffle his feet, grow distracted, and make it clear he had Komsomol business to do. A kiss for his mother, and then off. There was little contact, that last year, with the other two Musketeers or Lydia Ezherets. They were all busy, though none so busy as Sanya. "That year it seemed to me at times that my husband was a machine wound up for all eternity. It became a little frightening." Still there was time to fit in performances in amateur talent reviews at some of the Rostov schools and colleges. Sanya recited poetry and Natasha played the piano.

Meanwhile the world hadn't stood still. Trotsky was murdered with an ice pick in Mexico in August 1940; Hitler, Stalin's temporary partner, smashed his way through to the Channel; France fell; England was suffering the blitz and the imminent threat of invasion.

As Sanya prepared to contribute to Russian literature with an epic novel of the Revolution, he had no idea that Isaac Babel was dead; that Pilnyak was dead; the great Georgian poets Yashvili and Tabidze, dead; Pasternak, silenced; Mandelstam, dead; Akhmatova, ill and close to madness; Marina Tsvetayeva, returning from exile, in suicidal despair because her husband and daughter had been arrested.

All the great poets were silenced. Except for the hundred-year-old Kazakh poet and folksinger, Dzhambul Dzhabayev. He had been a major find, his poems—praising Stalin, Yezhov, etc.—widely translated into Russian. Shostakovich set some of his lyrics to music. But actually he hadn't written a word of poetry; his work was all the creation of a factory of versifiers. A Kazakh poet had been needed—just as a recording of Yudina had been needed—and so one had to be made. The only Russian word old Dzhambul knew was *vznos*, fee, as he squiggled his signature on a contract. He even said *vznos* when some children asked him for his autograph.[6]

Neither Sanya nor Natasha appear to have given much thought to the fate of Western Europe. It is neither surprising nor deplorable, exam revision tends to outweigh compassion. For Sanya it was an inevitable quarrel between capitalist regimes.

Natasha sat the chemistry finals together with Vitkevich. He failed to achieve honors because of his firm principles, to which she pays tribute in her memoir of Sanya. Nikolai was invited, in the paper on Marxism-Leninism, to answer a hypothetical question along the lines of "What would have happened if . . ." He declined, on the grounds that Lenin disapproved of such conjectural formulations. His mark was reduced. All the other chemistry students went to the examiners and demanded that he be allowed to re-sit. It was suggested to him that he write a statement requesting a re-sit on the grounds of illness during the exam. Koka refused, saying loftily, "You know perfectly well that's not the reason."

"To me," wrote Reshetovskaya, "the diploma incident showed Koka's character in its entirety."

There can be little doubt that Sanya would have shown the same rectitude. They were two of a kind. He showed his determination to follow his own path, at whatever cost, in a different way. Given his outstanding achievement in mathematics and physics, and his Komsomol record, he could have immediately entered Stalin's well-rewarded scientific elite. Instead, he planned that he and his wife would teach for a year in a village school, and then try to move to Moscow. He would finish the MIFLI literature course, and she would study at the conservatory. It is not clear whether he hoped his mother would come with them. Her TB was now quite advanced; late in 1940 she had attended a sanatorium in the Crimea.

He retained in later life some resentment that his mother, instead of exchanging Kislovodsk for Moscow, where she had studied, had chosen to live in Rostov. In Moscow, he told an interviewer, he would have had a purer model of Russian than in Rostov, where the language was "horrible." Living there in his formative years had held back his linguistic development. Only by miracle and hard work had he overcome the stiffness and clumsiness of his early style and learned the proper use of Russian.[7]

It is strange that he should blame the speech of Rostov for his early problems in writing. As if an American novelist were to lash out at a Mississippi childhood for having held him back from writing the Great American Novel; or James Joyce wishing he had grown up in London. Muscovites argue that southern Russian is truly deformed; yet, after all, Sanya could read—Turgenev, Tolstoy, Chekhov, Gorky: most writers learn by reading over and over their choice writers.

On 22 June 1941, he arrived in Moscow to sit his second-year MIFLI exams, and to plunge excitedly into the life of the longed-for capital. But history, as Herzen observed, has no libretto: on the same day Hitler, who also longed for Moscow, launched Barbarossa, the Wehrmacht smashing across the border along a two-thousand-mile front.

PART II

B a r b a r o s s a

1 9 4 1 – 1 9 5 3

SANYA AND NIKOLAI VITKEVICH, at the front, spring 1943. Their unexpected reunion was to cost them both dearly—yet would also give Solzhenitsyn his great literary theme.

11

O God of Battles . . .

An elephant attacking a host of ants . . .
—WEHRMACHT COLONEL

AT THREE IN THE MORNING OF THIS DAY, THE CALM OF THE SOVIET border had been shattered by the explosion and glare of six thousand gun flashes. Frontier guards, wrenched out of sleep, were still fastening their tunics as the German tanks ran them down. Along hundreds of sleepy miles, from the Baltic to the Carpathians, desperate appeals were radioed to headquarters—"We are being fired on—what shall we do?"—and were greeted with disbelief. Nazi Germany, since the 1939 nonaggression pact, had been Communist Russia's friend; when the Wehrmacht entered the working-class districts of Paris, French Communists greeted the invaders with raised fists and shouts of "Comrades!" Stalin had not believed—felt he *dared* not believe—the accurate warnings of the perfidious English and Americans, nor his own spies in the German command. So the blitzkrieg troops surging into Soviet territory were amazed to see Russian trains still heading west, bringing them supplies.

"What an appalling moment in time this is!" an English historian writes. "The head-on crash of the two greatest armies, the two most absolute systems, in the world. No battle in history compares with it. Not even that first ponderous heave of August 1914 when all the railway engines in Europe sped the mobilisation. . . . In terms of numbers of men, weight of ammunition, length of front, the desperate crescendo of the fighting, there will never be another day like 22nd June, 1941."[1]

Stalin, roused from sleep after a long delay, cowers into his chair as Molotov's report of his meeting with Ambassador Schulenburg sinks in. Germany is not simply countering a misunderstood concentration of Soviet troops on its borders; not demanding political or, at worst, territorial concessions: it has declared war. "The Great Gardener" looks as if he has personally been deafened and shell-shocked by those six thousand guns opening up, and the hail of bombs destroying the Soviet air force on the ground. He will become known, he croaks at length, as the leader who let all Lenin's achievements be destroyed; for he himself has waged war against his own people, and therefore it is inconceivable that they will be willing to fight against the invaders. He concedes that the Red Army commanders may be permitted to defend Soviet territory, but on no account may they penetrate beyond the border. As though, even yet, it may all turn out to be a bad dream.

All that power, that cruelty, has come to nothing . . . reflected Professor Mikhail Gerasimov, an archaeologist in far-off Samarkand. He was supervising the opening of the tomb of Timur the Lame, or Tamerlane, on this same day of 22 June. Legend insisted that if the medieval grave were violated there would be disastrous consequences. The good professor, still ignorant of Barbarossa, may have thought his country was already in a state of disaster and nothing much could happen to make it worse.

Timur, lamed by an arrow on his right side—you could see it in his skeleton, to which shreds of skin and russet beard clung still—and Stalin, with a deformed arm and webbed toes . . . Both had a piercing light shone in on them on that day. And for a time, the modern monster seemed to become mummified like his Mongol predecessor.

In Moscow, it was afternoon before the citizens were entrusted with the news of invasion, and an appeal by Molotov to rally to the government. At first the mood was of shock rather than panic; it even resembled a sullen calm. Young Sanya Solzhenitsyn, first-class physics and mathematics graduate from Rostov, arrived to take still more exams; stepped off the train at the end of the long journey; stretched his legs, breathed the fresh air; transferred his thoughts from the book he'd been reading to anticipation of pure pleasures in the capital—and encountered this strange uneasy atmosphere, an amalgam of calm, rumor, fear, a sick excitement.

When he realized that the Fascists had invaded, he rushed at once to a recruitment office. He felt, we can be sure, exaltation rather than despair. He was his own youthful father, cutting short his studies to fight for the motherland against the same brutal enemy; even the date was a simple transposition of 1914. Unfortunately the bureaucrats did not immediately share his sense of destiny, refusing to take him without his draft card. He would have to return to Rostov and enlist there. Sanya rushed to the station but found it in pandemonium. It was several days before he could get on a train, and then the journey home was agonizingly slow.

Upon arrival, he went to enlist in the artillery, his father's service; but this time he found his way barred on medical grounds: a slight abdominal defect he had had from birth, which had never caused him any problems. Maddeningly, just when Nikolai Vitkevich and other friends were being accepted for officer training, Sanya was told to wait, be patient. He burned to rush into the conflict. It was a just war, against the ancient enemy and against Fascism; he was certain of final victory. How could he look his father's image in the eye if he didn't take part? And—as he would later write to his wife while chafing in a camp behind the lines—"One cannot become a great Russian writer, living in the Russia of 1941–43, without having been at the front."[2]

But for the time being, as Hitler gobbled up great chunks of Russia, he and Natasha had to fall back on their prewar plan of becoming rural teachers. At the Cossack settlement of Morozovsk, halfway between Rostov and Stalingrad, Sanya settled to teach mathematics and astronomy to the village children, while Natasha would teach them chemistry and basic Darwinism. They found great pleasure in the excitement of children taught something new, and did their best to make the lessons interesting.

In the quiet, warm, moonlit September evenings, the young teachers would sit out on their porch together with their pleasant, cultivated neighbors, the Bronevitskys. Nikolai Bronevitsky, aged sixty, was one of those engineers, trained before the Revolution, whom Solzhenitsyn appreciated so much. His long, gentle face had a Chekhovian look, and in memory Sanya saw him as wearing pince-nez, though admitting he might not have done in reality. His flaxen-haired wife was even more quiet and gentle; still in her thirties, she seemed faded and middle-aged. Childless themselves, the Bronevitskys not surprisingly took to the intelligent, lively young couple, with whom they discussed the war situation. The tranquillity of the moonlit nights contrasted with the horrifying stories of rout brought by the trainloads of refugees heading for Stalingrad. Towns still officially in Soviet hands were described by these frightened refugees as already surrendered.

There was something about the way Bronevitsky referred to these towns as "taken," not "lost," that struck Sanya as a little odd. Almost as if it were good news. The old man probed, too, as to what they remembered of the years just past. Sanya and Natasha looked at each other curiously, and shrugged. They remembered hard work, and good fun. The university library, exams, theater, amateur concerts. . . . The Chekhovian engineer said, gently, hadn't they lost some of their professors? Weren't they put inside? Well, yes, the youngsters supposed one or two had been, and senior lecturers had replaced them. And students? Yes, some senior students had been jailed.

"And what did you make of it?"

Nothing. They had gone on dancing and studying.

"And no one close to you was—touched?"

They shook their heads. What strange questions he asked! Sanya thought momentarily of Fedorovsky, but—that was long ago.

Bronevitsky confessed he had been in several labor camps, and his health had been ruined. He spoke with blazing anger of the Dzhezkazgan camp, its water and air poisoned by copper. She was there too, said his quiet wife; they had met when they were permitted to go outside the wire. By miracle they were at liberty in Morozovsk at the outbreak of war, and had modest jobs.[3]

Later, Solzhenitsyn would remember how brave the old *zek* had been, in being so open, trying to nudge the naive young intellectuals in the direction of reality. But at that time it was to no avail. Even though they were serious-minded, and Sanya intensely interested in politics, they remained blind to the evil all around them. However, later on the memory of the couple helped him to see more clearly. He would lie on a bunk in some prison or camp and think of their sad, thoughtful Morozovsk neighbors.

By the middle of October 1941, Moscow was threatened; Russia seemed on the point of total collapse. General Guderian, master of the blitzkrieg tactic, sent an inquiry about winter clothing, since there were flurries of snow; he was told it would be sent in due course—it never was—and not to make further silly requests of this type: the winter, as it were, would not be necessary. There was panic and looting in Moscow; German artillery flashes could be seen and heard; government offices frenziedly prepared for withdrawal beyond the Urals. The German high command considered plans to put an electrified fence around besieged Leningrad, then destroy both city and citizens with a mass artillery barrage. The war was over—Goebbels told a foreign press conference in Berlin.

When a little-known general by the name of Zhukov was being appointed commander of the devastated western front, all available cannon fodder, whether men or horses, was being mobilized. Among them—at last—Solzhenitsyn. "How hard it was to leave home that day," he wrote to Natasha many years later; "but it was only that day that my life began."[4]

He found himself mucking out stables, in a camp 150 miles northwest of Stalingrad, with a crowd of elderly and sometimes sickly Don Cossacks from the Morozovsk area. From the very start, when the young intellectual entered the camp with briefcase in hand, he was the butt of jokes and humiliations. Once, his sergeant ordered him to pasture all ninety of the platoon's horses—although Solzhenitsyn could not even ride a horse. Knowing all the horses would escape into the steppe, he was forced to beg for some dirtier but more achievable fatigue.

A month after his enlistment, he learned that Rostov had fallen, and would have worried about his mother. It was a brief occupation; the Wehrmacht commanders had planned only to blow up the Don bridges and withdraw to a more holdable position; but Goebbels made so much capital out of capturing this "gateway to the Caucasus" that General von Kleist's Panzers were forced to try to hold the city. Their retreat, though of minor strategic importance, was the first Wehrmacht setback of the war, and therefore of symbolic value.

In the North, German commanders, their leather boots deep in mud, were thoughtfully rereading Caulaincourt's grim account of Napoleon's 1812 campaign; reminding themselves that he had started it on almost the same June date as Hitler. Snows followed torrential rain, along with fresh, well-fed, warmly clad Siberian troops skiing out from Moscow to drive back the exhausted, starved, and frozen enemy. On 10 December Guderian recorded that the temperature was minus 63 degrees Fahrenheit; men died while squatting to defecate, their anuses freezing up. The misery of the troops in summer uniforms and without fuel to burn was so extreme that many sought relief in suicide, clutching a grenade to the stomach. Goebbels announced, to the same journalists who had heard him say the war was over, that weather conditions had brought the advance to a temporary halt.

The winter of 1941–42 was not troubling Solzhenitsyn in his quiet behind-the-lines backwater; indeed, he always loved cold. Existence became more than bearable as he grew used to the rough old Cossacks and they to him. "On my name-day," he informed Natasha, "I've been shovelling manure: how appropriate!" He learned to ride bareback. Life was easy: no drill, no weapons to clean, no training. There was even time to read in the evenings. What did trouble him intensely was having to live such an unproductive, unheroic life. The Red Army was hardly making the best use of a physics graduate of great energy and intelligence. He wrote request after request to be properly trained and sent to the front.

Nothing had any effect. Then, in March 1942, a former mathematics student of Rostov University arrived as the unit's new political commissar. He was sympathetic to a fellow graduate, and arranged for him to take a packet to Thirteenth Military District headquarters in Stalingrad. At the same time a tank-corps lieutenant, recovering from wounds, asked Solzhenitsyn to take another packet to his corps headquarters, informing them of his whereabouts. The messenger was told to leave his stained smock behind and kit himself in regular private's uniform and greatcoat. On 23 March, Natasha had just finished breakfast and was reading *Molot*, the Red Army newspaper, when she saw a soldier, in greatcoat and fur hat, press his smiling face to the windowpane. Sanya! She rushed to the door and into his arms. He could stay, he said, until late the next night. Before he left for Stalingrad she gave him her photograph, inscribed "After half a year's separation, I bravely meet the new and even longer separation. It will not be a final one." Actually it would last, save for one snatched reunion at the front and some prison visits, for fifteen years. She returned to her teaching, and to passing the lonely evenings in new studies: geography, history, German, even astronomy—going outside at night to gaze up at the stars.

At headquarters, the fellow officers of the wounded tank-corps lieutenant who had sent a message via Solzhenitsyn were so delighted that they agreed to direct the messenger to artillery headquarters. There, the staff officers had the wisdom, on inspecting his papers, to post him to a course for battery commanders in a town called Semyonov. Radiantly happy, Sanya set off for artillery training, in the wake of such artillery officers as Isaaki Solzhenitsyn and Lev Tolstoy.

It took him a fortnight to travel a few hundred miles. Refugees and retreating troops caused chaos everywhere. This experience brought him up with a shock against the disaster that had overtaken Russia. Under orders from the Führer not to withdraw, the Wehrmacht had stood its ground— at immense cost—and by the end of winter the Red Army's counter-offensive had spent itself. The Wehrmacht began pushing forward again. Solzhenitsyn saw the consequence, in exhausted, dispirited men, shuffling toward the east, clogging the roads and railway stations. His heart went out to them, and he envied them their heroic suffering. His prewar scepticism about Stalin's leadership, in such contrast to his adulation of Lenin, became sharpened. In 1962 he would draw on the chaos of that fortnight's travel in a story called "Incident at Krechetovka Station." As in so much of his fiction, the main character, Zotov, was strongly autobiographical. However, the author set the events earlier—in October 1941—and made Zotov a lieutenant in charge of transport at a small station, rather than a private sent off to artillery school. The idealistic Zotov turns over a bedraggled, exhausted officer to the NKVD, mainly because he has suspiciously referred to Stalingrad by its former name of Tsaritsyn.

Uneasy about his action, though from a pragmatic point of view it is justifiable, Zotov is mainly tortured by the question of why the greatest military power in the world has been so overwhelmed; and what will be the end?

Cataclysmic though the situation was, it might have been even worse—and fatal for Stalin—if Hitler had shown an ounce of intelligent decency in his treatment of the overrun peoples. Instead, he inflicted savage cruelty and terror. "Confident in approaching victory," the Germans found it "agreeable to combine duty and sport; to bask in the glow of the crusader while enjoying the particular physical pleasure which so many Germans derive from the infliction of pain."[5] Later, fear and guilt, and sullen hatred at the countering barbarities, changed the motivation but by no means diminished the cruelty. Often the Germans were greeted as liberators; and, in places where an official ruled with some decency and tolerance, to all but the Jews—opening churches, and reintroducing free markets—on the whole those local people lived peaceably and even productively. The people of Kharkov, for instance, would long consider the two years of German occupation—despite their extermination of the Jews, which many indeed counted as a virtue—as the best years of their lives.

But tolerable governors were few. The Slavs were only a little less subhuman than the Jews. Koch, governor of the Ukraine, agreed with his superior Goering that "the best thing would be to kill all the men over fifteen years old, and then send in the SS stallions." Whipping Ukrainians to death in public places, day after day, was a favorite recreation. If a hundred "Communists" (that is, Slavs) were to be shot for the death of one German soldier, the means of execution, according to army orders, had to increase the deterrent effect. Firing squads should aim at or below the waist. (Otherwise, it was explained, children might escape execution altogether!) This practice meant that most victims were buried alive, in agony also from stomach wounds. Deterrence indeed . . .

Tragic Ukraine. The boy who in the famine sat day after day in his empty house may, a decade on, have been whipped to death or buried alive by Germans.

The fate of prisoners of war was terrible beyond words. The German high command ruled that there was no obligation to feed Bolshevik prisoners. As a result, according to Goering in a jocular memo, "After having eaten everything possible, including the soles of their boots, they have begun to eat each other and, what is more serious, have eaten a German sentry." The prison compounds were places of abandoned hope and utter misery just as certainly as were the extermination camps. Often no one entered the compounds except soldiers with flamethrowers. More than three million prisoners of war (three in every five) died from mass executions, forced marches, and starvation.

Stalin shared the blame with Hitler, for he had not signed the Hague Convention guaranteeing decent treatment of war prisoners. It was considered a crime for Red Army soldiers to surrender; and many officers shot themselves rather than be taken, fearing there would be reprisals against their families.

On the German side, the "ordinary" soldier was deeply implicated in the brutality, though the West, after the war, hid the extent of Wehrmacht atrocity. The barbarity could even (at least where Jews were concerned) be openly shared with relatives. Thus, a soldier called Franzl wrote to his mother that "yesterday we and the SS showed mercy towards every Jew we caught by just shooting them. Today it is different. So far we have consigned some 1,000 Jews to death, beaten with cudgels and spades."[6] (O that softhearted mother, pressing her son's letter to her warm bosom!) When Wehrmacht recruits were sent to the East, they entered a landscape of terror unimaginable to Bosch, a different world. Alan Clark has eloquently described the shock: "Once they had traversed the frontier of the occupied territories they were in a belt of country, up to five hundred miles across, where the septic violence of Nazism festered openly—no longer concealed beneath the trim roofs and *Gemütlichkeit* of suburban Germany. Mass murder, deportations, deliberate starvation of prisoner cages, the burning alive of school children, 'target practice' on civilian hospitals—atrocities were so commonplace that no man coming fresh to the scene could stay sane without acquiring a protective veneer of brutalisation."[7]

Fear of his own political commissars was only one reason for the fierce fighting spirit of the Russian soldier. Centuries of hardship and persecution had bred toughness; from the first, the invaders did not find the soft, sybaritic defeatism they had encountered in many of the French: here, if their officers were good, the troops fought tigerishly even in the opening weeks of rapid collapse. Moreover, when Stalin came out of his catatonic withdrawal, he cunningly appealed to his "brothers and sisters" to defend holy Russia rather than Communism. But above all the Germans forced the Red Army to fight "with insane stubbornness," "like wild beasts," because they gave them no alternative. General Guderian observed sadly, "We started to mistreat them much too soon."

What a comment on our century, Anna Akhmatova remarked with a grim smile to a friend in Leningrad-under-siege, that these are the happiest times of our life! Because for the first time the barbarians were not *within* the Russian people; or at least, not so openly. Of course, there were still millions in the Gulag. Akhmatova's son was released to fight in a punitive battalion—only to be rearrested after the war.

Nazism had turned slaves into patriots: a signal achievement. So, in March 1942, when Private Solzhenitsyn made his tortuous way to artillery school, Russia's plight was desperate but not—quite—hopeless. The elephant—in a German colonel's vivid metaphor—was still killing millions of ants; but the ants kept on swarming back onto him.

The arrival of a private, a raw recruit who had not even learned to salute yet, let alone received basic military training, astonished the Semyonov instructors. All their trainees were lieutenants or captains already appointed to be battery commanders. Solzhenitsyn was summoned to the CO, who suspected a trick. However, the private had shown himself capable of handling the technicalities, involving as they did a lot of mathematics, and the CO sent him on to proper officer-training school. Natasha was also on the move: Morozovsk being threatened by the German advance, the school was closed down and Natasha returned to live with her mother in Rostov, where she worked in a university laboratory making artillery fuses. Every fourth day the workers had to walk for hours across the steppe and there dig antitank ditches. The Germans were only thirty-five miles away, and there were constant bombing raids. Ironically, as Natasha observes in her account of their early marriage, she was closer to the front line than was Sanya. She had had no news of him; but then, on 2 May, Taissia, "as expansive as I was by nature," rushed into the lab excitedly waving a letter. "From Sanya! He's in Kostroma!"

Kostroma, where the Third Leningrad Artillery School was situated, is 180 miles northeast of Moscow. A river port on the banks of the Volga, it was a historic city. Plunged into the deliberate privations and brutality of an accelerated officer-training course, Solzhenitsyn still managed to keep a tiny corner of life for reading and writing, though facing hostility in so doing; he may, in these odd moments of privacy and reflection, have discovered that the people of Kostroma, in 1264, won a battle at Svyatoye Ozero ("Holy Lake") against earlier barbarians. The city later found fame as the cradle of the Romanov dynasty. Its dominating Assumption Cathedral, with a four-tiered belfry, was demolished in the 1930s.

The only escape from camp was a weekly march to the town bathhouse, and maneuvers in the countryside. On these welcome half escapes into nature, Solzhenitsyn found himself drawn to the bleak northern landscape, with its forlorn, decayed villages, even more than to the green meadows and woods of central Russia. He liked spareness and sparseness, uncluttered simplicity. At the same time, something unusual was happening to him, under the influence of being trained to be an elite. He was learning "a tiger-like stride and a rasping voice of command," and also enjoying not having to think for himself but just to obey orders.

While the summer months of training wore on, the Germans continued to make great gains. In July 1942, the battle for Stalingrad began; and Rostov came under fierce attack. Natasha, her mother, and Taissia managed to escape the panicking city, fighting their way onto one of the last trains out before the bridges were destroyed. Natasha found shelter for a time with her aunt Zhenia and a doctor cousin in Kislovodsk. The mountain spa town, with its "lovely fragrance" and association with her husband, seemed amazingly peaceful. They went to the theater and watched Dumas's *The Lady with the Camelias*.

But that peace did not last long. The German troops captured Rostov in only three days. Russia was shocked; the press openly attributed the disaster to "cowards and panic-stricken creatures."[8] General (later Marshal) Malinovsky was relieved of his command, though later exonerated. The Caucasus was open to the Germans, and with it almost the whole of the USSR's crude oil fields. Beyond them lay Turkey, Iraq, Persia, India.

Forty divisions poured south, and within a few weeks the swastika flew above Mount Elbrus, greatest of Caucasian peaks. Natasha, with her mother, aunt, and two cousins, fled again; they walked a hundred burning, dust-laden miles from Pyatigorsk to Nalchik. Natasha carried—this was wifely devotion—Sanya's manuscripts. The four women traveled from Nalchik to Baku, thence across the Caspian by boat. They had a two-thousand-mile train journey to Alma-Ata on the southern border of Kazakhstan. Their great journey finished in a town two hundred miles northeast, Taldy-Kurgan. Natasha's mother got a job as a store bookkeeper.

In occupied Rostov, a liquidation of Jews and other "undesirables" got under way. Tens of thousands were shot in a ravine called Zmeevskaya Balka. Other Jews were packed into gas-vans thirty or forty at a time; but this was less pleasant for the Germans because the victims emptied their bowels as they died. Some Russians betrayed Jews.[9]

Sanya's Jewish friend, Lydia Ezherets, with her boyfriend Simonyan, still a medical student, had managed to escape to central Asia. Simonyan later served on the western front, in Moscow, and in Japan.

The Soviet forces held the Germans at Ordzhonikidze in November. General von Kleist was permitted by Hitler to withdraw northward toward the Don. He held the line forty miles south of Rostov.

Rostov was a devastated city. Natasha's laboratory was destroyed, as was the house in Chekhov Lane where she and Sanya had lived, and his mother's house in Voroshilov Street. A student friend of Sanya's, Ferul Mazin, went to look; he saw one bare wall standing, and hanging on it was a map of the world—Sanya's map. . . .[10]

A letter from Sanya to Natasha, proudly signed "Your lieutenant," reached her in Taldy-Kurgan in late October 1942. Such postal efficiency, amid disaster!

The newly promoted officer still felt confident of ultimate Soviet victory: "For two summers Hitler has been trying to topple this boulder with the hands of all Europe. But he has not succeeded. Nor will he succeed in another two summers."[11] He worried about his manuscripts and academic records, and about his mother. In January 1943, he sent a telegram to "liberated" Georgievsk, asking his aunt Maria for news of her. His mother had indeed gone to Maria's, after the frantic escape from Rostov, and found Roman and Irina there too. She felt that Maria was mean, and kept her short of food, so she traveled back through German-held territory to occupied Rostov. There she found her home destroyed, including most of her poor furniture. She rented a fourth-floor room, without water or heating, and had to carry water and firewood up four flights of stairs. A bad attack of tuberculosis struck her down, compelling her to return to Georgievsk. Her actions suggest a woman at the end of her tether.

Sanya received no reply to his telegram. But at least he heard from Natasha, and knew she was safe in Kazakhstan.

With her unparalleled poetic power, Akhmatova—herself evacuated to central Asia, ordered out of besieged Leningrad—described the southeastward journey of so many; she followed painfully the almost endless track of her *zek* son, yet also felt assured of vengeance—against both tyrannies, presumably:

> . . . And already the frozen Kama
> Could be seen, and someone stammered
> "Quo vadis?" and before lips moved,
> Another panorama,
> With bridges and tunnels—the hammer
> Of the Urals pounded below.
> And under my eyes unravelled
> That road so many had travelled,
> By which they led away my son.
> And that road was long—long—long, amidst the
> Solemn and crystal
> Stillness
> Of Siberia's earth.
> From all that to ash is rendered,
> Filled with mortal dread yet
> Knowing the calendar
> Of vengeance, having wrung her
> Hands, her dry eyes lowered, Russia
> Walked before me towards the east.[12]

But by no means every Russian wanted the Germans to leave—especially those south of the Don.

12

Fighting for Lenin

Pride grows in the human heart like lard on a pig.[1]
—SOLZHENITSYN, *The Gulag Archipelago*

SANYA PREDICTED, IN A LETTER TO NATASHA, THAT THE PATRIOTIC war would pass into a revolutionary war with the imperialist-capitalist allies. He was willing, he told her, to die for Leninism. Given his ideological ardor, it is all the more extraordinary that the ex-*zek* Bronevitsky spoke so frankly on those peaceful, moonlit nights.

Now Morozovsk was in German hands, and Natasha learned that their former neighbor had been appointed burgomaster. Sanya's reaction to the news, like Natasha's, was "Filthy swine!" Twenty years later, writing *The Gulag Archipelago*, he makes a persuasive, and indeed moving, defense of Bronevitsky and other collaborators. Accustomed to believe that everything that appeared in the government's hate-filled propaganda about the West was lies, they naturally assumed that attacks on Nazi vileness were equally so. Also "the newspapers were forever changing their minds about the Hitlerites: at first it was friendly encounters between nice sentries in nasty Poland, and the newspapers were awash with sympathy for the valiant warriors standing up to French and English bankers . . . then one morning (the second morning of the war) an explosion of headlines—all Europe was piteously groaning under the Nazi heel."[2] It was understandable, therefore, that Bronevitsky gave the Germans a chance to show themselves as liberators.

Battery Commander Solzhenitsyn—by no means ready to understand in the middle of war—tried to explore the act of treachery in a short story with the Chekhovian title of "In the Town of M—." He was being moved around Russia—to Saransk, in central Russia, "three little houses in a flat field," he described it to Natasha; in February 1943, to the far north, the forests near Lake Ilmen, west of Novgorod; then, in April, five hundred miles south again to the river Neruch, near Orel. Still he was, maddeningly, being denied the crucial experience he thought necessary to a great writer in such an epoch—to fight. But at least the waiting around so characteristic of soldiering was giving him time to hone his writing talent. He armed himself with a field table and fold-up chair, and had his photo taken showing him seated at this, his pencil at ready. It looks a shade self-conscious. "The ideas are simply crowding on to my pen," he told Natasha. He would never lose the sense of being a soldier, continuing the battle with his pen, in rough conditions—preferably the open air.

By now the tide in the titanic struggle had begun to turn. After General von Paulus's surrender at Stalingrad, on 2 February 1943, the Reich would be fighting a defensive war. In April, the Germans claimed to have found a mass grave at Katyn, near Smolensk, and that the victims had been Polish officers, shot by the NKVD. The Polish government in exile believed the Germans. Stalin, deeply affronted by such a calumny, created his own Polish government in waiting.

In May, Sanya at last received a letter from his mother. He was relieved she was alive, but distressed to hear she had been ill with tuberculosis ever since an unhappy stay in Rostov. Sanya had been constantly aware of the danger to her from the Germans; "but for some reason, Natasha," he wrote, "I never expected it from that direction. Somehow I forgot to expect it." He told his wife that her, Natasha's, survival gave him something to live for. He also forbade her to wear lipstick; everything must be natural. Perhaps he feared the effect of her attractiveness. Deprived of men in her family, Natasha was probably not displeased by his masterfulness.

She knew he was not jealous of any effect she might be having on Kazakh men, in faroff Taldy-Kurgan: he was simply not the jealous type. Perhaps sexual frustration was making him censorious about women who "flaunted themselves." Actually he was drawn to feminine women, women who dressed to please a man. One of his most sensuous, sardonic, yet also envious, passages in *The Gulag Archipelago* records a *zek*'s reminiscence of a luxurious Moscow weekend in summer 1943. This man had been living a splendid life, in comfort, while others fought and died. "Do you understand what *dinner* is for a woman?" the *zek* inquired, his eyes sparkling. "For a woman it is absolutely unimportant what she had for breakfast or luncheon or what kind of work she does during the day. What's important for her is: her dress, her shoes, and her dinner! At the Prague restaurant there was a black-out, but you could go up onto the roof. . . . The aromatic summer air! . . . Next to you a woman in a *silk* dress. We have caroused the whole night long, and now we are drinking only champagne! . . ." His personal car waits to whisk them to his dacha in the pine woods. "Do you understand what a pine forest is like in the morning? Several hours of sleep behind closed shutters. We wake about ten—with the sun trying to break in through the Venetian blinds. All around the room is the lovely disorder of women's clothes. . . ." Then a *light* breakfast with red wine on the veranda, sunbathing and swimming. If it's a working Sunday, to the office (he is on "vital" work) to give a few orders. . . . [3]

The image of the women's clothes scattered around hints that Solzhenitsyn may have embroidered the narrative to match his own desires, for that image occurs frequently in his novels. For most of his twenties and thirties he had little enough chance of experiencing "a sweet disorder in the dress," which naturally would have appealed to the repressed instincts of the excessively ordered Sanya.

Deprived of Natasha, he was richly consoled in the spring of 1943 by meeting up with his dearest friend, Nikolai Vitkevich. One of his sergeants reported visiting a regiment that had just moved alongside theirs, as part of the buildup for the planned attack on Orel; and Solzhenitsyn realized it was the regiment to which Nikolai belonged. He jumped in a captured Opel Blitz and headed off to the next-door unit. He was directed to where he would find Lieutenant Vitkevich.

In a photograph taken around the time of their reunion, Sanya rests his arm on Koka's shoulder, and gazes warmly and emotionally straight into his friend's round, peasantlike face. Not for the first or last time we sense that, however much he desired women, Solzhenitsyn found a deeper spiritual and intellectual bond with close male friends. He and Koka almost immediately plunged back into political discussions, each drawing on the wealth of experience they had accrued since student days. Koka, an infantry officer, had been cajoled into joining the Party; Sanya was one of only two among the thirty officers of his battalion who declined to join. But Koka still thought along almost identical, anti-Stalinist lines as Sanya. They were like two halves of a single walnut, Sanya wrote in an autobiographical poem.

The two young officers, after days of discussion, astonishingly drew up a program for change, entitled "Resolution No. 1." They argued that the Soviet regime stifled economic development, literature, culture, and everyday life; a new organization was needed to fight to put things right. They were playing with fire, but seemed careless of the risk they were running. The government had downgraded the role of the political commissars in the army in favor of the purely military command, and this slight liberalization, won by the Red Army's success, may have lulled the friends into feeling secure.

Arrogance may also have played a part. "My power convinced me that I was a superior human being," Solzhenitsyn accused himself, looking back at those dashing days. Another of Stalin's rewards for the military (he who had been responsible for the deaths of more officers than the German army) was to restore their tsarist privileges. Badges of rank, abolished in the Revolution, reappeared; the Red Army now observed differences of rank more strictly than the British. In the U.S. and British armies, junior officers were paid three or four times more than privates; in the new Red Army, they were paid a hundred times as much. Sanya could afford to send money orders to Natasha and—less often—his mother.

The wiser Solzhenitsyn of the Brezhnev era lacerates himself for having enjoyed the trappings of his command: the orderlies leaping to pick up anything he had dropped; the rolls and butter in his separate bivouac; the right to address fathers and grandfathers in a demeaning style; to bawl men out and get them to do stupid punishments when they were exhausted.

An "anal" temperament might be drawn to play the harsh disciplinarian; aggression would always be one aspect of his huge energy; he would become expert at hurling verbal knives at his enemies, not unlike Grandfather Zakhar's knife threats against Roman. Nonetheless, Sanya was doubtless exaggerating his officerly arrogance. His men respected him, and he treated them as intelligent human beings. The specialism of his battery, which was to plot the position of enemy guns by analyzing their sound waves, meant that they often had time on their hands: even during a battle. Six separate listening posts were connected by phone to a central operator. Solzhenitsyn entertained and educated his men by having the operator read to them. Their favorites were *War and Peace* and a contemporary, down-to-earth mock epic of army life, *Vasily Tyorkin*, by Alexander Tvardovsky, a peasant's son. Sanya himself admired Tvardovsky's poem intensely, and thought of sending him a letter of appreciation.

Tvardovsky would one night start to read a story by Alexander Solzhenitsyn in bed, but within a few pages be so moved that he got up and dressed, feeling he could not dishonor such a writer by reading his book while wearing pajamas. But a lot would happen before then.

Sanya's own writing was consuming him in the time between military duties. Natasha complained she was not receiving enough letters from him. "Do you want me to become a writer or don't you?" he asked her.

No time for stories or letters on 5 July 1943, when the Germans, seeking to atone for Stalingrad, launched their offensive on the Kursk salient, ushering in the greatest tank battle in history. That which Solzhenitsyn had longed for was at last happening. And when he was later asked, by the merry *zek* recalling nights of passion in the summer of forty-three, if he knew what a *light* breakfast was, Solzhenitsyn nodded. "Of course I understand. It is still dark in the trenches, and one can of American pork stew for eight men, and then—'Hurrah! for the Motherland! For Stalin!' and over the top."[4]

For the first time in the war, the Red Army had been able to prepare for this battle unhurriedly and calmly. It had built up massive forces, and defensive fortifications stretched sixty miles behind the front, over a quiet landscape of valleys and copses, rivers, villages, and cornfields. General Rokossovsky's central front, to which both Solzhenitsyn and Vitkevich belonged, contained more artillery than infantry regiments: twenty thousand guns and 920 *Katyusha* multiple-rocket throwers. At the height of the battle, three thousand tanks were on the move at once. The Germans, despite their renewal of strength since Stalingrad, had felt in the planning more fatalism than confidence. If they could not knock out the Russians in the first few days, they never would. "Independence Day for America," a Panzer Corps chief observed gloomily, "the beginning of the end for Germany."[5]

The Red Army's artillery did its work expertly on the first day of battle. "Russian artillery was incomparably stronger in weight, numbers and direction. . . . The result was that many of the tanks were disabled by mines in the first half mile." Crews of disabled tanks were ordered to stay put and continue fighting: so became easy targets for the Soviet tanks. The next morning "the sun rose on a classic tableau of positional warfare, almost as if the Great War had been running continuously since 1917, with only the influx of more sophisticated equipment to mark the passage of time."[6] Brown smoke rose from burned corn and thatched roofs, and black, oily smoke from burned-out tanks; *Katyusha* rockets screamed above the chatter of small arms and the regular thump of the big guns. There was no German breakthrough over the next days and weeks. Elsewhere, the Western Allies invaded Sicily, then the *Duce* resigned. With the stalemate at Kursk, the war was lost for the Germans. Solzhenitsyn had chosen, or rather been chosen by, a decisive moment to fight his first campaign.

The Red Army counterattacked and, on 5 August 1943, Orel fell. Solzhenitsyn entered the city. Ten days later he was promoted to first lieutenant and awarded the Order of the Patriotic War, second class. He must have thought of his father's medals, buried in Rostov, and felt proud to have lived up to his memory. From now until March 1944 his unit was continuously in action as the Germans were driven back across European Russia to the Dnieper, fighting and dying in a bleak alien country, with that grim enemy, winter, coming soon.

Solzhenitsyn's battery operated with a good deal of independence, which suited him. He maintained tight discipline, and his unit was praised as one of the most efficient. Cool in the face of danger, he complained only that he had little time for his writing. Listening to the stories of his men, observing landscapes, diving into liberated towns—even, once, witnessing the execution of two Bronevitsky-like "traitors" in an atmosphere of drunken carnival—he wanted to record everything; his notebook became more vital than his revolver. Natasha, who had found a teaching post in her central Asian haven, and was rediscovering a tomboyish exuberance, was confronted in Sanya with a still-innocent youthful bravado. He wrote of taking up cigarettes, as it helped him concentrate on writing; of trying vodka. . . . An experienced soldier, who had presumably helped to kill scores of Germans, he was still the slightly prim, serious schoolboy who blushes at swearing and coarse jokes.

He was urging Natasha to return to Rostov. She was reluctant to abandon her teaching, but at last consented. He looked forward to their reunion during a ten-day leave he was granted, during a respite in the fighting, in March 1944. First, however, he went to Moscow, where he met up with his friends Lydia Ezherets and Kirill Simonyan. Simonyan, now a captain in the medical corps, was working for Lydia's father. Dr. Ezherets had moved from Rostov at the war's outset to head a well-known Moscow sanatorium. Currently it was a rest home for the top military. The three friends had a joyful reunion, and Sanya and Kirill sat up all night discussing politics. Kirill shared Sanya's views of Stalin, but not his enthusiasm for Marxism-Leninism. He still wanted to write, after the war, and hoped the five friends (the Three Musketeers plus Lydia and Natasha) could form a "commune" as they had always planned.

Dr. Ezherets allowed his daughter's friend to sleep in the luxury suite. "Do you know who used it last, Sanya? . . . Rokossovksy!"

So Sanya, who had dreamed of being a general, slept in a general's bed on this occasion.

Lydia, a postgraduate student in German literature, had offered Sanya in a letter to send on some of his stories to the writers Konstantin Fedin and Boris Lavrenev for an opinion. She was still waiting for a response, she told Sanya, who felt as if his whole future depended on their reply. If they said he had no talent, he wrote Natasha, "I'll tear my heart out of my breast, I'll stamp out fifteen years of my life."[7]

He took the train to Rostov and Natasha. But she was not there; her mother had fallen ill just before they were due to leave. Painfully disappointed, Sanya returned to his unit in Zhlobin, in Belorussia. He was fond of "sorrowful Belorussia," he would later write; "I became poignantly attached to its melancholy, sparse landscape and its gentle people."[8] As he arrived he would have looked for letters: from Natasha, from Koka. He wanted to tell the latter, especially, about his meeting with their two friends, and their political discussions.

But there was a quite unexpected return-to-sender. A money order to his mother in Georgievsk. It was marked "Addressee deceased."

The news was a hammer blow. We can imagine him walking out into the gray, bleak landscape; feeling unreal; lighting a cigarette, but not to help him to write, this time. Then guilt, guilt. Should he have done more for her? He had always moaned at her slowness, her indecisiveness; at carrying the awful burden of knowing she lived for him. And what had he done in return? He had not even bothered to go from Rostov to Georgievsk during his leave. Perhaps she would still have been alive; or, if not, at least he would have shown loyalty and love, and could have mourned at her fresh grave. There were more ways than Bronevitsky's to be a traitor.

He wrote to Natasha, addressing the letter to Rostov: "Mama has died. I am left with all the good she did for me and all the bad I did to her. No one wrote to me about her death. . . . Apparently she died in March."

But that turned out not to be the case. A letter, two months old, arrived from Aunt Irina. Taissia had died, she wrote, on 17 January—two weeks after Uncle Roman had died of a neglected ulcer. There was no money to pay a gravedigger to bury Taissia, so she had been laid in Roman's fresh grave.

The thought of his mother's poverty increased Sanya's guilt. He had sent her money, but not so much as he had sent to Natasha. However, he had not known she was quite so destitute.

At the end of the First World War, his father; now, at the beginning of the end of this war, his mother. The curious parallels continued.

Solzhenityn rarely talks about his mother, and has written very little about her: she whose every cough and turn in the bed he had heard for fourteen years. Her memory is too sacred to him, his friends explain.

When Natasha and her mother arrived in Rostov, by way of Moscow, she read Sanya's sad news and grieved too for Taissia. She had loved her vivacity, which shone through despite the illness slowing her up.

She could at least pass on some good news, received from Lydia Ezherets in Moscow: Boris Lavrenev had replied, saying he had found the stories "nice," and he had submitted them to the magazine *Znamya*. An established author could hardly use a less lukewarm adjective than "nice," especially to a frontline soldier; but his submitting the stories to a magazine was unexpected and encouraging.

Proud of her talented husband, Natasha reflected that it was high time they brought a child into the world. Now that he had lost his mother, surely Sanya too would want to pass life on. She wondered about her own father, lost to her; she had never known him. In Moscow, she had just been party to a very moving reconciliation. Visiting her uncle, Valentin Turkin, she and her mother, Maria—who had not seen her brother for thirty years—had been greeted so warmly by him that Maria had asked, "Volodya, now what about meeting your *own* daughter?" He blinked; his daughter, Veronica, was sixteen, lived only fifteen minutes' walk away, yet he had not seen her since she was a few months old. They got him to write her a note, and Natasha witnessed their spontaneously happy meeting, in which Valentin spoke to her as if they had been close all her life![9]

How Natasha longed to be greeted by her own father like that. . . . It would never be. But she would be with her husband soon, Sanya's letter promised. There were many women at the camp. He would send one of his men to collect her. Unconsciously, he wanted to relive that memorable episode in his father's war when Taissia came to the front and they were joined in marriage by the chaplain. And so, one May night, Natasha was roused out of sleep by her mother shouting, "Natasha, a sergeant is at the door!" Natasha threw on a bathrobe and went to let him in. While he had a meal and slept, Natasha dressed and at dawn went out to pace the streets, so excited was she at the prospect of being with Sanya again.

The next night she and Sergeant Ilya Solomin set out for Moscow. He had brought for her a field shirt with a wide leather belt, epaulets, and a tiny star that she fixed to a gray beret. Her Red Army pass certified that she had already served some time with the unit. She liked the intelligent young sergeant; especially when he praised his battery commander so highly. Ilya had sad eyes even when he smiled. It was little wonder; a Jew, his entire family had been wiped out in Minsk.

After staying with the Turkins overnight in Moscow, they set out west for Belorussia, and at last arrived at the complex of trenches. "Here we were, the two of us together. I was with my husband. In his dugout. Or was I dreaming?" She was not dreaming; but soon their intimacy was interrupted by the phone: Sanya was to bring his wife to the mess. She felt shy being with so many officers, but the vodka she drank for the first time in her life gave her courage. And there were other women, some picked up on the way, to serve as nurses or orderlies as well as "wives." Sanya, indeed, hoped Natasha would stay; with her chemistry degree she was amply qualified. He felt proud of her; their eyes kept meeting, as each talked with some officer or other. The front line had moved away westward, and to Natasha it seemed there was a relaxed, almost festive, atmosphere.

She and Sanya returned to his dugout. This May was exceptionally cold. They lit a stove. "Evening. Logs crackled in the stove." Her quiet way, surely, of implying passion as well as coziness, the scatter of clothes he had imagined and longed for. And bereavement often brings heightened desire.[10]

Afterward she said, "Tell me about your meeting with Koka." She still had a tender feeling for the boy who, she was convinced, had been in love with her—and still might be, a little.

"I'll read to you. 'The Sixth Course' begins with it."

"The Sixth Course" was a novel he planned, about students in war. The first five courses were at a university, the sixth was in battle. After running through his literary plans, he told her about his political discussions with Koka. Literature and politics were already closely entwined in Sanya's plans. Stalin, he and Koka believed, was diverging still further from Lenin's ideals. These epaulets. Alliance with England and the United States . . . The national anthem restored . . .

Perhaps of more interest to her were his views on the new marriage laws. These were designed to strengthen the family. At the Revolution, the laws of divorce and legitimacy had been completely relaxed. Now, an impending divorce had to be announced in a certain newspaper, with a delay of up to two years. The stigma of illegitimacy returned, with an effort to strengthen the family. Sanya no doubt agreed with Raisa Orlova, fervent Communist in 1944 and opposed to the changes: "People should be together as long as they were in love and should split up when love was gone. Nothing or no one should be an obstacle to that, least of all the state."[11] At this time, Solzhenitsyn's quarrel with Stalin appears to have been that he was too conservative; he even advised Natasha to buy the works of Marx, Engels, and Lenin, as he feared they might disappear after the war.[12]

And yet, for all his egalitarian and libertarian ideals, he seemed to enjoy making his men jump to it. He arranged for her to work at the switchboard, plotting distances; whenever he entered the trench, he expected her to stand to attention like the others. She declined; she was his wife. Her unreasonable attitude was undermining discipline, he said. She wanted them to have time to themselves, and this got in the way of his duties and also his all-important writing. It was bad enough having to share his writing and reading with his military duties—and now to have a wife to share it with too.

To judge by his later correspondence with her, he became annoyed with her domestic concerns, such as her desire to have children. How selfish it was, when their country was in a great conflagration—and he was attempting to become a great writer, like his hero of this time, Maxim Gorky! But their relationship remained, on the surface, warm: or so Natasha believed and believes. It was she who, after a month, proposed that she leave for Moscow, having read about postgraduate courses at Moscow University. The brigade was also about to have a new commander, General Travkin, who disliked having women in the front line. Sanya thought her ideas for a postgraduate course in Moscow were good. He embraced her warmly on saying *Do svidaniya*, then strode away briskly.

Her Moscow idea came to nothing; settling into Rostov once more, she took up a position as a laboratory assistant.

She left the battery just in time—the Belorussian front leaped into action. During nine days of advance Sanya hardly had time to jot down more than a few descriptive phrases. He was promoted to captain. Natasha rejoiced at the "swift, headlong, triumphant" advances of the summer of 1944; yet did Sanya plan to occupy *her*, entirely? It made her a little uneasy; he had been noncommittal too when she had talked of children. Yet of course what she most remembered was the excitement of it, and their happiness together. What an adventure!

13

Everything Is Allowed

But that was in another country.
—MARLOWE

IT WAS POSSIBLE, NOW, TO THINK OF A FUTURE. LYDIA EZHERETS was about to marry Kirill before he was sent to the front as medical officer. Natasha had come to feel quite close to her, she told Sanya in a letter, following her meeting with her in Moscow. Natasha was also in contact with Nikolai through letters; he chastised her for having been at the front; perhaps through having spent part of his childhood in a Muslim country he had strict views about a woman's place. If he felt jealous that Sanya had won her, he nobly suppressed the feeling. The great friendship of the Three Musketeers plus two girls had survived. Sanya, his wife knew, was in favor of setting up a commune together after the war, in Moscow or Leningrad. Whether seriously or not, she wrote saying: "Nadya Simonyan° is going to Leningrad. I have already written Lydia: Why not give Nadya the mission of looking for a place for us all to live?"[1]

Sanya felt closer to Nikolai than ever before: they were, he wrote Natasha, "like two trains that are travelling side by side at the same speed, and one could step from one to the other while they are moving."[2] With Koka alone did he feel a sense of seamless continuity, he said. It was a quietly vicious attack on her, and she felt it; she may have wondered to whom he was married. Could she be quite sure he would not take on board one of those camp followers she had met? Would he take up with some blond Polyak? Were his criticisms of the stricter laws on divorce a veiled threat?

Though Koka had been moved to another front, he and Sanya continued to discuss their anti-Stalinist "Resolution" in an exchange of letters, referring jokily to "the war after the war" in which they would carry out the program

---

°Sister of Kirill, she became a well-known composer.

drawn up in the—echoing the Tehran conference—"Big Two" conference they had had. Stalin was "the mustachioed one" or *pakhan*, the big shot. But as the autumn drew on Sanya complained to his wife that Koka's letters had dried up. Vitkevich, writing to Natasha, made the same complaint about Sanya. Sanya even sent one letter to him via Natasha, and that did reach him. He sent Natasha his photo; Koka's face was thinner than she remembered, and had the grim, haunted look of a front-line infantry fighter that she had not seen on Sanya's.

By the end of 1944, Sanya's battery was a hundred miles northeast of Warsaw, camped near Byalystok. He received a fuller, written report on his stories from Boris Lavrenev. He was complimentary, but regretted that *Znamya* had rejected the stories as not being sufficiently "positive"; "In the Town of M—," for example, tried too hard to understand the motivation of collaborators. The mixture of encouragement and discouragement no doubt heightened Sanya's frustration. How magnificently, he lamented to Natasha, he could write "The Sixth Course," if only there were the time!

He kept returning also to the conflict of vocation and domesticity that had reared up during her stay in his unit: she had told him she could not imagine their future without a child. Anyone, he now insisted, could produce and raise a child. "But to write a history of the post-October years as a work of art is something that perhaps I alone can do, and even then only by dividing my work with Koka, and perhaps with somebody else. That's how much this work is beyond the brain, body, and life of one person!"[3]

Koka, Koka again! Well, that was familiar to Natasha. But who was this "somebody else"? Certainly not she. Then Kirill? Or a woman? That blond Polyak . . . or just someone he was warning her she might have to share him with, one day. Because, for his work, everything would be allowed.

"Everything is allowed!" This was the sinister order of January 1945, parodying Dostoyevsky's *Demons*, issued by Stalin as the Red Army launched its offensive that would end in Berlin. They were to remember the sufferings of the homeland, and were encouraged to plunder—and worse. A private would be allowed to take home up to ten pounds in weight of booty; senior officers, several tons. And then, of course, there would be the plunder that would not need to be carried home, stored only in remorseful or licentious memory.

Solzhenitsyn read to his battery Marshal Rokossovsky's message: "Soldiers, sergeants, officers and generals! Today at 5 A.M. we commence our great last offensive. Germany lies before us! One more blow and the enemy will collapse, and immortal victory will crown our Army!" Then Sanya lectured his troops on the need to keep their discipline and self-control, and to show magnanimity. The ten-pound limit of booty would be strictly adhered to; he was revolted by the naked encouragement of greed and vengeance.

The army moved swiftly through Poland, then swung north, into East

Prussia, striking for the Baltic coast. As they crossed over the border there was no sign of the enemy. The Russians stared in amazement; how peaceful was this heartland of the German military tradition! Such orderliness in the landscape; a high road into every village; brick houses with sharply pointed gables, and barns made from solid timber. Steeples and towers . . . "An unknowable new planet."[4]

Soon the neat houses were ablaze; cows were bellowing dementedly in their burning sheds. Through the long nights "roofs met the skies" as the flames rose, with the crack of exploding tiles; and the Soviet columns poured ahead "like lava."

Fate and Brigadier General Travkin, the stern brigade commander, were taking him through the landscape that most powerfully ignited his imagination—the landscape of the Battle of Tannenberg. As a boy of seventeen he had written about these towns and villages, describing General Samsonov's agony when the Tsar's ill-prepared and, mostly, ill-led forces were launched to help the French save Paris. His father had been over this ground too. This was the catastrophe which, in Solzhenitsyn's view, led directly to the Revolution. The defeat obsessed him, and how weirdly his obsession had come to life! Entering Neidenburg, he found it ablaze—torched by rampaging Red Army men—as it was when Samsonov entered it.

A vivid passage in the poem *Prussian Nights*, his account of the 1945 advance, composed in a labor camp, describes his feeling of déjà vu. . . .

> I nursed inside me till I filled
> With muffled shouting, all the pain
> And all the shame, of that campaign.
> In the dark cathedral gloom
> Of one or another reading room
> I shared with none my boyish grief,
> I bent over the yellow pages
> Of those aging maps and plans,
> Till little circles, dots, and arrows
> Came alive beneath my hands,
> Now as a fire-fight in the marshes,
> Now as a tumult in the night:
> Thirst. Hunger. August. Heat.
> —Now the wildly lunging muzzles
> Of horses tearing at the rein,
> Now broken units turned to raving
> Mobs of men who'd gone insane. . . .[5]

Any doubts that he was predestined to write about August 1914 would henceforth have been stilled. He looked at Neidenburg, the flames turning the night almost into day, and *felt,* as a present suffering, the destruction of Samsonov's Second Army, near the town. He wrote to Natasha: "Am sitting not far from the forest where Olkhovsky and Severtsev were surrounded! . . ."*

Solzhenitsyn was part of two armies, fighting in two wars.

To add to the weirdness of it, his battery too found itself cut off and virtually surrounded. It happened on 26 January. As they were setting up listening posts near the village of Dietrichsdorf, they suddenly realized the woods were full of enemy infantry. A Wehrmacht unit, left behind in the hectic retreat, had abandoned vehicles and heavy guns in an attempt to make a swift, silent escape back to their lines. Solzhenitsyn reported the situation to battalion headquarters, but they did not believe him in the absence of howitzer fire and engines roaring. He sent his technical equipment, in the care of Sergeant Solomin and another NCO, along a path he considered the safer of two possible escape routes; he led the rest of his men out along the other. Both parties made good their escape, but Solzhenitsyn and Commissar Pashkin led a few men back to rescue a lorry containing their field kitchen, which had got stuck in the snow. They came under heavy rifle fire and had to scatter into the woods.

Solzhenitsyn wrote later, of this night, that he had had a sense of weightlessness, of "having merely visited this world, rather than being attached to it, of my body feeling strangely light and having been lent to me for just a while." There was a "sharpness of sensation that was not born of fear, but a rarer sharpness that comes when you swallow danger and when scenes of your past life go rushing through your head."

Part of the encircling enemy was Russian—Vlasovites.† They appeared, like white apparitions, or emanations from the snow, adding to his sense of being somehow detached from his body. "I watched as they suddenly rose from the snow where they'd dug in, wearing their winter camouflage cloaks, hurled themselves with a cheer on the battery of a 152-millimeter gun battalion at Adlig Schwenkitten, and knocked out twelve heavy cannon with hand grenades before they could fire a shot. Pursued by their tracer bullets, our last little group ran almost two miles in fresh snow to the bridge across the Passarge River. And there they were stopped."[6]

The Vlasovites—young men who fought for the Germans to escape from the death camps, to try and join up with the partisans, or in the vain hope that the Germans would allow them some say in their country's future destiny—fought with reckless courage because if they were caught they faced, at best, a hangman's rope. Solzhenitsyn once saw a trio of Vlasovites being marched to the rear; a T-34 thundered down the road toward the group, and one of the three threw himself underneath the tank.

Another image involving a Vlasovite would be etched, he wrote, in his

---

*These original names in what became *August 1914* were later changed.
†Lieut. Gen. Andrei Vlasov. Red Army officer; captured by the Germans in 1942, he subsequently led Russian forces against the Soviet Union. Executed in 1946.

mind forever: a security sergeant on horseback, driving a Wehrmacht soldier before him with a whip. The man was naked above the waist, and covered in blood. As the whip raised fresh bloody welts, he cried out to Solzhenitsyn in pure Russian: "Mr. Captain! Mr. Captain!" pleading for help. But Solzhenitsyn did nothing.[7]

It would have been hard indeed for a Red Army soldier to feel the slightest sympathy for a Vlasovite; and at least Sanya's spirit was independent enough to be aware of anomalies and paradoxes. Thus, exploring an abandoned East Prussian mill, he discovered that the departed miller was a spare-time writer with an admiration for Russian literature. An editor had returned a manuscript essay on Dostoyevsky with the comment that it was interesting but difficult to publish in these times. Captain Solzhenitsyn, following his own obsession, cut out from a book about the First World War some tiny photos of Tsar Nicholas II, Hindenburg, Samsonov, and other leaders.

His eyes bulged greedily, not before cases of French cognac, but in a post office before boxes of beautiful white writing paper! Enough to write on for a whole century, he thought—ordering his men to load the boxes aboard the truck, along with pens and pencils and other supplies of stationery, all incomparably superior to anything available in his own country.

He was disturbed by the sight of returning Russian prisoners of war— pitiably few compared with the numbers fallen into German hands earlier in the war. Why were they "the only people who looked sorrowful when all around were rejoicing?" Why did they form up in submissive columns, when the liberated prisoners from other countries were returning home as individuals?

Because of the headlong advance, the obsessional déjà vu, and the shock of what was to befall him, his memories of East Prussia have an impressionistic quality, almost like a sequence of cinema verité black-and-white stills. Since it was winter, there was more darkness than light; in *August 1914* we read that the "unnaturally white light of their headlamps gave a strange, dead look to the trunks of the roadside trees, to bushes, houses, barns, level-crossings, bridge-railings, waggons, and marching troops. . . ."[8] In *Prussian Nights*, it becomes a "dead light" illuminating the landscape. Nowhere in his autobiographical or semiautobiographical writings does he find the word "strange" such a fitting adjective. He felt almost separated from his body, not only because he was at times in danger of death, and a constant witness of extraordinary, terrible events, but also because he was, in a way, a ghost—of Samsonov, and of his father, Isaaki, Sanya.

And he projects a feeling, in *Prussian Nights,* that his bodiless presence is helpless to prevent atrocities: which indeed have been willed by Stalin. A dumbstruck housewife in a lonely house; the soldiers, laughing, friendly: "Get us some eggs then, Mum!" She does so; they shoot her, then her bedridden husband; only the young grandson escapes, leaping out of a window, and haring off pursued by bullets. . . .

His battery is held up in a traffic jam, and German refugee women are walking past them. One, "blonde and magnificent," in a reddish fur coat, smart shoes, and a knitted hat, strides along proudly, erect. She carries a briefcase. One of the soldiers makes her open it up. She tries to bribe him with a bottle of schnapps. He hurls it in the snow, saying, "You have a low opinion of Russian soldiers, young woman!" Snatching the briefcase, he shakes free a shirt, combs, letters, handkerchiefs, and "a snowstorm of photos."

Sanya—or at any rate the narrator in *Prussian Nights*, who is likewise a lover of fine paper—is in a car checking maps. One of his men leans in. "Yes? What do you want?" "—This photo, sir . . . The swastika." So her fiancé's probably in the SS. Nevertheless, the captain waves his hand, probably intending to say "Let her through"; but instead he sees the young woman fall, curl up like a small animal, and then gunshots ring out.

"In the thick of hell," Solzhenitsyn reflects, "who knows who's guilty?" The soldiers go unpunished; the message from Stalin has been "blood for blood." At least they did not first gang-rape her. The piercing white light of memory picks out a woman, wounded, just alive, beside a little girl, dead, on a mattress. "How many have been on it? A platoon, a company, perhaps?" The woman begs, "Töte mich, Soldat!" We do not know whether the narrator does kill her, as she asks, but he makes it plain there is no hospital where she could be helped.

By another weird coincidence, an officer who would become Solzhenitsyn's close friend, Lev Kopelev, was faced with a similar impossible choice, in the same sector. His flashlight, he writes, picked out a fur-hatted woman lying on a bed. She was moaning hoarsely. He saw that she had been stabbed with a Plexiglas dagger in the breast and stomach. There was nothing to be done for her. Out of pity and helplessness he ordered, "Sydorych, finish her off."[9] Conceivably, Solzhenitsyn drew on Kopelev's memory for the horrific aftermath of rape his poem describes. Kopelev's woman, though, is too far gone to beg for death, and there is no mention of a dead daughter.

In the poem's final, powerful episode, the narrator's sergeant major invites him to cast his eye over some women he has allowed to stay on in the billet. They are washing and ironing clothes, and looking after children. He makes his covert inspection; there is one, answering to the name "Anne," whose looks are passable. And, after all, he is no Erlkönig himself, to demand someone glamorous. The sergeant major brings her across the yard to where he is waiting. Suspecting but unsure, she wears an expression of gentle anguish. He makes it clear what he wants by slamming the door shut and ordering "*Komm!*"

Whether this is Solzhenitsyn himself, his imagination, or what some fellow officer has related, it is unmistakably rape, and an especially terrifying one, since the woman would have expected to be killed. The poem ends:

And after, unnaturally close
To the pale blue of her eyes,
I said to her—too late—"How base!"
Anne, that moment, with her face
Sunk in the pillow, in an unsteady
Voice that she could not control,
Begged, "Doch, erschiessen Sie mich nicht!"°

Have no fear . . . For—Oh!—already
Another's soul is on my soul. . . . [10]

Not the least strange feature of these three weeks of hectic advance, danger, and horror, is that he still had the inclination and energy to press home his private offensive against Natasha. "I saw how egotistical your love still was," he berated her with reference to her time in his battery, "how full of prejudices you still were about family life. You imagine our future as an uninterrupted life together, with accumulating furniture, with a cosy apartment, with regular visits from guests, evenings at the theatre. . . . It is quite probable that none of this will transpire. Ours may be a restless life. Moving from apartment to apartment." On the move at the time, he clearly felt the exhilaration of it. "Things will accumulate but they will have to be just as easily discarded.

"Everything depends upon you. I love you, I love nobody else. But just as a train cannot move off the rails for a single millimetre without crashing, so it is with me—I must not swerve from my path at any point. . . . " That train again: with Vitkevich's running exactly parallel, so that each could easily move to the other. . . . Harmony would only come, he warned Natasha, if she rose above her "completely understandable, completely human," but nevertheless "egotistical" desires.[11]

Like Kafka warning his fiancée, Felice Bauer, that she must not look forward to "heavy furniture" or frivolous dinner parties, and should not expect his company for more than an hour a day, Solzhenitsyn was setting out his supremely egotistical stall with a vengeance: take it or leave it. Kafka, however, describes his writing seclusion as being "a sleep deeper than that of death," and for a wife to tear him from it at night would be like tearing the dead from their graves. Solzhenitsyn's art, by contrast, seems to be a daylight one, despite its somber themes; we see him, not in a grave or vault, but sitting perkily at his table in the bracing outdoors. But both visions hint at a fear of the female world, fear of being dragged down into ordinary fertility. Fear of living with a dependent though sacrificial woman, hearing her every cough, every movement in bed. . . .

°"Don't shoot me!"

He was willing to share more of himself with Natasha than the narrator at the climax of *Prussian Nights* is willing to share with the politely raped German woman; but there would still be strict limits.

On 9 February 1945, ten days after he had led his battery out of encirclement, they were in a village east of Königsberg (Kaliningrad). It was not quite clear whether the narrow Soviet salient on the Baltic coast had cut off the Germans, or the Germans had cut off them. The mood was relaxed enough, anyway, for Master Sergeant Ilya Solomin to bring in a piece of blue velour to show to his captain. "I've no one to send this to, sir: why not send it to Natasha? It's large enough to make a blouse out of it."

Another NCO, answering a phone, said to Solzhenitsyn he was wanted immediately at brigade headquarters. He picked up his map case and strode off. Following an intuition, Solomin took into safekeeping a German ammunition chest containing books and Natasha's letters. Meanwhile, entering the office of Brigadier General Travkin, Sanya noticed a group of officers, most unknown to him, huddled in the corner. Travkin ordered him to hand over his revolver; Solzhenitsyn wonderingly did so, and saw his commander wind the leather strap round the butt before placing the revolver in a desk drawer. Gravely and in a low voice Travkin said, "All right, you must go now."

Solzhenitsyn was silent, puzzled: was he being sent on some special mission?

The windowpane rattled; only two hundred yards away shells were falling. "Yes, yes," Travkin repeated almost sadly, "it is time for you to go somewhere."

Two officers from the corner stepped forward and shouted: "You're under arrest!"

"Me? What for?"

Without answering, they ripped the epaulets from his shoulders and the star from his cap, removed his belt, and seized the map case. They turned him to march him from the room. "Solzhenitsyn, come back here!" Travkin ordered.

He twisted out of the two SMERSH officers' grasp, and turned to face his commander.

"Have you a friend on the First Ukrainian Front, Captain?"

"That's not allowed! You have no right!" the officers shouted. A colonel and a captain of counterintelligence, they felt confident they could shout at a general of the Red Army.

Solzhenitsyn understood everything at once. That this was about Stalin. Why letters to and from Koka hadn't been getting through. Travkin rose to his feet, leaned forward to shake Solzhenitsyn's hand, saying fearlessly and precisely, "I wish you happiness, Captain!"

For those few seconds, with great bravery, the stern and formal general crossed over the border. Solzhenitsyn would always treasure that handshake, saying it was the most courageous act he had seen in the war. For the prisoner—a captain no longer—the border crossing was immeasurable: from the immense privilege of command to being thrown into a concrete cellar overnight; at dawn, ringed by machine guns, ordered to "shit quickly" in a snowy courtyard littered with feces.

14

The Victory Spring

No one who has not been in jail knows what the State is.
—TOLSTOY

"THAT'S WHAT ARREST IS: IT'S A BLINDING FLASH AND A BLOW WHICH SHIFTS THE PRESENT INSTANTLY INTO THE PAST AND THE impossible into omnipotent actuality."[1] The first thought of his shocked brain, on being marched out of Travkin's office, was shame at having to go through the telephone room with his epaulets ripped off and without his belt. There was no chance to exchange a word with Ilya, who had been ordered to bring his belongings in a suitcase. He noted gratefully that Ilya hadn't brought the ammunition box containing forbidden books he had got hold of in eastern Poland, nor Natasha's letters. Solomin managed later to return the letters to her.

At brigade SMERSH headquarters, the prisoner's belongings were listed—all except a small scarlet cigarette case looted from a German, which the searcher waved away indulgently, allowing him to put it back in his pocket. They started off once more, heading by car for army SMERSH headquarters in the small town of Osterode.

Solzhenitsyn began again to feel light-headed and as if his mind were floating along beside the car, which sped through the level darkness. A flash of irrational elation—they were driving him straight to Moscow, to the Kremlin; he would be able to talk directly with Stalin, and get him to see that he must change his ways, change Russia! He didn't know this then, but Russia was a country where the boss could occasionally talk to a writer; Pasternak found himself, once, being rung up by Stalin, who asked him what he made of this poet called Mandelstam . . . whom still, eventually, he dispatched to die in the Gulag. . . . But Sanya's light-headed egoism is of a piece with his belief, in childhood, that his classmates would not exist if he were not at school. Something in him made him feel *magical* on occasions. And in time he would *make* himself magical, by a huge effort of will and energy, able to talk to leaders.

But not yet. He saw they were actually heading straight for the German lines. He wondered should he tell his captors. When he did so, they wouldn't believe him at first. They stopped the car to confer; just then a shell exploded ahead: the Germans could see their headlights from miles away. The SMERSH men jumped back into the car, did a frantic turn, and sped off the way they had come. Not trained to read maps, they asked Solzhenitsyn to navigate, and let him have a smoke.

At headquarters, in a former vicarage, he was searched again, and the same officer who had let him keep the scarlet cigarette case said, "Ah! Tried to get away with this, did you!" and pocketed it. Solzhenitsyn was flung into a small concrete cellar, stinking of kerosene. Three prisoners already filled the cell, lying on straw. He found they were tank officers—decent, friendly types, such as he had got to know well and respect for their straightforward natures. These officers had got drunk and chased, unsuccessfully, a couple of raunchy-looking blondes in a bathhouse. Everyone knew that if women were German it was almost a battle honor to rape them and then shoot them; but one of these girls happened to be the "campaign wife" of the local SMERSH chief. Later in the night, a fifth man was flung in on them, a Russian POW who had been sent over by the Germans as a spy, and who had immediately given himself up.

Next morning, after the toilet call in the yard under the scrutiny of machine gunners, Solzhenitsyn joined a small file of prisoners who were to be marched to the front headquarters at Brodnitz (now Brodnica), in western Poland. Six of the seven men with him in the file had had the letters "SU" (Soviet Union) painted in white on the backs of their threadbare greatcoats by their former German captors. Those letters had been essentially a death warrant in the event of capture. Perhaps three in every hundred Soviet prisoners of war came back; and their reward for all their self-sacrifice and suffering was the Gulag. They were traitors, just by surviving.

The seventh prisoner was a German civilian in his fifties, well fed and groomed, and wearing a black three-piece suit and overcoat.

As they waited to be marched off, the escorting sergeant gestured to Solzhenitsyn to pick up his suitcase. "I'm an officer," he objected; "let the German carry it."

Meekly the sergeant told the German to pick up the heavy case. The long march began. Squalls tore icy snow flurries from a black sky, chilling the prisoners to the bone. When the German could no longer carry the suitcase, the six "other ranks" took their turns carrying it. Only Solzhenitsyn, to his bitter shame later, did not carry it. At one point they encountered a transport column of empty carts; the soldiers who drove them, seeing the smart figure in a greatcoat with glittering buttons, spat at him and cursed him. "Vlasov bastard! Kill the rat!"

It took them two days, with an overnight stop, to walk the forty-five miles to Brodnitz. Solzhenitsyn was kept there for three days; then, with a lieutenant and two sergeants, he was put on an open goods train heading for

Byalystok. The sergeants each carried two heavy suitcases, loaded with booty that senior officers wanted transferred home to Russia. Most of the train was occupied by Russian women who had been rounded up and were being sent back as collaborators. At Byalystok, Solzhenitsyn and his escorts got onto an ordinary passenger train, and at Minsk transferred to the Minsk–Moscow express. By now, he was on familiar terms with his escorts, and had a reasonably comfortable journey; they removed the handcuffs, and the lieutenant bought vodka for him. The guards even winked and left him alone when he seemed to be getting friendly with a girl in Red Army uniform, coming home on leave. She was responding to his attentions until he whispered to her, "Rostov Sredny 27, Reshetovskaya," and implied that he was under arrest. The girl turned away in disgust, or disappointment, or both.

"No luck, eh?" commiserated one of the sergeants.

Sanya would ask himself why he didn't scream out, make his plight known in the most public way. In Moscow, the SMERSH escorts relied on him again to lead them to their goal: the former elegant residence of the Rossiya Insurance Company, in Lubyanka Square. There was little, now, that could be insured against in it. Its "black maw" opened to receive him.

Solzhenitsyn has described what happened to him, on entering the Lubyanka, in *The First Circle*. He has said that Innokenty Volodin's reception in the Lubyanka is based literally on what happened to him in February 1945.[2] He was never afraid of the literal.

He was taken down a flight of steps and into a passage lined on both sides with narrow olive green doors, very close together, each with a shiny oval number plate. This cellar had once been the insurance company's strong room, providing one of the reasons for the Cheka's choice of this building. A guard—perhaps the same "drab, elderly woman in an army skirt and tunic" whose glum face "looked up at Innokenty as though she had seen him here a hundred times"—fitted a long key into one of the doors and said, "In you go." It was the size of a broom closet; Russians call it by the English word "box." It held a small table and a stool, and they took up almost all the space; when Solzhenitsyn perched on the stool he could not stretch his legs out. To shoulder height, the walls were bright green; above that, a naked two-hundred-watt bulb illuminated dazzling whitewash.

There was intense silence, except, once or twice, the unlocking and locking of a nearby door. Every minute or so the peephole's shield lifted and a single, searching eye gazed at him. How long would he be kept in this hellhole. Until he died, maybe?

A broad-shouldered man in a gray overall suddenly entered, asked him his name, then took him into another room where he told him to strip. Standing, shivering with cold, the prisoner was subjected to a body search; "unwashed fingers" prodded inside his mouth, stretching first one cheek then another, and pulled down his lower eyelids. After checking nostrils, ears, fingers, and armpits, the warder ordered him, in a flat, dull voice, to take hold of his penis and move the foreskin back. He was ordered to spread his legs, bend, and touch the floor, then stretch his buttocks apart with his hands.

The man then searched his clothes—every seam, lining, and crevice—for about an hour. It would be hardly surprising if the fictional Innokenty's flash of sympathy for "the poor man—how sick he must have been of going through people's underclothes, cutting up their shoes and looking up their anuses year after year . . ." was originally Sanya's. But "the flicker of irony died down in him as he waited and watched in misery"; all the buttons and button loops, and all the gold braid and piping, were ripped off the tunic; and the pants lost their buttons too. The search yielded only a scrap of broken pencil that the warder contemptuously shook out of a boot.

Solzhenitsyn's uniform was left in rags; deprived of his suspenders, he had nothing to hold up his pants with; when he protested, the searcher muttered, "You'll get some string," and left.

He was sitting clutching his pants around him when a different warder, in a grubby white overall, came in and ordered him to undress again. He produced some clippers, gripped the prisoner's neck, and started pressing the clippers into his scalp. Solzhenitsyn raised his arms to have his armpits shaved, then the barber squatted to shave off the pubic hair.

When he left, the prisoner did not hurry to dress. He passed his hand over his head, feeling the unfamiliar stubble, and bumps he hadn't known were there.

This was, well and truly, the "poor, bare, fork'd creature," a man deprived of his entire identity. And not for an hour, a day, or a year, but perhaps forever. He was just pulling on his pants again when another warder came in, ordered him to undress, and inspected him for distinguishing marks. This visit was followed by one from a woman, who scornfully disregarded his nakedness, and asked him about lice and venereal diseases. When she had left, the first warder came and demanded to know why he still wasn't dressed.

He was taken to be measured, then for a toilet call and to wash. Even if he was moved only a few steps along the corridor, from room to room, he was commanded to put his hands behind his back. The warder guarding him clicked his tongue incessantly, as if calling a dog; but there was no dog; the noise was a warning in case some other prisoner was being moved. Rather than have two prisoners meet, one of them would be pushed into an empty box and told to face the wall while the other shuffled by. The impression was given that the whole vast building existed just to crush one man—but a man who was but a cipher, an anonymous face whom the warders had known for decades and who held no interest for them whatsoever. Whether he was naked, or in coarse prison underwear while his clothes were being "fried"—or even crouching in the toilet—females gazed at him with the same blank indifference. When his clothes were returned, they were crumpled and still hot, and did not seem his anymore.

Put back in his box, he felt exhausted. He put the stool on top of the table, and settled onto the floor. He was just dozing off when the door was flung open and a woman guard rasped, "Stand up! That isn't allowed!"

Next he was taken to be photographed and to have his fingerprints taken. Above the prints, he saw, was a line of writing: TO BE KEPT IN PERPETUITY. He shivered. "There was something mystical about it, something transcending man and his world."[3]

He asked for and was given a mug of water; and then, at last, was taken into a cell where there was a bench, and given a pillowcase and blanket. Though the regulation two-hundred-watt bulb shone down relentlessly, he was beginning to fall asleep when the door was thrown open with a crash and a warder shouted at him, "Arms outside the blanket!"

"What?"

"You mustn't have your arms inside the blanket. It's not allowed in here."

He found it astonishingly difficult to sleep with his arms outside; the human instinct is to hug the body when one sleeps. He tossed restlessly for a time, then, as the longed-for oblivion began to steal over him, he became aware of a series of bangings and shouted commands approaching down the corridor. His own door was flung open, and a warder stood there snarling, "Come on, time to get up!"

After the six o'clock reveille it was forbidden to fall asleep. Soon, reeling with tiredness, Solzhenitsyn was stumbling toward his first interrogation.

This took place in one of the Rossiya Insurance Company's grandest, most spacious rooms, the office now of Captain I. I. Yezepov. One wall was dominated by a thirteen-foot-high full-length portrait of Stalin. Solzhenitsyn heard the charge read out: he was accused of anti-Soviet propaganda under Article 58 of the criminal code, paragraph 10, and of founding a hostile organization under paragraph 11. The punishment prescribed in the criminal code could range from three years' deprivation of liberty to death by shooting. Yezepov had a copy of "Resolution No. 1," taken from Solzhenitsyn's map case, and copies of all correspondence between the accused and Vitkovich, Natasha, Simonyan, and Lydia Ezherets from April 1944 to February 1945.

Solzhenitsyn assumed that Nikolai was under arrest also. He was afraid for the others, whose letters lay on the desk. Every "perhaps," "I don't know," or "I've forgotten" became a "yes" to the cynical investigator. Sanya quickly saw that this would be no proper investigation; his guilt was assumed: he and Vitkevich, and possibly others, had been planning an anti-Soviet conspiracy.

He was taken back to the cell, and prevented from sleeping till night—and then, almost at once, the door slammed open and he was hauled out for another session of questioning. By the time he returned to his cell, it was almost dawn; and you couldn't sleep after six. If you had an undisturbed couple of hours before that hour, the banging of doors kept waking you—you were sure your own door was being opened. For the first four days, he had hardly any sleep.[4] In the great majority of cases, sleep deprivation was quite enough to break down resistance. There might be refinements, like letting the prisoner sit on a luxuriously soft leather sofa, with an assistant interrogator beside him who would kick him when he started nodding off. The Organs, as the security services were familiarly called, offered scope to investigators of a more active nature: such as the one who would run across the room and kick the prisoner in the genitals. In Moscow, Lefortovo and—the harshest—Sukhanovka were prisons that dealt with the hard cases, requiring less mild forms of "persuasion" than sleep deprivation, though that too went on; in Sukhanovka it could last for months.

This refined form of torture was excellent because it left no marks. And a creative interrogator could clinch a case by throwing in something unexpected. He could talk about a prisoner's wife, even show her through a peephole; then, later, let him hear some other woman screaming under torture, or even just a recording of screams. The prisoner was unhinged at the thought that it was, or could be, his wife. One female interrogator lulled her prisoner by questioning him in a polite, cultivated manner, then suddenly unleashing a stream of filthy abuse. Foul language could be very effective with religious people.

When Olga Ivinskaya, Pasternak's mistress and his inspiration for Lara in *Doctor Zhivago*, was in the Lubyanka in 1949, her interrogator demonstrated a surreal sense of humor. After months of sleep deprivation, she was promised a meeting with Pasternak. Overcome with joy, she was taken out to another building, and led down into a basement. She was thrust through a door into semidarkness; the door clanged shut behind her. She saw zinc-topped tables, motionless bodies covered by gray tarpaulin sheets, and over everything a sweetish smell. She sank down into a pool of water on the concrete floor, realizing she was in the Lubyanka morgue and terrified that one of the bodies might be Boris's. After a long time, she was removed, and told with an apologetic smile that she had been taken to the wrong room by mistake.[5] As a consequence of this and other traumas, she lost the child she was expecting by Boris.

If the intellectuals in the plays of Chekhov who spent all their time guessing what would happen in twenty, thirty, or forty years had been told that in forty years interrogation by torture would be practised in Russia . . . that a ramrod heated over a primus stove would be thrust up their anal canal . . . that a man's genitals would be slowly crushed beneath the toe of a jackboot; and that, in the luckiest possible circumstances, prisoners would be tortured by being kept from sleeping for a week, by thirst, and by being beaten to a bloody pulp, not one of Chekhov's plays would have got to its end because all the heroes would have gone off to insane asylums.

Yes, not only Chekhov's heroes, but what normal Russian at the beginning of the century, including any member of the Russian Social Democratic Workers' Party, could have believed, would have tolerated, such a slander against the bright future? . . . What had already become impossible under Catherine the Great was being practised during the flowering of the glorious twentieth century—in a society based on socialist principles . . . not by one scoundrel alone in one secret place only, but by tens of thousands of specially trained human beasts standing over millions of defenceless victims.[6]

These thoughts would come later. For now, he seemed to be the only prisoner in the Lubyanka, struggling to stay awake, his eyelids burning, and the warder, clicking as if to a dog, leading him to the big room with the portrait of Stalin. "The Kremlin mountaineer," as Mandelstam had called him in a poem that sealed his fate.

Yezepov liked to stand beneath that giant portrait, put his hand across his breast, and declaim his patriotic fervor.

Did he have a modicum of fellow feeling for a soldier? Or was Solzhenitsyn appearing to be cooperative, in an easy—indeed, almost a *genuine*—case? The latter, probably. After only four days, the prisoner was roused from sleep as if for another interrogation, but instead was told to bring his bedding and led on tiptoe down another corridor. The warder unlocked a cell door, and told him to enter. There were, to Solzhenitsyn's joy, three others inside, lying on metal cots, asleep.

"At the sound of the door opening, all three started and raised their heads for an instant. They, too, were waiting to see which of them was being called for interrogation. And those three heads lifted in alarm, those three unshaven, crumpled, pale faces seemed to me so human, so dear, that I stood there hugging my mattress and smiled with happiness. And they also smiled. And what a forgotten expression that was—after only one week!"[7]

They started talking, questioning. But one of them said sternly, "Sleep now! Talk tomorrow!"

And that was sensible.

While Sanya was taking part in the headlong advance through East Prussia, feeling how marvelously fate was allowing him to research for his great project, Natasha had the harder task of waiting, fearful that he might be killed or badly wounded at this late stage of the war. A letter came, at the beginning of March, and her heart lifted as she tore the envelope open. Then "a mountain of suffering"[8] fell on her. "You imagine our future as an uninterrupted life together, with accumulating furniture, with a cosy apartment, with regular visits from guests, evenings at the theatre. . . ." It probably won't be like that, he warned. He loved her, he loved no one else; but he was like a train that must not swerve even a millimeter or it would crash. She must love that train too, that unswervable destiny. "For now, you love only me, which means, in the final analysis, you love only for yourself, for the satisfaction of your own needs." His interests and hers had to be intertwined, like his and Koka's; she would have to rise above her "egotistical" plans for the future, or else. . . . He concluded the cold, hurtful letter with a postscript saying he had not had any letters from Koka, and that the Forty-seventh Army, in which Koka was serving, appeared to be heading straight for Berlin.

For a week she felt shaken and bruised by the onslaught. It was so unfair; she did not expect or want "accumulating furniture"; she was ready to make sacrifices; but she did want a loving family life, which meant a child. Was it too much to ask? Could a baby derail a train?

And then, a week later, this mountain of suffering was wiped out, to be replaced by an even heavier mountain of panic, as one of her postcards was returned overwritten with the words "The addressee has left the unit." She wrote to Arseny Pashkin, the commissar with whom she had become friendly during her visit to the battery, and to Ilya Solomin. Also to Kirill Simonyan, serving somewhere in East Prussia. He wrote back with the reassurance that she would have been informed if Sanya had been killed or wounded. A month went by in which Natasha lived like an automaton, keeping herself under reasonable control at work, weeping uncontrollably when she got home.

In April, her mother received a letter from Solomin. It struck them as strange that he should reply to her mother rather than Natasha, and the letter itself was part reassuring, part frightening: "Circumstances are such that I must now write to you. You are, of course, interested in Sanya's fate, why he's not writing to you, and what has happened to him. . . . He has been recalled from our unit. Why and for what reason I cannot tell you now. I only know he is alive and in good health, and nothing else. Also, that nothing bad will happen to him. . . . I ask you, please, not to worry, and to help Natasha."

Was Sanya on some special mission? More weeks went by, in which she was torn between hope and dread. It was also strange that Antonina Vitkevich, Koka's mother, had not heard from him for a long time. Why both of them? Was it just a coincidence?

Somewhere on the path to Berlin, almost the whole of Sanya's former battery was wiped out.

It is doubtful if Captain Yezepov, Solzhenitsyn's interrogator, thought of his career as an unswervable train, or his personal life as of subordinate interest. On one occasion he left Solzhenitsyn to stew over a tricky question while he telephoned his wife. "My dear, I'm sorry, I won't be home for dinner; in fact I'll probably be here all night—a difficult problem's come up." He stared straight at the prisoner as he said it, and Sanya's heart sank. Another night without sleep. Yezcpov put the phone down and returned to the attack. "This Simonyan: here, read this: he doesn't seem to reject the ideas in your last letter, does he? He seems his usual friendly self. . . ."

"Yes, but if you look at this sentence, he—"

"It's a friendly reply to you, isn't it?"

"Yes, but—"

"Yes," Yezepov recorded, before turning in his chair to pick up the phone, asking the operator to give him another number. His eyes sparkled as he purred, "Sonia, darling, I'll be with you in about an hour; we'll have dinner. . . . The chocolates reached you? Good. . . . Oh, not at all, darling— for you, only the best! . . ."

The sparkle still lingered in his eyes for a second as he turned to face the prisoner. It was a matter of indifference to him that his unfaithfulness had been revealed; he might have been talking to his wife and his mistress in front of a dog.

And Sanya felt a huge relief that this man was betraying his wife and so tonight would be occupied elsewhere. For himself, Sanya could imagine nothing more blissful than to be allowed to fall asleep and not be wakened until reveille.

"Looking back on my interrogation from my long subsequent imprisonment," he wrote in *The Gulag Archipelago*, "I had no reason to be proud of it. I might have borne myself more firmly; and in all probability I could have manoeuvred more skilfully. But my first weeks were characterized by a mental blackout and a slump into depression."[9] He was glaringly conscious that in his suitcase were several volumes of his war diary. Throughout the war he had tried to write down everything he saw and—more crucially— heard from others. The diaries, written in tiny, needle-thin writing in hard, light pencil, "constituted my claim to becoming a writer." He had named names, given dates; the diaries, if read by Yezepov, could be devastating for many men serving at the front. Solzhenitsyn deduced, from Yezepov's questioning, that he hadn't yet bothered to read the diaries. He was too lazy to plunge into that almost indecipherable script—unless he felt compelled to.

It therefore seemed the best tactic to hover fairly near the truth when Yezepov asked him about the letters to and from his friends. He tried to argue that he had been given to foolish, typically student soundings off about politics: essentially harmless grumbles. If he or his friends complained about the introduction of tuition fees, it was because it seemed a step away from Communist egalitarianism; if they criticized collectivization, it was because they wanted it to be carried out more successfully than hitherto.

"The only reason that these recollections do not torment me with remorse is that, thanks be to God, I avoided getting anyone else arrested. But I came close to it." There would be ill feeling toward Sanya in later times, utilized or created by the KGB; yet it is difficult to know how he could have dealt with the accusations much differently, given the correspondence Yezepov had in front of him. If Solzhenitsyn had behaved discreditably, it seems certain that others would have been arrested. Natasha, Simonyan, and Lydia Ezherets were not even taken in for questioning. Nor were the many soldiers mentioned incriminatingly in the war diaries. Solzhenitsyn was both relieved and stricken with despair when these diaries were burned, with his consent, in the Lubyanka furnace as being "immaterial to the investigation." It was a terrible thing, to see four years of his life, of his heart's blood, going up in flames, cast out as flakes of soot falling on the rooftop exercise yard—and to be *glad!*

On 2 May a thirty-gun salute roared out, and Sanya and his fellow prisoners wondered whether Berlin had fallen or Prague, since these were the only cities left uncaptured. It was in fact Berlin. Then, on 9 May, there was a thirty-gun salute for the fall of Prague, followed by a forty-gun salute. Lunch and dinner were brought at the same time and, as on 2 May, there were no interrogations. Captain Yezepov and his comrades were celebrating the great victory. (Perhaps his wife was saying to friends, "They work him so hard—even today he must work. . . .") After dark, the prisoners watched, in the small patch of their window that wasn't covered, the play of searchlights and fireworks. Outside, Moscow went crazy, three million people dancing, kissing, singing. But the Lubyanka, full of former front-line soldiers and prisoners of war, was silent: silent like a Western prison before an execution. At another prison, a young soldier-poet[*] wrote (or *thought*) of how the prisoners raised their heads from their bunks—"Oh, it's just a salute"—and then lay down again.

"And once again covered themselves with their coats."

A line worthy of Pushkin.

Those coats, Solzhenitsyn comments, which had been in the clay of the trenches, and been torn to tatters by German shrapnel. And adds: "That victory was not for us. And that spring was not for us either."[10]

Listening to the triumphant volleys celebrating victory in Rostov, Natasha cried with joy and grief. She remembered a letter of August 1944 in which Sanya had written: "The first instant—the news of the war's end—will be the brightest, the most blissful day in everyone's life."

Still there was no word of him. Only Solomin had had the courage to reply to her frantic inquiries. She who had always been bright and cheerful was incapable of smiling anymore. All her friends and colleagues knew her husband had disappeared, and sympathized with her.

On 25 June a telegram marked URGENT arrived from her aunt Veronica[†] Turkin in Moscow. It read: SANYA ALIVE WELL DETAILS LATER—VERONICA. Natasha felt a surge of happiness and hope. Perhaps he was in a special unit that had passed through Moscow. Two days later, another telegram: SANYA MOSCOW UNFREE ARRIVE OR ORDER TELEGRAPHIC TELEPHONE CALL MY ADDRESS—VERONICA.

Her aunt, speaking cautiously, her voice trembling, over the phone: "I took him a parcel today. . . ."

For the rest of that day Natasha could hardly stop crying. It was as if *she*

---

[*]Boris Gammerov. Solzhenitsyn and he would become friends.
[†]Her daughter, Natasha's teenaged cousin, had the same name.

were hemmed in by those cell walls. Yet, the next morning, she woke with a joyous heart: he was alive—nothing else mattered!

She walked along the street, her face alight, and did not even see a colleague who taught German. Shparlinsky caught her by the arm: "You've had news from your husband?"

She quelled her smile, dimmed her eyes, tried to look sad. "No."

"Ah!" He let go of her arm and moved past, muttering, "Frailty, thy name is woman!" She thought, his wife, or his girlfriend, must be giving him a hard time.

15

Education Sentimentale

From good to evil is one quaver.
—Russian proverb

"Are you from freedom?"

It was the first question asked of any newcomer to a cell. Had he come from outside? Could he give them news of the world?

And when Sanya was asked it—having spent an eternity in the two weeks and four days since his arrest—he replied, "No."

A great dramatic painter like Ilya Repin should have painted that scene, and called it *Are You from Freedom?* The open door; the young arrival in boots, greatcoat, winter hat half covering his shaven head, his arms enfolding a mattress, gazing in delighted astonishment at the three figures half rising from their bunks: removing handkerchiefs from their eyes, which are now screwed up to shield themselves from the brilliant lightbulb. . . . In the center of the cell, a table on which are a teapot, a chess set, and a small pile of books. There is a blue paper blind high up on one wall, suggesting there might be a tiny window behind it.

A rattle of keys woke Sanya from a dead sleep. Six A.M. Under the dazzling light, he and the others leapt up, made their beds, then sat on them. Talking was not permitted. It was the worst time for depression, those two hours before the day properly began; especially for those who needed glasses to read. Glasses were always removed at night. Two of the men in Sanya's cell were in that situation; they just sat on their beds like statues. Even if you had been interrogated all night, you were not allowed to nod off during those two hours; if you did, you were punished. You sat with your gloomy, oppressive thoughts, in stifling airlessness, under the relentless light.

The only activity in those first two hours was toilet parade. They were led out; in front, the duty prisoner carried, chest high, the two-gallon latrine bucket. At the toilets, each prisoner was handed two tiny bits of paper. It was of course often not possible to defecate so early in the morning; in which case the whole day, until six P.M. or even in some prisons the next morning, would be a torture; the prisoner would be robbed of the inclination to talk, read, think, or even eat the meager food.

At eight o'clock breakfast was brought around. And with that pound of unrisen wet bread, of a swamplike sogginess, the day began—life began! With it came a mug of tea and two lumps of sugar. After an inspection at nine, someone might be summoned for a daytime interrogation. That suggested the interrogator felt it was going well; otherwise he would wait for night, or the prisoner would be transferred to Lefortovo. If they were not required for interrogation, they could read—spectacles having been given back—play chess, talk. Late in the morning the reflections of a few rays of light might struggle in through the chink of window, and the artificial light would be turned off. The prisoners rejoiced because it meant that the exercise period was near.

For Sanya and his cell mates, this twenty-minute walk took place on the Lubyanka roof, overshadowed by the chimney that served the furnace and bore off his diaries and innumerable other testaments or works of literature. The walls rose around them to three times a man's height; the prisoners could hear, far below, the honking of car horns, telling them that life went on somewhere; but all they could see was the chimney, a guard in a tower above them, and—wonderful pathetic fallacy—"that segment of God's heaven whose unhappy fate it was to float over the Lubyanka."[1]

Still, they could breathe the fresh air, glimpse the sun. They were ordered to walk in pairs and not to talk. But they managed to converse in whispers. Sanya learned to seek out Arnold Susi, an Estonian lawyer. For twenty years between the wars Estonia had been independent. Highly regarded by his countrymen, Susi might have become Minister for Education in an independent Estonia, but the Red Army rolled into Tallinn in 1944. Susi, a liberal democrat, had been arrested with fourteen other leading constitutionalists. They were all charged under Article 58-2 with the criminal desire for national self-determination.[2]

Walking on the Lubyanka roof with this mild-mannered intellectual, who could speak fluent Russian, English, and German, Sanya received his first lesson in democracy. Susi spoke passionately for the virtues of a democratic parliament and constitution, such as his small Baltic country had drawn up from the best of European experience.

This brief exercise time was when—without fear of being overheard by a stool pigeon or a bug—the two men could discuss politics. Returning to the cell after that fresh air was, for them both, like being rearrested again.

Others took their place. At some point in the day "that unhappy segment of God's heaven" looked down on the shattered relic of Raoul Wallenberg, savior of Budapest Jews. He is believed to have been liquidated with poison in 1947.

Sanya also came to like and trust another of his cell mates, Anatoly Ilyich

Fastenko, a "beardless old man with black and very lively eyebrows." An Old Bolshevik, Fastenko had been a true, original revolutionary, imprisoned as early as 1904; he had served four years in irons in the Sevastopol prison, then escaped from Siberian exile with the customary ease of revolutionaries under tsardom. He had made his way to Paris, where he studied French, worked in the Longjumeau Bolshevik school, and knew Lenin. He moved to Canada and the United States, where he found the free-and-easy atmosphere astonishing. Clearly these peoples would not have, and not need, a proletarian revolution. After 1917 he returned home, but deliberately kept his distance from the new regime, opting to take a lowly job with *Pravda*. He had managed to survive, he and his wife, quietly until this year. Then a drunken writer in their apartment block had bragged of owning a pistol, and somehow Fastenko was brought in instead and nailed for terrorism. Also for having spied for the Tsar, and for the French and Canadian intelligence services.

He had no children. Every ten days his old wife brought in for him such food as she could scrape together—usually a piece of black bread, bought on the black market at a huge price, and some bluish boiled potatoes. "The sight of those wretched—and truly sacred—parcels tore at one's heartstrings. That was what this human being had earned for sixty-three years of honesty and doubts."[3]

On the face of it, Fastenko's fate confirmed Solzhenitsyn's belief that Stalin was the perverter of the Revolution. Yet—when Sanya was ready to kiss the cheek that had been kissed by Lenin—the Old Bolshevik disappointed him by failing to rave about Lenin's greatness. It offended Sanya that he was willing to be addressed as "Ilyich"; that sacred patronymic, when spoken on its own, should only ever refer to the great man. It was almost like blaspheming, to Sanya's ears, when Susi jovially asked, "Ilyich, isn't it your turn to take out the piss bucket?"

Fastenko advised the young man to remember Descartes's advice: "Question *everything*." Sanya was not yet ready to do so, and the relationship between the two men cooled slightly as time went on.

Sanya made sure he had nothing to do with the youngest man in the cell, Georgi Kramarenko, an airman. As soon as Sanya had entered the cell that first night, the young fellow had leapt up to help him assemble the extra cot brought in by the warder. He asked for tobacco, whereas the black-eyebrowed old man had asked for news. Sanya's "sensor relay," which he claimed never let him down throughout his time in the Gulag, clicked on. He had not yet come across the word *nasedka*, stool pigeon, that essential inmate of every cell. He would find that all stoolies resembled this first one, in tending to cadge from other prisoners, having an ingratiating manner, and receiving privileged treatment.

He saw Kramarenko in action with another newcomer. For one early morning, in that "brief, sweetly cerebral last hour before reveille," another prisoner was pushed in. Kramarenko jumped up to have a chat and cadge some tobacco; Sanya, Susi, and Fastenko did not bother to open their eyes. They heard a whisper, almost a sob, asking whether many were shot. When the time came to get up, Sanya observed a short, stocky man with a bulldog's fat jowls, who wore a general's uniform, and later absorbed him into his capacious memory.

Leonid Z., a bright peasant boy, had worked hard at school and entered an industrial academy in 1929, just when the widely cultured pre-Soviet engineers were being herded into the Gulag. He became the chief engineer for big construction projects outside Moscow. During the war he had been sent to Alma-Ata to oversee even grander construction projects. War made him rich. In recognition of the need for sacrifice he doffed his expensive suits in favor of a general's uniform. Women swarmed to him for the services and servicing he could provide; he had, he boasted, "uncorked" 290 of them, and regretted having been arrested before passing the three hundred mark. This Don Juan had no culture; read nothing in two months in the cell; believed there was a Canadian language.

He had grown overconfident in his Alma-Ata satrapy. What had finally brought his downfall had been a refusal to supply building materials for a prosecutor's dacha. His fellow prisoners assured him he would not get more than a *tenner* (a ten-year sentence), and would be an overseer in a camp; but he was entirely stricken. "All of us in the cell were deeply depressed, but none of us was so crushed as Z., none took his arrest as so profound a tragedy." He would sing a song about being "a tiny orphan," then burst into explosive sobs. Susi explained for Solzhenitsyn's benefit: "Cruelty is invariably accompanied by sentimentality. . . . For example, in the case of the Germans, the combination is a national trait."[4]

Every tenth day, the regulation interval, Z.'s long-unloved wife brought him bountiful parcels. After giving his cell mates a sandwich and twist of tobacco, he settled to the white bread, butter, red caviar, veal, sturgeon; then his tears would flood again, weeping for the wrongs he had done her: the love notes she had found, the women's panties he had stuffed in his pocket during some liaison in his car, and forgotten.

The contrast between this go-getting New Soviet Man and the Old Bolshevik Fastenko—the most cheerful in the cell, even though at his age he might never get out, never see again the wife who brought those bluish potatoes—was a telling one.

These varied characters began to give Sanya a glimpse of reality. Meanwhile, Susi and Fastenko were taking the measure of *him.* Susi remembered him later as a strange mixture of Marxist and democrat; and, in recording that memory, Solzhenitsyn agreed that things were wildly mixed up inside him.[5] The conflict had originated in the clash between the liberal, "Tolstoyan" beliefs of his home circle, and the conformist pressures applied to him at school. During the thirties, Marxism had won the battle; the cross had well and truly been torn from his neck.

Yet—probably to his own surprise—the liberal background was not wholly extinguished; had never been. He had probed more than was common, trying to go back to original sources; he had felt intuitively that the show trials were fixed. Unlike those many who thought "if only Stalin knew about this he'd do something about it," Sanya believed Stalin was the serpent in the essentially beneficent garden planted by Marx and Lenin.

Despite his reverence for "Ilyich," he had rather bravely declined to join the Party headed by Stalin. He was still promoted—a sign of how good a soldier he was; as a Party member he might well have become a colonel, like his fictional alter ego in *August 1914*, Vorotyntsev.

The exercise period divided their day. Then came lunch, brought at one. It consisted of a ladle of soup and another of a thin gruel, dumped onto flat aluminum plates. The famished prisoners became agitated at the arrival of the meal, wolfing the food down, until with time their stomachs shrank and they could eat it calmly. At four supper came—another ladle of gruel. At six they made another visit to the toilets, which could provide a blessed relief. Then evening could be almost an intoxicating time, as described in Solzhenitsyn's play *Prisoners:* "You wake up in the morning, sluggish from the straw, the stench, the numbness. The brain seizes up from a depressing lack of sleep. But towards the evening you get flashes of thought; your imagination is fired, you feel light, weightless, some kind of Nirvana, you know. . . . It's strange."[6]

No doubt purely physical things, such as lack of air, sleep, and food, played a part in the "Nirvana" sensation; but surely only a minor part. He was learning at last; learning among other things that life was more complex than he had thought. He even found good in Z., lamenting his sins toward his wife. Did he catch a glimpse of that other peasant boy who grew rich, then was brought low: the old man who crouched down in the corner of their shack in Rostov, sobbing and cursing?

Life in the cell had the unwavering course of an infinitely slow train moving back and forth over the same familiar track. Only the interrogations were unpredictable. And yet, "though the sixteen-hour days were short on outward events . . . they were so interesting that I, for example, now find a mere sixteen minutes' wait for a trolley bus much more boring. There were no events worthy of attention, and yet by evening I would sigh because once more there had not been enough time, once more the day had flown. The events were trivial, but for the first time in my life I learned to look at them through a magnifying glass."[7] Somehow he could be both depressed and vividly alive; a depressed person does not usually find events "interesting"; though, as the psychotherapist Michael Jacobs has pointed out, depression can free the mind from trivial distractions.[*]

They were moved into a larger cell so that a sixth prisoner could join

---

[*]Private communication to the author.

them. This prisoner, tall, thin, and with a yellowish, dead expression, stared uncomprehendingly at them for ages before he started to smile and croaked, "Peo-ple!" He had been kept in a box for three weeks, as compared with Sanya's four days. Yuri Y. had a similar background; he too was a "twin of October," his father a tsarist officer who had fought for the Reds in the Civil War. Yuri had fought bravely against the Finns, then was captured by the Germans and thrown into one of their hellish prison cages. Gradually, learning that Stalin had abandoned them, he went through the process of change that for Sanya was only just starting. He became a Vlasovite, hoping he could help to win freedom for Russia.

Sanya still could not stomach the thought of such treason—as he believed it to be—and still had faith in the October Revolution. Yuri disagreed that only in 1929 had the Revolution started to go wrong; he thought the corruption had always been there. They argued daily, so vehemently that they did not get close. But here too there was learning going on. After three weeks Yuri was taken out; Solzhenitsyn could never find out what had happened to him. Almost certainly a bullet or a rope.

His place was taken by one Victor Belov, a former Kremlin chauffeur, who believed he was the Emperor Mikhail Romanov. More reliably, the False Pretender shocked Sanya by describing the imperial luxury enjoyed in secret by the Kremlin leaders. Only Khrushchev,* he said, had egalitarian instincts, and treated his chauffeur as a friend.

Every ten days the cell door was flung open by an astonishing female figure "built like a horse," with a face so caked with white powder that it looked like a doll's mask, purple lips, and plucked, mascaraed eyebrows. Her arrival was the great event in their lives, for she was the Lubyanka's librarian. The biggest surprise offered by the Lubyanka was its library, which offered a richness of uncensored literature quite unobtainable anywhere else in what Akhmatova terms their "pre-Gutenberg" age. As the Vatican holds the greatest, most lurid pornography, so the Lubyanka held works that still acknowledged the human spirit. Their original owners would read no more.

The horselike librarian, fascinating to the prisoners in her repulsiveness, held the power to bring happiness or misery. The impassive mask would listen to their requests, then carry off for inspection the books they had just been reading. Were there, perhaps, pinpricks under certain letters, in an effort to communicate? If there were—or if her assistants said there were— the cell could be deprived of books for three months. "We were not only afraid," Solzhenitsyn recalls, "we actually trembled; just as we had in youth after sending a love letter, while we waited for an answer. Will it come or not? And what will it say?"[8]

The number of books she brought depended on the number of prisoners

---

*Then First Chairman of the Ukrainian SSR.

in a cell; so, five men, five books: a system, he wrote, that was more appropriate to a bread cutter than a librarian. Nevertheless, she would sometimes fulfill their order miraculously.

After the prisoners' trembling wait of several hours, the repulsive angel of the books returned; and, if she brought what they had ordered, or even if she had got hopelessly muddled but came with some unexpected gem, they no doubt found her supremely beautiful. According to whether she had brought treasure or trash, they decided to concentrate for the next ten days on reading or conversation. But of course a stimulating book often led to passionate discussion.

Here Solzhenitsyn first read the American Dos Passos, whose collage style of mixing real-life material with fiction would strongly influence him in writing *The Red Wheel*. The four Russian writers he mentions—Panteleimon Romanov, Pilnyak, Merezhkovsky, and Zamyatin—are as interestingly varied a group as Sanya's living fellow inmates.

Panteleimon Romanov (1885–1938), from the land-owning class, was a popular Soviet novelist and short-story writer in the twenties and thirties. His best-known work was *Tovarishch Kislyakov* (1930), somewhat freely translated for English readers as *Three Pairs of Silk Stockings*. Not that Romanov would have been likely to object to a touch of raciness—he enjoyed exploring sexual themes, especially the liberated code of behavior following the Revolution.

His fate—not necessarily because of his raciness—execution.

A much more significant figure was Boris Pilnyak (1894–1937). Pilnyak accepted the Revolution as a necessary act of destruction, but sought to keep faith with older humanist values. His novel *The Naked Year* (1922) brought him fame and privilege. He traveled widely in Europe and the Far East, and had friendships within the Kremlin. Among the first to guess at Stalin's unbridled lust for power, he revealed it, under the slightest of fictional masks, in a daring story called "Tale of the Unextinguished Moon." The story explored the death of a character closely and obviously based on the popular military commissar, M. V. Frunze, who died on an operating table on 31 October 1925. Frunze had had a stomach ulcer; Stalin—in comradely concern, according to his colleague Voroshilov—ordered him to have an operation. During the fatal operation it was found that the ulcer had healed of its own accord. There were rumors at the time that Stalin had ordered his death or at least hoped it might occur.

Pilnyak's story deftly portrayed the sinister isolation of his unnamed ruler. His headquarters "was steeped in silence, as if the silence had been hoarded for a century." He knows everything that goes on, in every artery of his kingdom. He is not personally cruel, simply icily indifferent to human fate. "Comrade Commander," he says to his victim, "you remember how we debated whether or not to send four thousand men to certain death? You ordered them to be sent. You were right. In three weeks you'll be on your feet. You must forgive me, but I have already given the order."

The story was published in the magazine *Novy Mir* in May 1926 and instantly suppressed. But Stalin, not yet supremely powerful, bided his time. A later and much more innocuous work, *Mahogany*, first published by a "White Guard" publishing house abroad, led to a vicious press campaign against Pilnyak. A mildly nostalgic novella became, in the familiar crude jargon of Soviet newspeak, an "intolerable crime," a "betrayal of the Revolution," "literary sabotage," a "disgraceful action." Factories from Minsk to Vladivostok joined in "unconditional and unanimous" condemnation of "intolerable Pilnyakism." Expelled from the Writers' Union, he disavowed his novella, and was permitted for a while to survive, though in a state of— quite sensible—terror. In 1937 he was taken during his child's third birthday party, and assured of a quick return. He was never seen again. Having once visited Japan, he was clearly a Japanese spy. . . . His wife and ex-wife were sent to Siberia, his children became outcasts. Sweet revenge for "Tale of the Unextinguished Moon."[9]

The old Rossiya Insurance Company would have considered authorship in this era a high-risk occupation.

Yet books by Romanov and Pilnyak lingered, like ghosts, in the prison where they had probably been shot.

The other two writers mentioned in *The Gulag Archipelago* managed to die naturally, thanks to exile, yet not peacefully, since they both remained tormented by longing for their country.

Dmitri Merezhkovsky (1865–1941), whose complete works were available in the prison, popularized French symbolism in the St. Petersburg of the 1890s, and married the symbolist poet Zinaida Gippius. They moved to Paris in 1920, living in their prewar apartment. His historico-philosophical books were like heavy port wine, his oratory, champagne. The memoirist Nina Berberova felt she wanted to kiss his hand whenever she heard him lecture. He and his wife became a kind of cultural grand duke and duchess of the Russian diaspora.

Berberova recalls him asking his wife which was dearer to her: Russia without freedom or freedom without Russia? After a moment's thought she said, "Freedom without Russia; and that is why I am here and not there." He agreed with her but added, gazing sadly into the distance: "But what good is freedom to me if there is no Russia?"[10] They both loathed Bolshevism so much they were almost unique among the émigrés in hoping the Nazis would win. Berberova's last memories of them in German-occupied Paris captures their tragedy: "He was very thin, very old. He ran in very small steps along the Rue Passy arm in arm with Gippius. When I went to see him three weeks ago, he was indifferent to everything (and to me). . . ."[11]

The purple-mouthed librarian could not have brought the most famous book of Yevgeny Zamyatin (1884–1937), *We*, written in 1920, because it was not published in Russia until 1988. Instead of Merezhkovsky's choice of freedom or Russia, *We* is set in a monolithic, standardized State of the future, which has chosen for its citizens (called Numbers) happiness rather than freedom. The ancients, choosing freedom, were constantly dissatisfied and crime ridden. Much of the work's energy comes from a tension between the sternly orthodox views of the narrator, D-503, and the sparkling unorthodoxy of his style. . . . "And then what a sky! Blue, unsullied by a single cloud (what primitive tastes the ancients must have had if their poets were inspired by those absurd, untidy clumps of mist, idiotically jostling one another about). I love—and I am sure that I am right in saying *we* love—only such a sky as this one today: sterile and immaculate."[12]

Though a Bolshevik, Zamyatin was horrified by the excesses of the Revolution. He believed in infinite revolutions. The ideas expressed in *We* were well-known in the Soviet Union, despite the ban on its publication. In 1929 a shortened version in Russian was published in Prague, leading to attacks on him mirroring those on Pilnyak. Probably thanks to an intercession by Gorky, Zamyatin was allowed to go into exile. Living in Paris, he kept much to himself, desperate to return. Berberova observed him marking time; understood "that there was no reason for him to stay alive . . . and no one for whom to write, and nothing to write about. . . . That he hated *them*, and *us* he slightly despised."[13] If he had to die prematurely it was not unfitting that he did so in 1937, as it were in sympathy with so many at home.

By gunshot or heartbreak, it didn't seem to matter.

Instructed by the living and the dead, Solzhenitsyn was starting out on a spiritual journey; and, in a way familiar to mystics, the hardships and depression he endured somehow opened up a way for the spirit to grow. He would look back on his first cell as akin to first love.

It was almost time to leave that "first cell, first love" behind. A week after the end of the war he was summoned to see Lieutenant Colonel Kotov, the overall supervisor of his case. Calm, well fed, impersonal, Kotov "yawningly" examined the dossier for fifteen minutes, then raised indifferent eyes to the wall and lazily asked if there was anything he wished to add to his testimony. Solzhenitsyn questioned the charge of setting up an anti-Soviet organization. After all, only two men, himself and Vitkevich, were involved, which was hardly an organization. Kotov sighed, spread his hands as though to say he wished he could help but . . . "What is there to say? One person is a person, but two persons are . . . people."

A few days later, Sanya was sent for by Yezepov, who gave him his statements to read over. As he read the various distortions, his blood boiled, he at first declined to sign; but then Yezepov threatened to start the whole investigation again, somewhere where collaborators were held; and that seemed unbearable. Better to get it over with. "Ahead was the promise of at least some sort of life."

In June he was told he was being moved to Butyrki prison. The parting from his friends was emotional. "Those people, who shared with you the floor and air of that stone cubicle during those days when you rethought your entire life, will from time to time be recollected by you as members of your own family," he would recall in *Gulag*.

In Butyrki, he found himself in a cell three times as big as the one he had left, and with three times the number of inmates. He was shocked to find Yuri Y., the Vlasovite, multiplied many times over, yet each with a unique and terrible story. There were also returned slave-labor peasants, and prisoners of war. Prisoners who had resisted all temptation to fight for the Germans, at the cost of almost certain death. They had survived by miracle, and through unbearable suffering, yet in Stalin's eyes their guilt was as great as the Vlasovites'. They had chosen a prison cage rather than death; and that was treason!

Solzhenitsyn reflected . . . England, where the workers were downtrodden viciously, had produced only one traitor in the war, Lord Haw-Haw. Russia, the Communist utopia, had produced hundreds of thousands! It made no sense. Or rather, it did, once you realized that all these men were not being sent off to camps for having done something, but rather to stop them doing something—talk to villagers about what they had seen in the West. Reproaching himself for having disregarded the pleas of the captured Vlasovite he saw being bloodily whipped, Solzhenitsyn now found himself standing up even for these men.

There were also many émigrés from the Civil War. They had lived in the West for more than two decades, but now their havens had been overrun by the Red Army or they had been sent back by the zealously cooperative Allies. Solzhenitsyn found that these sad people were not the seedy drug addicts of popular Soviet fantasy, but for the most part decent, patriotic, and far from reactionary Russians.

While he waited for some kind of trial, he was told he could receive parcels. Natasha's aunt, he thought, would be in the best position to bring them, since she lived in Moscow. She received a printed card informing her she could deliver parcels to Prisoner Solzhenitsyn, A. I. There followed the flurry of messages to Rostov, ending Natasha's ignorance at last.

Rumors of amnesty spread through the prison. On 27 July, he and another prisoner were called out after breakfast. The others ribbed them about soon being free, and to send them parcels. He knew it was an illusion, yet one could not help hoping. . . . Twenty men were led to the bathhouse, through a little emerald park in an interior courtyard. "The birds sang deafeningly . . . and the green of the trees seemed unbearably bright to eyes no longer used to it. Never had my eyes seen the green of the leaves with such intensity as they did that spring! And never in my life had I seen anything closer to God's paradise than that little Butyrki park, which never took more than thirty seconds to cross on the asphalt path."[14]

He was led in front of an NKVD major, who in a bored voice read out to him his sentence. Eight years.

16

New Jerusalem

I really do intend to go to the brick-works and start
working there very soon.
— TUZENBAKH, in *Three Sisters*

AUNT VERONICA WROTE TO HER NIECE IN ROSTOV: "SAW SHU-
rochka just once. She was returning with friends from her job of unloading
timber on the Moscow River. She looks marvellous. She is suntanned, energetic, cheerful, smiling from ear to ear, teeth sparkling! I'm very glad
she's in good spirits."[1]

Shurochka is the diminutive form of Alexandra. In *The First Circle* Solzhenitsyn would transfer Veronica Turkin's lucky glimpse of him to Nadya
(Natasha), and describes Nerzhin (himself) as sallow and emaciated like all
the other prisoners. A strong August sun burns down on them. He is smiling
as he listens to his gray-haired neighbor, and does not glance either at the
hills or at the curious bystanders.[2] It was indeed a lucky chance that Veronica spotted Natasha's husband: now at Krasnaya Presnya transit prison,
normally he had no respite from an overcrowded, stiflingly hot cell, but that
day he had jumped at the chance to join a casual work gang.

Natasha, lying prudently, had told all her friends and colleagues he had
been reported missing in action; she had discussed with her supervisor the
possibility of completing her postgraduate studies in Moscow. Not only
would she be closer to Sanya, at least temporarily, but she didn't know how
long she could keep the truth hidden in Rostov. He was so well-known
there and people kept inquiring; also, there were so many men not returning
from the war, causing a feeling of unease. Conveniently her professor was
leaving Rostov, and new arrangements for her would be necessary anyway.
He agreed to use his contacts in the chemistry department at Moscow University. She could go and talk to the professors.

So, while Sanya was still in Butyrki, she had bribed her way onto a plane
for Moscow, and persuaded a rather good-looking professor to admit her
so long as she passed her end-of-summer examinations. He would have been

unlikely to have been so accommodating if he could have seen her queueing outside the grim Butyrki walls to deliver a parcel.

Just before she left for the South again, to sit her exams, she learned that her husband had been sentenced to eight years in corrective labor camps, with rights to limited correspondence. Shaken, she went from the NKVD information center to Lydia Ezherets's, to share her sadness with their friend. Lydia—by now married to Kirill—took her to see a play, trying to cheer her up a little.° Natasha returned to Rostov, and on the same day Sanya was driven, in a Black Maria, or *raven*, probably marked "Bread" or "Meat," to Krasnaya Presnya.

A sprawling, chaotic complex, Krasnaya Presnya was the embarkation point for the infinitely far-stretched islands of the Gulag Archipelago. Every *zek* passed through it at some time. It was tied more closely to the Kolyma gold mines than to the life of "normal" Moscow—that Moscow which went to the circus or the theater.

Hitherto, in the Lubyanka and Butyrki, Solzhenitsyn had had the companionship of educated men, often idealists like himself. Krasnaya Presnya exposed him to a vastly more violent world, that of the hardened criminal. Natasha had once taught basic Darwinism, but one needed the experience of living with criminals to know it in the bone. Yet this halfway house between prison and labor camp seemed to him, in retrospect, invaluable; otherwise the shock of the camps would have been too great. He discovered in Krasnaya Presnya that thieves and cutthroats were of a higher order than the politicals. A rapist was still a Soviet man, "comrade"; Sanya was "Mister Fascist"—the criminals invented that term of abuse and the guards encouraged them to use it.

When Sanya and another "Mister Fascist" were pushed, the first night, into a cell crammed with over a hundred men, they crawled on their bellies under two bunks, hoping not to be bothered. But in the murk, they were aware of bodies rustling toward them "like big rats," and then hands, some belonging to boys of twelve, swiftly and silently stripped them of precious foodstuffs—lard, sugar, bread—that their relatives had brought them.

Sanya crawled out fighting mad, intent on hammering one of the thieves; but when he confronted the scarred and mountainous gang leader he meekly said that, in return for their food, they ought at least to be given bunks to sleep in. The gang leader agreed, and ordered a couple of his boys to move out of two bunks near the window. Not only had Sanya lost face, he also angered some of the politicals by the way he had got himself a bunk. He would blush, years after, at the memory of his behavior.[3]

Actually he had conformed straightaway to the Gulag morality. In order to survive, it seemed, you had to screw someone else. The most memorable

---

°J. B. Priestley's new left-wing play, *An Inspector Calls*. It fitted in with the end-of-war radicalism in Britain, which included widespread affection for "good old Joe" Stalin and swept a Labour government into power.

character he met in the transit prison was a "true son of Gulag" as such people were called—a veteran of many years and many camps throughout the Archipelago. This man, who happened to bunk down next to Sanya, owed his survival to having become a "special assignment" prisoner; he had a chit indicating he should only be used as a construction technician. The dominant expression in his face was one of cruelty and determination; Solzhenitsyn would discover that this was a "national" characteristic of the Archipelago; persons with soft, conciliatory expressions did not survive.

The veteran addressed a group of the new prisoners like a professor advising sophomores. From their first step in a camp, he said, others would be out to deceive and rob them. They should trust no one but themselves; there was no justice in the Gulag, and no altruism. The law of the jungle, of the taiga, prevailed. Above all, they must avoid general assignment work: the basic laboring work of the camps, to which 80 or 90 percent were assigned. If they were on general assignment, he emphasized, they were lost; they would be given impossible norms, would be constantly famished and exhausted, cold and wet. Most of these people perished. Solzhenitsyn was impressed by the lecture.

As he waited to see where he would be sent, he went on learning from the endless movement of people being processed. The staggering variety of characters streaming through—many of them willing to speak openly and frankly—was giving him a better understanding of what was going on, in himself and his people.

At last he received a letter from Natasha, and he replied. Natasha, opening the triangle into which he had folded his letter, was so overcome that she wanted to shout out. She read: "What indescribable joy the sheets written in your own hand gave me. . . . In this way I found out that you are alive, healthy, and free. To this day I don't know whether or not 'sir' has shared my fate." "Sir"—a reference to the Three Musketeers—was of course Koka. He was also concerned for Kirill and Lydia, and the reference to Natasha's being "free" indicated, as her mother spotted with alarm, that he had feared for her too. She was his "beautiful wife," whom he deeply loved, and whose youth had been spent mostly in waiting. He still hoped there would be an amnesty, and that in any case he would not have to serve his full sentence. But if he did, could he expect her to wait another eight years?

Whereas previously his dream had been to live in Moscow or Leningrad, in a commune, now he dreamed of going with her to live in a "remote, but thriving, well-provisioned, and picturesque village"; perhaps in Siberia or the Kuban, where his grandparents had lived; or along the Volga or the Don. They would both teach high school, and would spend the long summer vacations in Moscow, Leningrad, or Rostov.[4]

On completing her exams, she wanted to go back to Moscow in the hope of seeing him. First she had to get permission to leave her place of residence, and queue for hours for a ticket. It was now that Aunt Veronica wrote saying she had seen "Shurochka"; then sent another letter saying her latest parcel had not been accepted at Krasnaya Presnya; he had been moved, she didn't know where. A few days later: "Natasha, my golden one, truly you were born under a lucky star! How many envious eyes were fixed on me yesterday! You can calm down. Every Sunday you will be going from Moscow to New Jerusalem. This is a resort place, in a magnificent natural setting; it used to be called the 'Russian Switzerland.' You will see each other there."

He had been sent to a brick factory thirty miles west of Moscow, in the district of Zvenigorod. Two trucks took some sixty politicals out to the camp on 14 August 1945. They were bewildered to see the streets and houses decked with flags: Japan had surrendered, it was the day of final victory. At first sight the camp looked as attractive as Aunt Veronica's description had painted it to Natasha. The prisoners, starved of green, thrilled as they saw, all around the camp compound, gentle hills dotted with scruffy, pleasant-looking hamlets and dachas; and the white two-story factory itself, with a stone barracks for men and a wooden one for women, looked almost cozy. The surrounding barbed wire did not seem too constricting, set in such pleasant surroundings.

But the reality was a long way from the New Jerusalem.

And first there were the excited thieves and cutthroats, shouting, "The Fascists are coming! The Fascists are coming!"

It was late in the day when they arrived. The politicals queued to hand in their battered suitcases or other bags at the stores, then they were led into their stone barracks. It was a cavernous building containing no furniture whatever, only bunks. But such bunks! Four narrow boards, one pair at knee height, the other at shoulder height, held together precariously by two vertical steel posts about six feet apart. There was no mattress, nor bedding of any kind. The prisoners had to sleep on bare boards, and in their clothes and boots, since there was nowhere to put them and in any case they would have been stolen.

There were two additional sleep-depriving factors: if one of the four prisoners on a "wagonette" (as the structures were known in the Gulag) turned over, or climbed off or on, the whole thing shook, waking the other three; and since there were three shifts working the brick factory, and no attempt had been made to separate them in the barracks, there was an almost constant uproar of another shift getting ready to move out or in. Solzhenitsyn slept hardly at all that first night, and wondered if he would ever sleep again. Thieves roared out curses or laughs, playing cards; one of them leapt from top bunk to top bunk, landing on bodies, right across the room, crying, "That's how Napoleon went to Moscow for tobacco!" Then, having grabbed some tobacco, did the return journey, crying, "That's how Napoleon buggered off to Paris."

At a quarter after four in the morning, a bell rang out and guards shouted,

"First shift, up!" Solzhenitsyn wondered if some of the old folk in the "sleepy" collective farm near them, hearing the camp bell, recognized it as a bell from the former monastery, which had given the camp its name. Once, perhaps, this bell had roused monks to early prayer; but their self-imposed hardships would surely not have included getting up fully dressed and, without any time to wash, being herded with gummed-up eyes into a mess hall. Everyone else knew where to go in the murky, steam-filled chaos; he had to grope his way. At last he had his pound and a quarter of soggy bread, and an earthenware bowl full of black nettle soup; just a few leaves in the blackish water. No fish, meat, fat, or even salt. If tobacco was camp gold, salt was camp silver. His gorge rose as he tried to drink the repulsive soup. He looked up at the walls and ceiling; his eyes adjusting to the dim lamps, he read the slogan "WHOEVER DOES NOT WORK DOES NOT EAT!"

Nothing of a prisoner's life could be left in the barracks, no more than an ox can leave anything in its stall. Everything had to be put in store.

The prisoners stumbled out, and were formed up to be marched to the brickworks. The predawn August sky was paling; only the brightest stars were still visible. He could see Sirius and Procyon, the dog stars. Earthly dogs were barking madly, pulling at their leashes, wanting to get at the *zeks*.

The new *zeks* shifted rubbish heaps from one place to another, while it was being decided what to do with them. "The first day in camp! I do not wish my worst enemy that day! The folds of the brain are all mixed up because of the impossibility of absorbing the entire scope of the cruelty."[5] Several at a time, they were called into an office to be given their assignments. He had deliberately put on his despoiled officer's tunic—buttoned severely to the neck—and broad belt, even though he knew he would be pushing a wheelbarrow.

"An officer?" asked the factory director.

"Yes, sir!"

"Do you have experience working with people?"

"I do."

"What did you command?"

"An artillery battalion." (A battery seemed too small.)

The director looked at him with both trust and doubt. "And will you manage here? It's hard here."

"I think I'll manage."

"Okay, you'll be shift foreman in the clay pit."

Another former officer, a fresh-faced lad called Nikolai Akimov, was also appointed shift foreman. They left the office with a feeling of glad kinship. "What's he scaring us with?" Akimov asked. "There are no minefields, and no bombs dropping! Does he think we can't cope with twenty men!"

The clay pit was in a remote corner of the compound. The clay, which lay exposed in thick furrows, had to be loaded onto a car, which had then to be pushed along a trolley track to the pressing mill. Only at one point, at the rise out of the pit, was there a motor-driven windlass which lifted the truck mechanically. Toward the end of Solzhenitsyn's morning shift, within a day or two of his becoming foreman, a penalty brigade was brought in. They were criminals who had threatened the camp chief with a slit throat, in the hope of being sent back to Krasnaya Presnya. The gang immediately lay down in a sheltered spot, baring their short brawny limbs and fat tattooed stomachs, to sun themselves. Solzhenitsyn went up to them and ordered them to get to work. They laughed and told him to go fuck his mother.

He knew that if he ordered them to stand up they would stick a knife in him. He backed off, angry and confused. All the "sloggers" were looking at him, sizing up his response. Luckily the shift was at an end. Akimov took his place. Solzhenitsyn heard later he had been taken to the provincial prison hospital: he had upset the "cons" and they had smashed him in the kidneys with a crowbar.

Solzhenitsyn experienced a spiritual despondency in the clay pit deeper than if he had been digging the clay himself. He would go there at six A.M. and wander around feeling quite lost. He tried to lead, as the army had taught him to do, but from ignorance. The man who knew how to dig the clay and look after his men was the brigade leader, a nonpolitical called Barinov. Instead of quietly letting the brigade leader get on with it, Sanya bustled around like an officer, and Barinov did his best to humiliate him: constantly calling him over to solve a problem: how to re-lay the tracks; how to put back a wheel that had jumped off its axle; where to take the shovels for sharpening. His sarcastic cry was forever ringing out, "Foreman! Foreman!"

Though he did learn to keep out of Barinov's way, Sanya felt numb from his meaningless role, the horror of the nights in barracks, the starvation diet. Yet this Gulag "island" was not in Siberia, but close to Moscow.

He contemplated the prospect of eight years of this, always with the chance of having another term added on for no reason at the end; and found it unbearable. His mind, his spirit, were in total shock, and he didn't know how to recover. His dream was much more modest now than the high-school-teaching rural idyll, with long big-city breaks. Now . . .

Over there, beyond the barbed wire, across a vale, was a knoll. On it was a little village—ten houses. The rising sun illuminated it with its peaceful rays. So close to us—and the very opposite of a camp! (For that matter, it, too, was a camp, but one forgets that).° For a long time there was no motion at all there, but then a woman walked by with a pail, and a tiny child ran across the weeds in the street. A cock crowed and a cow mooed. And there in the clay pit we could hear

---

°That is, a collective farm, its peasants having no more legal rights than serfs, and with no religious rites or holy days.

everything perfectly. And a mongrel barked—what a lovely voice that was too! It was not a convoy dog!

And from every sound there and from the very immobility itself a holy peace flooded into my soul. And I knew for certain that if they should say to me at that very moment: That's your freedom! Just live in that village until your death! . . . Look at the sun every morning and harken to the roosters! . . . Are you willing? Oh, not only willing, but, good Lord, please send me a life like that![6]

Solzhenitsyn was responsible to the *zek* head of the wet-pressing plant, a middle-aged engineer in silicates called Olga Matronina. Her husband had been shot, and she had received eight years for being his wife. Yet she remained a fervent Communist, and even wore a red scarf around her head every day. Concerned that not enough bricks were being made, she doubled the workload expected. Solzhenitsyn declined to implement her demand, and she dressed him down in front of Barinov and the sloggers.

He was foreman for only a week or so before the position was abolished. With glinting eyes, Matronina ordered an equally delighted Barinov: "Put him to work with a crowbar and don't take your eyes off him! Make him load six cars a shift—make him *sweat!*"

There were prisoners who were known as "goners": they had visibly given up on life. Sanya could imagine that happening to him. When an NKVD lieutenant summoned him to his clean, pleasant room for a chat, and then asked him to write his autobiography, he was happy to oblige. He sat at a desk and, under the officer's benign gaze, wrote on smooth paper that he had commanded a battery, been decorated, and so on, feeling his ego recovering slightly. The officer was pleased with his piece, saying, "So you're a Soviet person, hmm?"

"Yes."

"Good. Come again in a few days." He did so, but the lieutenant had gone.

Briefly Sanya was moved from the clay pit to the factory floor, rolling away trolleys stacked with newly made bricks. The piles of bricks were insecure and sometimes fell on him; he burned his windpipe from breathing in fumes in unventilated drying chambers. But in his brief time there he absorbed one unforgettable image—that of a young girl, "a real genuine heroine of labour, though not suitable for the newspaper." As wet bricks, just mixed with clay and very heavy, emerged from the press, this girl, standing on a platform like a beauty queen, had incessantly to bend down, pick up a brick to waist or even shoulder height, then, without moving her feet, swing from her waist ninety degrees, to one side or another, and place the brick on a shelf. Moving at the speed of fast gymnastics, she did not pause for her whole eight-hour shift; for the first half of it, she never lost her smile.

She did it for an extra portion of bread and a small portion of semolina and water. Her ration was the biggest in the camp. But perhaps also, Solzhenitsyn suggests, she enjoyed standing up there, showing off her strong, bare legs below her hitched-up skirt, and the balletic grace of her movements. He, at least, obviously enjoyed her grace and energy, and his portrait of her in *Gulag* is one of his most moving and tender. She shines out in her almost carefree bravery; a flicker of eros against the blackness.

Though not sorry to return to the clay pit, because of the fumes burning him, he was not sure he could survive it. Toning down his fears, he wrote to Natasha: "The work loads of an unskilled labourer are beyond my strength. I curse my physical underdevelopment." Perhaps wishing to give her some hope, he told her he still thought there would be an amnesty.

And he was right: "All those who had burglarised apartments, stolen the clothes off passers-by, raped girls, corrupted minors, given consumers short weight, played the hoodlum, disfigured the defenceless, been wantonly destructive in forests and waterways, committed bigamy, practised blackmail or extortion, taken bribes, swindled, slandered, written false denunciations (but those particular people didn't actually serve time at all! . . .), peddled narcotics, pimped or forced women into prostitution, whose carelessness or ignorance had resulted in loss of life, all went scot-free. (And I have merely listed here the articles of the Code covered by the amnesty; this is not a mere flourish of eloquence.)"[7]

Also deserters were amnestied. Anyone who had fled from the front or not turned up at the conscription point; who had cowered in a hole, hidden by his mother throughout the war: provided they had given themselves up or been caught before the day of amnesty, these could walk free. One could see Stalin's reasoning for releasing them while making slaves of those who had fought heroically for their country and been captured: cowards are not dangerous.

Did he ever take his pipe from his mouth to smile, at the drollness of it all?

Women who yesterday had been dressed in rags and shouted obscenities were suddenly wearing polka-dot dresses and modestly walking to the railway station. And all over New Jerusalem appeared a new slogan: "For the broadest amnesty we shall respond to our dear Party and government with doubled productivity."

That is, those who were not amnestied would double their productivity, in gratitude for those who were.

Sanya had two special friends in the camp whom he had met in Butyrki, Boris Gammerov and Georgi Ingal. They had been arrested while still students at Moscow University, though Gammerov had already been a sergeant at the front, and been invalided out with shrapnel in a lung. He wore his threadbare army greatcoat, bullet-holed. He was twenty-two; his friend Ingal a little older. To Sanya they seemed a generation younger, and he refers to them in *Gulag* affectionately as his "boys."

His first conversation with Gammerov had been memorable. A newspaper had published one of the late President Roosevelt's favorite prayers, and Sanya muttered what he thought was self-evidently true: "Pure hypocrisy, of course." The youth, pale, yellowish, with a "Jewish tenderness of face,"[8] drew himself up and asked: "Why? Why should it be impossible that a political leader might sincerely believe in God?"

"Do you believe in God?"

"Of course."

Sanya was shocked. How could someone born fully in the Soviet epoch, in 1923, have a religious faith? He himself had long been an atheist—naturally. . . . Or was it natural? He admitted to himself that his comment on Roosevelt had not come from inner conviction, but was an implanted response.

Boris wrote poetry. Georgi Ingal was a prose writer; he had already almost finished a novel about Debussy, and at his arrest had been already a Candidate Member of the Soviet Writers' Union: on his way, that is, to a life of great privilege. In New Jerusalem he showed his determination by writing far into the night: sitting up in the top bunk wearing his padded jacket, sucking on his pencil. He had managed to get a job in accounts; Gammerov, too proud to try to influence anyone, was a laborer.

At roll call, which could go on for an hour or more, Sanya saw his "boys" with their eyes closed, and knew they were composing verses, or prose, or letters. Ingal was married, but his student wife "had not even worn out the shoes in which she'd gone with him that winter to the conservatory—and now she had left him. . . ."[9] Perhaps craving affection, he was writing to another girl he liked, but having to wish her well in her forthcoming marriage.

His crime had been to claim that his teacher, Yuri Tynyanov, a writer of historical novels about the Pushkin era, had been persecuted. Ingal had spoken emotionally and unwisely at Tynyanov's funeral in 1943. Gammerov had been part of a political discussion group at the university, of whom three had been pulled in. He was following a tradition: his father had been arrested and shot in 1937.

Now he and Sanya were laboring together in the clay pit; and a persistent autumn drizzle had set in. For three days it continued. Their tattered greatcoats were soaked through and their last front-line boots were rotting in the wet clay. Underneath his greatcoat Sanya wore ragged overalls, no longer his officer's uniform, which he had put in store. He could no longer try to set himself apart, like Matronina in her red scarf.

On the first day they joked about a character in Chekhov's *Three Sisters*. "Baron Tuzenbakh would have envied us now, Boris! Don't you remember, he dreamed of working in a brick-yard!"

"Ah yes—that's right." Boris straightened, to rest a moment. He was weaker than Sanya, and the sticky clay was growing heavier and heavier; he could hardly throw each shovelful up to the edge of the truck. He was thin and yellowish, and his features had grown sharp. His breath rasped; there was still shrapnel in his lung.

"Good old Tuzenbakh, eh, Boris! Wanted to work so hard he would throw himself on his bed and fall asleep at once!"

"After a good hot meal, of course, Sanya."

"Oh, naturally! And when he woke up his clothes would be washed, dried and pressed. . . ."

The shift ended at last. They went back to black nettle soup and a ladle of gruel; and slept in their wet clothes, shivering.

The next day, as the drizzle still fell, they could not get the clay to drop off their shovels into the car. They scooped it up with their hands and threw it in. Boris kept coughing; his wound was turning into tuberculosis. But he tried to talk about poetry. "Vladimir Solovyev* taught that one must greet death with gladness. Worse than here . . . it won't be."

Solzhenitsyn looked at him, and wondered if he would make it through the winter.

As the shift wore on, Boris was no longer able to talk. "Takes too much strength," he said. "Let's be silent and think to some purpose. For example, compose verses. In our heads."

Toward the end of the shift Matronina came; she had a dark shawl covering her red headscarf. She indicated with severe gestures that they would not leave until the brigade had fulfilled its norm. She left and the rain thickened. Red puddles formed, and the red spread up their boots, their coats. Their hands were so frozen they could no longer throw the clay into the cars. They went up on to the grass, sat down, and pulled up their coat collars round their necks. Sanya thought that, from the side, they must look like two reddish stones in the field.

The nearby village was hidden by the rain. Everyone else left to find some shelter; the half-filled cars were overturned. The two men, dragging their spades, which they must not lose, went to find some shelter by Matronina's plant, and came upon two *zeks* searching for something in a pile of coal. They found whatever they were searching for—a black-gray lump—and started eating it.

"What's that?"

"It's 'sea clay.' It's got no goodness but it doesn't do any harm; and if you eat it it makes you feel full. Go on, try it. . . ."

Matronina gave orders that the brigade should stay out all night. But the electricity went out, an escape was feared, and they were driven back, arms linked, through the pitch-darkness. Guard dogs snarled at their heals.

Gammerov died in the winter, in a hospital, from tuberculosis and exhaustion. Solzhenitsyn grieved, in later years, that he had not memorized any of his verse, which had seemed powerful and highly spiritual. Just that

---

*Religious and philosophical poet, 1853–1900.

one line which he quotes when recalling the victory celebrations of May 1945. It was Boris who wrote the verses about prisoners raising their heads, aroused by the noise, then deciding it had nothing to do with them. . . . "And once again covered themselves with their coats."

An epitaph for soldiers who should have returned as heroes needing treatment, good food, and recuperation, and instead were thrown into the bottomless pit of the Gulag. What circle of Hades for the perpetrator of such a betrayal?

17

V e t r o v

... And was accounted a good actor.
—HAMLET

GEORGI INGAL ALSO DID NOT SURVIVE THE CAMPS, THOUGH SOL-
zhenitsyn does not tell us where or how he perished. He presumably never
finished his novel about Debussy, nor wrote the many other things his talent
and determination would have insisted he write—had he not become one
of the sixty million or so victims of Soviet Communism. He did not get a
chance to love, or to have children and grandchildren. The unborn are also
victims.

Solzhenitsyn, too, found himself growing weaker in the clay pit. "In
prison we seemed to have grown weak, but here it went much faster. There
was already a ringing in the head. That pleasant weakness, in which it is
easier to give in than to fight back, kept coming closer." Unless it is a
rhetorical flourish in *Gulag*, his prayer, which a year ago had been for his
life to be saved from German shells and bombs, was now for death.[1]

But he was lucky. On 9 September 1945 the *zeks* were ordered to get
ready for a move. German POW's were being moved in to take over New
Jerusalem.

There is no more graphic illustration of the relativity of time than the
difference between Natasha's retrospective view of the New Jerusalem period and Sanya's. For Natasha, busy clearing up her affairs in Rostov while
awaiting the necessary permit to leave, it seemed no time at all between
her husband's arrival at New Jerusalem and word that he had been moved
on. In fact, he was just three weeks at the New Jerusalem camp. The accounts in *Gulag* make it seem like months, like years. Natasha's memoir,
with an understandable lack of imagination and a KGB-controlled editor,
summed up New Jerusalem with "the work was strenuous."[2]

She had been notified of an address—30 Kaluzhskaya Plaza, Construction
Site No. 121, Moscow 71—but knew no more as she traveled north. To

her astonishment Aunt Veronica, embracing her at the station, announced: "Sanya's already in Moscow. You will see him tomorrow. He is waiting." Her aunt had the gift of turning the Gulag into a romantic idyll. Thus, earlier, Sanya had been sunburned and smiling from ear to ear, coming from the river . . . next in a Swiss-style resort, where Natasha would visit him every Sunday. Now "he is waiting . . .": like a handsome, imperious lover brandishing a riding crop.

The next day Natasha took a bus out along busy Kaluga Street, to the south of the city. It was a street with a steady flow of limousines, some with diplomatic license plates.[3] She got off at the end of the railings that closed off Neskuchny Park, at the southern end of Gorky Park. Nothing except some discreet barbed wire above a wooden fence hinted at a camp; the figures in tattered overalls she glimpsed working high on a half-finished apartment block might just as easily have been free workers; indeed, there were free workers there as well as *zeks*. The guard room to the Kaluga Gate camp was like any ordinary entrance. She spoke to the duty guard, and was shown into a low-ceilinged room lined with wooden benches. She sat there for a few minutes. Footsteps—then, in the doorway, an even scraggier Sanya, shaven headed, his cap in his hands, smiling at her.

The guard was always present. Sanya begged her forgiveness for his last letters from the front. He wanted to cross out the lines that had upset her. He seemed to her to have changed, to have become more sensitive to her feelings.

"I'm lucky . . . I'm not on the general duties list. It's vital to keep off that." His faraway glance over her shoulder took in the clay pit, the sweeping rain, Boris coughing. "The lieutenant who interviewed me seemed quite a decent man. I told him I was a norm setter. . . ."

"And what's that?"

"I have no idea! They kept mentioning it at the last camp; I hoped it had something to do with mathematics. Anyway, he created a special post for me—production superintendent!"

"Sanya, that's wonderful!"

"Wait, wait! That was a week ago, I've been demoted to general duties! He was replaced, you see, and the new commandant felt I was—well, not aggressive enough. He's probably right. I'm painting and laying floors. It's not too bad. . . ."

His great stroke of luck was in being allowed to stay in the same privileged trusties' room, despite his rapid demotion. The room had single bunks for six prisoners, with a bedside table shared between two; and a half-legal electric hot plate. The room was kept locked by day, so personal items could be left there, avoiding the need to queue at a stores twice a day, and allowing more dignity. The miserable camp food could be supplemented by parcels. In Sanya's case, he received two parcels a week from Natasha. There was hunger in the population generally, in the aftermath of the war; and Natasha went short herself to get those parcels together for her husband.

He really was extremely lucky that the man appointed superintendent in his place was already in a trusties' room, so allowing Sanya to stay where he was, despite his demotion. Someone may have decided that he was worth working on, and so should be left some comforts that he might be loath to lose. In the room with him were an air force major general, a Ministry of Internal Affairs (MVD) general, a neuropathologist, an engineer, and a chairman of a village soviet. At the time, understandably, Solzhenitsyn valued only the comfort provided by the room; later, he would appreciate more the unique chance to be close to such exalted Soviet figures as the generals.

Jailed for corruption, Major General Alexander Belyayev stood out from everyone else in the camp for his height, bearing, short yet stylish-looking gray hair, excellent leather coat—the sort that saw only the inside of automobiles; but particularly for his air of not being present. "Even without stirring in the camp column he was able to demonstrate that he had no relationship whatever to all that camp rabble swarming about him. . . . Stretched to his full height he looked over the heads of the mob, just as if he were reviewing a completely different parade which we could not see. . . ."[4]

On first meeting Belyayev in the construction office, Sanya asked him for a light, expecting him casually to offer his cigarette to draw on; instead, he took an expensive lighter from his pocket and placed it on the desk. Every noon his wife would present at the guard house a vacuum container with a hot meal for him. He boasted that he didn't know which was the door to the mess hall. The former village soviet chairman, the peasant Prokhorov, brought him his bread ration in return for his portion of gruel. The general would fastidiously cut off all the crusts before he would eat the bread, then threw the trimmings in the slop bucket. Big-framed Prokhorov, a man of simple dignity, requested the crusts, but Belyayev ignored him. Sanya asked him why, and he replied, "My cellmate at the Lubyanka once asked me: 'Please let me finish your soup!' I was nearly sick to my stomach! I react very painfully to human humiliation!" Solzhenitsyn comments: "He refused bread to the hungry so as not to humiliate them!"

He was always blustering and complaining; it was painful for him to eat his wife's home cooking in front of five other people, he said. He loved to dominate conversation, though Solzhenitsyn noticed that this air force general never mentioned a single air battle, or even a single flight. Now an assistant norm setter, he expected deference from Sanya, and got it, even during the week or so when the latter was his superior. Solzhenitsyn wondered what he had been like *before* the humiliations of a Lubyanka box.

Yet he could not find it in him to dislike Belyayev; at least he laughed warmly when reading Gogol, and could make others laugh too when he was in a good mood. He needed some suffering to become a good man, Sanya thought. The other general there in a blue-gray MVD uniform, Pavel Zinovyev, was polite and restrained in manner, though essentially more sinister. With one "snakelike stare" he could stop you in your tracks from using the hot plate when he wanted to reserve it. He had been in charge of prisoners himself. Sentenced for corruption too, he had been punished more severely than Belyayev in having his savings confiscated; but had been allowed to choose this camp close to his fine apartment, in which his wife and daughter were still living. He too, out of pride, got Prokhorov to bring his food from the mess, though he could not disdainfully cast most of it aside as Belyayev did.

Solzhenitsyn, himself "a peasant at heart," liked best the two coarsest men in the room. Prokhorov, spokesman for the work brigades, did not go out of his way to be friendly, but also did not crawl. His service for the generals, which he needed to do to fill his big body, was done without a trace of servility. Solzhenitsyn felt Prokhorov could see through everyone, though he said little. The engineer, Orachevsky, spoke rarely, and was culturally ignorant; but he had a passionate devotion to the work of the construction site. He had been given eight years for being seen smiling at something in *Pravda*.

The sixth man in the room was serving as the camp doctor. This elderly man, Dr. Pravdin, disappointed Sanya most of all since he had matured under the civilized old regime; he should have been educated, fearless, and possessed of integrity, but instead he seemed childish and terrified. He scarcely dared take any decision for fear of having another sentence loaded onto him. Caring for the health of the prisoners was less important than pleasing the authorities. Perhaps it was appropriate that a neuropathologist should have developed weak nerves.

The generals dictated every aspect of life in their room—which became practically a model of feudal-Communist Russia, with the generals as aristos, the doctor as pseudo-intellectual, Orachevsky as hardworking mechanic, Prokhorov as peasant, and Solzhenitsyn as—in his ragged paint-daubed overalls—proletarian. He was the only non-trusty, and felt vulnerable.

Then one night Major General Belyayev was shaken out of sleep by a duty guard, who told him to get his things together. They took him off to Butyrki. He managed to send his roommates a note: "Don't lose heart! . . ." Evidently he meant because of his departure, Solzhenitsyn observes, though that seems a cruel and dubious assumption. . . . "If I am alive, I will write." He didn't write, from whichever distant island of the Gulag Archipelago received him. Solzhenitsyn heard a rumor he was fetching gruel, in the hope of getting a sip now and then. Perhaps, after all, fate made him suffer enough to become a good man.

In any case, his departure allowed Sanya to take over his position of assistant norm setter. He still did not quite know what it meant, but he multiplied and divided to his heart's content. He wore his captain's uniform again, wanting to stand out.

The senior guard, a young man who called himself Senin, used to drop in to the trusties' room, ostensibly for a chat about movies or literature. He had a soft voice and soft eyes, a very different style of person from the other guards. And indeed he was a fourth-year student at Moscow University, working for the MVD in his spare time. (Imagine, said Solzhenitsyn, a progressive student in tsarist times moonlighting as a jailer!) Fearing to meet fellow students in the street while wearing his blue shoulder boards, Senin always changed his clothes in the guard room.[5]

On one such visit he gestured secretly to Sanya to leave the room. Senin followed him after a discreet interval, and told him to report at once to the office of the security officer. He went with sinking heart: what if they had looked again at letters or diaries, and were going to slap another sentence on him? But the security officer was very pleasant, intelligent looking; inviting him to sit down (in a soft-padded chair) and asking him how he was finding camp life. Some attractive classical music was pouring out of a Philips radio on a bookstand; a shaded lamp stood on the desk; there was a small sofa. . . . The cozy room did not seem part of the camp world at all, and Sanya felt a yearning for the normality that evidently still existed somewhere *out there*.

Just as he was wondering where he had heard that beautiful melody before, he heard—as it were chiming gently with it—"Well, and after everything that has happened to you, after everything you have suffered, are you still a Soviet person? Or not?"[6]

After a long interval he replied, "The sentencing board said I was anti-Soviet."

"Oh, never mind that: How do you feel in your own heart? Are you still with us, or have you become embittered?"

He longed to tell him to go to blazes; instead, replied that he was still a socialist. That was good, said the officer; so he would be willing to help. . . .

"Help in what way?"

"If you overheard certain conversations, you might think it advisable to report them."

"I could never do that."

"Why not?"

"Well, because . . . it's not in my character. . . . I don't listen . . . I don't remember. . . ."

The officer leaned back and clicked off the music. Now it was in deadly earnest. There was the hint of Siberian cold. The pressure continued for an hour, two hours; it was long past lights-out, but the officer had no need to bother about that; this was his job. At length he switched to the subject of the thieves; Senin had told him Solzhenitsyn hated the thieves.

"Yes, I do." (Much more than the jailers did!)

"So if you heard some of them were planning to escape . . . You have a wife in Moscow: without a husband, she has to walk the streets alone, even at night; people on the street often have their clothes taken off them. You wouldn't refuse to report an escape plan, would you?"

Well, no, that was different. He could probably do that. And it seemed the only way out. A clean sheet of paper was thrust in front of him, and he

saw he would have to sign a statement that he would report any escape
planned by prisoners. "But we were talking only about thieves!"

"And who escapes except the thieves! I can't just mention thieves in an
official document; you're making it hard for me. You and I will know it
refers to thieves. . . ."

So he signed. And was told he would have to choose a pseudonym. He
could see the sly trap: a conspiratorial nickname would serve to confirm
him as an informer. His writer's imagination failed; the MVD officer—
perhaps thinking of the word for wind, rumor, *vetyer*—suggested Vetrov.[7]

Solzhenitsyn never reported anything. Senin used to ask him, "Well,
well?" and he would shrug and say the thieves disliked him and wouldn't
let him get near. Urged to spread his net wider, he insisted on the limits
agreed upon. No reasonable person can blame him for the slight concession
he made; it was far below the *norm* of compromise set by the frightened
Soviet populace; but Solzhenitsyn was not a "reasonable" man—it is part
of his greatness that he was not, however irritating the trait can be—and
in *The Gulag Archipelago* he expresses his shame for having compromised
so far, in order to keep his dry bed, his parcels and visits from Natasha.

His meetings with her had none of the leisureliness of his evening with the
MVD officer; nor, understandably, does he write about them. He still had
occasional bursts of optimism about an amnesty; he became "convinced
beyond doubt," she tells us in her memoir, that it had been agreed but for
some reason postponed. Commenting on his tautological emphasis, she
points out that there are never any gray uncertain areas for Sanya, only
acceptance or rejection.[8] In his more despondent times he offered to release
her from their marriage, to make a new life for herself. They had spent only
one year together since their marriage began five years earlier, and it might
be another eight years—or more—before they could be reunited. Misun-
derstandings were easy under the watchful eye of a guard, and Natasha
thought he wished her to be released. Eventually he assured her he desperately wanted her *not* to take him up on his offer and they both felt a
great relief.

His post as assistant norm setter allowed him to wander all over the
building under construction: a luxury apartment block for KGB officers.
Once he went up to what was then the top of the still rising structure. From
there he could see a panoramic view of Moscow. . . .

On one side were the Sparrow Hills, still open and clear. The future
Lenin Prospekt had just been projected and outlined but did not exist.
The insane asylum . . . could be seen in its pristine, original state. In
the opposite direction were the cupola of the Novodevichi Monastery,
the carcass of the Frunze Academy, and in a violet haze far, far ahead,
beyond the bustling streets, was the Kremlin, where all they had to

do was merely sign that amnesty which had already been prepared for us. . . .

But no matter how much of a greenhorn I was in champing at the bit to be out "in freedom," this city did not arouse in me envy or the wish to soar down onto its streets. All the evil holding us prisoner had been woven here.[9]

Those "free," ant-sized people scurrying around, eight floors below, were in a city and an empire gripped by ice. The Soviet Union had begun a relentless hate campaign against its former allies. On 5 March 1946, Winston Churchill announced somberly in Fulton, Missouri: "From Stettin in the Baltic to Trieste in the Adriatic an Iron Curtain has descended across the Continent." The Cold War had begun.

Within the Soviet Union's own borders, Stalin's war of the late 1930s against writers and the intelligentsia was unleashed again after a wartime lull. Akhmatova, poverty-stricken and ill, was one of the first postwar targets of the Great Norm Setter. Cassandra-like, she became fearful when, at two crowded poetry readings in Moscow, she was greeted with tumultuous applause; and, indeed, when Stalin was told about it he demanded, "Who organized this standing ovation?" A few weeks later she visited the Writers' Union building in her native Leningrad, and wondered vaguely why people there averted their eyes and pressed against the wall to let her pass. She bought some herring, and then met the writer Mikhail Zoshchenko in the street. "Anna Andreyevna," he groaned, "what can we do?" Not knowing what he was talking about, she advised patience. Arriving home she took the fish from its newspaper wrapping and read that Zhdanov, the cultural commissar, had attacked her and Zoshchenko viciously. She was a "nun-harlot" whose work breathed spiritual decadence and pessimism.

Stalin needed to stamp on a famous writer, as a warning to the intelligentsia that the comparative freedom of the war years was over. She was expelled from the Writers' Union, her forthcoming collection was pulped; far worse, her son, released from a Siberian camp to fight in the war, was rearrested.

Nadezhda Mandelstam describes meeting Pasternak at this time, in a street near a writers' apartment building. Fearing to be seen together, they ducked into a doorway to talk. In a low, gloomy voice he said if Anna was killed he didn't know if they could go on living.[10]

He had just written his intensely tragic "Hamlet" poem, beginning with Hamlet coming out onto the dark stage to face a thousand opera glasses, and ending with "Life is not so simple as to cross a field."

"We are living in Elsinore, Nadya."

The Kaluga Gate period is Solzhenitsyn's most Hamlet-like phase. At least, it seems so from his retrospective accounts in *The Gulag Archipelago*.

Whether at the time he had such a sense of isolation, guilt at behaving unworthily, we can't tell. There are certain factors missing from his picture of the Kaluga period that suggest he was undergoing crises of conscience and of identity. Notably he does not speak of friendship, nor of further spiritual learning. There is no Fastenko or Susi, no Gammerov or Ingal; no Kopelev and Panin of the next phase of the Gulag. In referring to the trusties' room, he excludes the peasant types, Orachevsky and Prokhorov, from membership of what he called a "chamber of monstrosities," but not himself. How hard it is, he would write, to become fully human; evidently he felt he had not yet achieved it.

This is, on the face of it, surprising. In Butyrki he had defended Vlasovites; here at Kaluga Gate he had been demoted from production superintendent to general duties because he insisted on maintaining decent safety standards. (Nor did he remain assistant norm setter for long, but went back to the painting brigade.) He made only a minimal compromise when under severe pressure from the security officer; in reality he gave nothing at all. So why the anguish? Why the feeling that he is a part of the corruption? It was not ignoble to want to stay alive, and to live under bearable conditions. It would have been extremely cruel to Natasha not to have tried, by a minor concession, to avoid being sent far away. Even Mandelstam wrote an ode to Stalin, in 1936, which may have saved his wife—who thereby was able to memorize and preserve his poems. Even Akhmatova praised Stalin, in a cycle called "Glory to Peace," to try to save her son. Solzhenitsyn has never published a single phrase that he did not believe in.

But that question of belief, of sincerity, is perhaps crucial. The Mandelstam and Akhmatova poems to Stalin are so obviously ersatz as to be laughable. Indeed, Nadezhda Mandelstam gives a very funny account, in *Hope Against Hope*, of her husband's agony as he tried in vain to be a conventional Soviet poet.[11] These efforts, in fact, honor poetry by being so ludicrously bad. No one with any taste could read the ode to Stalin or "Glory to Peace" without knowing at once they were totally insincere.

Solzhenitsyn, on the other hand, was not altogether lying when he agreed that he was still a "Soviet person." His privileged position at the Kaluga camp was extraordinary—to be appointed production superintendent, and placed in a cozy room with generals. And, though he fell as rapidly as he had risen, not once but twice, he was always in at least a semi-trusty position. He certainly did not gain the privileges dishonorably; arguably they were the consequence of sheer luck, an officer's uniform, and a confident manner upon arrival.

They may also, however, have been as a result of quite shrewd judgment on the part of the MVD. Arriving at Kaluga Gate, he was confronted by Junior Lieutenant Nevezhin, "a tall, gloomy hunchback." Nevezhin was actually over fifty, and had been demoted from a senior rank, possibly lieutenant colonel, for his tendency to feather his nest. He was an experienced

MVD officer. The autobiography Sanya had written at New Jerusalem was in his dossier; certainly Sanya became aware that the security officer who tried to make him an informer had read it. The chances are that Nevezhin spotted potential. He may have thought: here's a young man who has led soldiers in battle; he seems a good socialist who got into trouble because he doesn't think the present government is socialist enough; he still wants a Revolution. . . . Well, it's good that the young should retain their ideals. . . . He's eager to please; others have thought so too; otherwise he'd have at least a tenner and by now would be over the Yenisei. . . . We'll give him his chance. Norm setter?—Not enough; we'll create a new post, production superintendent. . . .

During the First Congress of Soviet Writers, in 1934, one of the less orthodox writers, Yury Olesha, spoke quite movingly of trying to understand the new, young Soviet man and woman; he wanted to ask, he said, "Who are you? What colours do you see? Do you ever have dreams? What do you daydream about? What do you feel yourself to be? How do you love? What feelings do you have? . . . Do you know how to cry? Are you tender? . . . What are you like, young man of the Socialist society? . . ."[12] It seems to me that Sanya, despite Natasha's finding a softening in him, was still broadly the rational, undreaming *Homo sovieticus;* still the young man who read Marx or Lenin after making love to his bride; who had no time for Pasternak's "irrelevant" poems.

There are no poetic images, relating to Kaluga Gate, of the depth and beauty to match the balletic girl of New Jerusalem, or the two red stones in a field. He may have been frightened by how close he had come to death, and shrunk back closer to his pre-arrest rationalist self.

The schizoid state was the normal state in Russia under the "bloat king" (bloated with blood, at least). No wonder Vsevolod Meyerhold had wanted a *Hamlet* with two princes. Everyone had to pretend that everything was wonderful; no one could admit, entering the office in the morning, that he had spent the night wide-awake, dry-mouthed from fear.

Even after Susi and Fastenko and Gammerov, Sanya could still say he was a socialist; would not deny that he was a Soviet man. What shames him, I think, about the Kaluga year is not that he pretended to be a Soviet man, but that in many ways he still was.

As at Elsinore, a company of players turned up unexpectedly. . . . The ancient tradition in which landowners vied with each other in the quality of their serf theater had descended to the Gulag; each cluster of camps had its troupe of *zek* actors, and the Moscow area had several. MVD officers interested in the theater would keep a close eye on the prisoner list in Krasnaya Presnya, ready to grab any talent passing through. Kaluga Gate had its own amateur theatrical group, to which Sanya belonged. When he heard that one of the traveling companies was going to be based for a while at Kaluga Gate, he was thrilled. He saw it as perhaps an opportunity to get admitted to its ranks. Of all possible roles in the Gulag this seemed the least unattractive.

He was thwarted in these hopes; nevertheless, he enjoyed the stimulus of the company's presence. There was a Latvian dancer with them, Izolda Glazunov, who was quite old; her dance seemed now divorced from the flesh, entirely in the world of mysticism and the transmigration of souls— in which she believed. Her husband, Osvald, was an actor in the troupe. They had both been given ten years for performing in German-occupied Riga. While the troupe was at Kaluga Gate, it was decided that Izolda was too old and must be replaced. Sanya saw her husband go almost crazy with grief after she had been carted off in a suddenly arranged and furtive transport, torn from him perhaps forever. The rulers of these *zek* players had held a mirror up to the worst excesses of nineteenth-century serfdom; but *then,* as Solzhenitsyn points out, there had been great and famous writers to call down God's wrath on the serf-owners' heads.

When the "professional" troupe had gone, he remained in the small amateur group—performing execrable plays labeled "for performance in the Gulag only"—but enjoying, as he had at school and university, appearing before an audience, seeing their stimulated faces, male and perhaps especially female. One of the rewards of the drama group was the chance it provided for men and women prisoners to mix. Easy enough for theatrical flirtations and affairs to develop in the free world, and all the more so in captivity. It happened to Sanya. One of the other performers, Anya Breslavskaya, became the basis for the character of Lyuba in his play *The Love-Girl and the Innocent,* the first draft of which was dedicated to her.° He later told Natasha they had had an affair, and that this was his only infidelity in all of his army service, imprisonment, and exile.

In *Gulag,* he writes compassionately about the fate of women in the camps. Anyone even reasonably attractive became a prey for the trusties. He describes one woman at Kaluga Gate of a swanlike beauty and dignity— a former Red Army sniper!—whom he watched being tormented into submission by a "fat, dirty old stock clerk" called Isaak Bershader. One pale, snowy evening he watched her knock on his door, her head bowed in shame and defeat.

Sexual love in the Gulag could be brutally down-to-earth. He mentions, for example, a camp where the men and women were separated by wire only, no armed guards; the men and women swarmed to meet at the wire, and the women knelt down in the position of washing floors. . . . Immortal eros, he suggests, was worth something, even in that debased form; the *zeks* were taking what happiness they could *while* they could. Yet also camp love often became intensely spiritual from the very difficulty of finding any op-

---

°His play *Respublika Truda* (Republic of Labor), 1981, YMCA Press, has a dedication to her also.

portunity for physical contact. "It was particularly from the absence of the flesh that this love became more poignant than out in freedom! Women who were already elderly could not sleep nights because of a chance smile, because of some fleeting mark of attention they had received. So sharply did the light of love stand out against the dirty, murky camp existence!"[13]

Once, from the fifth floor "chamber of horrors," he looked down at a secluded corner of Neskuchny Park and saw a lieutenant and his un-shy girlfriend copulating. Thanks to Natasha's parcels and to Anya Breslavskaya, Sanya was probably experiencing a reawakening of eros. The relationship between Nemov and Lyuba, in *The Love-Girl and the Innocent*, is marked by a kind of lyrical, innocent sensuality. Almost like first love on Nemov's side. Lyuba, when she has the rare pleasure of dressing up and making up for theatricals, moves almost into an erotic trance, and Nemov is utterly captivated by her childlike joy. A single kiss, or being handed her garments as she changes behind a screen, makes him tremble; he doesn't know what is happening to him.

In other respects Nemov is very correct and somewhat two-dimensional. Nemov echoes, in sound, Vetrov; also the Latin *nemo*, no one, and *nemyets*, German. At the play's conclusion, Lyuba is forced to give herself to the camp doctor; like the beautiful ex-sniper, she goes to her pursuer's cabin, her head bowed. She has begged Nemov to agree to share her; they can have secret meetings; otherwise he will lose *all* of her. Nemov prefers nothing to the thought of sharing her.

An intense romance, with desperate snatched caresses or even smiles—which perhaps came to be more longed for than the chaste, awkward, over-heard sessions with Natasha—may have been another reason for Sanya to feel guilt. Natasha had promised to remain faithful, and he was sure she was keeping to her promise; how ironic that he, in enslavement, was experiencing illicit passion! "O what a rogue and peasant slave am I!"

But most of his life was still backbreaking labor, laying parquet floors for ten hours a day; and constant gnawing hunger; and often cold and rain. Love was only a small light against the murk of Gulag existence. There was an intellectual void, as the site contained hardly any books. If he read while standing in the roll call, it was safest if it was a physics book rather than literature. And it was physics, and specifically nuclear physics, which brought his time at Kaluga Gate to an end. He was ordered to prepare for a move on 18 July 1946. He left his initials as a permanent record in the apartment block. It became a building full of ghosts for him; he could return to it, and say to himself, "There, a sniper like a fairy tale princess knocked on the door of a gross clerk . . . and there, I listened to classical music . . . and there . . ."

18

Stalin's Seminary

I love again the daily air we breathe;
Sleep comes in its proper time, and so does hunger. . . .
—PUSHKIN, *Autumn*

FATE AND STALIN NOW BROUGHT INTO SANYA'S LIFE TWO MEN WHO would become his close friends and who also incarnated, in an extreme form, the battle in his soul between the Communist believer and the skeptic. The road toward the meeting began early in 1946 at Kaluga Gate when, filling in a form, he described his occupation as "nuclear physicist"—on the grounds that he was a first-class physics graduate and had managed to read a book about the American atom bomb. Few things he wrote in his life would be more important than those two words of "job description."

Six months later, in July, he was told to pack his things and get ready to leave. He was driven first, in a *raven*, to a packed cell in Butyrki. He spent a hot, stifling night under the lowest bunk next to the latrine tank. In the morning, a distinguished-looking *zek*, Professor Timofeyev-Ressovsky, president of the "Scientific Society of Cell No. 75," invited him to give a talk. Sanya brazened his way successfully through the American A-bomb. In the two months he was in the cell, he experienced a sheer bliss in being able to sleep, and sleep again; and have two hot meals a day and intelligent conversation.

A frail, elderly man confronted him one day in a corridor and said, in broken Russian, "Do you remember me?" Squinting at him, Solzhenitsyn realized this was the German who he had insisted should carry his heavy suitcase on the march to Brodnitz after his arrest. He was embarrassed, but the German seemed pleased to see him. He had been given ten years' hard labor, and Solzhenitsyn was sure he would not see the Fatherland again.

In September, Sanya was sent to an aeronautical *sharashka* (prison scientific research institute) in Rybinsk on the upper Volga. Stalin had hit upon the shrewd idea during the thirties of arresting brilliant scientists and en-

gineers, scaring them with long sentences, then promising them good facilities and treatment, and possible parole, if they were prepared to set up
and head new research institutes. The Soviet Union's aircraft industry in
the war, for example, was created almost entirely by brilliant aeronautics
engineers such as Andrei Tupolev working in *sharashkas*. Without the distraction of family and social life, and with the strongest of motivations, the
scientists and engineers could throw all their energies into their projects.

After the Rybinsk *sharashka* he was sent to Zagorsk, outside Moscow. In
Rybinsk he worked in pure mathematics; in Zagorsk, as a librarian. Otherwise almost nothing is known about this year between Kaluga Gate and
Marfino, the *sharashka* near Ostankino Park, Moscow, to which he was
transferred in July 1947. The Marfino *sharashka* (which would become Mavrino in his novel *The First Circle*) was in a former seminary. A neoclassical
brick building terminated in a hexagonal tower enclosing a vaulted church.
It had borne the name Ease-My-Sorrows. Now it was "Special Prison No.
17." It was still in an unfinished state; there was a *zek* labor camp next door
providing the manpower to convert this house of God. Sanya was again put
in charge of the library, sorting and cataloging captured German scientific
material.

Soon after his arrival he met the man who would become the model for
the character of Sologdin in *The First Circle*. Descending a flight of stairs,
Sanya was struck by an unfamiliar form and face that reminded him instantly
of Christ. The stranger was also clearly straight from a camp. Sanya walked
out into the fresh air and the newcomer followed after a few minutes. After
some other *zeks* had spoken to the Christlike *zek*, satisfying their curiosity,
Sanya came up to him and startled him by saying, "As I was coming down
the stairs, what should I see in the darkness of the lobby but an image of
the Saviour Not-Made-by-Hand."[1]

Dmitri Panin was tall, with the bearing of a medieval knight; his face was
lean, with a short reddish beard and mustache, and radiant blue eyes. He
could have modeled for El Greco, he looked so spiritual and ablaze with
inner energy. Panin had been equally struck by his first sight of Solzhenitsyn.
. . . "The morning after my arrival, as I was drying my face on a government-
issue towel, an impressive figure of a man in an officer's greatcoat came
down the stairs. I took an immediate liking to the candid face, the bold
blue eyes, the splendid light brown hair, the aquiline nose. It was Alexander
Solzhenitsyn. . . ."

Very quickly they established friendly relations. Sanya listened in fascination to the story of a man who had already survived seven years in the
Gulag, under horrifying conditions. Panin, while not Christ, was a devout
Christian. Born to upper-middle-class parents in Moscow in 1911, he became an engineer. (So many engineers would help to shape Sanya's life.)
His view of the Bolshevik Revolution was very clear: "A huge country, basically Christian, had been made over into a nursery for rearing a new breed
of men under conditions of widescale terror and atheism. . . . The young

Communist state proceeded to mutilate and crush whatever opposed it, secular or sacred, to bury human life under atrocities."[2] He had witnessed some for himself as an impressionable child, during the Civil War.

He was arrested in 1940 after a denunciation by a work colleague, and sentenced to five years. When the war began, he welcomed the German army as liberators; then had the crushing disappointment of finding that Hitler too was a "cannibal." He was given another tenner in 1943 for "defeatist propaganda"; and endured unimaginable hardship in various Arctic labor camps. In 1941–42, before American relief supplies started to ease the food situation, he observed prisoners being killed off, by starvation, cold, and exhaustive work, with the efficacy of the gas chambers, though not their speed. In one logging camp of a thousand *zeks*, men were dying at a rate of eighteen a day; and as the body crates were leaving the camp, guards thrust bayonets through the heads just in case someone might be feigning death.[3]

But Panin remained indomitable and—it was clear to all who met him—with his moral spirit untainted.

Panin told his friend about an extraordinary fellow he had met in Butyrki on his way to Marfino, a man called Lev Kopelev. "I could never have imagined liking such a man, Sanya! . . ." They'd argued even in the cell. Kopelev was as devout a Communist—and even Stalinist—as Panin was an Orthodox Christian. But at that first meeting, the black-bearded young giant was opening a parcel from his family; he took out a loaf of white bread, broke it in half, and gave half to Panin. After seven years of the Arctic camps, Panin had forgotten what white bread looked like. "If Lev had given me only a tiny bit of it, I would have been rapturously happy. But here was half a loaf! His grand gesture affected me. . . ."[4]

He had also quickly realized that Kopelev was a brilliant linguist; and told him he would do his best to get him to the *sharashka*. Panin petitioned the *sharashka* authorities to that effect, and Sanya supported him, accepting Dmitri's recommendation on faith. Kopelev was an expert in German, among many other languages; and trainloads of German equipment and books were arriving at Marfino, demanding to be sorted.

Before long Panin was greeting Kopelev, and telling him what a bright, noble soul Solzhenitsyn was; a real personality; he loved him already, and was sure Lev would too. He led him to where he knew Sanya would be, engrossed in work. The two men met with a firm handshake and a smile. Kopelev has given his impression of that first meeting: "He rose to meet us. Tall, with light-brown hair, dressed in a faded army tunic. Intense light-blue eyes. Large forehead. Harsh rays of wrinkles over the bridge of his nose. One is uneven—a scar."[5]—That scar from his schooldays, which the KGB would try, twenty years later, to enlarge into evidence of anti-Semitism.

For other reasons than anti-Semitism, Sanya was a shade wary during his opening conversation with the huge, dark-haired, strikingly handsome Jew from Kiev; he admitted later he was suspicious because their military experiences in East Prussia had been so uncannily close. Sanya had probably heard his voice over the radio, and Lev had been arrested by the same branch of SMERSH. In his case he had been guilty of "bourgeois humanism: showing compassion for the enemy."

That warmed Sanya's heart; mistrust melted before the newcomer's attractive, openhearted personality. Here was another Three Musketeers, despite their vastly disparate beliefs and temperaments.

The building once called Ease-My-Sorrows did indeed ease the sorrows of its inhabitants, since the conditions were far better than in any normal camp or prison. This was especially true during their first months there in 1947 when Marfino was still being adapted. From starved parquet-layer, Solzhenitsyn had become a reasonably fed librarian, watching others laying floors. The *sharashka* inmates at first worked eight hours a day at most, and when they were off duty could stroll at will outdoors, under a century-old grove of limes. Sanya got into a habit that lingered, of pacing around a boundary fence—inside.

Their beds were comfortable, and every prisoner had a small bedside table. After lights-out at ten, only a blue-tinted bulb dimly burned.

And constantly there was talk, discussion, argument. Mixed with coarse expletives, so as to sound like everyday rows to an informer. But here was one institution in Stalin's Moscow where the intellect and imagination could range freely. It was still, in effect, a seminary, dominated by theology. . . .

Panin savaged Communism, and Kopelev, defending it angrily, called Panin a religious fossil. Sanya usually took a position midway between the other two. Often, though, he would leave them to it; they had the sense to know when he needed his own company. He needed it a lot. He was beginning to compose poetry, and also reading it much more widely than ever before: not only his favorite Yesenin, but Pasternak, Pushkin, Tiutchev, Gumilyov, Blok. His new friends shared that love, and also love of music; their radio gave them Mozart, Beethoven, Moussorgsky, Tchaikovsky, Chopin. . . . Sanya's taste was fairly romantic; he was grateful to Natasha for having taught him to appreciate the finer points of music, but he also enjoyed imagining a narrative or a landscape, so preferred the more programmatic composers.

They could even listen to the BBC World Service, which was not yet jammed. Yes, the *sharashka*, in its early period especially, was like a superior postgraduate hostel, almost an Oxford college. . . . Even perhaps a modest Manhattan Project, though they were only working on a walkie-talkie radio at first. . . . And the walls protected them from all trivial or carnal distractions. "The curtains drawn upon unfriendly night," in Yeats's phrase, they could sprawl on their beds descanting about art, politics, and religion, to their hearts' content. When the mood was on him—which was too rarely—Sanya could also be wildly funny, a subtle and deadly mimic.

At night they looked out of the window at the dense trees of the Botanical Garden. Southward toward the center of Moscow the sky was pinkish purple. They could catch few street noises, but heard the trains of the Riga and Yaroslavl railroads. In them were—as Kopelev wrote in a poem—"the sobs of station farewells, /The sadness of inevitable parting. /At night the distant horns sound/Calling to freedom, to freedom, to freedom."[6]

They had almost everything. Except freedom. It was probably Panin who said that they were in the First Circle of Hell.

Sanya and Natasha had their first reunion in July 1947. The meeting occurred under quite civilized circumstances. Since prisoners' families were not supposed to know where they were being held, the Marfino inmates were brought to the prison officers' club at the Taganka prison, and were issued special civilian clothes for the occasion. Natasha stood in the street, with other wives, waiting nervously. She saw, not some fearsome Black Maria, but a small bus draw up; the men who climbed out of it, looking "not a bit like prisoners,"[7] went immediately to their wives and embraced them.* In *The First Circle*, Solzhenitsyn compares the scene with ancient Greek steles, in which both the dead and those who mourn them are depicted: "The steles always had a thin line dividing the other world from this. The living looked fondly at the dead, while the dead man looked towards Hades with eyes that were neither happy nor sad but somehow blank—the look of one who knew too much."[8]

Nevertheless, Sanya and Natasha were able to reach each other across the dividing line; the meeting was joyful and tender; their love seemed to experience a resurrection. Natasha writes that the two years from summer 1947 were the happiest time of their separation. Actual meetings were very rare; but the couple constantly exchanged letters, and somehow, now that they were both "Muscovites," each keenly felt the life of the other.

Natasha had succeeded in becoming a postgraduate chemistry student with Professor Nikolai Kobozev. It was an honor to be under Kobozev, whose brilliant mind overrode a host of crippling ailments. At first Natasha had lived with the two Veronicas, mother and daughter; but her relatives' flat, spacious in prerevolutionary days, was shared with several other families. Wishing to spare them still more overcrowding, Natasha moved into a hostel. Surviving on a small grant, with food and clothing rationed, in poor, cramped accommodation, she was little better off than Sanya. Of course she was free; but could anyone be said to be free in Stalin's Russia?

For all the supposed secrecy, the wives of the Marfino prisoners knew where they were being held; Natasha, with Panin's wife, Yevgeniya, whom she had met on the first visit, made several trips to Ostankino Park. Hoping

---

*Later, such contact was forbidden.

to glimpse their husbands, they would gaze over a wall at the figures playing volleyball in the *sharashka*'s tiny yard; and once had to take to their heels when someone demanded to see their passports. How they must have giggled hysterically, from fright and excitement, when the danger was past! It was a comfort to be able to share the problems of being married to a political prisoner. Other than Yevgeniya Panin, few could be trusted to know that Natasha was the wife of an enemy of the people. It must have been particularly hard to have to hide the truth from the five girl students with whom she shared a shabby room. Their thoughts were filled with boyfriends: why wasn't Natasha interested in finding someone? . . .

Like Yevgeniya—indeed like most of the "political" wives—Natasha had been urged by her husband, from the very beginning, to divorce him and make a new life. Like most of the wives, she had indignantly refused, saying she would wait. Panin, according to Natasha in her memoir, demanded unfailing fidelity when Yevgeniya likewise declined to divorce him; Sanya kept shifting his position regarding fidelity, until Natasha wrote that they should "stop chewing on this theme"; her feelings for him had overwhelmed her for the rest of her life.

People had to work out their own individual solution, she reflects.[9] Fidelity was not necessarily a happy augury, nor was physical infidelity always an ill omen. She relates a moving story of one woman, "Vera Ivanovna," who felt she must preserve herself for her husband and yet also live a full life. Andrei "temporarily" (that is, for ten years!) released her from her vows. She was living with another man when news came that Andrei had been freed early because of ill health. The still young and beautiful woman rushed off to the distant camp, and brought back to Moscow an old, sick, skeletal man. They lived together for another sixteen years.

And there were wives, Natasha relates, who grew careworn and prematurely old during the waiting. The husbands, reunited with them, found that the dazzling new world of their freedom did not altogether fit with such stale, aged wives. . . . And the streets and workplaces were full of blushing, youthful women, looking for husbands and lovers. . . .

But in the summer of forty-seven, despite Sanya's imprisonment and the hardships of her life and of postwar Russia generally, Natasha was happy in her love and her work. She was finishing her dissertation, and by the autumn it was in the hands of Professor Kobozev. He pronounced himself satisfied with it, though she would have to spend many months preparing her formal defense for her doctorate. In January, Kobozev took her on as a postgraduate assistant. The wages were lower than her student grant had been; but at least she could remain in Moscow.

She and Sanya had a meeting on 20 June 1948, just three days before she was due to defend her thesis. They looked forward to their meetings like young lovers; he wrote to her that he went out into the yard after work, gazing up at the moon and imagining what they would say to each other.

His washed hair was in a towel rolled up like a turban: so that he would look good for her on the morrow. He thought that she, too, would be thinking more of their meeting than of her dissertation.[10]

The day of her defense was scorchingly hot, the temperature reaching ninety-five degrees; but the heat could not spoil her triumph, for with only two negative votes out of twenty-two she was awarded her doctorate. She was showered with bouquets; there was a banquet in the department dining room, and dancing; Lydia and Kirill brought champagne, and Natasha—ever fashionable—wore a gaily colored crepe de chine dress, made up for her by her mother. Sanya's absence was the only cloud on the celebration; yet he was close. Kirill and Lydia seemed to bring him even closer. An eight-year sentence—already a quarter over—would flash by!

Astonishingly, Nikolai Vitkevich—Sanya had given her the news at their meeting—was with him in Marfino. On hearing of his expected transfer from a labor camp, Sanya had feared a provocation to get his sentence increased; but when he came face-to-face with his great friend, all such fears were buried under the joy of reunion. He moved from a lower to a top bunk to sleep next to him. For several nights they hardly slept, deep in conversation.

Nikolai had been arrested near Berlin. Sentenced to a tenner, he had been sent to Vorkuta, on the edge of the Arctic Circle. There he had been set to work quarrying stone for the coal mines. Weakened by the backbreaking labor and poor food, he had become ill with scurvy.

After the initial exhilaration it gradually dawned on them that some of their intimacy had gone. Their paths had diverged. Nikolai, while still antagonistic to Stalin, had been quietened by the harsh conditions of the labor camp. Now he wanted to keep his head down and survive. He had differing reactions to Sanya's two new friends, getting on well enough with the old Party member, Kopelev, but detesting Panin, whom he characterized as a reactionary, religious troublemaker.

Probably Solzhenitsyn would have drawn away from Vitkevich in any case, even had there been no war and no arrest. Sanya needed enthusiasm, intellectual passion, in his closest friends. With Kopelev at this time he shared an intense interest in the Russian language and literature. Lev was put in charge of Marfino's "leisure" library, and made sure the existing stock of good fiction and poetry was supplemented by borrowings from the Lenin Library. He and Sanya were able to make for themselves a sanctuary; on a solid German rolltop desk stood a radio, a homemade electric cigarette lighter, piles of books and magazines. Sitting in a comfortable swivel chair, Sanya started to write, in stolen quarter hours, a long autobiographical poem, seeking to make sense of his early life. He urged Natasha to read some of the classic poets he was discovering. Declaring himself uninterested in foreign translations, he wished to plunge into Russia, as represented by her great writers.

Above all others, there was Dostoyevsky—read not for the first time, but never before with such sympathy for his patriotic and spiritual preoccupations. The position that Sanya was moving toward, at this great growing stage of his life, was one of total skepticism about everything; but inexorably his thoughts were leading him away from Marxism and toward the beliefs of his childhood world. Which meant, also, that Dmitri Panin gradually gained in influence upon him. It extended to Panin's habit of rising first in the mornings, and striding outside before breakfast to saw firewood in the company of the very Tolstoyan peasant-caretaker, Spiridon. On the coldest of winter mornings, Panin would stride about with no hat, his shirt unbuttoned to the waist, his topcoat slung over his shoulders; and as soon as the spring thaw arrived, he walked barefoot, seeking out the sharpest gravel and cinders. His asceticism appealed greatly to Sanya, always a lover of cold, and he was won over permanently to the early-morning routine.

The evenings occasionally—too occasionally for Panin, in retrospect—brought the relaxation of a poetry reading. He recalled in his memoir, *The Notebooks of Sologdin*, both his friends beautifully reciting poetry. He especially remembered prevailing upon them to read Mayakovsky. "Lev chose a passage from the poem 'A Cloud in Trousers,' and Sanya read 'The Vertebrate Flute.' Neither liked the poet very much; nonetheless, they recited him with great understanding. In my opinion the laurel wreath went to Sanya. With his dramatic talent, he enhanced the sound and sense of the lines by acting them out."[11]

More significantly, Panin pays warm tribute to Sanya's sense of humor and his readiness, against his nature, to be "idle" for the sake of friendship: "Solzhenitsyn," he observed rather unnecessarily, "is a man of exceptional vitality. . . . He often put up with our society simply out of courtesy, regretting the hours he was wasting on our idle pastimes. On the other hand, when he was in good form or allowed himself some time for a little amusement, we got enormous pleasure from his jokes, witticisms, and yarns. On such occasions the flush on Sanya's cheeks deepened; his nose whitened, as if carved from alabaster. It was not often that one saw this side of him — his sense of humor. He had the ability to catch the subtlest mannerisms, gestures, and intonations—things that usually escape the rest of us—and then to reproduce them with such artistry that his audience literally rocked with laughter."

The poetry readings and the humorous impressions were most common in the first six months, when the *sharashka* was still not fully operational and life was therefore more relaxed. The three friends were able to spend "many wonderful evenings" in the library. Sanya was able to show the most attractive side of his personality. If humor was one of his qualities that he too rarely allowed to emerge, even rarer perhaps was remorse—for one thing, he was usually too busy to indulge in it; but remorse too took possession of him during the time of his resurgent love for Natasha. It arose— he told her in a letter—after he had watched a film based on Pushkin's *Rusalka*.

Very rarely has he confessed to having been affected deeply by a particular work of art. *Rusalka*, one of Pushkin's compressed dramas, is close to primitive folktales about exploited love and vengeance. "The story of the faithless prince, and the miller's daughter who drowns herself and becomes a revengeful *rusalka* [mermaid], is . . . intensified by Pushkin's dramatic poetry to a point where we are compelled to experience what such a drowning and such a revenge might actually *mean*."[12] The scene that overwhelmed Sanya as an "agonising reproach" to himself was the opening one. The miller's daughter is in tears, longing for the prince who used to visit her every day. Now, as her annoyed father delights in reminding her, it is over a week since he came. "You've lost him, girl." She didn't have the sense to hold back, hold out for a money present to help repair the mill. . . . But his daughter still believes he will come; and her faith seems justified when they hear hoofbeats. The miller tactfully withdraws as the prince dismounts and greets the girl.

She is frightened by a certain formality in his greeting. "As much as ever, dearest. More than ever," the prince assures her, in answer to her anguished question. No, he is not sad, but full of joy to be seeing her again. Yet almost at once he plunges into the cynicism of lamenting that princes are not free as girls are, "to choose according to their hearts." God, and time, will comfort her. . . . He gives her a headband and a necklace, and a bag of gold promised to her father. The prince is about to leap onto his horse when she asks him to wait; she has something to tell him but has forgotten what it is. "Think," he commands her impatiently. Her thoughts wander distractedly, then: "Ah, I remember; today I felt your child move."

"Ah, poor girl!" he says; promises to see that she and the child are all right; he may even call to see them, in time; asks for one last embrace. Spurring his horse off, he says to himself: "Ouf! It's over—that's a load off my mind. / I expected storms, but it went off fairly smoothly."[13]

A few moments later, she throws herself into the river Dnieper. Her father goes mad. The prince wanders alone after his marriage, tormented by conscience.

Sanya had not deliberately left Natasha; but probably he remembered times when he had been relieved to part from her. And he had denied her desire for children. By the time they were reunited it might be too late. Kopelev had just been told another four years had been slapped onto his sentence. Panin had had his sentence doubled during the war. Even if Sanya escaped a similar penalty, Natasha would be in her mid-thirties by the time they could be together.

She reassured him she was not turning into "a cold and powerful" *rusalka;* she was happy in their love and in her work; and also had resumed her musical studies. Her piano teacher, Undina Dubova, had been a pupil of the famous Neuhaus; Natasha proudly told Sanya she had played in his presence, one day, and Neuhaus had expressed surprise that a "chemist" could play so well, so expressively. Sanya ordered his wife to become "a

great, brilliant pianist in these years!," adding that music was her true calling, and therefore her return to music might prove to be the real meaning
of her stay in Moscow.

In subtly downgrading her achievements as a scientist, he would certainly
have earned the approval of Panin, whose view of a wife's role was con-
descending even for a less feminist age. Yevgeniya had been married to him
for only three years before his arrest in 1940. "At that time [1947], she still
loved me very much," Panin wrote in his memoir. "Somehow the darker
aspects of life had bypassed her, not affecting her purity of spirit. She had
very little understanding of the world we lived in. I had never shared my
own thoughts and ideas about it with her. It seemed to me that between
the male and the female realms there was a sharp dividing line that one
had to observe: it was for the man to resolve life's more serious problems;
it was for the woman to look after the home and children, to involve herself
in art and religion. Now that I am in my declining years, I can see that my
view still holds true. Women are designed expressly for motherhood and
caring for the family."[14]

Even to the intelligentsia of Turgenev's era, Panin's views would have
seemed reactionary. More to the point, he seems heartless toward a woman
whose love had not wavered through seven years of separation.

Still less liberal was Vitkevich, who felt increasingly drawn to the Muslim
ideals of Dagestan, where he had spent some years of his childhood. For
him, now, any woman who became an actress or ballet dancer, letting herself be "pawed" by men on stage, was by definition a whore. He was enraptured when he could listen to mountain folk songs or the Azerbaijani
singer Beibutov on the radio. Kopelev, who became good friends with him,
pleased him by calling him by his Dagestan name, Jalil.[15]

Panin and Kopelev would divorce and remarry after their release. Natasha would both reject and suffer rejection. She and Yevgeniya both developed breast cancer in their later years. Natasha, ill in Moscow in the
nineties, would sometimes show visitors a snapshot of Dmitri and Yevgeniya
Panin taken after his release, and ask: "Who looks the older and more
haggard?"

And the visitor would have to reply, truthfully: "Yevgeniya."

Natasha gave her husband his copy of Yesenin's poetry that Ilya Solomin
had saved after his arrest. She wrote on it: "Thus will everything that is lost
return to you."

His thirtieth birthday approached; and with it a longed-for visit from
Natasha. It was a moment of almost pure happiness in the First Circle; and
though their meeting would be over almost before it had begun, the happy
memory of it would linger. He allowed himself to hope; perhaps the inscription in the Yesenin would come true.

Yesenin, the peasants' son: what a hooligan! Those lines that had so offended Panin. . . .

Look at the fat thighs
Of this obscene wall.
Here the nuns at night
Remove Christ's trousers.[16]

Sanya smiled. The scamp had daubed it on the walls of the Convent of the Passion! How could one not love such a poet!

19

Toward the House of the Dead

"Poor man, take this kopeck, for Christ's sake."
—PEASANT GIRL TO DOSTOYEVSKY

UNDER THE GAZE OF A BULL-NECKED WARDER IN A SOFT GRAY SUIT
who looked like a retired gangster, Sanya and Natasha held two separate
conversations that Sunday at the Taganka; one open and the other coded,
sometimes consisting only of a gesture. Both dialogues, fighting against
time—so little time, in the midst of many months of nonmeeting—were
subject to misunderstanding.

Sanya's brief smile, as he stood to greet her, made her feel jubilant,
though she had cried a little before entering the scruffy room, where pale
men in ill-fitting cheap suits sat nervously behind small tables. That smile
told her he loved her as much as ever. The warder would not allow them
to touch hands, but she wished her husband a happy birthday and took from
her bag some pastiles made by her mother. Though the room was cold, she
unbuttoned her new Astrakhan coat, hoping that her orange blouse would
brighten her face, which she thought must look gray in the dim light. He
cast his eyes over her in one long, roving look, which roused her; it was the
most important moment in the whole visit; she stretched over the table
toward him. He saw, though, how her breasts had grown thin, and said,
"You're very thin; you should eat more. Can't you eat better?" Speechlessly
she pleaded, You don't think I'm pretty any more . . . and he signaled back,
You're just as wonderful as ever!

"I do eat well," she lied. "It's just that I have such a busy life and I'm
always so harassed."

"In what way are you harassed?" he asked, trying vainly to push his leg
past the iron bar under the table, to touch hers. He was also asking, with
his eyes, desperately, Are you mine? Mine?

Her shining gray eyes replied, I am still the same. I haven't changed,
believe me. . . . Then, their luster dimming, she began telling him,

stumblingly, that she might be forced to do work that was classified as secret, and which would involve a rigorous security check. If she were to say her husband had been arrested under Article 58, she would lose her job and be refused her doctorate. Natasha lowered her eyes, licked her dry lips, and whispered, "I wanted to say—only you won't take it to heart, will you? . . . You once said we ought to get divorced—"

"Yes, of course!"

"Then you won't be against it . . . if . . . I have to . . . do it?" With a great effort she looked up at him, wide eyes pleading for forgiveness and understanding. "It would be . . . *pseudo*." She breathed the word rather than spoke it.

"Good girl! You should have done it long ago." His hearty voice became rapid-fire as he warned her that prison terms were elastic, they could stretch out forever; the authorities didn't sell tickets to the past; if only he'd learned to make shoes—that would really come in handy somewhere like Norilsk or Krasnoyarsk. Alarm on Natasha's face turned to horror, and she cried out, "No, no! Don't say that, darling!" He was taking away her hope. And now he was warning her, in the same rapid voice to deceive the retired gangster, that next year he might be sent far away, and all letters might be stopped. Her ears roaring from these nightmare predictions, she sought from him some look of pleading, some sign that he needed her to wait— for ten years if necessary; into Siberian exile, if necessary. But there was only a self-sufficient smile, and he was glancing around the room as if everywhere he found objects of fascination. He was always so self-sufficient.

He asked her to tell Panin's wife that he loved her, believed in her, and still hadn't lost hope. Panin had been deprived of visitation rights. Sighing, Natasha repeated the words to fix them in her memory. She knew that Yevgeniya too had had to opt for a divorce.

"Do what's best," Sanya's lips said; and Natasha's said sadly, "It suits you here." Her eyes added, You don't need me, you're happy in your man's world, as at the front.

When the warder announced time, they embraced across the small table. Her lips seemed to him to have weakened and forgotten how to kiss. The guard bellowed and grabbed Sanya by the shoulder. Natasha backed toward the door and said good-bye with the fingers of her ringless hand.

Returning in the bus to Marfino, then changing into a dark blue boiler-suit, he avoided his fellow prisoners. He needed to dwell on the touch of her fingertips, her womanly scent—that brief, unbearably sweet contact with the feminine world. Yet these bittersweet memories were overwhelmed by despair. He did not blame Natasha in the slightest; divorcing him was the only thing she could do. But—although now she might regard it as *pseudo*—events have their own inexorable logic; once having divorced him, she would find it easy to marry again. He believed they had met for the last time.

Such was the way Solzhenitsyn learned from Natasha that she was being forced to declare herself "unmarried." To be more exact, it is the way Gleb Nerzhin hears the news from his wife, Nadya, in *The First Circle*.[1] But we have it on Panin's authority that, in that novel, while it is by no means a photographic reproduction of life at the *sharashka*, Solzhenitsyn's character Gleb Nerzhin is "an extraordinarily truthful and accurate picture of himself"; and other inmates too are described with brilliant verisimilitude.[2] Only the thinnest veil, in fact, separates Nerzhin from Solzhenitsyn, Nadya from Natasha. Had the author set out to distance his novel's main character from his own reality, he would surely have avoided the coincidence of birthdays; and had he wanted to distance Nadya from Natasha, he would not have had the former telling Gleb she had performed with the celebrated pianist Jacob Zak—as Natasha once did.° Reshetovskaya has confirmed the essential accuracy of perhaps the most tragically intense and moving scene he ever wrote. Soviet reality was so extraordinary that fiction was unnecessary.

On his "thirtieth year to heaven" he was given the body blow of discovering that his marriage was over. It scarcely helped that her action was unavoidable; that, thin from lack of food, sexually starved, she too had been "crushed under the wheels of the grey prison van" as surely as he had been. For her part, she learned that he believed he might never be released, or only into harsh exile, like the Decembrists. And, full of smiles, he seemed almost happy about it.

His warning that he might not be allowed to remain in Moscow reflected a more severe regime in the *sharashka*. There were now watchtowers, a double barbed-wire fence around the perimeter, edged by a forbidden zone. Special guards from the Lubyanka were drafted in, and they had orders to shoot anyone straying outside the permitted area. The old seminary, at the start of 1949, began to look increasingly like any labor camp, with armed guards patrolling the corridors and judas holes in all the doors. The working day was lengthened to twelve hours; exercise in the yard was limited to a brief period before breakfast and lunch. At night the prisoners were locked in, the iron double doors sealed with wax and lead. Sunday was often a workday, with only the evening left free.

Russia as a whole was being sealed up with wax and lead, as Stalin's paranoia mounted. The tighter security at the university, which compelled Natasha to file for divorce, was a part of the same intensification of enslavement. Abroad, the Western alliance, soon to become organized as NATO, was flying in hundreds of planes a day in a desperate and successful effort to keep West Berlin under Allied control; Communism was triumphant in China, and threatening to take over Korea.

In what was now called "MGB Special Prison No. 1" the principal scientific aim was to create a "scrambler" telephone for the use of Stalin and

---

°Typically, Solzhenitsyn created a minimal difference: the fictional Nadya performed with Zak at a trade union concert in the House of Unions (Natasha performed there once, with other amateur players), whereas the real Natasha performed with him at the University Club.[3]

his aides. Solzhenitsyn and Kopelev were assigned to a special research group to study the phonetic properties of Russian. Unexpectedly they found the task absorbing, and so did not mourn too much the loss of their privileged position in the library. The new librarian was an attractive female MGB lieutenant. Needing to establish the relative frequency of all possible Russian syllables—there were, they found, almost a hundred thousand— Sanya and Lev prevailed on the lieutenant-librarian to get them a plentiful supply of contemporary literary works from the Lenin Library. A text would be read aloud slowly, and a team of ten prisoners would identify and note down the different syllables. Within three weeks, the researchers had succeeded in establishing that 3,500 of the 100,000 possible syllables were phonetically distinct. Just one hundred comprised 85 percent of all usages. Prison No. 1's new head, Colonel Anton Vasiliev, was so pleased with the progress being made that he invited the team to make a report to the institute's first scientific conference. He also allowed the team to move to the newly formed Acoustics Laboratory, in a large airy room, and to create their own comfortable space to work in.

Solzhenitsyn and Kopelev henceforth sat back-to-back, in a corner of the room cut off from the rest by benches and bookshelves. Having to listen through headphones to texts being read out in a small nearby booth, they found it easy to switch over to classical music. They had a small radio permanently tuned to the BBC World Service. As Sanya listened to Nekrasov being read aloud, or to the Polovtsian dances, or listened to a talk from London about Truman's astonishing presidential victory, his darting eyes observed pert-breasted MGB laboratory assistants flitting around the big room.

Despite the watchtowers, this was certainly not a Kolyma gold mine.

One evening Sanya was leaning back in his chair, his eyes closed, thinking about Natasha. The next day, 27 April, would be their ninth wedding anniversary. Was she still his wife? Her letters were as affectionate as ever. Some orchestral music coming from the Soviet Army Theater provided a background to his thoughts. Suddenly he jerked upright: the female announcer had just spoken her name! "Natalya Reshetovskaya will perform the . . ." He cried out in his excitement and sprang to his feet; Kopelev, behind him, jerked his head around in alarm. "What's up?"

"It's Natasha!"

"That's wonderful!"

He wrote to her in his bunk that night. "It was just as I thought it would be, Chopin and not Rachmaninov. I listened, and my heart was pounding. How I wanted to catch a glimpse of you at that moment!" He paused in his writing to gaze up at the spacious dome. The dim blue electric light gave a faint midnight impression of the scraps of angels, blue sky, and Cyrillic script that overtopped, with a crazy illogic, the silent prisoners. His pencil moved again over the rough page, telling her how he felt in his soul "as though we had seen each other on the eve of our anniversary."[4]

A month later, on 29 May, he had his first meeting with Natasha since the December visit. It was only in his letter handed to her on this occasion that he confessed the "darkest despair" he had felt at that darkest time of the year. It had given way to hope, and Natasha felt there was "a special, radiant quality" about this springtime visit. This time he carried back to the *sharashka* a bunch of lilies of the valley, and felt a sense of overwhelming relief at all being well with their love.

Natasha had caught a glimpse of her old friend Koka. Vitkevich caught sight of her too. His mother had come from Rostov and had been granted a visit on the same day as Natasha. She had attended a concert at which Natasha performed: the old Rostov loyalties were staunch.

Reshetovskaya does not tell us in her memoir why, on the day after the meeting with Sanya, she was "filled with complex feelings" and "thought [her] own private thoughts" as she conducted experiments in the laboratory. Was she starting to suffer from the strain of the separation? Was there, despite the radiance of their brief time together, some other face hovering in her mind? In any case, she tells us that her complex feelings and private thoughts turned to delight "when a fellow pupil of Undina Mikhailovna called me up and said that he happened to have an extra ticket for Sviatoslav Richter's concert. There was little time left. I quickly cut short my experiments and ran off to the conservatory."[5]

Almost certainly the delight sprang from the thought of Richter, not her fellow student. Increasingly, in her rather lonely private world, she found joy and consolation in music. She was to need that solace in the aftermath of the Richter concert, since on her arrival at work the next morning she was summoned by one of Professor Kobozev's deputies and reprimanded for having left a small ventilation window open overnight. Natasha responded that there had been several people still in Kobozev's office when she left, and the last one to leave should have closed the window. It was barred in any case. Nevertheless, said the administrator, the security service had taken a serious view of her lapse.

She went to the head of the Special Section to explain fully, and was heard out in silence. She assumed the matter was closed. Then, on 6 June, she was shattered to receive notice of dismissal from the university "on grounds of a slipshod attitude toward work, expressing itself in the fact that, upon leaving the laboratory, she left ajar the window and the door."[6] It looked as though some kindly informant had leaked the information she had wanted kept hidden. Natasha rushed to see Professor Kobozev, who was in a hospital outside Moscow in the care of Kirill Simonyan, recovering from a bleeding ulcer. Kobozev, a humane man—and a brave one, as he proved later in their lives—was upset at her dismissal, but felt he could not save her job; once the claws were in, they would not let go. He could and would, however, allow her to resign "for personal reasons," enabling her to find an academic post elsewhere.

Memories of her teaching days had been occurring frequently of late, and she decided to be positive about this misfortune and turn it to good. She started applying for teaching posts in and around Moscow. Meanwhile she was forced to ask her mother for financial help; her music teacher found her a pupil of her own. Unsuccessful in her quest for a chemistry post, Natasha for a while considered music as a career. Sanya was enthusiastic, urging her unrealistically to bypass the conservatory and become an immediate professional. "You will say there is no such way," he wrote, "but it must be found." A two-week holiday she had won at the university—that university which had dismissed her for being slipshod!—brought her the company of other young musicians at a House of Rest outside Moscow, as well as the stimulus of shared music-making, heart-to-heart talks, and tomfoolery. Her holiday companions encouraged her to enroll at the conservatory.

One had to earn a living, however; and she was not sure she wished to be a student again. A post as chemistry lecturer at a newly opened agricultural institute in Ryazan, a hundred miles southeast of Moscow, seemed to offer a promise of employment; with her application went a favorable report from the university and an enthusiastic recommendation from Kobozev. While she waited to hear if she had been successful, she translated articles from English and tutored a girl in chemistry. She heard from Ryazan—they did not want her. Forced to go the rounds again, she received an offer of a position as laboratory assistant at Gorky University. The chemistry professor, on a visit to Moscow, personally told her he was prepared to take her on for secret research, even though she admitted she was divorcing her husband, who was imprisoned.

She arrived in Gorky on 19 August 1949, and was immediately taken on the staff as of 1 September. The slight delay proved to be crucial. She was offered a substantial salary and expenses, promised a room on campus; in the meantime she was put up in a central hotel, with a broad window overlooking the Volga. It all seemed to her like a fairy tale after her cramped hostel room shared with several other girls in Moscow. She felt, suddenly, that she had a future. "I threw open the window. A gossamer pre-evening mist stretched along the Volga. Here and there a few lonely lights began to glimmer on the opposite shore. A fresh, cool breeze wafted in from the river. Then the lights were joined by others, and the river itself was gradually dotted with the moving lights of ships slowly sailing by. I was overwhelmed by a feeling I had not experienced for a very long time, the feeling of inner peace."[7]

She prepared for her work by rereading a two-volume chemistry textbook that Sanya had read while at Kaluga Gate; she strolled around the town and treated herself to meat dumplings; went to the movies. Then called at General Delivery on the off-chance there might be some mail for her. She found a telegram from Moscow friends: RYAZAN OFFERS POSITION ASSISTANT PROFESSOR.

Again confusion! What to do? . . . Just when the future here was opening out. But teaching offered her more than helping in a laboratory did; Ryazan was closer to Moscow, and above all the work was not classified, so she would not need to get a divorce! It still had not been made absolute.

Her Gorky chairman grumbled; offered her some teaching; but Natasha, still technically free to change her mind, was determined to look at what Ryazan had to offer. She called the agricultural institute long distance, and told them she would like to take a look before making a decision. Arriving on August 27, she found a quiet town that had preserved its ancient monuments and landmarks. The new institute, in a former boys' secondary school, was built on classical lines. She liked what she saw. The chemistry department chairman explained that the man they had selected had wanted something higher than an assistant professorship.

She accepted the post, and was assigned a cheerful white-and-blue room in the institute building. On 1 September she arrived with her luggage, which a carter loaded onto a wheelbarrow. She went with him at a snail's pace across the town. A note came from the deputy director, Naumov, before she had started to unpack: "Welcome! Your lecture is scheduled for tomorrow at 10:00 A.M. Can you do it?" Natasha, though dog-tired, stayed up most of the night to finish writing her introductory lecture, which she duly delivered to 150 students, the dean, and most of the faculty. "You'll do all right!" they pronounced at the end. It was truly a baptism of fire, and Natasha proved that not only Sanya was tough.

Briefly forgetting his fears of eternal exile after his sentence, he wrote to her: "For the first time, after all these years, a marvellous awareness has come upon me that somewhere, out there, a family home awaits me. . . . There is no home for me without you, home is only where you are the mistress of the house—there, where you live."[8]

Though she had chosen Ryazan rather than Gorky mainly for his sake, the unusual lyricism of her description of her "inner peace" as she gazed through a broad window at the Volga suggests that some part of Natasha was preparing for a life beyond Sanya—should it become necessary. Her sacrifices for him must have exhausted her. In Ryazan, amid the camaraderie of helping to shape a brand-new institute, she experienced "an ebullient, active life, quite unlike my two years in Moscow." Giving two lecture courses, performing as a pianist, accompanying a student choir, she had time only for four or five hours' sleep a night, and was happy. Her mother and an aunt took long vacations with her, and brought her favorite Rostov possessions with them.

Six months after her arrival in Ryazan, she was promoted to head of the chemistry department. Natasha now had a life of her own, was a woman of substance as well as talents.

There was little time to visit Moscow.

Solzhenitsyn was also becoming a de facto "head of department." Flinging himself with his customary energy into the fascinating task of analyzing speech sounds, he became, as Kopelev records, "an excellent commander of the articulation team—he was truly irreplaceable. This was understood by anyone who saw his work and could judge it objectively." In developing a theory and practice for articulation tests he was creating something that had not existed before. He worked "scrupulously, faultlessly, and conscientiously. He pronounced the 'diagnoses' . . . decisively, confidently, in some cases even with an awesome peremptoriness. His youth and army manners were showing."[9]

In reality Kopelev, six years the senior and awesomely gifted, was the official brigade commander. At first he smiled at Sanya's self-assertion and cockiness—some of which he saw as an attempt to impress some pretty girls who were among the workers from "outside." One *zek,* Sergei Kuprianov, a heroic survivor of the Leningrad siege, sentenced to twenty-five years for terrorism and counterrevolution, rebuked Kopelev for allowing Solzhenitsyn to dominate. "A boy, a snot nose, and he makes himself out to be a general. . . . Do it this way! And no chatter! . . . Take a look at him, he never smiles. All the time, he's so sullen, always huffy. In the whole wide world he's the only person he likes and it's mutual. He even picks his nose with extreme self-respect."[10]

"He's young, Sergei, and still ambitious. He was an officer almost before he could shave. But he's a good sort, you'll find out. Give him a chance."

But then Kuprianov, who had developed a device for listening in to the authorities, overheard Solzhenitsyn approach an engineer major with the suggestion that he—Solzhenitsyn—should report directly to him, bypassing the brigade commander. Kopelev suddenly felt distrust, even hostility; he said nothing, to protect Kuprianov, but Sanya could not help but be aware of coldness. He asked what was wrong, and Lev replied harshly, "You're not some broad that I have to be sweet to all the time! Do you know why horses don't commit suicide? Because they never clarify their relationships."

Theirs continued to be frosty for a time; but Kopelev couldn't keep up his hostility. "He had become too dear to me. He understood me better than anyone else around me, treated my work seriously and with good will. . . . He was more convincing than anyone else in confirming the meaning of my existence." He enjoyed Sanya's strong, penetrating mind, the unwavering concentration "as taut as a violin string"; and loved, like Panin, Sanya's too rare bouts of "unscheduled" fun. Important too was that Kopelev's younger, and only, brother had been called Sanya; he had died in battle in September 1941. Solzhenitsyn, who revealed when speaking of his childhood the pain of being fatherless, took his place.

Kopelev quarreled openly and quite violently with Panin, usually over religion. Their rowing came to a head when Panin one day took the side of D'Anthès, the slayer of Alexander Pushkin. A French Guards officer at the court of Nicholas I, Baron George-Charles D'Anthès had indulged in—at the very least—an indiscreet flirtation with Pushkin's wife, Natalya. Tormented by all the sniggers about cuckoldry, Pushkin challenged D'Anthès to a duel, and was mortally wounded. The nondescript Frenchman who killed Russia's greatest poet in the prime of his life has been anathematized by every patriotic Russian. Panin (who wished to reinstate duelling) argued that D'Anthès behaved strictly according to the code of honor; Pushkin, though a great genius, was an atheist, and therefore immoral.*

Panin had become more extreme in his denial of fleshly temptations. There were several women in the design department where he worked, and some of them played up to the handsome, gloomy, and unworldly prisoner. He forebade himself even to look at them; and if by accident he gazed at them for a moment too long, he condemned himself mercilessly. He would give away his dessert, saying, "Take it! I sinned today. For two—or even three—seconds I stared at a whore. So I have given myself penance."[11]

The female MGB officers, whose task it was to oversee and discipline the *zek* workers, were given regular lectures about not trusting these traitors and Fascists, however harmless they might seem. But some of these men were so handsome and powerful, and the young women were often unhappy. . . . So many husbands or lovers—actual or potential—had been slaughtered in the war; and those men who survived felt they could behave like pigs. . . . It was easy for a frustrated, unhappy girl to be tempted. One thirty-year-old mother of two, wife of an MGB colonel who was mostly either away somewhere or in a drunken stupor, caught Kopelev's fancy. Danger—to her far more than to Kopelev—heightened desire, and she also had a woman's pity for him. "Oh, how can it be," she said, "for a healthy man to be without a woman for ten years. Horrors! Poor thing! Well, all right, let's do it." For a while he was in love with her; their furtive affair lasted for over six months; she became pregnant and had an abortion. It wasn't that she was afraid of having a third child, she explained to Lev; but she was afraid of foreign blood; Jews had different skin even; see how hairy he was! Not that there weren't good people among the Jews. . . ."[12]

In line with his traditions, as a man and a Bolshevik, Kopelev devotes just over a page to this passionate relationship, compared with 240 dealing with the politics, work, and male relationships of Marfino.

The chemistry laboratory was headed by a woman called by Kopelev Captain Yevgeniya K., a widow with two children. Panin had known her and her older sister before the war, when both, he said, had been beautiful and of irreproachable morality; he could not understand why she had become a Chekist. Now, though she was still pretty, with intense gray eyes and reddish-brown hair, she had coarsened and grown broad in the hips; her severe lips held a perpetual cigarette. Swiftly she would put a stop to any flirting: "Hey, there! What are you staring at?—Ah, I see! Clara, do up your coat! And you—peeping Tom—you'd better go and jerk off, that's all

---

*Not quite accurate. Shortly before his fatal duel in January 1837 Pushkin told a friend that he had a new mystical conviction; nothing dogmatic; he simply believed in God.

you'll be getting. . . ." Yet this virago, who "strode heavily, solidly, like a man," became as soft as butter when she took Sergei Kuprianov into her office in the evenings. "It turns out she's unlucky, unhappy, falls in love easily. . . . Man, she's insatiable."[13]

There was, then, a varying dynamic of dominance and subservience. In matters of the heart, the female officers sometimes secretly trembled before the men whom they were supposed to discipline; sometimes, indeed, lay down and opened their legs to them. In *The First Circle*, Nerzhin has a romantic liaison with an MGB lieutenant called Serafina (Simochka). She is very short and plain; rather prim and proper—and unhappy; at twenty-five she has never been kissed. Then one day Nerzhin asks her to look with him at a microphone that has gone wrong, and "before she realised it, her cheek was touching his. . . . Their cheeks were on fire as they touched, but he too did not draw away! Suddenly he seized her head and kissed her on the lips. Simochka's whole body felt exquisitely faint. She forgot her duty to the Komsomol and to her country; all she could say was:

" 'The door's not shut.' "[14]

She risks her career and perhaps her freedom for the joy of brief meetings with him. They appear to be on the point of consummating their frail, poignant relationship when Nerzhin tells her he has had a visit from his wife; and he simply cannot betray her by continuing this relationship. He feels pain at Simochka's despair; she can only whisper that his wife won't wait for him. Perhaps not, he says, but she must have nothing to reproach him with. Having to wait for Simochka to struggle to find words, he reflects that men would have it out straightaway, not beat about the bush like this.

Since Nerzhin and Solzhenitsyn are so close in terms of their life history, it is all but inconceivable—indeed, it would run counter to artistic coherence—if the fictional figure of Simochka were not closely based on reality. Kopelev mentions a Senior Technician Lieutenant Anna Vasilievna (Anechka), a shy and homely girl who could sometimes look pretty when she smiled. She fell in love, he says, with Solzhenitsyn.[15]

Eros, then, was not entirely absent; and in this respect too Solzhenitsyn would appear to have occupied a position midway between Panin and Kopelev. But generally the friends lived in asceticism and study; and, like monks, they usually had much more important questions to discuss than the emotions beating in the hearts of Chekist girl-officers. Such as—how to behave toward a *zek* who one day sidled up to Kopelev and warned him and his friends not to get close to him. Because he was an informer. He explained that he had been in the Kolyma gold mines, where he had seen thousands shot without trial. He himself had been sentenced to death, but— he had signed. So, please, stay away from me. . . .

Kopelev told his friends, and said that in his view they should obey his wish. But Panin said it wasn't simple, it required solitary thought. And later, on their evening walk, they wait to hear him pronounce. "He strode between us, hands clasped behind his back, hunched up, pressing his forked dark-chestnut beard into his bare chest, red with the cold, his dark iconlike eyes flashing occasionally. . . ." He tells them they are both, spiritually, Christians: even though Sanya says he is a rational computer that doubts everything, and Lev insists he is a fervent Bolshevik-atheist. As Christians "we are obliged to fulfill that wretch's request exactly. . . . Yes, precisely, that wretch. Do not approach him anymore. We won't discuss him among ourselves—and certainly not with anyone else. But we'll treat him without hatred or disdain and as much as possible, help him. That is, help him from falling into temptation."[16]

Walking on slowly, heads bowed, whispering. Stalin's monks debating heaven and hell, salvation and damnation.

Actually Solzhenitsyn was deliberately slowing down his bodily movements, as 1949 moved toward its close, as a way of preparing himself for whatever might come: knowing that a *zek* must conserve his energy at all times. The warning of Simochka/Anechka may have begun to seem apposite; Natasha's letters were becoming more circumspect; though she had not divorced him, and was not on classified work, she felt it necessary to hide her marriage. Therefore she could not send parcels, and had asked her aunt Nina to take over that task. Sanya could read between the lines and see that the move to Ryazan, and her busy, fulfilling life there, had weakened their link.

He urged her to finalize the divorce and cease writing to him. Her well-being, he wrote, was more important than "this illusion about family relations which long ago ceased to exist." The words upset her hugely; he wrote them out of despair at enslavement that might have no end till death—easy to forget, in view of Marfino's comparative privileges, that Solzhenitsyn was an innocent man, a heroic patriot, yet he had been enslaved more completely than any nineteenth-century serf. He wrote, perhaps, in bitterness at Natasha's newfound confidence; perhaps in part genuinely from a desire to free her from entanglement to a doomed man. She wrote back to say that she totally rejected his advice.

They met in the Butyrki prison in March 1950. He confessed he had written his letter with his head, not his heart. It was a happy meeting, but at the end it became clouded as he said he regretted they had not had children. Natasha, saddened, said it was pointless to worry about it; it was probably too late to think of it.

It was easy to become used to Stalin's world, to forget that it was mad. What could be more mad than that these highly intelligent and decent men—inevitably engaged with the "interesting" problems they were set to work on—were helping the police state? The most clear-cut example of this came in the fall of 1949, when Colonel Vasiliev asked Kopelev to help nail a traitor. It had come to light, through phone taps on the American and Canadian embassies, that a Soviet diplomat was trying to warn the West of an atom spy in their midst, a spy who was planning to hand over atomic secrets to a Soviet agent in a Manhattan radio shop.° The identity of the informer was unknown, but the voices of three likely suspects had been taped. Kopelev was asked to compare the voices with that of the embassy caller, and find the guilty man. Seeing it as his patriotic duty to catch the traitor, Lev threw himself wholeheartedly into his task. A special "Laboratory No. 1" was created for him.

Fired also by intellectual excitement, believing it would be possible to establish "voiceprints" that were as unique as fingerprints, he took the considerable risk of involving Sanya. He, too, worked enthusiastically, quietly, to help develop a new science of "phonoscopy"—a method of identifying individual voices. They never quite reached that goal, but swiftly found the traitor. All their evidence pointed to a certain Ivanov, a diplomat who was about to be transferred to the Soviet embassy in Ottawa. He was already—it goes without saying—under arrest, with the two other suspects; and all of them could and would have been disposed of if the criminal had not been identified at Marfino; however, it was helpful to the security services to know it was Ivanov, in order to investigate whether he had any accomplices. It was found he had acted alone; Kopelev believes he intended to defect in Canada, and that he was acting out of desire for financial gain rather than idealism.

Certainly Kopelev himself was acting from sincere, if mistaken, motives; just as he had acted sincerely in the collectivization program. It is not known what Solzhenitsyn thought, at the time, about the morality of their actions. He may well have agreed with his Bolshevik friend that a balance of nuclear power must be achieved, and therefore it was justifiable to help the authorities in this case.

Panin would have been horrified had he known what they were doing. He himself, having completed his first tenner, had come to a turning point; his soul, so to speak, had reached a critical mass. He decided he could no longer help the regime in any way. He had worked intensively and successfully on a mechanical voice coder. His *zek* superior, the cultured and equally anti-Communist Professor Timofeyev, was confident they had solved the problem of creating a scrambler telephone, and that it would win them their freedom; but Panin burned all his drawings and papers. He no longer went to the design office but volunteered in the spring of 1950 to join the ordinary prisoners in raking up leaves and doing other odd jobs. He refused to work at all on Sundays, except to saw up logs. He read only what he wanted to read. As a result, his rations were reduced to the lowest category. He talked back at the guards. He knew it was only a matter of time before he would be sent to a labor camp, but he was unafraid, he knew that world already. Better they kill his body than his soul.

Sanya too, though avoiding such overt insubordination, began to act reck-

---

°Possibly Julius Rosenberg, who together with his wife, Ethel, was found guilty in 1951 of spying for the Soviets, and executed two years later in the face of widespread protest.

lessly. He became an expert complainer; just as Nerzhin gave his wife warnings with rapid-fire whispers, his creator and prototype would interrupt a roll call with a mercilessly well-aimed machine gun fire of complaint. It became a form of theater that the other prisoners looked forward to and enjoyed hugely; but the authorities were not amused.

He may have assumed that his mastery of the articulation experiments made him indispensable; but his reckless behavior demands some deeper psychological explanation. Given the task of assessing various models for a voice coder, he criticized the model, known as the "nine," created by Colonel Vasiliev, who was an accomplished sound engineer as well as Marfino's chief. Solzhenitsyn's strictures were not undeserved, but the special zest with which he savaged Vasiliev's design was hardly prudent. Cultivated and polite as he usually was, the colonel remarked: "So, Alexander Isayevich, you've buried my 'nine.' Yes, but what saddens me the most is that you bury it not like a dear departed who was close to many of us, but like a drunken bum who died under a fence."[17]

Sanya roared with laughter when relating this to his friends; but a few days later he was told he was being moved to the engineering design office to work with other mathematicians on cryptology. Refusing the transfer, he raked leaves with Panin till, on 19 May 1950, they were told to drop their rakes and go to the guardhouse. "You're moving out, you two: get your things together, double-quick!"

Sanya had time only to grab volume three of Dahl's four-volume Russian-language dictionary. He had come across Dahl in the Zagorsk *sharashka* library, and his dictionary and collection of Russian proverbs became sacred books to him. Vladimir Dahl (1801–72) had an earlier claim to fame. A friend of Pushkin, he had been with him at his death; had squeezed his hand as the feverish poet murmured, "No, there is no place for me here below. I shall die, it seems to be necessary." Dahl lived on, in a sense, to be a source of inspiration to a novelist at the other end of the "country of Russian literature."

Having given his notes, poems, the remaining Dahl books, and his precious volume of Yesenin to Kopelev for safekeeping, Sanya changed into his old army clothes. He and Panin braced themselves for the true Gulag. Sanya hugged Kopelev warmly; but the burly handsome Jewish Bolshevik and the refined ascetic Christian, still estranged by their quarrels, did not say good-bye to each other.

Kopelev passed Sanya's notes on to Anechka. Showing great courage, for she had a KGB husband, Sanya's former MGB "sweetheart" kept the notes safe, and was able to return them in 1956.

Had the notes been discovered, Anechka's fate might have been similar to that of an unknown woman in the Butyrki. Arriving there, en route to an unknown destination, Sanya and Panin heard an agonized female cry from a cell window: "Help! Save me! They're killing me!" Then it was choked off. After a month in the prison, the Marfino comrades found themselves mixed up with *zeks* of the 1949 vintage, many of whom had been given "a quarter"—that is, twenty-five years. They were all herded into a Stolypin, a type of convict transport invented by Nicholas II's minister of the interior. With narrow corridors running alongside a series of compartments, Stolypin cars superficially resembled a normal train; but they were completely windowless on the side where the prisoners were stowed—up to thirty or more, sometimes, in a compartment meant for half a dozen; while on the corridor side the barred windows were covered with blinds. Unless the guards who patrolled the corridor were humane enough to open a corridor window, allowing a brief draught of air, the atmosphere was stifling. The usual diet, for journeys of perhaps a month, was salt fish; since little water was given, the prisoners became tormented by thirst.

Sanya and Panin were lucky in having only fifteen *zeks* in their compartment; and the guards opened corridor windows and allowed the luxury of two toilet visits a day instead of the usual one.

They moved eastward in the wake of so many millions. A hundred years before, Fyodor Dostoyevsky had made the same journey in chains. At one point on the way a peasant girl approached him and held out her red, rough hand, saying, "Poor man, take this kopeck, for Christ's sake." Now, at a quiet station called Torbeyevo, Panin and Solzhenitsyn caught sight of a small peasant woman in the usual shabby clothing; her slanting eyes indicated a Mordovian or Chuvash. Suddenly the prisoners, who were lying on the top bunks, "sat up to attention: large tears were streaming from the woman's eyes. Having made out our silhouettes . . . she lifted a small, work-calloused hand and blessed us with the sign of the cross, again and again. Her diminutive face was wet with tears." As the train started to move again, she still went on making the sign of the cross, until she was lost to view.[18]

20

The Given Field

Cultivate the field that has been given to you.
—LEOŠ JANÁČEK

DRUMS ROLLED ON SEMYONOVSKY SQUARE IN ST. PETERSBURG. IT was 22 December 1849, and just an hour or so ago, on a frosty, overcast morning, Dostoyevsky and his fellow prisoners from the Petrashevsky "secret society" had heard that their sentence was not a few months of exile but death by firing squad. The young writer knew he had about three minutes to live; the first three of the twelve condemned had already been led to the stakes. A memory of Victor Hugo's "The Last Day of a Condemned Man" flitted through his mind. Then the sun broke through the massed cloud, and Fyodor's gaze was caught by the brilliant rays reflected from the gold spire of a nearby church. He was terrified, yet the worst thing was the constant thought, "Think if I don't die. Imagine that I am turned back to life, imagine how endless it will seem. A whole eternity! And this eternity will belong to me! Then I will live each minute as a century, without losing any of it, and I will keep an account of each minute and not waste a moment!"

The priest was assuring them that, although the wages of sin were death, physical death was not the end. Repentance could still bring them eternal life. Dostoyevsky and the others stretched to kiss the cross. And still the glittering spire seemed to represent his new, eternal spirit, and the thought of the timeless moment became so unbearable he wished they would shoot him at once.

Then a profound indifference stole over him. Everything—himself, his friends—seemed meaningless compared with that terrible moment when he would pass into the unknown, into darkness. "You've done your job, priest," one of the generals called out.

"We shall be with Christ," Fyodor said, embracing the aristocratic, once-handsome Nikolai Speshnev.

"A handful of dust!"

The first three, including the group's leader Petrashevsky, were hooded and bound to the stake; the firing squad had taken aim. An intolerable half minute went by. Someone came waving a white cloth and the soldiers lowered their rifles. A pardon from the Tsar. By the time the three men were unbound, one of them, Grigoryev, had lost his mind. Many of the others, Dostoyevsky included, remained locked for a while in apathy, indifference, gloom.[1] The onlookers, mostly people on their way to work, drifted away, disappointed.

It had all been a cruel deception. The Petrashevsky circle had pronounced the death penalty on tsardom, so Tsar Nicholas I had decided to show them what "awaiting execution" actually meant.

Even if the sentences had been carried out, the difference between tsarist and Bolshevik barbarity would have been as wide as Lake Baikal. There would still have been the priestly consolation, the opportunity to say good-bye to one another, and Christian burial. The comparatively few people executed under the tsars were permitted their immortal souls. This was not a bullet in the back of the neck of some broken wreck, in the Lubyanka cellars.

Many in Tsar Nicholas's entourage, including the Tsarevich,° were repelled by his decision to stage a mock execution, and suggested procedural alterations that would have reduced the mental torture. The sentences that were meted out in reality were not unduly harsh, since the court took account of the immaturity of the accused, and the fact that, thanks to prompt police action, Utopian dreams had not had time to turn to terrorist action. Dostoyevsky was sentenced to four years at hard labor and thereafter service as a common soldier.

For a man so incorrigibly urban as Dostoyevsky, the fate of exile to Siberia was in itself a form of death. He and his brother Mikhail were permitted a good-bye meeting. (How Felix Dzerzhinsky must have smiled at the quaint tsarist customs.) A blacksmith put iron chains on the prisoner's legs; he would wear them night and day for the next four years. Then he and two comrades, with three gendarmes, were placed in open sleighs and they set off. The journey even to the Urals was an enormous undertaking, across flat steppe in intense cold; when they passed over the mountains the temperature fell to forty degrees below, with a blizzard raging. Beyond them—that unimaginable "sleeping land," Siberia: one-quarter of the Asian continent, bigger than the United States, Europe, and Alaska combined.

A significant difference between Dostoyevsky's experience and Solzhenitsyn's, almost exactly a century later, was in the character of the prisoners by whom they found themselves surrounded. Almost all of Solzhenitsyn's

---

°As Alexander II, he instigated a law reform which "almost overnight . . . transformed the Russian judiciary from one of the worst to one of the best in the civilized world" (Nicholas V. Riasanovsky, A History of Russia, p. 377).

companions on his journey were politicals, with only a handful of thieves; Dostoyevsky and his two comrades found, in the transit center at Tobolsk, that they alone were political offenders, among hundreds of thieves and murderers. There were men whose crimes made his brain reel, such as the Tartar Gazin, called the "giant spider," who specialized in the slow murder of children. Hearing the howls, seeing faces full of spiritual apathy, blood lust, and sensuality, the writer could believe he was in the lowest circle of Hell.

Yet there was a more positive aspect to Siberia. It held no landowners and no serfs. Its bleak amplitudes paradoxically offered more freedom than the suffocating social system of European Russia. Many dreamed that one day there would be genuine freedom there—perhaps a federation with the United States. Some of this more liberated spirit had originated in Siberia's first famous prisoners: the remarkable young men known to history as the *Dekabristi*, or Decembrists, and their wives.

Following the death of Alexander I in December 1825, a group of officers, influenced toward liberalism by contact with the West in the Napoleonic Wars, tried to mount a coup. Pushkin, in exile on his family estate for blasphemy, would have been involved; ignorant of what was planned, he had set out for St. Petersburg, but turned back superstitiously when a hare and a priest crossed his path. While his friends were engaged in their ineffectual revolt on Senate Square, the great poet was writing one of his merriest narrative poems, *Count Nulin*. A hare and a priest saved him.

Five ringleaders of the abortive coup were sentenced to death by hanging, over a hundred to hard labor in Siberia. The harshness of the sentences (and again Dzerzhinsky smiles) lit a slow fire in Russia. Even the chaplain who listened to the condemned men's confessions called out "Lord bless the martyrs!" before fainting. The hangman brought from Sweden—Russia had none of its own—botched the execution, three of the ropes failing. After Muraviev-Apostol had crashed into the pit, he exclaimed: "Poor Russia, they don't even know how to hang properly!"

Wives were permitted to follow their husbands to Siberia, and eleven, out of a possible eighteen, chose to do so. (Under Stalin, they would have been criminals themselves. Anna Larina, after the execution of Nikolai Bukharin, found herself among four thousand "wives of traitors" in the Tomsk camp; and this camp was only one of several.) It was an astonishing act of self-sacrifice for young women, used to a life of luxury, to leave parents and even children for a living grave. The beautiful Maria Volkonskaya, only twenty-one, passed some of the time on the endless journey "singing and reciting poetry to myself—anything in French, Italian, or English that my memory could dredge up. Then I went through the Russian ballads my *nyanya* had taught me in my now, oh, so very distant childhood."[2] She could think only of being with Sergei, her beloved. Forests and steppes passed in a blur of unspeakable loneliness. When, at long last, she was led down into a mine, and confronted a shaggy, nonhuman creature weighed down by iron chains, "a feeling of exaltation and great pride swept over me. To the bewilderment of the guards, I knelt on the filthy floor and kissed the chains."

In time the Decembrists were allowed to live relatively free lives in Siberia. Their intelligence and idealism had an effect in Siberia far beyond their numbers. Four Decembrist wives, grown comfortably middle-aged but still cherishing those who suffered for freedom's sake, greeted Dostoyevsky and his two companions in Tobolsk; brought them a good dinner and New Testaments, in the bindings of which were tucked ten-ruble notes. Above all they brought the inspiration of their own endurance and survival, and their womanly tenderness.

Solzhenitsyn thought often of Dostoyevsky during his three-month journey eastward. In Omsk, he could almost see the old writer's ghost, in a gray convict suit with a yellow check on the back; his head shaven on one side. Dostoyevsky had been housed in a huge barracks, with a shit bucket giving off its foul stench in one corner. Solzhenitsyn was in a dungeon of the Omsk prison—once a military fortress built in the time of Catherine the Great. But the twentieth-century writer's mood was surprisingly cheerful; there was storytelling, singing, and other entertainment among the *zeks*. And, in general, Solzhenitsyn and Panin found a pugnacious spirit alive among his traveling companions, many of whom were Ukrainian nationalists. They refused to be cowed by the guards, and were able to win concessions.

Geir Kjetsaa, in his biography of Dostoyevsky, comments that Ivan Denisovich's good day would have been a bad day for Dostoyevsky. Crucially, Dostoyevsky could eat as much as he wished, and was able to supplement the prison food cheaply.

In Pavlodar, being marched through the street, Solzhenitsyn again saw the author of *Crime and Punishment* just ahead of him, dragging his chains.

Then, packed like sardines in lorries, with but a single toilet stop, the *zeks* of Stalin's paradise were bumped for eight hours across the dusty steppes of Kazakhstan:

> We crossed the Irtysh. We rode for a long time through water-meadows, then over dead flat steppe. The breath of the Irtysh, the freshness of the evening on the steppe, the scent of wormwood, enveloped us whenever we stopped for a few minutes and the swirling clouds of light-grey dust raised by the wheels sank to the ground. Thickly powdered with this dust, we looked at the road behind us (we were not allowed to turn our heads), kept silent (we were not allowed to talk), and thought about the camp we were heading for with its strange, difficult, un-Russian name. We had read the name on our case files hanging upside down from the top shelf in the Stolypin: EKIBASTUZ. But nobody could imagine where it was on the map. . . . [3]

Darkness fell, and then it was clear from the "enormous stars" that they were heading southwest.

Dostoyevsky too, at the end of his four years of hard labor, had traveled this way and seen the same stars, as he headed for Semipalatinsk, on the right bank of the river Irtysh. There, in the largely Muslim village, he was to join the punishment battalion for an indefinite period. The landscape he traveled through was dreary, treeless, and without grass; its monotony broken only by an occasional caravan of camels, or group of nomad tents. Yet, as a released prisoner, he felt exaltation. At the end of his life, he would tell friends he had never felt as happy as when he drove along the Irtysh "with the clean air around me and freedom in my heart."

Floodlights blazed down on the high wooden fence that marked the end of the journey for the *zeks*. Alsatians barked. All around lay the barren steppes of Kazakhstan in Soviet central Asia. Ekibastuz was one of a large complex of special hard-labor camps in this area, Karaganda, containing some sixty thousand male *zeks*. There was a nearby civilian settlement, like "a useless appendix to its prisons," as Akhmatova called Leningrad in *Requiem*. Above enormous double gates which opened for this transport there was no sign with the Russian equivalent of *Arbeit macht Frei*, and certainly there were no gas chambers and crematoria; but the whole atmosphere of Ekibastuz, as the newcomers got to know it, made the inmates abandon hope of release at the end of their sentence. The idea that they were almost certainly here forever was rammed into them. There were few thieves: those few occupied positions of privilege. The vast majority were politicals, and security was designed to be absolute.

Stalin had reorganized the camp system in 1948, attempting to rationalize it as an integral part of the economy. And perhaps a powerful weapon in a Third World War. At Kazan station, in the course of the long journey, Solzhenitsyn had heard a loudspeaker announcing that South Korea had started a war against the North, and that the North had penetrated the aggressors' front line ten kilometers on the first day. . . . Even as Solzhenitsyn began his time at Ekibastuz, in autumn 1950, Stalin was contemplating throwing the Red Army into the Asiatic war he had planned. A secret cable he sent to Chairman Mao asked: "Should we fear a Third World War? Probably not; we can easily beat the U.S., England, etc.; and best to do it now, before Japan re-arms to help the U.S." The atom spies had provided him with information which made it clear the West did not have enough nuclear bombs to destroy the USSR. Chairman Mao replied: "Good! Now is the time!"

Something or someone, fortunately, made Stalin cautious; the Soviet Union was not devastated by atomic bombs; all the same, a slow-working devastation took place, especially in Kazakhstan, where not only labor camps but nuclear testing sites and heavy industry were concentrated. Kazakhstan became a dumping ground for dangerous materials and unwanted nations. Around Semipalatinsk, Dostoyevsky's place of exile for five years, nuclear testing sites "have left half a million people ill with radioactive sickness, some of them—in Stalin's time—exposed intentionally as guinea-pigs. Over a region now riddled with unfissioned plutonium, some 500 bombs, exploded over forty years, have undermined a bewildered populace with cancers, leukemia, heart disease, birth defects and blindness. . . . All across this blighted country, lead smelters and copper foundries, cement and phosphates works still plunge the skies and waters in poisonous effluent, and some two million Kazakhs and Russians are rumoured chronically sick from the pollution."[4] So wrote a travel writer in 1994, the year of Solzhenitsyn's return to his homeland.

Stalin sowed the wind and innocents have reaped the whirlwind. The *zeks* of Ekibastuz saw only the immensity of flat steppe; were conscious of being pierced, not by radiation but by winter winds of unstoppable force and a temperature of minus forty. In these conditions, Solzhenitsyn did not try to become a trusty but worked for a year as a bricklayer. *One Day in the Life of Ivan Denisovich* would be based largely on his first winter at Ekibastuz. Bare existence on the edge of death; constant cruelty and bullying; starvation rations; misery without hope of relief: this was Ekibastuz. Yet there was spiritual blessing, Sanya found, in having had one's life stripped down to the bone; and a fulfilment in hard physical labor. At Kaluga Gate he had not been ready; now he was, and he could begin to live in the spirit of the late stories of Tolstoy, and even the Gospels. "He who loses his life shall find it."

This too was in the tradition of Dostoyevsky, who felt his life transformed by his Siberian experiences. "It was a good school," he wrote. "It strengthened my faith and awakened my love for those who bear all their suffering with patience. It also strengthened my love for Russia and opened my eyes to the great qualities of the Russian people." Even when bidding farewell to his brother, in St. Petersburg, he had predicted that his exile and suffering would be good for him as a writer: "I have been through a lot and will see and experience even more—you shall see how much I will have to write about."

At some indeterminate point at Marfino, Solzhenitsyn likewise realized the enormity of what had happened to Russia, and that Stalin had given him the opportunity—as nature or God had given him the talent—to explore this theme in all its terrible grandeur. Once he had grasped this, he could not but try to get himself moved from the comfortable *sharashka*. "The archipelago," he would later observe, "provided a unique, exceptional opportunity for our literature, and perhaps . . . even for world literature. This unbelievable serfdom in the full flower of the twentieth century, in this one and only and not at all redeeming sense, opened to writers a fertile though fatal path. . . . For the first time in history, such a multitude of sophisticated, mature, and cultivated people found themselves, not just in imagination, inside the pelt of slave, serf, logger, miner. And so for the first time in world history (on such a scale) the experience of the upper and the lower strata of society merged."[5]

It is this unique blending of artist and people that gives to Akhmatova, for example, her immense authority. A woman born into a privileged caste, she stood day after day outside Leningrad's Kresty prison, in an endless queue of other poor, shabby, and despairing people. "I was with my people in those hours," she states proudly in *Requiem;* "There where my people, unhappily, were." She can write, without any of the unconscious condescension so common among Western intellectuals, of "a woman with blue lips" in the queue, who "came out of the trance so common to us all and whispered in my ear . . . 'Can you describe this?' And I said, 'Yes, I can.' "

She had to hand the newly written verses of *Requiem* silently to her friend Lydia Chukovskaya, for her to memorize them, then would burn the page over a candle flame. Solzhenitsyn remarks on the tragic irony that so many of these "privileged" writers, those actually sent to camps, had "no pencil, no paper, no time, no supple fingers," but had jailers who searched their clothes and their orifices.

The *zeks* of Ekibastuz were allowed to have pencil and paper (and Sanya asked for pencils to be included in the parcels sent by Natasha's aunt Nina); but anything written down had to be shown to the authorities. For the most part he composed in his head, a method which virtually demanded verse rather than prose. Pushkin had been (as in so many genres) the originator of the verse novel with his *Yevgeni Onegin*; eventually the work created by Solzhenitsyn, entitled "The Way," contained twelve thousand lines, twice the length of *Onegin*. And every line had to be memorized as it was composed: an astounding feat. He was aided by a rosary that he asked some Catholic Lithuanians to make for him: he had seen them ingeniously making rosaries out of bits of bread, threads, and various dyes. The Lithuanians were amazed by his religious zeal, and happy to comply with his religion's bizarre demand that every tenth, fiftieth, and hundredth bead had to be distinguishable by touch alone. They duly made the hundredth bead in the form of a dark red heart. Waiting and marching, in the freezing cold, to and from the workplace, Solzhenitsyn counted his beads inside his wide mittens. Often the guards found the rosary, but supposed it was for praying and let him keep it.

Once a month he would recite to himself the whole *poema*. But it was not an ideal way to compose. It took longer and longer simply to ensure that he still remembered everything, and it was not possible to revise. When he did write down his verses, he was fearful they would be discovered. Once he pretended that a paper found on him contained a passage of Tvardovsky's *Vasily Tyorkin;* he got away with that, but knew that a much more incriminating page, which he had crumpled up and flung away before the search, was being blown about the camp. He tossed and turned sleeplessly all night. The subject matter would identify its author as a member of a team building the Disciplinary Barracks, and with so many Ukrainian speakers about it would not be hard to identify him as the culprit.

He prayed. The former atheist. Not with the rosary. And at five in the morning, as soon as they rose, dashed out to look for the crumpled ball. The wind took his breath away; he was practically blown about the camp. For an hour he searched in vain. He was in despair. Then, as the dawn glimmered, he spotted something white among a pile of boards; the paper had got stuck there. A miracle!

When their first winter had passed, he would recite outside to some of his comrades. Panin recalls: "Towards evening we would gather, sitting on our quilted jackets that we spread out on the drying ground, and would listen with rapture." For Panin, the poem was so overflowing with youth, strength, and purity of spirit that he regretted Sanya's later decision to publish only one section—chapter nine—under the title *Prussian Nights*. The *zeks* were proud that a writer of the highest quality was developing in their midst. There should be a monument erected to him, Panin suggests, while he is still alive, "and it should represent him in a dark quilted jacket and a fur hat with ear flaps, as a bricklayer taking a rest from his work on a new wall . . . his eyes gazing into the distance, his lips whispering lines of verse, and in his hands the prayer beads."[6]

The great Czech composer Leoš Janáček told a young composer, who was seeking his advice, to cultivate the field that had been given to him. This is what Solzhenitsyn now dedicated himself to doing.

21

Firebird

I loved you once; perhaps I love you still. . . .
—Pushkin

Sanya was luckier than his subsequent hero Ivan Denisovich in that he received regular parcels. Natasha's aunt in Rostov never failed him. Growing old, she needed help now to carry the parcels to the post office. Sanya acknowledged that he could never repay her kindness; his mother could not have cared for him better. Every month he received sugar, salt pork, biscuits, tobacco—the strong stuff that he preferred, butter sometimes, sausages, onions, and garlic. Just as important in the intense cold: felt boots, wool socks, and mittens; such items as toothpaste, needles and thread, a sponge, plastic dishes, a spill-proof inkwell, pencils; and books: he asked for the poems of Blok, the plays of Ostrovsky. It took great efforts to gather together all the items, and Aunt Nina's taking charge of it relieved Natasha of one duty among the many in her busy life. She was, after all, the breadwinner for all her family. Also, of course, she was spared the risk of exposure that sending parcels from Ryazan might have entailed.

She was permitted to write to Sanya once a month, but, cruelly, she could receive letters from him no more than twice a year. He was also allowed to send cards to Aunt Nina acknowledging the safe arrival of parcels. There could be no flow of communication, and Natasha began to feel emotionally isolated; even the few letters she received seemed to be echoing, in their passive tone, the vast distance between them. When she suggested coming to see him in her next summer vacation, he replied that it was out of the question. Only in three years from now might it be possible to meet. Meanwhile, there was no point thinking about the future; one had to find fulfillment in day-to-day living. This resigned, fatalistic person, who used the word god (uncapitalized) more and more frequently, was not the dynamic Sanya she knew. She recalls in her memoir:

"A feeling of great oneness in our inner beings was sustained in me from

1945 to 1950, and it even seemed to intensify. It was sustained by letters, by our rare meetings, by our inextinguishable love, about which we never wearied of writing to one another. No matter how rare our meetings in these years, not a single time had I encountered a person who seemed in any way a stranger to me. . . ." But now "Sanya increasingly became an unreal figure; he turned into a distant, beloved image."[1]

In February 1951, while Sanya labored at bricklaying in minus-forty cold, yet felt "high spirits," Natasha moved to a two-room apartment, with shared kitchen and bathroom, and her mother came north to live with her. Yet Natasha felt, more than she ever had at the hostel in Moscow, an intense loneliness. She saw everywhere so many happy families. If only she could have shouted to the rooftops that she had a man whom she loved, for whom she was waiting and would go on waiting!

Sanya felt pleasure at having got through his first winter of hard labor intact. His letter of March 1951 assured her his face was "lean, but fresh and ruddy," thanks to the freezing winds in the steppes. It was in this letter that he disabused her of her idea that she might come to visit in the summer, and told her they had to find the meaning of existence in day-to-day living.

Her response seemed to show that she was indeed becoming more patient, and enjoying day-to-day living more. He was pleased that she seemed to be finding satisfaction in her work and in her spare-time activities, such as the Mendeleyev Society. It was good that her mother had come to live with her; Maria would be a moral and physical support for her daughter, who had had to survive on her own for too long.

Maria, in far-off Ryazan, thoroughly agreed with that; she liked Sanya but felt he could offer no future. She liked the new assistant professor at Natasha's institute, secretary of the Mendeleyev Society, Vsevolod Somov, who started escorting Natasha home and stopping by for an occasional drink or a meal. A widower, Somov became increasingly attentive to his colleague, and at length proposed marriage. Natasha told him why it would be impossible; nevertheless, he continued to court her, encouraged by Maria. He pursued mother and daughter to Rostov in the summer and, when they went on to Kislovodsk in July to visit Aunt Zhenia, sent Natasha a letter that seemed to her to have come from a real person, not a remote image— that image to whom she had to write a letter. Never had it been so hard; after a few reticent lines she brought it to an abrupt end.

Somov came to meet their train, on their return to Ryazan. In his early forties, he looked much older; he had started to wear a hearing aid; but whereas Anna Karenina, at the end of her train journey from Petersburg to Moscow, involuntarily grimaced when she saw her husband's overlarge ears, Natasha felt only pleasure and gratitude on seeing Vsevolod. Such thoughtfulness counted a lot with a woman who had had to struggle through life unsupported. He escorted them to a taxi, where a bouquet of flowers awaited them on the backseat.

Here at long last was someone who wished to take care of her, Natasha felt. She had never known a father. That fall and winter she wavered. Letters to Sanya continued to be difficult to begin and a relief to finish. They troubled her, and she knew they would trouble him.

Feeling cared for by Vsevolod in almost a daughterly way did not prevent her also feeling maternal toward him. He needed a wife very badly. At first she and her mother had assumed he was on his own, but now it emerged that he had two sons. When the elder, thirteen-year-old Sergei, arrived in Ryazan he at once stirred Natasha's frustrated maternal hungers; the boy, who had not long since lost his mother, needed her love just as much as did his father; and she was moved to find him, after a time, taking to her.

Other pressures were moving her toward a new life: notably, another security form she was ordered to fill in. This time she decided to go through with the divorce, traveling to Moscow to complete the formalities. Legally obliged to announce the divorce proceedings in a newspaper, she chose the comparatively unpopular *Moscow Pravda*. A more personal and highly significant formality was handing over Sanya's manuscripts and notebooks to her cousin Veronica.

Veronica came to Ryazan to "inspect" Vsevolod, and approved. So did Lydia Ezherets, who was now separated from Kirill Simonyan, his homosexual tendencies having been mainly responsible for the breakup.

Sanya's letter of November 1951 did not get through to Ryazan; Natasha did not hear from him, except for the brief acknowledgments of parcels, between March 1951 and March 1952. Her memoir account of this reveals a troubled conscience: "The letter Sanya had written in November 1951 had not reached me, and now both of us stopped writing." Of course, he did not *stop* writing; he wrote whenever he could, but one of them failed to arrive. In any case the momentum toward a break was too great for the missing letter to have made a difference. She could not bring herself to write to him for his birthday, but sent only a greeting, wishing him "happiness in life." Around the time his letter of March 1952 arrived, Vsevolod and Sergei had moved in with Natasha and her mother. "Very simply, as of a certain time, V. S. and I became known to everyone as man and wife."[2] Apart from the fact that it would be another year before the divorce was made absolute, the situation was anything but simple; suddenly the lonely woman had a husband and a teenage son, as well as a live-in mother and a *zek* husband who knew nothing of these changes; knew only that, for some reason, she had stopped writing or perhaps her letters were not getting through. Natasha "quite simply" meant something like "It was a terrible thing to do, but . . ." She would never be good at expressing guilt frankly.

Sanya laid bricks for a power station, composing all the while; recited to his rosary. New heroes presented themselves. There was Tenno, a giant Estonian sailor, prince of escapers, who having done his solitary told the epic story of his weeks of freedom; how he had constantly seen dead Kazakh villages—destroyed either by Budenny's Red cavalry in the Civil War or the famine of 1931. Tenno and a companion had got beyond the Irtysh before recapture. There was someone else who escaped altogether: a former German or Hungarian officer, much respected in his work brigade, who one morning stepped calmly out of the column of men being marched to work, and walked straight toward the guards. His hands were in the pockets of his quilted jacket. The guards shouted a warning but he took no notice, and was cut down by a hail of bullets from an automatic rifle. No one knew why he had committed his "proud suicide," as the *zeks* later termed it, but his action had a profound effect.

Sanya's letters may have given a false impression of his well-being. There were times when he appeared to be on the verge of becoming a "goner" (*dokhodyaga*). Once, a reasonably decent officer, Major Sokholov, spotting that he was "on the way out," got him an indoor job, cutting up trees. Where a healthy man could use an ax once, Sanya had to use it three times. A norm setter in Sokholov's department called Gurevich spoke to a non-*zek* worker, Nefedov, about the need to take care of Solzhenitsyn: "He's a good man; in prison for nothing at all. . . ." And asked Nefedov if he would preserve the tiny homemade books in which Sanya was writing down his poems in his spidery script. Nefedov, to his great remorse, lost the books when he transferred to another hut.

Panin may have saved his friend. Panin had severed his links with his wife and family, and so from the beginning had not been receiving parcels; he had therefore thought it essential to avoid general duties, and was soon successful in that. For a time he was leader of a construction brigade, and when he found a more congenial position in the machine shop he managed to hand over the brigade command to his friend from Marfino days. Sanya now gained strength and had much more time in which to write; he had an excellent brigade assistant, a Chechen. He greatly respected Chechens— their family and religious values, bravery, and loyalty. It was impossible to find a Chechen stool pigeon—at least one who lived very long.

If Sanya was fortunate in once again finding a relatively comfortable niche, the men under his care were equally fortunate. The character of a brigade commander was a crucial factor in the struggle to survive. An unscrupulous brigade commander could flourish by driving his men into the ground; or, by dealing firmly with the authorities, in negotiating tolerable conditions and norms, he could weld his team almost into a family. The same leadership talents were called upon as Sanya had needed to show as a battery commander.

But if his situation at the front, so to speak, had considerably improved, the rear was giving cause for concern. Natasha's letter from Kislovodsk, his birthplace, had been short and felt somehow guarded. Her subsequent letters, as she started the new academic year in Ryazan, were little warmer. Well, it was hard for her; perhaps she was simply trying, as he had advised her, to be more stoical. Surely, though, her December letter, birthday letter, would be warm. . . .

No letter at all: just a card, wishing him—in a weirdly remote phrase—
"happiness in life." . . . Almost as if she would not be a part of that life!

He buried himself that winter of 1951–52 in his "writing," in books and
philology. Many *zeks* would recall him as the guy who always had Dahl
tucked under his arm. He and the great dictionary were inseparable; he
absorbed a page of it each day, delving into the beautiful roots of Russian
words.

He read the poems of the romantic poet Baratynsky, some Chekhov,
Wilkie Collins's *The Moonstone*, Goncharov's *Oblomov*. How pleasant it
would be, just once, to be able to lie in bed all morning and daydream, like
Oblomov! How pleasant to become involved with a plump, floury, motherly
peasant woman. . . . There were no women at Ekibastuz. He longed for the
sweet scent of Natasha's skin, her newly washed hair.

There were no women at Ekibastuz, Natasha knew; and this was one
reason why she did not write to tell him their marriage was over. Knowing
about her new husband would not free him to form another relationship.
If he merely suspected something was wrong, perhaps he would gradually
get used to being without her.

He could not believe Natasha would be unfaithful; and if anything bad
had happened to her, Aunt Nina would have let him know. He was in any
case not tempted to plunge into a narrative about love, its joys and pains;
nothing so nineteenth century. He knew what his theme had to be; and
love, and woman, were peripheral to it.

Prussian Nights, his almost dreamlike account of the advance at the end of
the war, had taken on a separate identity apart from the rest of his autobiographical poem, "The Way." His last months as a soldier were preoc-
cupying him, and gave rise also to two plays. *A Feast of Conquerors* was
written entirely in rhymed verse, and a longer play, *Prisoners,* partly so. *A
Feast of Conquerors* depicts a Red Army artillery unit's impromptu celebration dinner in an East Prussian country house. He was drawing on his
memory of just such a banquet in January 1945. Most of the play's characters are based on his former army comrades; and the "I" of *Prussian
Nights* (clearly in all essentials the author himself) becomes a lightly fic-
tionalized character, Nerzhin. Captain Sergei Nerzhin—fated to appear
again, only with a different first name and hugely enriched, in *The First
Circle*—is a battery commander from Rostov; his father, who fought in the
tsarist army, was killed six months before Sergei's birth: in battle, however,
not by his own clumsy hand on a hunting trip. Captain Nerzhin's wife, Lusia,
fled into the Caucasus just before Rostov fell, and from the mountains
managed to escape to Kazakhstan, "half dead," as Natasha had done.

This information about Lusia is conveyed during a powerful scene involving Nerzhin and a beautiful Russian girl, Galina, a friend of Nerzhin's
wife before the war. Galina and Nerzhin are astonished at this chance meeting in Prussia; and behave with the *tendresse* of former lovers or almost-

lovers, who wish they were not committed elsewhere. Galina, who is being investigated by SMERSH as a likely spy, confesses she is engaged to a Vlasovite officer. She has been in Vienna studying the piano (again that haunting piano theme . . .): "I am a woman born to be happy!" she explains. "I don't care what country it's in, and under what idiotic government. I can't stand uniforms. I prefer to wear a dress. I wouldn't exchange fashionable shoes for an aircraft gunner's boots, nor my silk stockings for a soldier's socks. . . . I want a home and family. How could such brilliant minds imagine that I want to drive a tractor? Maybe I was destined to be a butterfly. Perhaps I was born to be a Geisha girl. You can talk about equality for a hundred years, but you can have it as far as I'm concerned. We used to have quite a good time without it."[3] So don't talk to her about being *liberated* from the Germans!

Galina expects him to be horrified that she loves a Vlasovite—she has come to the front desperately trying to find her fiancé—but Nerzhin assures her he is cautiously sympathetic. Relieved, she then shows she is much more than a butterfly by launching into an impassioned attack on the USSR, calling it an impenetrable forest, without law, knowing only force and torture. On a neck chain she has a vial that she tells him contains poison; she will drink it rather than be thrown into a Soviet prison.

Unfortunately, after this early scene her role in the play dwindles, and her fate remains unknown; the play becomes little more than a political debate among the soldiers and security officers. Did Solzhenitsyn feel she was threatening to take over the play? It would have been better if he had allowed her to do so, since she is by far the most living character in this apprentice work.

Galina was closely based on a friend of Natasha's, Galya Kornileva, a music student. Taken off by the Germans, she graduated from the Rome Conservatory, but later married a Russian and returned to Rostov in the late fifties.[4] But at a deeper level Galina represents a feminine and pleasure-loving side of Sanya that he could not allow himself to indulge.

Solzhenitsyn's other play conceived at Ekibastuz, *Prisoners,* follows on closely, as it is set in the SMERSH headquarters at Brodnitz. His alter ego in this play is called Kholudenev, but he remains more a mouthpiece for ideas than a living reality. Rubin (Kopelev) of *The First Circle* makes his entrance in *Prisoners.* He suggests the imprisoned Red Army soldiers are successors to the Decembrists:* "But, friends, we're not the first to go back from a tidy Europe into an unwashed Russia. A hundred years ago other regiments felt nauseated at the thought. But then, on the impoverished and exhausted soil a wonderful flowering took place. . . . Now it's our turn, the turn of our generation. They did, though, crown their rebellion by reaching

---

*The play was first called *Decembrists without December.*

Senate Square, while we're arrested on the Asian border and are prisoners of SMERSH."[5]

In a later scene Rubin seems to negate these Decembrist sentiments by defending collectivization and the famine, arguing that the Revolution had to be ruthless in order to crush yesterday's tyrants forever; previous revolutions had practiced terror too timidly. This does not seem the same man who had seen himself and his imprisoned comrades as new Decembrists.

Weak in plot and characterization, *Prisoners* is moving as a threnody for many voices, representing prisoners of many backgrounds, including former White Guards and Vlasovites, who are now quite clearly presented as patriots, not pro-Hitler but anti-Stalin. An émigré White Army colonel, Vorotyntsev, would flourish later, in *August 1914*. It is hard not to see him as another incarnation of the author. His imagination needed always to work with, rather than against, the grain of actuality. The screaming woman of Butyrki utters the same desperate cry for help in this play.

At the end, the captives prepare for their journey to Pechora or Kolyma; the light fading, guard dogs mournfully howling. In the darkness, a voice asks who the dogs are howling for. Vorotyntsev's voice answers: "Never send to know for whom the dogs howl; they howl for thee." And the disjointed howling of the dogs grows ever louder.

He pored over that birthday card wishing him "happiness in life": what did it mean? But these purely personal concerns were overwhelmed by tension, and then violence, in the camp. Unrest had been seething below the surface for months; in other camps there were rebellions. Stalin's ploy in segregating the politicals and striving to break their will by the imposition of inhuman sentences and conditions had backfired, since men who despair may act desperately. In Ekibastuz, the arrival of a convoy of two thousand Ukrainian nationalists, young and rebellious by nature— they had mutinied in a camp farther north—brought a new fighting spirit. Colditz-style tunnels were constructed; stool pigeons were killed—forty-five in the space of eight months. The most common method was for masked Ukrainians to rush into a hut as soon as it was unlocked at reveille, and knife the stoolie in his bed. Those who still survived were terrified, and stopped informing.

Reluctantly the prison authorities made a few concessions, but soon struck back. They ordered the building of a high wall to split the camp in two, then separated the Ukrainians from the rest. On the non Ukrainian side was the jail, in which some of the fearful surviving stoolies had sought refuge. Now the *zeks* who took bread and gruel to the jail began to hear screams; the authorities had thrown some of the Ukrainians in with the stoolies, who were torturing and maiming them in revenge for the campaign of knifings.

On 22 January 1952 some of the *zeks* tore stakes out of the fence surrounding the jail and used them as battering rams against the window bars

of the stoolies' cell. When this failed, a barrel of fuel oil was rolled up from
the bakery. Three bucketsful of oil were splashed into the cell, but before
the attackers could set fire to it the guards in the watchtowers opened up
with machine guns. The *zeks*, most of whom were ex–Red Army, scattered,
zigzagging and keeping their heads down; but within a minute a dozen
bloodstained bodies lay on the ground.

The next day, something almost unthinkable happened in a camp full of
starved, skeletal men: a hunger strike. It was a spontaneous act; indeed,
since no one had organized the protest, Solzhenitsyn and Panin, unaware
of what was happening, were two of only three brigade leaders who led
their team out to work. Both bitterly regretted their thoughtless conformity.
After that they played a full part in the strike. Men who had received food
parcels pooled their supplies to give everyone a little something. As Solzhenitsyn would write in *The Gulag Archipelago,* these were not well-fed
prisoners but men for whom the loss of a three-ounce ration brought acute
distress. The most emaciated might easily slip into irreversible decline after
a few days, yet they too took part. Panin recalls the dramatic atmosphere:
"The chimneys in the mess-hall area stopped smoking. The camp zone now
made an eerie impression. The days were windless and freezing cold. The
smoke from the rows of barracks looked like long grey candles. There was
not a soul to be seen outdoors; a deathly quiet lay over everything."[6]

Although not suffering as badly as many others from hunger pangs, Sanya
was in pain. A few weeks earlier he had noticed a slight lump in his right
groin; it had grown to the size of a lemon, and during the hunger strike
became more and more painful.

The guards pleaded with the strikers to eat, and go back to work. The
Dzhezkazgan Mining Trust, which relied on this slave labor, would not be
pleased. On the fourth morning, some senior Gulag officials arrived; they
promised to accept complaints and eliminate causes of conflict. Some of the
strikers were for calling a halt, but the majority, including Panin, argued
that the pain of fasting for a few more days, to win their specific requests,
would ease their burden for years to come. It was agreed to continue. Solzhenitsyn said to Panin: "Your voice rang out like pure silver. Your whole
manner expressed conviction and faith in the rightness of our cause. This
was the finest day in your life."[7]

However, the solidarity was broken by early evening, when men from
Hut 9 were seen staggering toward the canteen. This hut was full of men
on general duties, and few of them received parcels. Many of them could
hardly walk. Nevertheless, some of their watching comrades wept in frustration and despair. One by one the other huts gave up.

There was a short-lived sense of victory. On Sunday 27 January the *zeks*
were given double rations, fresh bedding, a film show; they strolled around
discussing the great events. Two days later, officials flew in from Moscow,
Alma-Ata, and Karaganda to hold an inquiry. Solzhenitsyn and Panin spoke,
but more cautiously than they later cared to recollect; they would feel they

could have done more to express the grievances of their less articulate comrades. It was hard, even now, to overcome the slave mentality.

Gradually and predictably, the authorities imposed punishments. Solzhenitsyn escaped them by being taken into the camp hospital, where two *zek*
doctors diagnosed cancer and advised an immediate operation. The Ukrainian surgeon who was due to carry it out was sent away on a transport, and
Solzhenitsyn had to wait another two weeks. The growth was removed on
12 February, under a local anesthetic. The next day, as Sanya lay feverish
and in severe pain, Panin was being moved out, as a punishment for his
role in the strike. His journey ended at Spassk, known as "The Camp of
Death" because many were executed there, and thousands were incurably
sick and disabled. Kept in punishment cells, Panin was cheered by reading
on the walls of toilets: "Greetings to the heroes of Ekibastuz!" Threatened
with an addition to his sentence, he refused to be cowed, asking what was
a year, or ten years, compared with eternal life?

Solzhenitsyn too was thinking about eternal life. A sandbag placed on the
incision to prevent further swelling weighed on him like a giant slug. He
was burning up, while outside the frozen windows winter, late this year,
had come with a vengeance—it was fifty below. And death too might be
delayed awhile, or even for decades—the doctors assured him the cancer
had not spread—but it was unavoidable. Should you struggle to stay alive
at *any* cost? Rather, surely, what mattered was how you lived.

A doctor, Boris Kornfeld, sat by his bed one evening. The room was
otherwise empty, and unlit so as not to hurt the patient's eyes. Sanya could
not see the kindly doctor; but he heard him speaking of his conversion in
prison from Judaism to Christianity. All evening Kornfeld talked, ardently
praising Christian spirituality. Sanya listened with interest; though feverish
he did not hallucinate. He knew very little of Kornfeld; only that he had
not ventured out of the hospital for two months. This might possibly indicate
that he was a stool pigeon, in fear for his life, though it seemed unlikely.

The doctor spoke at length of crime and punishment—not Dostoyevsky's
novel but the abstract entities. It was late; the hospital was silent, asleep.
"On the whole, do you know," Kornfeld murmured, "I have become convinced that there is no punishment that comes to us in this life on earth
which is undeserved. Superficially it can have nothing to do with what we
are guilty of in actual fact, but if you go over your life with a fine-tooth
comb and ponder it deeply, you will always be able to hunt down that
transgression of yours for which you have now received this blow." There
seemed such mystical knowledge in his voice that the patient shuddered.

Without saying another word, Kornfeld rose, went out into the corridor,
undressed in a nearby ward, and went to sleep. Sometime in the night, he
was struck several times on the skull with a plasterer's mallet. Sanya was
wakened in the morning by the sound of running steps in the corridor. The
doctor died on the operating table, without regaining consciousness.

There were innocent men too who were thought mistakenly to be stool pigeons or who were killed for private reasons. Whatever the motive for Kornfeld's killing, Solzhenitsyn felt a solemnity in having listened to his last words on earth. And words of such meaning. . . . They became a kind of inheritance.

He felt grow in him, during that time in the hospital, a view of life which set him profoundly and definitively at odds with his youthful self, "October's twin." In *The Gulag Archipelago* he describes this awakening, which was a conversion experience analagous to the one the doomed Dr. Kornfeld had related to him:

"Gradually it was disclosed to me that the line separating good from evil passes not through states, nor between classes, nor between political parties either—but right through every human heart—and through all human hearts. This line shifts. Inside us, it oscillates with the years. And even within hearts overwhelmed by evil, one small bridgehead of good is retained. And even in the best of all hearts, there remains an unuprooted small corner of evil." All religions, he now understood, contain truth because they struggle with the evil inside a human being; whereas political revolutions "destroy only those carriers of evil contemporary with them (and also fail, out of haste, to discriminate the carriers of good as well). And they then take to themselves as their heritage the actual evil itself, magnified still more."[8]

Tolstoy was right, he continues, when he *dreamed* of being put in prison: needing it as a drought needs a shower of rain. And so, as Dostoyevsky had done a hundred years earlier, Solzhenitsyn blesses his prison for having nourished his soul. But immediately adds: "From beyond the grave come replies: It is very well for you to say that—when you came out of it alive!"

One reason for his survival was that, though Ekibastuz was a harsh camp, he had been lucky in having a light sentence and relatively favorable conditions. He has never sought to hide that; indeed has constantly emphasized his good fortune. When he left the hospital he did not want to resume his old job of brigade leader; he told Natasha, in his permitted March letter, that he was a softy intellectual who had read thousands of books but could not sharpen an ax or set a handle on a hammer. He therefore tried to become a carpenter, but instead was ordered to the foundry, to serve as a smelter's mate.

It was one of the most backbreaking jobs he ever had. A huge red-glowing furnace sat in the center of a high-roofed iron building; in sweltering heat and choking smoke, he had to stoke, chisel slag off the furnace, and lug moulds about. He was always running in sweat. The slogging labor and choking atmosphere must have reminded him of Matronina's pressing plant at New Jerusalem. He could still see that bright, smiling girl who continuously lifted the newly pressed bricks from floor to above her head. Yes, he'd been lucky. . . . And even here, in the foundry, he was lucky. The foundry manager was Vasili Brylov, a free worker, a good fellow who was forever improvising and scrounging with the well-being of his men in mind.

As a result of his almost Schindler-like genius, as well as the foundry's vital importance, they had double rations and a humane working atmosphere.

In his letter to Ryazan, to Natasha's silence, he told her about his operation, assuring her all the tumor had been removed and he was now fully recovered. His faith in God's will and God's mercy had greatly eased his path. Natasha received his letter (the first for a year, his last having gone missing) at about the time her new "husband" and his son were moving in. She still chose not to write back.

The parcels continued to arrive from Aunt Nina, paid for by Natasha. He wrote to the old woman begging her to tell him what was happening. She thought it was not her place to do so, and urged her niece to be honest with him. Natasha was fearful of distressing someone who had just had a cancer operation. There is usually, in such difficult situations, also a desire not to distress oneself. It would have distressed her to imagine him reading her letter. She preferred to blot him from her mind; it was easy to do, they had spent so little time together.

He must have brooded on her silence. Kholudenev in *Prisoners* bursts out at one point with: "I'm so randy I could howl like a wolf—for any woman!" And pure sexual hunger, all the stronger after his brush with death, might have counterpointed Sanya's bewilderment over his wife.

He went on pressing Aunt Nina to explain; and at last, in September, at Natasha's request the kind old woman wrote to him saying simply: "Natasha has asked me to tell you that you may arrange your life independently of her." Sanya, unreasonable fellow, declined to take this as the last word, and wrote to Natasha asking how was it possible that their marriage could terminate with "such an insignificant enigmatic phrase"?[29] He still hoped to rescue their marriage: no matter what she had done during the past two years, he wrote, she would not be guilty in his eyes. "Neither by my former behaviour nor my luckless life, which has ruined and withered your youth, have I justified that rare, that great love that you once felt for me and that I don't believe is exhausted now. The only guilty one is me. I have brought you so little joy, I shall be forever in your debt."

She at last wrote to say that she had a new family.

While one can feel sympathy for the course she had taken—it took a woman of rare character and depth of love to remain true to him for so long—it was barely forgivable to attempt to let silence, for almost a year, tell him the marriage was over. And the "permission" to live his life independently was absurd. How could he, a prisoner of the Gulag, live his life independently! The message was vague, graceless and brutal, lacking any expression of regret or affectionate memory. Only a cruel and stupid woman, or an evasive one bearing an enormous load of guilt, could have authorized that message; and Natasha was not cruel and stupid.

He was due to be released in February 1953. Despite all his urgings that she start a new life without him, he had kept hoping, and in the end

believing, she would join him in his place of exile. She would emulate the
wives of the Decembrists; and after all, he would not be in chains. He hoped
he might get taken on as a humble village schoolteacher, and to that end
he had asked Aunt Nina to send him mathematical textbooks; not the standard ones, but ones which would help him to teach with originality. Still,
he hardly dared let himself think of release; and he went cold when, one
day, he was summoned to see the security officer. Were they going to throw
an extra charge at him?

No, they wanted to ask him about an old Rostov friend, Kirill Simonyan.
The name gave him a jolt. He was asked to confirm his testimony in the
Lubyanka that Simonyan had anti-Soviet attitudes. It will be recalled that
Solzhenitsyn, believing at the time that his answers should bear some resemblance to the truth, had said everyone in his circle had minor quarrels
with Soviet policy. Now, it seemed, the highly successful Moscow surgeon
was being investigated. Sanya refused to confirm his previous testimony to
Captain Yezepov; rather he was glad of the chance to renounce it, saying it
had been extracted under duress.

The circumstances relating to Simonyan are obscure. Michael Scammell
suggests a possible sequence of events: Simonyan was being questioned
about homosexuality (a criminal offense) when the investigator stumbled on
Solzhenitsyn's 1945 testimony in the file. The innocuousness of Solzhenitsyn's comments is attested by the fact that Simonyan was not even called
in for questioning in forty-five. Ignoring Solzhenitsyn's recantation, the
MGB officer showed Simonyan the earlier statements, as processed and
garbled by Yezepov. Already frightened, Simonyan was horrified by a "betrayal," and from that day ceased to be Sanya's friend. He was released,
perhaps at a price. The interrogation—or the price paid for walking free—
weighed on him for the rest of his life; and he blamed Sanya.[10]

It still seems mysterious that an investigation into sexual offenses should
throw up some material from several years earlier: material regarded as of
minor significance even in those "carnivorous" times. Then, that the "author" of this minor material could be instantly traced to a distant camp in
Kazakhstan, and questioned again. This seems a ruthless efficiency more
characteristic of Germans than Russians.

Exile had flickered like an impossible mirage before Solzhenitsyn. But
he awoke one morning, to winter darkness and the knowledge that today
he would be released. Unless he was stopped at the gates and told his
sentence was prolonged or fresh charges were being laid: that did occasionally happen.

At the last, he had an experience similar to that of the prisoner of Chillon
in Byron's poem: of loving one's cell. "Only on the threshold of the guardhouse," he later wrote, "do you begin to feel that what you are leaving behind
you is both your prison and your homeland. This was your spiritual birthplace,
and a secret part of your soul will remain here forever—while your feet
trudge on into the dumb and unwelcoming expanse of 'freedom.' "[11] He and

some other released prisoners were marched under armed guard to the station, where, with hundreds of others out of the vast Karaganda complex, they were loaded onto a long prison train.

"All that was lost to you will be returned," Natasha had written on the copy of his Yesenin. On that train journey into the unknown, into a sentence of "perpetual exile," it must have seemed that almost everything had been lost. While fighting bravely for his country, he had lost his mother, then freedom and honor, sexual fulfillment, and a normal family life. All the hopes justified by his exceptional gifts and hard work had been dashed. He had been a slave to the state for eight years, and for the rest of his life, it seemed, would remain no better than a serf, tied to a Russian equivalent of a Yukon settlement. His wife had left him, almost at the end. He was quite alone. He had been brushed by death, who might come back.

Yet life can be stubborn. The beautiful Firebird of Russian legend cannot resist the great black Falcon who attacks her, but as her strength fails under his savagery her brilliant feathers float down, and glow even more richly, though becoming buried under leaves and grass.

PART III

New Worlds

1953 – 1965

SANYA AFTER HIS RELEASE from the Gulag in 1953, just prior to being sent into "perpetual internal exile."

22

F r e e   t o   B r e a t h e

We take the golden road to Samarkand. . . .
—JAMES EL
ROY FLECKER

SOLZHENITSYN'S SPIRITUAL JOURNEY IN THE GULAG HAD BEEN LONG drawn out—surprisingly so, perhaps, when we consider the impact on him of his first weeks of prison, all that he learned from conversation in his cell with such wise and experienced men as the Old Bolshevik Fastenko and the Estonian democrat Susi. This was followed by New Jerusalem: just three weeks in the clay pit, but an endless dark night of the soul; shared with Gammerov and Ingal, of sacred memory to him. . . . Gammerov coughing beside him, struggling to lift his spade, while contemplating death with gladness. "Worse than here . . . it won't be." The two half-dead *zeks* in the drenching rain looking like two reddish stones in a field, Solzhenitsyn imagines, creating one of his most powerful images. We might assume that at this point he must have totally freed himself from his Soviet past. In fact, he retained a degree of attachment to that old self; and clearly, when he looked back at his next, Kaluga Gate, period, he did not like what he saw. At Marfino, there was new growth, thanks to his free discussions with Kopelev and Panin; yet still he was capable of strutting and showing off, as Kopelev reveals in *Ease My Sorrows*. Solzhenitsyn himself sensed that if he was to move on from being "a rational computer that doubts everything" he would have to leave this too comfortable prison.

In the real Gulag at Ekibastuz, a slave of the Irtysh Coal Company, he reached the decisive moment of change; but not until he had been ground down to a state of mind as despairing as the New Jerusalem clay pits, by cancer and—probably, though he nowhere writes of it—the sudden *real* absence of Natasha.

Now, this new self was being moved through the dusty steppes of Kazakhstan toward an unknown place of exile. He was heading north, back the way he had come three years before. The transit camps flashed by—

Pavlodar, Omsk, Novosibirsk. Still the released prisoners were transported in overcrowded Stolypin cars, thrust into overcrowded cells en route, made to mix with criminals and with guard dogs growling. But at Omsk an amiable and amazed guard called out the names of the five prisoners coming from Ekibastuz, and asked them which god was working for them: for they were to go south, to where it was warm; to where there was rice, grapes, apples!

To where there was also a greater man-made desolation than anywhere else in Stalin's empire: radioactive dust, featureless cities built to house the slaves of heavy industry, and derelict villages. A million Kazakhs had died of famine at the end of the Civil War; and here the process of collectivization was unequaled in its cruelty. Out of a population in 1930 of four million, one million were dead, three years later, of starvation or disease, or killed by the Bolsheviks while trying to flee into China. The Kazakhs killed half their livestock, rather than let it fall into Bolshevik hands.

Stalin had replaced the dead Kazakhs with a million Volga Germans during the war; and this land of Turkic nomads, as big as western Europe, was now leavened with a host of other ethnic subgroups, including Crimean Tatars, Ukrainians, Poles, and Chechens from the Caucasus. Both in its exiled people—almost Kazekstan, Solzhenitsyn punned—and its pollution, it was "the waste-bin of Moscow's empire."[1]

By some incomprehensible throw of the dice in Moscow, the place where Solzhenitsyn was to be permitted to wither toward the grave was deep in the south, on the very border of Kirghizia. Skirting Lake Balkhash, the prison train arrived at Alma-Ata ("Father of Apples"), and saw the ice blue peaks of the Tien Shan, the Mountains of Heaven. Then they traveled west to the regional center of Dzhambul, midway between Alma-Ata and Tashkent. Arriving at dead of night, the prisoners were made to sit on the bare floor of a lorry, and driven off through the town. By the light of a waning moon they saw that amazingly they were passing through an avenue of Lombardy poplars! Where they had come from, on the Irtysh, the weather had been cruelly cold, as one expected in February; but here—why, it might almost be the Crimea! There was a spring breeze caressing their faces as the lorry jolted along.[2]

They spent the remaining hours of night in the town jail, though without the usual body search and bath. At dawn, on a red spring morning, they were led out to a waiting lorry. It drove through a cobbled street to the yard of the local MVD building, where some young lieutenants began processing the latest arrivals. Sanya was too absorbed in getting to know a new man on the lorry, who proved to be one of the oldest surviving Russian engineers, to inquire as to the best area and argue a case for being sent there; and so found himself in a group assigned to the Kok Terek district, a miserable patch of desert on the edge of the lifeless Bet-Pak-Dala of central Kazakhstan. "So much for the grapes we had dreamed of! . . ."[3] "District" is a relative term; as Solzhenitsyn observes in his *Gulag Archipelago* account, Kok Terek was bigger than Belgium.

A brown document was thrust at him to sign, and now for the first time he learned officially, though without surprise, that his exile was to be "in perpetuity." He and his comrades were then kept locked up in a small room for two more days, at the end of which they were marched back along the poplar avenue to the station. A train carried them for another whole day back the way they had come, toward Alma-Ata. Halfway there, they were turfed out, at the small town of Chu, and made to walk for six miles. Carrying suitcases and kit bags, dressed in anticipation of Siberia—Sanya in his threadbare army greatcoat and two padded jackets over long johns—the marchers were broiled. After another night in jail in the hamlet of Novotroitsk, they were picked up by another lorry and driven a further forty miles into the steppe. To right and left there was nothing but "harsh grey inedible grass, and only very occasionally a wretched Kazakh village framed with trees." Often they had to get down to heave and push the lorry out of muddy hollows. "At length the tops of a few poplars (Kok Terek means "green poplar") appeared ahead of us, over the curve of the steppe."

As the lorry bounced along between Chechen and Kazakh adobe huts, dogs pursued them in a cloud of dust; donkeys drawing little carts stood aside for them; from a yard a camel turned "slowly and contemptuously" to look at them. There were people too; the exiled *zeks* saw only the pretty dark girl in a doorway, the three Kazakh girls in flowery red dresses. A sea captain called Vasilenko, untroubled laundryman in Ekibastuz, shouted cheerfully: "This is okay!—We'll find wives for ourselves!" The lorry drove past the doleful emblems of Soviet provincial life—stores, tearoom, clinic, Soviet offices, Party headquarters, House of Culture—and stopped near the MVD-MGB building. The exiles jumped down, went into the yard, stripped to the waist, and washed the dust off them.[4]

Directly across the street Sanya saw a one-story building faced with incongruous Doric columns. A school. . . . His heart beat faster. A girl with waved hair, dressed neatly in a little wasp-waisted jacket, walked into the school. A teacher! How he envied her.

An MGB officer asked him to fill in another form. Sanya casually asked him where the District Education Department was, and the officer politely told him, and gave him permission to walk there. "And off I *walk*! I wonder whether everybody knows the meaning of this great free word. I am walking along *by myself*!"

Two fat Kazakh education inspectors were startled by this ragged Gogolesque apparition; even more so when he said offhandedly, "I should like a job in a school." They asked him in fairly good Russian what he had studied. "Physics and mathematics, at University." They started gabbling in rapid Kazakh. When they vanished into the director's office, Sanya noticed a middle-aged typist looking at him. Sympathy flashed between them— she too, a Cossack from Novocherkassk and a "terrorist," arrested in 1937, had passed through the Gulag and was now exiled in perpetuity. Quickly, speaking softly, she told him there was not a single mathematics teacher in

Kok Terek with higher education; and physics teachers were simply non-existent.

He was summoned before the director. Under a portrait of Stalin, a Kazakh woman, both feline and serpentine, assured him, amid lengthy discussions with her inspectors in Kazakh, that the schools were chock-full of mathematicians and physicists; there were no vacancies. As a stalling device, she gave him yet more forms to go away and fill in.

That night the MGB allowed him to sleep out in the open air. Donkeys brayed all night, male to female, and Solzhenitsyn sang to himself, I am free! I am free!

As he has since written in a prose poem, "Freedom to Breathe": "This, I believe, is the single most precious freedom that prison takes away from us: the freedom to breathe freely, as I now can. No food on earth, no wine, not even a woman's kiss is sweeter to me than this air steeped in the fragrance of flowers, of moisture and freshness. . . . We may survive a little longer."[5]

On the day following his seemingly abortive visit to the education office, he and his fellow exiles were allowed to look for private lodgings. He found a tiny room in an adobe hut, with an earthen floor and a small fogged window; for a bed he laid his padded jacket on the earth. There were no amenities, not even an oil lamp. But really, it was no worse than the shacks he had lived in as a child; and he rejoiced to be alone—in the dark; for nocturnal darkness, like the freedom to breathe, was a rarity in the Gulag.

He slept deeply, and was roused by his elderly landlady, an exile from Novgorod, who seemed agitated. "You must get up, young man," she whispered, "and go to the square—listen to what the loudspeakers are saying."

"Why? What's happened?"

"Just listen to the radio; I'm afraid to repeat what I've just heard."

He got up and hurried to the main square. A crowd of about two hundred people were gathered there; women were openly weeping and the old Kazakh men, visibly grief stricken, had removed their muskrat-fur hats. All over the empire there were similar gatherings, great or small, as people listened to radio announcements of Stalin's death. Only very rarely were more joyful sounds mingled with the sobbings; though this did occur at an apartment in the House of Composers in Moscow, where Shostakovich and other composers sat around a table, alternately sobbing and laughing.° In Kok Terek there was no laughter; the grief was genuine and simple: what would happen to them all? For the vast majority of the Soviet people, 6 March 1953 was as tragic a day as 22 November 1963 would be for Americans and many other Westerners.

°A scene that became etched in the memory of the eight-year-old son of the composer Leo Schwarz, today the painter Alexander Schwarz, who was crouched under the table, and which he later described to the author. The hysterical adults later found that a great Russian composer, Sergey Prokofiev, had also died that day.

Solzhenitsyn wanted to leap into the air, even dance a jig. However, his face, trained to meet every occasion, put on a mournful frown. Like a few young tractor drivers, however, he did not remove his hat.

After this wondrous gift at the start of his exile, he went in search of better accommodation. Katerina Melnichuk, the woman who opened her door to him, confronted a good-looking young man dressed very poorly. She could see at once he had good manners. He put his wooden suitcase down by the door and shook her hand. Her husband Jacov picked up the suitcase and said, "Oho, it's heavy! What have you got in there—books?"

"Yes, books," he replied, looking guilty.

Theirs was not the first house he had called at. Others had been frightened to take him. But Katerina and Jacov, even though their clay house consisted of just a tiny bedroom and kitchen, felt it would have been a sin to turn him away. Jacov made him a bed out of boxes in the kitchen, and offered him an oil lamp. They found, over the next weeks, that he burned the midnight oil, reading and writing; and rose early, at six, to go for long walks over the steppe; or to pace around the garden if the weather was bad. He would not wait for a potato to be peeled, but bit right into it, skin and all.

For a month he had no job, subsisting on potatoes, bread, and dripping, and two rubles' worth of hot broth each day from the tearooms. Yet he felt supremely happy, with so much time in which to write out and revise the poetry and drama composed in the labor camp. Then an MVD officer stopped him in the street, said "Come with me," and led him to the district consumer cooperative, a wholesale warehouse which supplied all Kok Terek's stores. An exiled Greek girl with sensational movie-star looks typed out an order making him "planning officer," for which role he would receive 450 rubles a month. Riches! His task was to help the cooperative cope with the annual reduction of prices (in most cases by a few miserable kopecks) that occurred on every 1 April. The fifteen free workers in the cooperative were sweating over their abaci; Sanya demanded, and finally got, a calculating machine.[6]

After a frantic week of repricing, none of the shops in Kok Terek were yet in a position to sell anything. The cooperative's obese and idle director ordered everyone to work for seventeen hours a day to make up time. Four hours' sleep was quite adequate according to modern scientific research, he said. They would work from seven A.M. to two A.M. the following morning, with an hour's break for dinner and another for supper. Sanya appeared to accept the ludicrous diktat as meekly as everyone else, but had no intention of letting his writing be sacrificed. On the first day of this regime, he quietly got up from his desk at five o'clock, and went home. He arrived again at nine the next morning.

Rather to his surprise, nothing happened to him. While everyone else became delirious with fatigue, he felt as fresh as a daisy, and went on writing. Even the roly-poly director looked the other way when Solzhenitsyn passed him. With Stalin's death the country was entering upon more uncertain times.

Stubbornly Solzhenitsyn kept trying to get taken on as a teacher. The superintendent of studies at the Berlik High School, a young Kazakh and local Party official called Zeinegata Syrimbetov, found the skinny, sunkeneyed man who approached him, in shabby army trousers and "boots that asked for food," rather a comical figure at first, but was impressed by his coolness and confidence, and even more by his astonishing academic credentials. The superintendent had been proud to be the only university graduate in the district; now here was another, and Syrimbetov was pleased rather than put out.

Too nervous at first to take a "political," he nevertheless kept seeing that tall, pale, blond-haired man in his mind's eye. What a waste! He sent for him again and asked if he might take a copy of his diploma to a Trade Union meeting at the Dzhambul Regional Education Office. Solzhenitsyn ran like the wind to fetch his diploma. Dzhambul's regional director duly agreed it was absurd not to use such a specialist, and signed an order appointing Solzhenitsyn teacher of mathematics, physics, and astronomy.

His first day as a teacher was 3 May 1953. "Shall I describe the happiness it gave me to go into the classroom and pick up the chalk? This was really the day of my release, the restoration of my citizenship: I stopped noticing all the other things which made up the life of an exile."[7]

The pupils' final examinations were almost upon them. The superintendent worried: what if Solzhenitsyn had forgotten his mathematics? He made him open the examination papers and answer the questions. His answers coinciding with those in the envelope, Syrimbetov and the other teachers grinned their relief and slapped Sanya on the back. Indeed, he would become the oracle for the other minimally educated teachers in Kok Terek, who often sought his help. It was easy, he would observe, to pass for a second Descartes in that place. . . .

He was not only brilliantly knowledgeable and intelligent, he possessed also boundless enthusiasm for his subjects and a desire to share his excitement with children. He continued to work with them after school, and visited them in their homes to discuss their progress. In Ekibastuz, when his column had been marched past a school, it had seemed to him "the supreme, heartbreaking happiness to enter a classroom carrying a register . . . and start a lesson with the mysterious air of one about to unfold wonders." He was one of those rare teachers who, on the evidence of fellow teachers and former pupils, *could* unfold wonders. Some, indeed, swore that teaching was his real destiny, not literature. Constantly striving to break away from routine methods he was, in fact, quite capable of using his literary knowledge to illumine mathematics or astronomy. "That reference in Tolstoy to the constellations," he might say: "is it true in terms of astronomy? What do *you* observe? . . ."

This was so different from the dead hand of the Soviet system of education. Also the children he taught were "very special." The children of exiles, with little hope of moving out of Kok Terek, and with desperately poor and narrow lives, they could only rise above their second-class status through education, and so they studied avidly. They were, besides, spared the distractions and dissipations by which urban children, "from London to Alma-Ata," were assaulted. (Most people today would regard the children of the 1950s—especially Soviets—as hardly corrupted by worldly dissipations; but Solzhenitsyn thought otherwise, at least when writing *The Gulag Archipelago*.)

He taught with unstinting energy and decisiveness; the children loved him, because he treated them as equals and never broke a promise; if they were unruly and he rapped out an order of "Attention!" like the officer he had been, they instantly froze—but from respect, not fear.

The children of the Berlik High School looked up, like hungry sheep, and Solzhenitsyn took a delight in feeding them. The pleasure did not waver, even though he was becoming more tired, and a pain in his stomach started to nag at him. He wondered if he was developing an ulcer.

There was a nagging pain in his soul, too: for companionship and intimacy. He too looked up and was not fed. He poured out some of his feelings to a newly discovered second cousin, Alexander Mikheyev. This Alexander, born in 1908, was the son of Anastasia, the younger daughter of Semyon and Pelageya Solzhenitsyn. Alexander (Sasha) had gone from the Sablia village school to a cobbler's last, had married, divorced, served in the front line—otherwise never left the North Caucasus. *Something*, then, was returned to Sanya. And Sasha had a sister, Liudmila, who could remember, aged five, Sanya's father, followed by a beautiful girl, pacing into the farmhouse, so handsome and erect, gazing around, his boots and spurs gleaming. . . . The hero home from war, and with a wife.

His father, in a moment of life, seen by someone still alive! . . .

Writing that he would like to meet him, Sanya confessed to Alexander in a letter of August 1953 that he felt very lonely, being without a wife or children. It was possible to live in Kok Terek, but very dull. "I don't know whom to marry, and it's very boring to be alone . . . ." He was not angry with Natasha, he assured Alexander, since he had spoiled all her youth, and all those years she had kept him going had helped to save his life. Casting his memory back to childhood, he recalled visiting Sablia, at the age of ten; but he remembered little.[8]

Strangely, in the same month that he wrote of his kind feelings toward his former wife, she had discovered his whereabouts from her aunt Nina and wrote to him. Spending her summer holidays on the Black Sea, perhaps attuned to a sad-sweet romanticism like Chekhov's heroine in "Lady with a Lapdog," she suggested they might have a spiritually intimate correspondence, and pictured their two lives ascending on two "parallel staircases."[9] Her image echoed his wartime reference to the two parallel trains, of his and Vitkevich's friendship.

When her letter came, Sanya was settling into a new home. He had rented—later to buy outright, thanks to his teacher's salary—an isolated one-room clay hut, whitewashed and thatched. Beyond his hedge of prickly pear and an irrigation ditch stretched the steppe, and in the far distance was the faint blue outline of the Chu-Ili Mountains. The physical isolation, all the greater in the fierce summer when there was no school, was conducive to writing; yet Natasha's letter must have made him realize afresh how lonely was his life, how sad he felt.

Writing on the old wooden suitcase that served as a table (later a skillful Ukrainian exile made him some furniture out of the local gnarled saxaul shrub), he replied that her letter gave him a feeling of joyous excitement. Her expressed wish for a platonic correspondence was evidently self-deception; in any case he could see no point in it, since it would involve her in deceiving another, and if he himself should marry, "if only for practical considerations," the correspondence would have to cease. But he would take her back if she would abandon her present life. He knew, he wrote, how weak he himself had been.

"That Sanchik [Sanya] whom you once knew and whom you loved quite undeservedly—that fellow would not have forgiven you. But the present-day Sanya doesn't even know if there is anything here to forgive. Probably I am even more guilty toward you. And, at all events, I did not save your life, but you have saved my life and more than my life." Whatever her decision, he would not be hurt or angry.

She wrote back to say she was upset by the contents of his letter, and by his total misunderstanding of hers. "I am completely satisfied with my present life and wish for nothing more." She would have to say farewell until such time as he, too, had achieved complete satisfaction "not only in your work but also in the personal sphere." In response to what appears to have been a tender and forgiving letter, Natasha's sounds insufferably sanctimonious—and perhaps not altogether honest to herself. If Sanya's sense of truth was like a laser beam, Natasha's was like moonlight on a stormy night. Clearly she wanted to believe she was perfectly contented with her unregistered second marriage; but since she would later admit she did not love Vsevolod—rather she loved her stepson—we may assume that Sanya's intuition of continuing involvement on her part was justified.

Their short-lived correspondence abruptly ceased. For friendship, Sanya was coming to rely on an elderly Russian couple. He had met Nikolai Zubov, a fifty-eight year-old gynecologist, soon after his arrival, and they had immediately forged a bond, with a feeling of being almost young together. This was probably, Sanya felt, because they were both on their own, without families. In Nikolai's case this was temporary; he was impatiently waiting for his wife, who had been in a labor camp with him but sent by mistake to a different place of exile.

Their "crime" had been that his eighty-year-old mother, with whom they had lived in a small town near Moscow, had given shelter for two nights to a Red Army deserter. The mother was deemed too old to arrest, but someone had to pay. Nikolai and Elena were given ten years and perpetual exile.

It was a year—and many frantic appeals to Moscow—before Elena arrived, and Sanya liked her too. The reunited couple were blissfully happy; for them, exile in Kok Terek was paradise. They were well educated and intellectually curious; so long as they had books, as well as each other and the freedom to breathe, they wanted nothing more. Nikolai had even made a kind of Eden out of his quarter-acre garden, planting it with apricot trees, vines, hops, and tobacco plants; it had a summer house and a central avenue. As a doctor, Nikolai worked twice as hard as many half his age; he was ready to go out at any time of the day or night to care for a patient.

They were joined by his immensely aged mother and a feeble-minded daughter, who was soon made pregnant by a local official. Nikolai had two other mentally disturbed children from a first marriage. Life was not easy for them, yet they had their love for each other and their spiritual resources. Getting to know Sanya was also a delight for them; they treated him like a son. He grew to love them too, and enjoyed the company of their two dogs, an Alsatian and a terrier, Zhuk and Tobik, taking them for long walks across the steppe. Tobik learned to bring messages, tied to his collar, between the houses.

Often Sanya shared his friends' simple meal. As summer began to soften into autumn, Elena became worried that Sanya was pushing away the food uneaten, and his clothes were hanging loose from his already spare form. His face gray with pain, Sanya admitted he felt worse, but still hoped he had gastritis or an ulcer. Nikolai had been giving him medicine. However, at last he agreed with his wife that something more had to be done, and insisted on sending him to a specialist in Dzhambul.

In a letter to his newly found cousin, Sasha, he expresses continuing loneliness. He lived alone, he wrote, on the edge of the hamlet. While step by step he was making his life more comfortable, he felt sad that he could not marry. Also this year, for the first time in his life, he was troubled by ill health: a torturing pain in his stomach.[10]

A slight breeze came from the direction of the Chu, and Solzhenitsyn, writing in the open air, took great gulps of it. Pain made him gasp, but he preferred pain and the freedom to breathe to a tranquil, pain-free bondage.

A few weeks later he rested against a boulder high up in the mountains, gazing down at Lake Issyk Kul. It stretched away east, boundlessly, ringed by snowy peaks that seemed insubstantial, floating. Issyk Kul, five times the size of Lake Geneva, is the deepest mountain lake in the world. A millennium ago, the Silk Road had snaked by it, bringing a flowering of trade and knowledge along its edges. Now it was asleep again. No one but Solzhenitsyn seemed present for thousands of square miles, though he had visited a nearby village in which an old Russian medicine man had sold him an infusion of the mandrake root.

In the intense silence, he imagined that deeper silence and blackness in the lake's depths; and kept hearing the words of the specialist in Dzhambul who had examined his X ray: "I can see you're a man who wants to be told the truth. . . . Well, I fear you may have just a few weeks. Perhaps three."

It was—he felt it himself—so sad; what had he lived for? Why had he been given this gift for writing? Fate had not allowed him to get very far with it. And love . . . Natasha . . . What had it all meant? A few *zeks* would remember him, and say, He showed such promise as a writer. He was sorry to let his pupils down.

Soon he would be less than a stone in the depths of Issyk Kul.

23

Shrinking the Cancer

All I want is . . . to sleep on a camp-bed under the stars . . .
to live just this one summer. . . .
—*Cancer Ward*

AT THE HOSPITAL IN DZHAMBUL, THE TESTS FOR A STOMACH CON-
dition had proved negative; but then an X-ray had revealed a tumor as big
as a fist growing from the back wall of the abdominal cavity. It might be a
metastasis of the tumor removed at Ekibastuz, or a new one. Besides the
dire prediction that he might have only weeks to live, he was given a cer-
tificate of admission to the cancer clinic in Tashkent. Instead of traveling
straight back to Kok Terek to start applying for permission to travel, Solzhenitsyn took the risky course—but after all, he was dying!—of dragging
his exhausted frame up into the mountains. He had heard, in Dzhambul,
of a healing natural medicine against cancer. It is testimony to his will to
live that he should have made such an epic journey—to try to get hold of
a mandrake root. . . .

It was his first journey since his student years not dictated by higher
authority; and his first ever that could be described as irrational. It is the
more regrettable, therefore, that he has nowhere chosen to describe that
heroic and illegal journey up into the aptly named "Mountains of Heaven."
In an Issyk Kul village he found, without too much trouble, the Russian
settler who possessed the medicine. The old man, after taking Sanya's
money, advised him to build up the dose gradually, drop by drop, over ten
days; then decrease it by a drop a day; after that he should leave an interval
of ten days before starting the process again. Any overdose would be like
taking poison, and it would be dangerous even to inhale the mandrake
infusion.

Returning home, the desperately sick man, unable to stand, sit, or lie
down without pain, felt his tumor swell, distending his stomach, almost
hourly through November and early December. He could not eat, and
found cancer as effective against sleep as the Lubyanka torturers had been.

He felt he had died psychologically already; had forgiven all those who had harmed him, if only because he had become indifferent to everything and everyone. For a couple of weeks in the middle of December his appetite returned, and he felt more hopeful; but before the last day of 1953, the day prescribed for his train journey west to Tashkent, he had worsened again.

He had to sleep (or lie awake in pain) that night in Chu station in order to catch the morning express. In *The Gulag Archipelago* he would write that he remembered clearly that night. It must have seemed a hopeless endeavor, to travel hundreds of miles in the hope of a miracle. Why not just take a little too much of the mandrake medicine? "It seemed as though for me life, and literature, were ending right there. I felt cheated."[1] Perhaps no other occasion in his life—not even his arrest in East Prussia—had seemed so completely without a glimmer of light. And the morning brought a near disaster; he had had to give up his identity card overnight to an MVD duty officer, who had later been carried away dead drunk. The identity card was nowhere to be found, and the express was only minutes away. Travel without an identity card would have been inconceivable. And his permit specified just *this* day for traveling to Tashkent, and no other.

Perhaps his life was saved, not by a folk medicine, but by an MVD officer who came strolling along the platform at that moment and who recognized him. Solzhenitsyn explained his predicament, showed him his travel permit, and the officer—imbued with a trace of seasonal good feeling—scribbled a note that should take him through all inspections.

Arriving in Tashkent on a cold, rainy day, he first had to go to MVD headquarters to hand in his permit, before traveling to the hospital. The oncological clinic refused to admit him without an identity card. As Kostoglotov was to do in *Cancer Ward*, Solzhenitsyn lay down and refused to move unless he was admitted. A doctor of German extraction, Irina Meike, saw to his admission on 4 January 1954. The very next day his treatment began. Dr. Lydia Dunayeva, head of the radiotherapy department, found the tumor to be a seminoma: a very rare form of cancer, usually occurring in middle-aged men. (Solzhenitsyn was thirty-five.) Dunayeva prescribed massive doses of radiation. He had, by the law of averages, a one-in-three chance of survival.

After two or three treatments he felt free of pain; after two weeks, the tumor was shrinking, he was eating well and putting on weight. But then came radiation sickness, loss of appetite, and a depression made worse by the effect of Sinestrol, a drug containing estrogen. Since seminoma mainly affected men, it was hoped that a female hormone might weaken its effect— a theory later proved to be false. It is clear from *Cancer Ward* that Solzhenitsyn suffered from a sense of being castrated. Kostoglotov suggests it by referring, in a letter, to his woman's dressing gown held together by his army belt. Shuffling in the hospital gardens, his face wrinkled and ashen, Solzhenitsyn, like his literary alter ego, felt bitter despair at ever being a man again, even should he survive.

All the greater, then, was the joy of feeling the sap rising again, the blood surging through him. His aged shuffle became less labored, and sometimes he walked beyond the bounds of the hospital, into the city streets and bazaars, to bargain for pickled cucumber and cabbage—which alone could relieve his radiation nausea.

That he defeated his cancer was of course a tribute to his own iron determination to live—subsisting somehow in the midst of despair; to the skill and compassion of the Tashkent doctors; and—to give the Soviet devil his due—to a relatively efficient system, allowing him (despite all the bureaucratic hazards) to receive the best available treatment within weeks, and without payment.

By mid-March he was discharged, with orders to turn up again in June. His cancer had shrunk to less than half its previous size, but he was not cured. Nevertheless, he left the clinic in a joyous mood, and wandered around the center of Tashkent for most of the day. He had not been in a city since his brief visit to Moscow in 1943; this experience, after his quiet life of exile and the confinement of the clinic, dazed him. Tashkent, with over two million inhabitants, mostly Uzbeks and Russians, was the third biggest Soviet city, and the greenest; by March, its trees were already in blossom.

During the Great Patriotic War, Tashkent had become a haven for the Russian intelligentsia. Though Bolshevism had superimposed triumphalist buildings and boulevards on the steep alleys and secretive courtyard gardens scented with almond or apricot, an enchantment still lingered; even a fifty-foot-high bronze statue of Lenin gazing fiercely out over the colonial city could not totally destroy its oriental charm, either for the wartime intellectuals and poets, or for the gaunt but revivified ex-*zek*. What astonished him most of all was a department store containing a vast array (after Kok Terek) of consumer goods. Unlike Kostoglotov, who could not afford the green-and-white-striped shirt he coveted, Sanya bought it.

He was astonished, too, to find a church that was open. For the first time since he had attended requiem mass with his mother for old Zakhar Shcherbak, he ventured inside a living church and gave thanks for having survived to see another spring.

Then he had to get to MVD headquarters, in an industrial suburb a half hour's walk from the nearest tram stop, to deregister; after which he made his way to the railroad station. There he recognized a rowdy gang as former labor camp criminals, and had the nightmare experience of seeing a drunken woman smash her baby's head against a stone floor.

The city that passed before his unseeing eyes as the train drew out would soon be transformed; for in 1966—a hundred years after the tsarist colonizers closed down the slave bazaar—a violent earthquake gutted half of Tashkent. Almost instantly the destroyed city bloomed with dozens of vast prefabricated tower blocks.

Unsure whether man or mandrake had shrunk his tumor, and whether it would swell once more, Solzhenitsyn detoured to revisit Issyk Kul and buy a further supply of the folk remedy. Arriving home at last, he was greeted joyfully by the Zubovs, their two frantically tail-wagging dogs, and not least his pupils. Once on his own, he dug up a champagne bottle in which he had secreted tightly rolled-up manuscripts. He had thought he would probably never see them again, and they themselves—his first-fruits—might never see the light of day. He gave thanks, this time under the vault of heaven.

To sleep out in the open, under the brilliant stars. . . . Just one more summer, O Lord! Then I should happily not wake again. . . .

He taught the position of those stars and constellations to his pupils, who came to his hut almost every night. Eventually they could identify almost every star. He gave himself to them with selfless energy—keeping in a special notebook, one for each class, a record of their likes and dislikes, their hobbies, their favorite subjects. Never in his life had he seen such eagerness to study as he saw in these deprived children of exiles; he was both responding to their eagerness and, of course, inspiring it. He would burst into a classroom like a whirlwind. Who could resist that enthusiasm?

A hobby of his own, which he was able to indulge thanks to his good salary (50 percent above the norm, since he worked thirty hours instead of the normal twenty), was photography. With his cherished new camera he photographed, through use of a timer, himself in his labor camp gear, wearing a snarling expression. It would become his most famous portrait. More importantly, he created microfilms of his manuscripts, and hid them in the covers of books. He put the books into packages that he addressed to Tolstoy's daughter Alexandra, now living in America, since he felt she would command respect, but did not send them.

In June, at the beginning of the summer vacation, he traveled to Tashkent once more. For all that he had been a stubborn, truculent patient, he was greeted warmly; doctors and nurses were delighted by how much weight he had put on and how well he looked. Radiotherapy was resumed, to reduce the tumor still further, but had to be interrupted when his white blood cell count dropped dangerously low.

The already slightly shrunken cancer of Stalinism likewise struck back at that time. Kengir Camp, in Kazakhstan, had followed the example of Ekibastuz and others to stage a mutiny. Eight thousand *zeks* had taken over the camp for forty days; believers of all religions held services, men and women who had corresponded secretly from their separate stockades met and consummated their love. Then, on 25 June, in the early dawn hours, tanks rumbled in, crushing everyone in their way. "The tanks grazed the sides of huts and crushed those who were clinging to them to escape the caterpillar tracks. Semyon Rak and his girl threw themselves under a tank clasped in each other's arms and ended it that way. . . . Faina Epstein remembers the corner of a hut collapsing, as if in a nightmare, and a tank passing obliquely over the wreckage and over living bodies; women tried to jump and fling themselves out of the way: behind the tank came a lorry, and the half-naked women were tossed onto it." Women who tried to shield men with their bodies were bayoneted. Others were shot. Some three hundred were killed.[2]

Almost simultaneously, Jean-Paul Sartre, reporting in *Libération* on his visit to the Soviet Union, was telling his interviewer that "Soviet citizens criticise their government much more and more effectively than we do. There is total freedom of criticism in the USSR." They did not travel abroad, not because they were prevented, but because they had no desire to leave their marvelous country. . . . Several years later the idiot savant confessed he knew it was a lie, but he hadn't wanted to embarrass his recent hosts.[3]

Sanya's blood count stabilized, and radiotherapy resumed. After almost two months of treatment—during which he read avidly, and wrote critical articles, never published, about Soviet authors—he was discharged as cured. He visited Tashkent zoo—an episode that went into *Cancer Ward*. Indeed, he conceived this novel that day, while on his way to MVD headquarters to deregister, though it would be eight years before he would write it. He was struck by the greater civility of the MVD personnel. Despite events at Kengir, the Gulag was softening; the arrest and summary execution of the KGB head, Lavrenti Beria, had left the security services confused and uncertain.

Nikolai Zubov relieved Solzhenitsyn's anxiety about his manuscripts by showing him how to construct a plywood box with a false compartment, and also fitted a secret container into his table. Solzhenitsyn's writing took place at the end of the day, when his pupils had gone and after he had done his household chores; and he spent all Sunday writing, unless he was required to help out at the state farm. He wrote a third play based on his Gulag experiences, called *The Love-Girl and the Innocent*. The "innocent" of the title was another Solzhenitsyn stand-in, Rodion Nemov. Like his creator at New Jerusalem, Kaluga Gate, and Ekibastuz, Nemov tries to survive but not at the expense of selling his soul. The Love-Girl, Lyuba, meets Nemov while taking part in amateur dramatics; like Anya Breslavskaya, to whom he dedicated this first draft.

Nemov cannot bear the compromise of sharing Lyuba with the camp doctor. Yet if she rejected the doctor's advances she would be forced onto a transport, taking her to almost certain death. The Gulag compelled its victims to such impossible choices between evils.

One Saturday evening in June 1955, a year after his second visit to Tashkent, Sanya invited Nikolai and Elena Zubov to visit him, and presented as a monologue the world premiere of *The Love-Girl and the Innocent*. He began to read just as darkness was falling; after a while he lit the oil lamp. The kerosene stank, as they had to keep the windows closed to muffle the sound. The Zubovs' dogs lay outside, and would have barked a warning had anyone stolen up, but still Sanya crept out between scenes to check. None of them ever forgot the magic of the occasion; it was, he recalled in *Invisible Allies*, "a steamy night in late June, majestically lit by moonlight in a way possible only on the open steppe. . . . That night the life of the labor camps reappeared before us in all its vivid brutality. . . . When the reading was finished, we went outside. As before, the whole steppe was suffused with boundless light, only the moon had by now moved to the far side of the sky. The settlement was fast asleep, and the predawn mist was beginning to creep in, adding to the fantastic setting. The Zubovs were deeply moved. . . . Elena—already fifty and leaning on the arm of a husband soon to be sixty—exclaimed, 'I can't get over how young we feel! It's like standing at the very summit of life!' "[4] Elena confirmed later, to Natasha, that she and her husband had been in a state of rapture, and it was one of the high points of her life.

Sanya was still realistic enough, on that entranced night, to take a note of the time elapsing, and was annoyed that the play was turning out to be overlong.

In that summer of 1955 he visited Karaganda, in a quest for a wife. Whoever was the potential bride, nothing came of the visit. But for a time he seemed almost desperate to find a wife. Once, it appears, he got on a train, heading for a girl recommended by some friends, but got off again, overcome by embarrassment. There were some pretty young teachers at the Berlik High School. He considered a Kazakh girl; also a Russian—with whom in fact he fell in love, and spent New Year's Eve of 1955 in her company. But she was a Komsomol enthusiast, and he feared she would betray him over his writings. That was the rub—his writings; whom could he trust with his life?

Before his first trip to Tashkent, when death seemed certain, he had written to a friend of his ex-wife's in Rostov, Irina Arsenyeva, begging her to come and take possession of his "belongings"; but the necessary euphemism had confused her and Kok Terek was far distant; she had not come, and he had had to bury papers in the champagne bottle, telling only the Zubovs of its whereabouts.

His underlying loneliness and desolation were revealed to two friends who came back into his life—Kopelev and Panin. They found him through a chance meeting, at TSUM, the Moscow Central Department Store, between Natasha Reshetovskaya and Yevgeniya Panin. Excited at bumping into her old companion of Marfino days, Yevgeniya described how she had traced her husband's whereabouts to Kustanay in northern Kazakhstan, traveled out there and found him—not alone. . . . Yet still she was bombarding the authorities to bring him back to Moscow. Kopelev, she said, had been released and was living here in Moscow; he and Mitya (Dmitri) were desperate to find out where Sanya was. Natasha gave her his address.

"He wrote to Mitya and me frequently," Kopelev recalled in his memoir, "and in some letters revealed the barely hidden depression and loneliness, the anticipation of approaching death, despair. We tried to comfort him as best we could, cheer him up; we looked for a wife for him."[5] This version of Solzhenitsyn is very different from the man who, by his own account, was enjoying some of the happiest years of his life. But of course the one did not rule out the other. And he did not trust that he was cured of cancer.

Yevgeniya Panin, too, tried to find him a wife—a Moscow student. And the Zubovs put him in touch with a niece of theirs, living in the Urals. Recovered health—he felt better than he had for ten years—brought naturally an intensification of sexual desire. It would have been impossible to have a relationship without marriage in the small and highly conservative Kazakh community. Two decades later he told a biographer that he considered that the greatest sacrifice of his life; he had stayed unmarried, following eight years in the camps, in order to preserve his manuscripts; and his celibate state might have continued indefinitely had he not been suddenly released.[6] Yet was it really impossible to find a trustworthy girl in Kok Terek? In truth—and perhaps his single-mindedness stemmed from his mother's sacrifice of a husband for him—the sudden flood of creativity would allow him no rival "object of desire."

Eros must have visited him through memory—of Natasha, and also of Anya at Kaluga Gate, his "Love-Girl"—and fantasy. The secret nape-shivering thrill of sexual contemplation is not dissimilar to the possessive excitement a writer feels when he or she sits and resumes the half-written story or poem; and perhaps, because of the sacrifice he was making, and his intense frustration, that quiet, secretive excitement became even more highly charged in his case. The thrill of writing *in secret* had to compensate for so much unlived life. And each night his secret passion had to be hidden physically—had to be stuffed in a hole, like Silas Marner hiding his wealth.

Unquestionably he had to be secretive; the more so in the years of writing *The Gulag Archipelago*. But secrecy became a kind of fetish too.

The snatched love affair between Nemov and Lyuba is the best-realized feature of *The Love-Girl and the Innocent*. While the play vividly portrays the external problems and venality of the camps, there is a lack of inner psychological complexity and tension. It is still an apprentice work. Had his cancer killed him in Kok Terek, we should not have heard of Solzhenitsyn. He might have cropped up in one or two camp memoirs as a man of striking personality and a writer of promise. But in the summer of 1955, when once again he was in touch with Panin and Kopelev, he began a novel which many regard as his greatest, *The First Circle*.

His quiet routine of school, writing, walks in the steppe, long, cooling, summer-evening swims in the river Chu, was suddenly threatened. He had to face the possibility that his perpetual exile might be temporary after all. Something was happening to the empire; it was hard to know what it was precisely, but even Kok Terek was awash with rumors. He bought a short-wave radio so that, with his windows blacked out, he could tune in to the BBC: "We were so worn out by decades of lying nonsense, we yearned for any scrap of truth, however tattered—and yet this work was not worth the time I wasted on it: the infantile West had no riches of wisdom or courage to bestow on those of us who were nurtured by the Archipelago."[7] This jaundiced view of the Western media probably does not reflect what he felt at the time; particularly, perhaps, when he first heard on the BBC about First Secretary Khrushchev's "secret speech" at the Twentieth Communist Party Congress, on 26 February 1956, in which he denounced Stalin's crimes. The speech, circulated within the Party, brought a shock wave infinitely greater than the earthquake that would devastate Tashkent.

Some local Party officials confirmed what he had learned over his short-wave radio. It meant that his great enemy, Stalin, had posthumously fallen, and the Gulag Archipelago was beginning to crumble. Here in Kazakhstan the local security officers, never as strict as those nearer the center, became still more relaxed in their treatment of exiles.

With uncertain joy came also unease. Words of consolation expressed by a friend to the Enlightenment writer Radishchev, exiled to Siberia by Catherine the Great, struck him forcefully: "Cut off from all men, remote from all the objects that dazzle us—you can all the more profitably voyage within yourself; you can gaze upon yourself dispassionately, and consequently form less biased judgements about things at which you previously looked through a veil of ambition and worldly cares." It was true for himself too, Sanya thought; and he contrasted his own calm existence with that of his friend Kopelev, living precariously in Moscow. He had been permitted to go there through a misunderstanding: Red Army collaborators had been amnestied, to match the release, following the German Chancellor Adenauer's visit of 1955, of their POWs—but Kopelev, of course, belonged to the *un*amnestied multitude who had simply fought for the motherland. . . . So Lev was fearful of every ring of the doorbell. Wasn't it better, Sanya mused, to stay where he was, in the wild steppe? After he had hidden his manuscripts, which he did every night, he slept like a baby.

Here, he could spend a whole hour watching ants display their wisdom. One morning they failed to appear to carry the loads of husks outside his hut to their winter store. Somehow they knew that the cheerful sunny sky would soon be filled with black clouds and rain would pelt the earth. After the rain the clouds were still heavy and black, yet the ants crept out of the mud-brick foundations of his hut to work—knowing for sure it would not rain again. "There, in the silence of exile, I could see with perfect certainty the true course of Pushkin's life. His first piece of good fortune was his banishment to the South, his second and greatest his banishment to Mikhailovskoye. There he should have lived, and gone on living, instead of hankering for other places. What fatal compulsion drew him to Petersburg? What fatality prompted him to marry? . . ."[8]

The truth was, Sanya had grown to love this land! Yet he could hardly fail to apply for a review of his case. And in April 1956 he received a letter from the regional MVD headquarters informing him that his sentence had been annulled and his exile lifted. He was free to go—wherever he wanted. He did not want to settle in a big city; and certainly Rostov, where he could have claimed a flat or room, held no appeal for him; Vitkevich was there, it was true, but the friendship no longer overrode other factors—most of all, that he craved the modest, peaceful greenery of central Russia, the Russia he had first seen and loved when drifting along the Volga.

He inquired about teaching posts in Vladimir and Kostroma provinces; and also wrote to Natasha, asking her if she would mind inquiring about jobs in the Ryazan region, but outside the city. He assured her that if he should move to that region there would be "no shadow cast on your life."

The gentleness and tact of that promise confirms an overall impression that, in these years of exile, Solzhenitsyn was an admirably well-balanced man: a devoted and brilliant teacher, much loved by his pupils; a devoted friend—and surrogate son—to the kindly Zubovs; and, in his own quietude, a writer whose dedication was unaffected by the danger it exposed him to, nor by the likelihood that his work would not be published in his lifetime. He was a man of rare virtue: truly therefore, in the deepest sense, a happy man.

It was a balanced writer's life too, apart from the lack of a woman—and that was not necessarily bad for his writing. He could daydream a lot, alone in a dream landscape of shimmering steppe, distant mountains. Granted more than the one summer under the stars that he had prayed for, he lived in a special kind of inner freedom, at peace. He had the stimulus and fulfillment of teaching eager pupils, which made the withdrawal to his secret life all the more delicious and creatively potent. He could idle away an hour watching ants—and find a beautiful prose poem arising from it. He was spared the doubtful blessing of a plentiful supply of research material, such as he would have during a much longer later exile. He had only a few books, memories, and imagination.

24

Time to Awake

As if it were Easter, and as if I were fourteen again . . .
—YEVGENIA GINZBURG, *Within the Whirlwind*

ONE DAY IN THIS EPOCH, THE MID-FIFTIES, OLGA IVINSKAYA RE-
ceived a phone call from her lover, Pasternak. His voice sounded shaken,
and he began to speak in a voice choked by tears. "What's wrong?" she
asked in alarm. "He's dead, he's dead, I say!" he groaned several times over.

He was speaking about Yuri Zhivago. The harrowing chapter in which
he suffers a fatal heart attack on a tram (not far from where later a son of
Pasternak would die at his car wheel) was now finished; and soon the whole
novel would be completed.[1]

Art, he wrote, is always meditating upon death and thereby creating life.

A boy with narrow Kirghiz eyes was forever coming into Zhivago's life.
He was his half brother Yevgraf. Yuri Zhivago "knew for certain that this
boy was the spirit of his death or, to put it quite plainly, that he was his
death. Yet how could he be his death if he was helping him to write a
poem? How could death be useful, how was it possible for death to be a
help? . . . Near him, touching him, were hell, corruption, dissolution, death;
yet equally near him were the spring and Mary Magdalene and life.—And
it was time to awake. Time to awake and to get up. Time to arise, time for
the resurrection."[2]

Over and over again, *Doctor Zhivago* echoes this call to awake, to arise.
. . . Just after Yuri, having told his love, Lara, that he cannot see her again,
decides he will see her just once more to take a more fitting leave, a night-
ingale begins to sing. " 'Wake up! Wake up!' it called entreatingly; it
sounded almost like the summons on the eve of Easter Sunday: 'Awake, O
my soul, why dost thou slumber?' " Though, in brutal fact, the spring thaw
in Russian cities yields dead rats, dogs, and tramps amid its sea of slush, in
Pasternak's masterpiece the Russia-wide thaw becomes the most potent
expression of the urge to turn death to life. . . . "At first the snow melted

quietly and secretly from inside. But by the time half the gigantic work of melting it was done, it could not be hidden any longer and the miracle became visible. Waters came rushing out from below, singing loudly. The forest stirred in its impenetrable depth, and everything in it awoke." The sky is drunk with spring and giddy with its fumes; it pours rain, which washes away the last of the armor plating of ice from the earth. Yuri, asleep in a train heading eastward into Siberia, "woke up, stretched, raised himself on one elbow and looked and listened."[3]

Easter, with its death and resurrection, its suffering and redemption, has always been the central festival and concept of Russian Orthodoxy. The Russian God, Jo Durden-Smith reflects, was very different from the Western one with "His orderliness, His timetables, His precise schedules of reward and punishment, His neat household furniture. The Russian God was older and more scattered and less interventionist; He did not seem, in fact, to be much interested in earth at all. . . . Eternity—where He dwelt at the focal point of the iconostasis—was a lot more important."[4] Russian history too is a matter, not of chronological events, but of deep ice ages and sudden, wondrous meltings. (And the rulers responsible for the darkest sufferings have been more revered and even loved than those who brought liberalization; there are no statues of Alexander II, liberator of the serfs, nor is Gorbachev well remembered.) The poet Osip Mandelstam, in infancy, burst into tears when he first heard the word "progress."

Communist theology, believing not merely in progress but in a material paradise *beyond* progress, was profoundly un-Russian, light-years away from the humble acceptance of experience expressed in the Zhivago poem "Daybreak":

> I feel for each of them
> As if I were in their skin,
> I melt with the melting snow,
> I frown with the morning.
>
> In me are people without names,
> Children, stay-at-homes, trees.
> I am conquered by them all
> And this is my only victory.

He spoke elsewhere, in prose, of "invisible threads of sympathy" linking the shining stars and a lone, exhausted cow homesick for its herd. That sense of the interwovenness of all life springs more naturally to the nonchronological Russian mind than to a westerner's.

In the mid-fifties, the Bolshevik snows were melting—a little. No writer has better conveyed the joy of that thaw than Yevgenia Ginzburg, at the climax of her two-volume memoir, *Into the Whirlwind* and *Within the Whirlwind*.

In her Moscow youth she had been a university teacher and eager Party member, with a husband and two children. Then in 1937 she was arrested for terrorism, and spent the next eighteen years in Kolyma. At last, after being reunited with her son, a grown-up stranger, she felt the changed atmosphere of the camps in one special, Pasternakian moment.... "Long-forgotten feelings, the smell of the earth in springtime, fragments of poems, a sense of oneness with the whole of creation.... As if it were Easter, and as if I were fourteen again...."[5]

When she had that experience she was returning late at night from an evening class she had been allowed to teach. One of her classes, just a year or so after Stalin's death, consisted of some of the security officers who had helped make life a misery. Now their master Beria too had been executed and disgraced, and they were frightened of what the next order from Moscow might bring. She reminded herself that most of the officers were really peasants, and managed to suppress the anger aroused in her by their jack-boots and epaulettes. She overcame *their* resentment at bad marks from a "terrorist" by means of an unpunctuated sentence from a decree by Nicholas II: "Execution impossible reprieve." "Well, would the condemned man die or not?" she asked them, and eventually showed them that it all depended on a simple comma. She gave them lessons on the literary classics, and eventually won their respect to the extent that they drew up a rota of escorts to conduct her home after dark. She recalls the commandant himself, a good-looking young man, interrupting her during their walk when she said she would be calling on him to get her documents stamped: "Do you know Molotov?" he asked her. Not personally, she said—but, yes, she had followed his career. "Well," he said thoughtfully, "his wife is in the same position as you.... She has to register.... In the same position ... in the same ..." He broke off decisively, adding: "I expect it'll soon be all over."

Russia was beginning to awaken, somewhat dazed, rising on her elbow to look and listen. It was probably a period, Ginzburg suggested, not unlike the first months of the Revolution: everyone having a constant, childlike expectation of miracles or horrors; and life, chaotic and merciless, whisking everyone away like scraps of paper in a rushing wind.

Within a short while Ginzburg was in an Ilyushin 14, on the first stage of the journey to Moscow. Crossing the Sea of Okhotsk alone took seven hours, and that was scarcely a start. The young woman of 1937 was now fifty. She remembered being ferried to Kolyma in the hold of the S.S. *Dzhurma*, the first prison ship to be used. In 1934, on its maiden voyage, it had been caught in the autumn ice and all twelve thousand *zeks* under hatches perished—a scene beyond imagination, even in the Gulag. On a later voyage, the prisoners burned to death in a fire; another time, several hundred girl prisoners, condemned for absenteeism from work, were subjected to mass rape by criminals. Between then and now, Ginzburg had endured all but the worst rigors (those belonged to the gold miners) of

Kolyma, a complex four times the area of France. Outside work, in star-vation rations, was obligatory if the temperature was above fifty below. For two months of the year the sun did not rise at all. In 1937–41 alone there were at least a million deaths.[6]

Having survived by some miracle, Yevgenia Ginzburg "remembered my first flight over the Sea of Okhotsk as a rare moment of illumination, when my soul was truly thankful for every blade of grass in the field and every star in the sky. . . . My whole being was not merely receptive but wide open to the cotton-wool clouds, the iridescent air stream. . . . I was eager to wel-come things half-forgotten, longed for, glimpsed at a distance in dreams—to welcome what we call *life*." When they had passed the Urals, trees, mead-ows, birds, the color of the sky—flashed into her memory and became real simultaneously, bringing a sweet, searing pain to her chest.

Home at last, she was moved by an encounter in a restaurant, where she and three other "grey beards" passed the time while awaiting rehabilitation documents. They talked so excitedly that three students at the next table started to pay keen attention. One of them got to his feet, came across and asked them, with a similar excitement: "Are you from there? From exile? Please forgive me, it's not just idle curiosity."

"Yes, we're from 'those' places. Very remote ones. Victims of thirty-seven."

Shattered by this encounter, the students sat for a time saying nothing, staring as though at ghosts. Then a girl said, "Just one moment," and rushed for the door. She came back carrying two bunches of gladioli wrapped in cellophane. She held them out to Yevgenia and the other woman present. The girl's eyes were full of tears, and even one of the men students had eyes that glistened.

"We were not heroes, only victims."

"You had the courage to endure."

Yevgenia was warmed by their sympathy. The young still had good hearts, it seemed.[7]

Sanya, informed in April 1956 that his sentence was annulled, finished the school year and sold his house. On 20 June he said good-bye to the Zubovs and other friends and took the train. He too felt overwhelmed on reaching the heart of Russia; though presumably without the dreamlike surreality that came with a return after almost twenty years. But as the train left behind the dusty steppe, crossing the Volga, and he gazed out at the Russian landscape from an open platform, tears streamed from his eyes.[8]

Certainly he did not share Ginzburg's "foolish euphoria"—as she herself termed it in her memoir—of believing this was the end of repression. In *The Gulag Archipelago* he praises her accurate memory but shows no mercy toward her—and her kind's—credulity in 1937. Most of her Stolypin trans-port to Siberia had consisted of similar zealous women Communists. At the Sverdlovsk transit prison baths they were driven naked between ranks of guards. Because they were unmolested, they spent the next stage of their journey singing with undiminished zest: "I know no other country/Where a person breathes so freely. . . ."

He points out too that these privileged men and women of the 1937 vintage were still very decent in clothes and manners as they were herded east. They were being sent to join the miserable remnants of their own victims of the early thirties, when many of them had been a part of Stalin's "shock brigade" to liquidate the kulaks. "The collective farmers and ordinary inmates had eyes and they immediately recognised the people who had carried out the monstrous cattle drive of 'collectivisation.' "9

But even if the great mid-fifties return home of the *zeks* had been, indeed—to quote Ginzburg's naive chapter title, which she was honest enough to keep in—"Before the dawn," no one could give back, to Solzhenitsyn or the voiceless millions, the life they had lost; the wives or husbands, the parents and children: including the children never born.

The whole empire was a graveyard. . . . From the permafrost and the slave ships of Kolyma to the shifting western border—Katyn, for instance, where the Polish officers had been killed, supposedly victims of the Nazis. Nothing disturbed, even after Khrushchev's speech, the even grimmer pine forest of Kuropaty outside Minsk. Here, where Solzhenitsyn's wartime sergeant, Ilya Solomin, lost his entire family to the Nazis, mass execution long predated Hitler. . . . From 1937 till the very day the Nazis started bombing Minsk, men and women were brought every day by lorry, lined up at the edge of deep graves, then shot in the back of the head. Some quarter of a million were shot at Kuropaty—and there were seven other killing fields around Minsk alone. . . .

Can these bones live?

25

In Search of Time Past

Hide, as with winter's ice, the streams
Of your emotions and your dreams. . . .
—Tyutchev, "Silentium"

That June in which Sanya arrived by train at the Kazan station in Moscow, Natasha had traveled south to collect the younger of her stepsons. Boris Somov was twelve; following his mother's death he had been cared for by relatives in southern Russia, and so Natasha was not close to him as she was to his elder brother, Sergei. Boris was only now beginning to call her Mama. In order to get to know him better, and to give him a treat, she took him on steamer trips up the Don and Volga to Moscow.

While they were sailing on the broad Volga, with grating music blaring over loudspeakers that made Natasha wish she could borrow Vsevolod's deafness, she was confirming in her mind her recent decision to marry him formally. The legality would give his two sons a real mother again.

Yes, she thought, as Boris did not flinch away from her arm round his shoulder—it's the right thing to do. . . . A weight fell from her.

Arriving in Moscow, they went to Lydia Ezherets, with whom they were to stay. After they had chatted awhile, Natasha went to phone Yevgeniya Panin, to arrange to meet. Natasha had forewarned her of her arrival with a postcard. Yevgeniya sounded ebullient—her husband had come back to Moscow and to her. Her voice softened: "Natasha, Sanya is here; he arrived two days ago. He wants to see you."[1]

That evening Natasha walked to the Panins' place on Deviatinsky Lane. She found it hard to climb the stairs, her legs like jelly. Yevgeniya met her at the door, and led her to Sanya. He was sitting at a round table with Panin, drinking tea. Both men stood up. The Panins soon left the room, and suddenly she and Sanya were talking. Although there were no guards present, it was as though they were again in the Butyrki meeting room, and he in his ill-fitting borrowed suit.

He was even thinner and paler than he had been then; and he had a yellowish tinge to his face, caused by the radiation treatment. To him, she seemed a trifle plumper, more staid and matronly; at thirty-eight, she had turned the corner into middle age.

After an hour or so he escorted her back to Lydia's, his hand under her elbow. It came on to rain, and they stopped to shelter in a porch, as so often they had done in their youth. They were suddenly very close, his face almost touching her wet, fragrant hair. He started to ask her why she had left him, with only a year to wait.

She mumbled, and turned her head away. She felt as if the past and the present were as confused as her own thoughts at that moment. Swallowing her words she managed to say shakily: "I was created to love you alone, but fate decreed otherwise."

"Not fate—a scoundrel who took advantage of you."

"He's not a scoundrel, Sanya; he's a kind man."

The rain easing, they walked on. "Will you come in to meet Lydia?"

"Another time. She'll understand."

He pulled out from his tattered army greatcoat a roll of paper, and thrust it at her. "Some poems. Please read them."

In the overheated apartment she did so at once. They were a lyrical sequence in her, Natasha's, voice, addressing her husband in the Gulag. The poetic letters spanned a year. The imagined Natasha asks him, at the onset of the first New Year, to remember that however hard his fate it will not be eternal. . . . "At the end of the road is your home,/And waiting for you there with love/Is your—always your—wife. . . ." *February* brings doubt, as she relates how she busies herself, yet life is senseless; she needs a hug from him, she is being told her beauty is fading; but "How can I look young, without you?/And you—won't you stop loving me?"

In *March* she reflects how she doesn't need the freedom he keeps offering her. *April* brings a brief lifting of spirits on their wedding anniversary. Ten years they have been married—nine of them apart. *July* tries to explain why she has not written for a long time. . . . "My dear, I persevered for a long, long time!/But now, I've no strength left. . . ." She laments the "Years, years, years apart. . . ." "Love me, love me!" she pleads; "I can't go on alone!/Understand, I need/Help, friendship, I don't know whose. . . ."

August is another poem of aching loneliness. He is never with her, though he is inside her; when she receives a letter from him she feels joy, and wants to write back; but knows that her page will be pawed by a censor, searching for an incriminating phrase or something to snigger at. The torn-off, damp leaves underfoot, in *October*, remind her of all the leaves of the calendar, damp with her tears, that she has torn off. Once, these had been bright, like the fallen leaves in the park; now, both the leaves of autumn and of the calendar are blown by an aimless gale, at random. Still, though she has come home wet through, she has sat immediately at the table to write to him, without changing her clothes.

It is New Year's Eve again in the second *December*. She will enjoy herself at a party, but in a coldhearted, indifferent spirit. "At midnight, hiding my lips in a glass,/I whisper, incomprehensibly to others:/'My love, we have waited a long time!/Less is left to wait, less is left for us to wait. . . . ' "[2]

The poems, on top of their meeting, affected her deeply. The last verse of the opening poem, in particular, tormented her conscience by its depiction of the ever-faithful wife waiting with love at home; yet later poems touched her heart by showing he was capable of compassionate understanding of her vulnerable, lonely situation.

The next morning, she tried to get the overwhelming impressions of the previous night out of her mind, deliberately doing everything at high speed. She told Lydia the meeting, and his poems, had opened up old wounds.

Arriving home in Ryazan, she found the self-confidence to say to Vsevolod, when they were sitting quietly together: "By the way, I met Sanya at Yevgeniya's."

Somov looked up sharply from his book.

"Nothing has changed because of it, Volodya," she assured him firmly.

As the days passed, however, she felt increasingly disturbed and conscience stricken: "quite simply"—life wasn't simple anymore.

Sanya revisited other ghosts from his past. The most sinister was the Lubyanka. He was seeking a full rehabilitation; from the KGB's information department on Kuznetsky Most, where Natalya and innumerable other wives had learned of their husbands' arrest, he had been led by an affable officer, dressed in civilian clothes, through the monotonous and terrifyingly familiar corridors of the prison, to his office. "You say you had Yezepov?" asked the man, on gesturing him to sit. "What a brute! He's been demoted. I was in counterespionage; we didn't have people like that."[3]

Looking through the file of letters that had incriminated Solzhenitsyn, the investigator laughed at some of the jokes about Stalin, praised the wartime stories: why not even try to get them published? . . . While viewing the friendly bureaucrat with caution—telling him, for example, that he had long since abandoned literature for teaching and had no interest in publishing his stories—Sanya came away convinced there had been a real change. Kopelev, indeed, was talking about the likelihood of there being a second Party, beside the Communists.

Soon after his arrival in Moscow, Sanya retraced, in more comfortable circumstances, the first part of the *zeks*' journey to Siberia. For the past year in Kok Terek, through the matchmaking auspices of Elena Zubov, he had been corresponding with her niece Natasha, a student living with her mother in the Urals. Sanya now spent two weeks with her and her mother; found the girl attractive, and proposed marriage. Natasha hesitated, though—frightened by such an importunate courtship; she promised to think about his proposal, and write him her answer. Then, she would come and visit him in Moscow, when they would decide what to do.

While Natasha-from-the-Urals was deliberating, he went in search of his southern roots. In Rostov he visited his ex-wife's aunt Nina to thank her for so faithfully sending parcels; and visited also his first Rostov home, the shack close to the lowering KGB building. The atmosphere in Rostov, he felt, was still oppressive by comparison with Moscow; Khrushchev's "secret speech" was here truly a well-guarded secret from all but a few. Sanya visited the ruins of the converted stables into which he and his mother had moved; the German bomb, he was told, had left his map of the world still hanging on the one standing, exposed wall.

He visited Taganrog, on the Black Sea, and found Vitkevich. Nikolai was surviving with difficulty by giving private mathematics lessons, while studying for a doctorate in chemistry. It infuriated him that Sanya had drawn attention to him again by seeking rehabilitation; he himself was quite content to stay in quiet Taganrog.

Sanya traveled into the Caucasus, to Georgievsk, where both his father and mother had died. He found his old aunts, Irina and Maria, with Maria's second husband, living in the small adobe house bought in 1924. Irina, so important to him in his childhood, lived in a tiny annex, surrounded by cats, whom she regarded as sacred animals. People were always bringing maimed cats to add to her brood. She still seemed utterly eccentric, but not in the aristocrat pistol-toting style of her youth; Roman's widow was living in squalor. Overwhelmed at seeing her beloved nephew again, Irina took him to the grave to which his mother had followed Roman within a fortnight. Sanya stood there a long time, thinking of his mother's carefree youth; her sparkling hopes; her early sorrow; her sad later life, sacrificing everything for him.

He promised to help Aunt Irina with a regular sum of money to supplement her meager pension; and asked her to write down an account of the Shcherbak family as she remembered it.

Impossible to find his father's grave, in a cemetery long since buried under a sports stadium. Reaching Kislovodsk, he managed to visit his baptismal church—St. Panteleimon—only a year before it too was to be demolished in the name of progress and Khrushchevian atheism. It was the feast of the ascension of St. Panteleimon, and the church was crowded: as it had been in his infancy when, held up high by his mama, he saw advancing through the hushed throng mounted troops he somehow knew bore them no goodwill: Budenny's Red cavalry.

When he returned to Moscow, he lived for a time with the Panins. The answer from Natasha-of-the-Urals was no: she was too young, wished to complete her studies. Natasha, his former wife, wrote him saying she loved him, and couldn't imagine how she could live without him. He wondered if this was just a passing mood.

But Natasha couldn't sleep, couldn't eat. The image in his poems about his wife waiting at home, at the end of the road, haunted and troubled her. Her new, unofficial husband, Somov, could see Natasha was drawing away from him, while swearing that her feelings were unchanged. Worried, he persuaded her to go on a boat trip along the Oka (they had their own motor boat). They spent August in a forest resort; but nothing could distract her from her turbulent thoughts; nor, when they arrived home, could her conscience prevent her from a surge of pleasure on seeing familiar handwriting on an envelope. "If you have the inclination, and should you find it possible—you can write me. My address, as of August 21, is . . . Vladimir Region."[4]

Lydia Ezherets advised her not to write back. Lydia knew all about unhappiness and change. There had been the shock of discovering Kirill's homosexuality, and the subsequent divorce. Her distinguished medical father, who had pulled a few strings after the war to obtain much-needed medicines for his patients, had been accused of speculation, and sentenced to twenty-five years in labor camps: in one of which he had died. She herself, as a Jew, had become tainted during the last years of Stalin's life, and prevented from teaching in Moscow. Forced to find posts in provincial towns, including Ryazan, she had got to know Natasha's new family quite well, and liked them. She did not want to see them hurt.

"It will be all right, Lydia; truly!" Natasha assured her. But then she burst into tears. Lydia held her and soothed her. Well, she had better sort her feelings out, one way or the other.

Natasha buried herself in her teaching and her piano playing. Music alone was able to console her. Though not for long—she had to steel herself to smile reassuringly when Somov's worried, haunted face appeared in the doorway. Miserably, later, he watched her picking at her food; the flesh was dropping off her.

Sanya had found a teaching post in the settlement of Torfoprodukt (Peat-produce), 130 miles east of Moscow. He had startled an education officer in Moscow by saying he wanted a post, not in a large city as was invariably sought, but in the wilds. Exploring several possibilities, he had found many picturesque places that were too remote even for his taste. Torfoprodukt had the advantage of being on the main Moscow–Kazan railroad. In all other respects it was singularly unappealing. Just as its name did violence to the Russian language, so its physical appearance was a desecration of the landscape. Where a dense forest had once stood was now a scarred desert of peat workings, a few drab 1930s huts and 1950-style glass-verandaed cottages surrounded a vast factory belching black smoke. A narrow-gauge track ran from the workings to the factory, and thence to the station. A workers' club blared music from a radiogram all day, and men staggered about in a vodka haze.

Fortunately, just over a hill, Sanya had stumbled on a peaceful hamlet called Miltsevo. A kindly market woman led him round the hamlet, trying to find him a place to stay; at last, with a sigh, she said, "We'd better try Matryona; only her place isn't well kept, on account of she's so sick."

The house had a steep shingle roof with an elaborately ornamental dormer window; four windows looked out onto the side where the sun never shone. The roof timbers were rotting. But nearby was a charming, typically Russian scene, as attractive as any in Miltsevo: a dammed-up stream under a bridge, two or three willows, a duck pond. His guide undid the latch and let them in. A woman nearing sixty lay prone on the stove, without a pillow. Her round face looked yellow and ill. Sanya saw flowerpots and tubs of fig plants on stools and benches.

She discouraged him from staying with her, saying, as she looked up at him from the stove, he would find more comfortable accommodation else-where; when her illness struck she was laid low for two or three days, and could do nothing for him. Even when she was well—"Don't expect any fancy cooking. . . ." To please her, he went off to try elsewhere, but came back; and this time found her up and about, and with something like a glint of pleasure in her eye at seeing him again.

He had settled in with her during the holiday months. They slept in the same room: she in a bed near the stove (which proved to be much more efficient at warming than at cooking), and he on a camp bed near the window. Over him he pulled his quilted gulag jacket. They shared the house with a lame cat, numerous mice, and innumerable cockroaches. Rising at four or five in the morning, Matryona would go outside to milk the goat, her only livestock; then she would go down to the cellar to pick out some small potatoes for their breakfast. Potatoes and barley, morning and eve-ning, were practically the only food. She had no pension, and the soil was poor.

Quickly she won his respect and affection by her simplicity, her courteous incuriosity about him, her total absence of insincerity, her refusal to moan, her quiet, hardworking courage. She had lost all six of her children early, one after another; never had there been more than one alive at any time. Though she struck him as more pagan than Christian, she lit the icon lamp on feast days and feast-day eves. For all her sufferings and hardships, she could disarm Sanya with a dazzling smile. He could put up with finding hairs, lumps of peat, or cockroach legs in his "tatie" soup.

In September he began to teach. Part of his annual salary was a lorry load of peat, which he gave to Matryona. He felt it should have been enough to see them through the winter, but she still went off with a sack under her arm, to dig up some for herself. Work was her infallible antidote against depression; and this too appealed to him.

He and his ex-wife continued to correspond, and with increasing warmth. Sanya wrote to tell her he was astonished at the shift in his feelings toward her during these two months, and had started to reflect that perhaps a new happiness was possible. He had forgiven her completely. Might they meet, so that they could sort out their feelings for one another? Since it was she who had ended their marriage, he thought she should take the initiative by coming to him; he suggested a three-day visit.

On a Friday evening in October, when Vsevolod was in Odessa at a

ceremony honoring a fellow professor, Natasha took the train to Torfoprodukt. Sanya, dressed in a brown overcoat and gray hat, was waiting for her
at the drab, rundown station.[5] He caught his breath on seeing her step out
of the train: she looked young again! Slimmer! Her whole face was aglow,
as in their youth!

"My God, Natasha! What's happened to you? You look marvelous!"

They walked on a lonely road across the steppe toward Miltsevo. "Over-
head the moon shone bright as ever. We stopped in the shadow of a neatly
formed haystack and kissed each other passionately. My head was thrown
back under the weight of his kisses and, as used to happen when we were
younger, my pretty brown hat with the tiny feathers tumbled to the ground.
Everything, everything came back at once. There was no need for words to
feel this, to understand, to believe in this passionate resurrection of an old
love."[6]

"But I still can't believe it. . . . How did you manage, since we last met,
to lose so much weight, to look younger and more beautiful?" he demanded.

Beyond everything—the lost appetite, the softer hair, the apricot-colored
crepe de chine blouse cut in his favorite style—it was the inner glow that
came from love, she knew; and, however sad it made her feel over Vsevolod
and her stepsons, this surely could not and *should* not be lost again.

She was introduced to Matryona, and was moved by her tact and discre-
tion. The peasant woman left them alone most of the time, and did not ask
any questions. Natasha eventually told her their story, and Matryona responded by relating her own unhappy love story. How the young man she
had loved and courted had not returned from the war of 1914, and even
tually she had agreed to marry his younger brother. Then her lost love had
turned up, having been a prisoner of war. . . . Matryona's yearning expression must have added to Natasha's conviction that she should follow the
dictates of her heart.

Sunday, 21 October 1956, was the name day of Sanya's mother, and they
felt, according to Natasha's account, inseparably close. Perhaps on this day
they made love for the first time in twelve years; in any event, they would
celebrate this date as marking their reunion. He wished her to leave Vsevolod, but warned her he was seriously and hopelessly ill, having a life
expectancy of only a year or two. "I need you in every way," she said: "alive
or dying." She would make the last years of his life beautiful, ease his
sufferings—or even give him the will to go on living.

From a remark she made to Veronica, her cousin, he had the stronger
doubts: "Ah, Veronica, how hard I had to work to win him back!"[7]

She still shrank from telling Vsevolod. She and Sanya corresponded, and
two or three times she revisited Matryona's house, their love burning more
intensely each time—at least in Natasha's memory. His warning to her now
was that she would have to subject herself to the same disciplined life that
he imposed on himself, for the sake of his writing. She did not mind that,
almost welcomed the chance to sacrifice and atone, was already poring over

the tiny spidery handwriting of the novel he was writing. It thrilled her that she was an important character in it as the wife of the prisoner-hero, Ner-·zhin.

He also gave her one of his plays to read. Noticing it was dedicated to Anya Breslavskaya, she inquired who she was. He told her. "We had an affair. It was the only one."

Natasha burst into tears.

"Don't cry. It was for the best. Do you think I could have forgiven you if *I* hadn't sinned?" And soon he was kissing away her tears.

At last she nerved herself to tell Vsevolod she was going back to Sanya. Vsevolod took the news badly. She knew she was causing him and his children enormous sorrow, but hardened herself to be cruel. Others could be harsh too: she endured the attacks of friends and colleagues. Nor did her mother approve; though Vsevolod lost some of Maria's support when he haggled over the division of their modest possessions. He moved out in November, into an apartment on Svoboda (Freedom) Street.

Among the most sympathetic to him of their mutual friends was Lydia Ezherets. He cried on her shoulder, perhaps literally—and they were to marry with bewildering speed.

Sanya paid his first visit to Ryazan on 30 December 1956. The next day they strolled around the town, oblivious to the bitterly cold weather. Calling at the civil registry, they found they could not immediately register their marriage since his passport contained no record of a divorce from her. They needed to go to Moscow, where notification of the divorce was dug up from the archives of the city court. Then Sanya returned to Torfoprodukt.

On 2 February their divorce was annulled, and on 6 February a military tribunal of the Supreme Court took the decision to annul the criminal charges that had led him to the labor camps. The decision was based on written evidence from former military colleagues, Natasha, Lydia—even Kirill Simonyan wrote supporting Sanya, though he was still refusing to meet him.

Another liberating event, on a later visit to Moscow, was the purchase of a typewriter, a Moskova-4. Natasha taught herself to touch-type, Sanya used two fingers, yet was the speedier in typing up his minuscule writing.

Natasha wrote a letter to her namesake in the Urals, thanking her for not accepting Sanya's proposal of marriage. That refusal, she wrote, was a gift of happiness to her.

There was one sad event. It happened that winter, when Sanya was serving out his teaching year at the Torfoprodukt school.

Widowed and childless after the war, Matryona had adopted her niece, Kira, to ease her loneliness. Kira was the youngest daughter of her "lost" sweetheart; so Matryona could imagine . . . Recently Kira had been married off to a railway worker in a village across the rail track. Unexpectedly the couple had acquired a plot of ground, but could not keep it unless they could build on it right away. Since it would be impossible to get the necessary timber so quickly, Kira's father demanded Matryona's help. She had willed to Kira a self-contained annex to her house: but why wait till then? Let it be dismantled now, and transferred to the new plot. . . . Matryona consented to have her house chopped up. One winter's evening Solzhenitsyn watched as the annex was severed from the rest of the house and loaded onto sleighs. The men were the worse for Matryona's homemade vodka. A tractor roared into action. Asking Sanya not to lock the door when he went to bed, Matryona went off in the wake of the carriers. Her tenant got down to work on his manuscript; wrote to Natasha; undressed, pulled his quilted coat over him, and slept.

In the middle of the night he was woken by loud voices approaching outside. He got up and saw men in uniform. It was unpleasant for a *zek* to be awakened by men in uniform. He learned that a terrible accident had happened. The party transporting the sleighs had been ploughed into by an unlighted train at a level crossing. Two men and Matryona had been killed instantly.

It was three in the morning when Sanya was left alone. He had to teach in a few hours; what could he do but try to sleep? He could lock the door now, Matryona would not be coming back. He lay down, leaving the light on. "The mice were squeaking so hard, it was almost as if they were groaning. They raced tirelessly up and down. My exhausted, confused mind could not throw off an involuntary sense of horror. I had a feeling that Matryona was moving about, bidding farewell to her home. . . ."[8]

The final tragic act of her life had occurred during the few months when her house sheltered a writer. A writer working in secret; one who deeply admired her; one who would be able to create out of the seeming poverty and hardship of her existence a brilliant and flawless work of art, his later story "Matryona's House"—scarcely needing to divert one iota from the reality.

After attending Matryona's funeral and wake, Solzhenitsyn moved in with one of her sisters-in-law, and was able to observe the greed, which had led up to the tragedy, show itself all the more nakedly as people fought over the dead woman's possessions.

He himself was preparing to merge his few possessions with those of Natasha. His move to Ryazan came at the end of the school year, in June. But first they spent some time in Moscow, visiting her relatives the Turkins: mother and daughter, the two Veronicas. The younger, who at the time of their marriage in 1940 had thought them a straitlaced provincial couple, and Sanya too self-absorbed to notice a pigtailed schoolgirl, had nevertheless treated him with kindness following his return from exile; she had written to him to say he was always welcome at Malaya Bronnaya Street. Solzhenitsyn had been touched by her letter and replied warmly. However, he had not felt able to take up the invitation until he and Natasha had become reunited.

The pigtailed schoolgirl, now in her thirties, married to her second husband, Yuri Stein, and with a two-year-old daughter—how life could move on if you weren't a *zek*—found Sanya gentle, serious, slow moving (the *zek*'s deliberate movements), and far more aged than she had expected. His hair was dull, his eyes lusterless. She sensed however that he had a new, steely strength underneath the gentleness, and she liked this Sanya much more than the arrogant newlywed of 1940. As for Natasha, she was bubbling over with happiness, it was clear—she simply could not do enough for her husband. It was like first love, the love that Turgenev believed "cannot and perhaps should not be repeated" . . . But Natasha was repeating it.

Indeed, how similar it all was, in a sense, to their first marriage! A sort of second honeymoon with the Turkins in Moscow, then starting to live together, with Natasha's mother, Maria, an important presence, as she had been the first time round. He immediately set to work brightening up the apartment with fresh paint and rewiring, using his camp experience. In so doing, and in changing the sleeping arrangements, he may have partly exorcised the ghost of Vsevolod Somov. Natasha may have been far more conscious of the accusing ghosts of Vsevolod's sons. With eighteen-year-old Sergei she had forged a sufficiently strong bond for their closeness to survive; Boris, however, had to unlearn a role he had only just begun to grow into.

Sanya and Natasha slept in the smaller of the two first-floor rooms comprising the apartment. Apart from the bed and a bedside table, the ten-foot-square room somehow also accommodated a spacious, impressive-looking desk for him and a small antique one for her. The walls were lined with bookshelves. Maria lived in a corner of the larger room, which also served as living and dining room. The kitchen and toilet were shared with their neighbors, two teachers of gymnastics. Though the apartment windows were overlooked in all directions by high buildings, the countryside was close, and there was a very pleasant, quiet backyard in which Sanya set up a table and bench under a shady apple tree. It was at this time that he wrote his prose poem "Freedom to Breathe": the first of many such pieces as he and Natasha began to explore the countryside.

"I don't remember ever having had such living conditions in all my life," he wrote to the Zubovs. Compared with the shacks of Rostov, army bivouacs, prisons, the camps, Kazakhstan's adobe huts, and Matryona's cockroach-infested home, this comfortable wooden house was indeed palatial. The photographs they took point unmistakably to his happiness with Natasha; he told the Zubovs in a letter: "Natushka and I are bound indissolubly to one another"; they meant all the more to each other, he wrote, in that they had no children; yet he had absolutely no regrets over their childlessness.

Having had a benign tumor removed, Natasha could no longer have children; Sanya had been told his cancer treatment had almost certainly made him infertile; pregnancy was impossible, and this may have allowed them to have freer sexual relations than early in their married life. Natasha hints that their sexual life was much better; and Sanya's letter to the Zubovs supports her belief that these years were happy for both of them.

Later, in less harmonious times, he would tell Kopelev the main reason for his going back to her was that she was "the only woman he could trust."[9] This is not exactly rearranging past reality—like the Soviet encyclopedist who replaced Beria with Bering Strait for a revised edition—but seems too dismissive of the part that love played. And one wonders if Natasha knew that her main attraction had been her trustworthiness.

But he *had* warned her, clearly enough, that their life would be quiet, with few entertainments, and that she must become docile. Before their remarriage he had given her Chekhov's short story "The Darling" to read—as apparently he had done with all his prospective wives. It depicts a woman who allows her life and character to be totally subjected to the will of her two successive husbands; and when the second dies, strives to serve in the same way her lodger's son. Chekhov's story is satirical, but Solzhenitsyn, agreeing with Tolstoy's approval of "the darling," took it in earnest, and told all his friends she was his ideal wife.

He wished his particular darling to give up most of the friendships she had made jointly with Vsevolod, and she complied. Even books, it seemed, might distract her from the task of helping him with his work. In the first months of their life in Ryazan, he was questioning her about her life in the Moscow hostel with her girlfriends while he had been in the *sharashka*, and also pored over her diaries of that time. In the second draft of what became *The First Circle* he completely changed his account of Nadia Nerzhin's life "outside."

In September 1957 he started to teach physics and astronomy at Ryazan's High School No. 2. The headmaster, Georgi Matveyev, had been totally won over by learning that Alexander Isayevich had served on the same wartime front. He soon realized he had hired a truly brilliant teacher. Once, he dropped in on his class, and became so fascinated by the lesson that he stayed till the end, completely forgetting why he had come. Solzhenitsyn showed so much energy and enthusiasm that we might wonder if this was the same man who struck Veronica Stein as listless, slow moving, and prematurely aged.

And when the day was over, his real work began. Each night, the rough drafts had to be burned, leaf by leaf, in the stove. Since this was in the communal kitchen, he and Natasha had to wait up late, till their neighbors, the gymnasts, had gone to bed.

Natasha, who still taught chemistry at the Agricultural Institute and earned a good salary—so allowing Sanya to teach for progressively fewer hours—also began to see the absorbed evenings in their shared study-bedroom as her real life. "After all, I loved my husband, I believed in him as a significant and extraordinary personality, and I wanted everything to be as he thought necessary. Totally aware of what I was doing, and acting completely of my own free will, I let myself dissolve in his personality. It was with utmost sincerity that I promised him to be 'a little darling.'" Imperceptibly an "impoverishment" in her life set in; yet she was for a long time unaware of it, since she had "a great deal of joy at home."[10]

Solzhenitsyn was no doubt recalling Natasha's self-abnegation when, in *August 1914*, Colonel Vorotyntsev asks himself remorsefully why he had been glad to leave his wife, Alina. For "he suddenly remembered how in Petersburg she had cleaned every speck of dust from his desk without moving a single pencil; how she had kept silent for hours, moving past his room without a sound when there was a special need for quiet; how, though she loved having company at home and visiting friends, she had refused invitations and had never begged to go out, so as not to let him see how disappointed she was. Suddenly he remembered everything good about her. . . ."[11]

Petersburg/Leningrad was the couple's destination in summer 1958; for Sanya it was his first visit. Meticulously they prepared card indexes beforehand on its history, art, and architecture, and consulted them earnestly during the six weeks of their visit. It was a kind of celebration of recovered health: he had suffered a relapse, and had had to go into hospital in the spring for two weeks of chemotherapy followed by outpatient treatment. He also continued to take mandrake root and another folk medicine, a birch fungus. Though by the summer he was feeling wonderfully well, for how long could he survive? Natasha, at his urging, had read up in the Lenin Library about his type of cancer, and predicted he might live another four years.

In that light, what courage and discipline he showed in his writing! And it is easy to understand her eagerness to serve him. She loved making small contributions to his book: giving him the name Mavrino for Marfino, Rubin (instead of his Tolstoyan "Levin") for Kopelev. And one day, in a rare hour of pure diversion on an ice rink, they were circling each other in slow, contrary circles, and she was musing about the book's title. He planned to call it *In the First Circle of Hell,* but that seemed cumbersome. The solution came to her in a skate's flash; and when they next glided toward each other she stopped him, placing her arms on his chest and saying, "Sanya, why don't you call it just *V'Kruge Pervom (In the First Circle)*?" He was thoughtful for a moment; then, resting his hands on her shoulders, smiled. "Perfect!"

His close friends of that First Circle were on the move domestically. Kopelev left his wife, Nadezhda, who had been another Marfino faithful, and married Raisa Orlova, once-fervent Communist and future dissident. Panin, who visited Ryazan and read the novel in which, as Sologdin, he appears, left Yevgeniya. Having converted to Catholicism, he had tried to browbeat his wife and their adolescent Komsomol son into doing likewise; the atmosphere had become poisoned. He left Yevgeniya a "letter of consolation" saying he loved her more than any other woman and wished to spend the rest of his life in a monastery. Instead, he married Issa Guinzberg, a Jew, and was allowed to emigrate with her to Paris in 1972.

I am reminded of a patient of Freud's who, discussing her middle-aged marriage, said, "When one of us dies, I shall move to Paris."

For the women outside the Gulag, it was not always wise to wait.

But for Natasha, who hadn't waited, life was brimming over. On the first October anniversary of their reunion, Sanya and his wife enjoyed a quiet evening, celebrating with a glass of light wine. Her diary records: "I am even frightened sometimes for our happiness, it's so complete!"

Their road, Kasimovsky Lane, was becoming less congenial, however. The yard of the Radio Institute next door was asphalted over and became used as a testing ground for motorcycles, while across the street a food warehouse was established, so that heavy lorries were constantly arriving or leaving. Indoors, however, there was an improvement. The two gymnastics teachers moved out, and Natasha's aunts, Nina and Manya, were invited to exchange their Rostov apartment for this accommodation. This they agreed to do, since they were getting too old to manage on their own. With their arrival there was no longer any need to wait till night to burn manuscripts. Maria continued to shop, clean, and cook, helped by Nina and Manya. In Natasha's hands was the autumn pickling and marinating; jars of cucumbers, tomatoes, plums stood in the cellar ready for the long winter. And Sanya, as he loved doing, swung the ax to chop up wood.

The house, naturally, revolved around him. So had the very first house of his life, in Kislovodsk—Mama, Aunt Maria, Aunt Irina, and Granny, all gazing down at him with anguished love. It was not uncongenial to be the object of so much caring.

And if, inevitably, the old women irritated him with their gossiping, it became all the more urgent to turn inward, into himself, into secrecy. He liked to shut the door on their female concerns, then feel the hairs at his nape stir as he confronted the virginal page. The difficulty of doing so, with so many competing claims on his time—not to mention the KGB—created an almost unbearable, and hugely creative, tension. In the words of Tyutchev's "Silentium," one of his favorite poems: "Know how to live within yourself. . . . Be silent, hide yourself. . . ." Hide your real self, even from those closest, as a zek conceals a broken razor blade in his sleeve.

26

D e a t h   o f   a   P o e t

He has turned into the life-giving ear of grain
Or into the gentlest rain of which he sang. . . .
—AKHMATOVA

DURING THE SUMMER OF 1959, WHEN THE SOLZHENITSYNS VISITED
Rostov to help the old aunts pack up a lifetime's possessions, they took the
chance to meet old friends. Vitkevich, who had got married, was back in
Rostov, working in the university chemistry department while completing
his Ph.D. dissertation. Natasha describes their meeting as the most important of many "joyous and heartwarming reunions" which made her and
Sanya feel young again. She felt proud and joyful to show friends from
prewar that they were reunited and very happy. Toward Nikolai she always
felt indulgent, but Sanya, on this visit, reacted differently to him, though
she does not seem to have noticed. What roused Solzhenitsyn's ire was a
discussion about Pasternak.

The Nobel Award, announced in October 1958, following the publication
in the West of *Doctor Zhivago*, had given rise to a vitriolic campaign against
him. *Pravda* had begun it, calling the novel "low-grade reactionary hackwork"; its author was "a weed" in the garden of socialism. The following
day, the Writers' Union voted to expel him. Vladimir Semichastny, Komsomol first secretary, compared Pasternak unfavorably with a pig, since he
had "fouled the spot where he ate and cast filth on those by whose labor
he lives and breathes." Pasternak renounced the prize, but the abuse did
not let up. It was suggested he might prefer to live abroad with his capitalist
toadies. Pasternak was nearly seventy and not in good health; the abuse
distressed him acutely. His mistress, Olga Ivinskaya, fearing a heart attack
or even suicide, persuaded him to write a letter to Khrushchev pleading to
be allowed to stay in Russia, since separation from it would be death.

Western authors and intellectuals, even those sympathetic to the Soviet
Union, protested strongly on Pasternak's behalf. Khrushchev would later
regret he had not permitted the novel to be published; yet, even though

Doctor Zhivago was not, as many in the West pointed out, overtly political, the Soviets were right in seeing it as a mortal enemy. Every page asserted a fidelity to something infinitely greater and more truthful than *any* political system, let alone a creed built on millions of deaths, slave labor, and a dead and meaningless language.

It appears that, during their Rostov meeting of summer 1959, Sanya expressed his disgust over the campaign against Pasternak, expecting Nikolai to agree. To Sanya's surprise, Vitkevich "didn't want to hear about it. 'Never mind about all that rot. Just let me tell you about the *fight I'm having* in my department!' (He was always locking horns with somebody, looking for promotion.) Yet the tribunal had thought him worth ten years in the camps. Perhaps one good flogging was all he deserved?"[1] This was how *The Gulag Archipelago* reported the exchange, no doubt one-sidedly; though Vitkevich was not named. The coarseness of the passage may reflect a later falling-out; perhaps at the time there was only a passing irritation on Sanya's part, unnoticed by Natasha.

Understandably Solzhenitsyn felt angry with ex-*zeks* who tried to forget their suffering. Such as "the old Leningrad Bolshevik Vasilyev. He had done two tenners, each with a five-year 'muzzle' (deprivation of civil rights). He was given a special pension by the republic. 'I am fully provided for. All praise to my Party and my people.' (Wonderful words: there has been nothing like this since Job glorified God: for his sores, the loss of his cattle, the famine, the deaths of his children, his humiliations—blessed be Thy name!) But he is no loafer, this Vasilyev, no mere passenger: 'I am a member of a commission for combating parasitism.' In other words, he putters away as far as his aging powers permit, contributing to one of the worst legal abuses of the day. There you see it—the face of Righteousness! . . ."[2] This is Solzhenitsyn at his merciless and inventive best.

The first idea of, and research for, *The Gulag Archipelago* occurred in the annus mirabilis of 1959; though he set it aside for the time being. After finishing a third draft of *The First Circle* he wrote, in just six weeks of May and June, the first draft of a short novel about life in a labor camp.

Then, during an unusually relaxing holiday in the Crimea, he began to write the story of Matryona Zakharova: that (unlike Vasilyev) truly righteous person. Indeed, his provisional title was based on a Russian proverb: "Without a Righteous Person No Village Can Stand." He put it aside after a few days; but a year later Matryona would return and he would write the story.

The Solzhenitsyns had traveled west from Rostov to the Crimea to meet up with the Zubovs. Sanya's close friends and confidants had been released from exile, and now lived in what proved to be a very bleak coastal spot called Ak-Mechet. In its sun-scorched bleakness it was actually little different from Kok Terek, and Sanya joked to them that it was simply Kok Terek next to a sea dug out by Komsomol enthusiasts! Elena was growing prematurely infirm, and was eventually unable to walk to the bench overlooking that sea; but they retained their serene contentment, listening to music and corresponding with friends. Sanya wrote them beautiful letters. They were overjoyed to see him again.

Having read earlier versions of his *sharashka* novel, they were eager to read the "final" version that he brought with him. He did not mention his latest writing, the short work entitled *Shch-854*. Probably this was because he felt he had merely turned it to the wall—as Titian used to say of paintings set aside to "mature." His unusually relaxed two-week Crimean holiday, consisting mostly of swimming, walking, and siestas, suggests he knew he had written something good.

They found hiding places for the novel, and for his plays and verse. "Guardians" were vital. One who proved utterly trustworthy was Natasha's old chemistry professor, Nikolai Kobozev. Constantly ill, in a wheelchair because of bone and spinal problems, he deeply impressed Sanya with his profound mind, as well as his simple Orthodox Christian faith. Kobozev's brother had died in prison; a sister-in-law of that brother agreed to store Solzhenitsyn's manuscripts somewhere far away. "I saw this woman only once and cannot even recall her name but shall always be grateful for what she did. . . . This was the most complete set of my manuscripts in existence. . . . Like a massive stone foundation, it underpinned all my activity by giving me the assurance that my works would survive, whatever might happen to me."[3]

From the beginning of September he began to revise *Shch-854*, completing it six weeks later. The images of Ekibastuz which he had been reliving intensely did not leave him; not for him any temptation to try to forget the Gulag. He has said that for five years he dreamed of nothing but the camps. Every year on the anniversary of his arrest, 9 February, he organized a "*zek*'s day," setting aside for himself the same meager ration of bread, sugary water, broth, and a ladleful of thin mush. By the end of that day he would already be picking up crumbs to put in his mouth, and licking the bowl. How vividly the old sensations sprang up!

He was fully at ease only with former camp inmates; and his eye was quick to see evidence of Gulag activity. At the train station in Ryazan, for example, he spotted a gap in the fence that never got repaired—and realized it was where the Stolypin cars stopped. Black Marias could pull up just outside, to load or unload prisoners, without most rail travelers being aware of it.

He visited the apartment block at Kaluga Gate, climbed to the second floor, and scrawled in black crayon on a white sill: "Labour Camp Division No. 121." On one occasion he endured the irony and torment of being required to give a lecture on physics and space travel to female prisoners at Ryazan's Corrective Labor Colony No. 2. As he walked with the education officer across the yard, shabby, dejected women greeted him obsequiously before he could greet them. While he was being entertained, he knew the women were being bullied into attending. Most of the young women in his audience were as angular and bony as old women, and their coughs, from the dampness of their prison, rasped throughout his lecture. There were also some fresh-looking, well-dressed women, obviously trusties. Their eyes never left him; not because they were interested in the cosmos but because they rarely saw a man. If he rested his gaze on them, and didn't listen to the coughing, he could get through the lecture. He wished he could vanish in smoke. Thank God he would be leaving shortly. . . . "For forty kopecks I shall ride home on the trolley bus and there I shall eat a tasty supper. But I must not forget: they will all be staying here. They will go on coughing like that. Coughing for endless years."[4]

On 30 May 1960 Boris Pasternak died. His funeral was an extraordinary and almost mystical event: perhaps the first indication that the omnipotent state simply could not overcome poetry. The official notice of his death was minimal; and the only advice as to the funeral was a handwritten scrap of paper anonymously posted next to the ticket window at the Kiev Station in Moscow, where passengers for Peredelkino, the writers' colony outside Moscow, bought their tickets. The sign read: "At four o'clock on the afternoon of Thursday, 2 June, the last leavetaking of Boris Leonidovich Pasternak, the greatest poet of present-day Russia, will take place." The sign was several times removed, and as often replaced by an unknown hand.

The Orthodox rites were performed at Pasternak's dacha, quietly, on the eve of the funeral. The next morning four leading pianists—Stanislav Neigauz, Andrei Volkonsky, Marya Yudina (she who had told Stalin he was a great sinner), and Sviatoslav Richter—performed there for several hours. Among the pallbearers who bore the coffin out were Andrei Sinyavsky and Yuli Daniel (later to be persecuted for their dissident writing), and Lev Kopelev. They emerged to a sea of grieving faces—friends, students, workers, and peasants. A Writers' Union official stepped out of a large black limousine and attempted to take charge of the coffin, but the students shouted him down. The people insisted on carrying the coffin to the cemetery.

The windows of the next-door dacha were curtained. The conformist writer Fedin lived there. He had been Pasternak's neighbor for twenty-three years, but for the past four years had not spoken to him. He had been in the forefront of the poet's assailants, while privately he had been known to weep over parts of *Doctor Zhivago*. He was now suffering from flu, it was said. . . . In a few years, Solzhenitsyn would experience his enmity, and would memorably compare his face with Dorian Gray's.

As the coffin was carried out, Kopelev's wife, Raisa Orlova, was standing directly opposite Olga Ivinskaya, and thought her overwhelmingly beautiful in her grief and her "humiliation." She had been prevented from seeing him in his last illness: but perhaps at Boris's behest, not his wife's, since he wished her not to remember him looking "a fright" without his dentures. Into old age he had retained a childlike beauty. In death, according to Orlova, "he was very handsome in the coffin, statuesque and with a resemblance to Dante."[5] Orlova observes that in Pushkin's Leningrad apartment there is a drawing of Pushkin in his coffin, drawn by the artist Bruni, while in Moscow there is a drawing of Pasternak in his coffin, drawn by the artist Bruni, a descendant. Russian writers are a close-knit family. . . .

There were plainclothes agents pretending to mourn, while eavesdropping and clicking their cameras; and there were foreign journalists just doing a job. All the rest of the four or five thousand crowding into Peredelkino's cemetery were there out of respect and love. Someone shouted: "He loved the workers." Another cry: "He spoke the truth." Yet another: "The poet was killed." (*Poét byl ubít!*) And the crowd responded: "Shame! Shame! Shame!" (*Pozór! Pozór! Pozór!*)

A young physicist read, in an anguished voice, the poem "Hamlet" from *Doctor Zhivago*; its final line a Russian proverb, "To live your life is not as simple as to cross a field." The poem's effect on some of the mourners must have been like signal beacons lighting up across a mountain range. They would have remembered how, for countless generations of Russians right back to Catherine's time, "the Hamlet question" had represented the search for meaning and justice in a corrupt society.

Someone in a work shirt said: "Sleep peacefully, dear Boris Leonidovich! We do not know all your works, but we swear to you at this hour: the day will come when we shall know them all." Whereupon a man in gray trousers called out severely: "The meeting is over, there will be no more speeches!" This time a foreigner indignantly said in broken Russian: "It will be over only when no one wishes to speak!"

The KGB's vengeance would come a few weeks later, with the arrest and imprisonment of Ivinskaya for a second four-year spell.

"He believed in eternity and he will belong to it. . . ."

"Glory to Pasternak!" And that loud cry was taken up by everyone.

As the coffin was lowered, the cemetery became one blaze of flowers, passed from hand to hand over the heads of the crowd, toward the grave. Afterward, the people refused to leave; poems were read or quoted by heart, on into candlelit night. People's lips could be seen moving, silently, in unison. Rain fell, but still the readings went on.

It was a very Russian way of saying good-bye to a great poet. Probably that homage to a writer could only have occurred in a society where repression was severe, though not quite absolute. Under Stalinism it could not have happened. In the calm consumerist democracies of the West, the people would not have wanted it, nor needed it, nor felt with such intensity.

27

R y a z a n s k y

It's time, my friend, it's time!
—PUSHKIN

THE HEART—AND ALL WHO KNEW HIM AGREED IT WAS A BIG heart—in Alexander Tvardovsky's large fifty-year-old body beat quickly. He was in bed, in his pajamas, a Friday night in December 1961, beginning to read a story that a copy editor had thrust into his hands: *Shch-854* by A. Ryazansky. Anna Berzer had said, "It's about a prison camp as seen through the eyes of a peasant"; she'd also offered him a manuscript by Lydia Chukovskaya about the Leningrad purges, which would no doubt be very good, but Tvardovsky had plucked this unknown Ryazansky's story from Anna Berzer's hands. He was a peasant himself, still at heart a barefoot boy in the meadows.

After reading just a couple of pages Tvardovsky put the story aside, got out of bed, and dressed again. He felt it would be an insult to the unknown author to read it in bed, in his pajamas. He went downstairs, and sat up all night reading the story, while his family slept. From time to time, in a daze, he went to the kitchen to make tea. When he had finished the story he reread it. When dawn broke he wanted to share his feelings with the world, but Moscow didn't rise at cockcrow as the old villages did; he had to wait. It didn't occur to him to go to bed.

Through all the compromises between truth and falsehood that he had been forced to accept over the years—years in which his journal, *Novy Mir*, fought the good fight for decent standards in literature—Tvardovsky had never lost his childlike wonder. He rejoiced as much over someone else's creation as over his own: especially if he could claim it for his beloved journal.

As the late dawn struggled through, he made phone call after phone call, spreading the good news. Second deputy editor Kondratovich was ordered to call the humble copy editor, Berzer, to ask who was hiding under a pseudonym: the immense and overstaffed power structure of a Soviet journal preventing him from calling Berzer himself. This inquiry led him to Lev Kopelev, and the excellent discovery that the author was an obscure schoolteacher in Ryazan. "I knew it!" Tvardovsky burst out to Kopelev on the phone. "I knew it couldn't be anyone who's had all the life squeezed out of them! . . . But why didn't you tell me yourself? Anyway, you should be proud to have such a friend. He's got a wonderful, pure and great talent. Not a drop of falsehood in it."

He read extracts to his wife over breakfast, then rushed to the office to get hold of more copies. It was a Saturday, the place was deserted except for cleaners, and Tvardovsky had to break into Anna Berzer's desk to get at four extra copies. He rushed off to see his friends. Solzhenitsyn observes that Tvardovsky had few friends—because he was talented, because he was *awkward,* because he was at heart a peasant among intellectuals; yet also, paradoxically, because he was a Soviet grandee, a Candidate Member of the Central Committee, leading a grandee's unnatural life. This December morning, he found two friends, one of them a *Novy Mir* author, Victor Nekrasov. "A new genius is born!" he announced. "Victor, go for a bottle! After all," he joked, "I was a colonel in the war, and you were only a captain!" Tvardovsky had been a war correspondent; Nekrasov had poured his horrific memories of battle into a powerful novel, *In the Trenches of Stalingrad*, which won him the 1947 Stalin Prize.

As the vodka was brought out, Tvardovsky remembered a similar occasion in Russian literary history involving a Nekrasov—Nikolai, the nineteenth-century poet who wrote powerfully about the hardships of the peasants: and he too had been an editor of a journal, *Sovremennik,* founded by Pushkin. Dostoyevsky had sent this earlier Nekrasov his first novel, *Poor Folk,* in 1845; Nekrasov rushed to the home of the critic Belinsky and told him, "A new Gogol has arisen!" Belinsky replied, "Gogols grow in your imagination like mushrooms." Now a later poet/editor said to a later Nekrasov, "Do you remember how one great writer went to see another great writer? I'm joking, of course, because I don't consider you a great writer. But a great writer has just been born, nevertheless."

They spent the rest of the morning getting drunk. Tvardovsky said his only aim in life from this moment was to get the story into print. He would go to the very top, to Nikita. "They say Russian literature has been killed; damn it, it's here, in this folder! . . . We've sent him a telegram; we'll take him under our wing. . . ."

In Ryazan, later that December Saturday, on the eve of his forty-third birthday, Sanya received a lightly coded telegram from Kopelev: "Alexander Trifonovich delighted with article—very much wants to see you—come as soon as possible—congratulations and regards." The schoolmaster-writer tried to stay calm, but kept repeating "How funny. . . . How funny. . . ." He greatly admired Tvardovsky as a poet; indeed, only a few days earlier Natasha had given him a copy of his latest narrative poem, *From the Far*

Horizon, and its artistry and honesty was reminding him of how his men in the artillery battery had loved the down-to-earth peasant-soldier in *Vasily Tyorkin.* Now Tvardovsky—he learned from a phone conversation with Kopelev—had lost a night's sleep reading his story about a peasant in a labor camp!

That night, *he* couldn't sleep.

He woke to birthday greetings from his family and a telegram in duplicate from Alexander Tvardovsky, inviting him to come to Moscow at *Novy Mir*'s expense.

On Tuesday, 12 December, a day when he was free from school teaching, he caught the 7 A.M. train for Moscow. He paused by Pushkin's statue as he crossed Strastnaya Square on his way to the *Novy Mir* offices—"partly to beg for his support, and partly to promise that I knew the path I must follow and would not stray from it. It was a sort of prayer."[1] He felt a strong anxiety over what he was risking: his liberty.

But above all, of course, he felt excitement. Was this the moment of change, the moment of destiny? Was it *"porá!"*—"It's time!" a familiar urgent appeal in Russian literature? It was high time for "It's time!"

Solzhenitsyn's path even to the editor of the Soviet Union's most liberal literary journal had been a long and difficult one. He had hidden away *Shch-854* like all his other writings, resigned to going unpublished in his lifetime. He had got on with his quiet life with Natasha. Writing to the Zubovs, he told them that Natasha, alone of all his potential wives, had read Chekhov's "Darling" and agreed without hesitation to abide by it.

In a shortened week—thanks to Natasha's salary—he continued to teach with enthusiasm and brilliance. Some at his school even proposed him for headmaster. But Sanya appeared at the last minute before the start of a class, and vanished instantly after.

Natasha was increasingly finding her enjoyment in helping her husband; though she was—by the admission of a relative who is now reluctant to accord her many virtues—an "excellent, creative teacher," her teaching became more of a chore, simply to earn money. Sanya wanted her to concentrate on her music, but here too she found herself coming up against a barrier. Probably she had reached the limit of her talent. She enjoyed playing Chopin as an accompaniment to his reading of the poems he had thrust into her hand, that rainy night in 1956. A recording was made of their performance, and Natasha never listened to it without feeling the wonder of their having come together again. They were living, she said, in "almost perfect harmony." She loved the summers, when they went exploring the countryside and the great rivers. His dynamic pulse had to slow a little on these trips.

Just as Sanya insisted to his wife that they only needed to buy books that were classics, so one should be economical with friendship. Natasha had given up, at his request, almost all her friendships shared jointly with Somov;

but one exception—because Sanya took to them—was a well-to-do Jewish couple, Veniamin and Suzanna Teush. Veniamin, much the older and now retired from his post as mathematics lecturer at Natasha's college, had turned from Communism to anthroposophy; but his intellectual interests were very wide. So were his wife's; Suzanna was warmer and more ebullient. Nature had symbolized the difference by making him immensely tall and bony, her, short and plump. Suzanna's lapsed Judaism matched perfectly well with her husband's lapsed Communism.

Sanya had decided very quickly to let them read *Shch-854*. He was desperate for intelligent and trustworthy readers. The story had an explosive effect on Veniamin. Weeping, he murmured, "Lord, now lettest Thou Thy servant depart in peace." He was so overwhelmed by the work that he lost all peace of mind, Sanya recalled.[2] "There are three atom bombs in the world," Teush said: "Kennedy has one, Khrushchev another, and you have the third!" It was music to his ears. Moreover, the Teushes proved capable of offering intelligent criticism.

For twelve years he had been happy to write in private, preserved from the compromises of submitting to editor and censor, and filled with creative joy. But of late his mood had begun to change. "I had written so many things, all quite unpublishable, all doomed to complete obscurity, that I felt clogged and supersaturated, and began to lose my buoyancy of mind and movement. I was beginning to suffer from lack of air in the literary underground. . . . When you have been writing for ten or twelve years in impenetrable solitude, you begin without realising it to let yourself go, to indulge yourself, or simply to lose your eye for jarring invective, for bombast. . . ."[3]

The critical suggestions by his new friends enabled him to make his camp story more reticent, less polemical, and therefore possibly more acceptable to the censors. But dare he risk it? After the persecution of Pasternak the atmosphere remained dark. True, there were signs of a bolder spirit abroad, young writers like the poets Yevtushenko and Voznesensky, whose independence of mind was not (or not yet) frozen by terror at the sound of an elevator whirring in the night. And Natasha, on a visit to Moscow, saw that the dreaded walls of the Butyrki were being torn down. But hope had been crushed many times before. The Butyrki might fall, but writers were still hounded: Vasily Grossman, for instance, a distinguished Ukrainian novelist, forced in 1961 to give up every copy of his epic novel *Life and Fate* to the KGB, and even his typewriter ribbon, or face arrest.

Nevertheless, the tone of the Twenty-second Congress, held in October 1961, had been surprisingly radical. Sanya had been impressed by the sincere, emotional tones of Khrushchev toward the end of his speech on the second day. He promised a monument to the memory of comrades who had been victims of arbitrary power, and ended his speech by giving expression to what Solzhenitsyn would later term Khrushchev's Christian aspect, his awareness of man's brevity: "Comrades! Our duty is to investigate carefully such abuses of power in all their aspects. Time passes and we shall die, since all of us are mortal, but as long as we have the strength to work we must clear up many things and tell the truth to the Party and our people."

Another speech that had moved and excited Solzhenitsyn was Tvardovsky's, who praised the reforms introduced five years before, and said that literature had undergone a period of moral regeneration and spiritual uplift as a result. However, writers were still not sufficiently showing the labors and ordeal of the people in a manner that was totally truthful to life. *Novy Mir*, he suggested, would be prepared to publish bolder works if only it had them.

"I read and re-read those speeches," Solzhenitsyn recalled, "and the walls of my secret world swayed like curtains in the theater, wavered, expanded and carried me queasily with them: had it arrived, then, the long-awaited moment of terrible joy, the moment when my head must break water?"[4]* He must not thrust his head out too soon, nor let the rare moment pass him by.

Surely the peasant Tvardovsky could not fail to be moved by the humble hero of his camp story. And wasn't Khrushchev a peasant, a *muzhik*, at heart too!

Still, he had not felt courageous enough to take his story to the *Novy Mir* offices himself; one November day he handed it over to Kopelev to deliver; and as it left his hand, he was gripped by agitation. He went to a hotel: which happened to be at Ostankino, right next to the Marfino *sharashka*. He spent three days at the hotel, reading a samizdat copy of *For Whom the Bell Tolls* which Kopelev had loaned to him: his first experience of Hemingway. At intervals he went out and paced the soft snow outside the Marfino fence; and felt the ghost of himself, as it were, pacing back and forth, back and forth, under the linden trees, *inside* the fence, overlooked by the watchtower—desperate for freedom. . . .

His agitation continued. It was still not too late to ask for the manuscript back. He had informed against himself!

But Hemingway's injured American hero, waiting bravely for death, would have made it hard for Solzhenitsyn to turn back, even had he really been tempted to do so. He returned to Ryazan. Raisa Orlova took the packet to *Novy Mir*, and the story he had preserved in secret for so long lay unread on a copy editor's desk for a whole week, for any hard-liner to pick up. Then Anna Berzer glanced at a few pages and was shaken. A colleague confirmed her feeling that this was an important work, perhaps a masterpiece. It must be read first by Tvardovsky, Berzer felt, otherwise his deputies would stifle it before it reached him.

The manuscript was appallingly scruffy and hard on the eyes: single-space type, without any margins, on both sides of the paper. She asked permission

---

*A reference to the dashing warriors emerging from the sea in Pushkin's fairy tale *Tsar Saltan*.

to have the story retyped at the journal's expense, so as to present the work in the best possible light. At present it did not bear the author's name; Berzer sent for Kopelev and asked him for a name. He thought of "A. Ryazansky" and the copy editor duly had it typed in beneath the title.

Then, at last, she approached various members of the board who, by protocol, had the right to read a work before it went to the chief editor. A tiny, intelligent, shrewd woman, she chose an approach calculated to put them off reading the story. So, she asked Gerasimov, who she knew hated camp stories, since they were trouble: "Do you want to read a story about the camps?" She invited Zaks, the managing secretary, who "asked only one thing of literature—that it not interfere with the comforts of his declining years,"[5] to read a page or two to see if he'd like to read it all. Zaks noted at once that the author was an unknown, and the first paragraph illiterate, and threw it back at Anna Berzer, mumbling "Busy, busy."

Now she had the right to approach the holy of holies. Tvardovsky did not care for her much; but she knew that if she offered him a Leningrad intellectual's novel of the purges, together with a story about "a prison camp as seen through the eyes of a peasant," Tvardovsky would be bound to pick the latter for his weekend reading. And so it had proved.

Tvardovsky had donned his pajamas, climbed into bed, picked up the story. And the first paragraph, which Zaks had found illiterate, made Tvardovsky's heart beat more rapidly. . . .

28

Launching Pads

The bird is free!

THERE WAS STILL A GHOST OF PUSHKIN WHEN SANYA MOVED ON from his statue and entered the *Novy Mir* building, since the journal's offices had once been a ballroom where the youthful Pushkin had danced. A more sedate literary figure greeted Sanya—second deputy editor Kondratovich. He tried to look imposing, but Solzhenitsyn summed him up immediately as a lightweight with no mind of his own. For his part, the bureaucrat may well have been startled that the visitor was quite so shabbily dressed—even for a provincial—and showing little pleasure at the honor being granted to him. Sanya had set out deliberately to appear the scruffy provincial teacher who had little time for writing; and he had schooled his features to stand fast against flattery and persuasion to compromise.

Kondratovich had written in a report to Tvardovsky that they almost certainly would not be able to publish the story; it was too pessimistic, and the language needed to be cleaned up.

"What else have you got?" he asked the shabby writer solemnly.

"I should prefer to leave that question to a later stage in our acquaintance."[1]

He also shook hands with Anna Berzer. Though at this time he did not know of her crucial part in getting his story to Tvardovsky, he took to her immediately.

Tvardovsky arrived straight from a meeting of the Lenin Prize committee. He greeted his guest with dignity. Knowing his appearance only from bad newspaper photographs, Solzhenitsyn took in that he was a big man, large in girth; but above all "I was immediately struck by the childish expression of his face—childish in its candor, even vulnerable in its childishness—not in the least spoiled, I thought, by long years at the highest levels of society, nor even by favours from the throne." He led Solzhenitsyn to the boardroom, where, together with other editors and managers, they sat at a long, antique oval table. Tvardovsky and Solzhenitsyn sat at either end, facing each other. The editor tried to be businesslike, but could not stop his face from beaming. He told his newly discovered author how marvelous his story was—perhaps even greater than *House of the Dead*, since Dostoyevsky had shown the people through the eyes of an intellectual, whereas here the intellectuals were seen through the eyes of the people. It was just one day, an ordinary day, even quite a good day, a day without horrors. . . . Tvardovsky's warmth was reaching across the length of the table, as if to draw the new author into his embrace. Benevolence was already turning to love; he could not have been prouder or more joyful if the story had been his own creation!

Solzhenitsyn kept his face solemn, as if he were completely unmoved by such praise; and answered questions evasively, not wishing to reveal too much of his life in Ryazan. . . . "Oh, you know, it's hard to say how long it took, when you're writing in odd gaps around your teaching. . . ." "Sixty rubles a month. . . ." (Mouths gaped at such poverty; he did not reveal there was also Natasha's salary.)

"We must draw up a contract," Tvardovsky said. "Of course I can't promise publication, and certainly can't set a firm date; but I'll do my best, Alexander Isayevich."

"Thank you." Was he really here? Was this happening to him? . . .

No one liked the story's title, *Shch-854*, a *zek* number close to Sanya's own. After some discussion round the table they settled on *One Day in the Life of Ivan Denisovich*. The author also promised to give his hero, Shukhov, a tiny hope of living in freedom one day; accepted a few corrections of Ukrainian; assured Zaks it was perfectly possible for a peasant to believe that God breaks bits off the moon to make stars. The mood was genial; Tvardovsky continued to be euphoric. His trusted first deputy editor, Dementyev, said nothing, however. Solzhenitsyn later read his report: "A difficult case: if we don't publish it will look as though we are afraid of the truth . . . but publication is impossible, because it does after all give a one-sided picture of reality." In spite of this reaction, Solzhenitsyn later found him helpful and constructive, a "likable fat-faced muzhik" with a genuine appreciation of good writing.

The other editor who thought, sensibly, that publication was very unlikely, Kondratovich, brightened when the author admitted under pressure that he had a few poems, prose poems, and a story about village life he could show them. "That sounds good," he encouraged; "after *Ivan Denisovich* you've exhausted the camps as a subject, wouldn't you agree? You'd do well to take the war as a theme." Solzhenitsyn's later comment carries a devastating irony: "A fife band thousands of mouths strong had been monotonously tootling its martial airs for twenty years, and still the army at war was an inexhaustible subject! Whereas the fifty millions who had perished in exile and in the camps could make do with one little grave mound—my story!"[2]

Arriving home that night, he seemed in a daze. Wordlessly he held up before four excited women a thick sheet of paper on which the word CONTRACT was blazened. Overcome, Natasha sank down onto a chair and burst into tears.

He returned to Moscow a week later to deliver the prose and verse he had promised. At a board meeting on 2 January 1962 he listened, astonished, to Tvardovsky's rambling and highly emotional monologue—interrupted occasionally by his own responses—explaining why it would be out of the question to publish the short story now known as "Matryona's House." Unlike the verse, which Tvardovsky described privately to colleagues as not worth reading, he loved Solzhenitsyn's portrait of a slatternly, illiterate village woman who was nevertheless, and unfathomably, good. Yet the story could not be published.

Berzer, who sat in on the meeting, and who was becoming Solzhenitsyn's close ally on the journal's staff, told him afterward she had never seen Tvardovsky in such an obvious turmoil of soul. Solzhenitsyn felt that the poet and editor's primary devotion, to Russian literature, with its devout belief in the moral duty of a writer, was in conflict with that other modern truth which he was also loyal to, the Party's truth. His ramblings were really an agonized internal argument. He attacked the story for showing village life at its worst, with everyone a degenerate or a vampire—then praised it for its truth to peasant speech and life. He praised its realism, pointing out that he appreciated nineteenth-century "critical realism" as much as "socialist realism."

He wished the story had acknowledged that decent generals and factory managers came out of the village, but then exclaimed: "I'm not saying you should have made Kira a member of the Komsomol; oh no." He found the narrator's attitude too Christian—then became fascinated by how *dobro* – "good," as in Tolstoy's "Children, the old man has told you a great good (*dobro*)"—had now been debased into meaning only "goods," property. At one moment he recalled how Stalin, contradicting Trotsky, had promised "not to plunder the village to pay for the building of socialism," but then paused, and looked at each person in turn around the table, asking in a perturbed way, "How, then, was it paid for?" No one answered him. He almost groaned as he exclaimed: "How could anyone possibly say the October Revolution was in vain?"

Solzhenitsyn leaned forward to gather up the rejected story, but Tvardovsky prevented him. "You might as well leave it for a while. Other people may want to read it. . . ."

Hugging him farewell, he added, "Please don't become *ideologically stalwart*! Don't write anything my staff could pass without my having to know about it."

To soften the blow of the rejection, he talked of various imaginative schemes to get *Ivan Denisovich* published; but really he had no idea how best to go about it. Solzhenitsyn promised to be patient; only young writers were impatient to see their name in print. He was grateful not to be in the Lubyanka.

Everyone at *Novy Mir* had by now read the work, and wanted to shake his hand; many were in awe of him. Indeed, he was increasingly becoming whispered about throughout Moscow's literary circles. One of the first to read *Ivan* was the popular children's writer Kornei Chukovsky; and he even wrote a report on it and sent it to Tvardovsky, thinking it might be useful to him. "This story marks the entry into our literature of a powerful, original and mature writer." He warned Tvardovsky—but in reality future censors—against trying to edit the text. Apparent eccentricities, he pointed out, were examples of the author's masterful use of Russian. Apart from a few near obscenities there was nothing that could not pass the censorship, since the story dealt with the past and was "totally dedicated to the glory of Russian man."

Chukovsky's statement gave Tvardovsky the idea of inviting comments from other writers, thereby creating a powerful tide of opinion in favor of publication. Some, including Ilya Ehrenburg, declined to comment; others were bolder. Samuil Marshak wrote that any Russian writer, or even reader, who read *Ivan Denisovich* would make greater demands on himself as a consequence; and that "it would be unforgivable to keep this from the reader."[3]

The secret fame of *Ivan Denisovich* was spreading. By early summer there were said to be some five hundred private and unauthorized copies in existence; there were readers in Odessa, Kiev, Sverdlovsk, Gorky. People were memorizing chapters and reading them at social gatherings. All this made the author's position far more vulnerable, even to the disastrous possibility of a Western publication. Devoted staff at *Novy Mir* were passionate in their frustration. One of them said to Solzhenitsyn, "If I had to sacrifice my career to get *Ivan Denisovich* into print, I would gladly do it." Such passion reveals a nobility of spirit that is the obverse of—and in a way dependent on—the dead letter of the Soviet state.

Trying to be patient, yet chafing at Tvardovsky's immobility, Sanya went on quietly with his teaching, and revised *The First Circle* for the fourth time. He chafed a little when Vitkevich and his wife arrived in Ryazan: Natasha had helped him to a senior lectureship in chemistry at the Ryazan Medical Institute. "They'll start visiting us," Sanya had groaned, on hearing the news of his appointment; "we'll have to exchange presents." Natasha, of course, was delighted. Sanya dutifully welcomed them on arrival and the two couples went on cycling trips together.

Other incursions from childhood he welcomed. Aunt Irina had come on a visit, and got on well with "our little old ladies," as Sanya called Natasha's mother and aunts. He had even suggested to his aunt that they find her a cottage in a pretty village. Irina considered it carefully, but decided she was too old to uproot from the Caucasus. Besides, how could she get all her cats on a train? "Cats," she wrote in a letter to one of the old ladies, "are the true followers of Christ. People, on the other hand, are far removed from the teachings of Christ."⁴ A wise old woman.

Sanya was becoming more interested in his father's family. On a visit to Mineral'nye Vody in 1962 he met two cousins—Sasha, with whom he had corresponded, and his sister Liudmila. Liudmila worked as a secretary in a vegetable depot. She told Sanya about two other brothers who had died of starvation in the famine of 1932–33.⁵ He learned also that of the two uncles who had vanished into Siberia at around that time—Konstantin and Ilya—the latter at least had survived, and was living in Yenisey. Sanya and Natasha were keenly looking forward to a summer visit to Siberia; they now resolved to meet Uncle Ilya.⁶

In late June, Sanya and his wife set off. During the weeklong train journey he found himself sitting beside a young MVD officer who was about to start work at the Irkutsk labor-camp complex. A likable young man in his way, he complained to his traveling companion how standards had fallen in the camps since Khrushchev's reforms, how insolent the prisoners had become. Solzhenitsyn expressed his sympathy.

The holiday makers fell in love with Lake Baikal, which indeed seemed to live up to the phrase "sacred Baikal" of a well-known song. But the trip was cut short because of a message from home: Tvardovsky had tried to contact him; a telegram awaited him at Krasnoyarsk. This was five hundred miles away, on their return journey, and meant they would not get to Yenisey to meet Uncle Ilya. Disappointed, the couple started the long homeward journey. The telegram at Krasnoyarsk read: "Cable immediately chances short visit Moscow re preparation manuscript for setting."

Arriving in Moscow in late July, Sanya found Tvardovsky in high spirits. He had sent the story to Khrushchev's first assistant, Vladimir Lebedev, together with the eulogies of Chukovsky, Marshak, and others. Lebedev, small, bald, in gold-rimmed glasses, appeared the image of a dry Soviet functionary, but possessed a decent library of officially banned books and was comparatively liberal. He was enthusiastic about the story Tvardovsky had sent him, and promised to recommend it personally to Khrushchev; however, Lebedev asked for some changes. The most important was that the ex-naval captain and Party member, Captain Buinovsky, should be treated less satirically, more positively. In addition, some of the camp slang should be toned down; and Lebedev didn't like the frequent references to the camp officers as "vermin." There should be more hopefulness, and an acknowledgment that Stalin was responsible for these crimes.

After Tvardovsky had informed Solzhenitsyn dispassionately of these changes requested by Lebedev, Dementyev launched into a *demented* assault in Lebedev's support, invoking the sacred isms of communism, patriotism, materialism—and above all that sacred "socialist realism" which demanded the reality of the wedding photograph or holiday brochure. *Ivan* had all too much of that "critical realism" that suited the prerevolutionary crushing of the masses. "By the end of his monologue Dementyev looked like a wild boar inflamed with rage, and if someone had put the 150 pages of my story before him just then he might easily have scattered it to the winds with his tusks."[7]

Tvardovsky was silent, waiting. Solzhenitsyn, his head bowed, thought of the *zeks*, his brothers, the camp rebellions, and felt shame that he had sought to argue with these men. "I've waited ten years," he replied, rising from his seat at the oval table, "and I can wait another ten. I'm in no hurry. My life doesn't depend on literature. Give me back my manuscript and I'll be on my way."

"Please, Alexander Isayevich!" Tvardovsky said in alarm. "You don't have to change anything. Just consider the suggestions quietly. It's just that we all very much want the manuscript to get through."

Dementyev subsided; he was silent. He traveled with Solzhenitsyn to Ryazan to collect the master copy, and was totally charming and friendly.

Working on the manuscript with the skillful and sensitive help of Anna Berzer, Solzhenitsyn found that the changes desired could be made easily, and perhaps even beneficially. He handed in the finished text, and waited. Another two months passed. In September, Tvardovsky was supposed to go to the United States, on a high-level exchange visit, but was prevented by illness. The American poet in the planned exchange was the eighty-eight-year-old Robert Frost. Though fiercely anti-Communist, the rumpled, down-to-earth poet got on famously with Russian audiences, the tearaway young Yevtushenko, and Khrushchev himself. Khrushchev met him at his dacha in Pitsunda, on the Black Sea coast, with Lebedev and the conformist poet Alexei Surkov. Frost chose his poem "Mending Wall" to quote in his gravelly New England accent. . . .

> Something there is that doesn't love a wall,
> That sends the frozen ground-swell under it. . . .

When Frost had been led away, Surkov and Lebedev started discussing *Ivan Denisovich,* and Khrushchev asked, "What's that? What are you hiding from me?" He demanded to see the manuscript, but Lebedev had left it in Moscow. Khrushchev ordered him to take a plane back to Moscow and get it. On his return, he read to his master a very "positive" description of Shukhov laying bricks. Khrushchev was touched at the careful way the *zek* husbanded his mortar. He wiped away tears; sent for Mikoyan to come and listen. Mikoyan was moved too. Khrushchev wanted to know why Tvardovsky didn't publish the story, and Lebedev explained that it wasn't so easy to get past the censors. "We see no reason why it shouldn't be published," Khrushchev said.

On their return to the Kremlin, Lebedev telephoned Tvardovsky and said, "Trifonich, there is justice in this world!" But still there was no definite word. Anxiety gripped everyone; Tvardovsky swore he would resign if permission was refused. Then, to Tvardovsky's amazement, he was asked to provide twenty-three copies for the Central Committee, to be sent the next morning. Since it would be impossible to type so many copies in one night, he decided to print a limited edition. Tvardovsky arranged for four of the *Izvestia* presses to print twenty-five copies overnight. Berzer and Kondratovich were placed in charge of four proofreaders and typesetters, who were sworn to secrecy about the astonishing text they were sweating over. At dawn the copies were bound in the journal's light blue covers and the plates locked away.

When members of the Presidium had read their copies, Khrushchev still had his work cut out persuading them to let the story through. He may even have needed two meetings. "There's a Stalinist in each of you," he is reported to have said; "there's even some of the Stalinist in me. We must root out this evil." In the end he took silence as consent, Mikoyan seconding his resolution to publish.

In October, Khrushchev summoned Tvardovsky to a personal meeting to announce the decision. The leader was in a sober, philosophic mood—as well he might be. In Washington, D.C., President Kennedy was pretending he had a cold, canceling all engagements, so he could consider the aerial photographs of Soviet missile sites on Cuba.

Khrushchev told Tvardovsky *Ivan Denisovich* was a life-enhancing work; though it would have been harmful if it were less well written. Some people had objected that the camp personnel weren't more sympathetically treated, but he had retorted, "Do you think they were running a holiday resort?" Tvardovsky took the opportunity to suggest that censorship of literature be removed altogether. "Kisses don't make babies, Nikita Sergeyevich. . . ."

In Washington, D.C., President Kennedy was saying to his aides, "We are very very close to war." Then, with a touch of bleak humor: "And there's not room enough in the White House bomb shelter for all of us."

"Books are circulating in illegal copies," Tvardovsky pressed Khrushchev; "what could be worse than that?"

Khrushchev seemed, to his guest, not unsympathetic to the abolition of censorship. But his politeness may have been out of courtesy to Tvardovsky, whose poetry he enjoyed and whom he deeply respected. After he had been forcibly retired, and was reading a lot, he said that he would never have allowed *The First Circle* to be published, but he did not regret allowing *Ivan Denisovich* through. Because Tvardovsky had told him more than once that "the story was a great work of literature and Solzhenitsyn a very great writer."[8] Solzhenitsyn would later complain that Tvardovsky had waited too long before actively trying to get his story published; but it appears that its publication owed almost everything to Khrushchev's great respect for his fellow "muzhik."

Nothing, of course, came of Tvardovsky's urgings about censorship.

Nor, fortunately, were the White House shelters needed. Some said that Frost's favorable report of his meeting had helped, by persuading Kennedy that Khrushchev was no madman.

Be that as may be, children could go on being swingers of birches.

On hearing the news of Khrushchev's approval of *Ivan Denisovich*, the *Novy Mir* staff jumped for joy, hugged one another endlessly, wept. No one did any work that Monday. Their happiness was pure; they gained nothing personally from the publication; nothing but their sense that Russia was beginning to reclaim its history and its soul.

Sanya was summoned from Ryazan to go through the page proofs. It was almost a year since he had read Hemingway in samizdat at a hotel near his old *sharashka*; now he was put up, at *Novy Mir*'s expense, at the luxurious central Hotel Ukraine. Lebedev had one last request: one of the characters, Tyurin, had said, "I crossed myself, and said to God: Thou art there in heaven after all, O Creator. Thy patience is long, but thy blows are heavy." Could this be omitted? Solzhenitsyn pored over the sentence in his hotel room. He was grateful for Lebedev's help, and wished to be obliging. Surely just one sentence . . .

But as he thought of the words, and remembered some of his friends, he wept for the first time over his story; and knew he could not take the words out. Unending despair had caused even some decent people to pray for an atomic war.

He was at Tvardovsky's home when a messenger brought an advance copy of *Novy Mir* issue No. 11, containing his story. Editor and author embraced, and Tvardovsky beamed and danced about the room, despite his bulk, crying out, "The bird is free! The bird is free!"[9]

29

F a m e

Now your hour has struck.—Pray!
—BLOK, *The Field of Kulikovo*

SHE SPOKE IN A DEEP, MEASURED VOICE: "YOU KNOW THAT IN A month you will be the most famous person on earth?"

"I know. But this will not be for long."

Russia's greatest living poet, Anna Akhmatova, was conversing with Russia's greatest living prose writer. Kopelev had introduced them; indeed, he seemed to know everybody. In her seventies now, she was stout, silver-haired, majestic. She had read *Ivan Denisovich* in samizdat, and found it overwhelming. She thought of her son, who had spent so many years in Siberia.

"Can you endure fame?" she pressed him.

"I have very strong nerves. I endured the Stalin camps."

"Pasternak could not endure fame. It's very difficult to endure fame, especially late fame."[1]

He told her he knew her great and highly complex work *Poem without a Hero* by heart. "I found it incomprehensible at first, but then all became clear." She read to him her sequence of the 1930s, *Requiem*, which had been published only in the West, "without her knowledge or permission." While admiring these tragic lyrics, he criticized them to her for dealing only with herself and her son, not the Russian people as a whole.

She found his prose "incomparable," but told him she found the verse he read to her—the sequence in the voice of a *zek*'s wife—lacking in mystery. She was being delicate; like Tvardovsky, she thought his poetry weak and sentimental. Stung, Sanya boldly told her that in her poems there was too *much* mystery—which displeased her.

However, the meeting did not disappoint either of them. Perhaps on her part there was a throb of painfully inappropriate desire. "A Viking came in," she recalled to Kopelev. "And totally unexpectedly, and young and kind.

Amazing eyes. I said to him: 'I want two hundred million people to read your story.' I think he agreed."[2] She who in her Petersburg youth had "fumbled the left glove/Onto my right hand" at grief over love, now burst out to her friend Lydia Chukovskaya, "Oh, Lydia Korneyevna, you should have seen this person. He is unimaginable. You have to see him for yourself, not just read *One Day*. . . . " In a poignant short poem from this time she writes that war and "plague" pass, but no one can cope with "the terror that is named the flight of time." The passionate Akhmatova certainly was aware of Solzhenitsyn's attractiveness, yet poignantly knew that for him she could not be more than an elderly poetess. Ah, if only she could come to him, just once, in the shape of the girl of 1913!

His respect for her work was enormous. When Kopelev asked him to name Russia's greatest modern poet, Solzhenitsyn said, "For me there is only Akhmatova. She is unique—magnificent. . . . I am convinced she is the greatest."[3]

Her shrewd warning about fame was echoed by Tvardovsky in a letter. He hoped that he would keep his head, not be carried away by the adulation he would receive; adding that at times he had been upset by his offhand reception of good news, but now he found such self-restraint reassuring. "You have undergone a number of ordeals, and I can hardly imagine you failing to stand up to this test."

Sanya did not take offense but was touched by Tvardovsky's tact and sensitivity. In his reply he again made the point that fame would be short-lived; and that he abided by the camp proverb "Don't let good luck fool you or bad luck frighten you." The greatest happiness "recognition" had given him had been the discovery, last December, that he—Tvardovsky—had found *Denisovich* worth a sleepless night.[4]

He also met the poet and prose writer Varlam Shalamov, who had spent seventeen years in Kolyma, and who was finding it impossible to get his searingly tragic *Kolyma Tales* published. Solzhenitsyn promised to do his best to help, but was unable to persuade Tvardovsky to publish some of the poetry. The meeting with Shalamov would have reinforced, if that were needed, his determination to remain true to his values—those of a *zek* and of a Russian writer. Toward Shalamov he felt humble, knowing he had plumbed depths of bestiality and despair, in the far northeast, beyond anything he had himself had to endure.

As publication day drew near, the atmosphere in Moscow was electric. Everyone in Moscow—every intellectual, that is—already knew about *Ivan Denisovich* and its author. It was clear that *Novy Mir* would sell out at once.

There can never have been such an atmosphere, such tension, excitement, and expectation, in the whole history of publishing. The official publication day was Saturday 17 November 1962, when subscription copies were sent out, and the staff could buy copies for themselves and friends. It was like it is in church, Tvardovsky told the author; people came in silently, handed over their seventy kopecks, took their copies silently, and left.

Even more extraordinary were the scenes at a plenary session of the Central Committee in the Kremlin Palace of Congresses. Beginning on 19 November, the congress was due to discuss Khrushchev's organizational reforms of industry and agriculture. Tvardovsky gave Solzhenistyn a rollicking firsthand account. Khrushchev had ordered twenty-five hundred copies of *Novy Mir* to be on display. He had harangued the assembly to read *Ivan*. "This is an important work," he told them. Forgetting the author's name, he called him "Ivan Denisovich" too. From then on, Tvardovsky reported, everyone had clutched two books: a red one, with their conference material, and a light blue one!

So the country's leaders, in their black Volgas racing down the center of Moscow's streets, their special stores, their luxurious dachas, found themselves—extraordinarily, unfamiliarly, often uncomfortably—becoming acquainted with one of those common men for whom the Revolution had been made. Not even one of the proletariat, but a man who came from what Marx described as "the idiocy of village life." One of the "dark people"; one of those whom the socialist founder Georgi Plekhanov described as "barbarian tillers of the soil . . . beasts of burden whose life provided no opportunity for the luxury of thought"; . . . "Fiercely and meanly individualistic," according to Lenin; "scum," according to Stalin, as reported by Khrushchev. Ivan Denisovich Shukhov.

His name, and something of his background, came from a middle-aged soldier in Solzhenitsyn's battery; he had not known Shukhov particularly well, but somehow he came back to him as an honest, decent fellow. The idea for the story arose one day when he was bricklaying at Ekibastuz:* "It was an ordinary camp day—hard, as usual, and I was working. I was helping to carry a hand-barrow full of mortar, and I thought that this was the way to describe the whole world of the camps . . . to gather everything into one day, all the different fragments . . . and to describe just one day in the life of an average and in no way remarkable prisoner from morning till night."[5]

The decision to see camp life through the consciousness of a peasant, though in the third person, which so appealed to Tvardovsky and Khrushchev, by no means gained universal approval. One of the story's earliest readers, Ehrenburg's secretary, Natalya Stolyarova, who had herself been in a camp, said to the author, "I don't understand why it wasn't written from the point of view of an intellectual." The dissident Leonid Plyushch both admits to the same puzzlement and rebukes himself for his earlier arrogance. For him, an *intelligent* called Buinovsky was the obvious hero: "The captain, it seemed to me, was a true Communist and intellectual, an invincible champion of justice

---

*In the West it is generally thought of as a novel, but Solzhenitsyn reserves this title (*roman* in Russian) for complex, polyphonic works exploring several destinies. He thought of *Ivan Denisovich* as a *rasskaz* (short story), even if a long one, though Tvardovsky persuaded him to accept the grander designation of *povest'* (tale).

who could understand the course of the Revolution and explain to the reader why Stalinism had emerged. Ivan Denisovich had lived like a work-horse before he was sent to the camps, and little had changed for him. As an intellectual and a Komsomol member inculcated with Stalin's contempt for the masses, I assumed that the true tragedy of the October Revolution could not be seen through Ivan Denisovich's eyes."[6]

Or in other words, only the kind of people who knew best what to do for Russia in 1917, and killed sixty million people in doing it, are worth listening to. . . .

Plyushch recanted, but his early dismissive view of Ivan Shukhov became respectably orthodox when Solzhenitsyn fell from grace. When the Ryazan branch of the Writers' Union voted to expel him, for example, an editor called Povarenkin claimed that "only one who is ideologically hostile to us could depict such an uninspiring character as Ivan Denisovich."[7] But the preference for an intellectual in Ivan Denisovich's place is sometimes heard in the anti-Communist West too. . . . "Surely," wrote Norman Podhoretz, "the impact of the story is weakened, not strengthened, by being told through a character whose life on the outside has been so full of hardship and deprivation as Ivan Denisovich Shukhov's and who has therefore become so accustomed to the kind of conditions he is forced to endure in the labor camp that he can end a day of unrelieved horror in a state of happiness over all the luck he has had in not suffering even more. . . . It makes identifying with Ivan Denisovich Shukhov (or entering into his skin, to use Solzhenitsyn's image) almost insuperably difficult."[8]

Such a criticism seems crass. True, Ivan Denisovich's life had been a hard one; and no one has more movingly described the desecration and destruction of traditional village life than Solzhenitsyn: the churches turned into barns or clubs; propaganda meetings designed to raise milk yields replacing the Angelus bell which "reminded man that he must abandon his trivial earthly cares and give up one hour of his thoughts to life eternal" ("A Journey Along the Oka"). But however hard had been Shukhov's life before, he had been with his family and his comrades, and there had been a degree of freedom. Solzhenitsyn had stood in New Jerusalem camp in 1945, gazing at the village on the nearby hill, and "knew for certain that if they should say to me at that very moment: That's your freedom! Just live in that village until your death! . . . Look at the sun every morning and harken to the roosters! . . . Are you willing? Oh, not only willing, but, good Lord, please send me a life like that!"[9] What arrogance, to imagine that Shukhov would not have felt the same longing! It is not so terribly far from Podhoretz's view to the idea that what happened to the peasants during collectivization was of less interest than the fate of intellectuals and Party members a few years later.

For a number of different reasons, it was surely right to have a common man as hero. There were thousands of Shukhovs for every one Buinovsky,

Plyushch, or Solzhenitsyn; their lives just as unique, precious, and inconceivable to others. As Solzhenitsyn has pointed out, his generation of writer-prisoners was in a sense "lucky," compared with those of the nineteenth century. The latter might have sympathized with the common prisoners but would be returning in due course to their privileged existences; whereas the zeks of Stalin's era were perceived as having endless sentences, so—educated or illiterate—all shared a common suffering.

It would have been easier for Solzhenitsyn to have had an intellectual hero; but that would have created a danger of his bringing in too many subjective impressions, memories, and experiences; the more difficult approach was also a liberating one: just as a poet who chooses to write in a strict form frees himself from all that will *not* suit the chosen form. In Solzhenitsyn's phrase, he chose Shukhov "as the line of greatest resistance."

Ivan Denisovich is a convincing character not only because Solzhenitsyn wore the same padded jacket and did the same common laboring—with the same sense of unreasonable yet uplifting pride in work—but also because this southern provincial, grandson of Zakhar Shcherbak, stood at a distance from the Moscow (or Manhattan) intellectual. He *could*, easily, enter into Shukhov's skin. He was secretive and cunning too, like the peasant, zek, hiding his true thoughts even from the trustful, open Tvardovsky: and glorying in it in *The Oak and the Calf*, his memoir of these years.

"There is no point expecting someone who's warm to understand someone who's cold." Taking Shukhov as his hero allowed the author to show the ways in which a man who is cold, who has no one to send parcels to him, no chance of a soft job, and no intellectual resources, can keep his soul intact. In the desperate world of the labor camp, the soul is preserved or lost, not by whether you remember chunks of poetry or can discuss Marxism, but by such matters as how you behave when someone is smoking a cigarette near you. . . . "Shukhov did not have a scrap of tobacco left, and today saw no prospect of getting any before the evening. He was tense all over in expectation, and now all his desire was concentrated on that dog-end, for which he felt he would be ready to give his freedom—but he wouldn't lower himself like Fetyukov, he wouldn't look at someone's mouth."[10]

It would, of course, have taken a brave reviewer to go against the Party line on *Ivan Denisovich;* but the enthusiastic critical reception was no doubt genuine in most cases. Most reviewers stressed the tale's Leninist orthodoxy; it was "Party-minded"; in *Pravda*, Vladimir Yermilov, a hack writer and opportunist, said that one's heart was wrung with grief and a light penetrated one's soul. He compared Solzhenitsyn to Tolstoy, and ludicrously predicted that "the fight against the consequences of Stalin's personality cult . . . will continue to facilitate the appearance of works of art outstanding for their ever-increasing artistic value." Presumably, this constantly rising productivity of "artistic value" would in a few decades produce works that would make Turgenev's *Fathers and Sons*—published one hundred years before *Ivan Denisovich*—seem like scribblings from the kindergarten.

Fathers and Sons and *Ivan Denisovich,* a century apart, encapsulate that century's experience. In his nihilist hero or antihero, Bazarov, the liberal Turgenev captured the essence of an outlook that would lead to the Revolution and the Gulag. In the words of Edward Crankshaw: "Bazarov's cold and immovable convictions that . . . humanitarian ideals are nothing but self-indulgent sentimentality . . . that the whole fabric of society must be rejected and destroyed in order that later generations may build anew on scientific lines, threw intellectual Russia into a tumult. . . ."[11] Like its twentieth-century counterpart, *Fathers and Sons* did not leave Russia's consciousness unaffected; it marked "the beginning of a long process whereby in ever growing numbers liberals who detested violence . . . found themselves nevertheless shamed by feelings of guilt into tolerating, if not actively supporting, such excesses." A century later, *Ivan Denisovich* portrayed the end result.

There were one or two reviewers who daringly hinted that Stalin's Russia as a whole was being shown as rotten, not just the camp world; and not necessarily only Stalin's. Ion Drutse, a leading Moldavian author, wrote in *Druzhba Narodov* (Friendship of Peoples) that Stalin had despised the masses, and there were still many "big cogs" who enjoyed having "little cogs" to order around. It hardly mattered which side of the wire you were on: "Are we not struck by the austere landscape of this story because we, too, as often as not, scanned the sky with morbidly strained eyes? Did we not also lay bricks, each in his own wall?"[12]

Ivan did not quite reach the two hundred million readers desired for it by Akhmatova; but the hundred thousand copies of *Novy Mir* vanished instantly, and within a few months a mass-circulation journal published at least 750,000 copies of the work, and another publishing house, Sovetsky Pisatel (Soviet Writer) brought it out as a book in an edition of a hundred thousand. All these copies too were instantly swallowed up. Someone decided that was enough, though millions more could have been sold. Solzhenitsyn was offered, and accepted, membership in the Writers' Union. This would allow him the privilege of using the closed sections of leading libraries, and also permit him to give up his teaching career without incurring a charge of parasitism.

Foreign translations, with their generous royalties, started to appear: two different English versions within a month of the *Novy Mir* edition. He was now, whether he liked it or not, a "celebrity"; and one day, by prior arrangement, a black Volga drew up outside his school and he was whisked off to a Kremlin meeting, at which Khrushchev was to address four hundred artists. Sanya had put on his scruffy provincial suit, as if to say, You can see I'm not Party material. . . . He had to go onto the podium to shake hands with Khrushchev and take the applause of the audience. In the interval, a short, intellectual-looking man in rimless glasses came up to him and asked him if he would sign his copy of *Novy Mir*. It was Lebedev, Khrushchev's helpful private secretary, and Sanya was happy to oblige. The television cameras were switched off as a seven-course banquet was served.

Not many years before he had faced exile in perpetuity, and lived in a mud hut on the edge of a desert. In the history of literature there had never been such a transformation.

Amid all the adulation nothing felt as good as the handshake of a former *zek*, especially one he had known. Sitting in the Moskva Hotel, soon after his story had come out, he was greeted by the Houdini of Ekibastuz, the big bruising Leningrad Estonian George Tenno. He soon became fast friends with him and his flaxen-haired part-Finnish wife, Natasha, feeling a spiritual kinship with them. Natasha too had pulled a tenner. Life outside was the anomaly. Explaining their rickety chairs, she said, "It isn't worth getting good ones; we're just living between prison sentences."[13]

Particularly welcome was a letter from a native Estonian, Arnold Susi, his cell mate in the Lubyanka. The first foreign-language version of *Ivan Denisovich*, in a cheap mass edition so that there was one copy for every four or five families, had come out in the still-unfree Estonian SSR. Susi and his family had spent years in Siberian exile after prison; now he was home but barred from living in a city. His wife had died, and he spent his time on the move between his son Arno and his daughter Heli.

The two *zeks* who had disputed while pacing the roof of the Lubyanka eventually met in a medieval university town, Tartu. Susi was frailer, grayer, but still the same courteous, sane, civilized man. Already well-disposed toward Estonians, Solzhenitsyn began to feel even greater warmth for them, so welcoming were they, so grateful for what he had written. Arnold seemed proud to introduce him, and everyone in Tartu seemed to want to shake his hand. "I told my family I'd met a genius in prison!" said Arnold. "I told them I was sure we'd hear of you, if you survived. You still believed you were a Marxist, I said, but that could change!"

Estonia would play a significant part in Solzhenitsyn's life over the next years.

Tvardovsky asked for, and Solzhenitsyn promised, loyalty to *Novy Mir*; but the promise to give him the first refusal of his work did not extend to his plays, and Solzhenitsyn's old love of the theater asserted itself. Oleg Yefremov, director of the Sovremennik (Contemporary) Theater in Moscow, was desperately keen to perform *The Love-Girl and the Innocent*. The author gave a private reading of it, and though members of the company found his reading somewhat hammy—and he, in his unstylish suit, looked like a dental technician, one actor said—the hardened professionals were very moved, and some were in tears after the first act. Yefremov was eager to put the play on within a month, rehearsing day and night and accepting authorial changes as they went along. But Solzhenitsyn was busy at school, and felt he couldn't let his amenable headmaster down. Tvardovsky, too, counseled caution with a theater company he thought somewhat questionable. Solzhenitsyn agreed he should be prudent at the time, but later felt that Tvardovsky had been jealous of this other outlet.

On New Year's Eve 1963, Natasha and her husband joined the theater's revelers at little tables set up in the foyer. Champagne flowed, firecrackers went off at midnight; elegant ladies flung their fur capes on the backs of chairs and, bare armed and almost bare bosomed, danced the twist. It was no doubt entertaining to have a brief taste of such sophisticated celebration; but Sanya would not mistake it for real life. He could not forget he had written to give a voice to those former *zeks* who were now writing to him in grateful droves. . . . "My face was smothered in tears," one woman wrote. "I didn't wipe them away or feel ashamed, because all this, packed into a small number of pages of the magazine, was mine, intimately mine, mine for every day of the fifteen years I spent in the camps." "I wept as I read— they were all familiar characters, as if from my own brigade. . . . Thank you once more! Please carry on in the same spirit—write, write. . . ."

That was the last thing he needed to be exhorted to do. Tvardovsky wanted him to relax a little, enjoy the moment of success, the breakthrough. Why not sit round the big editorial table, drink tea, nibble bibliki, and chat? "All writers do it!" he said jokingly. "They sit down for a quiet smoke like respectable people. Why are you always in such a hurry?" But Solzhenitsyn felt he had a lot of wasted time to catch up. He might have done better to listen to his editor. The best creative ideas don't necessarily come when a writer is hammering away at a typewriter, cramming a page with words. The idea for *Ivan Denisovich* came to him when he could do nothing except set one brick on top another. "Matryona's House" had also begun to be written at a brief time of mental recreation, the unusually relaxed holiday on the Black Sea coast.

Just *loafing*—Robert Frost could have told him—is essential for a writer.

Having been so sure that "Matryona's House" was unpublishable, Tvardovsky now decided this was a propitious time to publish it. He won Sanya's admiration too by suggesting changes based on his own profound knowledge of village life. Thus, "village carpenter" made little sense, Tvardovsky pointed out, since in a village everyone is a carpenter. Aspens do not grow around station buildings, because all the trees there are planted, and no one would ever plant an aspen. Berrying or mushrooming was pleasure, not work. The author was also persuaded to alter the year in which the story was set, 1956, to 1953, so that the harshness of the life depicted could be seen as belonging to the Stalin era. The change of year made nonsense of the narrator's claim that his return to Russia (presumably from the war) had been delayed "by a little matter of ten years."

Matryona herself is one of Solzhenitsyn's greatest portraits. She is slatternly, dirty, unthrifty, a poor housekeeper, and does not seem to follow any rational pattern of living. She won't even keep a pig, because she doesn't like the idea of fattening up a beast to kill it. When her house filled with smoke, instead of trying to save the house she rescued her fig plants. She helps her neighbors dig up potatoes for nothing, and loses all sense of time because she is so enjoying digging up such big potatoes. . . .

> Misunderstood and rejected by her husband, a stranger to her own family despite her happy, amiable temperament, comical, so foolish that she worked for others for no reward, this woman, who had buried all her six children, had stored up no earthly goods. Nothing but a dirty white goat, a lame cat and a row of fig-plants.
> None of us who lived close to her perceived that she was that one righteous person without whom, as the saying goes, no city can stand.
> Nor the world.

Olivier Clément, in *The Spirit of Solzhenitsyn*, observes that Matryona is a late representative of a Christian culture once common throughout Europe, in which everything had a beauty of its own: "sacred music and folk songs, clothes and houses, the objects of everyday life, the countryside of woods and fields, dotted with churches." The beauty did not have to be sought, but was everywhere, because everything was fully useful and yet "salted" by prayer, "taken up into the divine-human dimension so that heaven seemed to weigh upon the earth."[14] For Sergei Baranov, chairman of the Ryazan Writers' Union that expelled Solzhenitsyn in 1969, Matryona was an aberration: "Wherever did he find a woman so much alone," he demanded, "with her cockroaches and her cat and nobody around to help her? Where could one find such a Matryona? I was still hoping that Alexander Isayevich would write things the people needed."[15]

No one needs Matryona. . . . It is very strange, therefore, how Solzhenitsyn makes the reader feel sorrow at her death, and almost become aware, like her tenant, of her moving around the house in the night, saying good-bye. In this work, more than in any other, he takes us to a depth where political questions give place to the universal. Matryona's house could as easily be in Vermont or Cornwall; the prevailing political culture as easily capitalist or social democratic as Communist. Besides being a beautifully achieved woman in her own right, she is also, in a symbolic sense, the best part of Solzhenitsyn: his empathy and love for simple things, without the masculine ego and his frenetic activity.

Besides "Matryona's House," Tvardovsky was also going to publish a story called, originally, "An Incident at Kochetovka Station." The story concerns a young and idealistic officer, Vasili Zotov, who is in charge of troop movements at a small provincial railroad station during the chaotic retreat of 1941. The plot was based on a true event, narrated to Solzhenitsyn by a naval officer in 1944. Solzhenitsyn drew also on his own memories of his journey to Stalingrad, bearing dispatches, in 1942, and of the earlier nightmare of headlong Russian retreat. Zotov wants to scream aloud at the catastrophe overtaking his country. And where is the predicted Revolution in Europe? . . . Like Solzhenitsyn in the war he is "a stickler for precision"; his favorite author is Gorky and he is studying the first volume of *Das Kapital*. Unlike most young men he doesn't try to pretend he is not married, though he is being faithful with some difficulty.

The "incident" of the title occurs after the arrival of a middle-aged man who claims to Zotov that he has got separated from his unit while they were being moved to the rear. Zotov is drawn to the man's well-bred, courteous manner, and does his best to help him, until the stranger confuses Stalingrad with Tsaritsyn (its prerevolutionary name). Zotov thinks only a White Russian spy could be guilty of such an extraordinary lapse of memory, and informs the NKVD. He knows the man will suffer either death or a long imprisonment, and becomes haunted by the memory of the incident.

"Kochetovka" was the actual name of the small station where the original incident, as described to Solzhenitsyn, had occurred in 1941. However, since Kochetov was the name of Tvardovsky's main reactionary adversary (he was the editor of *Oktyabr* magazine), Solzhenitsyn agreed to change the title to "An Incident at Krechetovka Station."

The two stories, published in the January 1963 issue, were well received, and demonstrated that *Ivan Denisovich* had been no flash in the pan. However, the neo-Stalinists like Kochetov were fighting back. Khrushchev's position had been weakened by his diplomatic defeat over Cuba—and in any case *Ivan Denisovich*, with its realist style and peasant hero, had been something of a special case for him. Already at the December meeting where he had introduced Solzhenitsyn from the podium, he had denounced "formalist" artists, calling their work anti-Soviet, amoral, and useful only to cover urinals with. At a second meeting with artists in March, Khrushchev packed the Kremlin's Sverdlovsk Hall with Stalinists; in a long speech reported in *Pravda* and *Izvestia*, he made it brutally clear that artists must serve the state's ideology; he even had kind words to say about Stalin. *Ivan Denisovich* was again commended, but Khrushchev complained that publishers were being swamped by camp stories and memoirs, and this was dangerous. "It's the kind of 'stew' that will attract flies like a carcass, enormous fat flies, all sorts of bourgeois scum from abroad will come crawling all over it."[16]

The air was filled with "harsh invective and destructive hostility to anything that gave off the faintest whiff of freedom. It took only a short time . . . to recreate the atmosphere of intolerance we had known in the thirties, the atmosphere of the 'unanimous meetings' where savage beasts were trained and the doomed and flayed had only till nightfall to live. . . . [Khrushchev] had sent his billiard ball of a head rolling toward the Stalinist pocket. Just one more little push was needed."[17]

It was not a propitious time to contemplate putting on *The Love-Girl and the Innocent* at the Sovremennik; but that was just what Solzhenitsyn now wanted to do. He telephoned Lebedev, hoping he would again be an intermediary with Khrushchev—a highly optimistic move in the changed atmosphere. Lebedev sent on to his boss what is presumably a verbatim account of "the writer Alexander Solzhenitsyn's" words:

"I am deeply touched by the speech of Nikita Sergeyevich Khrushchev and would like to convey to him my profound gratitude for his exceptionally kind attitude toward us writers and to me personally, and for the high value accorded my humble work. My call to you is explained by the following: Nikita Sergeyevich has said that if our writers and other artistic figures get carried away by the theme of the labor camps, it will provide ammunition for our enemies, and huge, fat flies will fall on such materials like dung. . . ." He goes on to ask Lebedev for his "kind advice," "comradely advice," not an official ruling, as to whether he should give his play *The Love-Girl and the Innocent* to the Sovremennik. The prisoners in his play are not opposed to the camp administration but to unscrupulous elements in their own ranks. His "literary father," Tvardovsky, has recommended not giving it to the theater, whose director, Yefremov, has read the play and is interested in staging it.[18]

"I am now tormented by doubts," Solzhenitsyn reportedly continued. Bearing in mind Nikita Khrushchev's warning about labor camp material, he would like Comrade Lebedev's advice. If he agreed with Tvardovsky "I will immediately withdraw this play from the Sovremennik and work on it some more. I would be very pained if I were not to act as required of us writers by the Party and by Nikita Sergeyevich Khrushchev, who is very dear to me."

Lebedev informed Khrushchev that he had first checked with Yefremov, who had said they had no current plans to stage the play but felt it was suitable for production. On receiving and reading the play, Lebedev had expressed to Solzhenitsyn his "profound conviction" that in its present form the play was not suitable for staging, since it could be guaranteed to attract masses of those "fat flies." Lebedev concludes his memo:

"The writer Solzhenitsyn asked me, if the opportunity presents itself, to send his heartfelt greetings and best wishes to you, Nikita Sergeyevich. Once again he would like to assure you that he very well understood your paternal concern for the development of our Soviet literature and art and would try to be worthy of the high calling of a Soviet writer."[19]

If he is accurately reported in the Kremlin files, Solzhenitsyn could scarcely have gone further in flattery and obsequiousness toward a leader who had just (according to *The Oak and the Calf*) taken the country back almost to Stalinism.

Preparing to resign his teaching post in the summer, he wrote a pot-boiler—once again based on actuality—about a Ryazan school. Students and teachers at a poorly housed technical school give up their spare time for a year to complete long-delayed new premises. At the last moment the splendid new building is commandeered by a Moscow ministry for use as a scientific institute. The idealism of teachers and pupils has been betrayed "for the good of the cause." Tvardovsky published the story in the July issue. The journal *Literaturnaya Gazeta* began to snipe at the story over the coming weeks, attacking Solzhenitsyn for abandoning socialist realism in favor of critical realism. Kochetov's journal *Oktyabr* joined in with an assault on both "For the Good of the Cause" and "Matryona's House." *Novy Mir* defended its author. What was most depressing, as Michael Scammell observes, is that the literary quality of the stories was not considered relevant by either side.[20] "Matryona's House" was a masterpiece, "An Incident at Krechetovka Station" powerful, while "For the Good of the Cause" was a mediocre piece of reportage; but they were being judged purely by shifting rules of ideological soundness, nothing else.

In August 1963 Sanya and Natasha, on bicycles and laden with camping gear, visited a quieter battlefield, the plain of Kulikovo. There, in 1380, a quarter of a million Russian warriors had defeated the might of the Tatars, at enormous cost. And then on to another silent battlefield—Leo Tolstoy's estate of Yasnaya Polyana, where husband and wife had spiritually wrestled for decades; where, at the age of eighty-three, the old man just couldn't stand it any longer, and fled on a sleigh into the night. . . .

This cycling holiday, which also took in the ancient cities of Suzdal, Vladimir, and Rostov the Great, was—at least for Natasha—a necessary time of marital closeness in a turbulent year. He often had to be away from her; after he had given up school he more often *chose* to be away—not unnaturally wishing to have breaks from the three old ladies. But Natasha, working on at the agricultural institute, though without much enthusiasm, and organizing Sanya's files and press cuttings, was left behind too. "Suddenly, it seemed to me that I might fail to keep up with my husband, might lag behind him in that swift current and go to the bottom."[21] Though women were now fawning over him, there was no basis for her fear, she knew, beyond a woman's intuition. Their Ryazan friends and acquaintances told Victor Bukhanov, a reporter from the Novosti press agency, that they were an ideal couple. "God grant every family the same happiness." Bukhanov wormed no more than a couple of sentences out of his subject, but found his wife "cultivated and somewhat more open." He watched Solzhenitsyn chopping wood, dressed in his padded jacket, and felt that there was an essential and unforgettable connection between Solzhenitsyn and Ivan Denisovich Shukhov.[22]

If young would-be writers sent him work to comment on, as increasingly they did, he sent them back "Form No. 1." This pro forma letter regretted that they had not first asked his consent to send their work, said a superficial evaluation would be unfair and misleading, while a considered response would not be possible owing to the condition of his health and his late arrival on the literary scene. He had to place an extreme value on his time. He advised that they send their work to a magazine such as *Novy Mir*, and ended by wishing them all the best.

The pro forma letter was very understandable; he could have drowned under the unwanted attention to which he was being subjected. Yet he had himself sent work to authors, in his young days, and been grateful for their encouraging remarks.

There was loss; there had to be. He would never more be the author joyously alone with his creation. His abandonment of teaching, while giving him more time for research—and for the immense undertaking of *The Gulag Archipelago*—also denied him a healthy contact with the young. He was now a "professional" author: one who could rarely rest. One wonders if he anticipated this process when writing "Matryona's House"; her death, and her ghostly leave-taking of the poor possessions in her house—and of the narrator—seem close to what would soon be happening to Solzhenitsyn. Innocence was moving around stealthily, saying farewell.

At the end of 1963, with the royalties from *Ivan Denisovich*, he bought a green Moskvich car.

It was then that America lost her president and her innocence, and for two days a young man who had lived in Minsk, Lee Harvey Oswald, was the most famous person alive.

The editors of *Novy Mir* nominated Solzhenitsyn for a Lenin Prize, seconded by the State Archive of Literature and Art. He had no serious rivals. *Izvestia* carried an interview with the prototype of Captain Buinovsky, thought by Plyushch and others to be the rightful hero of *Ivan Denisovich*. The real-life captain, called Burkovsky, praised the truthfulness of Solzhenitsyn's story. *Pravda* published an essay by Marshak extolling *Ivan*. Sometime in March, however, the mood changed, and *Pravda* published a "selection" of letters from the customary blue-collar workers which said that *Ivan*, while it had quality, was not of sufficient stature to merit a Lenin Prize.

The artistic members of the Prize Committee were strongly in favor of Solzhenitsyn. Then S. P. Pavlov, First Secretary of the Komsomol, rose and said the prize could not go to Solzhenitsyn for political and legal reasons. Solzhenitsyn had surrendered to the Germans in the war and subsequently been convicted for a criminal offense. Tvardovsky leapt to his feet and said, "It's a lie."

"You will have to prove it's a lie," Pavlov said.

The agitated editor rushed off to consult Sanya, then went hunting in court archives. Meanwhile the prize committee, put under immense pressure, was finally forced to award the prize to O. Honchar, for a novel called *The Sheep-Bell*. This was announced to the world on Lenin's birthday, 22 April, 1964. While the Prize Committee was debating the nominations for other arts, Tvardovsky came in and read out the Supreme Court's decision on Solzhenitsyn's rehabilitation. The court had found, on unimpeachable evidence, that he had served his country courageously, displayed personal heroism, and inspired the devotion of his men. His only "offense" had been to speak out against the cult of personality.

Pavlov, having listened in silence, stood up and said in a syrupy voice, "Obviously I was wrong. I apologize."[23]

30

Love, Truths, and Microfilms

Nay, but this dotage of our general
O'erflows the measure. . . .
—*Antony and Cleopatra*

IN THE FIRST WEEKS OF 1964, WHEN IT WAS STILL GENERALLY AS-
sumed he would win the Lenin Prize, Sanya was researching in Moscow for
that vast project about the Revolution that had been interrupted by the
small matters of a world war and imprisonment. Delving into the Central
Military-Historical Archives in the former Lefortovo Palace, he unearthed
some documents relating to his father, one of which even identified the
Belorussian church in which his parents had been married. At the end of
January he phoned Natasha to tell her he was going to Leningrad, to work
at the "Publichka," the Leningrad Public Library. Sanya always enjoyed
Leningrad. Natasha was absorbed in her music at the time, practicing for a
performance of Kabalevsky's Concerto with a student from a music school.
Sanya wrote to say how well the research was going.

By now Natasha was not his only devoted female helper. One of several
others was a Leningrad spinster in her late fifties, Elizaveta Voronyanskaya,
who had just retired from her position as a scientific librarian. She had
written to him a worshipful letter; and met him later by appointment in the
"Publichka," having first watched him unseen for forty minutes, transfixed
by the way he kept tossing his pencil in the air and catching it without
lifting his eyes from his book. A lonely woman, she had much adoration
that needed an outlet. She did endless typing for him in her dark, cramped,
Dostoyevskian flat. Shostakovich was another whom she adored; she would
willingly scrub his floors and clean his overshoes, she said. Her passion,
apart from great men, was music. Especially requiems. She took the Solzhenitsyns to a performance of Mozart, and was in tears; she also gave them
a record of Verdi. In recognition of her intense nature, they knew her as
"Queen Elizabeth," or Q.

Now, in Ryazan, Natasha received a telegram from Q. saying, on Sanya's behalf: BEG PERMISSION REMAIN ONE WEEK LONGER. Then a letter came from Sanya himself saying he needed more time to complete his research. It was unthinkable to Natasha that they should be separated on her birthday, 26 February—he had always insisted they no longer had separate birthdays but must celebrate them as one being; she resolved to go to Leningrad and join him. However, a viral infection intervened and the trip to Leningrad was out of the question in the bitter cold.

In the end they met in Moscow on the twenty-fifth. Being a more intuitive creature than Karenin when he greeted Anna, she felt something was amiss, and said right away, on the railroad platform, "You're not mine anymore."

"That's not true."

He had brought her a pretty beige purse, but she didn't care for it. There was something not right, something strained in the way he was behaving toward her. Anyone but Natasha—with anyone but Sanya—might have suspected an affair; even their friend Suzanna Teush suspected something of the kind, and said to her when they were on their own: "Do you think he could be infatuated with one of the Sovremennik actresses?"

"That's the one thing I don't have to fear, Suzanna; he doesn't have the time!" They both gave a wry smile. "He tells me his creative work is my only rival, and I'm sure it's true."

"He seems to rely a lot on this Voronyanskaya woman. . . ."

"Yes; she even talked him into buying that awful sweater!" It was black, but with a flashy design—not at all his usual style.

After a few days Natasha returned to Ryazan; Sanya followed soon after. Maria, his mother-in-law, also found him entirely changed; nothing in the house that had once seemed to him a palace now gave him joy; everything made him irritable. The chimes of the clock had, as usual when he was due home, been stopped, so as not to disturb his work; but now they would sometimes ring out arrhythmically, as if conscious of a tense atmosphere in the house.

On being admitted to the Writers' Union he had been offered a bigger apartment in Moscow, which he had declined on the grounds that Moscow would be too noisy and its social life would suck him down. Perhaps he regretted that decision, Natasha wondered. Of course, he was getting to know quite grand people. The tension in the house kept mounting, till finally, unable to bear it, she demanded to know what was wrong.

"An act of betrayal has been committed in our home," he replied angrily.

She could not believe her ears. "By whom, Sanya?"

"Your mother."

"My mother! How has she betrayed you?" Had she, unwittingly, said something about his work that he thought might be dangerous? He would not tell her. Not there in the house. Later, perhaps, in Tashkent. They were due to take a train to Tashkent in a week or two, so that he could revisit the Oncological Clinic to research a novel to be called *Cancer Ward*.

They left Ryazan in winter and arrived in Tashkent to summerlike warmth. At the clinic he was welcomed as a distinguished guest; they had all been thrilled when their former patient became so suddenly famous. We knew him, we cured him! . . . He put on a white coat and was allowed to do the rounds with Dunayeva, the head of radiology, and other doctors. It felt false to him; everyone was acting a part.

"Well, now let's talk, Natasha," he said one day, in the restaurant of the Hotel Tashkent. Rain was lashing the windows. Gazing at her fixedly, he told her her mother had spoken much too frankly about his illness—a highly personal detail—to one of their visitors, a female science professor from Leningrad.*

Natasha knew at once the embarrassingly personal detail to which he was referring. "Well, if she mentioned that, it was . . . I can see it would annoy you."

"It was a betrayal."

"I'm sure Mama didn't mean any harm." Then a further thought struck her. "I find it very strange that this woman would *tell* you what Mother said to her. How could a mere acquaintance feel able to talk to you about such a thing?"

He was silent, still gazing at her. A sudden lurch in her heart. "Are you intimate with her?"

"Yes."

"She . . . has fallen in love with you?"

"Yes."

She smiled. A learned professor, in love with! . . . The next instant a flood of tears burst from her eyes. She heard him say he had not intended it to happen; she had helped him with his research, and would like to go walking with him through the villages of Belorussia and East Prussia, researching *The Red Wheel*. She had more stamina than Natasha and could rough it better. "You've helped me to create one novel. Permit me to allow her to help me create another!"

Brushing the tears from her eyes she said shakily, "I understand everything. My stage in your life has ended. Just let me go away altogether, go away from life itself."

"You must live, Natasha! If you take your life by your own hand, you will not only ruin yourself. You will also ruin me and my creative work." He seized her hands and raised them to his lips. And convinced her for a while nothing terrible had happened; he still loved her. His feelings for the two women were "two planes that could never intersect." For Natasha he had one feeling; for his Leningrad friend—something entirely different. . . .

(In other words: intense, passionate, romantic, lyrical, exciting, feverish. . . .)

---

*Actually she was a mathematician. Natasha, in her memoir *Sanya*, did her best to disguise her identity.

If she could understand that as a writer he needed to explore other relationships, he said, their relationship would deepen still further; because, to everything else would be added his gratitude and admiration that she had been willing to make such a sacrifice.

She seemed ready to accept, then again burst into tears.

The next morning, she couldn't eat breakfast, her throat was too tight. Then, while he was at the clinic, she had her hair cut and permed. Sanya was very appreciative; he was eloquent in his admiration for her beauty; for a short time she felt enraptured, ready to go along with anything. She had given him, for the past seven years, the comforts of a well-ordered house-hold, of music, of anticipating and fulfilling all his desires. Now he needed one more: "the comfort of an untroubled conscience." To be able to say, My wife has agreed willingly to this. . . . Shouldn't she try to provide that comfort for him too?

Could she not stifle the thought—lying in bed in Ryazan—that in East Prussia they were climbing into a sleeping bag and . . . ?

They strolled in a park adjoining the cancer clinic; the air was balmy and fragrant after the rain. His arm around her, he said, "You know, it's strange. *Then,* I had no woman in my life, but now—I have two. . . ." He suggested she start to keep a diary; it might be therapeutic for her. (And perhaps be useful for him later?)

They returned to frozen Ryazan. Her mother wondered why she had lost so much weight. It was hot, Natasha said; I didn't eat much. Sanya still let the old woman feel his silent censure, but her "betrayal" of him was never referred to.

Natasha still had a week of her holiday left, and went to Moscow. From there she wrote to him saying she had thought over everything carefully, and had decided she could not share him with another woman. He would have to choose. If he could not decide at once, he should move out of their house. She was tied to Ryazan through her job; he was not.

He wrote back a distressed letter in which he said he could not under-stand why he should be "chased out of the house for telling the truth." He had done enough traveling; he needed his home. Feeling some sympathy for him, she offered an alternative: she could have the house altered to make a separate study for him. They would have separate rooms until he could make a decision.

"Well, do that," he agreed.

She called in plasterers, painters, electricians, herself sewed curtains for the windows, a bedspread for the ottoman. For weeks he tried to suppress his longing for the other woman, as Natasha waited in dread and sorrow. Then he said, "She wouldn't suit me as a companion through life. You can destroy her letters." She removed the Leningrad professor's letters from File No. 21 ("The World of Scholars"), and destroyed them.[1]

Sometime later, he left a letter for her to read, should she feel lonely while he was away in the South. She read that their crisis was past, and it had convinced him more than ever that no one could be so devoted to him as she, no one live by his interests so much as she did; and with no one else did he feel so at ease and so good. There was a kind of echo of the message he had written on the back of his photograph, given to her on their wedding day: "Will you, under all circumstances, love the man with whom you have joined your life?" The question, it seemed, was who could love him with the greatest devotion, not whom he could love.

In *October 1916*, the sequel to *August 1914* in *The Red Wheel*, Colonel Georgi Vorotyntsev, Solzhenitsyn's alter ego, becomes acquainted with a very young (just over thirty) professor of medieval history in Petrograd. Professor Olda Andozerskaya has already appeared briefly in *August 1914;* there, talking to disbelieving liberal-minded students, she compares the Enlightenment unfavorably with the Middle Ages, which she says possessed an intense spiritual life. She is "a small, slim, unbending figure, looking from the back almost like a student except for a certain added elegance which was rather unusual for a member of the intelligentsia." She wears her hair piled high, a gray frock, high heels. She is very self-confident.² Vorotyntsev, in *October 1916*, meets her at the apartment of a noted Kadet politician, and the following day calls at her home. She lives on the embankment of the Neva, overlooking the Kamenni Ostrov.

He feels the spring of youth in his legs, and lightness in his heart. She leads him into a large room full of books, papers, and toys; on one wall is an icon of St. Olga, hung in the middle and without candles. They talk, standing face-to-face; she places her hands on his shoulders, close to his neck, looks up at him with her green eyes, and says, "God, what happiness that we still have people like you!" At that moment Vorotyntsev is lost. They have tea, then go out for a walk along the embankment in a bitter wind. They find a swing, and Olda climbs on and wants him to push her. "Harder! Harder!" The wind is so fierce it threatens to topple her; Georgi brings her to a halt. "Professor, you're just a girl at heart! If I had the right to, I'd call you Olzhenka."

"How splendid! No one's ever called me that. . . . It pleases me."

"So when may I call you that?"

"When no one can hear you."

"And when will that be?"

"Whenever you please."

He kisses her then, "on the lips, on the lips"; her bonnet goes flying.³

Next day he telephones; she tells him to come early, so the evening can be long. She couldn't sleep last night. When he arrives, she leaps into his arms, her legs embracing him, and he carries her—small, light—"into another room, the inevitable place." Their lovemaking is intense, passionate, inducing her to cry out in ecstasy; afterward, when they talk in bed lazily, she asks him if he realized, that first night, that she meets . . . others. . . . Georgi is shocked.

They discuss Stolypin, politics.

The days pass, in a dream for Georgi. The weather is bad, but he doesn't notice it. Olda obsesses him. She is never for one moment the same—in bed or out. Her skin, she confesses, is acutely sensitive; and her caresses, in turn, make his tough skin seem exquisitely alive and renewed, as if after an anesthetic. She asks him if it was ever like this with Alina. No, never, he replies. "Is she intelligent?" Even though her bed is full of ghosts, she can talk only of Alina! . . . "Well, she's not stupid; but she's no specialist." "Do you love her?" He avoids answering.

Toward Olda—who has no interest in children, despite her collection of toys, but loves cats—he feels an overwhelming gratitude; and toward Alina, no guilt—for he is a different man with Olda. She tells him she thinks he has more enthusiasm for making love to her than for saving Russia. Indeed, she is becoming his whole world. She seems a magical creature, and he is not surprised that she believes in astrology and the occult, despite being a scientist.

The only problem is that Alina's birthday, 27 October, is rapidly approaching; she is assaulting him with letters and telegrams; he must reply, explaining away his absence. At length she demands that he meet her in Moscow at the latest on the eve of her birthday. He discusses with Olda whether this means the twenty-fifth or twenty-sixth. Unquestionably the twenty-sixth, she replies. But he meets his wife, in Moscow, on the twenty-fifth.[4]

Olda's identity has always been a closely guarded secret among Solzhenitsyn's friends and relations, even those where the relationship has been broken; but her name was Olga Ladizhenskaya. Solzhenitsyn gives a blatant clue in the names. Andozerskaya contains the word for lake, *ozero*, while Ladizhenskaya almost contains the name of Petersburg's lake, Laduga— sometimes referred to as "Laduzhenskaya Ozero." The passage from *October 1916,* I am told on reliable authority, essentially tells the story of their meeting and love affair. Even the day of the month of the eve-of-birthday arrival in Moscow is the same in both cases. It must have been unpleasant for Natasha—among much that was deeply painful—to read that he considers her "not stupid," but clearly no match for the professor.

Ladizhenskaya was born in Petrograd in 1922: and so was forty-two in 1964, older than her fictional counterpart. A graduate of Moscow State University, she had a distinguished academic career in her native city, Leningrad. In 1969 she won a State Prize for her work and publications in mathematics, was made a candidate member of the Academy of Sciences in 1981 and a full academician in 1990. She is an honorary member of the German and Italian Academies. Few women have attained such eminence in mathematics. She has never married.

There can be no proof that any single incident in the "fiction," other than Alina's summons for her birthday, happened in the real affair. It would not surprise me, however—it would seem characteristic of his fidelity to the real—if Olga laid her hands on his shoulders, close to the neck, and told him it was happy for Russia that there were people like him; or that she wanted him to push her on a swing—or some similar girlish activity. He was evidently delighted by her mixture of acute intellect, rebellious views, unpredictability, and powerful sensuality. Olga awakened him sexually. When he and Natasha had married they were both, presumably, virgins; brought up in a rigidly puritanical society. The experienced Olga must have been a revelation: one that he wished to record, in the only passionately sexual episode in his entire work. "He describes her as crying out in bed," Natasha has said, adding, "I never cried out."[5] Olga may well have been the only woman—indeed, the only person—to attain "mastery" over him.

With that background, one can begin to interpret his behavior, as related by his wife, more sympathetically. He genuinely felt his marriage and his affair were two completely separate experiences; he was two different men with each of the women. He may have been struggling to express that when he chortled to Natasha that *then* he had no woman, now he has two; though very likely there was also a vengeful thrust—"You left me with nothing"—as well as immature vanity.

Sanya had had close relationships with only two women, his mother and Natasha. The affair that had swept him away *would*, without doubt, have been enriching for him, as a man and as a writer. He could also hardly be blamed if he smoldered with the knowledge that Natasha had thrown him over so heartlessly, when he was in a camp, whereas he was being honest about this affair, which entailed no threat to his feelings for Natasha—and yet she gave him a cruel choice.

In the end, he may have given Olga up because she threatened his peace of mind too much. She was emotional and dramatic. At one point she breaks the night's silence—Georgi lying at her side—by letting out a piercing hunter's cry. The feelings aroused by constant sexual excitement probably cut into the calm that—in Pushkin's words—is more important than ecstasy for creative inspiration.

He found her domineering—Chekhov's "Darling" was not for her. But the most important reason for giving her up is likely to have been the overwhelming nature of his passion for her. It threatened to penetrate all the defenses he had so carefully constructed. A woman who could make all one's skin feel so tender, so exquisitely responsive to the lightest touch, threatened to overflow the embankments. . . .

He could have turned into Shakespeare's unmanned Antony. He had no intention of allowing that to happen.

Strolling by the Neva with Olga, he would have passed memorials of Egypt, notably two sphinxes dredged up from the Nile in the Pushkin era. Pushkin wrote a fascinating story, left as a fragment, called "Egyptian Nights" (1824–30). A prose narrative set in Petersburg leads to a poem, "Cleopatra and Her Lovers." Cleopatra offers her bed for a night to any man willing to pay the price of dying at dawn. Three men offer themselves, and on successive nights make love to the queen, and die.

The brilliant poem is created and delivered impromptu by a visiting Italian *improvisatore*. Charsky, a gentleman-poet, was sitting at his desk writing one day when, unannounced, this ruffianly-looking Italian appeared in the doorway. The startled Charsky demands his business; the Italian begs for his support in becoming known in Petersburg society. Following a demonstration of the *improvisatore*'s astounding gift, Charsky promises to help him; the result is the performance, before an aristocratic assembly, of "Cleopatra and Her Lovers."

Sanya experienced his "Egyptian Nights" in Leningrad; but after a while it may have seemed to him that each night of passion was leading to death, in the sense of emotional exhaustion, and the loss of the sense of overriding purpose ("You think more of making love to me than saving Russia. . . ."); Olga Ladizhenskaya brought him delight at first, but then all that was dark, female and feline, oceanic, nocturnal, dreamlike, unconscious, unpredictable, dangerous, and immoral. In giving her up, he was acting virtuously, as well as sensibly. She wouldn't have suited him. But what she stood for, in his creative life, *improvisatore*-like, involved a real loss.

Breaking with her must have been painful. He was left with staid Natasha, who had bought an ugly, thick flannel nightdress. When he told her he didn't like it, she snarled, "Well, I don't care, it keeps me warm."*

And there were the three old ladies, grateful the home had returned to normal after Natasha's hysterical grief: appearing to Sanya, no doubt, like the three Fates.

That Easter, as he adjusted to a quiet life, Sanya entertained a guest. Tvardovsky had been more upset at *Ivan*'s not winning the Lenin Prize than Sanya; but his spirits revived when Sanya invited him to spend a weekend in Ryazan to read the manuscript of *The First Circle*. He had never before been invited there. On 2 May 1964, Easter Saturday (though, as Solzhenitsyn remarks, the religious festival would have meant nothing to him), in blue raincoat and blue beret, Tvardovsky briefly cast off the trappings of officialdom by buying his own train ticket to Ryazan. Sanya and Natasha met him, and helped him to wedge his large frame into their tiny Moskvich. Surprisingly it was Natasha's first meeting with Tvardovsky: suggesting how far she had been marginalized during Sanya's rise to fame.

She and the three old ladies of the house were impressed by their guest's courtesy and consideration, his intense blue eyes, and the "open quality of his face with its acquired sadness."[6] Fearful that he would be disappointed

---

*Actually Alina in *August 1914* (ch. 13), but Natasha acknowledges the incident. As she recalls him today, Sanya was "not a good lover." But she adds that his affair in Leningrad taught him that women can be different from each other in bed.

by *The First Circle*, he gently warned Sanya, over dinner, that every writer must expect setbacks.

The next morning he began to read the cramped typewritten pages. Natasha had placed a thermos of tea beside him, and he had brought his own honey to eat with the tea. Sanya, who made a point of not working when he had a guest staying, tinkered with the car outside, while Natasha worked in the kitchen garden. After lunch she played the piano. Tvardovsky tiptoed in and admired her playing. How nice to have a wife like that, who could sit down at the piano and play one thing after another! He tried to drag Sanya from a BBC broadcast to come and listen too.

That afternoon, as if inspired by the music, he started to show his excitement over the novel: forgetting to smoke, bobbing up and down in his chair; exclaiming to Sanya, who couldn't resist sneaking in occasionally to check how far he had read, "Great stuff! . . . So far, so far: I promise nothing!" At dinner his host reluctantly offered him cognac and vodka, and Tvardovsky soon lost control of himself, his eyes becoming wild, all whites.

The next morning he insisted on a bottle of cognac instead of tea, and his eyes were soon rolling again, and the novel again exercised its spell over him. "No, no—I don't believe you'd go and spoil it now!" he would chortle, as the amount still to be read diminished. "But you're a terrible man! If I ever came to power I'd put you away! . . . This is great, as good as Tolstoy and Dostoyevsky. So far, so far! When you're inside I'll bring you parcels! You'll even get the odd bottle of cognac."

Gloomily: "You know, there are islands in the Arctic where they've put all the cripples from the war. . . . I don't know, I don't know. . . . It's not an anti-Party book, that's the great thing. . . . Though I think you should tone down the Stalin passages. . . . This is wonderful, Alexander Isayevich—not a superfluous line! . . . *I* shall be put inside for publishing it! Even though it's basically optimistic."

He leapt to his feet and begged Sanya to play the role of an MGB interrogator, yelling accusations while the "prisoner" stood at attention. Sanya managed with great difficulty to undress him and get him to bed. But soon the household was awakened by the sound of Tvardovsky shouting and talking to himself, in different voices, acting different parts. Sanya came to him and saw him sitting in his underpants. "I shall go away and die soon," he said plaintively; then roared "Silence! On your feet!" and jumped up at his own command, with his thumbs along his seams. "Come what may, I can do no other."

When he had read in *Pravda* the result of the Lenin Prize ballot, he had said to Sanya despairingly *"Das ist Alles,"* the only time Sanya ever heard him speak in German. Now, a month later, he was echoing Luther. Sanya quieted him, sitting up with him for an hour. "He had a smoke, his face softened, and after a time he even began laughing, I took him back to bed soon after, and he caused no further disturbance."[7]

What is sad is not Tvardovsky's behavior but Sanya's prim disapproval of it.° He was the dissident, Tvardovsky the loyal Party member; yet it was the latter who came into the Solzhenitsyn house as a bizarre, unpredictable, theatrical, misbehaving *improvisatore*. And without some element of that embarrassing or shocking character, a writer is handicapped.

The *improvisatore* would make less and less frequent calls at Solzhenitsyn's house.

Two weeks after Easter, delivering a revised *First Circle* to the editor's home, Sanya found him recovered from his drinking bout. While the novel was being retyped, Tvardovsky would make sure all copies were carefully locked away, not wanting to run any risk of having the manuscript passed from hand to hand as *Ivan Denisovich* had been. Speedily the copies were prepared and circulated to the inner circle at *Novy Mir;* and on 11 June (Ascension Day) a solemn group met for the crucial discussions. "By the normal standards," Tvardovsky began, "this novel should be scuttled and its author arrested. But what sort of people are we?"

Kondratovich said, with familiar indecision, it was impossible to publish, and morally impossible not to. Tvardovsky pointed out sincerely—he would never have supported the novel otherwise—that the idea of Communism was not called into question. Timid Zaks wanted a second reading. Dementyev, clearly disturbed, said the writing was tremendous but "the novel plunges us into doubt and dismay. . . ." Lakshin, the youthful up-and-coming head of the criticism section, argued warmly for acceptance.

Within days a contract was drawn up. But the greatest obstacle, the censorship, remained. Tvardovsky decided to send the first quarter of the manuscript to Lebedev, hoping for his support once more. Back came his comment: "Bury it!"

"But Khrushchev—"

"—Is no longer enamoured of *Ivan Denisovich;* he thinks [Ivan's] brought him a lot of trouble."

That summer, the Solzhenitsyns loaded up their Moskvich and drove to Estonia. Apart from the Susis, his Leningrad helper Elizaveta Voronyanskaya, "Q.," was there; a yearly visitor, she had rented a farm in beautiful lake-covered countryside. It may have been awkward for Natasha, since Q. had sent her the telegram "explaining" Sanya's delay in Leningrad. Sanya had involved her in the deception. According to him, she had got in the way. Whatever the personal feelings, Sanya's writing came first. The two women, working in shifts, typed out a revised version of *The First Circle*. Sanya went off to a pine-covered hillside to write, using a tent if it rained. His soul felt eased in Estonia; for him it was a wonderfully relaxed and

---

°Compare Tolstoy's diary comment, after his guest Turgenev had drunk a bit too much: "Turgenev. Cancan. Sad."

productive summer. Life was lighter without passion. He was meditating *The Gulag Archipelago;* its form was conceived during that visit.

His thoughts turned to the future: how wonderful it would be to find a hideaway here in Estonia. . . . Susi came up with the perfect place—Haava, a farm near Tartu where he had stayed after his return from Siberia. The owner, a broad-shouldered, tough-minded widow called Marta Port, had sheltered the Susis and now did not hesitate to offer Sanya the chance to come there in secret whenever he wished. It was ideal: four spacious rooms, old-fashioned stoves, firewood . . . nearby, a shallow river and a wood.

They met Tenno and, through him, other ex-*zeks* with Tenno's resolve and discipline. A whole system was beginning to emerge. It would be needed.

In October 1964, Khrushchev was deposed. The former pipe fitter from a Donbass coal mine was pensioned off—a mild fate which, in itself, was testimony that he left the Soviet Union a better place than he had found it. He took to listening to the BBC World Service and Voice of America, and found them illuminating; he read a lot, including *The First Circle*, which he did not like. He was appalled by the invasion of Czechoslovakia in 1968, and deprecated the prosecution of dissidents.

His secretary, Lebedev, died soon after his master's downfall, and no one from the hierarchy attended his funeral except Tvardovsky. "In my mind's eye," wrote Solzhenitsyn at his most imaginatively humane, "I can see that sturdy, broad-backed figure bending sadly over little Lebedev's coffin."[8]

Made anxious by the accession of Brezhnev—and perhaps keen to escape his home—Sanya increasingly worked away from Ryazan: staying in Moscow with the Teushes, at Kornei Chukovsky's dacha in Peredelkino, and with an old peasant woman, Agafya, in a village he loved, Solotcha, thirty miles from Ryazan. He released his prose poems into samizdat, and soon they were circulating widely. In the month of Khrushchev's dismissal they were even published in the West, in the émigré magazine *Grani.* He was skirting the Rubicon.

Then he took several strides into the river. Transferring *The First Circle* to three rolls of microfilm, he gave them to a man enviably placed to travel freely between the Soviet Union and the West. This was Vadim Andreyev, son of a famous writer. Leonid Andreyev, a prerevolutionary socialist opposed to the Bolsheviks, had addressed from Finland a plea to the West to save Russia: then died in despair in 1919. His son still lived in the West but his heart was in Russia; indeed, he had requested and been granted Soviet citizenship. A writer and a diplomat, when he met Solzhenitsyn, who admired his biography of his father, Vadim was working in the UN Secretariat in Geneva.

Fearing a renewal of Stalinism, Andreyev agreed to smuggle the microfilms out. Urged to conceal them in a body belt, he wisely (and courageously) put the canisters loose in his raincoat pocket before he sauntered through airport customs.

The First Circle continued to be read secretly by a few of the author's friends, particularly those who had experienced the *sharashka* and who might well see a version of themselves in the text. Nikolai Vitkevich was given a copy to read at the end of 1964. On New Year's Eve, he and his wife were guests at the Solzhenitsyn house. Having perhaps drunk too much, Nikolai suddenly complained that Sanya was no longer open with him. Sanya responded that where openness between friends was felt to have ceased they should stop seeing each other. Nikolai then criticized the few chapters he had read of the *sharashka* novel for their tone of omniscience, their pretentious air, their lack of modesty. Disciples of Tolstoy and Dostoyevsky, he sneered, were even worse than the originals. The supper party grew as frigid as the weather outside. Next day, Sanya went round to the Vitkevich apartment and reclaimed his novel. When a baby was born to the Vitkeviches later in the year, Natasha begged her husband to congratulate them. No: Nikolai had attacked his novel, and he didn't see how the birth of a child was a greater event than the birth of a novel.[9] The friendship was over.

Nineteen sixty-four had seen the abandonment of a new and passionate love and an old and passionate friendship.

31

Dictating the Inferno

No sound of grief except the sound of sighing . . .
—*Inferno, IV*

THE TITLE OF THE NOVEL THAT HAD SO STIRRED TVARDOVSKY AT
Solzhenitsyn's home referred to the upper and least torturing level of the
Inferno in Dante's epic poem.

Dante was a sacred figure, a talisman and a messenger of hope to some
of the greatest modern Russian writers. In her poem "Muse" (1934), which
proudly asserts her calling in the midst of Stalinist terror, Akhmatova asked
the veiled woman who visits her at night, a flute in her hand: "And were
you Dante's guide/Dictating the Inferno? She answers: Yes." Fittingly, Akhmatova's last public appearance, on 19 October 1965 at Moscow's Bolshoi
Theater, was to celebrate the seven hundredth anniversary of Dante's birth.
Addressing the audience she said, "For my friends and contemporaries the
greatest, unattainable teacher was always the stern Alighieri."

Preeminent among those friends and contemporaries she was thinking of
the poet Osip Mandelstam. Anticipating arrest, he sewed a copy of the
Inferno into his jacket. One book, he said, was all he needed. He wrote a
prose work, *Conversation about Dante*, which his wife, Nadezhda, learned
by heart—all twenty thousand words of it.

Dante occupied Mandelstam's exalted place for several reasons. His
greatest work recognized—was built out of—a reality beyond materialism.
Its poetry was a supreme amalgam of substance and form. Mandelstam said
he only began to understand the structure of *The Divine Comedy* when he
examined the stones of Koktebel in the Crimea. He meant that Dante's
language was organic and multifaceted, in total contrast to the shrill and
colorless sloganizing that passed for language under the Bolsheviks. In the
manner of great poetry, any one of the terza rima stanzas was in an intimate
relation with the whole of the epic—and merged into the rest of life, love,
time, and eternity.

In the First Circle of the *Inferno* dwell passively the unbaptized and the virtuous pagans, knowing no torment except exclusion from God's presence. Virgil, Dante's guide, shows him Homer, Democritus, Plato, Ptolemy, Empedocles, Horace . . . a learned company. The First Circle does not lack intellect; nor, as we have found, did the Marfino *sharashka*.

Dante knew Siberia imaginatively. He speaks of the damned in the Ninth and lowest Circle whose first tears freeze to a lump of ice, so that their anguish has to turn inward. But perhaps Akhmatova was right when she said to her friend and memoirist Lydia Chukovskaya, "Our late Alighieri would have created a tenth circle of Hell out of this." *Late!*—so recently dead! . . . Lydia, who became close to Solzhenitsyn, saw him as a reborn Dante, who had brought "the living word from the nether regions."[1]

How different from the tortured forms of those millions of Kolyma skeletons were the "well-fed, well-dressed men with white hands," driven in a bus from the *sharashka* to meet their wives. These men were no longer very talkative, smiled sadly at their visitors, and assured them they had all they needed. Similarly the spirits in Dante's First Circle greet the living man in a kindly way; their eyes are grave and tranquil; they speak seldom and sedately. The grave, sedate spirits of the *sharashka* gaze at their wives across an invisible barrier: "The living looked fondly at the dead, while the dead man looked towards Hades with eyes that were neither happy nor sad but somehow blank—the look of someone who knew too much."[2]

Solzhenitsyn could hardly have identified himself more closely with Gleb Nerzhin, whose meeting with Nadya is the most powerful and moving episode in the novel. To take a few likenesses at random: Nerzhin and Nadya were also together for only a year before the war—their last year at University; he has previously been imprisoned at Kaluga Gate; he has always been an avid newspaper reader; Nadya has brought him a book of Yesenin's poetry, with the inscription "All that is lost shall be returned to you"; during the three December days that *The First Circle* occupies his birthday occurs; Nadya studies the piano and lives in a student hostel with several other girls; during the meeting, Nadya painfully mentions the possibility of a "*pseudo*" divorce. None of these correspondences is necessary to the plot, except the last. Most novelists, wishing to use their personal experience yet also create a distance, would without any difficulty have altered details. Nadya might become a violinist, or an amateur actress, and live with relatives; his birthday might be in May, and his favorite poet Blok; he has moved directly from a camp in the far North . . . and so on.

There was something in Solzhenitsyn that needed to go against that practice, to bring in real details even when to do so was inessential. So, in *October 1916*, not content with having the unfaithful Vorotyntsev pressurized by his wife's birthday, he must make their reunion, in Moscow, on the twenty-fifth.

In *The First Circle*, he obviously wanted it to be clear that Nerzhin and he are closer than identical twins. And yet, of course, Nerzhin is *not* Solzhenitsyn, from the simple fact that the former is a creation, and obedient to the rules of art.

Nevertheless, we can't help confusing the real and the fictional people in our minds; and, when we read the wonderful account of the couple's meeting, it is impossible quite to forget that "they" would later become bitter enemies.

Nerzhin's closest friends, Rubin and Sologdin, just as accurately mirror Kopelev and Panin. Rubin, huge in body and intellect, is still a staunch Communist, and indeed retains an affection for Stalin; while Sologdin, deeply religious, loathes Communism. Nerzhin hovers between the two positions, though he is increasingly drawn toward Sologdin's.

Around these four major characters there are a host of others, both inside the prison system and without. The main character outside, apart from Nadya, is a diplomat called Innokenti Volodin. He is indeed an innocent in the corrupt Soviet world, since he makes a courageous phone call to warn a well-known doctor not to hand over a medicine to a Western colleague, as it will spring a trap. Rubin is set the task of studying the voice print of the anonymous caller, to decide which of three suspects is the "traitor." Remorselessly the inside and outside prisons move closer, until finally they snap together, with Volodin's arrest and the start of the Lubyanka's process of dehumanization.

In the actual Marfino, Kopelev had been given the task of unearthing a traitor, warning the Americans of a Soviet spy in their midst, about to hand over atomic secrets. Kopelev was patriotically enraged, and committed himself to exposing the traitor. Few, in that era, would have felt any different.

Originally, Solzhenitsyn had kept close to the reality, but realized it would cost him any chance of getting the novel past the censors. In the course of "lightening" the novel from ninety-six chapters to eighty-seven—the version shown to Tvardovsky—an act of treachery became a humanitarian gesture: a warning to a well-known Soviet doctor not to hand over a medicine to a Western colleague, as the gesture could be used against him. This change had the beneficial effect of making the authorities' actions more unambiguously immoral; yet it was "rough" on Kopelev who, when *The First Circle* became widely read in samizdat, was known to be the prototype of Rubin: and hence someone who enthusiastically hunted down a man trying to do good. Solzhenitsyn did his best to overcome this by writing Kopelev a letter setting out the facts, and telling him to show it to anyone who might refuse to shake his hand. It was a barely adequate restitution.

Having read the novel carefully, Kopelev had less subjective criticisms to make. He felt his friend was far better at describing what he had experienced than what he had only imagined. He also, like Vitkevich, disliked the way he seemed to hold all truths in the palm of his hand. Somewhat stung, Solzhenitsyn pointed out tartly that Kopelev had believed *Ivan Denisovich* to be just a run-of-the-mill story. He felt he would be a "dead duck" if he was incapable of writing from his imagination, since one could not experience everything.

Kopelev's criticism, while not wholly invalid, does not really seem just. Most of the memorable episodes or images in *The First Circle* naturally belong to the experienced world of the *sharashka;* but they often involved an imaginative act of empathy. The author is, for example, wonderfully alive to the tremulous emotions of Simochka, the tiny MGB lieutenant who finds herself working with Nerzhin and falls in love with him. This, too, as we have seen, was based on personal experience; but Solzhenitsyn makes an imaginative leap into *her* emotions. He can bring to life her virginal excitement, in that moment when they bend together over a faulty microphone, and their cheeks touch. . . . "She nearly died of fright at the thought of what might happen next. She should have drawn back, but she went on foolishly looking at the microphone. There followed the longest and most terrifying minute she had ever known—their cheeks were on fire as they touched, but he too did not draw away! Suddenly he seized her head and kissed her on the lips. Simochka's whole body felt exquisitely faint. She forgot her duty to the Komsomol and to her country; all she could say was:

" 'The door's not shut.' . . ."[3]

The psychology of the end of their unconsummated relationship, when Gleb tells her he has seen his wife and his conscience won't allow this to continue, is perfectly observed. After urging him to realize that his wife won't wait for him, Simochka "thought with horror of how she would come home, say something offhand to her nagging mother and hurry off to bed. For months, she had gone to bed thinking of him. How humiliating to remember the way she had made ready for this evening! How she had scrubbed and scented herself!"[4] This, too, is imagination.

She hasn't the strength to ask him to go or to leave herself. Nerzhin finds her particularly attractive as a dim light falls on her sorrowful face; at the same time, having lived for so long with men, who get their explanations over briefly, he feels irritated at her sitting on in silence. "It was this absurd way women had of clinging to one."

In no way are the scenes in Nadya's hostel, in which he shows the mixture of sadness and frivolity in the girls' harsh lives, inferior to the *sharashka* scenes. Though one of Natasha's former roommates, given the novel to read in manuscript in 1964, was critical of the way only Nadya's suffering was fully shown; they had all suffered, not only the *zek*'s wife. She recalled one in particular, Olga Chaikovskaya, who had received news of her husband's death and her brother's, on the same day. She had struggled on, knowing she had a son to bring up.[5]

Solzhenitsyn probably *should* have explored the women of the hostel at greater length. It was not a failure of imagination, for the scenes that he did provide leave the reader wanting more. At home both with the movement of their minds and the rustle of their clothes, he was perfectly capable of creating memorable female characters; he just does not seem very interested in creating them—aside from Nadya, Matryona, and the two doctors of *Cancer Ward*. Nor are any of those quite Anna Karenina or Lara Guishar. Partly by choice and partly by fate, women played a peripheral role in his adult life.

Unlike Dante, who could accept that all his readers knew Hell existed, and did not need either to prove its horrors or to battle to bring down the Devil, Solzhenitsyn subordinated everything to the task of proving that Communism was evil and to be destroyed. Women, probably, did not seem particularly relevant to that great purpose. In artistic terms, it would surely have been more fruitful to have explored the women more fully while cutting down some of the male discussions, the Stalin chapters, the account of Mrs. Roosevelt's farcical visit.

In the next century of Alexander Solzhenitsyn the embattled politics of his work will fall away and become—as the Napoleonic Wars are in *War and Peace*—no more than the back-cloth for an exploration of human anguish, fear, courage, cowardice, desire. Already, before the end of the twentieth century, what is most moving about *The First Circle* is its brilliant depiction of experiences that seem timeless. Spiridon, the blind caretaker, has been unfolding and folding up a letter from his daughter countless times, waiting for Nerzhin to read it to him. Nerzhin begins to read the daughter's sad sentences but then is summoned to join a transport setting out for the East. The letter is forgotten as Nerzhin and Spiridon embrace. "With hands grimy with years of ingrained dirt," Spiridon put the letter back in his pocket and went off to his room. Then "he did not notice that he had knocked his fur hat on to the floor with his knee, and it stayed where it had fallen."[6]

Rubin, out in the prison yard at night, feels the "innocent, childlike touch of the cold snowflakes on his beard and flushed face," and closes his eyes to enjoy the intense feeling of peace. "At this moment he heard the long wavering hoot of a train from the railway which passed within less than half a mile of Mavrino—it was that special sound, so lonely and plaintive in the night, which in our later years reminds us of childhood, because when we were children it seemed to hold out so much promise of things to come."[7]

Such moments, full of truthful innocence, will ensure that *The First Circle* continues to be read when the Old Bolsheviks have become historical footnotes.

In September 1965 the KGB arrested *The First Circle*. "Arrested" was the KGB term.

Solzhenitsyn was working peacefully outside a little ramshackle wooden shack he had bought in a hamlet called Rozhdestvo, south of Moscow. There was no running water, electricity, or gas, the shack was flooded often by a little river, the Istya, at the bottom of his garden; but in summer it provided a wonderfully isolated, quiet, and picturesque spot in which to work. Natasha joined him sometimes on the weekends, but mostly he lived on his own. So far as he was aware, only his most trusted friends knew of his rustic hideaway.

On that September day, he heard an approaching car, and saw that its driver was Veronica Stein, Natasha's cousin, who had become one of his staunchest supporters. Her face, as she got out and came toward him, looked agitated. He soon learned the reason. The KGB had raided the Teushes' apartment and seized three copies of his novel; which he had entrusted to Teush only days before. For a few moments he was struck dumb by Veronica's news, and she saw the color completely drain from his face.

Worse news followed the next day when he drove to Moscow; the KGB had found the rest of his archive, which Teush had been hiding for three years. The confiscated works included his plays *A Feast of Conquerors* and *The Love-Girl and the Innocent*, besides early drafts of *Ivan Denisovich*. Teush had temporarily, over the summer holidays, entrusted the archive to a young Steiner disciple of his called Ilya Silberberg. The KGB had raided Silberberg's flat simultanously. Their discovery of *A Feast of Conquerors*, a play expressing sympathy for the Vlasovites, was especially horrifying. Solzhenitsyn feared imminent arrest. Arrest was in the air; he had learned also that Andrei Sinyavsky, a leading liberal critic, had been charged with smuggling out stories to the West. A less well known writer, Yuli Daniel, had also been arrested. The crackdown had come, and the politician thought most responsible for it was Alexander Shelepin, former KGB chairman, now in charge of the enforcement of ideological purity.

For Sanya, one of the most tormenting aspects of the seizure of *The First Circle* from the Teushes was that the copies ought not to have been there. They should have been locked away in the *Novy Mir* safe, where they had lain for the past year. Only days before, he had gone to Tvardovsky asking for the return of all the copies, saying he wished to make some grammatical corrections. It was an unconvincing lie; the truth was he had heard rumors that at an ideological conference in August he had been attacked for distortions in *Ivan Denisovich:* and Zhdanov, who had led the persecution of artists in 1946, was being praised. Tvardovsky had added to Sanya's fears by warning him of various unpleasant rumors about him: such as, that his newly grown beard was preparing the way for an escape, in disguise, to the West; and even that he might have served in the Gestapo in the war.

Solzhenitsyn had chosen to misunderstand the possibly half-joking warning as a personal attack, and would not permit his editor to keep even one of the four copies in the safe: as he had a right to do, since the journal had paid Solzhenitsyn an advance. Solzhenitsyn sent one copy to a journalist at *Pravda,* which he had hopes would publish a few extracts. (Strange, as Michael Scammell observes,[8] that he now distrusted Tvardovsky to keep his work safe, yet trusted *Pravda.*) He left the remaining three copies in a suitcase at the Teushes'.

His anger with the loyal Teush, his good friend, ardent supporter, and sensitive critic, is implied in this barely polite character assessment: "Teush was a thoroughly decent man, but alas, careless, a muddler, a happy-go-lucky conspirator;"[9] while, in pointing out that Silberberg alone among the Teushes' friends had been raided, he came close to voicing suspicion of deliberate betrayal on Silberberg's part.

He feared the KGB might already have gone through his Ryazan home; his life was by now too fragmented, as he observes in his memoir *The Oak and the Calf*, for him to know what might be happening there. Probably he would already have been arrested if they had known where to find him; now they would come for him, and the history of the Gulag would never get written; he had betrayed all the victims through sheer stupidity. . . . Such were his tortured thoughts. Luckily Tvardovsky, to whom he rushed in his first panic, was standing calmly behind his author. He suggested a protest letter to the new head of Agitprop, Demichev, who had met Solzhenitsyn not long ago, and been reasonably friendly once he had decided he was "not a second Pasternak." The letter was duly composed; Tvardovsky persuaded him to change "unlawful seizure" to "unwarranted seizure."

A crucial exchange took place in an elevator in a Moscow apartment block: Natasha handed to George Tenno a package containing a mass of notes and drafts appertaining to the embryonic *Archipelago*. Tenno made a smooth and skillful escape with it to Estonia, certain he was not being tailed. A day later everything was hidden away on a friend's farm. If that material had been lost, Solzhenitsyn wrote in *Invisible Allies*, "I am sure I would never have written the book. I simply wouldn't have had the patience or the ability to restore it: a loss of that magnitude is just too destructive and too painful."[10] Natasha, who might easily have been picked up, showed great courage that day—something that Solzhenitsyn might have acknowledged but has not.

Reluctant to return to Ryazan, he found a haven at the Peredelkino dacha of Kornei Chukovsky. In its spacious grounds "I strolled for hours through dark cloisters of pine-trees . . . with a heart empty of hope vainly trying to comprehend my situation and, more important, to discover some higher sense in the disaster that had fallen upon me."[11]

The seizure of his work had a devastating effect on him. It was harder to bear than his original arrest; it was

> the greatest misfortune in all my forty-seven years. For some months I felt it as though it were a real, unhealing physical wound—a javelin wound right through the breast, with the tip so firmly lodged that it could not be pulled out. The slightest stirring within me (perhaps the memory of some line or other from my impounded archive) caused a stab of pain. . . . Throughout this period I felt a constriction in my chest . . . a sickening tug somewhere near my solar plexus, and I could not decide whether it was a spiritual sickness or a foreboding of some

new grief. There was an unbearable burning sensation inside me. I was on fire, and nothing helped. My throat was always dry. I felt a tension that nothing would relax. You seek salvation in sleep (as you once did in prison); let me sleep and sleep and never get up again! Switch off and dream untroubled dreams! But within a few hours the shutter of the soul falls away and a red-hot drill whirls you back to reality. Every day you must find in yourself the will to put one foot in front of the other, to study, to work, to pretend that the soul can and must do these things, although in reality your mind wanders every five minutes: Why bother? What does it matter now? It is as though the world's clock has stopped. Thoughts of suicide—for the first time, and I hope the last.[12]

It is an extraordinary passage, probably the most intimate glimpse he allows himself to give his readers. He had admitted to feeling depressed in the first weeks of his arrest at the Lubyanka; but never made us *feel* the intensity of it. At that time he had been young, had come from the war, felt obscurely that through this experience he might one day be able to help his country. Now, however, there seems to have been a "dark night of the soul," without redemption. Even though there were other copies of his novel hidden in the Soviet Union—and, most reassuringly, microfilms of it in the West. It was not lost beyond all recovery, as Vasily Grossman had believed *Life and Fate* to be, when the KGB seized even his worn typewriter ribbon. And had gone to his grave in 1964 believing his epic novel was no more; though—perhaps thanks to someone at the KGB—a microfilm of it mysteriously turned up twenty years later.

In a depression, the self is being invited to look inward, to reflect on one's life. Sanya was not used to doing this: relentless duty always intervened. Now, in the dacha of the genial children's writer, Kornei Chukovsky, he was being given the opportunity—indeed, was being forced by the body and brain's exhaustion—to become still, to change as slowly as the autumn fruits and leaves.

His Muse was Matryona. She was displeased with him of late: all that fame—the car—women jostling for attention. . . . Replying to eager young writers with a pro forma letter, saying he was too busy . . . falling out with the man who loved him like a father, Tvardovsky. . . .

Old Matryona was moving about outside, grumbling that he had locked the door, when she had told him not to.

PART IV

Hostilities

❧

1965 – 1974

SANYA WRITING OUTSIDE HIS HOLIDAY DACHA at Rozhdestvo, at the end of the 1960s.

32

Into Battle

It is the cause, it is the cause, my soul. . . .
— *Othello*

TOO EXHAUSTED AND DESPAIRING EVEN TO READ IN THE EVENINGS,
he lay in the room reserved for him at Kornei Chukovsky's dacha, the lights
off. And went on brooding, his chest constricted, his throat dry, his mind
full of scorpions. His memory drifted to a journey he had made earlier that
year to the South. After visiting Aunt Irina in her Caucasian hovel, he had
driven to the Kuban, wishing to find Grandfather Zakhar's estate. It was
now a collective farm. He had wandered around the rooms and the grounds,
recognizing the place still, despite time and neglect, from photographs he
had studied. Coming upon the reservoir that had once supplied the house
with piped water, he asked two small boys playing there, "Why is it empty?"

"The water won't flow any more; the old owner, old Shcherbak, put a
curse on it."[1]

All the springs of creativity, energy, and joy had dried up in Zakhar
Shcherbak's grandson too.

Unknown to him, a modern Shcherbak had touched his life. This Shcherbak
was a KGB official, his formal title "Deputy Head of Second Chief Directorate of the Committee for State Security of the USSR Council of Ministers." He had provided for his chairman, V. Semichastny, an explosive
memorandum of Solzhenitsyn's opinions, obtained through secret surveillance. The lengthy and top-secret memorandum was presented by Semichastny to the Central Committee on 5 October 1965, together with a
commentary on *"The First Circle* and other unpublished works seized during a search 11 September 1965 at the home of his close acquaintance V.
L. Teush." The document bears the initials of fourteen Central Committee
members, including N. Podgorny, A. Mikoyan, M. Suslov, A. Shelepin, Y.
Andropov, and A. Kosygin—a dazzling constellation.[2]

Solzhenitsyn's reported remarks—probably made to Teush—were dev-astatingly incriminating. He spoke of a *Life of Lenin*, given him by an American journalist.° Sanya said he had spent five hours a day for two months reading it, but it had saved him several years of research. "Lenin was nothing but a serpent, a man totally without principles. He would lit-erally tell you he was on your side, but when you went to the door, he would shoot you in the back. Totally unprincipled. . . . Your hair stands on end when you read it. . . . You know, someday we'll take this up more thoroughly. . . ."

He relates how the rule of the soviets, or workers' councils, ended on 6 July 1918; the results of the elections were "systematically falsified." Today, there was a government without prospects, nothing functioned, there was paralysis. He was sure the republics would split off. . . . "Liberal people—I tell them it's all over for the Ukraine, it has to go." *"No, no!"* another voice protested. "Well, the Ukraine is a controversial issue. But about the western territories of the Ukraine, of course, there's no question, we must let them go." In the eastern part there should be a plebiscite in each region to decide nationality in a democratic way. "But how could there be any question about the Caucasus, the Baltics! On the very first day, if you want—whoever wants to leave, for God's sake, do so!" He was astonishingly prescient.

He declares his intention to have his books published at regular intervals in the West if he is arrested or harmed. At present he is writing *Archipelago*, which will be "an entire avalanche" when he releases it—probably between 1972 and 1975; earlier if there's trouble. He pours out his plans for the structure of the work, and an idea of its inclusive contents: for instance, it will cover collectivization. "No later than 1975 I will fire this terrible salvo. . . . I'll hand everything around and will publish over there (*laughs*). I don't know what will happen. Myself, I'll probably go to the Bastille, but I'm not despondent. . . . *Archipelago* will murder them. It will be devastating! . . . It's like lava flowing when I'm writing the *Archipelago*, it's impossible to stop. I think I'll finish the *Archipelago* by next summer."

The memorandum concludes with some comments—the only ones that might easily spring to the lips of a Western writer—about the slowness of (foreign) publishers in paying royalties.

The anonymously written commentary on the ideological content of *The First Circle*, in this first of over 150 KGB reports on him, is intelligent in its way, and written in an objective style. A reader today can almost imagine the KGB author accepts Solzhenitsyn's analysis of Soviet reality: for exam-ple, that the state itself "is a kind of appendage to the Gulag system, since there are no freedoms on the outside. . . ." And that "the building of so-cialism is above all a ruthless exploitation of people. . . ."

This "reviewer," turning to the play *A Feast of Conquerors*, quotes its

---

°By Louis Fischer (Harper & Row, 1964).

most powerful and anti-Soviet speech, in which Galina, the fiancée of a Vlasovite, calls the USSR an impenetrable forest, without laws, only the power to arrest and torture. The KGB commentator does not, rather strangely, mention the sympathy for the Vlasovite traitors, though this would have damned Solzhenitsyn even in the eyes of most liberals. It was noted, however, by the minor and conformist poet Alexei Surkov, who provided one of two "external" critiques offered to the Central Committee in January 1966. Surkov, in his negative review, said he felt "very sad" at what Solzhenitsyn had written; the second writer, Konstantin Simonov, expressed his "deep sense of pain." His criticisms of Solzhenitsyn's attitudes are quite bravely balanced by praise, both for *The First Circle*'s literary quality and for its depiction of life in a *sharashka*, which he believed to be truthful.[3]

One autumn evening Sanya was roused from his stupor by a cautious knock at his bedroom door. Dragging himself up, he went to open it. It would be old Kornei, telling him supper was ready. Kornei was proud to have him occupy a room in his dacha; preparing to meet him for the first time, back in the early days of *Ivan Denisovich*, he had put on a tie and jacket, saying that he was about to welcome Russia's greatest writer, so he must dress accordingly.

But tonight it wasn't Kornei; he saw a young woman, plain, unmade-up, her hair short and untidy; yet her dark eyes were lively and attentive. He "instantly sensed that help was at hand" at this first meeting with Kornei's granddaughter Elena (Liusha).[4] Liusha herself was in a depression at the time, following a personal loss, but had put on a cheerful face for the sake of a reportedly crushed man; she was surprised to find him looking "unbowed."

Liusha Chukovskaya was thirty-three and unmarried. She lived in a Moscow flat with her mother, another distinguished writer, friend and memoirist of Akhmatova, Lydia Chukovskaya. As though to escape the double literary burden, Liusha had studied chemistry, and was a senior researcher at the Moscow Institute of Organic Chemistry. On the weekends she came out to Peredelkino to act as secretary to her grandfather. Frail in health, she was blessed with "intensity of spirit." Kornei treasured her; she was thorough and accurate; just as important, she normally possessed great zest and a sense of humor.

She was soon offering Sanya helpful suggestions; he could use the flat she shared with her mother, either overnight if he had people to meet in the city, or to work in. As if this wasn't blessing enough, she offered to become his secretary: organize his affairs, type, meet people on his behalf—whatever needed doing. This astonishing offer took a huge weight off his mind.

It was good to feel he could have a base in Moscow. He had outgrown Ryazan. It was too far from the intellectual center, his house was too cramped for all his books; the lorries thundering to and from the new warehouse opposite, and the increasingly infirm old ladies, were bothersome; he could snarl at the former but had to be kind to the latter. Unlike manuscripts, old ladies seemed indestructible. In the spring of 1965 he had tried to move to Obninsk, which had many academic institutions. The suggestion had come from a new friend and admirer, the biochemist Zhores Medvedev; and indeed Natasha had accepted a post at the medical institute where Medvedev worked. However, the central authorities had seemed as determined to keep the Solzhenitsyns at a distance from Moscow as they had been to deny him a Lenin Prize, and the institute was forced to rescind the appointment. He may have learned to be grateful: Obninsk with Natasha and the three Fates was less attractive than a room at Peredelkino and another in central Moscow whenever he wished.

Natasha, understandably, was deeply upset by his almost continual absence from Ryazan. In Kornei's dining room one evening she told Sanya she would rather see him arrested than hiding away and deliberately choosing not to live with his family. He chose to interpret this cry of anger and pain as a serious threat, deciding he could no longer depend on her. He would have to set up a whole new secret system, to be kept hidden from her. Liusha was the obvious person to help him set it up.

If a depression sometimes encourages its victims to take stock of themselves, and perhaps alter course, in Sanya's case it seems to have led to a deepening of existing characteristics. He became even more secretive and mistrustful, drove himself even harder, became even more single-minded. Two years after the almost suicidal depression of autumn 1965, when he was writing about this experience in *The Oak and the Calf,* he was combative and superbly confident, a David against the state's Goliath. Any anger was directed outward; not only against his persecutors and enemies but against those who deserved, and sometimes received, his respect and affection, such as Tvardovsky. His attack on the state was at the same time a defense—of something in himself that must not be touched or threatened. Olga Ladizhenskaya had threatened it, and so had his depression; but he had conquered them both.

Conquering the depression involved literally an escape, to continue writing *The Gulag Archipelago* in his Estonian hideout.

Liusha arranged the Moscow exit. He walked from the *Novy Mir* offices to Liusha and Lydia's apartment, shaved off his beard, and descended with two suitcases to the street, where she had a taxi waiting. The apartment was under surveillance, the shaved-off beard not much of a disguise, and the KGB's carelessness or hesitancy would remain a mystery to him.[5] He kept silent as much as possible on the train to Talinn, speaking simple phrases in Estonian to the guard. In the camps he had been told he looked like an Estonian, and this may have helped.

Reaching his "beloved" Tartu, he felt already beyond Soviet borders. He avoided the hated language Russian; and though his mistakes and his accent gave him away, a Russian trying to master Estonian was such a rarity that he was always greeted warmly. Of course the feeling of freedom was an illusion, as the Susis reminded him.

After a predawn taxi ride he reached Haava, which had been made ready. And for two months he wrote, possessed. The Party poet Surkov would have been even sadder if he had known what Solzhenitsyn was now writing, amid the snow and pines and frozen stream of an Estonian hamlet.

He was made strong again by Estonia—even stronger than before. He would not forgive Veniamin Teush his carelessness; their friendship did resume after a few years, but was never so warm. Strength came from knowing "they" were backing off from a direct confrontation, and that *nothing* he said or wrote in the future could be worse than the plays they had already read. Had he known that they had transcripts of highly inflammatory conversations—including an outline of the *Archipelago*—and yet still hesitated to arrest him, he might have felt even more convinced he was untouchable.

A mysterious message from Natasha brought him back from Estonia a week before he had planned. Reaching Ryazan he asked what was wrong. She said, "Nothing—I'm just fed up: you've been away since autumn! To hell with the *Gulag!*" "Haven't you typed it?" "I'll type it when you're with me; not unless."

In the spring of 1966, he moved with her and the old ladies into a three-room flat in a well-built nineteenth-century house. Spacious and high-ceilinged, it looked over a busy square in the center of Ryazan. It still seemed too noisy; and it wasn't Moscow. . . . Fundamentally, the question was no longer where, but with whom.

Or rather, *without* whom. He no longer felt he had anything in common with Natasha. Until *Ivan Denisovich* and fame, he had been reasonably happy with her, grateful that she provided a comfortable home for him and served his writing. It may, even then, have irked him that Kopelev and Panin had managed to cast off their old wives as part of the fresh start, whereas he had taken back "damaged goods," so to speak. Fame brought adoring, intelligent, sophisticated women vying for his attention; he could have almost anyone he wanted. It was tempting. Poor provincial Natasha fell further into the background.

Apart from Olga Ladizhenskaya, there may have been other, and lighter, relationships. "He could be like a soldier moving through a village," a woman who knew him well, and respected him, commented. "His helpers worshiped him, and didn't mind that there were others." It was also very easy for the KGB to depict a respectable helper as Solzhenitsyn's whore. In 1978 a Czech writer called Tomas Rzhezach produced, in a spurious "biography," a list of Solzhenitsyn's supposed mistresses in these years.[*]

---

[*]*Spiral' izmeni Solzhenitsyna (The spiral of Solzhenitsyn's treachery*; Moscow: Progress, 1978) pp. 186–87. Rzhezach was a KGB agent. See pp. 463–65.

They included an underage schoolgirl, Lena F., who purportedly visited the Solotcha dacha as soon as Natasha had left to drive back to Ryazan; an "attractive, lively, intelligent" student of Reshetovskaya's, Natalya R.; and a married woman, Zoya B., whose husband cut up rough. . . . And there was the family Ch., mother and daughter, code-named by Solzhenitsyn the Princess and Liusha*. . . .

No credence whatever can be given to Rzhezach's "facts." Clearly the ultracautious dissident would have risked prosecution and disgrace by sleeping with an underage schoolgirl! And the attempt to involve the highly idealistic Chukovsky women, Lydia and Liusha, in some kind of ménage à trois is almost more laughable than it is scurrilous.

"The list of his lovers," writes Rzhezach, "would fill a whole telephone directory."—Besides writing *Gulag, The First Circle, Cancer Ward.* . . . Such energy!

Very likely—Natasha certainly believes so—there were a few diversions. Mostly Sanya cut himself off from his marital unhappiness by work, work, work: in increasing isolation even from others of apparently like mind: the "dissidents"—a word that came into existence at this time, the mid-sixties, with the beginnings of a protest movement.

The first-ever protest demonstration of the Soviet era, two hundred strong in Mayakovsky Square, demanded an open trial for Andrei Sinyavsky and Yuli Daniel, writers who had been arrested within days of the seizure of *The First Circle*. Sinyavsky, a leading critic for *Novy Mir*, had been accused of smuggling stories to the West. When their trial took place in February 1966, the accused did not plead guilty and repent, in the accustomed way, but defended themselves resolutely. Their words were broadcast by the BBC, and read eagerly in samizdat. The case gave rise to a storm of protest in the West.

Solzhenitsyn declined to join sixty-three prominent Moscow authors who wrote to the Twenty-third Congress of the Communist Party protesting the prison sentences imposed on the writers. He explained to Sinyavsky's wife that he "disapproved of writers who sought fame abroad." She was shocked.[6] Given that he was engaged in writing a work vast in scope and importance, his decision to concentrate on that, to the exclusion of all causes, was surely the right one. And what good would a letter do, he asked rhetorically, except make its authors feel warm about themselves? At a deeper level there was the feeling that he did not belong to this tribe of Moscow intellectuals, those ineffably superior people who, he felt sure, sixty years earlier would have been agitating for a socialist revolution. What liberals did not yet realize was that he saw himself as an outsider; in him ran the peasant blood of Semyon Solzhenitsyn and Zakhar Shcherbak—individualists who had pulled themselves up by their own bootstraps.

---

*In reality the "Princess" was the code name, not of Lydia Chukovskaya, but of another staunch helper, Natalya Kind.

There were those who began to fear he was turning into a less attractive person. The face which had seemed "soft" to Akhmatova seemed harder and more inflexible to some, now that he wore a beard. Vladimir Lakshin, one of his most ardent supporters at *Novy Mir*, observes that toward the end of the 1960s people noticed he was becoming even more miserly with his time, more peremptory and righteous in speech, better dressed and more dignified. The changes in him were gradual and subtle, Lakshin wrote; they seemed trivial; but he was no longer the direct, modest, firm yet cheerfully smiling teacher from Ryazan, in a homespun open-necked shirt.[7]

Akhmatova had asked him how he would handle fame. He had not been spoiled by it in the usual sense, but inevitably he saw himself as a public figure, Russia's opposition. There were invitations to speak to audiences. Often these meetings mysteriously failed to take place; but at the Lazarev Institute of Oriental Studies, he read two chapters from *Cancer Ward*, then used a question to rap out very swiftly (as Nerzhin had once done to Nadia) a prepared speech. "In a loud voice, and with a feeling of triumph and simple joy, I explained myself to the public. . . ."[8] There were shouts of "Yes!" when he demanded to know why he should not be allowed to read his work to them.

"You would have to live through a long life of slavery, bowing and scraping to authority from childhood up, springing to your feet to join with the rest in hypocritical applause, nodding assent to patent lies . . . to appreciate that hour of free speech from a platform with an audience of five hundred people, also intoxicated with freedom."[9]

He felt himself, for the first time, to be making history.

Liusha Chukovskaya could feel proudly that she was helping him do it. It was dangerous, but that made it the more exciting. She shivered a little, from fear or pleasure or both, as she watched him shaving off his beard in her kitchen, preparing to be smuggled out past the KGB watchers, the night he went off to Estonia. It also felt quite intimate. . . . Almost like being his wife.

She became totally indispensable, the undisputed head of his "counter-intelligence." Merely to summarize her voluntary work for him, as described in his moving chapter about her in *Invisible Allies*, is to become aware of a stunning devotion. In three years, 1965–68, she typed five massive books of his, a labor which included the almost impossible process of finding good-quality paper and carbon paper. She organized the hugely complex transfer abroad of the microfilms of *The Gulag Archipelago*. She typed out lengthy letters, of appeal or protest, and records of meetings, in scores of copies. Then she would deliver them, to other helpers, all of whom had their itinerary, according to Liusha's thorough planning. She took on responsibility for coordinating all communication with other assistants, including those in Leningrad. Everything and everyone coming from Leningrad passed through her apartment. She met people from the provinces whom he did not wish to rebuff but did not have the time to meet personally, and provided them with the books and papers they needed. She interviewed, using a dictaphone, eyewitnesses of the Revolution, then made typed transcripts. She even sent on his behalf a monthly parcel to Aunt Irina.

Such concentrated energy, Solzhenitsyn writes, was beyond the power of a single person, and could only be achieved as a result of her buoyant spirit. He never once suffered a delay because of her; everything ran with wonderful smoothness. She cut down on her hours of work at the institute, and on weekends her grandfather could not help noticing she had less time for him—deeply though she loved him.

When Kornei lay dying in 1969 she left his bedside to rush off to Rostov-on-Don because the complete *Gulag* was, by some mishap, in the hands of strangers. Returning in the train with it, she put it under the bottom bunk, and then had to endure the complaints of two old ladies whom she compelled to use the top bunks. Liusha pleaded a recent operation.

Did her grandfather look at her with reproach also, when she returned to his bedside?

Solzhenitsyn planned, for a time, to make her his literary executor. She and her mother were constantly watched by the KGB, a harassment that appears to have developed into ugly violence as the campaign against the author gathered force.

In the first four years of her most intense involvement, their work went "smoothly, harmoniously, without a hitch," he recalls. "In those years we were under such inhuman pressure from all sides that we never had a chance to talk about anything but the matter in hand." (*Never?* Wasn't there *once* when he could have opened a bottle of vodka and talked to her about her own life and feelings?) He admits he did not even always have the time to savor her charmingly apt sense of humor.

Then one day—he can't remember what prompted it—he said to her with "belatedly dawning amazement," "You must surely be doing all this for the *cause*."

And she gazed at him very directly and seriously and said, "No."

"No?"

"I do it for you."[10]

How astonishing that for four years he had not realized she loved him.

For him, the cause was everything. He still believed personal relationships should occupy only a twentieth of one's time and energy. When Natasha told him she would type *The Gulag Archipelago* if he were with her, but if not, it could go to hell—it was simply incomprehensible to him. Utterly illogical.

Echoing Freud, he might have asked in puzzlement, "What do women *want?*" The temperamental similarities with Freud are legion. Both were surrounded by female acolytes; both found it hard to forgive, and were inclined to anathematize former friends; they were autocrats who could charm and be marvelous company; led immensely disciplined lives in the service of a cause; were conservative as well as revolutionary; did not conform easily even within the circle of their fellow nonconformists.

Solzhenitsyn concludes his tribute to Liusha with these words: "My meeting with Liusha in that far-off autumn helped her emerge from a state of dejection. It led to her participation in a furious struggle. But that struggle consumed years of her life, took possession of her soul, and dragged her—at least in part against her will—into a tragic and uncharted orbit."[11] He was doubtless thinking of the attacks on her in 1972–73—a violent assault at the bottom of her stairs, a suspicious traffic accident that almost killed her. But did he know anything of what was going on within her heart?

"That's all over now," she said to a friend, who expressed amazement that her room held nothing but memorabilia of Solzhenitsyn.

33

Antiworlds

And let my works be seen and heard
By all who turn aside from me. . . .
—PUSHKIN, *The Prophet*

OLGA CARLISLE, A PAINTER AND JOURNALIST IN HER LATE THIRTIES,
had an almost mystical love for the land of her forefathers. Born in Paris
between the wars, married to an American, she had only in the past few
years been allowed to visit Russia, but her family background had instantly
opened the most distinguished doors. She had met Pasternak, Akhmatova,
Nadezhda Mandelstam, Kornei Chukovsky and his daughter Lydia, the artist
Neizvestny—and all had been pleased to welcome the granddaughter of a
much-loved writer, Leonid Andreyev. Her distinguished antecedents did not
stop with Andreyev; her maternal grandfather had been Victor Chernov,
leader of the Socialist Revolutionaries and a member of Kerensky's provisional government in 1917. The Cheka had tried to hunt Chernov down, at
Lenin's express order, but he had escaped.

On her fourth visit to Moscow, in April 1967, seeking material for a new
collection of Russian poetry in translation, she felt still the enchantment,
yet was also made uncomfortable by unexpected features. In the United
States, the liberal intelligentsia to which she belonged took it for granted
that the Soviet Union would gradually become more relaxed, despite recent
setbacks; yet their counterparts in Moscow seemed gloomy and pessimistic.
She found the dynamic young poet Yevgeny Yevtushenko, resting between
what he called "demanding, triumphal worldwide voyages," being given ac-
upuncture at his dacha by a Chinaman. Looking like St. Sebastian, Yevtushenko told her in a low, depressed voice that freedom was again being
crushed. His wife, who was knitting, pointed warningly toward the ceiling,
and he dropped his voice still further. Another unpleasant paradox for an
anti-Vietnam liberal in 1967: she was shocked to hear another dynamic
young poet, Joseph Brodsky, express grim approval of President Johnson's
escalation of America's involvement.

It was all very disturbing to a daughter of the Enlightenment.

Everyone in Moscow was talking about Solzhenitsyn, everyone seemed to be in awe of him. Samizdat copies of a novel called *Cancer Ward* were everywhere, and Olga spent a sleepless night reading it. She knew he lived in Ryazan, and so did not expect to meet him; but then a friend, Lev Kopelev, phoned her at her hotel and hinted that she might meet Solzhenitsyn if she came to a small party. She came, and as she climbed one of those somber Russian staircases she saw him above her, tall, wearing a blue beret and carrying a small rucksack on his back. He darted down past her, averting his eyes, but when she rang the doorbell he was suddenly beside her, smiling. When they got inside, they were formally introduced by their hosts, and Olga was quickly under his spell. He was so healthy, so alive! She couldn't help contrasting his vigor with the worn-out look of so many Moscow intellectuals, who stayed up too late drinking, smoking, and deciding the future of Russia. . . .

His eyes watched her intently. He was in complete ascendency over the others present. His voice was rich and idiosyncratic, embodying old folk sayings and labor camp slang. It matched the vigor of his mind. She could scarcely follow the flow of conversation, since they seemed to be using a sort of intimate code; but she gathered that he thought Tvardovsky would not be able to get *Cancer Ward* published, despite his promises; he spoke scathingly of him, calling him a drunkard.[1]

"I recognized you on the stairs," he said to the attractive French-Russian-American woman; "your photo is in Kornei Chukovsky's studio, which he's allowed me to work in. So I've been watched by you. You are less serious than in your photo." Later the same day, they met again at the home of Natalya Stolyarova, one of his helpers. At the end of the evening he escorted her back to her hotel. The streets were icy and he offered her his arm. She was aware of his strength, of the spring of his step. His face showed his age, but his walk was that of a much younger person. Relating to her how *The First Circle* had been "arrested," he showed her his rage by the tightening grip on her arm. The KGB was out to destroy him, he said; they would never forgive *Ivan Denisovich*. Everywhere, at every turning, there were huge banners in honor of the forthcoming fiftieth anniversary of the Revolution. He said to her, without pausing in his step, "I want you to see to the publication of *The First Circle* in the West."

As Olga went limp, he explained that she was to arrange for the translation and publication of the novel in such a way as to make as big a splash as possible. "Let it stun public opinion throughout the world; let the true nature of these scoundrels be known."[2]

They stopped. His sharp face faintly visible in the glow of a distant streetlight, he released her arm and searched her face, wanting to know whether she had fully understood. She had, and felt a huge responsibility, and a sense of fatality. "I'll do my best."

"It's a big book—my life. Of course, it will have to be done in absolute secrecy. You can imagine what would happen to me if you were found out."

They walked on, past a large area that was only rubble. "Old Moscow is being destroyed," she murmured; he barely nodded, continuing to outline his strategy.

They neared the Hotel Leningradskaya. A vast portrait of jutting-jawed Lenin, opposite the hotel entrance with its huddle of police spies, stared at her. She and the writer shook hands, and he vanished, with the stealth of a commando, down a side street.

She slept little that night. She realized their meeting hadn't been an accident. He had been well served by Vadim, her father; and perhaps he had come to like the dark, brooding looks of Vadim's daughter in the framed photograph at Chukovsky's dacha. He had learned that her husband, Henry Carlisle, was a former editor. She felt frightened, yet also exalted. She could do something worthwhile for Russia, something worthy of her grandfathers.

Flying home, she stopped off in Geneva to see her father. In his flat, which was like a little Russia, smoking Gauloise and drinking Italian coffee—so delicious after two months of the Russian kind—she told him she needed the microfilms. He paced the room, drawing on his cigarette, then said they must trust Solzhenitsyn's instincts, he was a former *zek*, and a very brave man. He brought the microfilms for her. She must be very careful; the slightest miscalculation on her part might kill him. She said she was only too aware of that.

At her home in Connecticut, she told her husband and waited to see how he would react. He listened gravely, then said it was an inviolable trust; it would be unthinkable to refuse; he would dedicate himself to it, with her, for as long as it took. It would be many months, they knew.

She read sections of *The First Circle* with the aid of a photographic enlarger, and knew that this indeed was a landmark in twentieth-century Russian literature. She engaged a near-neighbor, Thomas Whitney, an expert on Russia, to prepare a rough translation. At a May party in gracious and affluent New England surroundings, she wanted to speak of the novel to her friend "Phil Roth," but bit her tongue; then she and Henry were being invited into the presence of Cass Canfield, head of the publishing house Harper & Row, in the study of his country house. He listened, and questioned; would they have world rights? Olga thought that was Solzhenitsyn's intention, but of course the author would have to confirm it. There had to be absolute secrecy, which meant an unusual vagueness; not even the lawyers should be confided in at this stage. Canfield seemed to understand.

Nearing seventy, though looking much younger, "he would suddenly shift his gaze and, with extreme intensity, settle all his attention on you. . . ." So far, not unlike an older Solzhenitsyn! "His long fleshy face was full of shrewdness; his blue eyes made you feel like a blossom in the path of a humming-bird." It is not one of her most successful similes, yet its very fragility and awkwardness fits in with the sense she was beginning to have of "antiworlds"—the suffering of Russia in one world, and an American publisher and his shareholders in another.[3] She would have to be the bridge, as so often in her divided life.

Thinking of that first Moscow encounter, she must have remembered the "most extraordinary" meeting of her first visit, with Pasternak; of how he had held her arm lightly—not fiercely as Alexander Isayevich had done—to help her across a little wooden bridge.[4] And maybe, well-read as she was, seeing in her mind's eye the scene on the stairs when Solzhenitsyn ran down and then up, she recalled the moment in *Doctor Zhivago* when Yuri was confronted by his half brother, Yevgraf. . . . "Footsteps sounded above him. Someone came slowly half-way down the stairs, stopped as if hesitating, then turned and ran up again to the first-floor landing. . . ." Yuri raises his head and sees the youth.[5] Yevgraf becomes his savior yet also represents his death.

Olga Carlisle's initial sense of fatality would return, and grow stronger and stronger, threatening to overwhelm her.

Solzhenitsyn himself occupied antiworlds at this time. He seemed to be leading several different lives, and achieving enough for a dozen different men. Michael Scammell likens him to a Scarlet Pimpernel; another analogy might be with the Pied Piper, leading his enemies to their doom, his followers, his "children," toward eternity. He was also a one-man army; his conversation with Olga Carlisle was full of "salvoes," "explosions," and "bombs."

He was turning into myth—even to himself: after describing how, in the winter of 1967, his second in Estonia, he had revised and retyped fifteen hundred pages of *The Gulag Archipelago* in seventy three days, he exclaims, "It was not I who did it—mine was merely the hand that moved across the page!"[6] He was becoming a Christ figure, and in relation to the women who served him—as to his mother long ago there is a feeling of *Noli me tangere*. As Jesus to his disciples and to Mary Magdalene after his crucifixion, he would "disappear for a long time, only to reappear again as suddenly," Lydia Chukovskaya recalls.[7] "Wherever Solzhenitsyn happened to dwell and wherever fate cast him, he never for a moment ceased to be the absolute master of his own life. . . ." He pursued his own routine, his own schedule of work, broken down not just into hours, but into minutes. He and Lydia met only on "neutral ground," such as kitchen or corridor, and there were never any long conversations. That would have been relaxation, idleness. "It was as if, at a certain moment . . . he had sentenced himself to imprisonment in some strict regime camp, and was now rigidly enforcing that regime. He was convict and guard rolled into one, and his own surveillance of himself was, perhaps, more relentless than that of the KGB. This heroic task called for . . . an entire lifetime of toil with never a day off. And the main instrument of his labor was complete and well-fortified solitude."

Doubtless he treated her daughter Liusha in the same way.

Sometimes, Lydia wrote, he might leave a note, asking her if she would be free at nine; if so, they might listen to the radio together for twenty minutes. If they walked to the Peredelkino cemetery, he would be amazingly alert as to dangers on the path that might cause her to fall. He avoided the writers' village, except to go to the train station, preferring to walk among the pines on their land. When asked if he was not weary of walking back and forth, from one fence to the other, he replied, "No, I got used to it in the *sharashka*." She had the sense of a camp guard letting him out for two or three hours of exercise, whatever the weather, but doubted whether he was freed from his labors even then.

But he insisted on being no trouble to anyone else, doing his own cooking and cleaning. Though he was early to bed and early to rise, if she whispered in saying good night to guests, at midnight, outside his room, fearing to disturb his sleep, he would say sternly the next morning, "I shall be unable to stay here if I find that my presence is going to inhibit you."

At meals he still worked, listening to the radio and jotting notes. He would ask sudden, peremptory questions of her sometimes, often about literature, would listen carefully to her answer, perhaps ask a supplementary question, and then leave the room.

Lydia Chukovskaya had absolutely no time for those who blamed Solzhenitsyn for having absolutely no time. They said, "He only ever has time for himself." For himself! Chukovskaya echoes ironically; when he had to raise a "colossal structure, this majestic monument on a communal grave beyond the Arctic Circle?" He has forced us, she writes, to experience the fate of hundreds, even thousands of individuals, in a form which is perhaps unique in world literature. She felt proud to have helped him maintain his ferocious timekeeping, as he called it. Vividly she relates how the vertical scar on his forehead could deepen, emphasizing the straightness of his features—nose, hair, forehead—until it seemed that the *scar* was listening to her across the table, so intense was his concentration. Once, when he was angry on her behalf, she saw not a face, but a knife. However, as the tension eased and they even joked, he started to laugh merrily, and then his face became "round, rustic, even, I would say, somewhat simple," the face of "a fitter or mechanic, not long out of the peasantry." The scar seemed to have vanished, without trace.

These were rare moments of companionship. When he was at work writing, he was essentially alone, seeing only the phantoms of memory or *imagined* memory. Perhaps no writer has ever had such a gift of intense concentration, self-discipline, and ability to shut out everything and everyone.

In his second Estonian winter, he worked in a state of heavenly contentment. This year he could be more relaxed—if that is the word for such fiendish energy. Each day he went to bed exhausted at seven P.M., to wake up after one A.M. quite refreshed, and at once resume work. At nine A.M. he would stop, then move into a whole new day's work, finishing at six when he prepared a meal. When he became ill and was running a fever, he still chopped wood, stoked the stove, and did part of his writing standing up, with his back pressed against the hot tiles of the stove "in lieu of mustard plasters." His single goal, even should it cost him his life, was to finish the history of Russia's enslavement. Heli Susi, who came to the lonely farmhouse occasionally with supplies, "said that she had the impression that I no longer belonged to anything or anyone in this world and that I seemed to be moving all by myself in an unknown direction."[8] She would take away sections of the work for hiding. She taught German at Tallinn Conservatory, and had a son of fourteen, who prepared the microfilms of *The Gulag Archipelago*. Heli herself made many thoughtful suggestions from an aesthetic point of view.

Who can tell whether there lurks, behind the compliments to the daring and intelligent young woman—abandoned by her husband—who risked her freedom for his work's sake, an untold story? For her, caught up in the excitement of conspiracy, it would have been the most natural thing in the world to wish he were not quite so preoccupied when she came. For diversion, it seems, he chopped wood. And was, for ten weeks, a Stakhanovite writer working a double shift and no break for Sundays. Never had he been happier. All around, white snow, dark pines.

This was one antiworld, and the most important. "Silence, exile, cunning." An anti-Bolshevik conspirator; but also the monk Pimen in *Boris Godunov*, writing his chronicle, bearing witness.

Once more the KGB had no idea where he was—or even that he was missing. There was no mention of an unexplained disappearance when the Secretariat of the Central Committee discussed him on 10 March 1967; but the tone—even without the *Gulag*—was ominous. Yuri Andropov, the KGB's head, said, "He has written certain things, like *Feast of the Conquerors* and *Cancer Ward*, that are anti-Soviet in nature. We should take decisive measures to deal with Solzhenitsyn." He was rearing his head, he thought he was a hero, commented Semichastny, reporting that he was reading his work in public and had given an interview to a Japanese newspaper. (He had been doing something far more threatening that that!) Shauro: "He has been very active lately. His place of residence is Ryazan, but he spends most of his time in Moscow...." (If they but knew...) "Incidentally, he gets help from well-known scientists such as Kapitsa and Sakharov." Demichev said he was a crazy writer who should be resolutely opposed. He was spreading slander against everything Russian, said Grishin; and Semichastny proposed that the first measure against him should be expulsion from the Writers' Union.[9]

But nothing was done.

Upon his return in April 1967 from Estonia—bursting with health and energy, as Olga Carlisle witnessed—he plunged into a final revision of the second part of *Cancer Ward,* then went to see Tvardovsky to discuss the prospects of publication. They had not seen each other for eight months; the editor had been angry with him for allowing *Cancer Ward* to circulate in Moscow; Sanya had written to him asserting his right to be read. The reunion only served to deepen their rift. According to Solzhenitsyn's account: Tvardovsky said he had heard *Cancer Ward* had been published in the West. No, said Solzhenitsyn: just one chapter had been published abroad—by the Slovak Communist Party.... Tvardovsky was still deeply aggrieved: "You refuse to forgive the Soviet regime anything.... You have no genuine concern for the people! ... You hold nothing sacred! ..." And also: "I've been told you're always saying things against me...."

"*Against* you? And you *believed* it?"[10]

And reasonably so, on the evidence of Olga Carlisle: though, admittedly, she listened to him call Tvardovsky a drunkard a month after this rancorous meeting. Tvardovsky was feeling low, not having been reelected to the Central Committee, and having lost two aides, the trusted Dementyev and Zaks. They had been dismissed from *Novy Mir* by the Central Committee, without explanation or consultation.

That April, Sanya made himself invisible again for a month at Rozhdestvo, his primitive dacha on the small river Istya. Despite its lack of conveniences and its tendency to flood, he and Natasha had grown to love the tranquil spot. During this spring, he wrote there an exuberant literary memoir, 150 pages long, of his battle with the Establishment. It would eventually become the opening section of *The Oak and the Calf.* His reason for writing this apologia was because he was not sure he would survive for long in freedom; he was about to write to the forthcoming Congress of the Writers' Union, and knew his letter would "go off like a bomb."

The danger of being blown up by it himself was also why he had "primed" Olga Carlisle for an even bigger explosion. He was throwing himself with that huge energy into his other antiworld of political controversy and polemics. This was to be his private Battle of Kursk. He gave his wife and other assistants their instructions. No fewer than 250 copies were typed of the two-thousand-word-long letter, each personally signed; Liusha was mainly responsible for typing one hundred copies.... All 250 were posted from various Moscow districts, never more than two in the same box to outwit the postal censors. The recipients were carefully chosen: genuine writers (the majority), writers from non-Russian republics, and a few time-servers for confusion's sake, so as not to expose the decent people to KGB hostility.

Natasha tells us he played a recording of Beethoven's Ninth Symphony over and over as he composed his letter. It is a majestic plea for the Congress to discuss the "no longer tolerable oppression" of state censorship. "A survival of the Middle Ages, censorship has managed, Methuselah-like, to drag out its existence almost to the twenty-first century. Perishable, it attempts to arrogate to itself the prerogative of imperishable time—

that of separating good books from bad."[11] There was no provision for censorship in the constitution and it was therefore illegal. Remorselessly he catalogs the writers, from Dostoyevsky to Pasternak, who were censored and abused, and then at some point published and celebrated. Was it not high time this absurd and immoral process was ended? Literature could not develop in the categories of "permitted" and "not permitted." "A literature," he wrote movingly, "that is not the breath of life for the society of its time, that dares not communicate its own pain and its own fears to society, that does not warn in time against threatening moral and social dangers does not deserve the name of literature; it is only a facade. Such a literature loses the confidence of its own people, and its published works are pulped instead of read."[12]

He followed this general statement by urging the Writers' Union to begin, at long last, to defend the rights of its members. It asked them to consider the wrongs done to him, Solzhenitsyn: the seizure of *The First Circle* and his entire archive; the slanderous accusations that he had surrendered to the enemy and served the Germans in the war; the unscrupulous dissemination of a play written when he was in the depths of despair, forgotten by society, and which he had long since abandoned.

He concluded: "I am of course confident that I shall fulfill my duty as a writer in all circumstances—from the grave even more successfully and incontrovertibly than in my lifetime. No one can bar the road to truth, and to advance its cause I am prepared to accept even death. But may it be that repeated lessons will finally teach us not to stay the writer's pen during his lifetime?

"This has never yet added luster to our history."

"What a nice, quiet congress it's been!" observed Mikhail Sholokhov, summing up at the end. The presumed author of *Quiet Flows the Don* was probably being sarcastic. Carefully selected, the assembly had indeed been soporifically well behaved, but Sholokhov well knew that outside the main Kremlin hall there was no topic of conversation other than Solzhenitsyn's bombshell of a letter. He had not been exaggerating, it *was* a bomb; and it burst with most stunning force in the West. The KGB was thrown into confusion as *L'Unità*, the official voice of the Communist Party of Italy, extolled the letter and criticized the Soviet Union's treatment of literature. The Politburo could only give floundering instructions to their ambassador in Rome to meet with Comrade Longo, leader of the Italian Communists, asking them not to rock the boat of Communism.[13] The KGB produced a rather belated "biography" of the writer, inaccurate in only one small detail: it said his wife's father had died in the Civil War (the family's "official" version), whereas he had fled abroad. At a meeting in the Kremlin in July, Comrade Solomentsev said he had no doubt Solzhenitsyn should be debunked in the press, but would the Writers' Union be up to the task? There was a reminder of how negative had been the reaction to Sinyavsky/Daniel.

Solzhenitsyn, ignorant though he was of this Kremlin dithering, was overwhelmed by the response he was receiving, at home as well as abroad. About a hundred writers had replied to him agreeing that the issues of his letter should be openly discussed. Moreover, Tvardovsky was supporting him! Alexander Trifonovich was always taking him by surprise. It might still be possible, the editor said, for his journal to publish *Cancer Ward*. Solzhenitsyn found himself, with Tvardovsky, being offered the people's cigarettes and chocolate truffles at the Union offices.

Could *Cancer Ward* conceivably come out in the West, he was asked? Of course! he replied; it was always possible. There were so many copies floating around. . . . Consternation in the office; men coughing up their truffles. Please help to prevent that terrible thing, begged Tvardovsky, by letting Alexander Isayevich publish it here, in whatever journal he finds most to his taste. . . .

They saw no objection. . . . And thanked the novelist for coming![14]

But somewhere it was blocked.

During Natasha's summer vacation they set off in their car for a holiday in what had been East Prussia. With them was another of those highly cultured couples with whom they got on well, Yefim and Ekaterina Edkind. They enjoyed camping at night along the route of General Samsonov's—and Solzhenitsyn's—advances. He was researching again for the work which he still regarded as his life's main task, a historical-literary study of the Revolution. He planned to begin writing it in the autumn.

When he started it, he found that scenes he had written as long ago as 1936 could be used still, with only the style needing to be polished.

There was almost, that summer, a reconciliation with one of the great friends of his youth, Kirill Simonyan. Simonyan had written to him following the letter to the Congress, and it was arranged that Sanya should call on him. When he did so, there was no answer to his ring on the bell. He waited an hour, then returned to leave a note. Opening the letter-flap, he saw Simonyan's legs, motionless, in the hall. Evidently he had lost courage at the last moment. Sanya walked away, and they were never to meet.

The position with regard to *Cancer Ward* was that *Novy Mir* was ready to publish it but was waiting for permission. Solzhenitsyn wrote to the secretariat of the Writers' Union insisting that he would hold them responsible for the "senseless delay" of many months. He was invited, through Tvardovsky, to appear before them for a discussion. Tvardovsky told him there was hope, but the members had also been given *A Feast of Conquerors* to read, and there was much indignation about the play that expressed sympathy for Vlasovite traitors. Tvardovsky himself, like Konstantin Simonov, was still refusing to read a work disowned by its author.

On 22 September, he prepared to confront the Union's secretariat in the building that had once fictionally housed the Rostov family in *War and Peace*. In the chair was to be the seventy-five-year-old Konstantin Fedin. It was Fedin who had wept over passages of *Doctor Zhivago*, and been Pasternak's friend and neighbor, but who cut him dead after the Nobel storm, and hid away during the funeral.

If Pasternak was Hamlet, Fedin and another neighbor of Pasternak's, Alexander Fadeyev, were Rosencrantz and Guildenstern. Fadeyev, as Stalin's secretary of the Writers' Union, had liked Pasternak and possibly helped to preserve him; some thought the poet had had him in mind in creating Zhivago's helpful half-brother, Yevgraf. But he also signed away the lives of many writers. He became an alcoholic. In the wake of Khrushchev's sensational speech, Fadeyev had shot himself. Pasternak, after gazing down at the dead man in Moscow's Hall of Columns, said in a loud, clear voice, audible to everyone there, "Alexander Alexandrovich has rehabilitated himself." Then he bowed low before leaving.

Fedin and Fadeyev. . . . This is Solzhenitsyn's wonderful description of the former. . . . "On Fedin's face his every compromise, every betrayal, every base act, has superimposed its print in a dense crosshatching. (It was he who set the hounds on Pasternak, he who suggested the Sinyavsky trial.) Dorian Gray's sins all showed in the coarsening lines of his portrait. It was Fedin's lot to receive the marks on his face. . . . The face is bloodless under its patina of vice, a death's head smiling and nodding approval of the orators. . . ."[15]

One can see Stalin's, Dzerzhinsky's, Beria's outraged ghosts: why do you expose yourselves to these insults? Just get this bastard into the Lubyanka and torture him to death. . . .

An hour before the meeting to discuss *Cancer Ward*, Sanya had a much more painful experience to go through.

34

Life Against Death

Why on earth hadn't he gone to Vega?
He should have gone long ago. . . .
—*Cancer Ward*

TENNO WAS DYING, IN THE GLOOMY BLEAKNESS OF A HOSPITAL
ward. That brawny, Herculean man who had survived on the run for weeks
in the Kazakhstan desert, had shriveled from his cancer until his well-loved
striped sailor's jersey hung loose upon him; his face was a deathly skull;
pain was twisting his tortured body. Sanya, upon seeing him on 22 September 1967, took his hands gently in his; the arms, on which were tattooed
the words "Liberty" and "Do or Die" in English, together with an anchor,
looked breakably thin. Sanya had been with Tenno in Leningrad in the
spring when he fell ill. Believing he'd been poisoned by some bad sausage,
he tried starving himself; on the six-hour train ride back to Moscow, though
still unwell, he'd told merry stories about his amazing life. A few days later
he had been among the most active in posting copies of the "Fourth Congress" letters in various mailboxes around the city. But the "food poisoning"
wouldn't let up. For five months he'd been growing more and more ill,
yet—the bravest, most audacious of men—he wouldn't face his cancer or
the prospect of death. "They've now found it's a blockage in the stomach,"
his wife said, gazing at Sanya and giving a slight warning nod. "Now they've
found what it is, they can clear it up."[1]

"Good; it's about time! We need you up and about, George."

"I'll be with you," he whispered. "I've things to do still."

He had plans to murder Molotov.

So much a part of the *Archipelago*, Sanya reflected sadly, yet he won't
even see a typescript.

"So—tell me about today," Tenno said, trying to show some interest.
And indeed, Sanya outlined the battle ahead with such animation that
Tenno's eyes had a little light in them and he almost managed to smile.

"I think that one reason I fought such a good fight on that day," Solzhenitsyn wrote in *Invisible Allies*, "was that I confronted the fat-faced literary bullies having just come from the deathbed of a *zek*."²

There were some thirty secretaries of the Writers' Union present at the meeting to discuss *Cancer Ward*, from all over the USSR. He had to ask his neighbor who some of them were: "Who's that? . . . No, no, the one in between—the one with a face like a well-toweled plump backside with flashing spectacles perched on it." It turned out to be the Central Committee's representative, Comrade Melentyev. "So, that's who is secretly calling the tune. Just sits there scribbling. Scribble away! I'll show you what old *zeks* are made of!"³

The meeting lasted from three in the afternoon until eight, and would have continued had not Solzhenitsyn, rising, reminded them he did not live in Moscow and would have to catch his train. Tvardovsky had expressed a fear that he might explode with rage; Solzhenitsyn had told him he never lost control, the camps had taught him not to. If he blew up, it would be according to plan—if they arranged, say, that he would explode in the nineteenth minute, it would happen.⁴ He was still, in other words, an actor; and this would be a splendid stage.

A few extracts from his "Record" may convey some of the flavor:

KORNEICHUK (*after initial statements from Fedin and Solzhenitsyn*): How does he regard the wanton bourgeois propaganda that his letter provoked? Why doesn't he dissociate himself from it? Why does he endure it in silence? . . .

SOLZHENITSYN: I do not understand how one can be so sensitive to opinion abroad and so much less sensitive to live public opinion here in one's own country. Throughout my life, I have had the soil of my homeland under my feet; only *its* pain do I feel, only about *it* do I write. . . . My second letter is interpreted as an ultimatum: either print the story, or it will be printed in the West. But it isn't *I* who present this ultimatum to the secretariat; life presents this ultimatum to you and to me simultaneously. I write that I am disturbed by the distribution of the story in hundreds—this is a rough estimate; I haven't tried to count them—in hundreds of typewritten copies.

VOICE: How did this come about?

SOLZHENITSYN: My works exhibit one strange characteristic: people are forever asking permission to read them, and once they manage to borrow them they spend their own time, or money, on making copies, which they pass on to others. . . . The following is being said about me from the rostrum: "He was wrongly released, before his time was up." Whether I was wrongly released or not can be seen from the court decision of the Military Collegium. . . . It has been presented to the secretariat. . . .

TVARDOVSKY: It also includes Solzhenitsyn's record as a serving officer.

SOLZHENITSYN: And then the phrase "before his time was up" is used with great relish! After completing my eight-year sentence I spent a month in transit prisons—I feel embarrassed even to mention a matter so trivial in our country—then I was exiled in perpetuity without any formal sentence being passed, and I spent three years in exile, believing that I was doomed to be there forever. It was only because of the Twentieth Congress that I was set free—and this is called "ahead of time"! . . .

SALYNSKY: I shall speak of *Cancer Ward*. I believe that it should be printed—it is a vivid and powerful piece of work. To be sure it contains descriptions of disease in pathological terms, and the reader inevitably succumbs to the dread of cancer—a phobia that is already widespread in our century. This should somehow be eliminated. . . . And now a few words about moral socialism. In my opinion, there is nothing so very terrible about this. It *would* be horrifying if Solzhenitsyn were preaching *im*moral socialism. . . .

FEDIN: Alexander Isayevich, you must begin by protesting against the vile ends for which your name is used by our enemies in the West. In the process you will of course also have the opportunity to voice some of the complaints you've uttered here today. . . .

KOZHEVNIKOV: *Cancer Ward* evokes revulsion with its excessive naturalism, its piling up of all manner of horrors. . . .

SURKOV: I don't mind admitting that I am a well-read man. . . . I've even taken a sniff at Mikhailovsky and Vladimir Solovyov, with their naïve notion that economics can be made subordinate to morality. . . . This is not a physiological but a political story, and its whole thrust is ideological. . . . Of course, our reader is now so mature and so sophisticated that no silly little book is going to alienate him from communism. All the same, the works of Solzhenitsyn are more dangerous to us than those of Pasternak: Pasternak was a man divorced from life, while Solzhenitsyn has a bold, militant, ideological temperament, is a man with an idea. We represent the first revolution in the history of mankind that has kept unchanged its original slogans and banners. "Moral socialism" is philistine socialism. It is old and primitive, and [*speaking in the direction of Salynsky*] I don't understand how anyone could fail to understand this, how anyone could see anything in it.

SALYNSKY: I do not defend it in the least.

BARUZDIN: *Cancer Ward* is an antihuman work. . . .

ABASHIDZE: I have noticed him asking the person sitting next to him the name of each speaker. Why doesn't he know any of us? . . .

YASHEN: The author is not tortured by injustice: he is, rather, poisoned by hatred. People are outraged that there is such a writer in the ranks of the Union of Writers. I should like to propose his expulsion from the Union. He is not the only one who suffered, but others understand the tragedy of the time better.

KERBABEYEV: I read *Cancer Ward* with a feeling of great dissatisfaction. Everyone is a former prisoner, everything is gloomy, there is not a single word of warmth. It is utterly nauseating to read. Vera offers the hero her home and her embraces, but he rejects life. . . . Why does the author see only the dark side? Why don't I write about the dark side? I always strive to write only about joyful things.

SHARIPOV: I wouldn't make any allowances for him—I'd expel him from the Union. . . . Let him repudiate *Cancer Ward*. Our republic has reclaimed virgin and long-fallow lands and is going forward from success to success.

MARKOV: This has been a valuable discussion. . . . We await a completely clear answer from Solzhenitsyn to the bourgeois slander; we await his statement in the press. He must defend his honor as a Soviet writer. . . . The thing does have some worth on some kind of practical plane. But the social and political innuendos in it are utterly unacceptable to me. . . . As to the suggestions concerning expulsion from the Union—we should remember the principles of comradeship that are supposed to prevail, and not be unduly hasty.

SOLZHENITSYN: I am being criticised for the very title on the ground that cancer and cancer wards are not a medical subject but symbols of some sort. The texture is too dense, there are too many medical details for it to be a symbol. I have asked some leading cancer specialists for their view of the story, and they have acknowledged that from the medical point of view it is impeccable, and abreast of modern knowledge. . . . Some of those present may soon perhaps find themselves in a cancer ward and realise what sort of symbol this is. . . . I absolutely do not understand why *Cancer Ward* is accused of being antihumanitarian. Quite the reverse is true: life conquers death, the past is conquered by the future. . . . In general, the task of the writer cannot be reduced to defence or criticism of one or another form of government. The tasks of the writer are connected with more general and durable questions, such as the secrets of the human heart and conscience. . . .

SURKOV: You should state whether you dissociate yourself from the role ascribed to you in the West—that of leader of a political opposition in the USSR.

VOICES: Let him think it over!

———

SURKOV: Well, now we can relax over a few vodkas. I'll tell you what I really think. It may be that when the Soviet empire has gone the way of the Third Reich, *Cancer Ward* will come to stand even higher than *First Circle* among his novels. The latter is perhaps just a bit too enclosed, so to speak, within our political system, whereas the former, by dealing with something universal in human experience—cancer, pain, the certainty of dying—will never lose any of its relevance. Of course Solzhenitsyn was being disingenuous in claiming that the texture is too dense for the cancer ward to be symbolic of our society—clearly we're intended to see the analogy, and it gives it an added depth and somberness. . . . Yes, and indeed beauty, since it's a magnificently rich symbol. Nonetheless, it's the real cancer that's the main enemy. All the political plagues will pass, as our beloved Akhmatova said; but who can save us from "the terror that we call the flight of time?" . . . In three hundred years readers will still care about these characters, they will be angry with Oleg, for instance, that he chooses to disappoint both Zoya and Vera; and they will suffer with the radiologist, Dontsova, who knows she has a tumour herself from having absorbed too much radiation. . . .

SHARIPOV: I really liked Oleg Kostoglotov as a character! He's the sort of man we can do with in our virgin lands; he's a fighter! I haven't been able to read the whole of *First Circle*, my daughter took my *samizdat* copy when I was only about halfway through; but although it's clear that both Nerzhin and Kostoglotov ("bone-chewer," as he's so aptly called) are based on the author, I find the "bone-chewer" more sympathetic, more vulnerable, and therefore more human. He doesn't give a damn, because he thinks he's probably had it anyway. I enjoyed it when that Stalinist monster Rusanov asked him why he needed the light on, and he said "So I can pick my asshole!" He's a real soldier!

KERBABEYEV: What took me aback, and threw a new light on our friend Solzhenitsyn, was the amount of sex there is in it. Zoya, the nurse, she's really wonderful, the way she senses her own breasts. I made a note of the passage: "Zoya was aware of how clean and healthy she was, down to the last pore of skin and the tiniest toe-nail—in contrast to the decline and disease that surrounded her. She sensed with joy her twin, tightly-supported breasts, their weight as she lent across the patients' beds and

Apartment building in which the Fedorovskys, close friends of Sanya's mother, lived in the 1920s.

Sasha Kozhin, creator of a Solzhenitsyn museum in Rostov, standing in front of Sanya's childhood home, 1996. Sanya and his mother lived in this one-room shack for nine years.

Back of Cheka (KGB) headquarters in Rostov, close to Sanya's first home. He passed it daily on his way to and from school. Spent bullet shells from secret nocturnal executions are still sometimes found in the foreground area.

School photograph, 1935. Sanya stands next Nikolai Vitkevitch (second from left) in top row, while Kirill Simonyan is seated in second row. These close friends became known as the "Three Musketeers." To the left of Simonyan, her hair braided, is another close friend, Lydia Ezherets; and to the right is their much-loved literature teacher, Anastasia Grünau.

Sanya and Natasha, newlyweds, Rostov, 1940.

Sanya's last home with his mother, destroyed by a German shell.
(AUTHOR'S PHOTOGRAPH)

At the front, 1944, during a visit from Natasha. He was writing a novella about a girl at the front who exchanges letters with another girl back in her hometown. This work, like so many others, went up in KGB smoke.

Solzhenitsyn as a prisoner of the Gulag, 1946.

Solzhenitsyn used Lev Kopelev, left, and Dmitri Panin, right, as characters in
The First Circle.

Moscow, 1948. Natasha playing at a university concert. Sanya wanted her to devote herself to becoming a first-rate concert pianist.

Olga Carlisle, entrusted with bringing out *The First Circle* and *The Gulag Archipelago*.

(BARBARA HALL)

The explosion of grief and celebration at Pasternak's funeral in 1960 marked a turning point in Soviet history.

(ARCHIVE PHOTOS)

With his great supporter, the cellist-conductor Mstislav Rostropovich, at Rozhdestvo.

Alexander Tvardovsky, editor of *Novy Mir*, in 1961 shortly before he spent a sleepless night reading a story about the labor camps by an unknown author.

Solzhenitsyn casting earth upon the coffin of Alexander Tvardovsky, 1971.

Solzhenitsyn with his second wife, Natalya Svetlova, in England, 1974.

(*above*)
Solzhenitsyn arrives in exile,
February 1974. Fellow Nobel
laureate Heinrich Böll stands
at his side.

    (AP/WIDE WORLD PHOTOS)

(*right*)
Sanya at Norwich University
in Vermont, 1975.

    (AP/WIDE WORLD PHOTOS)

Sanya in the midst of his celebrated commencement address at Harvard in 1978.

Lev Kopelev and his wife, Raisa Orlova, arrive at Frankfurt International Airport en route to Cologne and dinner with Heinrich Böll, 1980.

Troitse Lykovo, overlooking the Moscow River, where Solzhenitsyn had a house built. Formerly the area was the home of such leading Soviet officials as Lavrenti Beria and Lazar Kaganovich.

Return to Rostov, 1984.

their tremor when she walked quickly." It made me feel . . . Well, I needn't tell you!

FEDIN: I remember that. I like the precision of her *tightly-supported* breasts. Could we have a window open perhaps?—it really is too early in the fall for central heating. . . . And the passage where Kostoglotov asks her to take her white coat off, and she does so for him, parading. . . . And all his wayward desires, that are threatened with extinction through the female hormone treatment, surge back: it's extremely moving. It makes me remember . . . when I was young.

SURKOV: Even at first, on arrival, when he's at death's door, it's a little bit of desire that shows us life isn't done for yet. When he lies down on the floor demanding attention, and Vera Gangart walks right up to him, and he sees her well-shaped legs tapering down to a pair of high-heeled shoes. Because she never dresses carelessly. And she says somewhere, sadly, to Dontsova I think, that she has nothing to save her good clothes for, she might as well wear them every day. There's no man in her life. The men have perished in the war or are in the camps.

KOZHEVNIKOV: The bone-chewer wants to call her Vega. A star. A tiny hope in the black sky of his and Russia's suffering. He desires Zoya and Vega, he's starved of life.

FEDIN: As we all are. That astonishing episode when a woman who is going to have her breast removed on the morrow offers it to a man's lips, for the last time! And done with such purity. Who the devil said the story was antihumanitarian?

BARUZDIN: I was speaking objectively, in Marxist terms. On a personal level I find it deeply humane. The women are all wonderful. Dontsova, going home to her ungrateful family, the way her lingering thoughts about her patients gradually turn to thoughts of cooking, shopping and washing-up at home that must be done. . . . I really felt I knew her from within, and sympathised with her. I hope she survives her cancer. The clinic needs her. Oh, and that quiet, middle-aged orderly, who cleans the floors silently under Kostoglotov's feet for two months, and he doesn't even see her; then he finds she's a *zek* too, and loves French poetry! Her husband's in a camp somewhere, her daughter died in exile, she still has a small son. Wait—I got a friend to type the story out for me: here a paragraph that almost made me cry. . . . "In her youth she might have been called 'Lily.' There could have been no hint then of the spectacle-marks on the bridge of her nose. As a girl she had made eyes, laughed and giggled. There had been lilac and lace in her life, and the poetry of the Symbolists. And no gypsy had ever foretold that she would end her life as a cleaning woman somewhere out in Asia." You know, I re-read that now and it again weighs on my heart. He's a great writer. But of course it's impossible to publish it unless he denounces the West.

FEDIN: Of course.

SURKOV: I still want to know *why* Kostoglotov didn't stay overnight with either Vega or Zoya? Or divide the night between them! After all, he's got his erection back, thanks to the blonde pressed against him in the tram. "He was impatient to see women and absorb them, in a way which he could never mention to them." Because he's been deprived of them for so long. And he writes Vega this letter which must have driven her crazy, poor woman, saying how he'd always craved to kiss her, even during the most intellectual conversations, but that one day she'd thank him for—what? His self-sacrifice? Damn you! she probably cursed him—why couldn't we have grabbed a little life while we had the chance, and let the future take care of itself!

TVARDOVSKY: I've listened with gratitude and amazement. It does seem artistically wrong that Oleg doesn't stay with either of them, I agree. It's as if, right at the end, he has to make the point that a *zek* can't be happy. But the only person stopping him there is himself. I will try to persuade him to think again about the ending.

   (*At least, Tvardovsky told a friend that a conversation of this sort happened after Solzhenitsyn had left to catch his train; but Tvardovsky was in one of his alcoholic hazes, and inclined to deadpan humor.*)

Sanya wrote up a lengthy record of the afternoon's meeting and took it to Liusha. "Could you make me fifty copies of this, do you think? . . . Ah, what would I do without you!"

He gave one of the copies to another of his assistants, Mirra Petrova, who was outside the main group because her path did not cross with theirs. Small, quiet, unmarried, with an almost boyish, otherworldly face, she was ready to give herself to a cause, like her Old Bolshevik father, a victim of Stalin. Her opportunity came when Sanya, having read to an audience some chapters of *Cancer Ward* at the archival library TsGALI, had requested feedback; of ten responses he had been astounded by one which, refreshingly, concentrated on Kostoglotov, his fate and his doomed love. The critique showed a level of perception that he expected to find normally only in good writers. He asked to meet this talented woman.

He was impressed by her fearlessness and independence; and was "struck by the specifically feminine point of view that I knew I lacked—a deficiency that in fact I had first perceived in this particular work. Her comments were like a whirlwind for the ever-shifting point of view they seemed to demonstrate, ranging as they did from disapproval of insufficiently high-minded depictions of women to objections that the portrayal was inadequately sensuous."[6] Now that he had moved from the camp theme he needed a woman's guidance and insight, especially it would seem on sensuality, and there was no one else who could provide them so well as Mirra Petrova. He had barely left her after his first visit when he felt a "nagging desire to continue the conversation," and indeed he returned "many dozens of times in subsequent years."

Devoted to the theater, especially Chekhov, she had a room in an actors' block, just five minutes from *Novy Mir;* he would often phone from their offices, then call around. She knew he needed some food, too, in his usually hectic excursion from place to place in Moscow. Nor was it just a snack; she was capable of questioning a woman who had cooked for rich people before the Revolution, and then producing for him—say—grouse in mulled wine, "in order to make such things easier to write about." Her decorative room revealed some of her passions—van Gogh, Thomas Mann, Tsvetayeva, and the much more minor Ehrenburg. (Solzhenitsyn teased her about that, and did his best to make her get rid of his portrait in her bookcase.)

Obviously the KGB were watching her; and Solzhenitsyn describes her as "cutting an attractive figure" as she signals to him with her purse that the coast is clear for him to leave. There may have been a romantic element; it is hard to imagine frequent discussions of a woman's sensuality, in such privacy, without a degree of attraction. Whether or not that is so, what he valued in going to her was that he could be a *writer* with her; she could evaluate, help him to choose between textual variants, for example in *Ivan Denisovich*. In addition she was an expert in the prerevolutionary period and could find the books and materials he wanted. She also typed the final versions of *Cancer Ward* and the full, ninety-six chapter *First Circle*.

And clearly he learned from her things about women that he could not learn from his wife. And perhaps had not had the time to learn from Olga Ladizhenskaya.

Mirra's only drawback from his point of view was that her tastes were too much within the mainstream of familiar "democratic intelligentsia" values. Increasingly that became a problem for both of them, and their friendship cooled. But it seems highly likely that something of Mirra Petrova is present in *Cancer Ward*, that she inspired—either intellectually or more directly—the richer colors in which the women in it are portrayed.

If only—one is tempted to think—he had allowed this influence to continue and had developed the feminine side of his psyche further. He touched upon the "secrets of the human heart and conscience" in relation to love and passion—but then drew back from them, as Kostoglotov drew back from Vega. If only he had not been possessed by his idée fixe of the Revolution, leading him to believe that he must now begin "the most important

book of my life." If only he'd allowed himself some rest—even some bore-
dom; stretched out supine, like Pushkin, on a billiard table, yawning and
taking potshots at the ceiling . . . so that the Muse might not always think,
Oh, he's busy, I'd better not disturb him. . . .

He went off, toward the end of 1967, to another of his much-loved secluded places, the village of Solotcha, deep in woods, thirty miles from
Ryazan. In the dark cottage of Agafya, a second Matryona, he surrounded
himself with pictures of Samsonov's generals. . . . But was paralyzed; in awe
of his subject. He found more things to add to *The Gulag Archipelago*
instead. The intense cold in Agafya's cottage gave a slight impression of
Siberia.

Back in Moscow, the chances of publishing *Cancer Ward* seemed
warmer; there were hints that Brezhnev would not object. An excited Tvardovsky summoned Sanya back. It was decided to set eight chapters in type.
The political temperature fell to zero again—and the type had to be broken
up. Sanya turned to Solotcha and *Gulag*, while a bereft Tvardovsky wrote
a noble and eloquent twenty-four-page letter to Fedin, pleading with him
to help publish the novel. He warned him that it might soon be too late,
since copies were bound to find their way to the West.

His devoted representative Olga Carlisle—not to mention cynical New York
lawyers—had that very concern over *The First Circle*. What if—a nightmarish thought—some other publisher suddenly came out with the book?
Solzhenitsyn had indicated that he would like it published by the end of
1968, so it was imperative, Olga felt, to meet him again. She was collaborating on an illustrated book about Pasternak's world, which gave her a good
excuse for returning to the Soviet Union so soon—five months—after her
spring visit. She arrived in late September 1967, and was to stay as usual at
Kornei Chukovsky's dacha. The snowy-haired, ruddy-faced old man always
warmly welcomed the granddaughter of his friend Leonid Andreyev. There
was a traditional jesting ritual of his offering her the hundred rubles that
Leonid had once loaned him and which he'd never repaid.

This could well be their last meeting, since Kornei was in his mid-
eighties.

Walking with her in the narrow Peredelkino lanes, he spoke about the
dissidents, and especially Solzhenitsyn. She did not know whether he was
aware of their closeness; but he lamented the harassment of him, and his
poverty; he was too proud to accept financial help, he said, but perhaps
Olga could find a way of raising some funds for him in the States?

Yet then he warned her against getting involved, saying that Sanya was
a man "possessed."[7]

When she made contact with the *oderzhimiy* writer, at another private
gathering, he soon led her away from the others out to a narrow balcony.
He seemed to her more confident than in the spring, his features less sharp;
and with his reddish beard he reminded her of some guerrilla leader, a

Castro or Che Guevara. Whether with hindsight or not, she would remember, thirty years later, a new imperiousness, a lack of kindness.[8] He started to pour out all sorts of plans for *The First Circle*, which were hard to reconcile with the businesslike arrangements drawn up in America, concerning translations, copyright, simultaneous publications round the world. He waved his hand dismissively, and spoke excitedly of salvos and crossfire.

Her voice a little shaky, she spoke of how vital it was, for his own safety's sake, that there be an unbreakable chain of authority, running secretly from him through her to Harper & Row, and then openly through them to publishers around the world. He must also assure her that no other copies would be released to the West, to avoid risk of piracy.

"Yes, yes, Olga Vadimovna, that is the best way. I approve." He laid his hands on her shoulders, and said emotionally, "I will show them! . . . We are involved in an unheard of adventure. You may not be able to return to Russia—it could be dangerous for you and for me. But in my heart I feel we shall meet again."

That winter, she and Henry shared the conviction of their friends in opposing the Vietnam War; but that cause had to take second place to preparing the novel for publication. They too were possessed, and drawn into a cloak-and-dagger world, becoming paranoid about security. The translator, Thomas Whitney, working a ten- or twelve-hour day in his Victorian barn converted to a Russian library, locked the manuscript in a safe at night, and also had his house guarded by fierce police dogs.

One cold moonlit night Olga dreamed that Solzhenitsyn was hiding in their house. Red Army soldiers in Civil War uniforms surrounded it, silently closing in on it, their bayonets glinting in the moonlight. She heard the shatter of glass as they broke in, the thump of their boots, the clanking of their weapons.[9] Waking up in terror, she saw the long black shadows across the moonlit terrace and they seemed to be moving closer. The terror did not subside; she feared something dreadful was happening to Solzhenitsyn.

35

T r a n s l a t i o n s   a n d   T r a n s i t i o n s

Where two or three are gathered together in my name . . .
—*St. Matthew's Gospel*

HE DECIDED* ON A BIG PUSH IN THE SPRING OF 1968—THAT FAMOUS
Prague Spring when it seemed as though Alexander Dubček's government
was going to give the Czechs "Communism with a human face." He, Liusha,
Q., and Natasha met in Rozhdestvo, where the three women hammered
away at typewriters to complete and edit *The Gulag Archipelago*. Liusha
was so speedy that Q. called her "the Paganini of the typewriter." Their
noble dedication does have overtones of chamber music, if not of primitive
Christianity. They completed the second volume in a month, before the
arrival of summer-cottage tourists in the surrounding dachas. Liusha had
already spent a month in Moscow typing up the first volume; then, during
June, she helped Natasha with volume three, though there was "not much
love lost between the two of them."[1] Natasha photographed the whole work
and transferred it to microfilm; he acknowledges that she did an excellent
job.

Another important helper was Ehrenburg's private secretary, Natalya Stolyarova—known as "Eva" in the Solzhenitsyn codebook. "Eva" was the
daughter of a famous Socialist revolutionary, Natalya Klimova, who took
part in an attempt to assassinate Prime Minister Stolypin in 1906. Stolypin
had not been harmed, but thirty people, visiting his dacha, had been blown
up and another thirty or so, including children, seriously injured. Klimova,
sentenced to death, did not beg for mercy, but the Tsar commuted her
sentence, and that of the only other convicted female, to hard labor for life.
Klimova charmed her wardress into allowing an escape. A terrorist once
more, she married another revolutionary, Ivan Stolyarov.

---

*Or rather "we decided." He informs us that whenever, in *Invisible Allies*, he uses "we," he
means—"for several years on end"—Liusha and himself.

"Eva," their daughter, was brought up in Paris but dreamed of living in Russia. She moved there in the thirties and was soon arrested as a "spy" and sent to a labor camp. Her contacts with the West made her an ideal helper for Sanya. He quotes without irony her sister Katya's remark that "Eva" had inherited her mother's vivacity, high principles, breadth of vision, and generous spirit: not a description that most readers, nor usually Solzhenitsyn, readily associate with blowing children to pieces. At any rate the daughter proved invaluable; she had persuaded Vadim Andreyev to carry the *First Circle* microfilms to the West; and after the spring typefest at Rozhdestvo she planned a similar migration for *The Gulag Archipelago*. The smuggler this time was Sasha Andreyev, Vadim's son, who was in Moscow on a UNESCO trip. The complicated transfer of the package to him was almost botched, the final exchange occurring in a car passing around the statue of Felix Dzerzhinsky in Lubyanka Square. . . .

For several days the conspirators did not know if Sasha had got away safely; they became sick with anxiety. Sanya was working, with less concentration than usual, on the original "authentic" version of *The First Circle*, with its nine extra chapters. All the windows of the Rozhdestvo shack were shut tight in the breathless heat of midsummer, to muffle the clack of typewriters. Then, at last, Liusha brought the happy news that the momentous work was safely delivered. Olga Carlisle had collected it from her brother, in a frenzied Paris that seemed on the verge of another revolution. "Big Fish," Sasha called the handed-over package. When his sister and brother-in-law got home to Connecticut, and were able to have the microfilms professionally processed, they settled down to read the work, and began to see that it was Big Fish indeed. Overwhelmed by the power of *The Gulag Archipelago*, Olga Carlisle came as close as she had ever been to a nervous breakdown.[2]

When Harper & Row announced the forthcoming publication of *The First Circle*, there were hostile critics who, recalling the author's outburst about foreign publications of *Cancer Ward*, accused Harper & Row of endangering his life. One eminent scholar and translator, Patricia Blake, excitedly told Olga at an exhibition of Neizvestny's sculpture that Solzhenitsyn would surely be killed if this work was published; she begged Olga to use her influence to stop it. Olga was in the painful position of not being able to explain that he *wanted* it to appear. At least, there were no legal battles, as there had been in both the United States and Europe, over who had the right to publish *Cancer Ward*. In the United States, Dial Press and Farrar, Straus & Giroux were bringing out competing editions.

The Carlisles, drained by the effort to edit *The First Circle*, almost dreaded the thought of editing the *Gulag* leviathan. But they felt honored too. Solzhenitsyn wanted it published if possible within two years. They were to let him know when the translation was ready, and he would signal when he wanted it published. But again there could be absolutely nothing in writing; nor did they know whether he wanted the work brought out in one volume or three; what to do about foreign translations; and always—after the worries about *The First Circle*—were there other manuscripts floating around?

It was a painful summer. Hot on the heels of Martin Luther King's death, Robert Kennedy, whom Olga Carlisle knew slightly, was gunned down. She had talked to him not long since about Solzhenitsyn; he had promised to read him and, giving her a copy of his own book, *To See a Newer World*, said, "With best wishes to you and those Russian writers you talk about so eloquently. And I'll be sure to read . . . that man! before we meet again."

August in Russia proved to be a turbulent month. Summoned by Tvardovsky to his dacha on the sixteenth, Solzhenitsyn found him in a buoyant mood. The BBC had broadcast and discussed his January letter to Fedin. Tvardovsky, instead of being frightened, seemed pleased; and amazed his guest by leaping up and saying, "We've missed three minutes! Let's go and listen!" And led the way to his radio to tune in to the BBC News. Could this be Tvardovsky?

Switching off, he murmured, "*There's* a radio station you can take seriously—absolutely without bias."[3] So warm did Sanya feel toward him that he told him about *Gulag*, and later showed him a precious copy; but Tvardovsky did not have the time to read it.

Back in Rozhdestvo, for many days and nights on end the writer heard the rumble of tanks and trucks on the road, heading west, but thought the Soviets were only trying to scare Czechoslovakia. When he heard the tragic news that the Soviet Union had crushed the tentative Czech reform movement he was stunned, like all his liberal friends; he began to compose a letter of protest, then backed away from it. It was a difficult decision, but what good would a letter do? Rather—wait, be prudent. . . .

On Sunday, 25 August, Tvardovsky could have heard the BBC broadcasting news of the brave demonstration of seven young people in Red Square. They had sat down, holding up homemade banners saying "Hands Off the CSSR" and "For Your Freedom and Ours." Among them was the poet Natalya Gorbanyevskaya, with her small child in a pram. The demonstrators were punched and manhandled into Black Marias—but they had been seen.

Mostly, the Soviet intellectuals felt a dreadful sense of oppression and helplessness, and did nothing.

On the day following the demonstration, Sanya came to Moscow to hold two meetings.[4] The first was with a twenty-eight-year-old mathematician, working for her doctorate, called Natalya Svetlova. The second, two hours later, was his first encounter with the great nuclear physicist Andrei Sakharov. He had recently shattered his professional career by writing, and putting into samizdat, an article arguing for a convergence between East and West, in the interest of world peace. He warned against the dangers of nuclear war, ecological catastrophe and world famine; for the Soviet Union he wanted freedom of conscience and expression, and democratization. His *Reflections* had been broadcast on the BBC; on 22 July it was published in the *New York Times*. He would never again be allowed into his place of work.

When Stalin died, Sakharov had written to his first wife: "I am under the influence of a great man's death. I am thinking of his humanity." At that time he had still believed that the Soviet state, for all its huge imperfections, represented a breakthrough into the future. That belief, he comments in his *Memoirs*, "shows the hypnotic power of mass ideology."[5] He had worked in a top-secret scientific city serviced by a slave labor camp. After he had achieved the highest honors for creating his country's first H-bomb, he began to be concerned for the effects of nuclear tests. By 1957, he calculated, half a million people had either died or would have their lives shortened by nuclear tests around the world. Now, twelve years on, his mature conscience had caused a small nuclear explosion in the intellectual world.

He admired Solzhenitsyn's work, and the former physics graduate was in awe of Sakharov's mathematical genius. They were to meet on neutral ground, the house of one of Sakharov's friends. But first, Sanya had to hold a kind of "job" interview with the young woman, Svetlova.

All summer, "Eva" had been saying to him, "You're wasting your strength, Sanya, on things that others could be doing. What you need are some energetic young people to help you. I could introduce you to some. . . ."

And truly, what energy he sensed in Natalya Svetlova, this "intense young woman, her dark hair swept forward above her hazel eyes! No trace of affection in her manner or dress" (unlike, say, the first Natalya, we can hear him add under his breath). He would discover that she "thought with an electronic rapidity." She loved music and poetry, was reading Akhmatova when only in her teens; and had done secretarial work for Nadezhda Mandelstam. She was acquainted with such dissidents as Gorbanyevskaya, Alexander Ginzburg, and Pavel Litvinov—grandson of the Soviet foreign minister—and had been within an inch of joining the demonstration. "Eva" had chosen wisely for him.

He met Svetlova at the small flat, near the House of Cinema, in which she lived with her little son, Dmitri, and her mother and stepfather. Alya (as Svetlova liked to be called) had married at twenty a still younger and even more brilliant mathematician, Andrei Tiurin, but they had separated amicably four years later. Svetlova explained to Solzhenitsyn that she would only be able to work for him for a couple of hours each evening, after putting her little boy to bed. He asked her if she would type out the complete version of *The First Circle*, and she readily agreed.

Her mother, Katya, was an aeronautical engineer, another fine intellect. Was he ever really close to anyone who didn't have a fine intellect? Probably his wife, despite her Ph.D. from Moscow University, *was* merely "not stupid" by comparison with so many others: a somewhat frightening thought. (Though Dmitri Panin refused to discount her intellect as others tended to do; he found her "brilliant in everything she touched—chemistry, music, photography—a vivacious, if somewhat moody, companion and a thoughtful, hospitable host"—perhaps because, when he knew her at the beginning of the renewed marriage, she was happy.[6])

Having been impressed by the new volunteer, Sanya was "charmed" also by Sakharov, with his gentle and candid look, his warm smile, his pleasantly throaty voice;[7] though it was a stuffily hot day, he wore a tight shirt collar and tie, and unbuttoned his jacket only in the course of their conversation, in the manner of an old-style Moscow intellectual. They both equally expressed their sense of helplessness in the face of the invasion of Czechoslovakia; Sanya told him about the demonstration and arrests in Red Square; and a few days later Sakharov tried to use what lingering influence he had by phoning the KGB head, Yuri Andropov, urging him to release the demonstrators. Andropov said he thought their sentences would be light. They were in fact given sentences of prison or exile of up to five years, and one was sent to a prison psychiatric unit.

Solzhenitsyn acknowledges in *The Oak and the Calf* that he was too insistently critical of *Reflections,* and admires the way Sakharov remained good-humored throughout the four hours they were together. Sakharov's account makes it clear he was being lectured: "I listened attentively as he talked away in his usual manner—passionately and with absolute conviction.[8] He summarizes Solzhenitsyn's disagreements with him as follows:

> Any kind of convergence was out of the question. The West was caught up in materialism and permissiveness, and socialism might prove to be its final ruin. The Soviet leaders were soulless robots who had latched onto power and the good life and would not let go unless forced to do so. It was wrong to differentiate Lenin from Stalin: corruption and destruction had begun on the first day of Bolshevik power. Sakharov's estimate of ten million deaths in labor camps was too low; Professor Kurganov had estimated sixty million deaths from terror, famine and related disease.
>
> It was a mistake to seek a multiparty system; what was needed was a non-party system; parties served the party bosses not the people. Scientists and engineers had a major part to play, but in the absence of an underlying spiritual goal any hope of using science to regulate progress was a delusion that would end with everyone being suffocated by the smoke and cinders of cities.[9]

Both the West, and most of the Russian intelligentsia, regarded Solzhenitsyn and Sakharov as almost identical democrats; but they were far from that. It was not that the former was trying to deceive anybody by a pretense of being liberal; the illusion came mostly from that peculiar complacent certainty, in liberal or left-liberal circles, that no other philosophical position is tenable. For a long time Solzhenitsyn did not realize, he wrote in *Invisible*

Allies, that the support he received from "progressive society" was but a passing phase based on a misunderstanding. He would find there was a wide gulf between his ideas and those of Liusha, even. People looked down on Orthodoxy, yet still praised him in his highly spiritual "miniatures," his prose poems, because it was fashionable to admire the aesthetics of icons, and even recognize the lyrical beauty of a church in a landscape.

He felt almost as distant from the ethical socialism and secularism of Tvardovsky and Sakharov—or, for that matter, Arthur Miller and Norman Mailer—as he did from Brezhnev. Perhaps the "enlightened" were ultimately more dangerous than the reactionary tyrants—because the latter forced you to look for truth and the spirit, whereas the former might make you content with "progress" and what in the late twentieth century we call political correctness.

It was turning out that Alya Svetlova, his youthful recruit, was actually much more on his wavelength than Sakharov. Even before Stalin's death, which had occurred while she was in high school, she had been starting to ferret out the true history of the Bolshevik Party. She had been able to use "suppressed" documents left behind by her grandfather, Ferdinand Svetlov, who had been a Bolshevik publicist before he himself was suppressed in 1937. The newest generation (Pavel Litvinov was another example) were rebelling against the ancien régime. Soon she was doing far more than typing yet another copy of a novel; her former husband too, Andrei Tiurin, with whom she was on good terms and who often called to see his son, asked to help in the struggle.

Alya proved to be as well organized and efficient as Liusha; indeed, "to describe her as businesslike would be an understatement; she worked with an alacrity, meticulousness, and lack of fuss that were the equal of any man. Her grasp of tactics, of how and when to act, was instantaneous—'computerlike,' as I called it—and from the outset she matched my own impetuous behavior at the time."[10] But there was nothing computerlike about her love of poetry, of which she knew a great deal by heart. To his delight he discovered she was skilled at editing and polishing literary texts. In choosing mathematics rather than the humanities, she had followed a pattern among independent-minded Russians, who knew that the sciences were taught more objectively.

She was an ideal helper; and soon became more than that. "The fourth or fifth time we met, I put my hands on her shoulders as one does when expressing gratitude and confidence to a friend. And this gesture instantly turned our lives upside down: from now on she was Alya, my second wife. . . ."

Strange, the reasons of the heart: with Liusha he had never, even for two minutes, been able to put aside the cause; yet with Alya, presumably, there were occasions when he forgot the Gulag and the Revolution almost completely. . . .

Liusha and Natasha did not need to feel jealous of each other anymore.

In *Alya*, a mutual friend reflects, "Sanya found all that was needful to him; she was educated, intelligent, witty, with a great many friends; she was small, shapely, and moved with grace. She worked conscientiously for him, and he could trust her absolutely with any secret. Independent-minded— no echo of Sanya—she was nevertheless of one mind with him in essence. She is a rare woman, and one in whom there has never been any vainglory."[11]

In the fall, *Cancer Ward* and *The First Circle* came out in Britain and the United States to an awesome salvo of publicity about the heroic, embattled author. While there were reviewers who noted that he was a traditional realist, an artist for whom Joyce, Mann, and Proust (or, we might add, Bulgakov and Pasternak) did not seem to exist, in general there was great acclaim, especially for *The First Circle*. Thomas Lask, in the *New York Times*, wrote that it was "at once classic and contemporary . . . future generations will read it with wonder and awe." Ronald Hingley, in the *Spectator*, described it as "arguably the greatest Russian novel of the twentieth century." Julian Symons of the *Sunday Times* called it "a majestic work of genius . . . a tremendously readable translation."

Translation—that was a sore point. The British publisher, William Collins, had refused to accept Harper & Row's version by Thomas Whitney, giving it instead to three translators, Max Hayward, Michael Glenny, and Ronald Hingley: pseudonymously, "Michael Guybon." And the author himself, when he had a chance to examine the texts, disliked all the translations. He prided himself on knowing English well enough to discriminate between a good and a bad translation, and he thought these were all highly unsatisfactory. This may have created his first doubts about Olga Carlisle. A year ago, he had placed his hands on *her* shoulders, in that gesture "expressing gratitude and confidence," but that was not a gesture he would repeat with her.

There were rumors that he was going to be arrested for publishing abroad, but he was confident he would not be. After Sinyavsky, Daniel, and others, they would find another way, he believed.

His fiftieth birthday arrived. In Russia, much is made of an artist's fiftieth birthday, but in his case, from the point of view of the press, he might not have existed. But all day, and indeed for a week before, telegrams poured in. Almost a thousand telegrams, letters, and other messages came for him, so that he felt moved, and also proud. "Let me scorn mock modesty and admit that I held my head high that week. Gratitude had caught up with me in my own lifetime, and I was conscious that it had not been lightly earned."[12]

Lydia Chukovskaya wrote: "In you the dumbstruck have found their voice. I can think of no writer so long awaited and so sorely needed as you. Where the word has not perished, the future is safe. Your bitter books both wound and heal the soul. You have restored to Russian literature its thunderous power." And Tvardovsky: "May you live another fifty years and may your talent lose none of its splendid strength. All else passes; only the truth will remain."

He chose to treat the day as a normal working one, except that he came out to have lunch with Natasha and some of his helpers. It ended, unfortunately, with a domestic row, witnessed by Veronica Stein. Sanya came out of his room to hand her a letter to give to Liusha. He explained he was going to Moscow for a few days and was telling Liusha he would like to stay at the Chukovsky dacha. Almost certainly, of course, he would be expecting to see Svetlova. His wife accused him of being selfish: why couldn't he go on a weekend so that she could be with him? A row broke out and continued until Sanya went to bed; Veronica, who was sharing a small bedroom with Natasha, heard her sobbing well into the night. She was right to feel jealousy, but wrong if she was focusing it on Liusha.

He made an elegiac visit to Talinn also before the year ended. Arnold Susi had died during 1968, as well as Tenno, and he wished to pay his respects to the great warriors. He met Heli Susi and together they lit candles and placed them on the graves of her father and George Tenno—buried close to each other near the ruins of a medieval cathedral. He said to his beloved comrades under his breath: "There are mines primed and ready to explode. . . ."

In February Natasha celebrated her own fiftieth birthday. Kopelev was their only guest: rather strangely, since she did not greatly care for him. She made Sanya's blood run cold by saying she intended to retire from her teaching position. For too long, she said, she had neglected to help him with his literary work. She could do a lot of his typing, and help him with the research for *August 1914*. Retirement, with a decent pension, would allow them to spend a lot more time together.

Perhaps the row on his birthday had been the last straw; she would make sure he had no excuse in future not to invite her to accompany him. He could not oppose her decision too openly; but the very thought of spending more time with her filled him with dread. He was completely committed to Alya. (And how strange it was that he used her name, "Alya Svetlova," in one of his boyhood stories!) Increasingly they thought almost in unison. . . . For years "I had dreamed in vain of finding a male friend whose ideas would be as close to my own as were those that Natasha [Alya] now came out with unprompted. . . ." It was wonderful to have a girl Echo. He loved her combativeness and courage too: "Let's *hit* them!" she would cry, after some gross violation. Not for nothing did she have a Cossack father.

When their relationship became known, there were backbiters who claimed she had charmed him away from his first wife with her sexual powers. Perhaps she blended the experience and passionate nature of Olga Ladizhenskaya—to a milder, less threatening degree—with sound common sense: too controlled to be a kind of *troll* draining him with sensual magic. In any case, an attractive new lover of twenty-eight is likely to have more erotic appeal than a familiar wife of fifty.

With Sanya, we can be sure, it was the meeting of minds that most counted. His words indicate how hard he found it to meet people who shared his beliefs. Above all, despite being Jewish on her maternal side, Alya was deeply, patriotically Russian, indeed an Orthodox Christian. She revealed "a deep-rooted spiritual affinity with everything quintessentially Russian, as well as an unusual concern and affection for the Russian language. This, together with her vibrant energy, made me want to see her more often."[13]

This shared Russianness is well brought out in an incident described by Sakharov. He, too, had a second wife of powerful ability and personality, Elena Bonner. ("A man chooses his first wife," a strong Russian woman told me, "but his second wife chooses the man!") Solzhenitsyn did not take to Bonner, believing she had too much influence over her mild and gentle husband. He thought she was pushing him to go abroad and abandon his responsibility to Russia; that she made him focus his efforts too much on the Jewish problem. Once, when Sakharov had written to support a Jewish appeal to the U.S. Congress concerning the right to emigrate, Solzhenitsyn sent him a note asking him if he would call on Alya. Sakharov and Bonner did so. Obviously speaking for Sanya too, Alya asked him how he could think of writing such a piece, when there were far more pressing problems. She cited the millions of collective farmers who were little better than serfs, denied the right to leave their farms and live and work elsewhere. "She disparaged our worries about Elena's children, saying that millions of Russian parents had no chance to give their children any sort of proper education. Outraged by Alya's lecturing tone, Elena burst out: "Don't give me that 'Russian people' shit! You make breakfast for your own children, not for the whole Russian people!"[14]

And yet—Alya's passionate speaking up for the voiceless Russians haunts the memory.

36

Doubles

Art is the heart's blood.
—EDVARD MUNCH

DURING 1969 SANYA LIVED FOR THE MOST PART AWAY FROM RYAZAN and his wife—his official wife, for it seems he regarded Alya Svetlova as his wife from the moment he placed his hands on her shoulders.

Not even his friends seemed to know about the affair. His double life was curiously echoed by a puerile KGB attempt to blacken his character. Word spread that he had turned to drink; he had been seen at a well-known restaurant, boozing and pestering women; an actress who had been "entertained" by him told Kopelev, who—knowing his friend's abstemiousness—decided to accompany her on another lunch appointment. As a result he and some cronies were able to frog-march the frightened impostor, an actor with a criminal record, to a police station; but the man was never charged. Later, Kopelev reported to Sanya that a second impostor, one so like him he was almost his double, had been seen regularly calling at a certain address where he obviously had a girlfriend. Sanya exploded—the address was Alya's![1]

—"We Russians are obsessed with doubles," a Russian poetess, with whom I was sharing a train journey, said to me. I had referred to the two Natalyas in Solzhenitsyn's life. "He is imitating Alexander Blok." She reminds me that Blok was torn between Liubov his wife and Liubov his mistress; the name appropriately meaning love. "But there are also the doubles of east and west, Slavophile and westernizer; Dostoyevsky and Chekhov; Solzhenitsyn and Sakharov; dark and light. . . . The luxuries our intellectuals depend on—apartments and dachas, special hospitals and stores—and their tender feelings for the dispossessed. . . . And there's Akhmatova, as you know, living with the art historian, Punin, in the thirties while his first wife—another Anna!—had the next bedroom and all three ate together. . . . Tiring of him, Akhmatova could say, 'Let's change rooms, Anna,' and the two women started moving their clothes, while Punin gawped like a goldfish!"

"But we have complicated relationships too, you know!" I reminded her.

"Of course; but our writers, our intelligentsia, think it's as natural as borshch; they embrace it as their fate! It's their punishment for the champagne and black caviar sandwiches on the 'Arrow.'. . . . They have to have Liubov and Liubov, Anna and Anna, Natalya and Alya. . . ."

We returned to our books for a while; then she threw her head back in delight, crying, "This Olga is very Russian!" I had loaned her Olga Carlisle's book about her Solzhenitsyn experience. The poet showed me the passage that had made her chuckle: Olga's account of an anti–Vietnam War march in Washington, in which she "ran" into Norman Mailer; had drinks with him and Robert Lowell at a hotel; talked about Herzen and the modern dissidents; marched with them then alongside a throng of student protesters; Mailer "delighted to be recognized," responding to the shouted greetings with a "gruff, friendly word"; he and Lowell deeply moved because "this new, concerned America was their child. . . ."; Olga being swept along in "a huge, warm wave of emotion. . . . Part of an immense, purposeful whole. . . . At this moment, the march and Solzhenitsyn's mission seemed to me a part of a single, proud enterprise."[2]

I chuckled too, saying, "She doesn't seem to realize he hated the protesters!"

"Of course! . . . But don't you agree she's so Russian?—dropping these big names of her friends, but feeling part of the masses!"

"It's how revolutions start," I said.

Another "double" she might have mentioned is that of Russian and Jew. The KGB waged a somewhat pathetic campaign to plant the idea that the troublesome writer's name was "Solzhenitser." "This is no mistake," a speaker at a Moscow lecture told a member of the audience who queried his pronunciation: "The person known to you as Solzhenitsyn is really Solzhenitser, and he's a Jew."

Embarked at last on August 1914 Solzhenitsyn completed his account of Samsonov's campaign and then, in the drizzle and slush of November in Ryazan, turned with savage joy to debunking Lenin. By a fitting coincidence Lenin's portrait had been installed opposite his house; he could gaze at him while committing his arch-blasphemy. Tvardovsky, who had read and admired the Samsonov chapters, would have been shattered to know that the "moral socialist"—as even his enemies assumed him to be—was an illusion, as pseudo as the drunken womanizing actor or the Jewish Solzhenitser.

On the morning of 4 November 1969, while the iconoclast was happily at work, there was a ring at his doorbell and he was confronted by a flustered secretary from the Ryazan Writers' Union. Taking care not to look him in the eye, she thrust a scrap of typewritten paper into his hand, before making a swift exit. He found he was being called to a conference on "the ideological education" of writers at three P.M. that very day. Convinced the sudden conference had something to do with himself, too tense to continue with the assault he was making on Lenin, he started pasting together some items which might be useful should he be attacked.

He arrived a few minutes early and spread out his papers and colored pencils on a table. Normally writers turned up at meetings an hour in advance, but on this occasion the room was eerily deserted, except for the acting secretary, Matushkin. He, too, avoided looking Sanya in the eye as the latter tried to make polite conversation.

Right on the dot of three, five writers, and half a dozen officials, rushed in. All the writers made a point of coming up to him and shaking his hand. One of them, Rodin, was obviously burning up with fever. "Why ever did you come?" Sanya inquired, appalled. It was soon clear why: he had been ordered to, so that there should be a quorum that could expel Solzhenitsyn from the Union. Rodin had been dragged from his bed, 120 miles away, and made to drive to the meeting. The branch secretary, Ernst Safonov, had actually volunteered to go into the hospital for an appendix operation in order to avoid the fateful meeting. A young poet, Markin, who gabbled a highly distressed speech, had been promised a new flat if he cooperated.

In their speeches calling for the expulsion of their colleague, the writers cited his failure to denounce Western exploitation of him, and also his "arrogance" in not helping young Ryazan writers by reading and commenting on their work. Given ten minutes to reply, but granted a further ten after a protest that this was "life or death," he rebutted both these charges; to the familiar accusation that he was too gloomy about his country's life, he quoted Nekrasov: "He who lives without grief or anger / Cannot love his native land." He rushed through his impromptu speech at the usual machine-gun speed for such emergencies, knowing that only what he actually *said* would carry an impact when he was able to convey it to samizdat.[3] He ended by repeating the promise he had given in his letter to the Fourth Congress, that he would fulfill his duty as a writer "from the grave even more successfully and incontrovertibly than in my lifetime."

When the vote was taken, five voted for expulsion, one (Solzhenitsyn) against.

The next morning, rising as usual at six, he switched on the Voice of America, not expecting anything in particular, but hearing almost at once, "According to private information from Moscow, Alexander Solzhenitsyn was yesterday expelled from the writers' organization in his hometown, Ryazan." The world had truly entered the electronic age. The Ryazan recommendation needed to be confirmed at a higher level, and he did not believe he could be expelled in absentia, or so precipitately. He was wrong; that very day, 5 November, expulsion was confirmed by the secretariat of the Russian Writers' Union. Enraged, he settled to dash off an open letter, which in part read:

> Shamelessly trampling under foot your own statutes, you have expelled me in my absence, expelled me precipitately, without even summoning me by telegram, without giving me even the four hours I needed to make my way from Ryazan and be present at the meeting. You have candidly revealed that the *decision* preceded the "discussion." Were you afraid of being obliged to grant me ten minutes for my answer? I am compelled to write this letter as a second best.
>
> Dust off the clock face. You are behind the times. Throw open the sumptuous heavy curtains—you do not even suspect that day is already dawning outside. We are no longer in that muted, that somber, that hopeless age when, just as compliantly, you expelled Akhmatova. We are not even in that timid, shivery period when you expelled Pasternak, howling abuse at him. Is this not disgrace enough for you? Do you want to make it blacker yet? But the time is near when each of you will seek to scratch his signature from today's resolution. . . . [4]

Ernst Safonov gained nothing from his emergency attack of appendicitis, being obliged to add his signature a month later. Only death or irreversible brain damage could have kept him both conscience free and in favor.

The Central Committee's Culture Department reported, on 13 November, initial responses to Solzhenitsyn's expulsion. Fedin predictably said it was a logical conclusion to what had taken place at the meeting he had chaired, two years before. Sholokhov pointed out that at that time he had "insisted on the expulsion of Solzhenitsyn from the Writer's Union." Alexei Surkov declared himself an implacable opponent of Solzhenitsyn in every respect. Alexander Kozhevnikov, who had been present at the Ryazan meeting, offered a distorted echo of Groucho Marx in commenting, "I already said at the meeting of the Writers' Union that I do not wish to be a member of the same organisation as Solzhenitsyn." Tvardovsky was reported as describing the expulsion of "an outstanding writer of our times" as inadmissible and incorrect. It would not be approved, he said, by Soviet and foreign intellectuals.

Five days later the Culture Department reported again. Bourgeois propaganda had raised an anti-Soviet uproar, making use of the author's own transcript of the proceedings. The *New York Times* had published his "open letter" on 5 November, whereas the original was not received by the Russian Writers' Union until 17 November. The tone of this letter had caused much indignation throughout the Soviet Union. Several writers, however, including B. Okudzhava and Y. Yevtushenko, had requested that the expulsion be reviewed before a plenum of the Union. The Moscow City Party Committee also reported to the Central Committee on the reaction of writers in the capital. The secretary, V. Grishin, was clearly alarmed by the extent of op-position to the expulsion. Yevtushenko is again mentioned, along with Lydia Chukovskaya and Lev Kopelev. The expulsion was "an insult to every honest writer," according to Vladimir Tendryakov and Boris Mozhaev, two serious artists who wrote about village life. It would be necessary, Grishin con-cluded, to intensify persuasive efforts with Moscow writers.[5]

Meanwhile Solzhenitsyn had decided it would be safer to leave Ryazan. Outside his house, beside the unblinking yellow eye of Lenin there stood, parked in a snowdrift, an even more watchful pickup truck with two men in the unlit cab, constantly surveying him. He felt unable to go back to his account of Lenin, and that block would continue for the next year and a half. It would be quite easy for the KGB to arrange a traffic accident for him out of the way here in Ryazan. He felt he should get out. It was probably a convenient decision for other reasons too. He said good-bye to Natasha, Maria, and the two aunts, and took the train to Moscow. This time he was heading for a new haven.

A former *zek*, a sixty-year-old woman, has described in a memoir an entertaining meeting she had on an overnight train journey from Leningrad to Moscow. Hoping for a staid female companion in the sleeping compart-ment, she was chagrined to find herself paired with a man, aged about forty. However, he proved so courteous, lively, and friendly—even helping her off with her coat—that she warmed to him and they sat talking all night, drinking champagne and eating caviar. He criticized a magazine she started to read, saying the writing was so predictable; he could only read authors who were not published. Solzhenitsyn, for instance. He rated him higher than Tolstoy; "but I guess you wouldn't agree."

"On the contrary, I respect his work a lot."

"He's no pitiful intellectual like Pasternak, Olenka." (After a few glasses they were calling each other by their familiar names.) "Solzhenitsyn would never beg not to be expelled."

The woman bridled at this, saying those times were different; it was brave then even to stay silent. He'd had no protectors—unlike Solzhenitsyn. And who did she think his protectors are? the lively fellow asked.

"Well, Chukovsky, Sakharov . . . and I suppose Rostropovich."

"You *suppose* Rostropovich! Let me tell you, after meeting him just once at a recital in Ryazan, Rostropovich invited him to live in his home and share everything! But what has Sakharov done? . . ."

His chance companion interrupted his heated speech by saying that Pas-ternak had not written the pleading letter to Khrushchev; an official and Olga Ivinskaya, Pasternak's mistress, had written it. "He wrote it out of love, Slava—for her sake."

"Yes, I see . . ." Slava said thoughtfully. "It was all because of women, naturally. . . . God, these women! Well, of course, that gives me a rather different picture. . . . But Solzhenitsyn would never have allowed himself to be run by women. . . ."

The "Arrow" arriving in Moscow, he hugged her good-bye, wrote down his phone number and full name, took his cello down from the rack . . . and only then did she realize he was Mstislav Rostropovich; and still she was not sure if he knew that she was Olga Ivinskaya.[6]

Kornei Chukovsky was dead; Lydia Chukovskaya was herself threatened with expulsion from the Writers' Union; Solzhenitsyn's relationship with Liusha had cooled because of Alya. So he decided to take up Slava Rostropovich's long-standing invitation.

As befitted a marriage of two international stars of the music world—the conductor-cellist was married to the great soprano Galina Vishnevskaya—they lived in one of Moscow's most elegant outer suburbs, a green, wooded area reserved for notables. "Zhukovka 1" housed the Party leaders and was impregnable; "Zhukovka 2," containing about sixteen spacious properties, had been built under Stalin for the top nuclear scientists. When two academicians moved out, Shostakovich and Rostropovich had been allowed to buy their properties. Recently the latter had built a separate flat, above a three-car garage, intended for a young Leningrad cellist who had, in the event, not turned up; it was perfect for Sanya. Now he would accept. The flat's self-sufficiency would increase his independence; it would mark a decisive break from Ryazan.

Galina, a beauty with a salty command of swear words, helped to carry a bed and other furniture from the main house into the flat, and hung some blue and white curtains, brought back from an American tour. Then she worried: was the design too abstract?

"Look, he fought a war and was ten years in prison and the camps, Galya! He won't give a shit. . . ."[7]

She looked out one morning and saw a battered Moskvich standing in the drive. He'd arrived, said Slava, moved his things in, and had now gone into the city; he'd be back in a few days. Galina tiptoed into the flat to see if there was anything else he might need. She found only a strange bundle on the bed. "I looked closer and saw that it was an old, black quilted jacket like those issued in labor camps, so worn out it had holes. It was wrapped around a thick pillow in a patched pillowcase. One could see that the patches in both jacket and pillowcase had been sewn by a man—they were pieced together with big, awkward stitches. All was neatly tied with a cord from which hung a dull aluminum tea kettle. It was as if a man had just returned from a concentration camp and was getting ready to go back. The pathos of it stabbed me like a knife.

" 'Slava, that's from *there*, isn't it?' " . . .[8]

A few days later she met their guest for the first time: "A light-haired, thickset man of middle age with a reddish beard, clear grey eyes that harbored a feverish glint, and a nervous, resonant voice." He thanked her for her generosity, and hoped he wouldn't crowd them. Reassuring him about that, she expressed a worry that the flat wouldn't be comfortable enough.

"Galochka," he replied, "I've never before lived in such luxury. For me it's the realisation of a dream. It's a marvellous place: the garden, the silence! A house and work—that's paradise—Lord above!" He had but one request: that she would let an old carpenter that he knew (doubtless an ex-*zek*) come and put up a table and bench far down in the garden—so that from spring to fall he could work out-of-doors.[9]

While his position was extremely precarious and difficult, Natasha's was in reality far worse. He possessed the secret love of Alya, the devotion of his helpers, and now the fiercely loyal friendship of Rostropovich. Thanks to him he had a comfortable and secure place to live. He could, of course, have been ejected from Zhukovka at any time, since he had no permit to live there; but "they" let him stay in a well-observed, well-bugged place. He had the sympathy and admiration of most of the Russian intelligentsia and of the Western world. He had the passion of his art.

Natasha had given up her job, in a desperate effort to keep her marriage together. For a long time he had virtually abandoned her—and even when they were together, what company was he? At fifty, she had lost her youthful attractiveness, becoming—in the words of Vishnevskaya—"a frail woman with a large head."[10] She had little apart from the three old sisters, who had lost their city on the Don but would never reach Moscow—and a sense of failure.

Galina gives a cruel portrait of Natasha, who had put pressure on her husband to let her live with him at Zhukovka the first winter. She struck Galina, when the couple first came to tea, as "an old maid from a provincial nest of gentlefolk. . . . She had never outgrown her role as the little, coldly proper young lady." When Galina and Slava were "engrossed" in conversation with Sanya, Natasha flitted away into the next room. She sat down at the piano and "began clumsily to play some Rachmaninov and Chopin, stabbing ruthlessly at the keys. Alexander Isayevich winced and dropped his eyes. Then he looked at Slava. "She might have refrained from playing in your presence, no?"

"I thought at the time," writes Vishnevskaya, "that it wasn't really so deplorable for a woman wanting to be 'interesting' to sit down at the piano and make music in the presence of a famous musician. But if she knew it was going to be embarrassing for her husband, that was another matter."

Sanya's disloyalty to his wife is appalling, and Galina's snobbery insufferable: the typical Muscovite intellectual's contempt for anyone from the provinces. She is the woman who is "stabbing."

The scene is fascinating psychologically; but it may never have happened. According to Natasha, she did not play the piano, in the presence of both Slava and Galina, for a whole year; Sanya had expressly forbidden her, since they were such great musicians. Then, one day, she came into the dacha when the Rostropoviches' daughter, Olya, was playing Chopin's Twelfth Etude. Olya asked her to play it, and she did so, though she had never played it before. She no longer felt that Sanya had any rights over her.

Galina and Slava came up to the glass door and looked in, surprised. Galina returned to the kitchen to cook mushrooms, while Slava listened to the end, then opened the door and embraced Natasha. "Natasha," he said, "you're a real musician!"[11]

It is an interesting example of the impossible art of biography. We all live in our own unique and semi-fictional novel.

Whether or not he was tolerating Natasha's presence, Sanya was always alone, it seemed to Galina. Looking out of her bedroom window in early morning, she would catch sight of him "pacing off the kilometers like a tiger—walking alongside the fence, back and forth, back and forth. Then he would go to the table quickly and write. After that, he would go back to pacing again for hours." An almost constant bonfire received all his rough drafts.

He lived on one ruble a day. She would find in the refrigerator nothing but a bottle of milk, a few eggs, a jar of sauerkraut, a boiled potato. When she scolded him, he laughed: he had everything—warmth, silence, and pure air. At first, she and Slava urged him to take his meals with them, and from time to time he would. "But he was as taut as a string. One felt that his ideas obsessed him, and pulsed feverishly within. He could not let go of them, he could not relax. It was a burden for him to sit at the table and waste precious time eating. And, after thanking us, he would make haste to leave."

His hosts were away performing a lot; and even when Galina was present at the dacha, she herself was inclined to solitude, and they would not come face-to-face with each other for weeks on end. Gradually, however, as a direct consequence of the couple's fervent support for the disgraced writer, they found their careers blighted. The foreign tours dried up, as did the concerts in Moscow and Leningrad.

Others too in the dissident camp were being persecuted, much more severely. In December 1969 Natalya Gorbanyevskaya, poet and editor of *Chronicle of Current Events*, which fought stubbornly for human rights, was arrested and taken to the Serbsky Psychiatric Institute. Here she was diagnosed as suffering from "sluggish schizophrenia." In February 1970 the dissident General Petro Grigorenko was arrested and—for the second time in six years—also incarcerated in a mental institution.

In May, Sanya's friend and supporter Zhores Medvedev was seized by a mixed group of police and psychiatric staff of the Kaluga Hospital. His violent arrest brought a storm of protest, and Solzhenitsyn broke his long habit of not becoming involved in individual cases by dashing off a fierce denunciation. "The incarceration of free-thinking people in madhouses is *spiritual murder*," he wrote; "it is a variation on the *gas chamber*, but is even more cruel: the torments of those done to death in this way are more evil and protracted."[12] Medvedev was saved by high-powered delegations and worldwide publicity, thanks to his international reputation as a geneticist.

In general, Soviet intellectuals were keeping their heads down, hoping that the freezing winds would spare them. The chief victims, other than Solzhenitsyn himself, were Tvardovsky and *Novy Mir*. Tvardovsky's protest on behalf of his most famous author had not gone unnoted. Another factor was his latest long poem, "By Right of Memory," in which the poet at last confronted with honesty the tragic fate of his father, a "kulak" peasant deported to Siberia.

Having had the poem rejected by the magazine *Yunost*, he decided to publish it in *Novy Mir*, but the censorship rejected it. He circulated proof copies, thus ensuring it would appear in samizdat. Then it was published in an émigré political weekly, *Possev:* probably planted by the KGB. Tvardovsky was invited to resign from *Novy Mir*. He refused. They sacked all his section heads, and replaced them with Party-minded hacks. Tvardovsky knew it was time to go. Sanya sat in the office with him, while other, lesser authors mooned about in the corridors. It was, fittingly, the anniversary of Pushkin's death, Sanya remarked.

Hearing of Tvardovsky's tearful farewell to his staff, Sanya was suddenly struck by a similarity to General Samsonov's farewell to his troops; and saw, beyond that, a resemblance in their characters. They had "the same inner greatness, the same bigness, the same purity, the same helplessness in practical matters and the same inability to keep up with the times. And also an aristocratic quality natural in Samsonov, paradoxical in Tvardovsky."[13]

In July, Tvardovsky celebrated his sixtieth birthday. There were the traditional encomiums in the press; but none of them mentioned his sixteen-year editorship of *Novy Mir*, nor his anti-Stalinist poem "Tyorkin in the Next World." Sanya sent him a telegram: "I wish you spacious days, precious discoveries, a happy creative life in your ripe years! Through all our constant quarrels and disagreements I remain immutably your deeply affectionate and ever grateful Solzhenitsyn."

Tvardovsky was always moved by any display of warm affection from Solzhenitsyn; he shut himself up in his study with the telegram, and sent a thank-you note back. So readily repelled by Tvardovsky's weakness and drinking and heavy smoking, Solzhenitsyn was rarely able to give him the love he craved. Yet at times Solzhenitsyn did feel that love for him; the two of them were curious doubles, but doubles nevertheless.

Later in the summer Tvardovsky suffered a stroke which left him half paralyzed. At the Kremlin Hospital he was treated for pleurisy, then it was discovered, after two weeks, that he had cancer and it was too late to operate. As with Solzhenitsyn sixteen years earlier, it was thought he had just a few weeks to live; the true nature of his illness was kept from him.

Natasha had her own memory of a cancer scare. The previous year she had had to have a lump—benign in the event—removed from a breast, and she was bitter that Sanya had not returned from a research trip to be with her. She suspected he was having an affair; probably with one of those panting assistants. In the vicious circle of a moribund marriage, she built up huge recriminations and suspicions when he kept her away from him; and on being allowed to join him again she would let it all out, which only served to anger him—and make the other Natalya seem all the more sweetly desirable. The moment his wife arrived, "everything would be gloom and endless conversations, and all my work would just slip from my hands until she left again." He knew he should have ended it years before, but there had always been another chapter to write first, another book. . . . [14]

Increasingly Natasha saw their marriage as having affinities with that of Lev and Sonya Tolstoy. That, too, had been stormy; yet, almost until the end, they had stayed together, and the world had no doubt that they loved each other. Sanya complained she was jealous; after the Leningrad affair she had obsessively queried his whereabouts, searched his pockets, tried to catch him out—but so had Tolstoy's wife: even to the extent of disguising herself as a peasant woman and trying to attract the master's attention, with the hope that he would prove her raging jealousy justified. . . .

At the beginning of August Sanya asked her if she would leave him to work alone at Rozhdestvo and return to Zhukovka. Reluctantly she agreed. She spent the month sorting his correspondence and planning her memoirs. And weeping a lot. When Sanya briefly visited Zhukovka on 26 August he was distressed to see her so unhappy. In the midst of another scene, he admitted he had been unfaithful, though without naming his lover. According to Natasha, he said, "Please understand me, I have to describe lots of women in my novel. You don't expect me to find my heroines round the dinner table, do you?" He told her he would move back to Zhukovka on 5 September. He suggested that she talk to Suzanna Teush, who had helped her greatly in 1964, at the time of his relationship with Olga.

When he left to drive back to Rozhdestvo Natasha was more distraught than ever. How much better it had been to suspect than to *know*. . . . She was beside herself with jealousy, imagining him in the unknown other woman's arms. . . .

She confided in an Orthodox priest, Father Vsevolod Shpiller. She should leave her husband for a while, Shpiller advised, and he found her a room in Moscow. She decided to move out of Zhukovka on the day of Sanya's planned return.

Before that happened, he had some news from Alya that rocked his whole world. She was pregnant. His treatment in Tashkent had not, after all, made him sterile. He had never wanted children, seeing them as enemies to his work; but now that his child was growing in his mistress's womb he was profoundly moved. Alya said she would happily keep his paternity a secret, and bring up the child on her own, if that was what he wanted. He felt it would be unfair on the child not to give him or her a name. He could not conceal his fatherhood. He accepted her suggestion that he should stay married to Natasha; she was too old to make a new life for herself and should not be abandoned. He settled to a writing task far more difficult than his letter to the Fourth Congress.

The woman of whom they had spoken, the letter informed Natasha, had just told him she was expecting his baby. He intended to admit he was the father. He hoped Natasha would not try to guess her name. She was not a passing fancy, but she was not trying to tear him away from his marriage. She was pleased to be having his child, but would not insist on marrying him.

She—Natasha—would be forever dear to him; she was in his blood and in his heart; that was why this letter was so hard to write. She could be proud of their long years together; these events did not cancel out the past. He would be responsible for her well-being for the rest of her life. Could she find the magnanimity that would make him her worshiper forever, and create beautiful, exalted relations that would last beyond the grave?[15]

Not knowing where Natasha would be—and perhaps thinking it advisable to have a sensible woman with her when she read his letter—he asked Veronica Stein to come to Rozhdestvo, and handed her the fourteen-page letter to pass on. Veronica did not have to seek out her cousin—the distraught woman came to her, on her way to the lodgings the priest had found for her. It was just before midnight on 5 September 1970. Yuri Stein was already in bed and his wife was in her nightclothes. Natasha was disheveled and hysterical; her cousin made tea for her and listened to her raging about Sanya: and still, Veronica thought, she does not know about the expected child. . . . There was no appropriate time for her to read such news; but Natasha did seem calmer after several cups of tea; and so Veronica thought she might as well get it over. She handed her the letter.

She skimmed through it, tore it into pieces, and rushed from the flat. In her dressing gown and slippers Veronica dashed out after her, and persuaded her to return, saying she would dress and go with her to her new place. While Veronica was pulling on her clothes she heard the front door slam; Natasha had left again. Veronica and her husband went out and searched streets and parks, without success. They dreaded what she might do in her present state; she had made several suicide threats.[16]

Suicide was in Natasha's tortured mind as she stumbled through the almost-deserted late-night streets. Her goal was the station from which the trains went to Zhukovka. *He* was due to arrive there; let him find her body. That would punish him . . . and the slut who had taken him from her. She managed to catch the last electric train. Perhaps the last journey of Anna Karenina flickered through her anguished mind. She too had felt a sense of triumph at how her death would hurt her lover, jolt him out of his indifference to her.

The train did not go all the way to Zhukovka; she had to walk several miles along the tracks. Her urge to die faded during the walk; a little hope was born, that when he saw her he might change his mind. Entering the empty apartment, she seized a knife and slashed her thumb, then wrote a short message in blood on a sheet of paper, which she stuck over Sanya's bed. Then she went to her room and slept.

When Sanya arrived early in the morning, he at once saw the message above his bed: the word "I," followed by a question mark, and with a cross through it. As though crossing out her existence. The blood and the weird squiggles were reminiscent of Munch's *The Scream*. Munch had described art as "the heart's blood." Here was Natasha's; as if she were saying to him, You can't hide behind the Gulag or the Revolution—I'm *your* victim!

A phone call. Wearily Sanya picked up the phone. His mind too was tortured. A bright Scandinavian voice: "You've won the Nobel Prize."

37

S a c r i f i c e

Finish, good lady! The bright day is done.
            —*Antony and Cleopatra*

INSTEAD OF DYING, NATASHA SUFFERED THE PAINFUL RELISH OF
trying to find out who his mistress was. At last it came to her that it must
be Natalya Svetlova, whom she had never met, and she challenged Sanya
with the name. After some time he admitted her intuition was correct. At
this meeting Natasha also found out that Katya, Alya's mother, was Jewish.
It surprised her, since he had always said he could never fall in love with a
Jewish woman.[1]

She now understood why Katya had stopped coming to visit, many
months ago; and remembered having remarked to him, lightly, during the
summer, "What a lot of Natashas there are around you!" And he had replied, "Even too many."[2]

It tormented her that, by his admission, the pregnancy was planned, by
which he presumably meant "hoped for"; whereas he had never wished to
have a child by her. He also spoke warmly of Alya's six-year-old son, Dmitri.

Sanya praised Alya's energy and competence as a helper. She had promised to go on helping him even if there should be another man in her life.
She would be his lifelong helper—unlike his Leningrad mistress of 1964,
who had refused such a promise.

This conversation took place at Rozhdestvo. Natasha had come to clean
up before the winter, and Sanya drove up unexpectedly. He was moved to
find her at work, and had tears in his eyes. She wished to prepare lunch for
them, but Sanya refused: he had too much work to do. Instead they sat
together on the bench, and talked. "Why didn't you let me develop my own
path?" she demanded. "Why did you get angry whenever I read books you
hadn't recommended? . . ."

"Yes, yes," he agreed contritely.

"Why did you prevent me from going to Moscow to continue my musical studies?"

"Yes, yes."

(She's right; but nothing can be done. And how will Vorotyntsev get out of the encirclement? . . . It will all vanish if I can't get to work soon.)

"How can I now recover from that, at my age, so as to make my life bearable?" . . .

Despite Alya's willingness to allow Natasha to remain his legal wife, Sanya's conversation increasingly touched on the subject of *razvód*—divorce—the word more frightening than any to her.

And then, one evening, she had an unexpected lightening of mood, and Sanya exclaimed at how much better she looked. "Be my mistress!" he urged—according to Natasha. And that night, she says, they slept together.

Next morning she was serving him an omelette when she saw there were tears coursing down his face. "You don't understand anything, my dear," he said; "love is returning."[3]

Her mind in a ferment, she returned to her lodgings in Moscow, but took the electric train out to Zhukovka on 3 October. He met her with the car; as they drove the familiar road to the Rostropovich mansion, she remarked with a laugh that she would be his dearest (most expensive) mistress—her room was thirty-five rubles a month! Steering one-handed, Sanya placed his right hand on her knee and said, "You *are* the dearest. We have survived so much."

For sure, he had not "seduced" her cold-bloodedly. He was trying to be compassionate, no doubt; and emotional turbulence can easily spill over into renewed—and brief—sexual desire. But now, following swiftly on his tender words, he was speaking again of divorce. "You'll destroy me if you don't agree to it!" he said, according to Natasha. She felt her own fragile hopes shatter.[4]

She fought frenziedly in retreat. At first he could see the child, but must give up the mother. Then, he could have the mother too, but she begged him not to divorce her. She hurried from one friend to another, pouring out her grief and anger, asking them to intercede with Sanya. He was impervious to all entreaties. Alya would have a child; she, Natasha, had none; if she would allow a divorce he would go down on his knees . . . their relationship would reach new spiritual heights. Natasha replied that she was not a saint.

It was an insoluble situation: a woman who could not live without him, and a man who could not love her enough to live with her anymore, and felt that his happiness demanded that he turn to his new love. Natasha went to see the Kopelevs and the Teushes, begging them to plead with Sanya on her behalf. She prayed on her knees before God that her marriage might be saved. Veniamin Teush did talk to Sanya and had some effect. Sanya told him he had not persuaded him, but shaken his resolve. Natasha thanked God for this mercy, and wrote to her husband that she would love his future child; only, please don't divorce me. . . . He read her letter, and said there was nothing new in it.

"She is gnawing into my liver," he told Veronica.[5]

Into this grievous clash of opposing desires burst the Nobel announcement. A telegram from the Swedish Academy on 10 October 1970 informed Solzhenitsyn that the prize was being awarded to him "for the ethical force with which he has pursued the indispensable traditions of Russian literature." Responding to it, he wrote that he regarded the decision as a tribute to Russian literature and "to our troubled history." The adjective made it clear there could be no question, in his mind, of playing down the politics of the Nobel Committee's choice. He had already indicated that he intended to come and receive the prize on the traditional day, insofar as this depended on him. He had added, pointedly, that he was well, and the state of his health would be no obstacle to his making the trip.

When Tvardovsky, partly paralyzed and hardly able to speak, heard about the Nobel Prize he startled his nurses by shouting out, "Bravo! Bravo! Victory!"

From the Western press, including leading Communist newspapers, came a torrent of praise for the new laureate. The Soviet press, which predictably condemned the "darling of Western reactionary circles," could cite only the most obscure left-wing newspapers in support of its own line. Glavlit, the Politburo's censorship agency, gave a full and thoroughly depressing survey of the views of reputable Western left-wing parties and newspapers: for example, L'Humanité (France): "the great writer and his wonderful books . . ." Volkstimme (Austria): "the son of Lenin's revolution, who has guarded the great democratic tradition of Russian literature . . ." Kansan Uutiset (Finland): "They [his life and his novels] help us to better understand human suffering." The gloomy survey concludes laconically: "All these newspapers have been confiscated by the Glavlit controller and prevented from going on sale."[6]

For Sanya, the most precious words of congratulation came from Vladimir prison, where zeks who had known him in the camps managed to smuggle out through the stone walls of their cells a letter signed by no fewer than nineteen men: "We hotly dispute the Swedish Academy's claim to have been first to appreciate your valor as a writer and as a citizen at its true worth. We jealously cherish our friend, our cellmate, our comrade of the prison trains. . . ."[7]

It is easy to criticize Solzhenitsyn for his treatment of his wife; but what cannot be gainsaid is his absolute commitment to the zeks, and they knew it. For those millions, no flaws in his character could chip away at the granite strength of this man, who would always be a hero to them. They knew he would give everything for them.

What also has to be understood is the emotional and physical toll that his writing of Gulag, and his exhausting and heroic campaign against the state, must have taken on him; if he seemed, or was, egotistical, narcissistic, almost childish at times in his demands on others, this was in part, surely, an effect of depletion, of needing to be replenished by others. Also, we do not have his version of what happened in his personal life. We have Natasha's; and she was not above putting a favorable gloss on her own behavior. From her own account, he was prone to tears around this time—his emotions overwrought. Close supporters of that time—even those with whom he has since quarreled—still argue vehemently in his defense.

The Nobel ceremony was due to take place on 10 December. Despite his initial statement of intent, Sanya was increasingly unsure if he should go—presuming he was granted an exit visa. The problem was that he might not be allowed back. The Academy had expressed the hope that he and his wife could come. Natasha, who was entrusted with sending off his reply, said to Veronica that she could easily have added the words "I can come with my wife," but had not done so.[8] One of the great stresses of the past months, when he had heard rumors that he might win the Nobel, had been the possibility of finding himself in the West, prevented from being joined by anyone but his legal wife. Now that he knew Alya was pregnant, this was an even more horrifying scenario.

Following the announcement of the award, Natasha felt an upsurge of hope; she was not only genuinely thrilled for Sanya's sake, but seemed to think the triumph would totally alter their situation: surely he would not want scandal at such a time, with the world's spotlight on him, on them both. "Aren't you going to congratulate me?" she asked Veronica. "Half the prize is due to me." She had moved back into Zhukovka to deal with his mail.

Natasha might have seen the possibility of exile as having its advantages. She would miss her mother and aunts, and friends, and Russia . . . but she and Sanya would be thrown together, would face the TV cameras together; he would need her more than ever to create a home somewhere. . . . There would be no problem about money, with so many royalties sitting in Western banks, and now the enormous Nobel award. . . . *That* woman and the baby would be forever banished. . . .

The Kremlin and Lubyanka were urgently considering the government's options. In a top-secret memorandum,[9] KGB chief Yuri Andropov quotes a selection of individual responses, ranging from Firsova, an actress from Novosibirsk ("If it were in my power, I would kick him out of the country— that would be one less piece of scum to deal with. . . .") to Yevtushenko, who wrote thoughtfully and bravely: "This is going to be a story with a tragic ending in any case: whether he is allowed to go and then return, or go and not return. There is only one way out of this situation, but nobody will dare choose it: recognize Solzhenitsyn, restore his membership in the Writers' Union, and afterward, just declare suddenly that *Cancer Ward* is to be published." Yevtushenko has often been criticized in the West for being too "adaptable," but the KGB records show him to have been absolutely firm in supporting Solzhenitsyn.

On the question of a visa, Andropov's initial recommendation was cautiously positive: "The KGB believes that if Solzhenitsyn officially applies for permission to visit Sweden to receive the Nobel Prize, we could comply with his request. As to the matter of his return to the Soviet Union, a decision should depend on Solzhenitsyn's behavior abroad. If Solzhenitsyn decides to stay abroad, it is hardly expedient, in our opinion, to take any measures to bring him back to the Soviet Union."

On 14 October Solzhenitsyn wrote to Mikhail Suslov, one of the Kremlin's hard-liners, reminding him they had met in 1962 and the minister had expressed sympathy with his work. He proposed that the atmosphere surrounding the award could be transformed for the better if *Cancer Ward* could be released for immediate publication, and an edition of his collected stories prepared. He, Solzhenitsyn, would then submit his recently completed novel *August 1914* for publication. This novel could not possibly present any problems for the censorship, since the "Samsonov catastrophe" had been caused by the paralysis of the tsarist military command.[10]

On the same day, when he seems to have been in an optimistic frame of mind, he said to Natasha suddenly, over dinner at Zhukovka: "I am becoming more and more attached to Alya. Could you not sacrifice yourself . . . for the sake of three people?"

She did not reply, but made up her mind instantly: Yes, I can. Yes, I must. . . . Saying she was going to play the piano, she left to go to the "big house." He followed her somewhat uneasily, wishing to give her his blessing; but hearing her speak to someone on the telephone, in a calm voice, he was reassured, and retired to his work. Actually she was ringing someone to cancel an appointment on the following day. Then she went to the Rostropoviches' grand, and played over and over, passionately, the first movement of Beethoven's Third Piano Concerto. Manly and strong, it would strengthen her resolve. Returning to their apartment, she found Sanya in his bed reading. She told him she was going for a walk. She went to Ilinskoye station, where she wrote to her best friend, Suzanna Teush, posted the letter, and walked home. There she bade Sanya a last "Good night," imprinting his image in her mind. He lifted his head, said "Good night," and made a wide sign of the cross.

She filled a glass of water and carried it to her bedroom. Deciding not to undress—they would try to revive her, and would have no time to make her decent—she got into bed. Hurriedly she wrote to Sanya, asking that she be buried at Rozhdestvo; and to Veronica, telling her what clothes to bury her in. Then, taking out two packets of sleeping pills from deep inside boxes of vitamins, she swallowed the pills with the water, until all thirty-six were gone. Feeling lighter, relieved from suffering, she curled up in her usual way to sleep. The last thing she was aware of were the strong blows of her heart.[11]

. . .

Next morning Sanya realized he had not heard her moving about in her room, at her usual hour for getting up; nor was there any sign of her after he dropped a heavy book on the floor. Entering her room, he found her unconscious, with saliva dribbling from her mouth. Realizing she had taken an overdose, he ran to a nearby dacha where he knew there was a medical orderly tending a terminally ill academician, Igor Tamm. The orderly came and gave Natasha an injection, while Sanya rang Veronica. At her suggestion he then called the Kopelevs. "How could she do this to me?" he raged at Lev; "how *dare* she do this to me?" . . . The Kopelevs arranged for two discreet doctors to come from a nearby writers' clinic. Sanya was reluctant to have her moved to a hospital, fearing the resultant publicity, for attempted suicide was a criminal offense. However, the doctors had no choice but to insist. The comatose woman was taken by ambulance to a nearby hospital and put in a private room.[12]

Twenty-four hours later, she emerged from the black hole just long enough to hear a doctor, leaning over her, say, "Aren't you glad your friends were able to save you?" and to shake her head from side to side. Some time later, surfacing again, she recognized Veronica. Bursting into tears, she demanded to know why she had been saved; she had truly wanted to die. In fact, if the first tablets she had swallowed had not paralyzed her esophagus, she surely would have died. She was interviewed by a woman police doctor who, not recognizing the names Reshetovskaya and Stein, had no idea that this was anything more than a humdrum domestic affair, and so agreed not to press for any action to be taken.

Natasha was removed to the psychiatric ward of another hospital. Veronica, Suzanna, and other friends took turns sitting with her. Sanya, still feeling "How dare she do this to me?" kept away. He had offered her reasonable terms, he told Veronica, and she had tried to destroy him. He felt no more obligation toward her; he washed his hands of her. But he did agree to see her, on 26 October, when Veronica told him she was much more reasonable and would agree to a divorce. Though only days earlier she had been full of plans for her and Sanya, with Veronica's help, to found a museum at Rozhdestvo. This must have been a time of wavering sanity for Natasha. Wearing a fresh dressing gown and makeup, she showed her husband off to her fellow patients in a public ward; and in front of them she announced her husband was taking her home. Over the protests of a doctor, who said it was too early, she insisted. The author of *Cancer Ward* should not have disapproved of disobedience toward officialdom.

He would not, however, take her to Zhukovka. Since her mother was staying in Moscow with the Steins during this emergency, Natasha agreed to spend the night there. She was willing to go with Sanya to Ryazan the next day, to instigate divorce proceedings. On the way to the station she changed her mind: she would not divorce him. Then, on the train, she was amenable once more; it was so nice to be traveling with him, she said; it was like a second honeymoon. Sanya, sitting opposite, went on correcting some chapters of *August 1914*. Handing her some pages, he said, "Read them! These are the chapters in which I used your Rostov research. How well you did that! Such an abundance, I couldn't use it all. . . ." She experienced his words as caresses. If only the train would never reach Ryazan. . . .

The journey proved futile. No official was willing to take responsibility for setting a divorce in motion, for such a famous miscreant, without orders from above. He returned to Zhukovka and the unresolved question of whether to go to Stockholm; Natasha went to stay with friends, promising to return for a divorce application after the November holidays.[13]

With the suavity of a Western publicity director, though considerably more frankness, Yuri Andropov was outlining in his top-secret KGB memorandum the latest developments in Solzhenitsyn's life and relationships:

It has been established that some time ago Solzhenitsyn started living with Natalya Dmitrievna Svetlova, born 1939, who is a postgraduate of the mechanical and mathematical department of Moscow State University and is now pregnant. On 15 October 1970, Reshetovskaya took an overdose of sleeping tablets and was hospitalised and diagnosed as "poisoned." Right now she is undergoing medical treatment at the psychoneurological department of Moscow City Clinical Hospital No. 1.

Solzhenitsyn tries to keep the true situation of his family secret. According to available evidence, Solzhenitsyn lives in the dacha of M. Rostropovich, the cellist, in the settlement of Zhukovka in the Odintsovo District of the Moscow Region. There he is putting the final touches to his manuscript entitled *August 1914* in which events are described dating from the beginning of World War I.[14]

But Andropov's knowledge is much more intimate. Of interest—he reports for the benefit of Comrades Brezhnev, Chernenko, Kosygin, Podgorny, Shelepin, Suslov, and others—is Reshetovskaya's opinion of her husband's personality. She had said the following:

My earlier vision of my husband has been totally destroyed. Previously I believed he was absolutely unique and extraordinary. He always mesmerized me. Everything was fine until he became famous.

Success always spoiled him. He no longer needed other individuals. Whatever the company, he was always the center of attention. And why not? He was the hub of the universe. All that interests him in other people is what he can get from them and use for his own purposes. The horrible thing is that everybody bowed down to him, and he got terribly spoiled.

It recently emerged that he has taken to philandering. When it happened the first time, I said: If she is a serious woman, you can go to her, but my life will be ended. "No, under no circumstances are you going to ruin my career and me," he answered. I felt incredibly miserable. He had been telling lies to me all these years. I practically abandoned normal life for his sake, you know. Rules and regulations of incredible harshness. He gave me no latitude. If I picked up a book to read: "Don't read it! Read my outlines or read the encyclopedia. . . . Read what I wrote in *Novy Mir*. . . . Don't watch that movie. . . . Throw that newspaper out of our home altogether. . . . Don't listen to the radio," and so on. It was nothing less than the suppression of my personality.

Our relationship became too excruciating. He who calls on people to tell the truth, who stands up for the truth in all his works, and at home all lies! On the one hand, he's afraid I'll commit suicide, on the other, he would like us to break up.[15]

Reading this "quotation" in 1995, in the Russian edition of the KGB documents, Natasha was greatly distressed, wondering when and how the KGB had recorded those words. Probably they were spoken to one of the doctors interviewing her after her suicide attempt; but of course there were "ears" everywhere.

Meanwhile the turbulence over the Nobel Prize continued. The editor of *Pravda*, M. Zimyanin, sent to the Central Committee an open letter from Rostropovich, who had released it to the world's press. Rostropovich knew his letter would get him and his wife into even deeper trouble, but with his usual bold honesty could not resist supporting his friend against the attacks in the Soviet press. He asked why the comments of one or two insignificant Western newspapers had been quoted, bypassing such renowned Communist titles as *L'Humanité, Lettres françaises*, and *L'Unità*. Why was the Nobel Prize just dirty politics when awarded to Pasternak and Solzhenitsyn, but a proper recognition of genius when awarded to Sholokhov? Why were lessons not drawn from the abuse leveled at Shostakovich and Prokofiev under Stalin, when now they were acknowledged to be giants of Russian music?

The comparison with Sholokhov was given added force when the Swedish embassy, on government orders, refused to countenance the possibility of an award ceremony at the embassy—an alternative that Solzhenitsyn had asked a friendly journalist, Per Hegge, to explore. It was a long time since the Swedes had taken on the Russians at Poltava in 1709; then, Charles XI, warned he faced impossible odds, said that if an angel were to descend from Heaven and tell him to go back, he would not; the modern Swedes showed the white feather immediately in the face of Soviet pressure: the duty of the embassy was to maintain good relations with the local authorities. The shocked Hegge reminded Ambassador Jarring that five years before he had given an official dinner for Sholokhov at the embassy and personally congratulated him. What would the world think?

Learning that Solzhenitsyn was thinking of donating the monetary award (about $225,000 at that time) to the Vietnamese Children's Aid Foundation, the Soviets also pressured the Vietnamese government to refuse any such offer.

By 20 November Andropov had hardened his position dramatically against the writer, seeing him as a dangerous and defiant opponent of the Soviet system. "If Solzhenitsyn continues to reside in the country after receiving the Nobel Prize, it will strengthen his position, and allow him to propagandise his views more actively. . . . He will continue to play the part of an internal émigré publishing his works abroad. His name will be used by hostile circles as a rallying cry for anti-Sovietism."[16] If, on the other hand, he was expelled, or his visa revoked during a visit to Stockholm, there would be a short-lived outcry but he would lose the advantages of being an ambiguous figure, an internal émigré. Andropov drew up the draft of a decree revoking Solzhenitsyn's citizenship, on the grounds of his denigration of Soviet society and his becoming a tool of the most reactionary anti-Communist forces.

In the same memorandum, Andropov—who was said to live so close to Solzhenitsyn at Zhukovka that the two men could wave to each other when they got up in the morning—proposed one further vicious refinement of persecution:

"Meanwhile, we must not overlook the fact that doctors have concealed a suicide attempt by Reshetovskaya, Solzhenitsyn's wife, and criminal proceedings should be instituted concerning this matter."

Sanya summoned Natasha to Zhukovka on 30 October: "I shall expect you whatever the weather." When they were in his room, he asked her to swear before the cross that she would not end her life. "Unless you obliterate me from life," she replied, rising from her knees. That is to say, by divorce.

No, she must swear it under *any* circumstances, he insisted.

They drove together to the much-loved primitive dacha at Rozhdestvo. There, knowing there was work to be done shutting it up for the winter— but for whose sake?—she burst into tears. An angry scene followed, in which he warned her that if she took her life it might harm Alya. "When you were swallowing the pills," he told her, "she felt something was wrong in her womb—it was telepathy."[17]

My God! thought Natasha—even my death becomes a matter of whether it's good or bad for her and her child! . . . She felt weak, and could eat no food, only milk. The day was ruined. Sanya was disappointed. "I thought it would be like—then . . ." he said, referring to the day when, according to Natasha, they had slept together—26 September.

His remark has the ring of sincerity. Perhaps a very complex calculation was going on in his mind. It may be that he hated the way in which an overpowering love was forcing him to betray Natasha, his vows, and the teachings of the church. Part of him perhaps would have given anything to be out of Alya's spell. And it may have appeared that only a divorce, and marriage to Alya, might begin to revive his former feelings for Natasha, who would have the charms of "the other woman." If only Natasha would let him begin to wear *Alya* like a forgettable knapsack on his back—while he brought happiness to his mistress, and therefore could ease his conscience. . . .

But Natasha's bad day at Rozhdestvo spoiled this dream, if such it was.

Alone again, Natasha reread his early letters promising undying love for her, and saying a writer should not have children. They confirmed to her distraught mind that she ought not to allow him to commit the sin of putting away his wife. She traveled to her mother and aunts in Ryazan, to friends in Riga, and all around Moscow, showing his letters to all and sundry. And praying, praying, praying.

A year or two before meeting Sanya, Alya Svetlova had been baptized into the Orthodox faith. Her godmother was a family friend, the great pianist Maria Yudina—who had dared to pray that Stalin be forgiven his great sins. A Jew who had become a devout Christian, Yudina was an extraordinary and exotic woman. She always wore a black pyramid-shaped dress and a large pectoral cross. Unpredictable and imperious, she was capable of interrupting her passionate performances to recite Pasternak or some other unacceptable poet. With a face that looked maidenly, in contrast to the masculine force of her playing, she was sometimes compared to the Mona Lisa. She had been banned from performing abroad, but never arrested.[18] Her flamboyant personality seemed characteristic of her native city, Leningrad—at least, of the Petersburg of Blok, Akhmatova, and the *Ballet Russe*.

Natasha had had some piano lessons from Yudina—despite Sanya's having warned her that his wife's playing wasn't good enough—and they too had become friends. Sanya had made her promise not to tell Yudina that her goddaughter was his mistress, for whom he wished to divorce Natasha. Natasha had therefore kept away from her; but one day the grand old lady phoned her, and said, "I feel I'm dying. I want to embrace you for the last time. Come to me."

The apartment was small, because Yudina gave away her money to the poor. The two women kissed. Yudina's rich gray hair seemed like a halo around her head. She asked her visitor what was wrong; and then, who the woman was. For a long time Natasha would not answer, but Yudina kept insisting. At last Natasha thought, To hell with him! He's always ordered me to do or not do this or that. . . . And dropped hints. The old lady was deeply upset. She made the sign of the cross over Natasha, for the last time.[19]

She promised to write to Sanya. But soon after, before she could do so, she died. Her words might have had an effect.

When Natasha heard on the BBC that Solzhenitsyn would not be attending the Nobel ceremony in Stockholm, she felt relief. Because it meant she would see him again, his "blue eyes," if only in a divorce court. . . .

She began, as an attempted therapy, to write a memoir of their love.

On the night of the Stockholm ceremony, Sanya sat with Rostropovich and a few friends, celebrating abstemiously as always. The short statement he had sent was read out without its final sentence, which asked those at the banquet to remember there were prisoners on hunger strike. Russia's was not the only censorship.

He felt tired. Tired from fighting on all fronts. Yet the memoir he continued to write from time to time, *The Oak and the Calf*, gives an impression of someone in a constant state of exhilaration, joy in the battle. And almost nothing of the exhausting struggle going on in his personal life.

On the penultimate day of 1970 Alya gave birth to a son, Yermolai. Rostropovich became his godfather. Galina Vishnevskaya met Alya for the first time at the christening, which took place at the Nechayannaya Radost Church. At the celebration lunch at Zhukovka, Galina was able to get her first good look at Sanya's new companion, and was very impressed. "She was thirty, in full bloom, a strong woman and the personification of a good wife and mother. . . . I realised that such a woman would follow him into the fire without thinking twice."[20] Much better than a provincial old maid with an overlarge head.

It must have been painful for Alya, too, to know how much Natasha was suffering. But she no longer, presumably, urged him to stay married to Natasha. Alya's willpower equaled her lover's; on first meeting him she had said to a friend, "That's the man for me! I was very fond of my husband, but until now I never knew what love was."

After the birth of their son, she found herself dismissed from her research post, while her mother also lost her engineering job. Paradoxically, they were able to move into a larger, four-roomed flat in Kozitsky Lane, off Gorky Street.

In February 1071 Solzhenitsyn and Rostropovich visited Tvardovsky at his dacha. The desperately sick man insisted on standing to greet them, helped by his daughter and son-in-law, one on each side. Sanya could see that his right side was paralyzed. "Get-ting ol-d-er," he managed to bring out. "A smile that his lips could not quite complete expressed regret, perhaps a great sadness."[21] It was the longest sentence he spoke; Sanya was not sure if he was apologizing for aging himself or was shocked at how much older his friend looked.

When Sanya, still hoping to get Tvardovsky's opinion of *August 1914*, showed him the typescript, he found his voice again to ask: "How many . . . ?" It was not possible nor necessary for him to finish the question; it was "How many pages of type?" (For how many months would it run in

Novy Mir?) Sanya felt none of the customary agony of trying to converse with someone suffering from partial aphasia; for Tvardovsky,

> instead of losing his temper to no purpose . . . showed by the unchanging look of kindly acquiescence in his eyes his submissiveness to a higher power above us all which we, his companions, also recognised, but which did not in the least prevent us from understanding one another and being of one mind. A. T.'s powers of active response were paralysed, but kindly feeling streamed from his eyes unstemmed, and his face, exhausted as it was by illness, still retained its old, childlike expression.
>
> When A. T. was particularly anxious to finish saying something and could not manage it, I helped him out by taking his left hand—which was warm, and free and alive. He squeezed my hand in reply, and in this way we understood each other well enough. . . . Understood that all was forgiven between us. That all the bad things, the hurts, the troubles, might never have been.[22]

Perhaps the tender, healing quality of this meeting carried over to a reunion with Natasha on her birthday, 26 February. According to her, he wept, was filled with remorse, and said how relieved he was she had swallowed sleeping pills and not the mandrake root infusion that would have been fatal. She wanted to return to Zhukovka, but he persuaded her to let a year pass. He promised not to seek a divorce during that year, so that she could regain her strength and begin a new life.

Paying another visit to Tvardovsky in May, he was surprised and delighted to find him much improved. He could now move his left leg and left hand (which, Sanya notes with wry disapproval, kept reaching for cigarettes); his facial movements were almost as expressive as of old; and best of all, his speech was easier. He had read *August 1914*, and pronounced it "marvelous," reinforcing the word with movements of his head and eyes, and by moaning.[23]

Did he realize that the portrait of the tragic General Samsonov, with his bigness, his clumsiness, his innocence, his inner greatness, was based on himself? Probably not. In any case, Solzhenitsyn's overt portrayal of him, in *The Oak and the Calf*, is a great achievement. It is overharsh; yet somehow that seems almost deliberate, as if the author wishes us to take sides with the erring Tvardovsky against his too censorious judge. At any rate, his account of his last meetings with him would not be nearly so moving in their reconciling tenderness had Tvardovsky been sentimentally drawn.

In June, YMCA Press, Paris, brought out a Russian-language edition of *August 1914*. The KGB reported that all the sympathetic characters were White Guard types, the ideas were Tolstoyan in a distorted form, and there was nothing about the class struggle.[24] Even some of the writer's friends who had read it, including Svetlova and Chukovskaya, had expressed negative opinions about the literary qualities of this work.

Assuming that the KGB had good information, one wonders whether Svetlova told Sanya to his face about her doubts? And did "Chukovskaya" refer to the older woman, Lydia, or her daughter Liusha? Certainly Liusha was dismayed when she read the manuscript. What was the point of stirring up the past? But with her customary energy and conscientiousness she circulated the text and encouraged people to write essays on it, which she published as a collection in samizdat.[25] Sanya seemed more than usually anxious to hear people's views on this new departure in his writing.

In the polarization of sympathies always created by a marital breakup, his circle of friends and helpers held firm. And he had Veronica, Natasha's cousin, staunchly with him. Natasha was distraught to hear through friends, a few weeks after her suicide attempt, that Veronica had broken with her because of her "bad character." She was possessed, Veronica was said to feel, by a "hysterical love" for Sanya. On the day Natasha heard this reported to her, she learned that Veronica, her closest contemporary relative, was at the Sovremennik Theater with Sanya.[26] It plunged her deeper into despair—and was followed by passing a store selling baby carriages.

Her pain was indeed dreadful. But Veronica and others saw that her behavior was making Sanya distraught, and might blank out the voice of Russia's conscience. Brought up, like Sanya himself, to place family relationships below the great political and moral questions, they tended not to be sentimental about marriage. If love had gone, they felt, what point was there in maintaining a shallow form? They could also see that Natasha never took any blame for what had happened; and contrasted this with Sanya's nobility in Ekibastuz and Kok Terek, when he accepted responsibility for Natasha's desertion of him for another man.

38

Burnt by the Sun

A scratch! A scratch!
—*Romeo and Juliet*

SANYA'S FEAR THAT AT ANY MOMENT HE MIGHT BE SEIZED, AND SENT abroad or into distant internal exile with only Natasha permitted to accompany him, was a realistic one. As we have seen, many in the Politburo, including Andropov, were pressing for such a move; a document depriving him of citizenship had been drafted. But there were people opposed to such a draconian measure, so for the moment nothing happened.

The Minister of Internal Affairs, N. Shchelokov, even argued in a memorandum of October 1971 for an easing of the author's situation. The memorandum went directly to Brezhnev, who underlined several key sentences. Shchelokov made eight numbered points, which may be summarized as follows:

1. He is a major figure in the ideological struggle, a reality impossible to ignore. He is a reactionary banner for anti-Soviets.

2. "Objectively, Solzhenitsyn has talent. He is a literary phenomenon." It would be useful to have his pen serving the interests of the people.

3. We must analyze past mistakes in dealing with artists, including Solzhenitsyn. He was made a member of the Writers' Union for *Ivan Denisovich*, and praised to the skies; he was thrown out of the Writers' Union for *Cancer Ward*, "which was written from the very same ideological position." Such inconsistency weakens us. " 'The Solzhenitsyn problem' was created by literary administrators who should have known better."*

4. Writers who are "shaky" need to be watched, monitored, and guided. "Yelling at them, giving orders, and hounding them are ineffective methods." His works could have been published here after painstaking editing.

---

*Underscored text indicates Brezhnev's underlinings.

"One way or another, work such as these can be edited down and published so that subsequently they can be hushed up." Don't force them to publish abroad. If we publish them here, sufficiently edited, there is no interest abroad. "In this case, what needs to be done is not to execute our enemies publicly, but to smother them in embraces. This is a basic truth, of which those comrades who manage literature should be aware."

5. "In the Solzhenitsyn business we are repeating the same glaring errors that we committed with regard to Boris Pasternak." Pasternak is a major Russian writer, even more significant than Solzhenitsyn. It was a glaring error to attack him over the Nobel Prize. "*Dr. Zhevago* [sic]" should have been "edited down" and published here, thus minimizing foreign interest in it. It is impossible today to conceal a work, in view of modern communications. "We must take these facts into account. Unfortunately no one is taking them into account. It is time for our publishing houses to understand that today they must not reject literary works, but transform them." Pasternak is now being described as a great writer. This puzzles people. They wonder, Will the same thing happen with Solzhenitsyn?

6. Many of our writers emigrated because we treated them too inflexibly. "We demanded of them things which they could not deliver by virtue of their class affiliation and their class upbringing. . . . Our attitude toward the creative intelligentsia should be more flexible, more tolerant, and more judicious."

7. Fairly soon Daniel and Sinyavsky will be released. Interest in them will increase because we have made martyrs of them. We have not removed the problem they have caused but aggravated it. We don't need to aggravate the "Solzhenitsyn Problem" in the same way.

8. How then should we deal with him? We should let him go abroad to receive the Nobel Prize. "Under no circumstances should the issue of depriving him of his citizenship be raised." We should work toward the goal of having him conduct himself with dignity while he is abroad: so that he says he has no differences with the Party, only professional differences with his literary colleagues. Then, give him an apartment without delay. Take care of his needs. "One of the higher-ups needs to sit down and talk with him, to remove the bitter taste that his persecution has, no doubt, left in his mouth. In a word, we need to fight for Solzhenitsyn, not toss him out. We need to fight for Solzhenitsyn and not against Solzhenitsyn."[1]

The tone of Shchelokov's memorandum is positively civilized; and only one word in the full text, "scum," of Daniel and Sinyavsky, seems to come from the normal crude Soviet lexicon. It is hardly conceivable that Solzhenitsyn would have said he had no quarrel with his government, only over professional matters with fellow writers; but undoubtedly there would have been far less interest in him in the West if his novels had been published at home. He had himself proposed a modus vivendi—publish *Cancer Ward*, and prepare a collection of his stories.

Unfortunately, there were not many Shchelokovs in the Kremlin. The minutes of a meeting of a Secretariat chaired by Suslov on 7 October 1971 referred to the memorandum, but limited the brief discussion to the question of whether the rogue author might be allowed to live with "his new wife" at her flat in Moscow, where he could be watched more effectively. No conclusion was reached.[2] At least he was not deported; Natasha did not face criminal charges; and the press was silent in response to the provocation of the appearance in the West of *August 1914*.

But August 1971 might easily have settled the Kremlin's dilemma in a highly satisfactory way. . . .

Natasha was staying at Rozhdestvo. Unwilling to meet her there, Sanya decided to drive south, to do some more research on the First World War and Civil War period. He hoped to find some old men who had witnessed those events, and also to visit and talk to Aunt Irina, whom he had not seen for eight years. Galina Vishnevskaya was horrified that he was going to drive his old Moskvich, and warned him it could fall to pieces on the way. Also— who could know what the KGB might arrange? It would be easy to set up a "traffic accident." Why not take the train—or better still stay at home? . . . But he would not heed her warnings. He was going with a friend who was a mechanical engineer; everything would be fine. They would be back in two weeks.

Three days later she was boiling coffee when she saw Sanya; he was on the point of collapse, having to cling on to things to stop himself from falling down. She dropped everything to help him. His face was contorted with pain, his whole trunk and legs covered in huge blisters. Getting him into bed, she learned that in the heat of the South—though he had scarcely left the car—he had swollen up and developed blisters all over his chest, back, legs, and arms, and started vomiting. Fearing to take him to a local hospital, his friend had put him on a sleeper to Moscow and rung Alya's mother, Katya, asking her to meet the train and bring someone to help her with him. Katya had gone to the Kursk station with a young engineer with whom she worked, Alexander Gorlov, and found Sanya still in his bunk, barely able to move. They had had great difficulty getting him to Zhukovka.

Galina phoned an oncologist she knew well, who came at once. He was puzzled and alarmed by his patient's condition. It looked like some extreme form of heat allergy. He should go to the hospital without delay. But after discussion with Galina and Slava the specialist agreed it might be better to let him be taken care of by them. The summer was very hot and humid, and they had a cot set up for him in the shade.

In her memoir, Galina comments that she could not imagine such a strong allergy existed, to cause so violent a reaction. Her grandmother had not suffered worse blisters when the stove had set fire to her dress and burned her from head to toe. Sanya told the Rostropoviches he'd scarcely been out of the car apart from going to eat at lunchrooms. Could they have put something in his food, he wondered? . . . But it appears he told Veronica that on the day it had started, the car heater had come on and jammed; finding the heat intolerable, they had got out to try to disconnect the hoses. Wearing only shorts, he might have suffered sunstroke then. Since catching malaria on his honeymoon, he had been sensitive to heat and the sun.[3] Too much sun is also the explanation he offers in *The Oak and the Calf.*

Despite his agonizing condition, he was practical enough to ask Gorlov if he would go to Rozhdestvo to collect a spare part for the Moskvich. Gorlov agreed to go. The next day, Katya rushed in to Galina and said, "Please come! Something's happened: Sanya's in a state, and I don't know what to do!" Galina flew out and found Sanya raging; Katya had learned from Gorlov, at work, that he'd had a terrifying experience at Rozhdestvo. He had found the door ajar, its lock broken, and heard voices inside. Pushing the door open, he saw nine men in civilian clothes, engaged in a search.

He had demanded to know what they were doing. They slammed the door behind him, beat him, pinioned his arms, and dragged him outside, face down, toward a car. Fearing he would be beaten to death, he shouted for help, and people came running. The man in charge produced his red KGB card, and the local people melted away.

Gorlov was taken to the Naro-Fominsk police station, and warned that if he talked about this he would never get to defend his doctoral dissertation, and his son and wife would suffer too.

The incident was duly reported by Andropov in a memorandum of 16 August.[4] While the KGB had been conducting a stakeout, he noted, one Gorlov had been detained. "For purposes of confidentiality he was told that the stakeout at the dacha was organized in response to a warning about a planned robbery. Solzhenitsyn, who at the present time is in a state of anxiety due to fears that his social origins are going to be exposed in the press, used this event as an opportunity to prepare and distribute another in a series of letters to the West. (Text enclosed.) . . . Solzhenitsyn will be informed that the participation of the KGB in this incident is a figment of his imagination, and that the whole episode was purely of a law-enforcement nature. Therefore he should have contacted the police in the first instance." Andropov finally asks the Ministry of Internal Affairs to make sure the police confirm the "robbery" version.

Solzhenitsyn's open letter to Andropov, written from his sickbed, leads up to his (true) version of what happened with a passage that expresses his cold fury:

> For many years, I have borne in silence the lawlessness of your employees: the inspection of all my correspondence, the confiscation of half of it, the tracking down of my correspondents, their persecution at work and by state agencies, the spying around my house, the shadowing of visitors, the tapping of telephone conversations, the drilling of holes in ceilings, the placing of recording apparatus in my city apartment and at my cottage, and a persistent slander campaign against me

from the platforms of lecture halls when they are put at the disposal
of officials from your ministry.

But after the raid yesterday, I will no longer be silent. . . . [5]

In line with Andropov's memorandum, Colonel Berezin of the KGB rang
the Rostropovich dacha and asked Galina, politely, if he might speak with
Solzhenitsyn, on the subject of his letter. Since Sanya was too ill to get up,
Alya came in his place; she heard the colonel explain that, on Andropov's
personal word, he could assure her the KGB had had nothing to do with
what had happened.

Gorlov was not altogether happy to find his name blazoned in public as
a consequence of Solzhenitsyn's open letter. Both men were offered apol-
ogies—by the police—for the unfortunate "violation of citizens' lawful
rights." But Gorlov subsequently lost his job and *was* unable to defend his
dissertation. He emigrated to the United States in 1975.

Andropov's comment that Solzhenitsyn was nervous that his social origins
were about to be exposed in the press is puzzling. Such an "exposure" did
take place, in *Literaturnaya Gazeta* of 12 January 1972, but Solzhenitsyn
appears to have been taken completely by surprise by it. The *Gazeta's* article, headlined "*Stern* Magazine on Solzhenitsyn's Family," was a rehash
of a somewhat dubious interview with Irina Shcherbak in Georgievsk, by
Dieter Steiner, which formed the basis of his *Stern* article of November
1971. Andropov's words must indicate that he knew the old woman was
being investigated by KGB officers with a view to "promoting" a visit by an
amenable foreign journalist. Steiner, who did not speak Russian well, could
never have traced Solzhenitsyn's aged aunt without help; and indeed, Georgievsk, like most of the USSR, was closed to westerners.

In reality Irina was visited by three men who spoke excellent Russian.
One of them may well have been Victor Louis (real name Vitali Levin), an
unsavory literary entrepeneur who had been given a license by the KGB to
cause mischief: he had hawked an early pirated copy of *Cancer Ward* to
the West, and broke in on Solzhenitsyn's privacy at Rozhdestvo, seeking an
interview and photographs. Immensely privileged himself—he had married
a rich Englishwoman who attended Moscow's Anglican church—he spread
lies about Solzhenitsyn's supposedly opulent lifestyle. Whether or not Louis
was involved in this operation, the three men made five visits in all to Irina.
Steiner did meet her, and had his photograph taken with her against the
background of her mean little clay hovel.

August 1914 had been published in Russian, in June 1971, by the YMCA
Press in Paris. The *Stern* feature linked the interview with Irina to the
novel, in which the Shcherbak family appeared as the Tomchaks, and the
rich and beautiful Irina was given her true first name. Steiner records the
old woman as bewailing her poverty—amply confirmed by the one whitewashed room, three yards by two, in which she lived with her dog (and
many cats, though he does not mention these). After fifty-three years under

the commissars, she says bitterly, she has ten rubles a month in pension from the state, and fifteen sent to her by Sanya.

Literaturnaya Gazeta's version of the *Stern* piece excluded the complaints about Communism, but made full use of the old woman's barbed descriptions of the Shcherbak family. They were, she asserted, a "family of boors"; landowners of their kind lived like pigs: nothing but drunkenness, cards, and debauchery. Old Zakhar, a loudmouth, beat his wife and would pull a knife on Roman, Irina's husband, whom she had been compelled by her father to marry. Sanya's mother, Taissia, was conservative, arrogant, and ridiculous. In marrying Isaaki Solzhenitsyn she ensured that "money married money," for his family was wealthy too.

Following Irina's account of the death of Sanya's father, Steiner comments that it was reportedly an accident, but was "probably" suicide because the Civil War had begun and the Reds were executing landowners.

The old woman did not approve of Natasha—whom she described (falsely) as the daughter of a Jewish businessman—because she had not followed her husband into exile but went to live with another man. This had upset Sanya. After his rehabilitation he'd got a good teaching job in Ryazan, and Natasha wanted to move back in. Irina had told him, when he came to her to ask her advice, she only esteemed wives who followed their husbands into exile. All others were mistresses. But Natasha had plagued him into taking her back. Now he had left her for a younger woman.

Irina had last seen her famous nephew a year ago. He had sent her the money for a visit. On arrival at Ryazan station, she saw Sanya and Natasha withdraw into the station building, hiding from her because she was so poorly dressed. . . . If she had had the money for a ticket she would have gone back to the Caucasus straightaway, but she only had twenty kopecks left. . . . She had meant to stay three months in Ryazan, but left after seventeen days. Sanya and Natasha and her relatives lived, she agreeably confirmed, a privileged existence, regularly visiting Moscow for plays and concerts. In her last letter to Sanya she had written, "Sanya, you are not treating me well; I always see before my eyes the dear little boy I carried in my arms so often. . . ."[6]

One glimpses a mixture of reality and confusion. The idea that her hosts were ashamed of her dress, and hid themselves, is clearly a delusion; but no doubt the Ryazan household in 1970 would not have had a relaxed and happy atmosphere.

His sudden severe illness, the KGB-*Stern* operation, and the stakeout at Rozhdestvo may not have been isolated occurrences. In the Moscow monthly *Sovershenno Sekretno*, no. 4, 1992, a professional KGB agent, Colonel Boris Ivanov, gave an alternative explanation of Solzhenitsyn's mysterious illness. Solzhenitsyn published a fuller version as an appendix to *Invisible Allies*. Ivanov served the security services for more than thirty years in the north Caucasus, in Georgia, and in Lithuania. From 1967 to 1976 he headed one of the subdivisions of the ideological directorate in the Rostov KGB administration.

His narrative is serious and unsensational. One day early in the 1970s he was summoned from his office by the shrill ring of the special "black" or "boss" phone, which rarely carried any message except a simple: "Please step into my office." It was so on this day. Passing through a slightly darkened reception room, through the massive double doors, he announced his presence. The KGB general looked affable; with him was a middle-aged stranger in a double-breasted gray suit. The general introduced Ivanov and the stranger, and motioned to the former to sit down. He then warned him of the top-secret nature of the business in hand. The writer Solzhenitsyn, he said, was traveling to their region for unknown reasons. The comrade from Moscow had been sent in connection with that. Ivanov knew all Solzhenitsyn's former links in Rostov, so who better to help out? A car had been laid on, hotel accommodation arranged.

Ivanov felt uneasy. Why hadn't Moscow just handed the task of keeping track of Solzhenitsyn over to Rostov? He knew Solzhenitsyn had outstanding conspiratorial talents, and that there was a whole operations unit of the KGB set up to counter him. Its primary task was to block the dissemination of his works. Ivanov's task had been to gather all the information he could about his Rostov background: to be his biographer, in a sense. . . . He found, among many other things, that "the young man had been gifted, conscientious, and literally lived according to a schedule. Girls liked him for his intelligence and straightforward personality but thought his reserve and remoteness excessive and a little absurd." One of Ivanov's responsibilities was to acquaint visiting foreign writers with material that could compromise Solzhenitsyn. It is very likely, therefore, that Ivanov was involved with the *Stern* article. A few years later his directorate helped Natasha to publish and distribute her memoir.

Invariably there was advance warning of people to be helped: but not in this case. Of course it could have been because Solzhenitsyn had made an unexpected move. Anyway, Ivanov and the gray-suited man went to the Moskovskaya Hotel, where a luxurious suite had been reserved for the visitor. They came down to the cafeteria, Ivanov took his companion to a favorite viewing spot, and studied the menu. A young man entered, glanced across, and sauntered to the counter. Ivanov felt the two men knew each other. The gray-suited man asked Ivanov about his time in Lithuania, and whether any "special actions" had been taken there.

After dinner gray-suit summoned a black Volga, and he and Ivanov were driven northward toward the town of Kamensk. They stopped by a dense pine forest, where the surveillance unit which had followed Solzhenitsyn from Moscow was contacted. The target and his friend were camping in the forest. Ivanov was scornful of the way the gray-suited man, who had revealed himself over dinner as a recent upper-echelon recruit from Komsomol administration, did not know how to move quietly through a forest.[7]

They drove on to Novocherkassk, where the local KGB had arranged hotel rooms. In the morning they were kept informed every five or ten minutes of their prey's movements. The word came that they had reached Novocherkassk, had parked in Yermak Square, and were walking to the cathedral, where a church service was taking place.

"Have you ever seen Solzhenitsyn?" asked gray-suit.

"No."

"Do you want to?"

"Naturally."

The worshipers in the cathedral were not many in number, but were devoutly listening to the choir, crossing themselves, seeming to Ivanov full of inner peace. The two KGB men moved forward, their hats in their hands. Then gray-suit nudged Ivanov. "I saw a kneeling middle-aged man with a large open forehead and a horseshoe-shaped reddish beard. Oblivious to his surroundings, he was crossing himself and making prostrations, while a lanky man about fifty-five stood next to him." Ivanov could not tear his eyes away; he confesses that he felt "deeply shocked" by what he saw. While he believed everyone had a right to profess his own religious beliefs, the sight of such an intelligent man making prostrations disconcerted him.

The honesty of that "confession" is very persuasive as to the honesty of the whole account.

The KGB men did not linger in the cathedral. On the way out gray-suit asked Ivanov what he thought. He did not reply. Several hours later, after they had been apprised of various calls the "target" had made, they heard that he was in the main street and about to enter a store. At once, with great urgency, the driver of the Volga was ordered to head for the center. Gray-suit nervously ordered the driver to stop several times on the way; he would get out and dash off somewhere for a moment. At one such stop he met up with the stranger from the Moskovskaya's cafeteria in Rostov. Ivanov saw the two men gesturing as if disagreeing over something. He got out to join them, but the third man was off toward the store; entering as Solzhenitsyn and his friend left, the "third man" turned on his heels and followed them. Ivanov asked his chief if he could be of assistance.

"Possibly. . . . Let's go."

It was a procession: first Solzhenitsyn and friend, then the third man— short, sturdily built, with dark close-cropped hair—then Ivanov and gray-suit. In a while the two in front entered a large food store; the others followed. There were five of them now in the same confined space. The third man stood close behind the target, who was in line in front of the pastry counter. Ivanov had his view of what happened next partially blocked by gray-suit, but clearly remembers "the movements of the third man's gloved hands, and an object of some kind that he held in one of them. In any case, something I could not understand was taking place next to me, right in the middle of Novocherkassk. The whole operation lasted only a couple of minutes."

The third man left the store. Ivanov followed gray-suit out. In the street the latter smiled, and said quietly, "That's it. It's all over. He won't last very long now."

Sitting in the car, almost purring with satisfaction, he said, "The first attempt failed, you see, but on the second pass everything went okay." He looked at the driver and stopped short.

The two agents parted in Rostov. Ivanov's mind, he says, was in turmoil. He kept his mouth shut, to preserve himself and his family. He had no idea what happened to Solzhenitsyn as a result of the "second pass"—though obviously the writer had not died. No doubt Ivanov wished to bury the episode in his mind; otherwise a few inquiries would have ascertained that Solzhenitsyn was seriously ill for two to three months. Ivanov heard that gray-suit was later sent abroad, and "needless to say, tourism was not the purpose." The actual hit man never crossed his path again. Ivanov concludes his confession by saying that the events have weighed on his conscience for two decades. "It is time we looked one another squarely in the eyes."[8]

Solzhenitsyn was asked by journalist Dmitri Likhanov to comment on Ivanov's story, and his answering letter was published in the same issue of *Sovershenno Sekretno*. He wrote that it clarified the mystery of what had happened to him. He gave Likhanov an account of his movements that are presumably more accurate than the rough outline that appears in *Galina*. He and his friend had arrived in Novocherkassk at 10 A.M. on 8 August 1971. It was a Sunday; they had gone to the cathedral, as Ivanov had said. At this stage he felt fine. After the service they went through the town and visited some stores. He had no awareness of being pricked; but by the middle of the day he felt his skin aching all over the left side of his body; he felt worse and worse as the day passed; by morning he had developed huge blisters. His friend took him to a clinic, where it was decided, probably unwisely, to puncture the blisters. They drove on, bypassing Rostov, heading south; but when they got to the rail station at Tikhoretskaya he was in too much agony to go any further, and his friend put him on the train for Moscow. He got back on 12 August.

Alya wrote to Likhanov also, stressing the seriousness of Sanya's condition at that time, and the agonizing pain he had suffered for many weeks. He could not even bear a light sheet on him. She confirmed that these events took place in August 1971; Colonel Ivanov had mentioned a different year, 1973, but later agreed he had probably erred in this.

Likhanov quoted an extract from the published notes of Dr. Nikolai Zhukov, who had attended the patient from 23 August. He found him suffering a high fever, needing to have a heater turned on in the evenings since he was shivering so much. Zhukov confirmed that the condition was both serious and mysterious. Likhanov contacted Dr. Yevgeni Luzhnikov, a specialist in poisons, and described to him the symptoms of Solzhenitsyn's illness. Replying at once, Dr. Luzhnikov observed that the symptoms as described were typical of skin poisoning by ricin, a highly toxic poison made from castor-oil seeds. Ricin, injected, would cause the skin to become red and swollen; this could spread and affect even the bones; the victim became highly feverish. A dose of more than three milligrams could cause death. The sores were difficult to treat, and the whole healing process could take two to three years.

The Politburo and KGB had an affection for poisons injected under the skin. According to former KGB head Semichastny, writing in the magazine *Ogonyok*, Brezhnev had hinted to him that it would be easier to poison Khrushchev than oust him from power. Pavel Sudoplatov, organizer of Trotsky's murder and an expert in "special tasks," believes the Swedish diplomat Raoul Wallenburg and many others were dispatched in that way: as was the dissident Bulgarian journalist Georgi Markov. Before his death in London in 1978, Markov spoke of having been jabbed by an umbrella while crossing Westminster Bridge. In his right thigh was found a highly toxic pellet. The KGB provided the training and the toxin—produced probably in Toxicological Laboratory No. 12 at the KGB Research Institute of Higher and Advanced Technologies.[9] According to Oleg Gordievsky, ricin was the toxin used.[10]

Solzhenitsyn, in 1992, did not take issue with any factual details presented by Ivanov, with the single exception of the year. Ivanov had to have been present to have known of the visit to Novocherkassk and to its cathedral, followed by a walk around town. His sober account is not that of a fantasist adding a hit man and a death plot to a humdrum surveillance operation, but of a man wanting to tell the truth at last.

Likhanov claims to have seen a report by an unidentified KGB officer stating that he had burned in the Lubyanka, on 3 July 1990, 105 documents of the now redundant operation "Spider," relating to Solzhenitsyn.

The murder attempt, if such it was, must surely have been with the knowledge and agreement of Andropov. For a long time he had been urging strong action, to no avail. He may have decided to scotch the serpent once and for all. He was right to see him as a highly dangerous enemy. It would have been easy to persuade an initially skeptical and angry West—societies desperate for détente—that the Soviets would not be so foolish as to *invite* opprobrium. Andropov would have been ready to assure the Politburo the KGB was not responsible.

Conceivably they may have wanted to frighten him with a nonlethal dose; but that would have been hard to judge, and Solzhenitsyn did fall seriously ill. The likelihood is that some factor weakened the toxin slightly; it had had to be carried from Moscow to Novocherkassk.

In 1994, former KGB General Oleg Kalugin, Chief of Counter-Intelligence, confirmed in his memoir, *Spymaster*, that an agent applied a poisonous substance to Solzhenitsyn in a store, in the early seventies, with the aim of inducing a heart attack.

Had death occurred, the dissident movement would have been shocked and devastated; but Solzhenitsyn would undoubtedly have spoken even more eloquently from the grave than in his life; within months *The Gulag Archipelago* would have been released in the West, as his last, greatest, and world-transforming work. Preserved from later controversy and *The Red Wheel*, he would have been almost divinized. His tragically premature death would have entered myth, like John F. Kennedy's; there would have been ceaseless speculation about possible KGB plots; but most sensible people would have concluded that the great liberal writer had died naturally—burnt by the sun.

In September 1971 Nikita Khrushchev "died that most unnatural death for an Old Bolshevik, a natural death." "When I die," he once announced jovially after a false report of his death, "I shall inform all foreign correspondents myself." But when his actual death came, no obituaries appeared, no information about his funeral. Yet the word spread, just as it had done before Pasternak's funeral, and on the morning of 13 September people began to gather outside the gate of the Novodevichy Cemetery. They were mostly old people, *zeks* who had "come back to life" thanks to Khrushchev's speech. It was apt that the Soviets were preventing unauthorized people from entering the cemetery by hanging a large notice, "Cleaning Day," above the entrance. Nikita was murky himself, but he changed Russia with his Cleaning Day.

Solzhenitsyn acknowledged this, one day when he paused in front of the grave during a walk through the cemetery. After hesitating, he placed on the grave a single flower.

A few weeks after Khrushchev's death, on 18 December, Tvardovsky died. So famous a poet had to be given a state funeral. Which meant, as Sanya's post-funeral elegy recalled, "in the guard of honor we see the very same seedy deadbeats who once hunted and harassed him with unholy cries. Yes, it's an old custom of ours dating from the time of Pushkin: dead poets must fall into the hands of their enemies." Entry to the Writers' Club on Herzen Street, where the farewell ceremony was to take place, was limited to Writers' Union members and family, but Sanya arrived very early, and no one dared stop him. Tvardovsky's widow invited him to sit with her in front. All the speeches, by reliable hacks, none of whom had been close friends, had been censored; none mentioned the last ten years of his life. Solzhenitsyn was seen making the sign of the cross, as if to safeguard the dead man from the evil powers.

When the meeting was declared closed and everyone except family and close friends had been asked to leave, a young woman in the middle of the hall rose to her feet and transformed the occasion by exclaiming in a clear voice: "Why are you closing the meeting so soon? Is it possible that no one is going to say that we are burying our civic conscience here? That Tvardovsky was forcibly removed from his work, that he was compelled to leave *Novy Mir*, that his last poem was not published? That they shut his mouth before he shut it of his own accord?" Vigilantes shouted at her, trying to drown her voice, but she was already pushing her way toward the exit, a scarf thrown over her head. None of Tvardovsky's friends ever found out who she was.[11]

As with Khrushchev's funeral, buses did not stop that day opposite the Novodevichy Cemetery. Mourners, many of them old or infirm, had to walk back a mile or more from the Luzhniki stadium. They found the cemetery cordoned off by barriers and a whole company of soldiers and a squad of police. Students protested in vain that Tvardovsky was a national poet. An elderly gentleman pleaded that he had known Tvardovsky ever since the war.

"This is outrageous!" someone shouted. "Even worse than Pushkin's funeral!"

A policeman, coolly: "Oh, so you were there, were you?"

Well, yes . . . all educated Russians were there. . . . They remember how the people who loved Pushkin shivered outside St. Isaac's Cathedral in Petersburg, only to find closed doors, because the actual funeral was taking place in a tucked-away church overflowing with "an apathetic crowd of epaulets, decorations, spurs and sabers, lorgnettes, high headdresses and white gloves. . . ."[12] They remember the body, trussed up in canvas, being sledded off in the dead of night, across the gleaming snow.

Lakshin, formerly of *Novy Mir*, and Solzhenitsyn escorted Mrs. Tvardovsky to the grave. His fur hat in his hand, Sanya bent to kiss the corpse. The whole foreign press corps in Moscow was present, and cameras flashed, catching his every movement and expression.

There were those present—especially Lakshin—who thought he hogged the limelight, treating the solemn occasion as a photo opportunity. They would later quote the cool note he sent to Tvardovsky's younger daughter declining her invitation to a private leave-taking on the eve: "No, my whole day is already planned out. I'll come to the lying-in-state at the Central House of Writers tomorrow, as I have already noted in my diary."[13] The unruly son would attend the funeral only on his own terms. But in doing so he made certain that every literate but ignorant westerner knew the name Tvardovsky, and that he had been on the side of the angels, and had died.

Nonetheless, clearly Lakshin felt the deeper personal grief; and so the cameras turned on Solzhenitsyn offended him—hurt him in the soul. He remembered a very different Tvardovsky. In the book he would write in anger to counteract the portrait in *The Oak and the Calf*, he claims Solzhenitsyn simply did not understand Tvardovsky's humor. He recalls meeting the editor at the Moscow airport, after the latter had made an official trip to Italy in company with Sanya's old enemy Alexei Surkov. Lakshin saw with surprise that Tvardovsky was alone. "Where's Surkov?" Lakshin asked. "He chose freedom," Tvardovsky replied—then collapsed with laughter. *I Chose Freedom* was the title of a memoir by Victor Kravchenko, who had found asylum in the United States in 1944. Actually Surkov had got off in Kiev. In Lakshin's view, Sanya was incapable of understanding such deadpan humor, and misinterpreted much.

Lakshin also quoted the editor as pronouncing a kind of epitaph on Sanya: "His poor old skull couldn't stand the strain."[14]

Of fame, he meant. But it was not so simple as that. It would have been very easy for Solzhenitsyn to have been mildly controversial after *Ivan Denisovich*, but to have been reasonable, made compromises, and enjoyed the wealth, the dachas, the women. He did not. He wrote *Gulag*. A man who could write and fight with demonic energy could not also be your clubbable nice guy from next door. Tvardovsky knew that; and he loved him.

39

Encounter Battles

In tragic life . . .
No villain need be: Passion spins the plot.
—George Meredith, *Modern Love*

The instinctive shock felt by KGB officer Ivanov on seeing the great writer prostrate himself before God was shared by others too, brought up as good children of the Enlightenment. To find that a writer believed passionately in Chairman Mao, or Stalin, or Ho Chi Minh, was acceptable to the liberal mind; but if he believed passionately in God it caused a frisson of discomfort and doubt. Olga and Henry Carlisle, meeting a "messenger" they had sent to Solzhenitsyn, hearing him enthuse, "A splendid man—a giant of a man—a deeply religious man!" were reduced to silence; they had been aware that Orthodoxy was important to Solzhenitsyn, but the thought that his Christianity came across so powerfully at a first meeting took them aback.[1]

Sanya continued to try to be charitable to his stubborn wife, but still she refused to act like a saint. If indeed he wept with remorse during his reunion with her on her birthday, 26 February 1971, and promised to give her a year in which to gather strength before he sought a divorce, his restraint did not hold out; for the next time they met, in October, at the tail end of his "allergic illness," he told her Alya and the baby had moved in to Zhukovka with him and he was going for an immediate divorce. He would give up to Natasha his share of the Ryazan flat; the grand piano and other furniture; the money in their savings account; and a new Moskvich.

On 25 October, he submitted a formal petition, which was heard in Ryazan on 29 November. Natasha asked for a postponement on the grounds that the rights to the Rozhdestvo dacha could not be settled by the Ryazan court. But her highly emotional pleas made it clear that a disputed dacha was not the real motive. She quoted from his letters to show that their love was eternal, and their childlessness not her fault but his. She told the court she could never be reconciled to the fact that the man who had been, and would always be, closest to her was now abandoning her when she was on the brink of old age. Leaving her alone with three old ladies, ranging from eighty-one to ninety-three years old. "Throwing her into a void" was out of character for him; it had to be the result of a "temporary delusion," and soon he would come to his senses.[2]

Sanya leapt to the conclusion that the KGB had browbeaten the judge into granting Natasha's plea for a six-month adjournment; but it would have been a callous judge who could have observed her almost frenzied grief without wishing to show sympathy. Indeed, to have requested a few months' delay does not seem unreasonable. Sanya, coldly furious, told her she had won "six dead months"; there would be no contact.

He left Natasha's letters unopened; her mother wrote accusing him of being unbelievably cruel; she could not have expected his response: a letter of almost two thousand words, written with a *Gulag*-like ferocity on the subject of Natasha. He was acting merely from self-preservation, he began. For the past seven years, since the fall of sixty-four, his marriage had been Hell; he looked back at them with horror. After every parting there had been a "scene"; she had held two pistols to his head: "I'll kill myself" and "I shall go mad!" She had boasted that he feared her more than the state! Had cost him more strength than all his writing and other labors; mentally these years had been worse than the labor camps—a psychological catastrophe. Seeing her now made him ill for days after, preventing him from working. He would NEVER return to her—NEVER UNDER ANY CIRCUMSTANCES. . . . (Capitals, exclamation marks, and underlinings begin to appear more and more densely, and one can sense an almost ungovernable rage.) In a late snowstorm of exclamatory phrases he reveals that she had told him, in 1964, that she had not loved him until 1944. When all that time he had thought himself loved! And was now going off to war—to death, perhaps—leaving her in her comfortable bed! *Six years of lies!*

Is it fanciful to imagine that in that oddly self-pitying passage we can hear the cries of the small child left behind in Kislovodsk, his mama evidently not loving him? There is very little pity for *Natasha*'s aged mother in his letter. She must have been shaken by it. And unmistakably he did feel he had gone through seven years of Hell. Only now, he wrote, did he have a feeling of light in his soul; love had come to him too late—but he was not going to let go of it.[3]

He *might* have said to the old lady, "Natasha chose a good year in which, with your encouragement, she divorced her *zek* husband for another man; a year in which I had no idea what was happening until the message that I might arrange my life independently; and in which she (and you) had no fear that I might turn up at your door threatening to go mad or commit suicide. . . ." But he did not; he spared her his savage irony.

One of the people Natasha asked to intercede for her with Sanya was Dmitri Panin. Sanya accused her, through the intercessor, of an insatiable vanity that had created a fantasy world. He did not have the time or energy to correct to friends the slanders she was spreading about his supposed despotism. She had been too self-absorbed ever to understand him. Their marriage was dead; he loved another woman.

The chivalrous Panin was among the few who continued to support Natasha, against those who thought the great writer was being ground down by the exhausting conflict, or who simply found Natasha's behavior embarrassing. Nonetheless, Panin and his new Catholic-Jewish wife Issa had a cordial farewell with Sanya before leaving for Paris: part of the limited Jewish exodus permitted as a contribution to détente with the West in the early 1970s.

In the same exodus, Veronica and Yuri Stein left, to settle in the United States. Sanya himself briefly fell out with them, accusing them of not defending him against two biographers, David Burg and George Feifer. He was already beginning to fear intrusive Western "rascals" who went around "making up fairy tales" or "collecting lavatory-wall gossip."[4] His annoyance with Veronica was not long lasting, and she remained his warm friend and defender.

Another deep friendship had gradually weakened in the course of a long separation, that with his old Kok Terek friends, the Zubovs. Nikolai had paid a brief visit to Moscow in 1969 and they had met at Rozhdestvo; however "we were no longer on the same wavelength," Sanya observes, as in those days when each of them could grasp the other's meaning at a word. In 1971, he had encouraged a visit from Natasha to the elderly couple, hoping they could talk some sense into her. He came to regret her visit, thinking it responsible for the interest the KGB took in the old couple later; however, "at the time I could not have imagined into whose clutches our divorce would drive my wife nor that she was on the verge of becoming (or had already become) more dangerous to me than any spy, both because she was ready to collaborate with anyone against me and because she knew so many of my secret allies."[5]

There were acquaintanceships that never ripened into friendship. On each side of the Rostropoviches, in their not undistinguished road, lived Sakharov and Shostakovich. The nuclear physicist lived in a two-story brick house, cramped inside, with hordes of relatives from his two marriages. When he fell out with the state he pure-mindedly gave back his life's savings, 150,000 rubles. Losing his right to an official car, his own car commandeered by his children, he could be seen, wrote Galina, lugging heavy bags of groceries home at night from the station. He was a gentle man, and too willing, Sanya thought, to waste his strength by supporting every cause, every individual. Despite their respect for each other, the two greatest dissidents never really hit it off.

Rostropovich tried his best to bring about a friendship between composer and writer, but their experiences and characters were totally different. Shostakovich was no tough brawler. "Tell him he shouldn't take on that Kremlin gang, Slava; a writer has to work. He should write—he is a great writer."[6] Shostakovich would have liked to have created an opera out of "Matryona's House," a superb subject for his genius.

There was one new friend with whose mind and temperament the writer felt completely at one. True to a pattern in Solzhenitsyn's life, Igor Shafarevich was a brilliant mathematician, appointed a full professor at Moscow University at twenty-one. Mankind was on the verge, Shafarevich believed, of a spiritual renaissance. Now in his mid-forties, he was "tackling" socialism, with a "freedom and humor of which the Western world, hypnotised as it is from the left, is today incapable." Above all, he loved Russia with all his soul.[7] Another who became his friend and trusted helper at this time was a young historian, Vadim Borisov.

Henceforth, anyone who did not share a common bloodstream and heartbeat with Russia would be unlikely to win Sanya's warm friendship. He would have felt more fellow feeling for a Communist patriot than a social democratic internationalist. His unsuccessful attempt to persuade conservative-Communist newspapers and journals (*Pravda*, for example) to publish him, in preference to Tvardovsky's "liberal" journal, had been a sign of this tendency.

In February 1972 he composed a *Lenten Letter to the Patriarch*, in which he urged Patriarch Pimen of Moscow to act with greater courage in the face of the atheism under which the Orthodox Church was forced to bow. To most liberal-minded Russians, Orthodoxy was an irrelevance. For the first time, Liusha Chukovskaya, his devoted helper, rebelled against him by adamantly refusing to type the *Letter*. "After more than six years of working together, it became apparent that we did not think alike."[8]

The spirit of Russia was at the heart of *The Red Wheel*, of which he was now writing the second "knot" (exploration of a crucial historical period), *October 1916*. The fact that his imagination was immersed in war must have affected how he felt and behaved generally. He was totally the general, writer, and priest—Russia's conscience—he had dreamed of being in his boyhood. In the battle with the state he continued to feel exultation—so different from Shostakovich, whose splendid memoir, *Testimony*, ends with a heartrending admission of depression, overwhelming grief, a miserable life. Solzhenitsyn gives the impression that he *needs* the conflict in order to be fully alive. He speaks of the "encounter battle" that was going on, defining that term as the chance meeting of warring armies. In this case, he says, on one side (consisting of Sakharov and himself) there were two columns, neither of which knew anything of the other's movements and plans. His constant military metaphors give tremendous élan to his writing. With what exuberance—like Dickens describing a Christmas feast—he spreads before us the mouthwatering banquet of his projected "novel": "After a long illness I had just plunged into my work on *October 1916*—which turned out to be a vast subject, a double 'Knot,' if not a treble one: this because I had omitted, for the same reason of 'economy,' the undoubtedly necessary *August 1915*, and skirted around the whole political and spiritual history of Russia from the beginning of the century in Knot I. The arrears had mounted up and now threatened to burst the bounds of the story, to overwhelm it. I wanted only to work. . . ."⁹ Such a gargantuan appetite: and he envisages some twenty knots!

He broke off to write his Nobel lecture, still undelivered. The secretary of the Swedish Academy, Karl Gierow, wrote reporting on a meeting with Ambassador Jarring. Alas, Jarring regretted, the lecture couldn't be given at the embassy—there was no suitably spacious room. . . . In his reply, suggesting that the investiture might take place in a private apartment (Svetlova's flat), Solzhenitsyn makes frisky play with Jarring's absurd excuse: "The apartment is, it is true, certainly no more spacious than the Swedish Embassy, but forty or fifty people can be fitted in quite comfortably by Russian standards. . . ." Gierow thought this a good idea; Solzhenitsyn took great care with the guest list, and jokily invited Furtseva, the ultraconformist Minister for Culture. She was not amused. The ceremony was arranged for Easter; the great centerpiece of the Orthodox faith would add insult to injury. On 3 April 1972 Andropov noted "Solzhenitsyn's mistress Svetlova and her relatives are buying up dishes and food in large quantities for the guests invited to the reception . . . Easter cakes, dyed eggs, etc."¹⁰ It was all in vain, as Andropov points out—for Gierow had already been denied an entry visa.

After a lull, Andropov was targeting Solzhenitsyn again; though not with ricin. In a report to the Central Committee of 27 March he again summarizes the writer's activities and concludes: "An analysis of Solzhenitsyn's behavior throughout his entire conscious life indisputably proves he has deliberately and irrevocably embarked on the path of struggle with the Soviet government and will wage this struggle regardless of everything."¹¹ For the second time in fifteen months, the KGB chairman presented a draft of a revocation of citizenship.

Three days later the Politburo met to consider his report. A measure of Solzhenitsyn's importance, indeed his power, is that a discussion of what to do with him involved them in a survey of the entire state of the Soviet Union. The gerontocracy knows that *he* is the formidable enemy; an army in his own right. Clearly troubled, they have to cheer themselves up, with the Politburo's version of primitive Zulu battle chants before an attack on a tiny but better-armed garrison. . . . *Brezhnev:* "It was good to hear Comrade Andropov's report. . . . The moral and political condition of our society is good and healthy. Our people are dynamically moving forward toward the cherished goal of communism. . . ." *Grishin:* "It is really true, comrades, that on the whole our situation is a good one. This is the clear judgement from Moscow, our capital city. . . . There really is unity among our people and we are proud of that. . . ." *Ponomarev:* "Ethnic groups in our country are drawing closer and closer in every way. . . ." *Suslov:* "The situation in the country truly is quite good as Comrade Brezhnev has said. . . ." *Demichev:*

"Our artists' and writers' associations are ideologically strong. . . ." *Podgorny:* "The Soviet Union gets stronger and stronger from year to year in all respects. . . ."

If only they knew what to do with this wretch Solzhenitsyn. . . . Brezhnev blames a slackening of vigilance, of that "truly Bolshevik-style struggle" on "the scum of human society" which is poisoning the healthy atmosphere. He warns against nationalism, as a breeding ground for anti-Communism. Victor Grishin, First Secretary in Moscow, agreed with that, mentioning the Baltic republics and the Ukraine. And Zionism . . . If Jews from all over the country were to be allowed to leave for Israel, "we should not do it through Moscow . . . because they come here with their pianos and their cars and have big send-offs at the airport. And this is done on a grand scale. I think this should stop." As for Solzhenitsyn, *he* should be removed too, certainly from Moscow. He was "a true degenerate": this from a bureaucrat who liked to have a fully equipped brothel connecting with his office. Solomentsev supported the call for more ideological warfare against nationalism, said that young people were being affected by the dissidents, and blamed Khrushchev for discovering "that scum" Solzhenitsyn. Suslov added his warning about bourgeois nationalism, agreed that Khrushchev—and Mikoyan—were much to blame for the Solzhenitsyn phenomenon, and that he should be removed from Moscow; whether into internal or external exile he was not sure. Podgorny agreed that Solzhenitsyn was capable of doing great harm, but—for fear of bourgeois propaganda—did not think he should be expelled from the country. Kosygin argued for a political-educational approach rather than a punitive policy. Comrade Andropov, he said, should decide how to handle "these people" (Sakharov and the dissident Pyotr Yakir had also been mentioned). In what was perhaps a warning to Andropov not to return to Stalinist methods, Kosygin added that they should be dealt with "in accordance with our available laws." If he [Andropov] should resolve it wrongly, "then we will correct him." Had Kosygin picked up rumors of the assassination attempt?

"That is why I am consulting with the Politburo," Andropov said blandly. He and Podgorny were delegated to make concrete proposals; but there had been no strong support for expulsion from the Soviet Union, and Podgorny had argued against it. Andropov's second draft, revoking Solzhenitsyn's citizenship, was again consigned to the Files. He must have felt intensely frustrated.[12]

The question of legality had been brought up by Brezhnev himself, after Solomentsev had called for expulsion; it seemed that no actual law had been broken. . . . Comrade Stalin must have turned in his niche of the Kremlin wall. With the benefit of hindsight a reader of that transcript could say, They're finished.

On the very same day, 30 March 1972, Solzhenitsyn was executing a far more confident and effective operation, intended to counter the propaganda of the *Stern* and *Literaturnaya Gazeta* features on his class background. He had invited two experienced American journalists, Hedrick Smith of the *New York Times* and Robert Kaiser of the *Washington Post*, to interview him in Alya's flat. Zhores Medvedev had helped to set up the meeting, communicating with both parties in code, and carrying out reconnaissance sorties with the journalists under cover of darkness. When Sanya, shortly after noon, unbolted the door to let them in, they confronted a man who did not behave like an icon but someone who was warm and engaging and immensely dynamic—bounding out of chairs, moving athletically across the room. They noticed, journalistically, that his steel molars flashed when he smiled; he had something of a paunch under his pullover; his hands were stubby and powerful, a worker's hands, and an index finger had a dark tobacco stain. He introduced the Americans to Alya and the baby. In the words of Andropov's surveillance report of 3 April: "At the very beginning . . . Solzhenitsyn's mistress warned the correspondents that someone might well be eavesdropping on them, in view of which the rest of the exchange was largely carried out by writing notes."

The pleasant informality of the welcome vanished as Sanya placed before the Americans two copies of a twenty-five-page manuscript. All the questions and answers were there; he wanted it published in full.

Smith thought of walking out; but contented himself with muttering to Kaiser, "This is outrageous." They informed Solzhenitsyn that this wasn't how interviews were conducted in the West, where journalists liked making up their own questions. Several hours of negotiations followed. With Svetlova's help, they struggled through the seven-thousand-word text. "Not even the President would get this much space," they said. Solzhenitsyn finally agreed to some cuts, and to their posing some questions of their own, on condition that a Swedish journalist—and a blond Swede amazingly was conjured up, instantly, from somewhere in the flat could print the whole interview in the wake of the American publications.

The Americans were grateful for Alya's diplomacy and sense of humor, and dazzled by Solzhenitsyn's intense blue eyed gaze and "radiant smile." (The smile switched on for photographs with Alya and Yermolai, but vanished for solo pictures.) Above all, they were overwhelmed by the force of his personality. Had they known that twenty-three members of the Politburo had simultaneously quailed before that personality, they might not have been surprised.

The interview had a strong effect in the West. He evoked indignation at the way his wartime service was being distorted by a whispering campaign. "The word went round, 'Solzhenitsyn voluntarily surrendered to the Germans! No, he surrendered a whole battery! After that he served as a policeman in occupied territory! No, he was a Vlasovite! No, he served in the Gestapo itself!' Outwardly all is calm, there is no harassment, but under the skin there is this cancer of slander. *Novy Mir* once organised a readers' conference in Novosibirsk, and someone passed Tvardovsky a note: 'How can you allow someone who worked for the Gestapo to be printed in your magazine?' "[13]

Vividly he described the poverty of his childhood; he had only recently (a slight exaggeration) discovered what running water in an apartment meant. Through cold and damp and overwork, his mother had caught tuberculosis and died at forty-nine. He said the Solzhenitsyns had been ordinary Stavropol peasants, working the land themselves, with a few horses and oxen, a dozen cows, and two hundred sheep. His maternal grandfather had started as a peasant, but thanks to his energy and industry had become "quite rich." He had supplied the country with grain and wool, and had cared for his workers so well that after the Revolution they voluntarily supported him for twelve years until his death. "Let a state farm director try begging from his workers after his dismissal."

The greatest fury was on behalf of his father, a "Narodnik and Tolstoyan" imputed to have been "a cowardly suicide 'out of fear of the Reds'—before he had seen the firstborn son he had longed for, and when he had lived only briefly with his beloved wife! The judgement of a reptile."[14]

"Solzhenitsyn is becoming more impudent," Brezhnev observed, as he opened another Politburo meeting on 14 April. "We should take the most resolute steps to deal with him."

"I think he should be stripped of his Soviet citizenship," Andropov declared. And Kosygin was now prepared to go along with that. But Podgorny was away; they would have to wait a few days. . . . Something should be done about Rostropovich too, Kosygin added. Andropov had reported that the cellist-conductor had held discussions with the U.S. ambassador and at the West German embassy. At Easter, with his wife, he had spent five hours at Zagorsk, the pre-Communist home of Orthodox Christianity, taking part in the ritual. "We've given orders to stop his foreign tours," growled Brezhnev, "but still he's touring all over the world."[15]

In July 1972, the second court hearing of the divorce petition was heard. According to Veronica Stein, quoting from memory, Sanya's petition made the following points:

When Natalya Alexeyevna ruptured our first marriage, I was a speechless prisoner not even informed about the divorce. There was no "second side" heard. Then, she had been ready for "eternal separation." . . . She has used more energy—soul and intelligence—to write speeches against me than to build up our marital life. . . . She blames her actions on illness, but in reality she lacks the will to keep her nerves in order. . . . Each meeting after the separation was a tremendous darkness and shock. I couldn't work unless I was away from her. . . . She claims herself that when she was young she didn't love me, she received my courtship without love and married me without love. . . . The first three years of the second marriage were happy. But they became filled with mutual irritation. She spoke freely about our problems with all who would listen. . . . She never understood the depth of my vocation. She lived beside me without penetrating into the meaning of the work at all. . . . I tried to be patient. I asked her to look for a solution. But she was busy only with her self and her feelings. It all took away from my work. In court she has repeated her fantastic inventions which she spreads in Moscow society; she has lots of free time and uses it all to describe her version of the family breakup. . . . [16]

She was using his letters, except those from 1965–69 which she had burned, to further her literary career; he demanded that they be returned to him. She was prepared for him to live with his new family, but insisted that she be still legally his wife. This seemed to him "ugly, impossible, and contradictory to the definition of marriage given by law."[17]

His petition was again denied. He came home to Zhukovka in great distress, and immediately wrote to the Supreme Court requesting a review.

Galina tried to comfort Alya, who was expecting her third child—her second by Sanya. Although a strong young woman, she suffered from difficult pregnancies, and she had circles under her eyes and pains in her belly. She was philosophical about yet another postponement: "Why all this fuss? I've told him already we can just go on the way we are. I don't need anything. It can't be easy for her. I understand."[18]

One evening Galina was sitting with them on their porch when the phone rang. She picked it up, and heard a woman ask for Alexander Isayevich. "Who's speaking?" Galina asked.

"I'm Alexeyeva, his wife's new attorney. I have to talk to him about an important matter."

Galina handed the phone to Sanya. "I don't know you," he said, "and I have nothing to say to you." She begged him. The matter couldn't be put off; nor could it be spoken about over the phone. Could he come to Moscow tomorrow? No, he said.

"Then I'll come to you at the dacha. It has to do with your divorce; it's very urgent." After checking with Galina, he agreed; and said he would meet the three o'clock train.

The next afternoon Galina saw him come back alone from the station. She hadn't turned up. He had waited for the next train too. No sign of her. A few days after that, an old woman handed Galina a letter, which she said a man had asked her to pass on. Seeing it was addressed to Sanya, Galina handed it to him. He opened it, read it, and flushed with anger. He handed it to Galina, and she read:

"Stop your grimy proposals—I want nothing to do with you. . . . Knowing full well that as your wife's lawyer I did not have the right to meet with you under unofficial circumstances, like a provocateur you tried to lure me to the dacha. . . . You wanted me to fall into the trap you had set, and you would have advertised to the whole world that there had been another scandal. . . . Your true identity as an intriguer will be recognised by all your friends, to whom I am sending a copy of this letter. . . ."

Several friends did receive copies over the next few days. Then Galina saw Natasha's new Moskvich draw up at the gate. She shouted to Galina that she needed to talk to Alexander Isayevich. Galina went and told him, suggesting he bring her into the main house, since Alya was in a vulnerable condition; she might easily start to give birth.

While they waited for him, Natasha said to Galina, "What should I do to keep him from divorcing me? Give me some advice."

"Natasha, you shouldn't do anything. Alya will have their second child in two months. You have no children."

"I won't give him a divorce. He can live with her—but I must be his wife."

"But how can you want such a humiliating position?"

"Because if they send him out of Russia, I'll go with him."[19]

Sanya arrived; Galina stood up to go, but he asked her to stay as a witness. He gave Natasha her attorney's letter to read. She denied all knowledge of it. Galina felt she was playing a role she had been taught to play, and doing it badly; that she hated him, and was on the point of losing all self-control. Natasha complained that he'd forgotten how they'd suffered together during his imprisonment, how she had waited for him.

"No, *you're* forgetting that you married someone else while I was in a camp. I never held it against you, I'm simply reminding you, since you brought it up."

She fell on her knees. "Forgive me!"

Galina could stand it no longer, and left. Late that night, Natasha came again, with the attorney. She asked Galina to fetch Sanya. He and Alya were already in bed; she knocked softly, and his head, like a specter's, appeared at the window. "Natasha's here again, with Alexeyeva. Can you come?"

She went back and sat with the visitors. Natasha was pale; Alexeyeva, very young, "a humpback without a hump," with a large head and no neck, stared at the floor. When Sanya came in, he walked slowly across the room and sat down quietly. He had been living at Zhukovka for many years, but only at that moment did Galina understand what he had been through. "I was filled with pity for that great man." He must have entered like that every time he had been summoned for an interrogation, she thought.

Breaking the silence, Natasha said she had brought Alexeyeva to confirm that she—Natasha—had known nothing about the letter; and to tell him how it had come about. In a toneless, weak voice, the attorney asked for forgiveness; she explained that she had arrived on the three o'clock train as arranged, but as soon as she stepped out onto the platform two men had grabbed her and pulled her back onto the train—KGB agents. They had brought her back to Moscow, to the Lubyanka. They kept her for six hours and forced her to write the letter. Then, day after day, they had bullied her into promising to prevent the divorce and to discredit him in the eyes of his friends. Otherwise, she would lose the right to practice law. What could she have done? What should she do now?"

"Write down everything you've told us. Only, don't pretend you've never been to the Lubyanka before: they recommended you to her."

To Galina's amazement, she started to write. Her first version was unsatisfactory, a mere apology for "misunderstanding" his invitation to the dacha; the second time, she recorded events faithfully, and signed the confession. He said he would publish it to the world if she continued to spread the slander, otherwise he would do nothing with it.

Galina "wanted to smash that drab face of hers and throw her out."[20] That seems to lack understanding and compassion. The girl's career was at stake; she had weakened, yet repented quickly; for her to confess on paper that the KGB had forced her to write a slanderous accusation was brave. It requires even more courage for the "poor in spirit" to risk persecution.

In America, another hurt woman, and her angry husband, were filing a kind of divorce. Some time before, Solzhenitsyn had put all his business affairs in the hands of a Swiss lawyer, Dr. Fritz Heeb. This new complication had caused endless problems for the Carlisles, who never quite knew if they or Dr. Heeb held the right of decision over Western publications. To complicate matters further, Dr. Heeb did not understand English very well; Heeb and the Carlisles just couldn't make sense of each other.

Having gathered, from various sources, that Solzhenitsyn no longer had good feeling toward her, Olga Carlisle wrote saying that either she should hold worldwide responsibility for *The Gulag Archipelago* or she would turn over all authority and responsibility to Dr. Heeb. The "triangle," she and Henry believed, was unmanageable.

On a flight from Paris she felt, in the timelessness of moving westward with the sun, a sudden deep sorrow and depression, recognizing that Solzhenitsyn, to whom she felt she had given five years of her life, had repudiated her.[21]

In Moscow, the granddaughter of her friend Kornei Chukovsky, Liusha, was perhaps also feeling, not precisely repudiated, but less needed. Solzhenitsyn had been going to make her his literary executor; but with Svetlova's arrival on the scene that idea had been abandoned. Liusha still worked hard for him, and suffered for it: one night she was attacked by an unknown man in the lobby of her apartment building. He knocked her to the concrete floor and began choking her. She managed to free herself, and he fled. With a KGB surveillance squad just twenty yards away the attack was unlikely to have been a random one.[22]

In September a second son, christened Ignat, was born. In October, Natasha and her successor met, at the former's request. She asked Svetlova if she ever thought of her, and she replied that she did; she herself was on good terms with her first husband, and had thought the same would be true for the Solzhenitsyns. She was sorry for the grief she had caused. "Forgive me! Forgive me! Forgive me!" she said three times, emotionally. Influenced by this, and by the birth of another child, Natasha wrote to the Supreme Court saying she withdrew her objections to a divorce. But her note to Svetlova, with a copy of her letter to the court, annoyed Alya, and she replied with a cool note which upset Natasha in her turn. She might have withdrawn her consent to divorce; but at this time her mother, now aged eighty-two, suffered a heart attack. She died in December; on her deathbed she made her daughter promise to go through with the divorce.

In grief for her mother now as well as her marriage, Natasha could not keep her silence. The question of Solzhenitsyn's poverty or wealth had been much aired in the press. In his interview with Smith and Kaiser he had emphasized his poverty. As a result, an American novelist and screenwriter called Albert Maltz, highly successful in the Soviet Union, had offered to let him have his ruble royalties. Bernard Malamud and Robert Penn Warren likewise offered to help. Solzhenitsyn had expressed his gratitude to Maltz, and consented to accept the money, but strictly as a loan. He had no roof of his own, and had had to sell his old car, he wrote. This exaggerated picture of poverty had been countered by a Novesti journalist, Semyon Vladimirov, writing in the *New York Times*, who spoke of Solzhenitsyn's Rozhdestvo dacha, three cars, and two comfortable flats available to him. Zhores Medvedev, in the same newspaper, denounced this version as absurd.

Natasha then poured scorn on Medvedev's version, in a statement released by KGB-controlled Novosti to the *New York Times*. Her former husband was wealthy, she said; his lies and betrayal had led to her attempting suicide, and that had been partly responsible for her mother's "premature" death. She was planning to publish her memoir, giving a true picture.

Two weeks later, the *New York Times* carried a further statement from her, complaining that Novosti had taken advantage of her state of grief by getting her to sign her name to comments that they had added.

Understandably she felt bitter that Sanya had not seen fit to defend *her* against Aunt Irina's attacks on her character. It would have cost him nothing to have done so, in a sentence or two, during the Smith-Kaiser interview. She asked him to rectify the omission, but he would promise to do so only "posthumously." In that case, she informed him, she would have to defend herself by publishing, through Novosti, her memoirs.[23] It is probable, though, that she was relieved to have a justification for doing so. Writing her memoirs gave her something to do.

On 15 March 1973 they were divorced in Ryazan's registry office, "by consent."

One can't help overhearing, with sadness, Nadya Nerzhin murmuring to her husband, "It would be . . . *pseudo*."

Her behavior over the divorce had brought him torment. Yet not the least torment must have been his knowledge that, without wishing her harm—indeed, trying to be kind and generous—he had completed what she had failed to do in her suicide attempt. Since their remarriage she had lived in his shadow, lived only for him: he had seen to that. He took away from Natasha her reason for living and her status as Solzhenitsyn's wife. He left her with financial security, but otherwise with few independent friends, and a home in Ryazan occupied by old ladies she had to take care of. As she had pointed out to him, she had few inner resources she could call upon to make her life bearable. She plunged into eight years of depression.

This was Natasha's version of her circumstances; no doubt it was true, but not quite the whole truth. Some things she chose to keep hidden.

With his ex-wife on his conscience, Sanya would find it virtually impossible henceforward to explore fully, deeply, reverently, a female character in his "fiction"; and fortunately the gratefully accepted burden of history in *The Red Wheel* offered him a convenient alibi for avoiding totally—as he had avoided in part before—the female psyche, and love.

40

C a s u a l t i e s

She should have died hereafter . . .
—MACBETH

SANYA AND ALYA WERE MARRIED IN APRIL 1973. SHE WAS AGAIN
pregnant.

For the period April 1972 to July 1973 there are no documents in the
KGB Files. But there were anonymous letters to the newlyweds, in the
form of stuck-on bits of colored paper, intended to frighten them. The first
demanded $100,000; another said: "Well, bitch, you never came! Now
you've only got yourself to blame. We'll *straighten you out*. Just you wait!"

The rift between Sanya and Olga Carlisle deepened. Olga's letters angered him: because it seemed to him the Carlisles were treating the *Gulag*
as a commercial commodity; and because they could not see that sharing
responsibility with Dr. Heeb, with clearly demarcated tasks, would increase
security. Also because their chosen translator, Thomas Whitney, was being
so slow. Olga had said Whitney had a complete first-draft translation and a
substantial part in more finished style.[1] To which Sanya responded that a
translator should not ever need to make a first-draft literal translation—
which is not what Olga had written; "first draft" and "literal" are not the
same. The best thing to do, Sanya wrote, was to burn Whitney's "greatly
unfinished" translation, after paying him off for what he had done.

"In other, earlier times," Olga replied, "I would have asked my father to
avenge my honour on receiving your letter of April 5, 1973, knowing of
course that he would do everything possible to avoid killing a great Russian
writer in a duel!"[2] Despite her light tone, she felt wounded and outraged.
That he could insinuate that she was governed by commercial considerations! She who had given her soul to his work, for years. She told him she
could not go back on an agreement with the translator, made with his au-
thorization. "You do not seem to understand that our circle was (and still
is) cemented, not by a love of dollars, but by a love of Russia." The reason

she and her husband were withdrawing from the editing of his book was that they realized their work had not satisfied him.

In June Dr. Heeb visited the Carlisles in the United States. They explained to him that volume 1 of *Gulag* was ready; they had spent all winter editing the translation; volumes 2 and 3 were translated but not yet edited. Solzhenitsyn had previously indicated he wanted volume 1 to come out before the other volumes. Dr. Heeb, according to Olga, asked for the Russian text, and carried it off in a black leather case. Heeb claimed he had asked for the translation and was refused it. That was, Olga claims, "an outright lie." Later in the year Heeb requested that the complete translation be sent and—far from its needing to be burned—wrote in October to say the translation was acceptable, with minor adjustments. Whitney then worked on a final text with Michael Scammell and a Harper & Row editor—the Carlisles keeping to their resolution to become uninvolved.°

In Moscow that June in 1973, Liusha Chukovskaya was again the object of—almost certainly—KGB violence. She was riding in a taxi in the multiple-lane Sadovoye Ring Road when a truck traveling alongside made an inexplicable ninety-degree turn and crashed into the right side of the taxi. The force of the impact should have killed her; as it was, she had a major concussion and needed prolonged medical treatment. For weeks she could not walk by herself, and could not concentrate enough to read or even think properly. Her mind jumped from topic to topic. Yet even in the first hours, badly injured, she had the presence of mind to call Natalya Stolyarova ("Eva"), who rushed over and took possession of secret documents and the keys to her flat. The truck driver had been arrested; Liusha turned up at the court hearing to plead with the judge not to send him to prison, for he had two children; but the court set him free very quickly on the grounds that he belonged to a special military unit.[4]

Trying to lift some of the pressure off the Rostropoviches, Solzhenitsyn moved his family to a dacha at Firsanovka, just outside Moscow; but, finding it hard to work there owing to low-flying aircraft, he went off to Rozhdestvo to write, at a time when he knew Natasha would not be there. "For weeks on end," he recalls, "I had to leave my little boys and my wife, who was near her time, in an unprotected dacha at Firsanovka. . . ."[5] He did not, of course, *have to*, in any practical sense; but he reflects that he had never given in to sensible reasons for not writing, even when he was in transit jails without a pencil, dying of cancer, or in an exile's hovel after a double teaching shift; and he did not intend to start finding sensible reasons now. Alya, who had a similar iron determination, would not have wanted him to.

If he had let his writing be interrupted, he affirms with pride, he would

---

°When Whitney, perhaps at Solzhenitsyn's suggestion, hosted a party for the writer on his way home from his controversial Harvard address of June 1978, the absent Carlisles—away on a vacation—were offended by what they saw as a lack of tact, and collaborative friendship faded, sadly, into cool distance.[3]

not be able to say, at fifty-five, that he now had no more than twenty years of work to get through. . . . [6]

Has any other major writer—Shakespeare, Goethe, Dostoyevsky—thought in terms of a "production norm" that has to be got through before death? But if the twenty years shrank to twenty minutes, courtesy of the KGB . . . he was ready to die, rather than betray his principles. Andropov, playing Boswell to his Johnson, reports to the Politburo on 17 July 1973 Sanya's words to his eleven-year-old stepson, Dmitri: "For us life is a never-ending struggle. There is no one in this country whom the government hates more than me. The government is all-powerful. They have the world at their feet. And I am sitting right under their nose. But Mama and I have never given up anything without a fight. And we never will give up. We would rather die. That is why we will always be fighting to the very end. We will never compromise, since compromising has destroyed human-ity. . . ."[7] He told Dmitri to behave with dignity if he himself was taken; he must not bend his knees to them, nor ask them for mercy.

Very likely he knew there were secret listeners. Andropov's report con-cludes by saying that the KGB is now gathering information with the goal of pressing criminal charges. The Gulag threatened once more.

Sanya and Alya had indeed agreed, solemnly, that they were ready to sacrifice their own lives, *and even their children's*, rather than betray the *Gulag*. The KGB concentrated, however, on weaker targets, in particular his elderly helper in Leningrad, Elizaveta Voronyanskaya, "Q." Some work-ers were moved out of her communal apartment and a nurse, who proved to be a niece of a prosecutor, moved in. Two young women came about a private typing job, took away samples of Voronyanskaya's typeface, and never returned. That summer Voronyanskaya and another helper, Nina Pakhtusova, took a holiday in the Crimea, where the former became naively trusting of a minor poet who showed an interest in discussing Solzhenitsyn. Voronyanskaya's flat was doubtless searched in her absence: Andropov's re-port of 16 July 1973 contains a long extract from her "memoirs" concerning *The Gulag Archipelago*. From the time its author asked her to type a copy, in 1967, she had been mesmerized by it, and her fascination had led her to be indiscreet, mentioning it to friends, as well as describing it at length in her memoirs. "If the human race doesn't commit suicide in a fit of mad-ness," she wrote in a passage quoted by Andropov, ". . . not one thinking person will pass by this Everest of Russian literature, which embraces the unfathomable suffering of the people, revealing the hidden, unbearable life of half the Russian people during fifty years of Communist rule."

Way back in 1965, Sanya had warned the KGB involuntarily about this work, saying in a bugged conversation that *The Gulag Archipelago* would "murder them," would be "devastating!" Yezhov or Beria would have had *him* murdered at once, but their milder successors had "allowed" him to write it, during those joyful Estonian winters; and the KGB still did not have a copy; indeed Andropov was referring to it as a "novel." The secret circle of helpers had done its job magnificently. But now the KGB scented blood; the two ladies were seized as they got off the train at the Moskovski station at the end of their holiday on 4 August. Pakhtusova was interrogated for five days, following a search in her flat which unearthed, according to the KGB, 192 documents, including her friend's memoirs (*KGB File*, 10 August 1973). Pakhtusova did not give an inch during the interrogation. She "was allowed to bump into Q once, in the toilet. Haggard, with inflamed lips and feverish eyes, Q whispered to her, 'Don't resist. I've told them everything.' "[8]

Sanya was at Rozhdestvo, saying good-bye to his beloved little shack before he signed it over completely to his ex-wife. It seemed sensible to give it up to her, since he intended once more going "into battle." He writes with powerful emotion of the moment of leave-taking: "I will not deny that I wept. Nowhere is Russia so real, so solidly present to me as in this patch of land on a bend of the Istya, the familiar woods, and the long clearing nearby. Never, and nowhere, have I written so easily, and perhaps I never shall again." However exhausted or disgruntled he was when he arrived, "some soothing influence emanated from the grass, the water, the birches and the willows, the oaken bench, the table on the brink of the little river— and in two hours' time I was able to write again. It was a miracle."[9]

Independently he and Sakharov chose this time to go on the attack. Sakharov, in a press conference on international problems, called the USSR "one great concentration camp, one great restricted area." Sanya gave an interview to Associated Press and *Le Monde*. He spoke of the threats to his family; in the winter of 1971–72, he said, sources within the KGB apparatus itself had hinted that there were preparations to kill him in a car accident. (Obviously he could not mention the recent "accident" to Liusha.) He described the continuing persecution of the Rostropoviches. He unleashed a passionate denunciation of the kind of state that could think Sakharov a helper of foreign intelligence, and General Grigorenko and Vladimir Bukovsky (dissidents being "treated" as "schizophrenics") criminally insane. Of the former he says: "The unyielding General Grigorenko requires incomparably more courage than is demanded on the battlefield, to spurn daily, after four years in the hell of a prison psychiatric hospital, the temptation to buy freedom from torment at the price of his convictions, pretending to see wrong as right."[10]

It was another gripping performance, another *written* interview, as Andropov noted; but that only made it the more effective. In the Russia of this period, it was generally the worst who lacked all conviction, and the best, preeminently Solzhenitsyn and Sakharov, who were full of passionate intensity.

Then, for Solzhenitsyn, catastrophe: the Leningrad KGB discovered a copy of *The Gulag Archipelago*. It was in the attic of a flat belonging to a former Vlasovite, Leonid Samutin, one of the helpers. Q. had been forced to give his name; Samutin, in his turn, had been forced to reveal the highly inadequate hiding place of the momentous work.

No copy of it should have been in Leningrad at all. Q. had been asked to burn it; and in the fall of 1972 she had sent to Solzhenitsyn "a dramatically vivid account of how she and Samutin had lit a bonfire, and then, with crimson and yellow foliage falling around them and to the accompaniment of her sobs, they had burned the priceless manuscript to the last page."[11] She had lied; she could not bear to destroy the work that meant so much to her.

Now, thanks to her folly, *The Gulag Archipelago* could have been lost; for she had had no idea there was a copy in the West. Sanya would be arrested, and perhaps the most important work ever written by a Russian would join all the burned manuscripts. And people she had named would perish too.

Released from interrogation, she returned to her dark, Dostoyevskian flat in Romenskaya Street. She tried to commit suicide but was prevented. In hospital she explained that she had tried to take her life because of giving testimony against Solzhenitsyn. As soon as she was discharged from the hospital, on 23 August, she hanged herself.[12]

This is according to Andropov's memorandum of 4 September. There was no reliable report of her after the snatched few words with her fellow prisoner. Pakhtusova, warned not to tell anyone of her arrest, often walked along Romenskaya, but the windows of her friend's flat were always dark; and when she rang the doorbell, no one came. Evidently this was during the time Q. was hospitalized.

The only anecdotal information on what happened came from the nurse, her dubious neighbor. According to her, the old woman had come home after five days of interrogation, in an agitated state, and remained in her room, repeating over and over that she was a "Judas." She suffered some kind of a heart attack, and the nurse took her to hospital. She was discharged after a week, and soon after, hanged herself in her dark, fetid hallway.

The KGB informed a second cousin, an illiterate woman called Dusya; Voronyanskaya had been brought to death, they told her, by the intelligentsia. Illiterate Dusya might have been, but she showed initiative in finding her way to an apartment where she knew a good friend of her cousin lived: Samutin. That was the first any of the circle knew of her death.

A few mourners attended her funeral, which took place on 30 August in one of Leningrad's ugliest cemeteries, Yuzhnoye . . . "A vision of depressing uniformity, a huge churned-up vacant field with the type of clay that clings to your shoes when it rains."[13] (Not unlike the clay works at New Jerusalem.) Motorized carts delivered the coffins to the assigned plot, with the mourners keeping up as best they could: a true socialist cemetery, Solzhenitsyn observes. At the wake, the neighbor-nurse drank a lot, and said Voronyanskaya's body had knife wounds and blood. Murder can't be ruled out—

certainly Solzhenitsyn has never done so—though suicide remains more likely.

Liusha, still suffering severely from the effects of her car accident, was further shattered by the news from Leningrad, and her mind again lost all the concentration it had been slowly reclaiming. She expected to be arrested any day; and there was the further anxiety wrought by a garbled message. Liusha and another helper rushed to Firsanovka with the news that the *archiv* (archive) had been seized. The next day, 2 September, clarification came from Leningrad. Still weak, Liusha took a taxi, right across Moscow and north to Firsanovka, to deliver one letter of the alphabet: *archip*, not *archiv* . . . their short form of *The Gulag Archipelago*. An unbelievable disaster.

"Liusha," Solzhenitsyn relates dramatically, "her mind clouded by her injuries, now needed to solve increasingly complex problems, with the dark mystery of Q's death tormenting her like a beak hammering on her vulnerable head. She tried to put together the contradictory pieces of evidence, quite plausibly expecting to share Q's fate, and in this state of extreme stress she really needed to meet with me for several hours a day in order to talk things over. It was a genuine need, and I had an obligation to her, yet precisely because of the extreme danger, this was a period when I could not spare a minute for meetings and conversation as I scrambled to take countermeasures and to salvage manuscripts." No longer able to sustain the high pitch of intensity required of her for so many years, she now needed sympathy and encouragement. Lacking it, "Liusha was overcome by a feeling of abandonment, abandonment in a hostile world."[14]

His own immediate problem was how to deal with the seizure of *archip*. On 3 September he traveled to Moscow to see Alya. She was expecting their third child any day. After describing what had happened he said to her, "We'll have to detonate it, don't you think?"

Without a moment's hesitation: "Let's do it."[15]

The next day, by means of a coded out-of-town call to a Swedish journalist, Stig Fredrikson, he arranged an evening meeting with him. At the meeting he made a statement for the Western media, announcing the existence of his *Gulag* and its seizure. He gave a secret instruction that the work should be published as soon as possible.

And at that point, in strong contrast to Liusha, he became euphoric. The work was safe, in the West. Even if he fell at this moment, it would be published. He was in "a merry mood, a martial mood," characteristically recalling a battle of 4–5 September 1944 when apparent defeat was turned into victory. "Not for a single hour, not for a minute, was I downhearted on this occasion. I was sorry for the poor, rash woman whose impulse—to preserve the book in case I could not—had brought disaster upon it, upon herself and upon many others. But I had enough experience of such sharp bends in the road to know from the prickling of my scalp that God's hand was in it! It is Thy will! . . ." But for this apparent disaster, the work would have continued to be delayed. God had intervened to say: "Sleepest thou, idle servant? . . ."[16] This was the moment, he wrote, the great moment, the engagement for which perhaps he had been living.

In *Solzhenitsyn and the Secret Circle*, Olga Carlisle understandably points up the uncomfortable disparity between the suicide of his distraught assistant and the elation of Solzhenitsyn. "At no moment," she writes, "is the intensity of Solzhenitsyn's sense of mission more evident." One suspects that she may be mentally adding "and ruthlessness" after "sense of mission." Ruthlessness there may be; but we should recall how the adrenaline was flowing, and also how betrayed he and others must have felt as a result of this woman's indiscretion.

Hereafter he could feel sad for her, and pray for her; now was the moment for action, energy, single-mindedness, the elation of battle. The woman was a casualty of war, and by her own rashness. He and Alya prepared themselves for the worst possible scenario. There was already a clamor of support in the West for the dissidents. He was sure Andropov was feeling his blood turning to ice in his veins, knowing that publication would be fatal for the system. He would be wondering how to stop it. Their most likely option was to kidnap the children—posing as gangsters, probably—and use them as hostages. Well, that wouldn't do them any good: "our children were no dearer to us than the memory of the millions done to death, and nothing could make us stop that book."[17]

But these were not the red-blooded days of Stalin, when children were routinely arrested and sometimes even executed. Nowadays, every attempt was made to pay lip service to legality; Andropov even acknowledged, at a Politburo meeting, that Solzhenitsyn had a legal right to live in Moscow; he was forced to search for reasons to justify excluding him (*6 August*).

Instead of seizing his small children, the KGB tried to offer him an inducement through his ex-wife. Natasha asked if she could meet him at the Kazan station. He records their encounter in detail in *The Oak and the Calf*. She asked him if he would meet certain people to talk things over.

"What for?" He was cold; he knew what was coming; he recalls his years in exile of "furious longing" for a woman, someone he could trust with his books; and how, after coming back, "I had given up and gone back to my former wife."[18] Was this how it had *really* been, in which case it was cruel treatment both of her and, particularly, her stepsons? Or was it how he would *like*, now, to think it had been?

"Well," she said, "the immediate purpose would be to discuss the possibilities of publishing *Cancer Ward*."

Of course, there would be conditions. Such as, he must promise not to publish anything else for twenty years. . . .

But *Cancer Ward* had long been superseded; all the intellectuals had samizdat copies on their shelves already.

"You're a fanatic," she said; "you have no thought for your own children.

. . . If something happens to one of them, I suppose you'll say that's the KGB too. . . ." And, as if this was not provocative enough, she told him that in her memoir she had succeeded in explaining his character, defending him, helping him. "She had taken it upon herself to explain me! She who had never understood me, never never read my heart, never anticipated a single action of mine . . . had presumed to explain me to the secret police! And in partnership with them, to the whole world. . . ."[19]

Yet, in her muddled and unhappy way, she did wish to defend him. An interview she gave to *Le Figaro* early in 1974 must have been arranged by the KGB, since Ryazan, where it took place, was closed to foreigners. They must have expected her to be hostile, but she defended her ex-husband by saying he had been unswervingly loyal in his early years, and in the army; and the "unfortunate" *A Feast of Conquerors* had been written when his anger was justified; moreover, he had later repudiated the play. Asked about their life in Ryazan, she replied that his high school pupils had had excellent relations with him; he had been well liked. Everything he undertook he did with seriousness. As soon as school was finished, he raced home to get down to his writing.

She felt, she said, that his tragedy had started when he could not get *Cancer Ward* and *The First Circle* published in his own country. He had never wished to have his work first appear in foreign editions; this phenomenon had created a difficult and complex situation and affected his state of mind—which began to resemble his state of mind in the camps. This is an honest and far from stupid viewpoint.

Concerning *Gulag*, she drew attention to his own remarks that the work was a literary investigation—but went much further in saying it was not a scientific or historical investigation. He was relying on camp folklore, with his tendency to follow his instinct, his first impressions, and then permit no doubts to enter his mind. In contrast, she said, her old professor, Kobozev, always *preferred* to find results that were inconsistent with his theory.

This particular "theory" of *Gulag* greatly understates the essential truth of Solzhenitsyn's findings, but it is not a malicious point of view. Indeed, it is impossible to read the *Figaro* interview and not respect her attempt to be fair, under the most difficult external circumstances and with so much pain in her heart. Only at the end, the journalist related, did her voice reveal her emotion by falling to a whisper. She did not wish to discuss the marriage breakup, she said; "all that is very painful. It happened to me not when I was twenty, or thirty, or forty, but when I was fifty—too old to start one's life afresh." Her eyes filled with tears; the silence hung oppressively, then she went to her piano and played some Liszt.

Le Figaro itself found the interview "curious" in its moderation, and wondered if it signaled a more moderate official attitude to Solzhenitsyn. It only signaled that Natasha still cared for him.[20]

In the winter of 1973–74 he was living at the Chukovskys' dacha in Peredelkino. On 28 December, eating a light lunch and listening to the BBC, he heard that the first volume of the Russian language edition of *The Gulag Archipelago* had come out in Paris. It was ten days early; always imaginative in using special days, he had asked for it to appear on 7 January, the Orthodox Christmas. But he was not disposed to criticize his publishers, who had worked night and day to bring it out.

He heard the news calmly, still forking cabbage into his mouth.[21]

He burned his hand on the stove. He went into the city for treatment. He celebrated the publishing event with his wife and a few friends. He felt—and later he broadcast the statement, and many newspapers printed it on 21 January, which he knew, though they didn't, was happily the anniversary of Lenin's death—"I have fulfilled my duty to those who perished. . . . 'We need groan no more, our bones can rest from aching: the word has been spoken, and heard. . . . ' "[22]

41

D é j à V u

There is no happiness on earth, but there is peace
And freedom. . . .
—PUSHKIN

GOD HAD ENABLED HIM TO ACHIEVE HIS GREAT WORK. MORE RE-
mained to do, his epic history of the Revolution; with God's help he could
achieve that too. He felt, in a sense, invulnerable. God had saved him from
German guns, the Gulag, fatal cancer. The infant in the Kislovodsk villa,
circled by loving anxious women, survived, despite all the perils outside the
walls.

Stepan was born, his third son in as many years. "*Bring forth men-
children only.*" *Women were overemotional, disturbing creatures; they could
float out from the icon, hover over your head—half comforting, half threatening. They could be treacherous. They should be steel hard, soft only in
serving you. Even mathematicians could be overemotional—my God, yes!
But Alya wasn't like that. . . . She would stay; not like the woman in Kislovodsk, the woman in Ryazan.*

His part in God's plan was to devote every moment, and all his strength,
to writing. After the christening of Stepan, when everyone sat down to a
celebration meal, no one considered it odd or unsociable that after fifteen
minutes Sanya looked at his watch, made his excuses, and left. Everyone,
on the contrary, admired his single-mindedness; for his devotion to his work
was a devotion to truth and to Russia.

He came out of his workroom into the dining area, and in the pale January
light saw Liusha standing there. She was not often at the dacha, and the
unexpectedness of the image took him back eight years, to the day he had
confronted her in just this way for the first time. Then, in the depths of
depression, he had been grateful for her gentle warmth; now, she launched
into an immediate raging tirade against him, thrusting a sheaf of notes she

had made into his hands. He was lost for words against such a torrent of anger. Anger that was also anguish.

He had asked her to type up three essays intended for a collection to be called *From Under the Rubble*. Shafarevich, Borisov, and other Russian patriots were to contribute. Like his earlier *Letter to the Soviet Leaders*, his three essays exalted the values of conscience and religious faith above Western notions of democracy. Liusha had been forced to type such sentiments as these: "In the long history of mankind there have not been so very many democratic republics, yet people lived for centuries without them and were not always worse off. They even experienced that 'happiness' we are forever hearing about, which was sometimes called pastoral or patriarchal. . . . They preserved the physical health of the nation. . . . They preserved its moral health, too, which has left its imprint at least on folklore and proverbs—a level of moral health incomparably higher than that expressed today in simian radio music, pop songs and insulting advertisements: could a listener from outer space imagine that our planet had already known and left behind it Bach, Rembrandt and Dante?"[1] Under the tap-tap of Liusha Chukovskaya's incorrigibly progressive fingers appeared the suggestion that "the autocrats of earlier, religious ages, though their power was ostensibly unlimited, felt themselves responsible before God and their own consciences." And: "the absolutely essential task is not political liberation, but the liberation of our souls from participation in the lie forced upon us. . . ."

Such ideas flew directly in the face of what a modern political historian has called "the leading moral illusion of the twentieth century: the notion that in the modern age the principal arena of the moral life, the true realm of good and evil, is politics."[2] For most intellectuals, ideas and ideals of patriotism and religion were, almost literally, unthinkable. Liusha had become so enraged that she started to make notes, found that too slow, so moved to a dictaphone, her voice shaking. She then turned her spoken comments into disordered notes—and rushed to Peredelkino to tell him in person how unspeakably shameful the essays were. She dropped all trace of the intellectual restraint and sobriety typical of her. He recognized—it is perhaps his only acknowledgment of Freudian concepts—"a certain degree of emotional substitution was involved . . . as can happen in arguments with women, where annoyance in one sphere is transferred to an entirely unrelated one."[3] Her outburst so exhausted her, weak as she still was from her car accident, that she had to go and lie down.

She was also being forced to confront a misgiving almost too hard to bear: "could she have sacrificed so many years and her best efforts in the service of this? Would it not have been infinitely more appropriate and more loyal to have helped her grandfather in the last years of his life? And now to help her mother, who was going blind and whose work had become a constant struggle?"—An increasing one, since the indomitable old lady was expelled from the Writers' Union on 9 January 1974. Lydia reacted much less negatively than her daughter to Sanya's essays, finding them remote from her interests but not offensive. She retained a great affection for him, and her vivid portrait of him as "convict and guard rolled into one," with a "more relentless surveillance of himself than that of the KGB," relates to this period.

Over the more personal aspect of Liusha's pain, he felt remorse. "I was grieved by the realisation that all too much had been neglected over the years and that it was now far too late to set it straight."[4] She continued to help him, and indeed asked for work. It must have been hard for her to overcome the addiction. The concluding paragraph of his chapter on her in *Invisible Allies* strikes a portentously somber note: "My meeting with Liusha in that far-off autumn helped her emerge from a state of dejection. It led her to participation in a furious struggle. But the struggle consumed years of her life, took possession of her soul, and dragged her—at least in part against her will—into a tragic and uncharted orbit."

Another helper, Mirra Petrova, had for some time been perturbed by what she felt to be the rightward drift of his writing in both *August 1914* and *October 1916*. She liked the military chapters and the depiction of Samsonov in the former, but hated the privileged Tomchak family (in essence the Shcherbaks), and any mention of religion. He learned from her reactions the strength of the contemporary appeal of "democratic intelligentsia values," those which had briefly gained power through the February Revolution.

While at Peredelkino he had his last meeting with Kopelev. Kopelev tactlessly brought an American publisher of Russian authors, Carl Proffer, to Peredelkino without an appointment; Sanya showed his displeasure, and both of the old friends from Marfino were "grim-faced and taciturn" as they parted.[5] Kopelev had already annoyed the writer by—in his view—swinging back to his former Marxist sympathies. Solzhenitsyn quotes a Russian proverb: "Even fire can't clean a barrel that has once held tar," and in almost the same breath accuses him of a lack of steely resolve, of having put him in danger with careless or unscrupulous copying of manuscripts, of writing a verbose attack on the *Letter to the Soviet Leaders*, and of becoming his "fierce and abiding foe."[*] Despite all this, "I did not lose my affection for Lev. Who could ever forget his huge, shaggy figure, his forthright, magnanimous impulses? He was generous toward all he met and, except when he lost his temper, kindly too."[6] That was a judgment that everyone who knew Kopelev—who died in 1997—shared.

No one could say that Sanya was "generous toward all he met." Natasha's description of his character, in *Figaro*, as "complex, contradictory and inconsistent" seems fair. He seemed to exemplify the characteristic of modern man described by Yeats: "More substance in our enmities/Than in our love"; yet his unequaled gift for savage vituperation is a major and glorious feature

---

[*]Like Freud, he had a tendency to make opponents out of his male friends but, despite disagreements, retain his friendships with women.

of *The Gulag Archipelago*, so we should be grateful for it. Sanya needed his powers of invective to awaken the West; for, as he potently observes, more than a mere factual account of the Soviet horrors was required to offset the exculpatory tendencies of Western intellectuals.

Just two weeks after *Gulag*'s publication in Paris, Soviet ball-bearing fitters and sewing machine operatives were giving vent to their indignation in *Pravda* and other newspapers. For example: "I wouldn't even want to argue with him because he doesn't deserve having anyone argue with him. All our Soviet reality . . . fully exposes him as an untalented scribbler." "I'm an ordinary worker, a mother of two children. . . . This scum should have no place on our Soviet earth. . . ." "If it were up to me, you'd finding nothing left of him. . . ." "A coward and a deserter . . . alien to the word motherland. . . ." "How long do we have to tolerate . . . ?" "A renegade, an ideological saboteur . . ." "Literally choking with pathological hatred for his native country, the socialist system and Soviet people. . . ." "A rich speculator . . ." "In the daylight, all reptiles look disgusting." Former KGB director Semichastny had compared Pasternak unfavorably with a pig; Solzhenitsyn was still further down the evolutionary scale.

His wife was subjected to a constant stream of abusive and threatening phone calls. Among them: "Isn't that Vlasovite dead yet?" "The man I idolized is the scum of the earth." "Some of us have done time without betraying our country—get it? We won't leave that son of a bitch above ground much longer." Near the Svetlovas' flat off Gorky Street, where they were living that winter, a poster denouncing "the traitor Solzhenitsyn" was put up; it bore a yellow skull and crossbones on a black background. A few of the abusive phone calls arrived at Peredelkino, and threatened the ailing, almost-blind Lydia Chukovskaya.

Nikolai Vitkevich, now a full professor in charge of the chemistry department of a large research institute in Bryansk, a Party member, was summoned to Moscow to read Solzhenitsyn's statements following his 1945 arrest and interrogation. Vitkevich professed himself shocked by what he read, and denounced his childhood friend. He himself, Vitkevich said, would never have brought others, his friends and even his own wife, into his confession, by doing which Solzhenitsyn had earned himself a lighter sentence, eight years instead of ten.

In fact, Vitkevich had been better off, since he had not been subject to "perpetual exile." He had arrived back in Rostov a year before Solzhenitsyn's exile was commuted; and, of course, but for Khrushchev, the exiled writer might still have been a schoolteacher in Kok Terek twenty years later. He reacted with justified pain to Vitkevich's accusations; and pointed out mordantly that he was being accused of having been a good Soviet citizen in cooperating with the authorities.[7]

Simonyan, who had been shown Sanya's prison statements in 1952, was also put under pressure to write a denunciation. It seems he was able to avoid doing so for the present, but must have promised to write an "exposé."

A friend reports entering Kirill's office and seeing him holding his head in his hands, weeping.[8]

Solzhenitsyn gave an interview to *Time* magazine, in which he denied that *Gulag* was intended to damage détente and to bring back the full rigor of the Cold War; but there must not be conciliation with oppressors, only between peoples. To counteract the vicious campaign in the Soviet Union, the Western media were loud in their support for him. The BBC and Deutsche Welle began broadcasting extracts from *Gulag* in Russian. Copies of the book, smuggled in, were already circulating in Moscow. German and Swedish translations appeared almost immediately; what angered Solzhenitsyn was his conviction that the English translation was not yet ready. The more publicity there was in America, the less likely it would be that the Soviets would feel strong enough to arrest him; but the Americans had only reports of the work, not the work itself. He would remark in *The Oak and the Calf*, "two or three soulless, mercenary products of a Western upbringing made a mess of everything that I had sent out at the Feast of the Trinity in 1968. . . ."[9] Whether "soulless" and "mercenary" justly characterize the attitude of the Carlisles to their precious responsibility must be doubted. Both are adamant that volume 1 was ready for publication in 1970; they awaited only his signal.[10]

In his own country Solzhenitsyn was courageously supported by Sakharov, by the historian Roy Medvedev, twin brother of Zhores, and by Lydia Chukovskaya. Sakharov said the new work was the stone that would finally shatter the wall dividing mankind; Medvedev—who remained a Leninist, and thereby incurred Solzhenitsyn's disapproval—called it a unique contribution to world literature and "completely authentic" in its basic facts; Chukovskaya said he had restored names to a host of victims and re-endowed events with their true weight and meaning. These utterances were drowned by the protests of ball-bearing fitters and sewing machine operatives.

Sanya knew that the end of January and beginning of February were dangerous times in his life—he had been arrested then, had been transferred from prison to camp then, had had his operation then; but once through it he could breathe more easily. He wrote in his diary on 7 February. "Forecast for February. Apart from attempts to discredit me, they aren't likely to do anything, and there will probably be a breathing space."[11]

The next day, a Friday, Alya phoned him to say there had been a phone call summoning him to the public prosecutor's office. She had refused to accept the summons, finding some technical defect in it. He was probably just going to be warned, he thought; it had happened to Sakharov. He decided to stay and work at Peredelkino for the weekend. On Monday he went to Alya's flat. A second summons came; he returned it with a typed note attached saying he refused to be questioned by any agency of a lawless state. He and Alya discussed what he should do if he were arrested and put in prison. If he was allowed to write, he thought he might attempt a history of Russia for children; but he was sure he would not survive more than two years. After a sleepless night, he worked on some correspondence, and pushed five-month-old Stepan, in his stroller, in the yard. Igor Shafarevich came, bringing the manuscript of his new work, *The Socialist Phenomenon.* They went upstairs to discuss *From Under the Rubble,* in which Shafarevich was involved. There was a ring at the door; Alya answered it; two men from the public prosecutor: "We have to clear this matter up; it won't take long." Leaving the door on the chain, she went upstairs and told her husband. He came down and unlocked the chain, whereupon the two men forced their way in, followed by six others who had been hiding round the corner.

Arrest. For all his preparations, he was in a state of "witless shock." He put on his old Kazakh sheepskin coat and shabby flat fur cap. He forgot to say good-bye to anyone but his wife. They kissed at the door, the KGB looking on, and blessed each other. "Look after the children."

Down the stairs, not feeling them under his feet. The car had mounted the sidewalk and its rear door was already open. He sat inside and two men sandwiched him. Four men with him, and four in a car following. Turning onto Pushkin Street, to slushy thawing Strastnoy Boulevard. The left lane meant they were not heading for the prosecutor's office but Lefortovo prison. Suddenly he simply had to rub his throat near the windpipe with two fingers, to massage it. His escort on his right said nervously, "Keep your hands down!"

"I know the rules. I have nothing to stab or cut myself with."

Somehow the rubbing seemed to make him feel better.[12]

They drew up in the yard of the Lefortovo and he was ordered to get out. He did so unhurriedly, slinging his galoshes bag over his shoulder so that it looked like a beggar's bundle. Up the steps, through the entrance hall, into a "box" for body searches. As if he had never left it. A businesslike searcher cheerfully told him to undress; and for all his determination that if he were arrested again he would refuse to cooperate, he found himself obeying. The *zek* mentality took over: order is order. The arrest had unnerved him; he had not expected it. He was sitting on a bench in his underwear when a glossy, sly-looking, gray-headed colonel came in. "Why aren't you on your feet?" he demanded. "I'm Colonel Komarov, commandant of the Lefortovo Maximum Security Prison."

Sanya had imagined this moment in many different ways; but always in a cell. Sitting on his bed, he would invite the officer to "come and sit by me." Or he would say, "Political prisoners did not stand up for prison officers in old Russia. I don't see why they should in Soviet Russia." Or—it took great honesty to admit this—he would "innocently stand up when the key rattled in the lock and pretend that I had been on my feet before they came."[13]

But now, taken by surprise in the frisking room, schooled by long *zek* habit to obedience, and having decided he should husband his strength for interrogation—he stood up.

. . .

He was given a coarse undershirt, a black prison shirt, and a real suit; then he was taken to the prison's second floor. He looked out for the iron landings and staircases of American jails, but everything was covered with dingy canvas sheets, so that "it was rather like a circus by night, hushed and gloomy between shows." Expecting solitary confinement, he was surprised to find himself in a cell that was one-man in size, but with three beds; two young men were lying, puffing at cigarettes; the air was already dense with smoke. He asked to be put in a single cell, as—a reformed smoker—smoking bothered him; and was told politely that his request would be noted.

The cells had not changed; still the revolting gray lavatory pan; the black bread on the shelf; the bright light set in the ceiling, guarded by a wire cage; the judas hole.

He talked to the young men, arrested for currency speculation. They were still dazed, whereas Sanya was relieved to find he did not have the reactions of a novice. Already he was pacing, four short steps from wall to wall in his laceless prison shoes.

He is hungry, not having bothered to have lunch, but taking Stepan for an airing instead. The lads offer him some of their bread, and he picks pieces off it. It's awful but he will get used to it. He is overcome by his normal evening lassitude, probably increased by shock; his usual bedtime is nine, and he "sees nothing wrong with eight," but here the official bedtime isn't until ten. He lies down without undressing and on top of the blanket, since those are the rules; he feels the blood rush to his head because his pillow is too low. If only he had his sheepskin coat; besides, the lads warn him it gets so cold at night he will be done for without an overcoat.

He shouts, and the serving hatch is opened. "It's time my clothes were brought back; surely they're disinfected by now?"

"We're looking into it."

A few minutes later, the door opens to let in an officer bringing a second blanket, brand-new from the store; the lads stare at this granddad, bearded like an Old Believer, who's been put in with them: is he some VIP, to get this special treatment? Behind the officer with a blanket comes a lieutenant colonel. "Would you come along?" he asks. Ah, the nighttime interrogation. . . . Sanya follows him. It's not far. He is taken into an office. A small, sharp-featured man says in an abrupt, piercing voice: "Solzhenitsyn?"

"The same."

"I am Malyarov, Deputy Prosecutor General of the USSR!"

"I've heard of you."

The tiny, self-important man tells him he is being charged under Article 64 with treason. He asks the prisoner to sign the arrest document, but he declines, saying, "I shall take no part either in your investigation or in your trial. You must carry on without me."

Back in his cell; the lads ask him what he will get. Should he tell them? Up to fifteen years, certainly. But of course there's also death by shooting.

He slips his shoes under his pillow: an old *zek* trick to keep thieves off, but here it's to raise his pillow slightly. Before he can wonder whether it's okay to put his arms inside the blanket, and cover his eyes with a towel, the hatch is rasped open and he hears: "Get your shoes down on the floor!"

He bunches up the pillow as best he can, breathes deeply the foul and almost nonexistent air—and sleeps.

"It's easy enough going to sleep in the evening, but not to get back to sleep after you wake up for the first time. All the troubles of the day force their way in at your first awakening, you feel a burning pain in the chest, in the heart; how can you possibly sleep? It wasn't the currency speculator somewhere behind me, sighing, tossing and turning, smoking through the night, it wasn't the light from that diabolical bulb clawing at my eyes—it was my own miscalculations, my own false moves: how they flood into the brain at night, wave after relentless wave."[14]

He has promised Alya he will survive for two years, until all his books have been published; but that was under the assumption that he would have air and silence and a chance to write. Here, he doesn't think he will last two months. Yet he can review his life with detachment. It has been worthwhile. He thanks God for what he has been able to achieve.

It was not cold in the cell during the night; he thought, later, they had probably raised the temperature specially for him. The rattle of the serving hatch woke him. All the doors banging—out of bed, look lively! Here's a brush—get sweeping! But how lenient they had become . . . once you'd dressed and made your bed, you could lie down on top of it again. They brought plenty of disgusting black bread, and hot water, slightly discolored with something or other; and a bit of "Fidel's dark granulated stuff" to sweeten it. And gruel! He couldn't believe it: gruel for breakfast! "Almost a mess-tin full—six or seven times the Lubyanka lunchtime portion in the old days. . . ."[15] So salty it was almost uneatable; he thought humorously of protesting that he needed a salt-free diet for his blood pressure.

The young prisoners asked him about the camps. How did he know so much? Who was he?

"Did you ever read something called *Ivan Denisovich*?"

"N-no. But I remember some talk about it. Is that you, then—Ivan Denisovich?"

"No, I'm not the man. . . . But did you ever hear the name Solzhenitsyn?"

He was telling them so that, if he disappeared, they could speak of meeting him. They recalled something in *Pravda*; were embarrassed, since *Pravda* had called him a traitor.

The lieutenant colonel stood in the doorway, beckoning him. He was led downstairs to one of the admission boxes and told to put on the clothes that were lying on the table: overcoat, sealskin cap, spotless white shirt, a tie, shoelaces. . . . "What do I want these for? Just give me my *own* things back!"

The officer looked uneasy. "Later, later. . . . Right now it's quite impossible. . . . Right now you're taking a journey."

Memory flashed back to a scene in his brigade commander's office in 1945. He too had said, with embarrassment, "You're going on a journey."

Was it some nightmare of repetition? Blok had forewarned him: "You'll die—and start again all over, / And everything you'll see repeat: / Night, the canal's icy ripples, / The chemist's shop, the lamp, the street." Noticing there were tiny white specks all over his suit, from his lying on a blanket, the lieutenant colonel summoned a lieutenant with a clothes brush; and both lieutenant and lieutenant colonel took turns brushing him down, front and back.

The special valeting made his confidence jump. Just as, in 1945 on the eastern front, he had leaped to the conclusion that he was being driven to Moscow to talk with Stalin, so now he knew that at last he was going to meet the Politburo. They might even be ready to discuss *Letter to the Soviet Leaders,* in which he had told them they could keep their positions so long as they abandoned Marxism-Leninism and introduced morality and law. "The conversation would be a serious one, perhaps the most important in my life. There was no need to plan it: I had carried a plan in my heart and in my head for a long time. . . ."

He put on the gleaming white shirt, but refused to wear the tie. Time passed. The lieutenant colonel apologized for the delay, and asked him to wait a bit longer. . . ." Sanya saw by his gestures that he meant "in the cell," and he was led back to it.

The young prisoners were astonished by his transformation. Pacing up and down, he rehearsed his conversation with the Politburo. Something told him that, given two or three hours, he could budge them, shake their certainty.[16]

But when he was summoned again, it was not the Politburo he faced, merely Malyarov; the public prosecutor solemnly pronounced a decree depriving him of citizenship and expelling him from the Soviet Union.

"I can only go with my family. I must return to my family now."

Malyarov stood up. Walked like an actor to the center of the room. "Your family will follow you."

"What guarantee have I?"

"Who would want to keep you apart?"

It was Thursday, 14 February. The day for lovers. Once again there were two cars, with eight officials, including a doctor who had been carefully monitoring his health in prison. The direction they were taking through the slushy streets indicated they were heading for Sheremetevo Airport. He protested that he couldn't go by plane, but the doctor said civilly that the plans couldn't be changed; he would be with him, with the necessary medicine.

For the last time: *The Union of Party and People is indissoluble!*

Their route took them along Third Tverskaya-Yamskaya Street, and he thought of his helper in years past, Professor Kobozev, Natasha's former boss, whose gloomy, cluttered flat overlooked this thunderously noisy street. He saw the passageway down which he, Sanya, often had entered furtively, bearing manuscripts to be hidden.[17] Always in desperate ill health, Kobozev had lapsed this past year into a semi-comatose state and was close to death. One of the most brilliant, wide-ranging minds Solzhenitsyn had ever encountered; he should have visited him more often. . . . Too late.

Glory to the Party of Marxism-Leninism! . . .

Sanya may have reflected, as the car charged up the bleak highway toward the airport, that many things were on the point of death; and this was one way of cutting short the death agony. Never again, probably, would he see Natasha, nor hear her angry, hysterical, demented voice. Never again have to feel remorseful, handing over work to Liusha for typing. Former friends who now attacked him would be left far behind. There would be those he would miss; Shafarevich, Borisov, Rostropovich . . . but Slava would resume his foreign travels, they would meet occasionally, no doubt. Depending on where he was going: he still had no idea where they were sending him. But really, it was for the best not to have the distraction of friends; they expected one's time. It would be enough to have his wife and children.

He knew Alya would be doing everything possible to rescue manuscripts, to alert the Western press, to raise Cain generally. They'd find it hard to shut Alya up.

Workers of the World Unite! . . .

The plane had been delayed for three hours. The passengers were exhausted and irate. European air controllers had been told the problem was fog. The VIP prisoner was ushered into the forward cabin, where he was encircled by seven fresh plainclothesmen and the familiar doctor. The doctor showed him medication still in its factory wrappings, to assure him it was not poison. The agent who sat between him and the window was solicitous. "Haven't you flown before? It fastens like this; look, have a sweet or two—they really help at takeoff." The smiling blue-uniformed stewardess holds out the bowl of sweets.

They taxi past buildings and aircraft in the gloom and slush. The last of Russia. He is leaving Russia for the second time; the first had been in a frontline truck, with the advancing Red Army. He had returned to Moscow in the custody of three KGB men; now he is leaving Moscow in the custody of eight. It was like his arrest in reverse, he reflected.[18]

The aircraft took off with a shudder. He crossed himself and bowed to the receding land.

Through the clouds, over the clouds; "dazzling sunlight on fields of snowy cloud." It was like a fairy tale; here he is taking coffee and biscuits from the smart stewardess—and in his pocket is a crust of black Lefortovo bread. Others are huddled under that pitiless naked bulb. "O Lord, if Thou res-forest my life to me, how can I reduce those cells to ruins? . . ." Like the child in Pushkin's *Tsar Saltan,* imprisoned in a barrel and thrown into the waves, he had pushed against the wood and burst out.

It's two in the afternoon; the day does not seem to darken; he finds they are on a course between Minsk and Kiev. Does this mean . . . Vienna? His mind drifts; he does not have to think. "Perfect equilibrium. Hang there, and realise that life holds few such hours. However you look at it, it's a victory. The calf has proved no weaker than the oak." He stands, and heads back to where he imagines the lavatory is, causing consternation behind him and a stampede to bring him back. "It's in the nose." They prevent him from shutting the door.

He asks the friendly, helpful doctor if he would mind telling him his name and patronymic. The doctor freezes; says curtly, "Ivan Ivanych."

> . . . The merry vessel runs,
> Past the island of Buyan
> To the land of King Saltan . . .

He hangs there in heaven, the plane seemingly motionless. It is deeply painful; but also in a way exhilarating, a rebirth. The purity of those snow fields, under such pure blue! If only he had his notebook. . . .

> And the land they all desire
> Is sighted already from afar . . .

The plane drones steadily and he half drowses.

Images from Pushkin fairy tales . . . Tsar Nikita and his forty vagina-less daughters . . . *Tsar Saltan* . . . "Are things foul abroad, or fair? . . . Seen any wonders anywhere? . . ." A knight in shining armor emerging from the Black Sea . . .

PART V

Iron Curtains

1974 –

ROSTOV, 1984, Sanya was "Russia's conscience" to many, but others asked, "Who is Solzhenitsyn?"

42

The West's KGB

Nel mezzo del cammin di nostra vita . . .
—Dante

ALYA, WHOSE FLAT HAD BEEN CRAMMED, ALMOST FROM THE MO-
ment of arrest, with supportive dissidents and friends, and Western journalists who helped her smuggle out dangerous papers, received a phone
message to say her husband was being deported, and was at that moment
on a flight to the West. Red-eyed, worried about little Stepan, who had
fallen ill, as well as Sanya, she said, "It's a great misfortune. I really won't
believe it until I hear his voice."

Solzhenitsyn's mood on the plane changed suddenly. It happened when
he looked around at the KGB men. They really were thugs; a few of them
had certainly killed. Suddenly he knew what was in store for him. How
could he, an old *zek*, have been taken in! My God! Soon, in "nervous,
neutral Austria," an embassy car will pull up right to the steps of the empty
plane, and he will be manhandled into it. In a few days' time he will be
found dead at the side of some Austrian highway.

He must try to be as casual as possible, pretending he has not guessed
their intention—which now is transparent and needing no verification; it's
the KGB way. He struggles with his school German to form a sentence he
can cry out in the few seconds between plane and car. . . . "*Herr Polizei!
Achtung! Ich bin Schriftsteller Solchenizyn! Ich bitte um Ihre Hilfe und
Verteidigung!*"

The engine hum changes and they are dropping toward the snowy clouds.
Into the swirling gray, and at last through. He sees a winding river, neither
broad nor narrow. The Danube? There are fewer parks and open spaces
than he expected of Vienna, and more industry. He hates the sickening
drop toward the ground, and crosses himself. The wheels touch, then taxi,
slowing. A large building bears the words *Frankfurt am Mein*.

They halt. "Put his hat and coat on him! Get him out!"

He is still rehearsing his German sentence. One of the killer thugs thrusts five hundred–mark notes into his hands. "To whom do I owe this?"

"You don't, you don't . . ."

He is told to walk out and down the ramp. A crowd of about two hundred people await him, clapping. Cameras flash, the handles of movie cameras are turning.

A smiling federal minister shakes his hand; a woman comes forward and presents him with a bouquet of daffodils. "Welcome, Herr Solzhenitsyn . . ."

> *Near is your fate, your destiny,*
> *This princess, that you want—am I . . .*

Accompanied by Peter Dingens, a former press attaché in Moscow, he is ushered into a Foreign Ministry black Mercedes. For the first time, as they swing out of the airport: *Thank you for flying Lufthansa . . .* The limousine gathers speed. *Probably the best lager in the world . . . For discreet family planning counseling ring . . . Girls play safe with a Hettner sport bra . . . The cigarette that's cool as a mountain spring . . .*

Neon traffic signs and reflector signals took the place of the blazing East Prussian farmhouses of his last foray into German territory. Twenty-nine years ago to the day he had been freezing on an open railway wagon between Brodnitz and Byalystok, heading back for the Russian border amid hundreds of other "traitors" and "collaborators," both men and women. Now he is being borne at high speed along the autobahn, cushioned by high-powered German technology.

The road climbed into the Eifel hills west of Bonn, to the hamlet of Langenbroich, where the limousine halted. He was being hugged and kissed by his old friend, the writer Heinrich Böll, and shown into his cottage. A left-wing Catholic, Böll had a cherished portrait of Rosa Luxemburg on the wall, and a sympathetic book about the Baader-Meinhof gang on his coffee table. It marked the beginning of many ironies.

"The wolves want their prey, my friend! We'd better go out one more time. . . ."

There were 106 residents in the hamlet, and the journalists, photographers, and TV crews there on this cold evening outnumbered them. Solzhenitsyn thanked them all, said he had been in prison only that morning, and wanted to phone his family. "Please leave Mr. Böll and myself in peace tomorrow," he said.

But of course they did not go away. Sanya could see their shadowy forms flitting past the windows, trying to peer in. The yard is bathed in arc lights. The wolf pack is silent, respectful, waiting. They admire him—and want good copy, good pictures.

Calling home, he was relieved to hear Alya's voice. "Are my pencils safe?" he inquired. He spoke with her for thirty-five minutes; faintly he heard the sound of classical music, soothing their children to sleep in the next room.

There may have been a brief disagreement; she and his dissident friends apparently thought better Siberian imprisonment or exile than deportation to the West. From the viewpoint of the political struggle they were undoubtedly right; a Nobel Prize winner languishing in Verkhoyansk or Novosibirsk would have had enormous mythic power.

Sanya did not agree. Yes, it was very painful to be cast out of Russia. In one sense the front-page headline of the English *Guardian*, "The most bitter fate for a writer," was true, or at least it contained a truth. But the author of the article, the literary editor W. L. Webb, was wrong in saying that exile was "the sentence Solzhenitsyn most feared." When he had been taken back to his cell after being told his fate, "my steps seemed lighter all the time; my feet touched the floor more lightly. I was soaring, floating up from this tomb. By this morning, I had reconciled myself to the idea that I had two months to live, and even *that* two months under interrogation. . . . And suddenly I was not ill at all. I was guilty of nothing. I was bound neither for the operating table nor for the scaffold. I could go on living!"[1]

For a quarter century, from the moment when a scrap of incriminating paper was being blown about the Ekibastuz camp, he had been on a ski run down a fearsome mountain. He had begun to feel divinely guarded, and had deliberately skied close to the precipice. But the strain had been enormous. he only realized the enormity of it when his career was brought to a sudden halt. Then, instead of hurling him into an abyss, *they* had sat him on a safe, relatively pleasant ski lift. A sense of relief, even euphoria, was inevitable, and mitigated the shock and pain of exile.

Living for him meant writing. He was an infinitely tougher character than Pasternak; with a sense of selfhood that, in childhood, had made him wonder whether his school and schoolmates still existed if he was home sick, and which now felt capable of carrying Russia with him. Give him his pencils, his books, his writing desk, his wife and children, and somewhere wintry to live—and he would survive well enough. Certainly there would be no worries about money; it was reckoned that his lawyer, Heeb, had banked over a million dollars for him, more than a year before his expulsion. Four countries swiftly offered him asylum: West Germany, France, Britain, and Norway.

He had been moving away, psychologically, emotionally, from his dissident "neo-Kadet" allies for several years; in a sense, Andropov was giving him the chance that many people yearn for in midlife—to throw everything up, to cast off all that is stale and used up, and to move on. And he had no responsibility for it; no one could blame him for selfishly moving on. . . .

In pointing out minor inconsistencies in the writer's account of the process of expulsion, Michael Scammell raised the question of whether Solzhenitsyn not only knew that he was going to West Germany, but may even have requested exile rather than a Soviet trial. The official version of the West German government has been that on 13 February the Soviet ambassador to Bonn phoned a Foreign Ministry official asking for an interview to discuss an important matter. The next morning the ambassador informed the official that his country was expelling Solzhenitsyn—who had selected Germany as his preferred country, and asked to stay with Heinrich Böll. Böll was the only Western author he knew personally. Willi Brandt was told of the request, and assented. In a speech of 2 February he had introduced the subject of Solzhenitsyn, saying he would always find a ready welcome in Germany. The German line is that the Soviet ambassador's request was the first inkling they had of the expulsion.

The opening up of the KGB's files allows us to look some way into the minds of the Soviets in the month between the publication of *Gulag* and the expulsion. At a two-hour meeting of the Politburo on 7 January, Brezhnev described *The Gulag Archipelago*, which he admitted no one had yet read, as a "contemptuous anti-Soviet lampoon." The author had encroached on everything they held sacred, so they had every right to imprison him. Podgorny and Kosygin spoke in favor of a trial and an internal sentence, the latter mentioning Verkhoyansk as a suitable place, since it would be too cold for foreign reporters to go there. We shouldn't be afraid of severe measures, Kosygin went on; after all, "Let's take England: hundreds of people are done away with there." Andropov: "I think Solzhenitsyn should be deported without his consent. At one time Trotsky was expelled and nobody asked for his consent." Brezhnev, after saying the author had already served a sentence for "gross violations of Soviet law"(!), instructed the KGB and Prosecutor's Office to develop a procedure to bring him to trial.

At this stage the decision was evenly balanced between deportation and an internal sentence. Andropov spoke vaguely of asking Iraq or Switzerland if they would take him.[2]

West Germany was a desirable asylum for the writer, from the Soviet point of view, since it would appear to fit in with his supposed affection for Fascists, Vlasovites, and so on. Therefore Brandt's indirect offer of asylum, in a comment that was apparently added as an unscripted aside in his speech of 2 February, came as a gift from the capitalist heaven. Tass immediately cabled the reference to Moscow. Andropov phoned Brezhnev, and in a letter to him of 7 February stated that *Gulag* was evoking a certain sympathy among the creative intelligentsia, and there could be no more delay in finding a solution. Therefore, today, Comrade Kevorkov was flying out for talks with Egon Bahr, Brandt's most trusted aide, to try to negotiate the deportation. It should be possible to expel the writer on 10 or 11 February. If for some reason the plan fell through, he should be arrested not later than February 15. The Prosecutor's Office was ready.[3]

It is quite possible that Brandt's aside was not a complete surprise to Andropov. Indeed, very likely he duped the "right" country to offer asylum. The Bonn government was riddled with Stasi agents; three months later Brandt would be forced to resign when it was found that a close aide, Gunter Guillaume, was a Stasi spy. It would have been simple to plant the idea that the Soviets had all but made up their minds to send Solzhenitsyn to Siberia, but that a humanitarian gesture from Brandt *might* make them consider the humane alternative. An aide told a *New York Times* reporter that Brandt's words had been carefully chosen, following hints that the writer might face severe punishment.

But it does seem that there was nothing absolutely cut-and-dried about his fate until a few days before the arrest; and no question of his having *opted* for deportation in general or for West Germany in particular. As for the choice of Böll, it is likely that his name came up in the discussions between Kevorkov and Bahr. The KGB knew of the German writer's visits to Solzhenitsyn during trips to the Soviet Union; though they may not have known that in 1965 he had smuggled out a subversive screenplay and poetry at a dangerous time, and kept them safe for years; nor that in 1972, to Solzhenitsyn's "undying gratitude," he had witnessed every page of his will, and smuggled that out too.

Those generous and courageous acts—though in actuality Böll risked far less than Natasha, who did *not* earn his "undying gratitude" when she was photocopying and handing on *The Gulag Archipelago*—seemed far to outweigh his leftist politics; the cherished Rosa Luxemburg, the coffee-table Baader-Meinhof. Sanya even quotes his friend's description of the gang as "youthful idealists, driven to the point of despair," without the slightest hint that he disapproved of such radical-chic tolerance of violence.[1]

For his part, Böll must still have believed Solzhenitsyn was a socialist. His review of *The First Circle* indicates an astonishing capacity to equate the evils of East and West. . . . "It was written for the liberation of Socialism. We have not the slightest cause to gloat over *The First Circle* as depicting Stalinist outrages, absurdities, and entanglements. We have more reason to wonder whether a Western author could be as brilliantly successful in revealing the world of the unsuspecting and the world of the silent sufferers within our own tangled complexities. . . ." (Surely a Nobel laureate should have found more apt nouns for a dictator responsible for tens of millions of deaths than "outrages, absurdities, and entanglements.") In his review of the just-published German edition of the first two parts of *Gulag*, there are sentences which, had they come from Kopelev or Tvardovsky, would have made Solzhenitsyn explode with rage: "We should not for a moment forget that it ends in 1956. . . . While no sensible person can wish for an overthrow in the Soviet Union, we all see a change as desirable. . . . Since the author shows no trace of self-righteousness, this book should be no cause for self-righteousness on the part of any of its readers. We should not forget either this or the fact that it ends in 1956. . . ."[5]

Yet here they were, shoulder to shoulder, strolling in the orchard of the converted stone farmhouse for the cameras, two democratic socialists together. . . . And a third soon joined them. Dr. Heeb flew straightaway from Zurich. A stolid, ultrarespectable Swiss burgher, the lawyer was nevertheless a staunch socialist; his father had known Lenin, Trotsky, Rosa Luxemburg. Sanya greeted him with a friendly bear hug; and just as warmly embraced

Janis Sapiets of the BBC Russian service, thanking him for the Orthodox services. Sapiets, a Latvian-Russian, was allowed five minutes with him in the dining room. The exiled writer, in his shirtsleeves, had an exercise book before him, in which he had been writing. He struck Sapiets as "inwardly so calm. Eyes and voice are calm. He speaks in low, quiet tones."[6] His calmness and serenity struck others. Per Hegge, who had helped him often in Moscow, observed, "He looks far less sad than I think he is."

But he became tetchy when the waiting horde, milling around, babbling in half a dozen languages, kept demanding that he talk to them. When would he give a press conference? "Never, never!" he replied, at his third appearance for photographs. "In the near future I will not answer a single question. I will not give a single interview. I have said enough in Moscow." Langenbroich had never known anything like the noise, delirium, and publicity of that day. "With Solzhenitsyn and Böll, two percent of us are Nobel Prize winners," one resident joked. Village children brought flowers, and Sanya thanked them. A postman brought letters and telegrams. In the clear, cold sky, swooping toward the sheep-grazed hills, two Phantoms of the Bundeswehr periodically screamed their welcome. It was not one he cared for.

But over the next few years in the West, he *would* speak and hold interviews; and in a sense he was conquered by the West. He would find, perhaps too late, that he had possessed more inner freedom in the Butyrki cell, the *sharashka*, at Ekibastuz, in the silence of the Kazakh steppe, and when burning his manuscripts at the end of the day in Ryazan. In the West, he would be overwhelmed by the psychobabble of "opinions," the locust host of commentaries, the conformism to party or pressure-group lines disguised as democracy. He would find—what he had always suspected—that Mandelstam's phrase "the unclean goat-smell issuing from the enemies of the word" could apply to societies other than Stalin's. Probably he had not considered a problem that had exercised Gogol—that where there was no censorship, writers could lose their sense of cunning, or never develop it. Even *he* had tried to be publishable in the Soviet Union; and had been helped by Teush, Anna Berzer, and others to be more artful, in both senses of the word. He was immune to the West's self-indulgence materially; less so in his writing.

After his refusal to speak to the particular locust swarm that had descended on Langenbroich, he was heard to say querulously, "I have to hold talks." One was with his old friend Dmitri Panin. Now living in Paris, Panin had published his memoirs in 1973. He had kept to the agreements he had made with Sanya concerning what might and what might not be written about him; but he had called the book *The Notebooks of Sologdin*—his fictional name in *The First Circle*. Solzhenitsyn now accused him of exploiting his name in the West, and asked him to leave, saying he no longer wished to have anything to do with him. Several months later he heard that Panin had had a heart operation and that the medical bills had drained him

financially; he sent him a check, which Panin returned. The two men ne__
met or corresponded again.[7]

Though we have only Panin's version of what happened that day in Langenbroich, it appears that Solzhenitsyn acted with unbelievable cruelty. And
the logic by which a mere title was so much more exploitative than portrayal
of Panin as the major character Sologdin, in a novel read by millions, is
hard to grasp.

One more pre-*Denisovich* friend had proved unworthy. There were few
left.

Despite his affection for German orderliness, the exile did not wish to live
there. Norway, where he was offered a house set aside for artists, appealed
to him because of the people's independence and the cold climate; but first
he would go with Fritz Heeb and take a look at Switzerland. The city of
Lenin drew him. Heeb wished to fly, but Sanya refused to undergo that
experience again, so soon. No, he would not even take a helicopter as far
as Cologne. As a result, a motorcade that a president would have found
extravagant wound its way down the mountain roads and onto the autobahn.
Cologne itself was brought to a standstill by the endless procession, which
refused to stop at red lights.

It was impossible to visit the cathedral, as he wished to do, since the
crowd of reporters, photographers, and sightseers was too dense. He could
only look at the east side from the roof of the post office. The train from
Cologne to Zurich was likewise packed with journalists, with more climbing
on at every stop and waiting for them at Zurich. They could hardly get from
train to car. Heeb's flat was besieged; when Sanya went onto the balcony
in the evening to get some air, he faced a sudden ambush of arc lights and
cameras.

They followed him even into the hills; finally, driven mad, he turned on
them and snarled: "Go away! You're worse than the KGB! I want to be
alone."

The Garboesque wish, and the comparison with the KGB, made it the
best sound bite (as a later generation would call it) he had yet given the
press, and soon it was being flashed around the globe. Andropov might have
allowed himself a brief smile.

Indeed he was probably already feeling content. He had assessed the risk
soberly. "Either way [deportation or arrest] there will be losses," he had
warned Brezhnev. "But unfortunately there is no other way out, since Solzhenitsyn's impunity is causing us more damage within the country than
would be caused internationally if he were deported or arrested." It was a
realistic and intelligent assessment. And the immediate response in the West
could have been far worse; in Britain, the *Guardian*, thought of as the voice
of the left-liberal intelligentsia, possessed of an ineffable moral relativism,
actually *praised* the Soviets in its leader of 14 February, saying "the Soviet

government has behaved humanely, especially if it turns out to be true that Solzhenitsyn's family will be joining him." "Especially if" implies that it would still have behaved quite humanely even if the family could *not* join him. The same leader also showed how hard it was to make liberals take the evils of Bolshevism seriously—even after Robert Conquest's *The Great Terror*—by speaking of a reign of terror worthy of the worst tsars . . . thereby demonstrating yet again how needful was the intense passion of *The Gulag Archipelago* to hammer home the reality to Western dolts.

Among Western authors, Graham Greene was one who spoke out strongly; he said writers should boycott the Soviets, ghettoize them. Overall, anger was tempered by relief that worse had not happened. Zhores Medvedev, now living in London, having had his citizenship revoked during a foreign trip, commented that he had expected Solzhenitsyn to have been tried and exiled in his own country, in Siberia. He doubted if the deportation was legal. (He, too, would fall into the pit reserved for ex-friends, criticized for being an apologist of the Soviets, his book *Ten Years after Ivan Denisovich* described in *The Oak and the Calf* as "vapid.")

In Moscow, amid an orchestrated chorus of relief that the traitor was gone, there were protests from the—now badly weakened—dissident movement; while the more mainstream Yevtushenko, so often maligned for timeserving, sent an immediate telegram of protest to Brezhnev, in which he said that while he disagreed with Solzhenitsyn on many points, *Gulag* contained "terrible documented pages about the bloody crimes of the Stalinist past."

It must have pleased the Politburo that the people who mattered, the Western leaders, were reacting cautiously. President Nixon had Watergate problems; he wanted a détente-promoting visit to Moscow, which Secretary of State Kissinger was to set up by a visit of his own the next month. It was clear from Dr. Kissinger's remarks that he had no intention of letting a troublesome writer wreck these plans. "The administration is deeply concerned," he said; "but we are delighted that Mr. Solzhenitsyn is not in some of the difficulties that were feared yesterday." No, détente would not be affected; it was essential, because of the inadmissibility of nuclear war.

In Ottawa, Premier Pierre Trudeau said Solzhenitsyn was welcome to live in Canada as an immigrant, but the government had no plans to offer him political asylum. In Britain, Prime Minister Edward Heath, preoccupied by an election and a crippling miners' strike, said in an election press conference that Britain was concerned, in tones that suggested he was not about to threaten a missile strike. Labour's soon-to-be prime minister, Harold Wilson, said his party had protested to the Soviet ambassador, but wished there would be as much condemnation when a right-wing government did "this sort of thing."

West Germany's Christian Democratic opposition criticized Brandt for having given the Soviets an opening with his "unscripted aside," and wondered if he had connived at their action. We now know there was a real problem over the question of who would receive Solzhenitsyn; Brandt's offer was humane in its effect and, doubtless, intention; but it helped the Soviets to deliver a devastating blow to the small band of dissidents, who had now lost their most powerful and charismatic personality.

Not letting the grass grow under his feet, the exiled writer left Zurich for Norway on 17 February. Remember he had been in Lefortovo on the fourteenth: his energy was staggering. Again he was besieged everywhere, and still he refused to spend ten minutes with reporters, which might have satisfied them. The crowds in Copenhagen, where he took the overnight ferry, were as big as those in Zurich. They applauded him. In Norway he considered a few houses for possible residence, enjoyed the snowy mountain solitudes, and pronounced the film of *Ivan Denisovich*, starring Tom Courteney, which he watched there, as decent and honest, just not Russian.

Back in Zurich the friendly mayor Sigmund Widmer found for him a detached three-story villa near the city center, and also, since living there seemed to make him uneasy, offered him the use of his farmhouse in Sternenberg, the mountain village where he had shouted at the reporters. The landscape reminded him, he told Widmer, of the North Caucasus, where he had been born. He spent the weekdays here, buying provisions in the local store, returning to the city on the weekend.

It was at this house, "a typical European suburban villa," shaded by large trees, that Olga Carlisle called on him, on the first day of spring, a brilliant cold blue day, with the surrounding mountains like a landscape by Paul Klee. On a visit to Geneva, she had written to him asking if she might call, and he had replied at once offering an appointment, and adding in a sentence that chilled her—that if the English translation of *Gulag* had appeared in January they would not have dared throw him out of Russia. He was blaming her for the worst possible fate for a Russian writer, she thought. The villa's gate was locked and there appeared to be no doorbell. The house was too far to shout. She banged on the gate with her fists.[8]

At last he came and opened the gate, shook her hand, invited her into the garden. He looked vigorous; she felt a surge of gladness. But soon she saw how much had changed. "The youthful, dynamic man I had met in Moscow was now an imperious figure, part military, part ecclesiastical, with a priestly beard and eyes more scrutinising than ever. For an instant I had the feeling of being a junior lieutenant reporting to a commander in chief, an acolyte entering the presence of a prince of the church. His greeting was markedly cordial, but I knew at once I was no longer a friend." As he led the way to the house along a narrow path, she was struck by his "carefully bridled exhilaration. I could sense it in his springy walk, the carriage of his head." She had the impression of "a closely guarded sense of triumph."

Under a tall tree he unexpectedly sat on a seat, said to excuse him, it would take but a second, and scribbled a note. Then he was up, showing her inside. They sat in a dark, cool room stacked with books and papers. She asked after his family.

"Very well. I speak to my wife every day on the telephone. Little Styopa has been ill but he's better now."

"And when are they expected to reach Zurich?"

"My wife is packing my archives. She will not leave the USSR unless the archives are allowed out too. That is final. Because of this, Olga Vadimovna, the date of her arrival is not known."

She tried to explain why the delay in *Gulag* was not of her doing. If only he had allowed the work to remain in her hands, it would be out by now. She spoke firmly, controlling her anger. The details were complex, but she knew every one intimately; they were engraved in her heart.

His face seemed to relax, and he led her into the kitchen, where he struggled with the still-unfamiliar electric stove to boil water for tea. She brought a box containing a rich assortment of cookies, which clearly delighted him. His face darkened; he criticized her; she fought back; he seemed grudgingly to accept her account as true. Then he got up and paced, and spoke of salvos and counterattacks and victories. "The KGB burnt my camp jacket," he said. "Alya went to try to retrieve it but it was too late. They are fetishists, these policemen. They must have thought by destroying my old *bushlat* they were destroying me." He touched his new blue ski jacket, resting over his chair. "I miss it."

Suddenly his voice rose again: "Olga Vadimovna, had *The Gulag Archipelago* come out in time, they never would have dared expel me! I had a fabulous strategy worked out. . . ."

He spoke at length, and joyfully, of the books he intended to write. She had to return to Geneva, where she was staying. He walked her to the trolley-bus stop in the gray, moist twilight. Hands in the pockets of his ski jacket as he walked away, he showed his ability to blend into the landscape, the vanished *zek*.

A week later, the problem of the archives apparently solved, he was ready to welcome his family. With the help of Liusha and others his wife had managed to pack up everything and get "dangerous" material ghosted out of the country. The government granted exit visas for Alya's son Dmitri, and Katya, her mother. Sanya had also requested a visa for Aunt Irina; but not surprisingly she decided not to leave Georgievsk for Zurich. Liusha promised to act as go-between in making sure the old lady was all right.

At an emotional farewell party on 28 March attended by dissidents, some Western reporters, her ex-husband, and other friends, Alya spoke with a blend of sorrow, determination, and dedication: "It is painful to part from Russia, painful that our children are condemned to a life without a homeland, painful and difficult to leave friends who are not protected." They could remove her husband bodily, but could never separate his spirit from Russia. "And even if his books are now set ablaze on bonfires, their existence in his homeland is indestructible, just as Solzhenitsyn's love for Russia is indestructible. My place is beside him, but leaving Russia is excruciatingly painful."[9]

43

Friendly Fire

His vocation—he knew no other—
was to change the course of history. . . .
—*LENIN IN ZURICH*

FOURTEEN HUNDRED POUNDS OF LUGGAGE WENT WITH SANYA'S family: the innocuous part of his library and archive, and his favorite old-fashioned desk, given to him by an admirer of *Ivan Denisovich*.

As he met them at the airport, he at last changed his watch from Moscow time.

An armored car with a machine gun, and police with automatic rifles, greeted the plane. Dr. Heeb's car, with Sanya in the passenger seat, had been allowed onto the tarmac; behind a fence reporters and photographers jostled for position. Allowed onto the plane to greet his family in private, Sanya emerged with Yermolai and Ignat (Yermosha and Igonya) on either arm, his wife beside him, with the recovering Stepan (Styopa) in a portable cot. It made a good pose. A reporter called: "All's well that ends well?" He answered, "Yes."[1] That was the only word they were getting.

Just before his family's arrival, Sanya had penned a note to Olga Carlisle and sent it to her Paris address by way of his Russian-language publisher, YMCA Press. Olga received it, unsealed, as she was preparing to fly home. She read, over a coffee at a bustling workers' café, where once Russian painters had gathered: "Olga Vadimovna, I am very sorry that during the week you were able to come to Zurich, Dr. Heeb was absent and I had no information to counter yours during our conversation. Upon his return I have learned: that in June 1973 he requested that you give him the English translation, but you answered that you could not do this without Tom Whitney's consent and in view of the lack of final readiness of the translation; that in October 1973, having received three volumes of 'translation,' Dr. Heeb was not informed—and has learned from me only now—that this was a so-called 'unedited translation,' and that the work of your collective on Volume 1 was never shown to him."

She could hardly believe what she was reading. She knew that Dr. Heeb had requested only the Russian text, not the English translations, in June 1973; she knew she had explained, over a lunch, "painstakingly and repeatedly" for his imperfect English, that only one volume was so far edited; and knew that, when she had asked the Harper & Row lawyer to put the work on volume 1 at Dr. Heeb's disposal, she had been told that he did not want it.

But was the confusion Dr. Heeb's? Or Solzhenitsyn's? It was impossible to tell.[2]

Actually the relations between Sanya and his lawyer were not particularly warm. After the first encounter at Böll's house there were no more bear hugs. The Russian did not take to Heeb's dry decorum, nor to his socialism. Finally Sanya dismissed him as his lawyer, following a blazing row involving also an Italian agent and a French publisher. Sanya decided Heeb was incompetent at handling literary affairs. Heeb was left feeling wounded and bitter; and perhaps Olga's broodingly Slavic lips twitched in a mirthless smile.

There was as yet no hint of that breakup when Alya joined her husband: but he was already, she found, enmeshed in political controversy; already a "dissident" among the Western intelligentsia. To the thousands who hero-worshipped him, he was the indomitable fighter for democracy and human rights; the great majority assumed that his works were—as Böll had expressed it—for the liberation of socialism. But now the shock and disillusionment that had overcome Liusha Chukovskaya and Mirra Petrova was to become widespread. On 2 March YMCA published the Russian text of his polemic *Letter to the Soviet Leaders*. Translations followed at once. The whole fifteen-thousand-word text appeared in the *Sunday Times* of London, while the *New York Times* devoted a full page to it. For the first time Solzhenitsyn addressed the public in his own voice, free from any aesthetic constraints, and the assumption that, like Sakharov and other dissidents, he yearned to transform his country into a liberal democracy was swept away. Harry Schwarz in the *Saturday Review/World* put it in terms Americans could easily understand: "No one . . . can doubt that if Solzhenitsyn had been an American citizen in 1972 he would have voted for Richard Nixon against George McGovern. . . ."

The *Letter* made it clear that both West and East were monstrous consequences of the false turning we know as the eighteenth-century Enlightenment. The West, steeped in trivia, complacency, and materialism, was facing catastrophe. Probably it still had enough flexibility to save itself, by realizing that the doctrine of material progress was false. Earth's resources were finite; the "endless, infinite progress dinned into our heads by the dreamers of the Enlightenment cannot be accomplished on it."

Russia had, above all, to cast off the dead weight of Marxism, "that murky whirlwind of *Progressive Ideology* that swept in on us from the West at the end of the last century and that has tormented and ravaged our soul quite enough." Mother Russia must turn inward, abandoning its interference in the Third World, withdrawing from its Eastern European empire, including the Baltic states. It should concentrate on its national heartland, Siberia and the Northeast.

There, in that still virgin land, Russia could avoid repeating the disastrous errors of the twentieth century—industry, roads, and cities, for example. He wanted towns that were human and friendly; houses with gardens and which were no more than two stories high. "And if anybody has to dive underground at crossroads, let it be the vehicles and not the old, the young, and the sick." Collective farms should be abolished, as should compulsory military service.

Many of his environmental suggestions have since become the orthodoxy of "green" politics. Since then, we have seen Chernobyl, the death of the Aral Sea. His ideas may still seem Utopian, but can no longer be dismissed—as they were by many commentators at the time—as proof that he was slightly crazed.

He was not, he said, convinced by that "democracy run riot" of the West, where every four years there was a paroxysm of party against party. These parties represented only differing interests, and had no strong moral foundation. The system led to weakness in the face of shifting, random majorities, not to mention determined evil, such as terrorist campaigns. Better an authoritarian government, with an observed constitution, freedom of expression, and a modest use of state power, than a "democracy" of cynical and valueless opposing parties always needing to please the most influential part of the electorate. What was more important was to have a grass-roots democracy, and he advocated bringing back the soviets. They "were in no way dependent upon ideology"; they arose out of the people and consulted them closely.

So long as an authoritarian order did not degenerate into tyranny, there was much to be said for the stability it created. The old order in Russia had preserved intact its people's spiritual health, thanks to the moral foundation of Orthodoxy. He believed that, today, Christianity was "the only living spiritual force capable of undertaking the spiritual healing of Russia"; but he did not ask for it to have special privileges. He did not even ask for Marxism to be outlawed.

However close to the truth might have been his analysis of party politics and the dominance of influential groups, no one wished to question anything so fundamental. Yet, far from being antidemocratic, he was attempting to strip democracy of its ingrained injustices, by espousing the rights of local communities.

Nor was he, or is he, a "nationalist" in the sense of wanting aggrandizement. Quite the reverse; he wanted Russia to cast off its empire. Responding to critics, among them Sakharov, he pointed out that he was calling for peaceful withdrawal of the Soviet Union on a scale far exceeding that envisaged by détente, yet he was being accused of being a nationalist! He believed passionately in nations as embodying the character of a people.

It was profoundly unfashionable to attach a mystical value to nationhood. America had its flag saluting, to be sure, but America was a melting pot of races. Solzhenitsyn was attacked for his questioning of Enlightenment values, just as inevitably as Darwin was attacked for arguing that we are descended from apes. It was just unthinkable not to be enlightened. . . . Also, of course, his polemical style was so much less subtle and sensitive than his imaginative writing. "His vocation was to change the course of history," as he writes of Lenin, that earlier exile in Zurich.

Tatiana Tolstoya, in an essay of 1992, finds many similarities between Lenin's ideas and Solzhenitsyn's. Both had a place for soviets, forms of local "self-determination." "According to Lenin, socialism is a matter of inventory and control; according to Solzhenitsyn, the future of Russia is a matter of inventory and control. For Lenin, there is the wisdom of the party. For Solzhenitsyn, there is the wisdom of the elders. For Lenin, the intelligentsia is 'shit.' For Solzhenitsyn, it is filth, pus, hypocrisy. . . . Solzhenitsyn believes that 'party rivalry distorts the national will.' Lenin thought much the same and destroyed all parties save his own."[3]

This seems specious; Lenin despised Christian or bourgeois morality, and believed in getting what he wanted by terror. Lenin's "dream" and Solzhenitsyn's have nothing in common.

The *New York Times*, his firm supporter for so many years, attracted his special rage by finessing a "scoop." At Dr. Heeb's request, Michael Scammell had offered them the English translation of the *Letter*. They had declined, but sent a correspondent to the YMCA Press in Paris, claiming (according to Scammell) that he had authorized them to give them a copy of the Russian text. They then got three of Scammell's friends in London to translate that text. In so doing they found that Solzhenitsyn had originally, in the text sent to Brezhnev, put forward a stronger anti-Western slant. He had toned the *Letter* down for Western consumption, omitting—for example—the belief that America was "ungovernable."

At the time, many sensible Americans might have agreed that it was. It was a turbulent era. A war had been fought and was about to be lost. Leaders had been gunned down. Of the last three presidents, the first had been assassinated, the second pulled out of a second term because of the hostility to war in Vietnam (for Solzhenitsyn, a vital war against Communism), and the third resigned in disgrace—for what seemed, to many Russians, a trivial offense, brought down by a campaigning liberal establishment. In *Lenin in Zurich*, Lenin reflects on the effect of the ongoing European war on Russia: "An anti-Tsarist campaign will be mounted by socialist newspapers in various countries, and the excitement of Tsar-baiting will spread to their neighbours on the right, the liberals—that is to say, to the dominant section of the press throughout the world. A newspaper crusade against the Tsar! In this connection it is particularly important to capture public opinion in the United States."[4] Overtones of Watergate are audible.

Solzhenitsyn's original *Letter* mentioned a particular famous case in which, in his view, liberal pressure had damaged the state: the Ellsberg trial, "in which a judge, flouting his obligatory independence in order to pander to the passions of society, acquits a man who, during an exhausting war, steals and publishes Defence Department documents." Daniel Ellsberg, convinced of the immorality of his country's conduct in Southeast Asia, had copied the secret official history of the Vietnam War and passed it to the *New York Times*. In May 1973, a federal judge dismissed all charges against him on the grounds of government misconduct: a break-in to Ellsberg's psychiatrist's office.

Olga Carlisle recalls in her memoir a dinner party at which Ellsberg and his wife were present. When conversation turned to the just published *Lenin in Zurich*, Ellsberg was all concentration. He confessed that Solzhenitsyn had been one of his inspirations when he decided to release the Pentagon Papers. At the time he read *The First Circle*, he was working for the Rand Corporation, engrossed just as Solzhenitsyn had been in a not dissimilar institute. Of course, he was not a prisoner, but he felt isolated. "I even felt a parallel between our predicaments, and eventually the time came when I too had to leave the safety of my work and speak out."

Then one day he learned that Solzhenitsyn was singling him out as a traitor in time of war. He was shaken; he remained deeply affected by that. He had tried to emulate him; of course, in far less dangerous conditions. Nor did he mean to compare the Soviet regime with the American. And yet . . .[5]

It is a poignant juxtaposition: the Russian and the American dissident. They simply don't understand each other. For Solzhenitsyn, the mortal defensive war against Communism was humanity's last stand; it took precedence over everything; over an American liberal's conscience leading to notoriety, over a Russian woman's leading to suicide. Both Ellsberg and Voronyanskaya had broken trust in this most vital of battles.

His accusation of American weakness seemed to be borne out by the extreme pusillanimity of the White House toward him. Nixon, a man clinging to a reed in a torrent, had no words of welcome for him. Secretary of State Kissinger made sure Solzhenitsyn remained frozen out after Nixon's departure. Annoyed by American press reactions to his *Letter*, Solzhenitsyn was slow in visiting the United States. When he finally reached Washington, D.C., in June 1975, to deliver a speech to union members, the White House remained silent. Ford did not invite him round because, an aide said, the Russian was here "promoting his books," and the president felt he ought not to support a commercial venture. (This, a week or so after President Ford had posed with a beauty queen and Pelé, the Brazilian soccer star.) Later the reason was changed to Ford's not wanting a meeting "without substance." Ford's intellect presumably could find nothing of substance to talk about with the author of *The Gulag Archipelago*.

One State Department official tried to explain to some student interns that this man—a man who had fought the Nazis and the Bolsheviks, demanded freedom of speech and religion, the rule of morality, grass-roots democracy, ecology before profit, an end to military conscription, and an end to the Soviet empire—was ideologically akin to Himmler. "Let's face it, he's just about a Fascist," he remarked.

Simon Winchester, the English *Guardian*'s Washington correspondent, praised Ford for his "reality and integrity" in denying a hearing to the "shaggy author," the "hairy polemicist" who had become the "darling of the redneck population" after talking for an hour and a half to thousands of "sagging beer bellies." The politically correct *Guardian* would instantly have sacked Mr. Winchester had the "shaggy" writer he attacked been a Sikh or an Orthodox Jew, or if, instead of "sagging beer bellies," he had referred to an audience of "slit-eyed Asians"; but these insults were fine.

The great majority of Americans, beer bellies or not, told the White House in no uncertain terms that Solzhenitsyn had been treated disgracefully. The White House backtracked, but it was too late.

Nothing must endanger détente. The Americans and Soviets were due to link up in space. Most Democrats concurred with the policy. The Politburo must have been laughing its head off—America was truly spineless! If only Kissinger and Ford had been in charge during the Cuban crisis. . . . As though the Soviets would have canceled détente if Ford had offered Solzhenitsyn a martini!

The deportation was paying off, in several different ways, and Solzhenitsyn was contributing mightily.

Andropov reported the satisfying news that "Solzhenitsyn's family is currently suffering serious hardships in everyday life. For example, Solzhenitsyn's wife stated in a phone call to her Moscow friends that the conditions of life for Soviet citizens in Switzerland are bad, and tried to persuade them 'not to come here of their own will.' "[6] There could hardly have been material hardships; but Alya felt the loss of her country more keenly even than he. She was more isolated, and knew no German. Sanya was away at the farm during the week, writing. Alya, as well as continuing to be her husband's secretary and assistant, had also to worry about the health and happiness of four children. She coped staunchly, as she always would.

Mayor Widmer and his wife befriended her; Mrs. Widmer started to learn Russian, and took her off walking in the mountains. Sanya joined them whenever it was not too hot. The four of them would sing Russian songs as they hiked. The Russian couple also relied on their new friends for a social life—Sanya was unusually willing, indeed eager, to go to dinner parties arranged by them so that they could meet local people. Perhaps his distance from his former wife, psychologically as well as physically, was allowing him to feel more relaxed.

He enjoyed seeing democracy working at the local, small-scale level in Switzerland. Visiting Bern, soon after his arrival, to meet the Minister of Justice concerning residence, he was impressed that the square, right in front of the Bundeshaus, was crowded with peasants and farmers and market stalls—so different from the vast, empty squares around most government buildings in the Soviet Union. Still more impressive was his visit to Appenzell, a village on the Austrian border, for the canton elections. He told his guide, the editor of *Neue Zürcher Zeitung*, he wished to keep out of the limelight; but when he went to church—it was a Sunday—everybody recognized him; and on his emergence he was being applauded and asked for autographs. When he explained he only signed books, the village bookshop was opened, and copies of Solzhenitsyn at once sold out.

He was impressed by the ritual of the elections, with all the men carrying swords or daggers as a sign of their right to vote. His guide apologized for the reactionary views expressed in some of the speeches; for example, there was strong opposition to giving full voting rights to some Italian residents. "That's all right," their guest assured him; "if these people want to stay on their own and don't accept foreigners, that's all right by me, and you don't have to excuse it."[7] He was impressed by the way in which, by a show of hands, in ten minutes, all the policies were decided—conservatively—for the next year: no foreigners, no new taxes, no increase in the unemployment benefit. "It was the voice of the people. The question was irrevocably decided—without newspaper articles, without television commentaries, without senate commissions. . . ."

Appenzell's "mayor," Raymond Brogher, made a speech in which he boasted that the canton had kept its election procedure fundamentally unchanged for fifteen hundred years; it had never succumbed to the "madness of total freedom," believing that neither the individual nor the state could be guaranteed freedom without discipline and the preservation of honor. What mattered was not a beautiful constitution but the quality of the officeholders.

It was all sweet to the Russian's ears; it reminded him of the old soviets. He said at the postelection banquet that he was a fervent admirer of Swiss grass-roots democracy, which had grown "not out of the ideas of the Enlightenment but directly out of the ancient forms of the commune."[8]

He was waved off by the honored populace, leaving the village in its ancient enchantment, a fairy tale of alpenhorns and apron skirts, where the men decided matters without fuss and the women bore children and baked bread.

His former wife's shadow fell on him briefly, in the summer of 1974, when an Italian publisher brought out her memoirs (*Mio Marito Solgenitsyn*). Aggressively midwifed by Novosti, it painted a hostile portrait of him as a selfish egomaniac; and it was clear that Novosti had exploited the bitterness of a woman who was left with very little in her life except Novosti's short-lived interest. They had made savage cuts and changes late in the process without her knowledge or approval, she claimed. Even so, there were gleams of genuine feeling and memory showing through the distortions—the more so in the later English version, *Sanya*, where she managed to restore a little of her text. Hostile though the Natasha/Novosti book was, it was still too generous toward him for it to be published at home. To his credit, Sanya decided to stay silent. "What fools they are," he said. "If they had left it to her, she would have done me far more damage."[9]

He began to associate with some dissident Czech émigrés, thanks to a married couple whom he met early on and who were happy to be helpful. Dr. František Holub claimed to be a linguist who had been working in Romania on a Czech-Romanian dictionary; others said he was a diplomat. His wife, a native Russian, had worked for Pragokonzert, the organization responsible for musical tours. They had left Czechoslovakia after the Soviet invasion of 1968. According to Mayor Widmer, Mrs. Holub turned up at Solzhenitsyn's house one day, soon after his arrival, to offer the traditional Russian bread and salt.

Many of the Czechs to whom they introduced him were supporters of "socialism with a human face," and had been Party members; on some of these the famous exile did not make an altogether favorable impression. Andropov learned that he had appeared "an arrogant tsarist chauvinist."[10] No doubt the informant had emphasized the negative—others were honored and impressed.

Among those who turned up at the Holubs' city-center flat to meet the great man was a young writer called Tomas Rzhezach. He had done two surprising things: emigrated with his wife after 1968, which no one had expected, given his mediocrity and orthodoxy; and produced, after talentless years, a good spy novel. Possibly some Novosti editor had coached him line by line, in the manner of Western editors with illiterate celebrities. The Holubs introduced the starlet extravagantly and absurdly as "our Czech Solzhenitsyn." Rzhezach was not popular with the other Czechs because he had joined the exodus very late; but Dr. Holub explained to his compatriots that Solzhenitsyn had asked for him to be invited because of his fluent Russian. It was indeed fluent, and the two men talked for some time. The Russian, usually slow to trust, loaned him *Prussian Nights* to translate into Czech.[11]

Rzhezach took off back to Prague, leaving his wife and debts but taking *Prussian Nights*. Warned by the Zurich police that the Holubs were not all they appeared, the exile cut them from his life; but does not seem to have discovered that the "Czech Solzhenitsyn" owed his excellent Russian to having spent five years at a counterespionage college in Moscow. Where was Sanya's usually infallible intuition?

Presumably through Rzhezach, the KGB learned that Solzhenitsyn had no intention of lying low. He had plans to help organize the dissident movement more effectively, he told the Czechs, and had founded a "Russian Social Fund," financed by the royalties from *Gulag*, to assist the families of political prisoners. He planned to fight Communism by influencing the Soviet intelligentsia and youth, whereas Sakharov put his trust in international public opinion. Solzhenitsyn considered him—according to the Zurich source—"a crazy and irresponsible person."

Letting the three Czechs into his life was a rare lapse. People who visited him were instructed not to tell anyone. Secrecy was as natural to him as breathing; he liked to sit in the middle of a web of intrigue and have charge of all the independent strands: the KGB code name for him, "Spider," was well chosen. They might still, so easily, arrange an accident . . . But in fact it was Dr. Holub who had a fatal road accident.

Two deaths relating to the melancholy saga of Olga Carlisle (whom he calls "ill-starred" in *Invisible Allies*) occurred at around this time. His first glimpse of Olga's parents had been in October 1964, at which meeting he had found the sixty-year-old Vadim to be "a gentleman of the old school—reserved, rather dry, a man of complete integrity."[12] He and his wife had felt honored to be asked to smuggle all his work up to and including *The First Circle*, on microfilm, through the customs. It was for Russia, her literature, and her camps—Vadim's own brother had been imprisoned. In the years since, the Andreyevs had sent many gifts—medicine, baby food, a tape recorder, stationery. The Solzhenitsyns visited them at their Genevan home, bringing an enormous box of chocolates as a token of gratitude.

Sanya also brought, writes their daughter, "a somewhat muffled confirmation of his displeasure with our performance in his service." The old couple were too stunned at first to take it in. "He is at best a Soviet character," Olga Carlisle believes. "Civilized Russians do not do such things." Having seen Alya's "managerial" bearing in a TV documentary, she wonders if his wife had encouraged him to proclaim their daughter's "dishonor." Eventually "my father wrote him a letter defending our honor, but on the day this letter reached Solzhenitsyn in Zurich, my father died of sudden heart failure. My mother received a letter of condolence from Solzhenitsyn. It explained why he had not revealed* my villainy to my parents when they had last met: 'I understood that it would have been painful for you to learn the disagreeable truth, evident to all in America who have had anything to do with this affair.'

"My mother died shortly after. She who had been so brave as a girl in the Lubyanka and as a young woman under the German Occupation, spent the last months of her life in a state of depression. . . . In her mind the ruthless Bolsheviks had once again overwhelmed the naïve SRs." She who had been interrogated by Dzerzhinsky in her youth, and devastated by Solzhenitsyn in her old age, "died believing that after six decades of Communism there was no hope for Russia."[13]

The Andreyevs had done him great service; could Sanya not have let

---

*Revealed more clearly, she means, presumably.

them go to their grave in peace? Why was it so necessary to tell them their daughter had not come up to the mark?

He would probably say the truth, as he saw it, demanded that he speak out; and that same imperative of truth, possibly with more substance, caused him to sponsor the publication in Paris of a book by a deceased Soviet critic. The work argued that Mikhail Sholokhov had plagiarized most of *And Quiet Flows the Don* from Fyodor Kryukov, a Cossack who had died in the Civil War. Sanya contributed an introduction. Could Sholokhov have completed the first volume by the age of twenty? And could an *inogorodni*, a Russian outsider, have been capable of penetrating the Cossack world, even in its style, so authentically? The case against Sholokhov's sole authorship is indeed strong, although Kryukov's authorship has not been established.

A great Russian exile, seventy-five-year-old Vladimir Nabokov, was living with his wife at the Palace Hotel in Montreux. Though regretting that Nabokov had given up writing about Russian themes, Sanya admired his talent greatly, and had proposed him for the Nobel Prize in 1971. Nabokov wrote him a note of welcome to the West and extended an open invitation to visit. In the fall of 1974, planning a driving trip that would take them through Montreux, Sanya wrote to Nabokov, asking whether he and his wife might call on a certain day. If so, could he please confirm the arrangement? No response came, unsuccessfully they tried to phone; when they reached the Palace Hotel, they slowed the car at the end of the drive, decided he might be ill or too busy, and drove on.

Inside, the Nabokovs were sitting in a private dining room, silent, wondering, while waiters poised to serve lunch for a party of four. An hour passed; the lunch grew cold; still they waited, in vain. A few weeks later Nabokov expressed his distress and puzzlement to another recent exile, Vladimir Maximov. Maximov proceeded to Zurich to see the Solzhenitsyns. When he discovered they had expected a confirmation, he phoned Nabokov and explained the misunderstanding. But Solzhenitsyn and Nabokov did not speak on the phone, and never met.

Olga Carlisle too had waited—for an agreed signal from Solzhenitsyn, a request for the works of Corneille—before launching volume 1 of *Gulag*. According to her, it had never arrived; she had even vetoed a suggestion by Harper & Row that they go ahead and publish, because the signal had not come. Yet he was convinced she had let him down, and thereby caused his expulsion from Russia.[14] Freud—who had a similar "misunderstanding" causing a nonmeeting with Jung in 1912—might have said of the Nabokov-Solzhenitsyn debacle, "They weren't too unhappy not to meet"; and of the absent signal, "He kept hoping he wouldn't have to take the risk of exploding his bomb."

A number of other dissidents beside Maximov left the Soviet Union in this period; the most notable, Sinyavsky. In July 1974 the Rostropoviches were given permission to go to the West. Galina parted with especial love and agony from a sobbing Dmitri Shostakovich—he was terminally ill, and they knew they would not meet again—and the bare stage of the Bolshoi, which she embraced full length. When *From Under the Rubble* was published in Paris in November 1974, Shafarevich, the principal coauthor, spoke at a press conference in Moscow. He strongly criticized the recent waves of migration—excepting Solzhenitsyn, because he had had no choice—which were denuding the country of its culture. The voluntary exiles had not been able to stand the pressure that believers had endured for decades; they lacked the necessary spiritual qualities. He singled out Sinyavsky, for a phrase in a recent émigré article: "Russia, you bitch, you'll pay for this too!" ("This" referred to her treatment of the Jewish population.) Well, said Shafarevich, Sinyavsky was absolutely right to leave for somewhere he could be more comfortable.

It was felt that Shafarevich was speaking for Solzhenitsyn; and indeed the latter had criticized voluntary exiles for running away, in a TV interview with Walter Cronkite. Two days after Shafarevich's press conference, speaking at his own press conference in Zurich, Solzhenitsyn also criticized Sinyavsky's remark, calling it a blasphemous and impermissible slur on "Mother Russia." Sinyavsky's satirical, abrasive style did not appeal to him—but also Sinyavsky, in the same article, had disparaged literary realism as being dated, and said the "flowering of prose" in twentieth-century Russia had not yet occurred.

Rostropovich wrote an open letter to Shafarevich in the émigré press, pointing out that he had faced artistic and spiritual extinction had he stayed in Russia; his exile was therefore hardly voluntary. He was too polite to add that he had suffered persecution entirely because of his help for Solzhenitsyn. It must have galled him to read Sanya's response to another counterattack, that of the émigré dissident Pavel Litvinov; everyone must have the right to emigrate, Sanya wrote, but it was "in all places and at all times a weakness, an abandonment of one's native land to the oppressors." The first two mass waves of migration, at the end of the great wars, had been "grand popular movements," but this third one was just a "thin slice" off the Jewish migration to Israel. And those who went should not use their freedom to make "malevolent attacks" on the motherland—another jab at Sinyavsky.

Perhaps he enjoyed the bursts of "friendly fire" at some of his old allies because for most of his time in Zurich he was living inside the dogmatic and aggressive skull of Vladimir Ilyich Lenin. Living here enabled him, miraculously, it seemed—to commune with his ghost, follow in his footsteps. It was natural, therefore, to go back over the Lenin chapters in different "knots" of his vast history, and enrich the portrait. Since it would be many years before the separate knots would appear, it made sense to publish the Lenin chapters as a separate work. So the idea of *Lenin in Zurich* was born.

Though ideologically Lenin and Solzhenitsyn are scarcely on the same planet, the Lenin of the book does strikingly remind us of his creator. There is the almost brutally insistent energy—the first sentence is "Yes, yes, yes, yes! . . ." He is crushed into a rigid working timetable: "A single wasted hour made Lenin ill." His womenfolk—the obedient, economical wife, Nadya, and the exciting, distant mistress, Inessa—"reading his looks and his movements right, did not pester him with trifles. . . ." Nadya would even go walking with them, à trois: as Solzhenitsyn had once proposed to Natasha. Lenin too had always refused to compromise; could make do with little food; was self-centered, knowing a lot of people but conveying the impression—through Solzhenitsyn's laconic, dynamic style—that the world revolved within his bald dome. He is a prophet, changing the world is his only vocation; only few will listen, so he is short-tempered and intolerant.

Nikita Struve, Solzhenitsyn's YMCA Press publisher, asked him in an interview of March 1976 whether there was something of himself in Lenin. He denied it, saying, "My sole task is to create the living Lenin, just as he was, ignoring all the official haloes and official legends. But to say that I am drawing on myself in creating Lenin is an utterly superficial assertion. I am drawing exclusively upon *him* himself."[15]

This seems to me both true and not true. Everything is genuinely determined by Solzhenitsyn's highly convincing sense of Lenin's psychological reality; yet that reality is so close to the author's, at so many points, that it is obviously much more than as he described it to Struve—building up psychological and everyday experience so as to understand another person in their own setting. How could Solzhenitsyn *not* have felt it was *he* who felt ill if an hour was wasted; he who was uncompromising, abstemious, secretive, needed women but only "in their place"? It is a striking fact that many of his most successful literary creations are embodiments of himself, to varying degrees: Nerzhin, Kostoglotov, Vorotyntsev, Ivan Denisovich Shukhov (Sanya without education), and Lenin (Sanya without conscience).

In his childhood and youth, Lenin had been his idol. Even in the Lubyanka cell he had found it blasphemous when someone said, "Ilyich, go and empty the piss pot!" And now? Responding to criticism from Boris Souverine, who had known Lenin, he wrote: "How can anyone blacken Lenin's name more than he himself did by ordering the execution of peasants for failing to clear away snow? . . . What can anyone say about Lenin and Trotsky . . . that would be worse than simply recalling how they created the first and greatest totalitarianism the world has seen, and how they devised the methods of mass terror, including the technique of drowning people imprisoned in barges (thus anticipating the gas chambers)? . . ."[16]

He wrote *Lenin in Zurich* out of a highly charged tension: drawing his character to a considerable extent out of his own psyche, but with the knowledge that Lenin had laid down the foundations of the Gulag Archipelago. Solzhenitsyn had written in the work of that name that the line between good and evil ran through every human heart; Lenin was the dark side of his own heart.

But not everything in *Lenin in Zurich* is dependent on the powerful evocation of Lenin and his world. At the opposite extreme from Solzhenitsyn's polemical writing is his amazing gift for metaphor, for symbolic images, which can take us into a deeper reality in an instant. For example: "The dark water from the depths of the lake runs unhindered through the fisherman's net, and Inessa with her concept of free love was not to be caught in the net of class analysis."

At last, in June 1974, the English-speaking world was about to read a work that was both momentous history and a work of literature in which the creative water poured inexhaustibly through the fisherman's net.

44

Arkhipelág Gulág

> The police made a prisoner stand barefoot on an iron floor
> at a time of intense frost; the man died in hospital, of which
> Prince Meshchersky was president, and he told the story
> afterwards with horror.
> —HERZEN, *Childhood, Youth, and Exile*

> I was remembering my friends, and all I saw was corpses,
> mountains of corpses. I'm not exaggerating,
> I *mean* mountains. . . . I'm grieving all the time.
> —SHOSTAKOVICH, *Testimony*

WAS THERE EVER A MORE ASTONISHING, ATTENTION SEIZING, PER-
fect opening to a major work than the disarmingly homespun beginning of
the preface to *The Gulag Archipelago*? . . .

"In 1949 some friends and I came upon a noteworthy news item in
Nature, a magazine of the Academy of Sciences. It reported in tiny type
that in the course of excavations on the Kolyma River a subterranean ice
lens had been discovered which was actually a frozen stream—and in it
were found frozen specimens of prehistoric fauna some tens of thousands
of years old. Whether fish or salamander, these were preserved in so fresh
a state, the scientific correspondent reported, that those present immediately broke open the ice encasing the specimens and devoured them *with
relish* on the spot."

Solzhenitsyn proceeds to imagine the astonishment of the small readership of the journal, as they contemplated the thought of still fresh salamander flesh, but says that even fewer could have known "the genuine and
heroic meaning" of this "incautious" report. He and his friends (the Marfino
zeks) understood at once, and could visualize the frenzied scene as the ice
was broken up, and chunks of the prehistoric flesh were dragged to the
bonfire to be thawed and bolted down. "We understood because we ourselves were the same kind of people. . . . We, too, were from that powerful
tribe of *zeks*, unique on the face of the earth, the only people who could
devour prehistoric salamander *with relish*."[1] He straightaway introduces the
reader to the concept of the Gulag as a country, an "amazing country."
"Gulag" is an acronym for *Glavnoye upravleniye lagerei* (Main Administration of the Camps), and it appears that Solzhenitsyn was the first to use
the word as an independent noun. After his introduction of that powerful

metaphor of Gulag = country, he at once, still within the first page, further defines and enriches it by identifying that country as being in the form of an archipelago; an archipelago of which Kolyma was "the greatest and most famous island," its "pole of ferocity."

Yet, amazingly, many people did not even guess at the presence of that archipelago—which psychologically was fused into a continent. Only those who had been there knew it properly and they, on returning from it, were stricken dumb. When a bit of the truth was revealed, it was sealed up again because "if you dwell on the past you'll lose an eye." But the proverb, he pointed out, goes on to say, "Forget the past and you'll lose both eyes."

Someday, he predicted, the Archipelago would be brought to light, like— another beautiful comparison—"some improbable salamander." *He* could not be so bold as to relate the Archipelago's history, but he has been entrusted with personal reports and letters, and has absorbed his own eleven years there. He has come "almost to love that monstrous world. . . ." He will try to give some account of the bones and flesh of that salamander— which he declares is still alive.

Metaphor, Aristotle claimed, was the soul of poetry; and Mandelstam had that essence in mind when he wrote that poetry was like an airplane that, in midair, could launch a second plane—while itself flying on—and then that second plane could launch a third, and so on. There is no finer example of the exuberant creativity of metaphor than the preface to—the Russian title has even more bite—*Arkhipelág Gulág*. From frozen salamander to Gulag and its "tribe" to Archipelago—to the whole of "monstrous" Bolshevik Russia as a giant salamander. . . . Despite the horror of the subject matter, the exuberant creativity of Solzhenitsyn's metaphoric sense has an intoxicating effect on the reader. *Here*, one feels, is a writer with the courage, force, and genius to destroy the Medusa by gazing at the monster in the mirror of art.

It is worth reminding ourselves of the extent, in brutal round numbers of deaths, of the horrors he set himself to evoke. Professor I. A. Kurganov, an émigré statistician, analyzed official statistics and came up with a total of some sixty-six million deaths in the war of the state against the people. Dmitri Panin, in *The Notebooks of Sologdin*, on the basis of his own and friends' researches, arrived at the following estimations, which bear out Kurganov's figures:[2]

Years	Cause of Death	Victims (in millions)
1917–21	Shootings, tortures	6–12
1922–23	Famine in the Volga region and other areas	7.5–13

1922–28	Destruction of the old social classes, the clergy, and believers	2–3
1929–33	Liquidation of kulaks; organized famine	16
1934–41 (up to outbreak of war)	Mass executions in prisons and camps; starvation in camps; artificially created epidemics	7
1941–42	Destruction of *zeks* through hunger and overwork	7.5
1943–45	Death in Stalin's wartime camps	5
1946–53	Death in Stalin's camps after the war	6

This gives, at the lowest estimates, almost sixty million. No one, Solzhenitsyn asserts, has seriously disputed Kurganov's figures; the most cautious estimates say that at least forty-five million died.

Add the thirty-one million now officially admitted to have been lost in the Great Patriotic War: a fifth of the population! (When and where, Solzhenitsyn asked, had a people ever laid down so many in a war?)[3] Add the living dead, who somehow survived with breath still in their bodies, but with lives and family relationships shattered; add the grief-stricken relatives of victims, and the millions of young women who never had the chance to become wives and mothers. It becomes clear that when Akhmatova spoke in *Requiem* of "a hundred million of my people" crying through her "tormented mouth," she was not using hyperbole.

Easy to understand how Shostakovich, seeing mountains of corpses, was overwhelmed by a sense of the unbearable gray despair of his life, in which "there were no particular happy moments." What is astounding is the absolute vitality of Solzhenitsyn that allowed him to begin his threnody for sixty million with a piece of savage black humor and startling poetic metaphors.

Only a man given to extremes—one who could withdraw for two winters into the Estonian wilderness, without thought for anyone, and write *double shifts* each day, for month after month—could have created this work. Had he been gentle, friendly, "nice," like Sakharov, he could never have written it. Had he lolled congenially in bars with Tvardovsky and the *Novy Mir* editors he could never have written it. Sakharov himself, though knowing more than most about the Gulag, found his first reading of the work a "shattering experience." It happened right after New Year's Day 1974; Dmitri, Svetlova's teenage son, paid the Sakharovs an unexpected visit. Elena

Bonner offered him a glass of tea, but he refused; they could see he was bursting to tell them something. He went to the bathroom and returned with a book he had hidden under his clothes: the first volume of the Russian text, smuggled in from Paris.[4] It is a rather touching scene, showing that Solzhenitsyn did truly value Sakharov, despite their differences. Minutes after receiving the gift, Sakharov and his wife were "devouring the masterpiece." "Angry, mournful, sardonic" are the adjectives Sakharov finds to describe Solzhenitsyn's style; all are true; but there is also a grim exultation in his own power to testify with such brilliant, unstemmable *ferocity*. He had no scrap of doubt: if people could only read his book, Communism would start to die, the great salamander would twitch a few times and lie still.

Who can say that he was wrong?

The Archipelago metaphor provides the formal scheme of the work and recurs in many of the chapter titles. Thus: "The Ships of the Archipelago," "The Ports of the Archipelago," "From Island to Island," "The Archipelago Rises from the Sea": this chapter, in Part III, an account of the history of Solovetsky Island, a monastic foundation in the White Sea. It had been used as a tsarist prison; from the sixteenth century to the end of the Romanov dynasty, it had held a total of 316 inmates. The Bolsheviks, on 28 October 1929, *killed* that number in a single night. Solzhenitsyn also uses the cancer metaphor that had touched him so closely, by calling one chapter "The Archipelago Metastasizes."

Gulag is a highly repetitive work. As he himself observed, "Nothing but the same thing over and over again." He has been entrusted with the experiences of hundreds of men and women who have written to him or talked to him; he cannot be false to their momentous experience just because of "the tedium of it all!"[5] As Joseph Brodsky observed, "We can only welcome the fact that he had enough aesthetic intuition—paradoxical though it may seem—to reject the 'sense of moderation' bred in us by nineteenth-century literature."[6] Solzhenitsyn is by nature an immoderate writer; and in the theme of the Gulag he found a subject exactly suited to him.

Gulag is a work totally devoid of egoism. He allows the voices of his comrades, dead and alive, to tell their own story. He is merely their chronicler. Though he was working alone, in that Estonian farmhouse and elsewhere, we feel the presence of others, ghostly voices; he becomes their medium. Through a multiplicity of styles, as Elisabeth Markstein has observed, "one might say that the material itself had *begun to speak*."[7]

The work becomes not simply a chronicle of overwhelming barbarity—though that would have been more than enough—but a work of profound spirituality. The normal values of life are overturned. Here, for example, is the author describing how he was being transferred, a single prisoner with two guards, in normal transport from one of the "paradise islands" (*sharashkas*) to another. . . . You hear strange and insignificant conversations, he writes, "about some husband who beats up his wife or has left her; and some mother-in-law who, for some reason, does not get along with her daughter-in-law. . . . You listen to all this, and the goose pimples of rejection run up and down your spine. . . ." The only one alive there, you realize, is incorporeal *you;* all the others are mistaken in thinking themselves alive. . . .

> And how can you bring it home to them? By an inspiration? By a vision? A dream? Brothers! People! Why has life been given you? In the deep, deaf stillness of midnight, the doors of the death cells are being swung open—and great-souled people are being dragged out to be shot. On all the railroads of the country this very minute, right now, people who have just been fed salt herring are licking their dry lips with bitter tongues. They dream of the happiness of stretching out one's legs and of the relief one feels after going to the toilet. In Or-otukan the earth thaws only in summer and only to the depth of three feet—and only then can they bury the bones of those who died during the winter. And you have the right to arrange your own life under the blue sky and the hot sun, to get a drink of water, to stretch, to travel wherever you like without a convoy. So what's this about unwiped feet? And what's this about a mother-in law? What about the main thing in life, all its riddles? If you want, I'll spell it out for you right now. Do not pursue what is illusory—property and position: all that is gained at the expense of your nerves decade after decade, and is confiscated in one fell night. Live with a steady superiority over life— don't be afraid of misfortune, and do not yearn after happiness; it is, after all, all the same: the bitter doesn't last forever, and the sweet never fills the cup to overflowing. It is enough if you don't freeze in the cold and if thirst and hunger don't claw at your insides. If your back isn't broken, if your feet can walk, if both arms can bend, if both eyes see, and if both ears hear, then whom should you envy? And why? Our envy of others devours us most of all. Rub your eyes and purify your heart—and prize above all else in the world those who love you and who wish you well. Do not hurt them or scold them, and never part from any of them in anger; after all, you simply do not know: it might be your last act before your arrest, and that will be how you are imprinted in their memory![18]

It is hardly surprising that he felt the "infantile West" could teach him nothing. Yet this wise, compassionate, and spiritual Solzhenitsyn seems to have more in common with the internal exile in Kok Terek—that lonely but immensely attractive man who gave himself unstintingly to his school-children—than with the later warrior who fought the state and various unsatisfactory individuals.

No matter; he became hardened, he made himself into an entire army. And he never lost sight of the fact that, while *he* could "bless" his prison, because it had rid him of the evil illusions of his youth, millions of others had simply been destroyed by it. If not killed, their health wrecked, as happened to Shalamov. Solzhenitsyn had offered to coauthor *Gulag* with Shalamov, but the survivor of eighteen years in Magaden did not have the strength. He had scarcely enough strength to smile when he read, in the *Notes of Maria Volkonskaya*, that the Decembrist prisoners in Nerchinsk had a norm of 118 pounds of ore to mine and load each day: his own daily norm on the Kolyma having been 28,800 pounds.

The English and French translations of *The Gulag Archipelago*, volume 1, appeared finally in the spring and summer of 1974. The muddle that had characterized the history of the English version carried on right up to publication. Michael Scammell, working with Thomas Whitney on the latter's rough draft, had no idea that a revised and edited version of volume 1 already existed, nor that Olga Carlisle was in any way connected with the process. Five years after the Carlisles received the manuscript with instructions to prepare it for publication, Scammell found himself with just three weeks to revise almost seven hundred pages.

Inadequacies of translation did not lessen the huge impact made by the work's long-heralded appearance. W. L. Webb of the *Guardian* wrote that "To live now and not to know this work is to be a kind of historical fool missing a crucial part of the consciousness of the age." Vast numbers of people seemed to be taking that message to heart; two million copies of the American paperback alone were published. The work was "the most powerful single indictment of a political regime ever to be levelled in modern times . . . The Soviet leaders cannot, just by ignoring it themselves or attempting to smother it with falsehood, consign it to oblivion or cause it to remain without consequences. It is too large for the craw of the Soviet propaganda machine. It will stick there, with increasing discomfort, until it has done its work" (George Kennan, *New York Review of Books*).

But it was intellectual France whose craw became most immediately uncomfortable. Indeed its love affair with the Soviet Union never recovered. Some of its aging leaders had seemed, after Khrushchev's revelations and the suppression of Hungary, to be waiting unconsciously for a coup de grâce: Nina Berberova has mordant pages describing how such committed Communists as Sartre and de Beauvoir, Aragon and Elsa Triolet, had sunk into the gloom of old age, fear of death, and loss of faith. "What shall we do?" Sartre asks his lover. "Where shall we go? Whom shall we be with?" Yet, clinging on, they condemn the repression of Hungary, then visit Moscow determined to meet only, de Beauvoir confessed, with the privileged class. (And Solzhenitsyn magnificently refused to meet them.) The last rites: street demonstrations against de Gaulle by aged comrades who marvel at the thrill of traveling by metro—they have only ever used taxis. But now—even before *Gulag*—de Beauvoir mourned, "A whirlwind is carrying me to the grave, and I am trying not to think."[9]

Such pampered idealists may have found personal extinction less unbearable than the whirlwind of *The Gulag Archipelago*. It seems fitting that when Solzhenitsyn looked for an image that might bring home to readers, especially in the West, the size of the farthest Gulag "island," its "pole of ferocity," Kolyma with its hundred camps, he declared it was five times the size of France. Cozy Left Bank sidewalk cafés suddenly vanish in an endless expanse of permafrost.

45

T r a v e l s   a n d   B r a w l s

Pray God we too never have to make words, words, words,
the very marrow of our bones instead of the marks on the side of
the tube of the sixteenth brand of toothpaste now on sale.
—DENNIS POTTER[1]

IN DECEMBER 1974 HE WENT TO STOCKHOLM TO COLLECT HIS Nobel Prize. At the award banquet he thanked the Swedish Academy for having given him enormous support in his struggle with his persecutors. In his long-delayed address he spoke of literature as condensed experience, the living memory of nations. Art had always triumphed in the struggle with lies, and always would. "The simple course of the simple brave man is not to participate in the lie and not to support lying actions. Even if they come into the world and reign in the world, let it not be through me."

He gave an exuberant four-hour-long press conference. He was not against democracy, he said, but wished it to be soundly based; Russia would have to move toward it "smoothly, cautiously, and slowly" after the breakup of the Soviet system. To a question about Amnesty International he replied that it was a noble idea, but unfortunately its much-vaunted even-handedness was a sham: in the West and the Third World, information was so easily attainable, and in the East so hard to come by.

He moved through the Western world: no longer seeing the lying red banners proclaiming the eternal union of party and people, but the myriad trivial lies proclaiming that life was less good without this particular car, toothpaste, or lager. Everywhere entering—and stirring up further—a media babble.

The French Communist newspaper *L'Humanité* had fought hard to establish him as a cold warrior who wished to destroy détente; it had chosen to attack one of his most vulnerable areas, his defense of Vlasov. On the day after the writer's arrival in Zurich, *L'Humanité* had even echoed Soviet crudity in running the headline: "Solzhenitsyn Vacationing in Switzerland." However, this campaign by the hard-line, unreformed Communist Party of France failed abysmally. When he visited Paris in April 1975 and appeared on the leading TV book program *Apostrophe,* five million people tuned in—twice the average number of viewers—and were captivated by his blazing sincerity and his charm. According to *L'Express* he was "a new prophet, the herald of a great religious movement." For *Paris Match,* "a genius . . . the equal of Dostoyevsky." When *Gulag* came out in May, it achieved instant and massive success. The left was forced to acknowledge that the camps were not merely an error that Soviet Communism had corrected. The file was not closed. In 1976 the French Communist Party, biting the bullet, condemned the contemporary camps in the Soviet Union, and also the punitive psychiatric hospitals. Even more centrally, it was forced to dissociate itself from the "dictatorship of the proletariat." "All of this can be attributed to the dramatic upset in French public opinion, particularly among the left, occasioned by the reading of *The Gulag Archipelago.*"[2]

"Poetry makes nothing happen . . ." Yet Solzhenitsyn's great work, a modern epic, overturned a religion—that Sartrean faith which for half a century had strained at every gnat that came from America while swallowing every camel from the Soviet Union. It was symbolically fitting that Sartre went blind in the year of *Gulag's* original publication, 1973. He and his kind had been guilty of a worse moral blindness than that of Oedipus, for they had actually adored the monster and its plague.

"It will forever remain one of the ironic lessons of history that the moral force which finally shattered the influence of Sartre and the French Left on their own home ground came not from any effective dissent in the intellectual capitals of the West but from a heroic survivor of the very system whose evils they had long denied." The publication of *Gulag* "reduced this whole tradition of political falsehood to ideological rubble."[3]

Within two weeks of his highly publicized and sensationally successful visit to Paris, he was flying very discreetly to Canada. Alarmed by the ease with which the KGB had palmed the Holubs off onto him, he was looking for a more remote home; moreover one that would be less claustrophobic than Switzerland, with its beautiful but lowering mountains. In between visiting Orthodox communities—which encouraged a rumor that he had chosen to become a monk—he explored possible properties in Quebec and Ontario. He refused all interviews, but agreed to a brief meeting with Pierre Trudeau, the prime minister. His only public address in Canada was a three-minute message for the Ukrainian service of Radio Canada International. He reminded his "dear brothers" that his grandfather had been a Ukrainian, and castigated the West for having ignored the fate of the six million dead in the famine of 1933.

Attending the Easter service in Montreal's Orthodox cathedral, he was approached by a Russian with whom he had already had some correspondence: Professor Alexis Klimoff. Klimoff was "obviously awed," but found Solzhenitsyn very kind and friendly. From this chance meeting a friendship developed, and Klimoff became a valued translator.[4] Alya joined her husband midway in his Canadian visit and they proceeded westward to British

Columbia and thence to Juneau, Alaska. For the first time he was on American soil. A century ago, it had been a Russian colony: in 1867 the U.S. Senate, by a single vote, had overcome the opposition of those who claimed the territory was "an utterly useless land of perpetual snow," and bought it for $7.2 million. Sanya enjoyed the harsh climate and the company of Bishop Gregory, spiritual head of the Alaskan Orthodox Church. At Old Sitka, the couple visited the ruins of the Fort of the Archangel Gabriel, founded by the first Russian governor, Alexander Baranov, in 1799—year of Pushkin's birth. Tlingit Indians had destroyed the fort soon after it was built. Now, Solzhenitsyn was introduced to Orthodox Christian Indians, who inducted him into their clan.

One motive for visiting Alaska, he had told the bishop, had been the spell cast on him by Jack London in his childhood. On moving south again to California he made a pilgrimage to London's home there. A more pragmatic pilgrimage was to the Hoover Institution on War, Revolution, and Peace, at Stanford University, which held the richest archive of twentieth-century Russian history in the West. He was made an honorary fellow, which allowed him to use the Hoover library whenever he wished. It would be invaluable, he felt, in the research for his historical sequence; in his own country, these documents were suppressed.

For several days he stayed as a guest of a community of Old Believers in Oregon. As a nonmember of the sect, he was prohibited from entering their church. He admired their stubbornness in this respect, just as he had approved of the rural Swiss denying voting rights to foreigners. It was clear the Old Believers had transplanted successfully to this remote corner of the new world.

Toward the end of June 1975 came his visit to Washington, D.C.—the White House's non-invitation, and a speech at the Hilton Hotel to an audience of twenty-five hundred members of the AFL-CIO, America's main trade-union organization. He spoke in Russian from notes—his words simultaneously translated. Michael Scammell suggests he was carried away by the enthusiastic reception to indulge in demogoguery and gross flattery of America;[5] but there was surely little more than truthful courtesy in the tribute: "The United States has long shown itself to be the most magnanimous, the most generous country in the world. Wherever there is a flood, an earthquake, a fire, a natural disaster, an epidemic, who is the first to help? The United States. Who helps the most and unselfishly? The United States. And what do we hear in reply? Reproaches, curses, 'Yankee Go Home.' . . . But none of this takes the load off America's shoulders. Whether you like it or not, the course of history has made you the leaders of the world. Your country can no longer think provincially."[6]

On 15 July he addressed an audience of some eighty congressmen at a reception in his honor held in the Senate Caucus Room. Twenty-five senators of widely differing political views, who included Henry Jackson, John Glenn, Hubert Humphrey, William Buckley, and Adlai Stevenson, had sponsored the meeting. Senator Jackson expressed the American people's admiration and respect for his literary work and his courageous support for human rights. Responding, he told the congressmen, "Your country has just recently passed through the extended ordeal of Vietnam, which exhausted and divided your country. I can say with certainty that this ordeal was the least of a long chain of similar trials which awaits you in the near future." Fortunately, this cheerless prophecy, at least in terms of military conflict, did not come true.

In early October the Senate unanimously adopted a resolution from Senator Jesse Helms to confer honorary citizenship on the Russian. The resolution passed to the House Committee on the Judiciary for its recommendation. At this stage the State Department stepped in, strongly recommending against the resolution. It pointed out that the only foreigner so honored previously had been Winston Churchill, who had differed from Solzhenitsyn in manifesting a "commitment to aid and affect America's destiny." Solzhenitsyn was indeed a man of courage and a great and inspiring writer, but the Nobel Prize had been the appropriate confirmation of that.

The resolution died. It seemed a vindictive act on the part of Kissinger. After all, the Russian writer grieved over America's defeat in Vietnam, whereas many native Americans rejoiced. Yet the argument that, unlike Churchill, he had made no commitment to aid America's destiny is not without merit. Certainly most of the liberal press was not happy with what they saw as his dangerous attacks on détente, his air of being a wild religious mystic, and would have approved the State Department's churlishness.

Kissinger was angered, and threatened to resign as Secretary of State, when pro Reagan Republicans persuaded President Ford to include a Solzhenitsyn plank in the 1976 campaign for reelection. Later, however, perhaps noticing that the Reagan supporters had been irked by the Ford-Kissinger cold-shouldering of the exile, Kissinger let it be known that he had become a Solzhenitsyn enthusiast. . . . "Henry Kissinger," wrote his conservative friend William Buckley, "shortly after Gerald Ford became President, sat down to read a chapter or two from *Gulag Archipelago*, having up until then read only Solzhenitsyn's *Cancer Ward*. He found the book so engrossing, he ended by reading it all. He then read through *Ivan Denisovich*, and *First Circle*. He then took *Gulag* to President Ford with the recommendation that he read it. One does not know whether Mr. Ford did so."[7] Recalling Lebedev urging Khrushchev to read *Ivan Denisovich*, we may reflect on this apocryphal scene as a farcical echo.

Jimmy Carter won the 1976 election for the Democrats. During the campaign, aware of Democratic feeling against Solzhenitsyn, Carter did not mention him; after his election, he said he intended to meet him, and criticized Ford's and Kissinger's failure to do so. However, the political situation changed again. Khrushchev remained the only supreme American or Soviet leader whom Solzhenitsyn met.

He was depressed by what he saw as a fatal loss of will by the West.

Everywhere, it seemed, the West was losing or had lost the struggle against Communism. The Helsinki human rights agreement of August 1975 had in no way caused the USSR to lessen its campaign of hatred against the West, but westerners—including journalists in the Soviet imperium—seemed terrified of breaking the accord's spirit by any harsh criticism of the Soviet regime.

By the time he reached Britain, in February 1976, his gloom over the state of the world left him little time for either diplomatic niceties or tourism. England, in any case, does not seem to have touched his imagination; perhaps it seemed too small, cozy, and crowded, its climate too temperate and damp. Oxford and Stratford-upon-Avon seem to have left him cold; in the former, he declined to visit the colleges but spent most of his time discussing translation with H. T. Willetts. Willetts became one of his best English translators; when the reader comes to his translation of the third volume of *Gulag*, the sense of increased vividness and expressiveness is unmistakable, compared with the earlier volumes translated by other hands.

Staying at a small hotel in Windsor, under false names, the Russian couple admired the castle but spent most of their time in their room. Refusing to eat in the dining room, they snacked on bread and salami bought at nearby shops. Sanya wished to make his own tea, but their French electric element would not plug into an English socket. The hotel manager offered to send up tea whenever they wanted it, but his famous guest, saying he often needed tea in the middle of the night, would not hear of a maid being troubled.[8]

Moving to London, he was filmed standing on the steps of the National Gallery, but had no time to go inside to view the pictures. He declared Trafalgar Square worthy of a capital city. At Television Centre he ignored the top brass waiting for him in the executive dining room, preferring to watch the end of a videotaped film on Eastern Europe; and at the Russian Service, offered good wine, asked for Coca-Cola, which his hosts did not have. Then he delivered a peremptory speech, rather in the tones of a bossy headmaster addressing his sixth form prefects, reproving the BBC for its declining standards in its Russian service, and informing them how they might do better in the future. They should provide more pure information, for a people bombarded with lies; should broadcast to the minorities, for example in Estonian, Latvian, and Ukrainian; should offer more religion. Christianity was the most vital form of dissent in Russia, and some communities were two or three hundred miles from a church. The BBC could bring the church into their homes. Conceding that the English would find it hard to empathize with this need, he said, "In your country, religion is more . . ."

"Subliminal," an apologetically subliminal BBC accent prompted; and the Russian agreed.[9] Indeed, Matthew Arnold's "sea of faith" had ebbed away exceedingly from England. If Solzhenitsyn was depressed by the worldwide advance of Communism, Britain was depressed more narcissistically by its slow, well-bred decline from imperial and wartime glory. Both the main political parties, Labour and Conservative, differed little in believing that not much could be done, other than to cushion the worst deprivation with the provisions of the welfare state. Industrial unrest was rife.

Solzhenitsyn visited the House of Commons and heard the PM and Leader of the Opposition debating the question of emigration from Eastern Europe. The exile already had little time for Labour Prime Minister Harold Wilson, who had reacted to his expulsion with the glib remark about also disliking right-wing repressions. The Opposition Leader was now, remarkably, a woman, Margaret Thatcher. Supercilious Tory grandees and contemptuous left-liberal commentators alike waited for the inevitable banana peel that would return her to oblivion. She was highly, absurdly patriotic, and unenlightened about managing national decline; she could not last long.

Onto this sleepy, gloomy stage stepped Solzhenitsyn, with a BBC Panorama interview conducted by Michael Charlton, and its effect was galvanizing. Five million watched the original broadcast; fifteen million, the size of the audience for a popular comedy show or "soap," watched its repeat.

Clearly the prophetlike Russian's call to "stiffen the sinews, summon up the blood" struck a chord for many Britons. He attacked the abandonment of the responsible use of freedom in the West. A people under assault from IRA terrorists heard him denounce "this universal adulation of revolutionaries, the more so the more extreme they are! Similarly, before the Revolution . . . people in good positions, intellectuals, professors, liberals, spent a great deal of effort, anger and indignation in defending terrorists. And then the paralysis of governmental power . . ."

He expressed his despair at the way in which the West had strengthened totalitarianism in the East by giving up "all its world positions." As a result, it was no longer possible to talk about evolutionary change in Russia, as he and Sakharov had both hoped might happen. Asked why people in the West were beginning to feel uneasy about him, he claimed it was because he was pointing out there was an irreconcilable contradiction between good and evil; westerners wanted compromise, a comfortable life. England in 1939 had fortunately not thought in this way. . . . "If moral considerations were not applicable to politics then it would have been quite incomprehensible why on earth England went to war with Hitler's Germany. *Pragmatically*, you could have got out of the situation, but England chose the moral course and experienced and demonstrated to the world perhaps the most brilliant and heroic period in its history." How his views of that conflict had changed since, as an ardent young Communist, he had thought the Western war an irrelevance of last-gasp capitalism.

Nothing would happen unexpectedly in the Soviet Union—he mistakenly predicted—but the West might collapse at any time, purely because of its failure of will and courage. Even the journalists in Moscow, given the right of freer movement, were no longer reporting the persecution of dissidents. Reminded by his interviewer of Bertrand Russell's famous words "Better red than dead," Solzhenitsyn struck back fiercely: "All my life," he said, "and the life of my generation . . . we have all had one standpoint: better to be dead than a scoundrel. In this horrible expression of Bertrand Russell there is an absence of all moral criteria. Looked at from a short distance these words allow one to manoeuvre and continue to enjoy life. But from a long-term point of view it will undoubtedly destroy those people who think like that. It is a terrible thought. I thank you for quoting this as a striking example."

In a BBC radio broadcast (28 March 1976), Solzhenitsyn lashed out at the West's embrace of socialism and "progressive" ideas. He excoriated Britain for having declined to help save Russia from the Bolsheviks at the end of the First World War, and for treacherously handing back to Stalin more than a million Russians and Ukrainians at the end of the Second. No other Western country had received such a savaging from its Russian guest; he seemed even to take pleasure in heaping insults on his polite hosts. . . . "For some twenty years Britain's voice has not been heard in our planet; its character has gone, its freshness has faded. And Britain's position in the world today is of less significance than that of Romania, or even . . . Uganda."

The tabloid *Daily Mirror* responded with the headline "Solzhenitwit," describing this "millionaire Russian exile" and Cold War prophet as a "Britain-basher" (25 March). Serious commentators ranged in their views of him from the *Guardian*'s scornful James Cameron ("Solzhenitsyn, the one-man Armageddon") to *The Times*'s adulatory Bernard Levin ("We who have just seen the greatest man now alive . . ."). Levin sought to assure Solzhenitsyn (*Listener*, 1 April 1976) that the heart of the British people was as sound as ever; the columnist had received a flood of letters saying "Thank God someone has said this, somebody has expressed what *we* are feeling, rather than these unrepresentative people who command so much of the public voices in this country." Britain's recovery of the Falkland Islands, in 1982, may be said to have validated Levin's contention: moral and physical courage—in the face of the usual chorus of appeasers—restoring freedom to the islanders and democracy to Argentina.

His thoughts moving to his next destination, Solzhenitsyn referred, during his "lecture" to BBC World Service staff, to the emotional way in which a BBC journalist had reported the execution of five Basque terrorists by the Franco regime; their leavetaking with their relatives had been "heartrending." *Our* feelings about that, said Solzhenitsyn, were to say to ourselves, Lord, at least there was a leavetaking! Untold numbers of completely *innocent* people had disappeared in Russia without a leavetaking—even a heartrending one.

Perhaps for the very reason that Spain had not yet become a progressive democracy, he seemed to respond more warmly and spontaneously there. He recalled, at a press conference, how in his youth he and his friends had been passionately caught up in Spain's Civil War. And yet, now, he realized it had cost far fewer lives than Russia's, and led to an infinitely milder form of government. He was finding that Spaniards were not tied to their place of residence, they could travel abroad freely, newspapers from all over the world were on sale at kiosks. . . . "If we had such conditions in the Soviet Union today, we would be thunderstruck, we would say this was unprecedented freedom. . . ." He believed there was only totalitarianism of the left; right-wing dictatorships were less than total.

These comments were quoted and misquoted elsewhere in the West, and attracted a hostile reception. But he told the Spanish he wanted to escape from the tyranny of left and right; the crisis facing mankind was not political but spiritual. The French Orthodox priest Olivier Clément, in *The Spirit of Solzhenitsyn*, points out that Solzhenitsyn believed the bases of industrial civilization—overemphasis on production, exploitation of nature, and gigantic technostructures that deprive man of his humanity and despoil the environment—scarcely seem to differ in East and West.[10]

Nothing demonstrates more clearly the gulf that separated Solzhenitsyn from the prevailing values of both hemispheres than his feeling—unspoken but clear—that authoritarian Catholic patriarchal Spain, separated from Enlightenment progressivism, was a more sympathetic country in which to live or to visit than West Germany or Britain.

The Oak and the Calf, his zestful memoir of the years of fame and persecution, came out in Russian, and copies found their way into the Soviet Union. The memoir, in which Sanya comes across as a kind of Arthurian knight, pure and without fault, caused deep distress to Tvardovsky's daughter Valentina. She wrote him an open letter, bitterly accusing him of injustice and ingratitude to her father. Vladimir Lakshin, Tvardovsky's assistant at *Novy Mir*, also took up arms on behalf of a man whom he had regarded as a father.[11] He found it hard, he wrote, to recognize the weak, drunken man portrayed in the memoir as Tvardovsky, and found it almost as hard to recognize the irreproachable, strong, always virtuous Solzhenitsyn.

"But I raised a monument to him!" Solzhenitsyn said to Michael Scammell, as if bewildered by these criticisms. A daughter, still mourning, could hardly be expected to view his portrait objectively as literature. Naturally she saw her father portrayed too often as a slobbering, staggering drunk, trapped between his love of the Party and love of good writing.

Solzhenitsyn should have understood. He had made his feelings clear about biographers and memoirists: the information they gathered was no different from the results of police spying. "I regard the publication of such biographies during an author's lifetime as ill-mannered and immoral, especially since they are bound to involve living people who are exposed and have much to lose from such publicity. I can defend myself against such publications in no other way than by asking authors, editors, and publishers to respect my right to privacy."[12] Admittedly Tvardovsky was not alive, but those closest to him were, and were bound to be distressed. And indeed he went on to write quite revealingly about his living helper, Liusha Chukov-skaya, in *Invisible Allies*. Liusha may not have wanted her emotions so publicly, if discreetly, paraded.

The Oak and the Calf is much less egotistical than it appears. He does truly see himself in it as merely an instrument of God. In placing at the center of the book a knightly figure, a St. George blessed so that he can destroy great evil, he creates in the reader a mood of exultation. It is a book of archetypes: Solzhenitsyn–St. George at the top; Fedin and his kind, the Dorian Gray wolf face, in the depths; in the middle, the flawed tragic hero, Tvardovsky—who finally conquers his own worse self. Nevertheless, Solzhenitsyn laid himself open to the charge that he understates the efforts being made by other dissidents. For example, the anonymous woman who so courageously stood up and denounced Tvardovsky's persecutors, at the end of his memorial service, is not mentioned in *The Oak and the Calf*.

A "memoir" that came out of the KGB swamp was a twenty-three-page pamphlet entitled *Who Is Solzhenitsyn?*, by Kirill Simonyan.[13] It was published in Danish by an obscure left-wing publisher in an obscure Danish town. Besides an accusation of anti-Semitism, Simonyan claimed that his former friend had engineered his own arrest in the war in order to avoid further fighting. He also claimed to recall Sanya's mother telling him her husband had committed suicide in 1918 out of despair over the Bolshevik victory.

Simonyan wrote it under severe pressure. The heart attack that killed him before the pamphlet came out may have been a form of suicide too, in a way. His death was a sad loss to medicine, for he was accounted a great surgeon. Sad also is the thought of that happy fellowship of their student years, involving Simonyan, Vitkevich, Lydia Ezherets, and Sanya, not simply fading gently with time, but being turned into acrimony. For this, the Soviet state carries the blame.

46

The Dissident

A plague o' both your houses . . .

THE SIMPLE FOLK OF CAVENDISH, VERMONT, SITTING IN A BRIGHTLY painted school gymnasium on a February evening in 1977, politely avoided looking at the silent strangers in the front row: the stern-looking, burly, bearded man in a brown overcoat, and two women next to him—one, in her thirties, and one of about his age, around sixty. The villagers had seen the bearded man before, on TV, in newspapers; that made him a celebrity. So there was a stirring of excitement, unusual in the annual town meeting. It had been a long time since the burning of witches in New England.

Word had got around that this Russian writer and his family had moved last fall into the old Hoffman house and farm, up the steep long dirt track of Tracer Brook Road, northwest of the village. The only evidence of anyone living there, for these several months, had been the tall chain-link fence, topped by barbed wire, that had sprung up all around the fifty-acre property; and, behind the further screen of pine and birch, the sound of hammering and building, as reportedly two or three dozen workmen had set about renovating the old house. Of the rumored famous owner there had been no sign, until now.

There had been a lot of grumbling about the fence. Hunters—and here, almost every man was a hunter—felt they had a right to go where they wanted. As their own New England poet, Robert Frost, had written: "Something there is that doesn't love a wall . . . Before I built a wall I'd ask to know / What I was walling in or walling out, / And to whom I was like to give offense. . . ." But the newcomer, it seemed, followed the darker creed of the neighbor who would growl, "Good fences make good neighbors. . . ."

"Dear friends and neighbors! . . ." The bearded Russian had stood up and turned to face the audience; his incomprehensible words had been translated by the elder of the women, who stood up also. This woman looked, because of her age and babushka roundness, more suited to being the writer's wife than the younger woman; indeed, some in the audience wondered if this younger woman, Alya, was their daughter. . . . The fluent translator was in fact his secretary, Irina Alberti, daughter of a Don Cossack Civil War émigré, widow of an Italian diplomat. Through her, Sanya informed two hundred craning people—about a sixth of the village—that he had chosen to live in Cavendish because of "the simple way of life of the people, the countryside, and the long winters with the snow which reminds me of Russia." It was hard to be an exile, he said; "God has determined for everyone to live in that country where his roots are. As a growing tree sometimes dies when transplanted, the spirit of a human being also is stifled when it is removed from the place of its roots. It is a very bitter fate to think and look back at one's own country. My country, by the way, is Russia, not the Soviet Union—which is not at all the same thing. . . . I was born in the year of the Bolshevik revolution; I shall soon be sixty; but in all my life before I have never had a permanent home. . . ."[1]

That was not strictly true; the house in Ryazan had seemed almost *too* permanent, short of an arrest.

"Sometimes I wasn't allowed to even live with my family. For many years the Soviet authorities chased me from one place to another, and at last they expelled me from my homeland." He warned them about the sickness of Communism; it could easily spread to other countries. For himself, he knew he was not beyond Soviet reach, even in peaceful Vermont; and unfortunately there would be inconvenience caused to the villagers. "My fence, I know, prevents your snowmobiles and hunters from going on their way—I am sorry for that and ask you to forgive me, but I had to protect myself from certain types of disturbances. In Switzerland, during the past two years, I had visits from KGB agents. And even here, I have had death-threats pushed under my gate. . . ."[2] He saw their faces, concentrated, respectful, even awed in an impassive way. Their plain and sober, check-shirt-and-overalled lives could scarcely take in the drama of a writer threatened with death by the KGB.

—Yet you did not need to be a dissident Russian writer to receive death threats; the capitalist world of hype and bestsellerdom could attract plenty of crazies, as John Irving was soon to find out: his famous novel *The World According to Garp* would draw for its author more than a hundred death threats.[3]

". . . Of course, a bit of fencing with some chicken-wire on top isn't going to keep KGB agents out!" Sanya said with a wry twitch of his lips. "But it keeps away people who just want to see me. Journalists who think they should know every detail of my life and have pictures of me published. . . . I know they are a bother to you too; and for this I am sorry. All my life consists of only one thing—work. And the characteristic of my work does not permit sudden interruptions and pauses. Sometimes a five-minute interruption, and the whole day is lost." Hundreds of people came to see him in Zurich; people from different nations; they came without invitation and without writing to him beforehand. "So for hundreds of hours I talked to them and my work was ruined. I had no means of stopping them. So please bear with my fence, and if you can help us to preserve our privacy we shall be very grateful. The Russian people dream of the day they can be liberated from the Soviet system; and when that day comes, I will thank you very much for being good friends and neighbors, and I will go home."

He smiled, sat down, leaning a little toward his wife. The good Cavendish folk stood to applaud him, and many came to shake hands with the couple as they prepared to leave. Deciding to go before the town meeting got properly under way, Sanya missed a demonstration of sturdy, practical democracy not unlike the canton election meeting he had attended in Switzerland.

He had first given thought to living in Vermont in 1975, during his journeys through Canada, Alaska, and the United States. A three-day visit to Norwich University, at the invitation of its Russian department, had impressed him, and he took to the state's climate and countryside. He had asked a young architect called Alexis Vinogradov to look out for a property; and quite quickly Vinogradov was contacting him in Zurich with an account of the Cavendish property. Sanya authorized him at once to buy it, renovate it, and build an additional library-studio. The property cost the new owners $150,000, and a further quarter million was set aside for the improvements. In the summer of 1976 the Solzhenitsyns asked for, and were granted, a permanent residence visa. Almost a year after the original purchase in the fall of 1975, they moved in.

Irate with Solzhenitsyn for reportedly saying he had felt out of place living in the banking capital of Europe, *Blick*, a Zurich newspaper, revealed a few financial details from his tax returns. In 1974 the newly exiled author had declared an income of $320,000 and savings of $1.8 million. By 1976, by which time he owned the Vermont property, the declared income had fallen to $155,000 and savings to $1.4. Uncomfortable he might have been in the home of banking, *Blick* sarcastically commented, but he was "comfortably bedded financially." *Publishers Weekly* reported in 1976 that some thirty million copies of his books had been sold throughout the world, in more than thirty languages. The first volume of *The Gulag Archipelago* alone had sold eight to ten million copies.

All the royalties from *Gulag* were going to the Russian Social Fund, set up by Sanya and directed energetically by Alya. The fund was no token gesture; between April 1974, at the fund's inception, and February 1977, when its administrator in Moscow, Alexander Ginzburg, was arrested for alleged currency speculation, Solzhenitsyn had provided the ruble equivalent of $300,000, and this sum had helped fifteen hundred political prisoners. His declared income (for Swiss tax officials) of only $155,000 for 1976 excluded huge royalties from *Gulag*, set aside for the fund. That omission displeased the Swiss tax authorities.

Throwing himself passionately into supporting Ginzburg, even hiring a well-known American lawyer for the legal defense, Solzhenitsyn declared Ginzburg had had no dealings with foreign currency; the currency allegedly found in his flat must have been a KGB plant. At the end of May 1977, Solzhenitsyn and his wife spoke out to the Western media against the increasing brutalism of the Soviets. Alya claimed dissidents were being attacked in the street and beaten up. Some were being thrown into jail for a time as a warning; and there were murders that were not investigated. Dissidents' friends were being harassed and abused; and conditions in the labor camps were worsening.

The Soviets had punished Alya for her work for the fund in the only way available to them—by stripping her of her citizenship.

The decision to move to America no doubt had many causes. For all Sanya's desire to be a country dweller, he had grown used to being near the center of power—and liked it. Switzerland had a tenacious democracy, but was removed from the power struggle. America, the superpower, also gave him a sense of *prostránstvo*—space. And possessing, for the first time in his life, a spacious estate, he may have felt he was beginning to recover that plenitude which he associated with Grandfather Zakhar's rich, bustling, productive estate in the Kuban.

Outside his fifty-acre world of birch and pine, he saw chaos and approaching disaster. "A World Split Apart" was the theme and title of a lecture he gave at Harvard University in June 1978. Only two days before did the *New York Times* report that Alexander Solzhenitsyn was scheduled to give the commencement address on 8 June. Between ten and fifteen thousand people endured a drizzly rain in Harvard Yard to hear him speak. They heard a lecture that seemed to take almost everyone—perhaps surprisingly—by surprise. He said little or nothing he had not been saying for the past four years; but Harvard had not been listening, or he had not gathered his thoughts into such a coherent whole. The commencement address, in the words of Ronald Berman, had the kind of impact made by Churchill's speech in Fulton, Missouri, warning of an Iron Curtain descending across Europe; and it set off "an avalanche of critical misunderstanding."[4]

After the briefest of congratulations to "this old and illustrious university," Solzhenitsyn evoked the Harvard motto, *Veritas*; but not, as many must have expected, to compliment the university on having been faithful to the truth; instead, he allowed it to lead into a dire warning about the West's loss of courage. The planet was dangerously split, a physical and spiritual fight for its survival had started, and yet the West's screens and publications were full of prescribed smiles and raised glasses. What was the joy about? He offered his audience "a measure of bitter truth."[5]

With characteristic fearlessness he denounced, at the very altar of the liberal establishment, the pacifists who "became accomplices in the betrayal of Far Eastern nations, in the genocide and suffering today imposed on thirty million people there. Do these convinced pacifists now hear the moans coming from there?" he asked in thunderous evangelistic tones. "Do they understand their responsibility today? Or do they prefer not to hear?" But this was not a diatribe against Communism; indeed, he claimed that decades of suffering in the East had produced "stronger, deeper and more interesting characters than those generated by standardized Western well-being." His target was modernity itself, the flight from the spiritual world, beginning with the Renaissance, which had produced a dazzling technology, the full achievement of the rights of man, "even to excess"—but also "moral poverty . . . the calamity of an autonomous, irreligious humanistic consciousness."

He looked at times like Lenin, at times like Fidel Castro—punching the air to hammer home his points. The numerous pacific, irreligious humanists in his bedrizzled audience became punch-drunk; they weren't used to being harangued. Especially by a dissident whom they had, at a distance, applauded and deeply admired. And you could see he was enjoying their discomfiture. *"All right, you self-righteous bastards, you thought I hated* Communism! *Well, Communism came from the likes of* you! . . ."

A destructive and irresponsible freedom had been granted endless space, he thundered. Society had scarcely any defenses against the abyss of human decadence. He gave the example of motion pictures full of pornography, crime, and horror—considered to be part of freedom. The press abused their wide freedom by observing only the letter of the law, without moral responsibility to its readership or to history. There was no censorship of any obvious kind in the West, and yet "fashionable trends of thought and ideas are fastidiously separated from those that are not fashionable, and the latter, without ever being forbidden, have little chance of finding their way into periodicals or books or being heard in colleges." The journalists and the professors planning minority- or women-oriented syllabuses seethed: how *dare* he suggest there was any censorship in America? . . .

Having lived most of his life under a Communist regime, he continued—moving on to the lawyers and law professors—he knew that a society without any objective legal scale was terrible indeed; but "a society with no other scale than the legal one is also less than worthy of man." Where men are governed by purely legalistic relationships there is an atmosphere of "spiritual mediocrity."

The tilt toward freedom had sprung from "a humanistic and benevolent concept according to which man—the master of this world—does not bear any evil within himself, and all the defects of life are caused by misguided social systems, which must therefore be corrected." And yet one saw that the West, where the best social conditions had been achieved, had more crime than the destitute and lawless Soviet Union.

Man had emancipated himself from the moral heritage of Christian civilization. "Two hundred or even fifty years ago, it would have seemed quite impossible, in America, that an individual be granted boundless freedom with no purpose, simply for the satisfaction of his whims. . . ." But that is what had now occurred in the West. And in the East?—Communism, Marx had said, was "naturalised humanism"; one indeed saw in socialism and Communism a boundless materialism, freedom from religion and religious responsibility (and even, in Communism, aggressive atheism), and a concentration on social structures.

The world, in other words, was not split between West and East, good and bad; both West and East were on the same side, the wrong side, of the disastrous split that had occurred when rationalism became the guiding light for humanity. "Is it true that man is above everything?" he asked finally. "Is there no Superior Spirit above him? Is it right that man's life and society's activities should be ruled by material expansion above all? Is it permissible to promote such expansion to the detriment of our integral spiritual life?"[6]

Harvard's liberal intelligentsia, most of them furious as well as wet, stood up and cheered him.

The *New York Times* editorial writers expressed their anger politely. "Mr. Solzhenitsyn's world view seems to us far more dangerous than the easygoing spirit which he finds so exasperating. . . . Life in a society run by zealots like Mr. Solzhenitsyn is bound to be uncomfortable for those who do not share his vision or ascribe to his beliefs." What he considered softness and weakness, the *Times* saw as "tolerance of many ideas, humility before the ultimate truths, a recognition of the responsibilities imposed by our awful power. When our leaders have departed from these quiet virtues, as in Vietnam, the result has been terrible damage, to others and to ourselves."[7]

The *Washington Post* accused the Russian of "gross misunderstanding of western society, which has chosen to organize its political and social and cultural affairs on the basis of a respect for the differences among men." He used tolerance and diversity, which were "the splendors of the West," to attack those very virtues. His speech would provide ammunition for the American Right; he was speaking for "boundless cold war."[8] One of the *Post*'s syndicated columnists, George F. Will, expressed the dissonant view that the screechings of the liberals were a sign of "intellectual parochialism," and observed ironically of the *New York Times* that its "spacious skepticism extends to all values except its own." Solzhenitsyn's ideas, he observed, were broadly congruent with the ideas of Cicero, Augustine, Aquinas, Richard Hooker, Pascal, Thomas More, and Burke.

Other voices spoke, somewhat condescendingly, of Solzhenitsyn's otherworldly mysticism, and the resemblance of his ideas to those of Dostoyevsky and the nineteenth-century Slavophiles; by imputation, therefore, he was enmired in reaction. No one pointed out a strong affinity to a great Russian modernist writer, Pasternak: for example, in the thoughts and emotions he gave to Lara as she weeps over her lover's coffin. . . .

Never, never, not even in their moments of richest and wildest happiness, had they lost the sense of what is highest and most ravishing—joy in the whole universe, its form, its beauty, the feeling of their own belonging to it, being part of it.

This compatibility of the whole was the breath of life to them. And consequently they were unattracted to the modern fashion of coddling man, exalting him above the rest of nature and worshipping him. A sociology built on this false premise and served up as politics, struck them as pathetically home-made and amateurish beyond their comprehension.[9]

It seems rather sad that two of the great liberal newspapers of America could not even begin to grapple with the central question raised by Solzhenitsyn, in an echo of the more lyrical Pasternak, but could only celebrate skepticism and diversity.

After his Harvard address, and the award to him of an honorary degree, the newly elevated Doctor of Letters (Harvard) returned to his Cavendish hideout: the gate locked. Upset by the subsequent attacks on him, and in any case conscious that he was a writer, not a politician, he withdrew from the public arena. He was rarely seen. Reported appearances were more like apparitions, like those of Christ after the Crucifixion.

There was a low-life version of Judas, in the year of the Harvard speech: Tomas Rzhezach.° The Czech writer who had ingratiated himself with Solzhenitsyn in Zurich wrote a "book" about him, Spiral' izmeni Solzhenitsyna (The spiral of Solzhenitsyn's treachery). Progress publishing house issued it in Moscow, calling it a translation from the original Czech. In a foreword the publishers claimed the author had belonged to the inner circle of Solzhenitsyn's friends in Zurich; his book was "strictly objective," and exposed the image of the writer cultivated by bourgeois propaganda.

Rzhezach began by stating that he had written "not the biography of a writer but an autopsy of the corpse of a traitor." He drew on the most questionable sources and his own fantasy to create a picture of a villain without a single redeeming feature. This Solzhenitsyn is driven by two motives only: vanity and fear. Rzhezach uses—in a literal sense—the tragic Simonyan as the main accuser. The great surgeon had been dead for two years by the time the book came out in 1978. His "views" of Solzhenitsyn, as expressed to his KGB-trained Czech interviewer, are the same as those in his pamphlet Who Is Solzhenitsyn? Sanya, he confirmed, had been terrified of death in battle. There was certainly fear in the air—Simonyan's, not Solzhenitsyn's.

The unwholesome Rzhezach tries to mimic the style of Western "exposures," with a staccato buildup to the astonishing revelation. Thus, at the

---

°In Czech, Řezáč; but pronounced Rzhezach, and spelled accordingly in Russian references to him.

front, after having lost his battery through cowardice, Solzhenitsyn is over-come with terror. . . . "He might perish . . . might be killed. . . . This thought Solzhenitsyn could not endure. Not in any circumstances! Especially now that the war would not last a year, but only months—perhaps only weeks. At such a moment he did not wish to die. And yet Soviet soldiers were dying. The battles were becoming fiercer. . . . Therefore into his head was born the most perfect and the most fiendish plan ever conceived—a plan of saving his own life. . . ."[10]

It involved writing antigovernment letters to Simonyan and Vitkevich, knowing they would be opened by the censors and he would be arrested. . . . Simonyan received Sanya's inflammatory letter in the winter of 1943–44; so the fiendishly brilliant schemer had to wait out at least a year of hard fighting before his cunning plan bore fruit in February 1945. . . . A fact that somehow escapes the KGB biographer's attention.

Solzhenitsyn, Rzhezach claims, fully expected there would be an amnesty after victory; but then, when he was charged with an offense that might carry a death penalty, fear made him betray all his friends. . . . (So why weren't Simonyan, Lydia Ezherets, and Natasha arrested?) In the camps he became an informer, under the name of Vetrov, and actually betrayed the insurrection at Ekibastuz. (If he had done such a thing, he should of course have been praised by Rzhezach for his loyalty to the state, not condemned.) In internal exile he became a clock-watching teacher and a hack writer. He betrayed his country and his wife. He was even betraying his future wife, Svetlova, when she was carrying their first child, by sleeping with a priest's daughter. . . . He had betrayed his mother during the war by not bothering to visit her during a short leave, but instead sleeping with an old Rostov girlfriend. . . .

And so the book goes on. In the West, now, Solzhenitsyn was a war-monger.

Rzhezach is a fool as well as a knave. If he had written with the appear-ance of wishing to be balanced, and therefore praised the occasional virtue in his subject, his book might have been more effective black propaganda. He could, for example, have given Solzhenitsyn credit for being an excellent and enthusiastic teacher, a fact that no one disputes. In this book, however, he is a lazy teacher who spends the minimum of time with his pupils and none with his colleagues.

Look now upon this picture, now on this. . . . First: a Soviet doctor who was visiting the United States sought out Solzhenitsyn, and told him: "I have a message for you from Kirill Simonyan. He told me not long before he died, 'If you should meet Solzhenitsyn, tell him I'm so sorry. They hounded me, threatening to reveal all my intimate secrets and destroy my career. . . . I was weak. I never cease to suffer from my guilt.'"

Solzhenitsyn said to the doctor: "I knew that, of course. I always pray for Kira."[11]

The second, from Rzhezach's text: "Having concluded my conversation with Kirill Semyonovich Simonyan, I said to him: 'My dear professor, I can't write all that. It would look like slander. Tell me something good, something positive, about Alexander Isayevich, for the sake of objectivity.'

"He looked at me with an understanding and slightly sorrowful expression.° 'He was an excellent mathematician,' he said with unusual firmness."[12]

KGB General Oleg Kalugin gave a copy of Rzhezach's book to British spy Donald Maclean, and relates that he returned it the next day with a note saying: "Thanks for the gift. But please don't send me any more trash. It's an insult to me."[13]

Somewhere today, one assumes, an aging Czech hack sees that book on his shelves. He knows it is one of the most corrupt, lying, and meretricious books ever written— too despicable even for the traitor Maclean; even *Mein Kampf* was cleaner, being at least sincere. Does the author sign copies for friends? Do his lovers think his breath smells slightly of the grave?

°That at least one can believe.

47

A Zone of Quiet

"Hey, aren't you that Russian writer, Solzhenitsyn?"
"No, I only look like him."
—CONVERSATION IN A LIBRARY

CAVENDISH, IN THE BLACK RIVER VALLEY, SURROUNDED BY densely forested mountains, has a becalmed air. Here is the silence, soft glowing light, predictable four seasons, and predictable snow that attracted the exiled writer to it. Its residents live for the most part in neat clapboard houses, farmhouses straggle up the lower slopes; the population figure of just over a thousand has scarcely varied since the Civil War. In the aftermath of that conflict many French Canadians moved in, bringing a Roman Catholic leavening to the predominantly Protestant English stock. Polish families came, and some Finns, their origins gradually smudging away into the common destiny of rural, respectable New England.

Nothing much ever happened there. Solzhenitsyn's appearance at the community meeting was the most exciting event since a visit from President Calvin Coolidge in 1928.[1] A native of nearby Plymouth, Coolidge came to look at the extensive damage caused by flooding of the Black River. He arrived a year later, said very little, and left. The village is evidently the kind of place in which great men say very little.

There was not much that humble Cavendish people could say to the reporters desperate for scraps of news about their famous resident. . . .

"You don't even know he's here, really. . . ."

"He stays up on his hill. . . ."

"His wife and children always say good morning or wave. . . ."

"They're not bad neighbors. They keep a nice place. . . ."

Appreciating the need for privacy, conservative New Englanders knew he had had books banned by the evil Communists, and were happy to give him peace and space. Cavendish folk had not had an urge to ban books since its library board watched solemnly, in 1881, a dreadful French novel called *Camille* being ritually burned.[2]

While Russia was experiencing a century of mass deaths, famine, and terror, tiny Cavendish lost just nine men in two distant world wars. The profound changes taking place were not obvious in the landscape. An affectionate local history makes the point that there were fewer amenities in Cavendish toward the end of the twentieth century than at the beginning. The railroad, a century old, no longer has passenger trains, only freight; buses run less conveniently, and it is virtually impossible to live in the village without owning a car. Dairy farming, which with woolen mills and sawmills historically comprised the local economy, had by the mid-1980s almost completely died out. The last mill had closed in 1958. Still Cavendish has not become a ghost village of commuters, if only because of the doubtful virtue that many people are retired. There are many small-time home-based businesses: the engraving of guns, the selling of tulip bulbs, weaving, pottery, and a winery. There is no local doctor. Increasingly, through satellite dishes and computers, residents belong to a global village as well as a Vermont one.

But still the prevailing reality of Cavendish is—to quote a title of Robert Bly's—"silence on snowy fields."

That is what Sanya required: "quiet and lots of light," as his wife told a reporter. He needed nothing else; her husband insisted he had enough of everything to last him the rest of his life. "I can't even persuade him to buy shirts and pants." Completely indifferent to cold, he could happily work in a cold room. Indifferent to food too, he could eat the same thing day in and day out.

Very few journalists now were granted an entry into the writer's life. The one American journalist, a freelance called Andrew Nemethy, who in 1983 drove up the narrowing dirt-track road through increasingly dense trees to the chain-link fence and the electronic surveillance, had a feeling of awed privilege; even had he been working for a more combative magazine than *Vermont Life* he would have been unlikely to write anything uncomplimentary. But in any case the Solzhenitsyns insisted on reading and approving— and where necessary changing—his text.

Nemethy described "a spacious and modern two-story wood house surrounded by a cleared yard and dense woods. Adjacent to it, nestled in the trees, is a small, airy three-story brick-and-wood library and study where the Russian author does his writing. The three-acre compound also contains a guest house, garage and small pond. The rest of the property, all forested, is, as Mrs. Solzhenitsyn put it, a 'zone of quiet.' "[3]

The reporter, accompanied by a photographer and a former editor of the magazine, was greeted by Alya, the three sons, and the author's secretary – no longer Mrs. Alberti but a man, Leonard DiLisio, who was to act as interpreter. They had emerged from the house to greet their media guests, smiling and offering their hands. "We were ushered into the high-ceilinged living room and invited to sit on a large, L-shaped sofa that faces the room's massive brick hearth. A big picture window framed a distant mountain range, and in the adjoining kitchen, a sign of the Solzhenitsyns' hospitality, a freshly made Orekhovy torte (a Russian nutcake), waited to be served with espresso coffee. Ignat, who is already accomplished at Mozart and Beethoven, was studiously practicing piano in the children's room and the pleasant sound of his music filled the house as we started talking."

Alya conducted the interview, in the presence of her mother and three sons; Sanya was at work. Later he turned up for the photographic session, which lasted an hour, chatting amiably and showing an obvious love for his children.

Nemethy described the interview with Mrs. Solzhenitsyn as beginning, in a typical late-summer Vermont fashion, with chat about gardens. " 'We have very, very good tomatoes, and cucumbers and Boston lettuce too,' Mrs. Solzhenitsyn told us proudly. Dried dill hung in the kitchen, and the garden also had oregano and basil growing in profusion."

According to one guest, the living room, which held a piano, a photocopier, and two modern couches, did not feel lived in; it was a comfortable but impersonal space for receiving visitors.[4] The real life of the home went on elsewhere: in the kitchen with its large table where the family, including occasionally even Sanya, had their meals; in the library-study where, in the months too cold for him to be outside, he worked from eight in the morning until ten at night; in the children's classroom; in the room where, on an IBM computer, Alya labored at setting and printing her husband's collected works. She sent the pages to YMCA, in Paris, where they were offset.

The whole residence, in Nemethy's account, seemed as perfectly harmonious and well constructed as the Mozart and Beethoven that young Ignat was already beginning to master. These fifty acres were like a Dark Age monastery; or like Kitezh, the Russian city that sank beneath a lake when the Mongols came, so as to continue its secret life. Everyone sprang out of bed early; by seven-thirty the children were breakfasting with their grandmother, Katya, who had taken charge of the domestic side of things. She led the children, before the meal, in a long traditional prayer, which included a plea for Russia to be saved from its persecutors.

Katya got the children off to school, then drove to fetch provisions or worked in the garden. Alya set type, saw off unwelcome visitors, dealt with the fund for dissidents, answered the phone. She made sure the children learned a Russian poem each day. Sanya found time to teach them mathematics and physics, subjects in which the local schools were sadly inadequate. He also found time to chop wood, or play tennis—gracefully but slowly and inexpertly, it appears—on the court he had had constructed. The children could watch one cartoon a week on television.

At weekends friends such as Rostropovich came to stay; and during such periods Sanya would take supper in the house, to talk. Normally he never stopped for lunch and often worked on during supper too—food would be brought to him. He wrote in longhand, mostly standing at a lectern, since sciatica made it more comfortable to stand.

Life was in no way luxurious. The adults took all their meals except supper in their own time, informally, before hurrying back to work. Stern duty and a tidy, quasi-Germanic order prevailed. Yet the obsessional writer had everything he could want: it wasn't surprising he felt he would need nothing more until he died—except for Russia, which Alya told Nemethy they missed more painfully each passing year. He created; Alya typeset and was his unfailing guard and intermediary. She was even polite and pleasant to the neighbors. If someone unknown spoke into the intercom outside the magic circle, she would inquire as to his business and say, "I'll ask him at dinner and get back to you."

"I have excellent relations with American libraries," Sanya told another privileged journalist, a French television reporter. Microfilms of texts needed for *The Red Wheel* flooded in from Stanford. With *Americans*, as distinct from their libraries, Sanya appeared to have an absence of relations.

He had no need. There was little need to venture outside his private, and infinitely more pleasant, Marfino seminary. He left the estate only to visit research institutes and libraries: Columbia, Yale, and Dartmouth, as well as Stanford. The obsessional writer had the perfect wife, the perfect mother-in-law. And well-behaved children whom he doted on. The remarkable Alya shared his sense of mission, and somehow did not grow sour at taking second place to his work.

This was a life far from the mess and grime of Matryona's house.

If there was any kind of mess, or even tension, it did not appear in *Vermont Life*. We are presented with a picture window, like that which looked out from the L-shaped sofa to a mountain.

Socialist Realism had given rise to many such portrayals, without shadows. In Solzhenitsyn's books, after *Denisovich*, the heroes are usually unshadowed by vices too. Indeed, but for being anti-Communist, his books up to *August 1914* observe the Socialist Realism canons, being realistic, concerned with social defects but in a positive way, possessing an upstanding hero, and intended for a mass audience. The *Vermont Life* Solzhenitsyn is the hero figure of *The Oak and the Calf*, with his family, not the drunk, tormented Tvardovsky.

According to a later editor of *Vermont Life*, Tom Slayton, the Solzhenitsyns showed themselves to be "super control freaks" during the negotiations for the profile. Through the office of the governor of Vermont, Richard Snelling, they had insisted on complete control even of the photography: where and how to set up and shoot, and the arrangement of the family. However, the magazine had been extremely pleased with the profile and the photographs, and was grateful to Solzhenitsyn for having consented to the piece. The issue had sold out.[5]

In the event, the Solzhenitsyns had no cause to object to very much in the original text; they argued mainly over nuances, Nemethy says, and the required changes were duly made.

Two years later in 1985, at a time when the Russians were reported to be applying for citizenship, an editor for another Vermont newspaper, the *Times Argus*, took Solzhenitsyn to task for his treating a gentle and genteel magazine, grateful for its rare scoop, as though it were *Pravda* at the height of a hostile campaign:

> It seemed to us at the time that the Solzhenitsyns' demand for edit-ing—read censoring—rights to anything written about them hinted of a deep-seated and probably misplaced paranoia. And we found it cu-rious that the demand came from a man who was jailed in his home-land and eventually exiled because of his determination to expose the truth as he saw it, not as it was distorted or blunted by the totalitarian government he despised.
>
> Would Solzhenitsyn allow subjects of his work to screen his writing before publication to assure it conformed with their own self-images?[6]

It was a shrewd question; the man who had called passionately in an open letter for the abolition of censorship in the Soviet Union was not in a good position to insist on controlling what benign *Vermont Life* wrote about him. And he had taken a robust line in writing about the weaknesses of Tvardovsky and Voronyanskaya.

The unfortunate "Q." was not forgotten by the author whom she had unwittingly betrayed. In a footnote to his chapter on Voronyanskaya in *In-visible Allies*, he informs us that every August he plays in her memory the recording of Verdi's *Requiem* that she had given him. In 1985, a Swiss follower of Rudolf Steiner by the name of Joanna Fischer wrote to him that Voronyanskaya, a person previously unknown to her, had begun to "visit" her frequently, begging her to let Solzhenitsyn know that she was in urgent need of his help at present. "Of course I pray for her," he concludes, "it goes without saying. . . ."[7]

If this sounds uncomfortably sanctimonious, Michael Scammell, during a four-day interview for his biography, was able to prise from him an ex-pression of distress and—almost—remorse over his abandonment of Na-tasha:

"As always, every family story is incredibly complicated and confused. Each side can marshal a thousand arguments, and each person is unavoid-ably guilty—it's always that way. . . . That's why it is the sort of thing that doesn't allow of a simple solution or a simple paraphrase. All that can be said in the most general terms, when you take a bird's eye view of it . . . is that we were both wrong to get married, especially the second time; we should never have done it twice. . . . But of course, so many feelings and memories are invested in any joint life together. And it's terribly painful when it breaks up. . . ."[8]

Yuri Andropov must have heard something similar from a bugging device; for he would inform people that "Solzhenitsyn says he made a mistake (twice) in marrying Natasha."

"Natalya . . . and I would never have parted," Sanya told his authorized English biographer, "if we hadn't had such an awful life the last five years. . . . I was ready for any sort of peaceful coexistence, but she wouldn't have it, she couldn't imagine the seriousness of the danger, she was sure we would never split up."[9]

After a combative passage in which he recalled the folly of her thinking she could wage war against him, he continued: "If she had simply said, if she had behaved, so to speak, like a wounded bird, I would never have thrown her over; it would have been impossible. I understand that it's wrong to abandon women at that age, I know it. It's terrible, absolutely terrible. It's a weight that will be with you till the end of your days; you'll never have a clear conscience again. It will always be here inside . . . and it's very hard. . . ."[10]

Deeply hurt by his published references to her "treachery," Natasha wrote to him in 1980 a letter in the form of an additional chapter to her ever-expanding memoirs. In it, she denied collaborating with the KGB, and described how she had been outraged by finding that her original text had been cut by a quarter and grossly distorted. She had struggled with some success to lessen the damage for the American and French editions. But Sanya needed to continue believing in her treachery: after telling Scammell it was very hard, suffering the guilt of his actions toward her, he added, "but it's easier, too, because she went to the KGB—when she cooperates with the KGB and publishes her book, it makes it easier for me. . . . Then I no longer feel that remorse, that awful remorse. . . ."

He would become gloomy at such confessional times, Scammell recalls; doubtless gazing at the brooding Vermont pines, the exile spoke of old men in the Orthodox religion who desperately tried to pray away their sins, which were beginning to strangle them; then he quoted a Russian proverb: "You are born in a clear field, but you die in a dark wood."[11]

The biography, when it appeared in 1984—monumental, exhaustively researched, and immeasurably enriching the world's knowledge of Solzhenitsyn—did not please its subject and those closest to him. It seemed to them much too sympathetic to Natasha. Scammell had found her extremely cooperative in answering questions, whereas Sanya, after interviews over several days, had put up the barriers to his English guest—understandably, for he had work to do. It was not surprising if Natasha's side seemed more generously, or at least fairly, represented in *Solzhenitsyn*. Also Scammell, like so many others, had become uneasy about the Russian's political views; and his biography, naturally, reflected his unease. "I ended up parting company with him," says Scammell, "when I stood up to him about his politics."✻

✻His alienation from Solzhenitsyn by 1997 is revealed by further comments reported in the PEN Newsletter of May 1997: "He became very tyrannical. He discarded all his friends of earlier years: he could not stand anybody of any stature around him; he was surrounded by sycophants,

Sanya's long, acrimonious dispute with Olga Carlisle reached its climax with the publication of the English translation of *The Oak and the Calf*. In a footnote he named the "dry, mercenary people" who had held up the publication of *Gulag* in the West, and added that the Carlisles had taken a sum equal to about half the worldwide royalties of *The First Circle*. Hearing that he was planning to issue fresh accusations, the Carlisles took out a two-million-dollar lawsuit in San Francisco, charging him and his American publishers, Harper & Row, with libel and invasion of privacy. The action was dismissed on 4 October 1980, on the grounds that, even if the author's charges were false, they were an expression of opinion rather than allegations of misconduct. He had been preserved by the First Amendment. The Carlisles felt—she claims in *Under a New Sky*—that their legal action had succeeded in its aim of preventing further attacks.

Olga Carlisle records that she and her husband received an average of under twelve thousand dollars a year for six years' work; and claimed no agency fees for *Gulag*. If her figures are accurate, their remuneration does not seem excessive by American standards. True, her life or liberty had never been endangered—as some sympathizers believed, assuming *she* had been involved in the smuggling; and Solzhenitsyn could point to westerners who had aided him without thought of reward. Most outstandingly, Whitney gave his services as a translator without recompense, as a contribution to Russia, the homeland of his deceased wife.

It may not be easy to understand why the Carlisles had to expend so much time and energy, over several years, on the smuggled-out texts; but Olga reasonably cites the endless negotiations with publishers, lawyers, etc., that were involved, and the fact that Whitney's translations were "very rough indeed, demanding very extensive 'editing'—essentially rewriting and totally reworking from the Russian. (For obvious reasons our names did not appear on the translations.)"[12] One thing is surely beyond dispute, given Olga Carlisle's pride in her distinguished family: that she was above all possessed by a love of Russia.

The Cavendish folk loyally kept reporters and the idly curious away from their famous recluse; a sign in Joe Allen's store proclaimed "No directions to the Solzhenitsyn home." Through the Reagan decade, the writer faded from the public eye. References to him in the press were brief and increasingly tucked away. In September 1979 the *Burlington Free Press* reported that he had passed his driving test in Rutland. His interpreter-secretary, Leonard DiLisio, had helped him with the written test.

His wife had got a ticket for speeding, during the time of home hunting. Perhaps fast driving was a form of rebellion on her part, a memory of imperfect, wild, free—within the overall enslavement—youth.[13]

---

and still is. . . . . The people who loved and admired him all moved away, or were pushed away; and the people who were left were second-rate flatterers."

The family's application for American citizenship turned into something of an anticlimax. Their decision to become "American" may have been a sign that they were resigning themselves to having to spend the rest of their lives in exile. On 24 June 1985, in Rutland, three rows of reporters and photographers awaited the famous bearded prophetlike face. It did not appear. Only Alya came, with Yermolai, aged fourteen. Alya said her husband was ill; but a family friend told a *New York Times* reporter the whole family was well, answering hesitantly "It's hard to say" when asked why the author had not attended.[14] Sanya, in fact, never became an American citizen.

Despite two hours a day coaching in Russian from a tutor, from early childhood, and their mother's suckling them on the Russian classics, the young Solzhenitsyns were as American as most other immigrant children. In 1983, two Soviet visitors, a historian and the deputy foreign editor of *Izvestia*, found a serene half hour watching a Russian class at the Green Mountain High School disturbed by an eleven-year-old's incisive probing in faultless Russian. At the end of the battery of questions about disarmament, they walked with him outside and asked his name. Yermolai Solzhenitsyn. In an interview later the *Izvestia* man, Yuri Bandura, said he was "a fine boy. . . . We talked to him as we would any other American boy." Of the boy's father he observed that the Soviets no longer thought of him; he was a forgotten man. "He just does not belong to us. He did not love us. But there's no bitterness."[15]

Like his two younger brothers, Yermolai was considered "wicked smart" by his teachers, graded three years ahead of others of his age. That may have been an understatement; Alexis Klimoff, visiting to discuss translations, found the teenagers studying subjects at a level ten years ahead of their peers. A priest from the Orthodox Church at Claremont, Father Tregubov, instructed them in religion for a while. It was all part of the rich and rigorous demands placed upon them.[16] At age twelve, Yermolai helped his mother by setting one of his father's works on their IBM computer. He would go on to spend a year at Eton, the elite of England's public (that is, private) schools. Young Sanya, Komsomol activist, could never have imagined he would send his eldest son to Eton. After this "finishing school" experience, Yermolai studied Chinese at Harvard.

Ignat, at eleven, made his solo debut as a pianist with the Windham Community Orchestra. The blond and round-faced boy performed Beethoven's Piano Concerto No. 2. His mother, grandmother, and brothers were among the audience of two hundred who gave him a standing ovation; his father did not attend, though he came to later recitals.

Ignat would proceed to the Curtis School, in Philadelphia, the most prestigious music school in the country. Like Yermolai, he also studied for a while in England. His father must have valued English education, even if he was not drawn to the English.

Dmitri Tiurin, Alya's son by her first marriage, was away at boarding school. Aged fifteen in 1979 when Scammell met him, he was already "a broad-shouldered, dark, and handsome boy about six feet tall, with his mother's prominent Russian cheek-bones and broad forehead."[17] Slightly aside from the family, it seems, and mad about machinery, during his holidays he spent most of his time driving tractors, diggers, and bulldozers for a neighboring contractor. The villagers would catch sight of him, when a little older, driving an old Cadillac hearse.

The brilliant, high-achieving boys were encouraged to lead a balanced life. When they were young, they enjoyed a large nursery, a sandpit, and swings in their own forest wilderness. When older, they had a basketball net over the garage door, a tennis court, and a large pond they could swim in. Television, which their father hated, was strictly limited but not banned. They had happy, mutually loving parents, and their father, despite his murderous timetable and need for solitude, found time to play tennis with them and tutor them; and they obviously shared warm relations. They had the stimulation of meeting interesting people who came as guests: Rostropovich often—one of few friends from the past where the mutual warmth remained unabated; and a new friend, Senator Patrick Moynihan from New York.

The picture-window portrayal of ordered harmony offered by *Vermont Life* is probably—almost maddeningly, for the rest of us who have muddled lives—close to the truth. Here was a productive hive, a rich simplicity: a mixture of the *sharashka* and Grandfather Zakhar's overflowingly productive estate. Sanya and his loving disciples farmed the grain of the spirit.

Michael Scammell has given us an account of a typical day in the exile's life: he rose between five and six, went for a swim in the pond, ate breakfast alone, then did some household chores or read until eight. Now began his writing day. For all but four months of the year he wrote away from the house, in a summer house—a wooden tin-roofed cabin by the pond and waterfall. Outside was a wooden bench and table. It was a charming spot, with the pond mirroring the colorful trees, and the waterfall glinting. The cabin held a bed, an old refrigerator, and a hot plate, and there was a small bathroom. Food was usually brought to him and he cooked it himself; he often stayed the night there. "He retained many of his bachelor ways, and his style of life was hardly different from what it once had been in Kok Terek, and then again in his various hide-outs. . . ."[18] Against the rear wall of his cabin leaned a Tolstoyan scythe: he loved scything the grass, as he had learned to do at Rozhdestvo, as much as he loved sawing logs.

From eight in the morning until five, he wrote almost without a break. If he wound his way up through birch, sycamore, and pine to the house, to take his evening meal there, this was no cue for relaxation: the evening would be devoted to consultations with Alya or with a guest, correspondence, and further reading. He would be in bed by ten.

Alya worked as hard. She was in a noble tradition of wives who sacrificed themselves for their husbands: the Decembrists' wives, and Sonya Tolstoy who, without an IBM computer, recopied successive drafts of *War and Peace* seven times. Alexis Klimoff found himself "just completely over-

whelmed by the amount of work that [Alya] had been able to do." Apart
from raising the children, doing her husband's public relations, organizing
the fund set up to aid dissidents, and typesetting twenty volumes, "she was
also his—if you wish—his research institute. She did a tremendous amount
of legwork for him. So, together, the amount of labor they were able to
channel to good ends is remarkable, extraordinary."[19] Though athletic, a
former sculler for the Soviet Union and a fine basketball player, she usually
could not find the time to partner her husband at the tennis he so enjoyed.
She explained to Scammell: "He doesn't realize how frantically busy I am,
and when I have a bit of time to spare, especially with him, I don't want
to spend it playing tennis."

Throughout the household, Scammell observed, there was a constant
sense of serious effort; each member worked in his or her own way, and at
his or her own pace, to serve the common purpose. There would be whispered huddled meetings, entailing a breaking off of a task to deal with
something urgent. It gave an air of secrecy and mystery to the place. Guests
were enjoined not to reveal to anyone that they had been invited. The
closed-circuit television monitor hummed in its little room, and the intercom occasionally crackled, as some arrival was interrogated. All this created
a sense of excitement, of partaking of some kind of spiritual Manhattan
Project. The work was not wholly concentrated on one man; they invited
people to send in their memoirs of Russia to the library, and much effort
went to establishing the library as an important center for preserving the
memories of otherwise unknown Russian lives. Alya typeset some of the
most interesting memoirs for publication by YMCA.

The years passed, monotonously in a sense, serenely. The Slavic snows
arrived early and departed late. The research library, cubist in structure,
air-conditioned, built up its store of necessary, terrible memories. Microfilms of rare historical documents needed for *The Red Wheel* continued to
arrive from Stanford. Above all, the aging man wrote, wrote, wrote; twelve
or fourteen hours a day, seven days a week. For a writer of his temperament,
it was almost perfect happiness; with no cloud in the sky except the brooding, half-suppressed remorse over the wife he had abandoned, and grief for
lost Russia. His maternal grandfather's paradisal and productive estate had
been destroyed by the Bolsheviks. Sanya, on his estate, was writing the
momentous work that would explain to future Russians why it all happened.

On his desk was a photograph of his soft-featured father, in uniform.
How difficult it was to imagine him, to *become* him! That Isaaki was young
enough to be his grandson. . . . He feels a vague yearning. Tolstoy was
luckier; at least he cherished a single memory of his mother's face, bending over him tenderly. Eighty years later, Tolstoy still felt the anguish of
loss. . . . "I walked round the garden this morning and, as always, thought
about my mother, my "mamma," whom I don't remember at all, but who
remains for me a sacred ideal. . . . And as I walked along the avenue of
birches and approached the avenue of walnut trees I saw the imprint in the

mud of a woman's foot, and thought about her, about her body. And to imagine her body was beyond my powers. Anything physical would defile her. How good my feelings were towards her! How I would have liked to have the same feelings towards everyone: women and men. . . . It's possible. I'll *try*. . . ."[20]

The reflected trees are dimming in the still pool, the snow dulls on the pines, the Green Mountains beyond are shadowing. Sanya's hand moves in tight crabbed lines over the page. Still so far to go. He had planned twenty knots, and he's only on the fourth! Five years of his life for every single year of tsarist Russia's in her death throes, of his father's, nearing its end too. . . . This evening he will work on, sleep here. Alya will understand.

He puts the red pencil down, and picks up the blue. A different color for a different phase of the endless work.

48

The Relentless Wheel

One final legend, and my chronicle
Is finished: the task ordained by God. . . .
—PUSHKIN, *Boris Godunov*

OF COURSE THE LIFE OF THE WRITER, SEEMINGLY SO BALANCED AS
seen through the picture window of his wife's account to a Vermont journalist, would strike most people as incredibly *un*balanced. Most writers
and their families have vacations, go to the movies, dine out with friends,
have brunch out on a Sunday, take in a baseball game, flirt at parties, get
drunk. . . . Sanya, for fifteen years, devotes himself to his work virtually every
day, and almost every hour of each day; he is reminiscent of the monk
Pimen in *Boris Godunov*, writing story after story, legend after legend, in
his cell, so that long after these dark ages some other monk will find his
chronicle and learn the truth of Russia's history. "The Revolution needs no
historian," Lenin had replied to Gorky's request that a historian's life be
spared. Ilyich had not reckoned with Sanya.

Was there ever any lightening of the atmosphere? Did any of the three
adults ever take a glass of vodka too much and tell an off-color joke? The
children liked American football, and brought their girlfriends home. No
doubt Alya and her mother, sensible and practical, made sure there was not
too much of a hothouse atmosphere for them to grow up in; however,
certainly as far as Sanya's life was concerned, the myth of the completely
possessed writer was essential truth. He worked, almost the entire waking
day. For Russia.

The two women eased his burden. He never had to answer a phone call.
"He for God only, she for God in him . . ."—there is a touch of John Milton
in this Russian. For Katya, a highly qualified aeronautics engineer, the sacrifice of her own career for the sake of overseeing the home and garden
and the boys was not small. Even though she spoke little English, she had
more contact with the local people than her daughter or son-in-law, since

she did the shopping and commuting, and struck everyone as a warm, kind person.

Alya appeared, to one local person who met her several times, Susan Smallheer of the *Rutland Herald,* not at all warm. "I'm a newspaper reporter, and she was always 'How can I manipulate this person?' . . . That was my overwhelming feeling. . . . She's very almost-mannish . . . not mannish in the sense of being asexual, just not a really feminine figure. . . . Very protective and calculating. She was very manipulative of the *Rutland Herald*. When it served her purpose, she would talk to the *Herald,* and when she had bigger media fish to fry, we were put off."[1] No sensual, troll-like Olga Ladizhenskaya, evidently; but a superb manager. And that, ultimately, was what Sanya wanted.

Doubtless she *was* calculating with the press. Warmth was something you bestowed on family and close friends, not newspaper reporters: this was probably her attitude.

As the years passed, and the relentless wheel of the work started in his youth kept turning, how real was she to Sanya as a *woman*? Her remark that, when she had some rare personal time with him, she preferred not to spend it playing tennis, suggests that *he* would have been happy with a set of tennis. How did she manage to stay in love with him? (No one who knows them doubts that she is.) "It is the cause, it is the cause, my soul. . . ."

At least she knew that her writer, general, priest was not caressing some Gypsy girl when he slept in his personal Cavendish Kok Terek. What had proved illusory for Natasha, that she had no rival except writing, was utterly true for Alya; and his writing was inseparable from the great cause to which she was as devoted as he.

All the same, locked into this cosmic cottage industry, did she *never* feel like screaming?

He would say that never in his life did he enjoy such perfect conditions for his work as in these Vermont years. But perhaps they were too perfect for the good of his imagination. Permitted to flow on endlessly, from day to day, week to week, year to year, when did he have that enforced disturbance from routine that the Muse requires in order to nudge her artist in a different direction?

With the willing servitude of Alya and Katya, he had created a kind of earthly paradise. No nineteenth-century gentry writer—Turgenev, say—had such problem-free conditions, for there was no bustling or decaying estate to manage. Problems from the past, which can weigh down a writer's soul, could be put out of mind, thanks to that Iron Curtain. He had been able to create a domestic environment, with the help of architects, that exactly suited him. And yet . . . Where was the tension, the inescapable conflicts within oneself or one's life, that are needed to goad a writer? He lived essentially alone—with that *norm setter* who kept telling him, Hurry! Hurry! You have just twenty years to write this, *and it can't be any shorter. . . .*

If he relaxed for a few days, if he ever "chilled out"—to use one of his sons' ironic Americanisms—who knows what might happen? Maybe an idea for a story that would divert him from his task; maybe some uncomfortable thought or memory forcing its way up like a determined sperm to the womb of his mind. So better not stop.

Snowed under by microfilms that offered new information about Stolypin, Nicholas II, or some tsarist colonel's memoirs, what opportunity did the creative unconscious have to make the pondlike surface of his mind tremble? What did he, a great writer of fiction, want with all those documents? "I have an excellent relationship with American libraries. . . ." Novelists sometimes need the services of a good library, but that should not be at the center of their art, as one suspects it became for Sanya.

Fiction, indeed, played little part in *The Red Wheel*. Essentially it is a work of history; and since history has largely been made by men, women play a very minor part in this vast work. The feeling for women that—instructed by Mirra Petrova—he was beginning to develop in *Cancer Ward*, and which promised an extra richness in his art, no longer seems important to him or relevant to what he is doing. One is inclined to think a late-life passion, some brief Nabokovian mixture of anguish and eros in anonymous motels, might have done far more for his art than fifteen years of rare archival material flooding in.

Nikita Struve, his émigré Russian editor, asked him in a 1976 interview if it bothered him to face criticism for allowing reality to preponderate over imagination. His response was: "It really can't be helped, I really cannot envisage any higher task than to serve reality—i.e. to recreate a reality which has been crushed, trampled and maligned. And I do not consider imagination (*vymysel*) to be my task or goal. I have not the slightest desire to dazzle the reader with my imaginative powers. Imagination is simply a means by which the artist can concentrate reality. . . . All that was needed was to recreate everything as it was. Well, not absolutely identically, for then—this is the familiar principle of art concentrating reality—for then it would not be art at all; it would be too long, and no man can relive the lives of thousands of others."[2]

Struve had *Ivan Denisovich* particularly in mind. Solzhenitsyn's answer is absolutely convincing in regard to that work; as also to *The First Circle* and *Cancer Ward*. The reality of Stalinist Russia rendered the fictive imagination unnecessary. "All" that Russian novelists of the Bolshevik century needed to do was to follow the grain of reality; concentrating it, as Solzhenitsyn says, through the shaping power of art—of artistic form. In those works in which he dealt with Stalinism his imaginative power is supreme. When future centuries wish to know what it was like to live in Stalin's Russia they will surely read a handful of poems by Akhmatova and Mandelstam; *The Master and Margarita* and *Doctor Zhivago*; the memoirs of Yevgenia Ginzburg and Nadezhda Mandelstam; and they will read *Ivan Denisovich*, *The First Circle*, *Cancer Ward*, and *The Gulag Archipelago*.

There are other powerful works—but those few would be enough to depict the age.

For Sanya, however, those books of a single decade had been essentially diversions preventing him from resuming the work begun at eighteen, in Rostov. And Struve, who had published the Russian version of *August 1914*, sensed that this ever-burgeoning work would hardly be a *concentration* of reality. Sanya confirmed that it would be of enormous length: "Since its main dramatis persona is Russia as a whole, it is a vast narrative. No matter how much I compress it—and even if God grants me another twenty years of life—I shall still only just succeed in finishing it."

He had succeeded in crystallizing the history of the Gulag in two or three years of intense effort; yet the years from the beginning of the First World War to collectivization were bound to take another twenty years at the least! And he could only compress it into two decades by eschewing a sequential narrative in favor of certain crucial actions ("knots"), such as—in *August 1914*—the Battle of Tannenberg. He explains: "I generally select points which seem to determine the course of events. . . . And I give a dense and detailed account of those ten or twenty days. Then comes an interval before the next 'knot' begins. That is how the idea of the 'knots' came about."

Struve, who had flown straightaway to West Germany in February 1974 to meet his exiled hero and quickly formed a warm friendship, asked a question which troubles most readers of *August 1914*: "Isn't it hard to correlate the family scenes in the novel with its historical dimension? In *August 1914*, the military epopee rather tended to force out the novelistic part."

The destruction of Russia's army at Tannenberg, Solzhenitsyn explained, had seemed to him a fitting representation of the whole of the disastrous war. This was where he had started even in 1937; and in 1969, when he had returned to it, he found no reason to alter what he had written except stylistically. He had allowed himself to make the first "knot" an entirely military one, not because he wished to write a military history but because it had to represent the war. "So far," he told Struve, whose heart may have quailed—"very little of the plot has concerned the family, the personal side. And, in fact, they never will occupy the foreground." The personal fates of individuals always seemed very important to the characters themselves, but they did not always have much influence on history. His true protagonist was "Russia herself."

Over the coming decades the "unimportant" human characters, based on his father and mother and other members of his family and circle—these figures already, at the first, dwarfed by the great events of war—would fade further. Similar in its conception to *War and Peace, The Red Wheel* has no Natasha Rostov, Pierre, or Prince Andrei.

The exiled writer confessed he had many possible themes for novels and stories, jotted down in embryonic form. "So they will never be written?" Struve asked—sadly perhaps. "I'm afraid not, because my main theme is driving me on, and there is little enough time left in my life as it is."

Both *Cancer Ward* and *Ivan Denisovich* had started as notebook jottings which might never have come to anything if he had become distracted. They had not *demanded* to be written. In the case of *Cancer Ward*, the all-but-forgotten idea recurred to him in 1963, after the publication of *Ivan Denisovich*, when he began wondering what he might write that he could submit openly to *Novy Mir*.

Sanya is unconsciously confessing that he is no longer listening to the Muse—who comes at night, as she came to Akhmatova; or at unexpected moments of the day; and who needs mental space within "her" artist for the ideas to germinate; but Solzhenitsyn had no time.

It is too strong to say that the seventeen years of almost perfect peace in Vermont were a catastrophe. Randall Jarrell defined a poet as someone who stands out in a thunderstorm under a tree, hoping to get struck by lightning; and if he is struck five or six times, he's a genius. Solzhenitsyn had stood out under the lightning and been struck five times (I include "Matryona's House"). Yet it seems almost certain that his art in later life has suffered acutely from his having had his prayers—for tranquillity and good research facilities—answered.

If only he *could* go back to writing in shorter forms, he told Struve; but unfortunately this work demanded to be written. There had not been a single coherent literary account of the years preceding the Revolution. The last eyewitnesses were dying off but it was still possible to question some of the living. "The whole fabric of life as it existed before and up to the revolution has been destroyed, and my generation may well be the last which can still treat this material as something other than history, which can write about it not purely in the form of a historical narrative, but drawing upon the vestiges of living memory."[3] His own childhood memory, he added, was imbued with elements of prerevolutionary life; the "breath" of those times still came to him and helped him "process the material."

It is an odd phrase for a creative writer to use: to *process the material*. In 1976 he did not realize what a vast array of material would be at his disposal over the predicted twenty years; and under its weight memory would find it harder and harder to breathe. The *material* was now of greater importance than the thrill of creating unknown worlds through his moving hand. When he tells Struve "The material keeps flowing in, vast quantities of it. . . . The work is excessive, very demanding . . ." there seems to be already (even before the American archives started avalanching toward him) an absence of the almost demonic joy he had taken in assembling the elements of the Gulag and reforging them into the rapier of his imagination. He speaks now more like a bureaucrat in charge of the production of pig iron. It involves "an inordinate amount of work—my own and that of my helpers. . . ."

Whereas his intention had been to deal with the Bolshevik seizure of power, and take the work on into the late twenties, he has stopped at *March 1917*. Only four of the projected twenty volumes were written. In the words of one of his American translators, he "ran out of steam." He was disappointed in the lack of feedback he was getting; but that, as Alexis Klimoff has observed, is because the books are "massive, massive, massive."[4] He was taking so long on each "knot," constantly adding new material as he "processed" it, that the period he was studying was moving away at a much faster rate.

His artistic aim, he told Struve, was to penetrate as deeply as possible into the psychology of historical figures, and to show them from the inside. Fictional characters had only a minor role, that of creating an atmosphere of everyday life.[5] Tolstoy's object in creating Pierre, Prince Andrei, and Natasha Rostov was obviously far more than to create an atmosphere of everyday life. We have to respect Solzhenitsyn's different artistic principles, but the downgrading of fiction to the "second plane" surely impoverished the work.

August 1914, the first "knot," begins with scenes and characters that can formally be described as fictional, though it is clear, even from their names, that they are essentially depictions of family members—father, mother, grandfather, aunt—as he imagines them in their youth. He acknowledges their reality in his note to the English translation (1989). Sanya Lazhenitsyn has pacifist Tolstoyan ideals, and is even described as meeting the old man at Yasnaya Polyana; but when war breaks out he feels "sorry for Russia" and sees it as his duty to enlist. Traveling north on the Baku mail train, he catches sight of a well-cared-for, densely planted estate, and glimpses through the trees a young woman in a white dress, standing on a balcony. It is, by a Zhivago-like coincidence, Irina—sister-in-law of Ksenia Tomchak (Taissia Shcherbak), who will become his bride and the mother of his to-be-famous son.

After some sixty pages, the fictional-personal is replaced by the epic events of history. When Sanya returned, in the spring of 1969, to the great conception begun thirty-two years earlier, Natasha saw at once that her husband was lost in his imagination. Arriving home after a trip to Moscow, she was met by a preoccupied Sanya at the Ryazan station. He did not attend to her excited prattle; "It's as if I'm in a dream," he said. "He was in other years, living in the world of his heroes," she recalls.[6] No doubt—already attached to Alya and hardly overjoyed at his wife's return—he was grateful to have other worlds to live in.

The hero he was mainly inhabiting was General Samsonov. Some of his own misfortunes he was now able to turn into blessings. The battlefield which had obsessed him in youth he had himself fought across in 1944: the ultimate research trip. And he had known someone who had many of Samsonov's virtues and weaknesses: Alexander Tvardovsky. Bulky, awkward, honest, Samsonov had done his best to serve Russia, despite its leaders' corruption. Tvardovsky, son of a peasant, had done the same. Both were destroyed by corrupt leaders.

Samsonov, in his suicide by shooting, touches the fate of Sanya's father. In Knot 2, *October 1916*, Sanya Lazhenitsyn confesses to a priest that he is tormented by the guilt of killing. He sees only one way out, he says: to be killed. There, perhaps, we have Solzhenitsyn's interpretation of his father's death: not strictly suicide, but carelessness born of an unconscious death wish; an expiation.

Overwhelmingly, *August 1914* is an account of a single battle. Solzhenitsyn demonstrates a masterly control over the mysterious changes on a battlefield—changes that seem to take place by their own mysterious logic rather than the decisions of generals. There is repetitiveness, but an epic grandeur too. During an August holiday, sixty years on, I was gripped by the novel's vast scope; while the rest of my family swam on an English beach, I lived entirely within the forest of Tannenberg. This was indeed a Tolstoyan intensity.

The English-language version of the "original" *August 1914*, appearing in 1972, attracted respectful but unenthusiastic reviews. The enormous battle scene was indigestible to many readers, including most women—and, to many liberal Americans revolted by their own nightmarish war in Vietnam, unattractive. "White" Russians did not like his depiction of a corrupt tsarist system leading almost inevitably to war and disaster. There was admiration at his mastery in dealing with vast numbers of men in action; and agreement that the account of Samsonov's last hours was a magnificent piece of writing, the high point of the book. But even the brilliant war scenes seemed encumbered by too much detail; while the scenes of private life were sparkling with life but too fragmentary.

"It is . . . from the appearance of *August 1914*," Solzhenitsyn noted, "that we must date the schism among my readers, the steady loss of supporters, with more leaving me than remained behind. I was received with 'hurrahs' as long as I appeared to be against Stalinist abuses only; thus far the entire Soviet public was with me. In my first works I was concealing my features from the police censorship—but, by the same token, from the public at large. With each subsequent step I inevitably revealed more and more of myself. . . . And in so doing I should inevitably lose the reading public, lose my contemporaries in the hope of winning posterity."[7]

Still in the Soviet Union when the first "knot" was published abroad, Solzhenitsyn had written much of the second, *October 1916*, and was planning the third, *March 1917*. Yet even this early, he was aware of falling behind in his epic, of incompletion: "*October 1916* . . . turned out to be a vast subject, a double 'Knot,' if not a treble one: this because I had omitted, for the sake of 'economy,' the undoubtedly necessary *August 1915*, and skirted around the whole political and spiritual history of Russia from the beginning of the century in Knot I. The arrears had mounted up and now threatened to burst the bounds of the story, to overwhelm it."[8]

A decade later, *October 1916* still had not been published; but in 1983 a new Russian version of *August 1914* came out, as volumes 11 and 12 of the *Collected Works* that had begun to appear in 1978 as a joint "Vermont-Paris" undertaking.

The revised version did not reach the English-speaking world until 1989. Faithful readers were astonished to find that the novel they had eagerly read in 1972 had been only a first draft; the new text had more than three hundred additional pages, many in small print. In order to gather in what he had been forced to leave behind at first draft; the "political and spiritual history of Russia from the beginning of the century," he had added long discursive portraits of Nicholas II and Pyotr Stolypin, accounts of revolutionary figures including Stolypin's assassin, and a chapter on Lenin. To confuse the reader even more, the Lenin chapter and others placed in later knots had already appeared separately (the English version in 1976) under the title *Lenin in Zurich.*

The artistic unity of the original *August 1914,* strained but intact through the intensity of concentration on a brief time period and a single battle, was now shattered. The large chunks of Stolypin and Tsar Nicholas made their appearance arbitrarily in a text that already (to quote Dr. Johnson on *Paradise Lost*) "no one would have wished longer."

Solzhenitsyn explained in a note that in spring 1976 he "worked at the Hoover Institution in California and assembled a great deal of information on the story of Stolypin's assassination." In a sense, an assassination took place in the Hoover Institute that spring. An artist died. He became, instead, a kind of obsessional "hoarder"; nothing was to be left to the reader's imagination.

Exile from his great theme, Stalinism and the Gulag, had exposed his major weakness. Whatever its origins—and I suspect it was born early in his life—an overpowering repression would not allow him to penetrate below the conscious level of his mind. In his earlier works this did not matter, for he was able to externalize his unconscious: the savage, *Inferno*-esque vision of *Gulag* is, in a sense, a projection of his own repressed violence—on a gargantuan scale, because of the intensity of the repression. Lacking a strong fictive sense, he could never have invented an Inferno, as Dante did; he didn't need to, because this Russian Inferno *existed*. He hacked the salamander out of the ice. No one else in world literature, ever, could have done it.

But by his Vermont years it was done. He could only have continued to be a major novelist by being able to explore, at a personal level, the heart's dark forest. A Vermont farmer, and great American poet, Robert Frost—with whom he has certain things in common, such as conservative, patriotic views, and a love of swinging the axe—was not afraid to confront his darker self, without becoming "confessional." Solzhenitsyn—so enormously courageous against external threats—would never have had the courage to turn a remorseless light upon himself, as Frost does in "Home Burial," for example. There, in a tragic domestic setting based on Frost's own loss of a child, the poet *becomes* both the unsolaceable wife and the insensitive husband. Solzhenitsyn could not find that kind of creative power—because finding it would have meant exposing his psyche to too much feeling. That is why his poetry failed; and why, after his great creative decade, he became a historian.

An historian with axes to grind. Among them his belief that Stolypin, Nicholas II's prime minister, could have saved Russia had he not been murdered in 1911. He depicts Stolypin in terms that evoke Christ.

> From 1910 . . . terrorists no longer found an enthusiastic and grateful welcome even in intellectual households. . . . Stolypin could turn his attention to preventing the pollution of the Neva by effluents and to the provision of free tea for down-and-outs in night shelters. Blessed with exuberant good health, he could never find enough work to do. No one ever saw him jaded. . . .
>
> The Kadets [liberal democrats] no longer dared revile Stolypin and stopped attacking him altogether. They tacitly accepted the new situation—just as long as they did not have to give the victor credit. He had carved himself an inexplicably strange niche: too much of a nationalist for the Octobrists, too much of an Octobrist for the nationalists, a reactionary to all on the Left yet practically a Kadet to the true Right.

For all that, everyone had got into the habit of tolerating him, since the country was calmer and they saw that "it was possible to live a quiet life in Russia."[9]

The portrait of Stolypin, and account of his assassination, takes up 245 pages in small print: novel sized, but a hagiography—perhaps not undeserved. Where have we seen, in another figure, enormous energy, with ideas that appealed neither to liberals nor the official establishment?

Stolypin's measures *against* terrorism ushered in what came to be called the "Stolypin terror." Solzhenitsyn's reflections on the liberal horror that greeted the tightening-up bring out clearly his abhorrence of the intelligentsia of the prerevolutionary years: "these draconian measures aroused the unanimous wrath of educated Russian society. There was a spate of newspaper articles, speeches, and letters (one from Lev Tolstoy) arguing that no one should ever dare to execute anyone, not even the most brutal of murderers. . . . Even telegrams of sympathy to officials hurt by revolutionaries were invariably greeted with indignation by the liberals. . . . Yet, whether Stolypin was brutalising Russia or not, terrorism declined. . . ."[10]

Reviewing the enlarged *August 1914* for *The New Republic*, Tomas Venclova, a Lithuanian writer and Yale professor, observed: "Of course, the number of Stolypin's victims was infinitely smaller than the number of Lenin's and Stalin's victims. But that is arithmetic. In their ruthlessness, in their contempt for the rule of law, Lenin and Stolypin were, to a degree, two sides of the same coin."[11] Such an equation would be viewed by

Solzhenitsyn as an example of moral blindness, typical of the liberalism he rejected.

Conscious of his own debt to Solzhenitsyn from the time when he read him in secret, Venclova writes what he "would prefer to avoid: *August 1914* is a pitiful failure, artistically and intellectually. . . ." The enlarged work was certainly a failure in artistic terms, but hardly a "pitiful" one. Venclova exaggerated probably because he shared the intelligentsia's sense of betrayal at the rightward shift in the author's ideas. The reviewer quoted an anonymous former friend and helper of Solzhenitsyn who "once said to me in genuine horror: 'He managed to cheat all of us. He deceived two generations.' " The contempt he was now expressing toward the turn-of-the-century liberals could rankle with their successors eighty years later. He seemed to believe the intelligentsia, tolerant of terror, relativistic in their morals, were as responsible for the Revolution as the corrupt autocracy and even the Bolsheviks! This ruthless, dogmatic, obsessed Lenin of literature could not see what was apparent to all liberals—that liberalism was, by its very nature, good.

Venclova praised the masterly description of trench life, the consummate account of Samsonov's end, and the striking images that could be found "on almost any page"—scarcely evidence of a *pitiful* failure. He thought the depiction of the main "fictional" hero, Colonel Vorotyntsev, was successful. Vorotyntsev is, we recollect, the Solzhenitsyn alter ego, torn between his wife and mistress. In *October 1916,* his frozen emotional state reflects, on the personal level, the paralysis of Russia.

Always a conservative in his art—as he now appeared to be in his ideology—Solzhenitsyn tried in *The Red Wheel* to take on board some of the modernist techniques of Western novelists. From Dos Passos, whose novel *1919* he had read in the Lubyanka, he borrowed the technique of introducing cinematic sequences with sound effects, camera directions, and montages of prerevolutionary headlines, slogans, and advertisements. None of it works very well.

Much more interesting, to readers of Russian, was his somewhat strained attempt to move the trite language of the Soviets back toward the richness of Church Slavonic. He uses, in Venclova's words, "uncommon morphemes and compounds, wild gerunds and adverbs, shocking ellipses and syntactical inversions. They look very strange, to put it mildly; but they are, for the most part, theoretically possible in Russian." For translators it would have been impossible to give an impression of these stylistic features, and none attempted to do so.

With so much added to the original version, there are also subtle textual differences. For instance, in the original version, when Vorotyntsev realizes guiltily that he is quite glad to be leaving his wife in order to return to his regiment, he recalls the earlier times with poignant questions. . . . Why had his skin apparently hardened, so that he had "ceased to register the passing touch of the least little hair? . . . Where was the thrill of excitement at the sight of her soft, light, scented clothes?" Why were their kisses "less tender and urgent"? Now, after lovemaking, Alina asked him at once to take his weight off her, and talked about domestic matters. She had even bought an ugly flannel nightdress; and when he objected that it was ugly she had replied that she didn't care, it kept her warm.[12]

In the later text, the wistful, sorrowful questions have turned into emotionless statements: "It was as though his skin had become coarse and insensitive, had ceased to feel every stray wisp of hair. He found himself becoming indifferent to her soft, flimsy, fragrant garments. . . ." The down-to-earth realistic detail of Alina's (and Natasha's?) behavior after lovemaking is replaced by a generalization: "Love's rituals became flat and tiresome." The ugly, thick flannel nightdress has also vanished.[13]

The changes seem to mark a process of withdrawal, on the author's part, from the erotic field. Not that he had ever been completely at home in it; but in *Cancer Ward* his erogenous nerves had gained in sensitivity. Now they seemed coarsened again, like Vorotyntsev's skin. Of course, between the first version of *August 1914* and the final version lay the divorce and the hostility; probably he could not bear the still-erotic tone of the original passage.

A few chapters of *March 1917* return to Vorotyntsev's love affair with Olda Andozerskaya, closely based, as we have seen, on Sanya's affair with Olga Ladizhenskaya in 1964. Granted a few days' furlough, Vorotyntsev has to choose between Moscow and Petrograd (Petersburg)—that is to say, Alina or Olda. He hurries to Olda's embrace. Strike-ridden wintry Petrograd is in a state of chaos. With Olda, first at her dacha on the city's outskirts, then at her apartment, he experiences the joy of love—"what other woman had given him a tenth of the joy that Olda gave?"—but grows gloomy because constantly she lectures him, questions him, and hectors him on how he should be firm with Alina. He realizes that, even if he were free, he would not marry Olda; she is too demanding, too in love with power.[14]

Eros—"the salient between the garter-straps," as a former Moscow actress called it, seeking to compare Sanya the warrior and Sanya the lover is almost absent from *The Red Wheel*. So indeed is spiritual love between the sexes. In its vast, chaotic entirety, as imaginative history, the relentless *Red Wheel* has an undeniable grandeur. There is much unfashionable wisdom in it, and brilliant evocations of Duma meetings. It is drenched in a love of Russia, not as superior to other nations but as a unique embodiment of the spirit. Russia's uniqueness of "personality" is, as he sees it, a defense against anti-human abstraction. He wanted humanity to learn from history before it was too late. That was an honorable motive for an aging writer. It was not ignoble to keep pointing out that people throughout history have been able to lead decent, spiritual lives, even under benevolent autocracies; and that in a democracy it is possible to be enslaved to materialistic death and false ideals; not stupid to argue that the Enlightenment, elevating man's reason above God, has been responsible for mass deaths in the name of ideology. When the Nazis built Buchenwald, they left untouched at its center Goethe's favorite tree.

Just the same, he ought not to have got rid of Alina's thick flannel nightdress.

49

The Jewish Question

—Hath not a Jew eyes?

SINCE IT HAS BEEN SOLZHENITSYN'S FATE TO EMBRACE ALMOST ALL of his country's experience in the twentieth century, it was almost inevitable that he would become involved in Russia's perennial "Jewish problem."

Venclova, in his politely scathing review of *August 1914*, expressed serious misgivings about the portrayal of Stolypin's assassin, an anarchist called Dmitri Bogrov. Bogrov was described as weak and cowardly, a "spineless intellectual," attached to luxury and self-pitying. "He always seemed exhausted, perplexed, out of spirits. His voice was cracked, and sometimes quavery, like that of someone with lung trouble." Serpentine imagery accompanies him; after he has mortally wounded Stolypin, "the terrorist's black back was wriggling away up the aisle." Solzhenitsyn was depicting, according to Venclova and many other critics, a stereotypical Jew.

In contrast, Stolypin was "strongly built, a fine figure of a man with a rich, deep voice. . . ." "He had a constant anxious awareness of all Russia as though it were there in his breast . . ."

Venclova comments: "Perhaps those embarrassing stereotypes have a certain foundation in historical evidence. But in the context of art they smack of myth. Of ugly myth."[1]

We may see a certain politically correct squeamishness in that remark, which comes close to telling the artist he must avoid historical truth. But the reviewer also pointed out that, though Bogrov had been given the Russian name Dmitri by his Christianized father, Solzhenitsyn prefers to call him Mordko (Mordecai) Bogrov.

Unlike Venclova's temperate discussion, which more or less clears the author of being anti-Semitic "in the vulgar sense," but rather a "fundamentalist" of the rooted life as distinct from rootless people of the diaspora, Lev Navrozov's earlier assault, in 1985, following the Russian language publication of *August 1914*, was hysterically violent. An émigré from 1972, Navrozov denounced Solzhenitsyn's "xenophobic trash." He is "a Soviet small-town provincial who doesn't know any language except his semiliterate Russian and fantasizes in his xenophobic insulation"; *August 1914* was as intellectually shabby as *The Protocols of the Elders of Zion*—but that turn-of-the-century forgery, purporting to show that the Jews were plotting world domination, was actually "superior" in its language to the Solzhenitsyn. . . . His style shows a "comical ineptness"; Navrozov writes that when *Ivan Denisovich* appeared he thought its author might develop into a minor novelist, but Khrushchev's use of him to strike the Stalinists, and his subsequent persecution, made him strut like a bearded Tolstoy, so "this semiliterate provincial, who has finally found his vocation—anti-Semitic hackwork—has been sensationalised into an intellectual colossus. . . ."[2]

Navrozov's almost comical venom and exaggeration completely undermine his argument. More serious notice had to be taken of Professor Richard Pipes, a distinguished Harvard Russian specialist and writer. Pipes argued that Solzhenitsyn distorted Bogrov's motives by depicting him as acting entirely in his capacity as a Jew, whereas "the historical Bogrov was a Jewish renegade, not acting as a Jew at all. Every culture has its own brand of anti-Semitism. In Solzhenitsyn's case, it's not racial. It has nothing to do with blood. He's certainly not a racist; the question is fundamentally religious and cultural. He bears some resemblance to Dostoievsky, who was a fervent Christian and patriot and a rabid anti-Semite. Solzhenitsyn is unquestionably in the grip of the Russian extreme right's view of the Revolution, which is that it was the doing of the Jews."[3]

In August 1984 Radio Liberty broadcast to the Soviet Union a talk by an expatriate Russian poet and scholar, Lev Loseff, in which he offered a literary and psychological analysis of Solzhenitsyn's Bogrov. The talk brought angry letters to Radio Liberty's management. What offended some Radio Liberty personnel was that the words "snake" and "degenerate" had been applied to Bogrov, while Stolypin was a "Slavic knight." Some of Solzhenitsyn's imagery had been compared by Loseff to parts of *The Protocols of the Elders of Zion;* that work had been characterized accurately by Loseff as vile—but this was clearly, his accusers suggested, simply a stratagem. It had also to be borne in mind that Soviet listeners heard the broadcasts through heavy jamming, and so would be unlikely to appreciate subtle distinctions.

Radio Liberty staff member Lev Roitman declared the program's "propaganda of racial hatred" an insult to any decent person. It would have led hundreds of thousands of Jewish listeners in the Soviet Union to "an odious conclusion." The program's producer, Georg V. Schlippe, just as angrily demanded an apology from the accusers. Professor Loseff, a pen name for Lifschutz, responded with dignity, pointing out that he was himself a Russian Jew, and had tried only to analyze Solzhenitsyn's attitudes and imagery.

He had studied the text very carefully, and come to the considered conclusion that, while the snake imagery has sometimes been used by anti-Semites, Solzhenitsyn intended the snake to represent rationalism. The conflict was philosophical, not racial. Loseff expressed the hope, as a Russian Jewish writer and concerned American citizen, that their "high-pitched insults and threats" would not succeed in getting their real target, the novelist, banned from their transmitters.

Replying to a piece of journalism by Christopher Hitchens entitled "Liberty for Jew Baiters," Loseff pointed out forcefully: "I am not an anti-Semitic commentator for Radio Liberty but a Russian poet and critic and professor of Russian literature at Dartmouth College in the USA. I also happen to be a Jew who had to leave Russia due in great measure to officially sponsored anti-Semitism."[4]

It was a very confused, very Russian, row, which ended in new guidelines being handed down to Radio Liberty producers. Professor Loseff felt that the consequence for him was to have an offer of regular appearances on the station withdrawn.

Solzhenitsyn had some powerful supporters; among them was the writer Elie Wiesel, a survivor of Auschwitz, where he had lost almost all his family. Completely exonerating Solzhenitsyn, he explained "he is too intelligent, too honest, too courageous, too great a writer. For Solzhenitsyn to be an anti-Semite would be wholly out of character. I am only disturbed by what seems to be an unconscious insensitivity on his part to Jewish suffering." Told later that Solzhenitsyn's attitude was simply that Jews were not "his subject," Wiesel said: "Well, I understand that. As a Russian, he is concerned mainly with Russians the way I'm concerned mainly with Jews."[5]

Rostropovich was prepared to *swear* that his friend was no anti-Semite. Alya told the *New York Times* the accusation was "absolutely absurd"; her husband had been surrounded in Russia by Jewish friends, both in and out of the Gulag. She was herself half Jewish, the reporter duly noted.

The whole Radio Liberty controversy generated more heat than light. It was fueled by Russian enmities, and the impossibility of conducting any balanced debate upon the sensitive subject in the wake of the Holocaust.

The charge of anti-Semitism had first been superficially raised in specialized Jewish journals and the *Jerusalem Post* in 1972. Five years later Mark Perakh, a scientist, extensively analyzed the matter in *Midstream*, the publication of the Theodor Herzl Foundation. Perakh claimed to find that, while individual Jews in Solzhenitsyn's fiction were in general fairly presented, their role was nearly always negative. Thus, in *The First Circle*, three major Jewish characters, Rubin and Kagan among the inmates, and Roitman among the administrators, were all in some way defenders of evil. Perakh's argument seems hard on Solzhenitsyn, since both Rubin (Kopelev) and Roitman are shown as "decent" people. Hard on him, also, was the argument that the lack of significant Jewish characters in *Ivan Denisovich* and *Cancer Ward* was in itself suspect. The writer was damned if he included Jews, and damned if he didn't.

It was true that the three Jews in the early play *The Love-Girl and the Innocent* were presented as disgustingly greedy, cunning, and manipulative: Shylocks of the camp. One, a fat and dirty bookkeeper adept at corrupting women prisoners, was modeled on Isaak Bershader, a *zek* trusty of Kaluga Gate. Bershader emerged again, as it were, in *Lenin in Zurich*, in the revolting guise of Lenin's rich paymaster, Israil Lazarevich Helphand (Parvus). Parvus was "a revolutionary of the new type, a millionaire revolutionary, a financier and industrialist. . . ." "There he stood—such as he was, in his flesh and blood: with an immense gut, an extended dome-shaped head, fleshy bulldog-like physiognomy. . . ."

Undoubtedly two of the men Solzhenitsyn blamed most for the Revolution were Jews, the "weakly, snakelike" Bogrov, who ended what he considered Russia's last best hope of progress; and the repulsively fleshy Parvus, who financed the Bolsheviks. They are not attractive portraits. But doubtless they were not very attractive personalities.

When volume 2 of *The Gulag Archipelago* appeared, it was seen that the six Gulag villains whose photographs the author chose to include were all Jews: Aron Solts, Naftaly Frenkel, Yakov Rappoport, Matvei Berman, Lazar Kogan, and Genrikh Yagoda. Solzhenitsyn explained they were the only ones whose photos he could find.

As Perakh admitted, there is a wholly positive Jew in *August 1914*, Arkhangorodsky. Modeled on a friend of his mother in Rostov, he is one of those archetypes of decency for Solzhenitsyn, a cultivated engineer. Calm and patriotic, he argues with family members angry at injustice that revolution would be ruinous: "No one with any sense can be in favour of revolution, because it is just a prolonged process of insane destruction. . . . And the bloodier, the more protracted the revolution is, the more dearly the people have to pay for it—the better its claim to be called a 'Great Revolution.' " At mention of the anti-Semitic Black Hundreds, his voice starts to tremble; between the Black Hundreds and the Red Hundreds, he says, there is only a handful of practical people trying their best.[6]

Notwithstanding this honorable and honest Jew—and Solzhenitsyn's greatness as a writer and a battler for truth and justice—Perakh believed that on balance his work did show a negative attitude toward Jews.

Naturally, as we have seen, the KGB also got involved with the "Jewish question." First of all, it tried to persuade people that he was Jewish himself, his real name Solzhenitser. Next it tried to show he was an anti-Semite; Kirill Simonyan "remembered" that Sanya's scarred forehead was the consequence of a fight in class after he had called a fellow pupil a Yid.

The reality, according to Solzhenitsyn, was that he had defended the right of another pupil to *say* whatever he liked; for this offense he had been arraigned before a Pioneer court. The gash on his forehead had come from a separate fight.

And then there had been the occasion when a group of Pioneers had ripped the cross from his neck. Since most of the Pioneers were Jewish children, the incident must have been full of complexity. One may imagine that as a reborn and imprisoned Orthodox Christian he might well have looked back in anger. Those boys must have played a part in turning him against his family "White" background to become an enthusiastic young Communist. What the sociologists term "peer pressure."

Personal childhood experience merged into the broad picture of Jewish domination of the Bolshevik takeover. It is politic today to play that fact down, but it is surely undeniable. Richard Pipes, who criticized Solzhenitsyn for anti-Semitic tendencies, is a balanced scholar on the issue: "The number of Jews active in Communism in Russia and abroad was striking: in Hungary, for example, they furnished 95 percent of the leading figures in Bela Kun's dictatorship. They also were disproportionately represented among Communists in Germany and Austria during the revolutionary upheavals there in 1918–23, and in the apparatus of the Communist International."[7] Including such leading figures as Trotsky, Zinoviev, Kamenev, Sverdlov, and Radek, the first Politburo was three-quarters Jewish. Seventy percent of the Cheka was either Jewish or Latvian. Pipes seems here to be backing up what he elsewhere implies is a far right myth.

Hugo Koehler, part of a U.S. intelligence mission sent to observe the Civil War, wrote that "the Jews are in absolute control . . . the great mass of officials are Jews. . . ."[8] And the same officials or their successors were overseers during collectivization. During the Terror, Jews were as much the target for repression as any other race; and probably only Stalin's death prevented a mass deportation of Jews.

Under tsardom Jews had suffered savage pogroms and discrimination, which made them, almost inevitably, outsiders. Solzhenitsyn fully recognized this. In *October 1916* Sanya Lazhenitsyn defends Jews against the anti-Semitism of another platoon commander, who has accused them of preferring administration to the perils of the front line. Sanya tells him there are brave and intelligent Jews, but the state, in treating them as less than full citizens, is to blame for their reluctance to defend Russia in the Tsar's army.

Moreover, as Prof. Dr. W. W. Krysko observed sympathetically: "It was not a matter of great note that Jews were playing a large role in the re-making of Russia, because Jews represented the only group of people destined by their own history to lead a New Order which was going to . . . promote international brotherhood."[9] Intelligent and dynamic, Jews played as predominant a part in the Bolshevik Revolution as they played in the creation of psychoanalysis, modern physics, and modernism in art.

Solzhenitsyn can hardly be blamed for detesting the kind of "international brotherhood" that was violently imposed on Russia. Only the thought control of political correctness could characterize this as anti-Semitic. The charge is absurd, as his wife said. Arkhangorodsky's Jewishness is immaterial to Solzhenitsyn; what mattered was that, despite injustice, he was happy to work patiently for a better Russia, rather than go down the ruinous road of revolutionary destruction. As for the Bogrov-Stolypin section, those forty pages have to be combed assiduously in order to find images that might seem anti-Semitic. The racial identity of the terrorist is relevant only insofar as he was partly motivated by seeking vengeance for the pogroms—and feared that Stolypin's reforms would be bad for Jews if they succeeded in shoring up the tsarist state.

Understandably incensed by the accusations, Sanya wrote to *New York Times* reporter Richard Grenier a letter in which he asserted that he was dedicated to the study of history "just as it was." This was necessary "in order not to repeat the horrors that humanity perpetrated on itself in the twentieth century—all types of revolutionary and ethnic genocide." His critics had arbitrarily accused him of anti-Semitism because, in prerevolutionary Russia, a period his work was dealing with, "a Jewish question existed and was a burning issue. But at that time, hundreds of authors, including Jews, wrote about this; at that time, precisely the omission of mentioning the Jewish question was considered a manifestation of anti-Semitism—and it would be unworthy for an historian of that era to pretend that that question did not exist."

The charge of anti-Semitism was "base"; he went on to consider the term itself: "This word, just as other labels as well, has lost its precise meaning from thoughtless use, and different publicists in different decades understood it differently. If a biased and unjustified attitude toward the Jewish nation is understood by this term—then I tell you assuredly: not only is there no—nor could there be—'anti-Semitism' in my work, nor for that matter in any book worthy of being called *literature*. To approach a literary work with the measuring stick of 'anti-Semitism' is vulgar, an underdeveloped understanding of the nature of a literary work. By this measuring stick Shakespeare could be proclaimed 'anti-Semitic,' and his creative work struck out."[10]

What he opposes, with every bone in his body, is the belief that nationhood does not matter. Socialism's aim, said Lenin, was to abolish the distinction between nations, to bring them into fusion. Rosa Luxemburg, leader of the German Communists, said, "I have no separate corner in my heart for the ghetto: I feel at home in the entire world wherever there are clouds and birds and human tears." It appears to be such a rational philosophy, so enlightened—indeed, proceeding straight from the Enlightenment—that, as Vadim Borisov observed in an essay in *From Under the Rubble*, severe moral censure was addressed to Russian writers who could not overcome the "base instinct" of loving their country.[11] To lose one's sense of nationhood, to lose the right "*simply to love* the land of our birth blindly and unpremeditatedly," as Solzhenitsyn put it in the same book, was for a people to risk losing their historical memory and even the language in which that memory is embedded.

In the modern Soviet Union, on the evidence of his irritation with Sakharov's wife, he felt the minority cause of Jewish emigration took unfair precedence over the suffering of the Russian people, who had nowhere to go. He may have resented, at least unconsciously, the primacy given to the six million over the sixty million. But he greatly admired the state of Israel; the passionate commitment of its people, and its bedrock of religious values. He was for "God and country," though never in a chauvinist or imperialistic way.

He just knew where home was. . . . There is a striking photograph showing the writer with his three young sons on the Cavendish estate. Crouching with them on a large boulder, he is pointing away over the photographer's shoulder. Their eyes follow in that direction. He was telling them that *there* was where their country was, and this boulder was a flying horse that one day would take them home. They never forgot that lesson.

There seemed no chance of realizing his dream of returning. The Cold War was burning fiercely in the year of the Radio Liberty controversy, 1984—Orwell's year. The Soviets were fighting in Afghanistan; President Reagan had called the Soviet Union an "Evil Empire"; hundreds of thousands protested at the siting of medium-range missiles in Western Europe; a peaceful South Korean airliner, straying off course, had been shot down over Sakhalin Island; the Soviets boycotted the 1984 Olympics in Los Angeles after the American boycott of the 1980 Olympics in Moscow.

According to KGB defector Oleg Gordievsky, the Soviet Union developed a paranoid fear, around this time, that the West would start a nuclear war. Kryuchkov, the KGB head, warned his agents around the globe to be on their guard: capitalism was fearful of plunging into collapse, seeing Communism sweeping the board in the developing world.

The paranoia began to lessen when Andropov died, thanks in part to British Prime Minister Margaret Thatcher. Although they had christened her the Iron Lady, the Soviets were impressed by her sensitivity during the funeral service for Andropov (she did not chatter like other Western leaders, and remained respectful even when the coffin broke open); and also by the profound political sense she showed during post-funeral discussions with the new leader, Chernenko.[12] Another geriatric, Chernenko did not last long. Mikhail Gorbachev replaced him.

Chernobyl exploded. Radioactive dust spread over the Ukraine and beyond Soviet territory. Man's lust to dominate nature was being rewarded. A huge area around the wrecked nuclear power station became a desert, uninhabitable perhaps for generations.

Newspeak continued in the Kremlin sanctum; on 2 November 1987, at the Palace of Congresses, Gorbachev addressed a mass television audience as well as foreign Communist icons—Honecker of East Germany, Jaruzelski of Poland, Castro of Cuba, Ceauşescu of Romania. The occasion was the seventieth anniversary of the October Revolution. "Neither the grossest errors nor the deviations from the principles of socialism that were committed could turn our people and our country from the path they embarked on in 1917," Gorbachev assured the millions. "The socialist system and the quest and experience which it has tested in practice are of universal human significance. It has offered to the world its answers to the fundamental questions of human life and appropriated its humanist and collectivist values, at the center of which stands the working-man. . . . In October 1917 we departed the old world and irreversibly rejected it. We are traveling to a new world, the world of Communism. We shall never deviate from this path."[13] The transcript announced *"Prolonged and stormy applause."*

They were indeed "traveling to a new world," but the rest of that sentence was less certain. As Freud dryly observed when told the Revolution would result in a period of chaos followed by an earthly paradise, "I half believe it."

50

The Broken Wall

How Sultan after Sultan with his Pomp
Abode his Hour or two, and went his way.
                                                          — *The Rubáiyát*

THE SPHINX OF HISTORY BLINKED, AND IT ALL VANISHED. THE IR-
reversible Revolution was no more; the gross cancer stopped growing, began
to shrink, then rapidly imploded—a miracle, like the one that had occurred
in a Tashkent cancer ward. The crucial moment came in November 1989
when dazed, joyful East Berliners strolled, as if sleepwalking, through a gap
in the wall into West Berlin. Something there was that didn't love a wall.

"The Union of Party and People is Unbreakable!" All those red buntings
assuring the world that *this*—Communism—alone was not subject to mu-
tability but was immortal: just souvenirs now, and museum items.

Even in Gorbachev's speech on the seventieth anniversary, recognizable
human language had occasionally broken through the heavy jamming of
newspeak nonsense. "The guilt of Stalin and those close to him before the
Party and the people for the mass repressions and lawlessness that were
permitted are immense and unforgivable . . . even now we still encounter
attempts to ignore sensitive questions of our history, to hush them up, to
pretend that nothing special happened. We cannot agree with this. It would
be a neglect of historical truth, disrespect for the memory of those who
found themselves innocent victims of lawlessness and arbitrariness."[1]

The prose was hardly Turgenev; but it belonged to a world—foreign to
Bolshevism—in which language is connected with meaning and sincerity; a
reluctant reformer, Gorbachev nevertheless opened the way to Communism's destruction by encouraging glasnost, openness.

True to Russia's history, works of art had been at the forefront in creating
this Easter of the spirit. Tens of millions had flocked to see a Georgian film,
Repentance, a surrealist exposure of Stalinism, in 1986. Even Gorbachev, it
was said, wept on seeing it: as Khrushchev had wept over *Ivan Denisovich*.[2]
Banned books started to blossom, like desert flowers after rain: *Doctor*

Zhivago, 1984 (in 1987), Akhmatova's *Requiem*, Vasily Grossman's long-lost *Life and Fate*; even Nabokov's *Lolita*. "It's more exciting right now to read than to live," said Tankred Golenpolsky of the State Publishing Committee.

During 1987 church bells rang out in Rostov, for the first time in fifty years.

Surely the time was ripe for Solzhenitsyn's works to be published. But he was still anathema to many conservatives because of his insistence that Lenin had begun the terror. To accept that would be to consign the whole Communist period to perdition. It was too much, at first even for Gorbachev.

In summer 1988, the loyal Liusha Chukovskaya wrote a short article appealing for Solzhenitsyn's citizenship to be restored, and sent it to a weekly journal, *Book Review*. Bravely its editor published it. Thousands of letters and telegrams of support poured in.[3] The momentum was unstoppable. Early in 1989, two newspapers, in Latvia and Lithuania, published "Live Not by a Lie," an essay that had appeared in samizdat just before his exile. In April the essay was published again in a small Moscow journal, *Twentieth Century and Peace*. In remote Kuban, another small journal began to publish a three-part "guide" to his work, consisting mostly of close paraphrase or quotation.

The editor of *Novy Mir* tried to persuade Solzhenitsyn to permit his journal to publish *The First Circle* and *Cancer Ward*; but the author was adamant that *Gulag* must appear first. He got his way—not before a last-ditch battle by the conservatives in the Central Committee and the censorship. At last, in October 1989, the first long extract from *The Gulag Archipelago* ran off the *Novy Mir* presses. The journal published one-third of the work in three issues. In so doing it added a million to its readership; some three million copies were sold. The state-run publishing house Sovietski Pisatel announced a collected works. Interest in Solzhenitsyn was enormous.

1990 became known as "the year of Solzhenitsyn."

Olga Carlisle was able to return to the Soviet Union at last, to visit her family; and among the joyful signs of thaw she found right-wing and anti-Semitic ideas that disturbed her greatly. Some of those who promulgated those ideas were calling for Solzhenitsyn's return. A true servant of the Russian earth, he was contrasted by far right speakers and writers with "depraved cosmopolitans" like Andrei Sinyavsky. Visiting the grave of Pasternak with a friend, she was told the great poet's profile had had to be cleaned, because it had recently been defaced. Olga felt sickened, and wondered whether "the grim prophet from Vermont" knew what kind of apologists he had in Russia? "Was it all said without his knowledge?"[4] The answer clearly was—yes. He had no knowledge of, nor would he have approved of, praise from extremists.

In the summer of 1990 he wrote down his ideas on the way forward for

Russia, and this long polemical essay was published by *Komsomolskaya Pravda*, a large-circulation daily. In 1991 the work appeared, under the title *Rebuilding Russia*, in English. His views on what constituted "Russia" had remained consistent since a KGB listening device heard him argue for the dismemberment of the Union and the liberation of annexed states. By 1990 that heresy had become an inevitability. Solzhenitsyn wished to see Russia, the Ukraine, and Belorussia forming a union of closely related peoples: the ancient "Rus." It would not be a question of *allowing* the Baltic states, the Transcaucasian states, the central Asian states, and Moldavia to leave; it was imperative that they did; at risk, if Russia clung on to empire, was the "spiritual and physical salvation of our own people."[5]

The Bolsheviks had played fast and loose with national boundaries, considering them of little importance. Kazakhstan had been permitted haphazard expansion; the northern half was essentially Russia. That would need to be adjusted; but of much greater concern to him was the position of the Ukraine and Belorussia. "I am well-nigh half Ukrainian by birth, and I grew up to the sound of Ukrainian speech. And I spent the greater part of my front-line service in sorrowful Belorussia, where I became poignantly attached to its melancholy, sparse landscape and its gentle people."[6] Addressing them therefore as "one of their own" he begged them to accept their unity with Russia; for all three had sprung from "precious Kiev." The Ukraine had suffered horrifically under Communism; but did this justify lopping the Ukraine off from a living organism? If their people genuinely wished to separate, they must be allowed to do so: but the area was so ethnically heterogeneous that the choice would have to be made on a local basis.

When the Ukraine opted for independence, and Kazakhstan declined to allow Russia to carve up its territory—however valid Solzhenitsyn's argument—he would become increasingly vocal about the "twenty-five million Russians [who] all of a sudden live outside Russia."[7]

Rebuilding Russia shows him as an anti-imperialist; and his dreams for the internal organizations of the new Rus ally him with the "greens." He wanted a return to the manufacture of durable goods. . . . "Today (in the West) we see a numbing sequence of new, ever new and flashy models, while the healthy notion of *repair* is disappearing. . . ."[8] (Cynics might have asked why his son Ignat drove a sporty new black Probe car rather than a battered old Chevrolet—but boys will be boys.) He wanted a decentralization of power, with about forty strongly self-governing regions, each with its culturally vital city. Only such dispersion could promote construction and repair of towns, villages, roads.

The young would have to be protected from America's "cultural imperialism," self-indulgent and squalid "mass culture."

His most trenchant criticism was reserved for Western-style democracy. He approvingly quoted Karl Popper's remark that one chooses democracy not because it abounds in virtues but to avoid tyranny; and the Austrian statesman Joseph Schumpeter's definition of democracy as "the surrogate faith of intellectuals deprived of religion."[9] The democrats of the February Revolution of 1917 had wrecked everything. Nationwide elections were especially open to question in a country as vast as Russia, for such a system results in voters "not knowing their deputies, a situation that benefits the smoothest talkers as well as individuals with strong behind-the-scenes support."[10] He was also struck by the preponderance of jurists and lawyers in most parliaments: a "jurocracy," in fact. Another drawback of democracy was that a well-organized minority could hold sway over a disorganized majority.

He remembered with admiration the sight of local democracy at work in Switzerland, and even to a minor extent in Cavendish. He wanted a democracy rooted in local elections, like the tsarist *zemstvos*. Such forms of local government would be likely, of course, to give rise to more conservative principles being applied. "European democracy was originally imbued with a sense of Christian responsibility and self-discipline, but these spiritual principles have been gradually losing their force. Spiritual independence is being pressed on all sides by the dictatorship of self-satisfied vulgarity, of the latest fads, and of group interests."[11] He disliked the very idea of political parties and "professional" politicians; they distorted the national will, and offered ideology at the expense of the personal, the individual.

In his most impassioned statement he decries the very practice of politics: "Political activity is by no means the principal mode of human life, and politics is hardly the most sought-after enterprise for the majority of the people. The more energetic the political activity in a country, the greater is the loss to spiritual life. Politics must not swallow up all of a people's spiritual and creative energies. Beyond upholding its *rights,* mankind must defend its soul, freeing it for reflection and feeling."[12]

A man or woman not enslaved to contemporary values might consider his remarks, upon reflection, as wise.

He emerges as a strong Russo-centered patriot (but not nationalist or imperialist); a conservative "green"; a defender of the less articulate and educated against the urban and urbane professional politicians. . . . This is not a program of far right politics, though it may be an unattainable vision.

The spiritual life underlay the worldly activities of the Solzhenitsyn household. Once a month an Orthodox priest came to hold a service in the private chapel on the first floor of the "working house"; and each morning the family prayed before its icons. Lent was strictly observed, as were the children's saint's days.

Alexander Isayevich went on writing in longhand, for eternity and against time. He had not yet reached the Revolution and the subsequent ambiguous death of his father, nor would he ever reach it.

His great friend Vadim Borisov had been appointed his agent in the Soviet Union, with the task of getting a definitive collection of his works published, in the desired order. Rostropovich, returning to Moscow in 1989, had said he had vowed not to come back until Solzhenitsyn was able to do so; but the writer had given him his blessing, and a message: he would come home when all his works were published freely in the Soviet Union. His citizenship had been restored by presidential decree, and his membership of the Writers' Union was restored too, in July 1989. After the vote readmitting him, the Writers' Union secretary, Vladimir Karpov, declared he had never seen such unanimity. "Not since we voted to expel him!" someone cried.

Borisov, whose academic career had been seriously harmed as a consequence of his support for Solzhenitsyn, found himself in the dreamlike situation of flying first class to New York, to meet his friend again after fifteen years. Collected from the local airport by Alya, Borisov saw for himself how undefensive the famous fence was, and found a relaxed, homely atmosphere. They should think about returning home, he urged; following the publication of *Gulag* he would possess huge authority. But Sanya, unlike Lenin, did not seize the moment. A charge of treason still lay against him, he pointed out; if there were a sudden reaction—as indeed almost happened two years later—he could be in danger. Sanya before had never feared danger, and in reality he did not fear it now; what held him back was that *The Red Wheel* still had some way to roll.

Back in Moscow, Borisov continued to organize the publication of his friend's works. There was enormous demand. Some seven million copies were published and sold. Gorbachev acknowledged in a televised session of parliament, in September 1990, that Solzhenitsyn was undoubtedly a great man; however, he advised the writer to stop cutting up the Soviet Union with "his scissors and his plough," and dismissed his political views as being "immersed in the past." The words that carried weight, though, were those that admitted, to a hushed chamber, Solzhenitsyn's greatness.

On 18 August 1991, hard-liners in the Kremlin staged a coup d'état, arresting Gorbachev at his opulent Black Sea dacha. Within three days Boris Yeltsin had jumped onto a tank in front of the Parliament building, appealing to the troops to support reform, and the bungling conspirators lost their nerve and the country. The intelligentsia, the young, and others with reasons to be hopeful about life were in ecstasy; though the babushkas went on stoically standing outside the metros at night, hoping to sell a few flowers or groceries. "No likely end could bring them loss / Or leave them happier than before."° What did it matter, to them, who the Tsar was?

"In August of 1991, my wife and I were incredibly excited to watch Dzerzhinsky's statue taken down outside the KGB building," Solzhenitsyn told reporter David Remnick. "That, of course, was a great moment for us.

°W. B. Yeats, "An Irish Airman Foresees His Death."

But I was asked at the time, 'Why didn't you send a telegram of congratulations?' You know, I felt deep inside that this was not yet a victory. I knew how deeply communism had penetrated into the fabric of life. . . ."[13]

On 21 September the chief Soviet prosecutor, Nikolai Trubin, found "no proof whatsoever testifying to any crime committed by Alexander Solzhenitsyn." The decision was made public through Tass. Immediately Sanya issued a statement saying that now there was no legal obstacle to his returning home—and he would do so. But first he must complete his writings, since in Russia he would become immersed in other concerns.

He had always—crazily, it seemed—insisted he would one day be able to go home; though he now admitted that in the early 1980s, when Andropov was in power, his confidence had waned; it had been a gloomy time. But now, the way was finally clear. . . . Except for *The Red Wheel*. Amid his rejoicing at the fall of Dzerzhinsky's statue, did he feel a twinge of anxiety that he had been writing about a dated Revolution? That people might now be much more interested in the current one?

Yevgeny Yevtushenko said the public prosecutor ought to have personally apologized to such a great writer; the dry official pronouncement was not enough. And the next day Trubin sent a telegram to Cavendish.

In June 1992 Alya, with two of their sons, stepped onto Russian soil again at Sheremetyevo Airport. They were greeted with flowers and embraces by a small crowd of friends and officials. She had come to prepare her husband's homecoming, she told the press. It would be the last move of his life, and it had to be well prepared.

Since the shock of arrest in 1945, he had always prepared meticulously for any eventuality.

By now the former Soviet Union was disintegrating. While welcoming the secession of non-Russian peoples, he must have grieved that the Ukraine and Belorussia chose to leave; and already there were quarrels between the Ukraine and Russia.

Alya had another, and primary, task besides planning their new home: to legalize and find premises for the Russian Social Fund, which had hitherto had to work unofficially, and in earlier times perilously, to help former *zeks* and their families. All of the royalties from *The Gulag Archipelago* continued to go to this fund.

Boris Yeltsin was in Washington that same month, discussing arms control and economic help for his country. He also found time to telephone Solzhenitsyn in Cavendish. He spoke in tones of penitence about the writer's persecution, and said Russia's doors were open to him. The writer told Yeltsin he supported his reform program, and urged that steps be taken as soon as possible to let peasants own land.

Toward the end of 1993 the decision was made: they would return home next May. Sanya made no farewell tour around the United States, but visited

Western Europe. He bade farewell to old friends in Germany and Switzerland; visited his publisher Nikita Struve in Paris; and had an audience with Pope John Paul II in Rome. At the International Institute for Philosophy, in the Liechtenstein village of Schaan, he called in his speech for "a saner, more limited role for modern technology, a search for spirituality that would allow men and women to move beyond self-absorption and fear of death."[14] His tone was mellower now; his rhetoric, according to David Remnick, was now leavened by "a pleasant, almost New Age modesty."

He also spoke at Lucs-sur-Bologne in western France, at a ceremony marking the Vendée massacres in the French Revolution's Reign of Terror. Revolutions, he said, destroyed the organic structures of life, cut off the best lives while giving free rein to the worst. He would not wish a "great" revolution on anyone.

Almost simultaneously, Ignat Solzhenitsyn was performing Shostakovich's Piano Concerto No. 1, with the National Symphony Orchestra of Washington, conductor Mstislav Rostropovich, at the Moscow Conservatory. The audience, overflowing into aisles and stairways, applauded heartily, and young girls leaned over the balcony to shout "Ignat! Ignat!" Others ran up to present flowers. Russian music had so often been the only secret language through which Russians could express their innermost feelings. The conductor André Previn has written that one of the most unforgettable events of his musical life was a performance by the London Symphony Orchestra in Moscow of Rachmaninov's Second Symphony, during which he saw members of the audience "openly and unabashedly weeping." Coming out of the stage door afterward into the icy street, he saw people still waiting; from among them a young woman came forward and, in a mixture of broken English and French, thanked him for the Rachmaninov. Then she gave him "a token of her gratitude to Rachmaninov": an orange.

That young Soviet woman, who had nothing to give but an orange—for which, as Previn observed, she had doubtless queued for hours—somehow seems richer than her counterpart in the West.

After his performance in freer time, Ignat Solzhenitsyn told journalists, "Not a day has gone by that we have not thought about coming back." Rostropovich described Ignat—who had been born at his dacha and was his godson—as possessing astounding talent.

Later, Rostropovich and the orchestra gave a free performance in Red Square, to a crowd of 100,000 people. The "1812 Overture" was performed with booming cannon fire and the Kremlin bells ringing. Boris Yeltsin, whom Rostropovich had firmly supported during the attempted coup, waded into the crowd before the concert to shake people's hands.[15]

Sanya would find a Russia transformed—not always to his liking. Pushkin's statue faced a McDonald's. The West was moving in. Send us your trivia, your TV game shows, your dazzling trash, your pornography! Russia was begging.

Public opinion was now being polled. In renamed St. Petersburg, 18 percent of those polled wanted Yeltsin for president; 48 percent wanted Alexander Solzhenitsyn.

Russia was bubbling—with hundreds of political parties, Mafia-type "hoods" from the Caucasus, and weird sects reminiscent of unreal, surreal Petersburg of Blok's time. A woman calling herself Maria Devi Khristos, aged thirty-three—the age of Christ at his death—was said to have 144,000 Ukrainian followers in the cult of the White Brotherhood, many of them children and teenagers. Three days before the world was due to end—according to Khristos—she was urging her followers to emulate her by killing themselves. The Kiev police arrested her and many disciples during violent scenes in Kiev's St. Sophia Cathedral. Khristos's husband was described, at the time of his arrest, as being dressed in a gray pullover and anorak, with matted filthy hair and a large scar across his forehead. He recognized only his wife's authority: "She is omnipotent." A late-twentieth-century female Rasputin.[16]

As Akhmatova had written of the year 1913: "Are the last days close upon us? . . . / Slogan writers, false prophets . . . / As in the past the future is maturing, / So the past is rotting in the future—A terrible carnival of dead leaves" (*Poem without a Hero*).

1993 also was a time that was beginning to have no time for heroes. Only salesmen. Heroin instead of heroines.

The Solzhenitsyns started to go home. It would take a long time. In February Sanya took his formal leave of Cavendish at the annual town meeting, just as he had said hello to it seventeen years earlier. Few people had seen him in the meantime. He presented the library with a selection of signed books, and received in return a memorial plaque. The village folk were probably more excited by the presence of a true celebrity, TV commentator Mike Wallace, and several camera crews from CBS's *60 Minutes*. They would remember the day Mike Wallace and CBS came.

Mike Wallace later gave his impressions of his meeting with the great man. He had found him "utterly self-absorbed, incredibly self-absorbed. He genuinely believed he had the Holy Grail and anyone who didn't understand that just didn't understand." He scarcely listened to the questions, his mind being made up already. "Everything in life was business, everything was hard work. His days were numbered, and he had very important work to do." Wallace found Alya "extremely attractive, interesting, indeed fascinating; a woman of immense intelligence; the ultimate protector and keeper of the flame; his handmaiden." It was obvious the children adored both parents.[17]

The youngest son, Stepan, was Sanya's interpreter on that occasion. He was now a junior at Harvard, studying urban planning. Ignat might have been right in saying, in Moscow, not a day had passed when they hadn't thought of returning to Russia; but in fact the sons were grown up and thoroughly Americanized. Ignat, when not studying piano and conducting at the Curtis Institute of Music in Philadelphia, was jetting around the world, to triumphant reviews. He drove his Probe at high speed, played loud rock music, and wore shades because his eyes were weak.* Yermolai, student of Chinese, had part financed his studies at Harvard, in true American style, by taking a part-time job as a bouncer in a Cambridge bar. He wanted to be a businessman in China.

Ignat and Stepan both had warm feelings for Cavendish, and for Vermont generally. The former was also quite at home jet-setting. He seemed to Susan Smallheer of the *Rutland Herald* more standoffish and self-protective than Stepan, who was shier. When Stepan attended the 1996 town meeting, "people just treated him like any college kid."

David Remnick, visiting for an interview with Solzhenitsyn and finding Ignat and Stepan home on vacation, gives a vivid impression of how Americanized they had become, and also how relaxed they seemed to be about their father. Asked if he ever stopped working, Ignat replied, with a smile, "No, he's never said, 'Today I'm just gonna chill out, get a job, and blow off this 'Red Wheel' thing.' Not one day."

Stepan added: "Chilling out is not exactly his thing."

"So, why can't the West get over this?" Ignat asked, becoming serious. "Why is his working all the time such an annoyance?"

"They assume he must be weird," Stepan said.[19]

Amidst the preparations for leaving—another kind of departure. Alya's first son, Dmitri, who had damaged an eye in a serious traffic accident some years previously, was running a business in New York restoring and selling Triumph and Norton motorcycles. Aged thirty-two, apparently in good health, he was living with his wife, Sabrina, and their six-month-old daughter Tatiana. The young man was charged with careless driving and disorderly conduct in Vermont, and had to pay a small fine. Soon after, in the early hours of 18 March 1994, his wife found him slumped on the bathroom floor, dead. Susan Smallheer of the *Rutland Herald* heard rumors of a drug overdose, but found the New York medical authorities unwilling to give information. According to the family, Dmitri had died of a heart attack. Sanya's secretary, Leonard DiLisio, and Father Andrei Tregubov, who officiated at the funeral, told reporters that most men in Dmitri's family suffered from congenital heart disease and died young.

The Solzhenitsyns wanted Dmitri to be buried on their Cavendish estate, but Vermont state law required a survey of private land before permission could be granted, and apparently there was insufficient time. The funeral took place at Father Tregubov's church, the Holy Resurrection Russian Orthodox Church in Clarement, New Hampshire, fifteen miles from

---

*In 1995, while driving with his sister-in-law Sabrina Tiurin and her two-year-old daughter, Ignat turned his Probe over twice on Interstate 91 in Massachusetts. Minor injuries were sustained. Ignat was cited for speeding and dangerous driving.[18]

Cavendish. The church overflowed with mourners. Alya, Yermolai, Ignat, and Stepan were in a church familiar to them, for they had regularly come for services; Sanya, however, had never been there, having preferred—perhaps because services were in English—to wait for Father Tregubov to visit him at home.[20]

Dmitri, an Orthodox Christian though unorthodox in his life, had in earlier years driven a Cadillac hearse around Cavendish. Now, still young, the Manhattan restorer of vintage motorcycles was being laid to rest in a Russian cemetery in a New England town. The snow-covered earth, too, seemed Russian, as the mourners—who included Dmitri's father, Professor Andrei Tiurin, and his second wife—sang "Eternal Memory." For Alya and her first husband, the sorrowful afternoon must have been filled with a sense of more deaths than that of their son.

Returning to Cavendish, Alya may have been grateful there was even more work than usual to occupy her. Four hundred packing cases started to be filled. Only the writer's desk would remain behind.

In that spring of 1994, Moscow bookstores were selling good quantities of novelized versions of the Charles Bronson movie *Death Wish*, an Italian TV series *Octopus*, and a Mexican soap, *Simply Maria*. Stephen King was a big best-seller. A British journalist, looking for copies of Solzhenitsyn, found nothing in the fiction section at House of Books, Moscow's biggest bookstore. A girl told him he could try the secondhand section. There he found a used copy of *Cancer Ward* and a small volume of short stories, so old that the store was glad to unload it for eighty-five rubles (five cents). At Book World he found no Solzhenitsyns at all. The market in Russian literature had collapsed.

His Moscow editor, Sergei Dubov, was gunned down by a Mafia-style assassin as he left his home one morning: murdered not because he brought banned classics to the masses but because he financed this with more lucrative advertising and lonely hearts magazines, money-spinners that some "businessman" craved sufficiently to have their owner removed.

The West was moving east with the Solzhenitsyns.

Also largely forgotten amid the piles of *zhenski roman*, or romantic fiction, was Natalya Reshetovskaya's fourth memoir, *Otlucheniye* (Excommunication). She had been able to publish this one without KGB nudging. Based on diaries and letters of 1968–70, the dramatic years marking the end of their marriage, it was sentimental, self-justifying, highly partial—and yet lively, at times loving, and moving. . . . By no means a classic memoir, no rival in style or depth of thought to the memoirs of Nadezhda Mandelstam or Yevgenia Ginzburg, yet pulsing with "the heart's blood."

Natasha was living in a small apartment off the Leninski Prospekt in Moscow. Suffering from cancer, she was in a twenty-year-old time capsule, surrounded by portraits and other mementoes of her life with Sanya. Her latest memoir showed her still bewildered and tortured by his changing moods of those years when he had met another, younger Natasha. . . .

On 8 October 1968, preparing to go off to Moscow for a few days, he says to her suddenly: "Do you remember today's date? This was the date when I first took your hand. . . ."

Her heart became warm. That was in 1937—thirty-one years ago! "It seemed as if we had never been parted. Our past and our present closed ranks together, creating the impression that we have been together our whole lives. . . ."[21]

To celebrate her fiftieth birthday, on 26 February 1969, she and Sanya went to see Turgenev's *A Month in the Country* at the Ryazan Dramatic Theater. She was touched that he waited till the end of the *second* act before suggesting they leave. The next day, seeing her off at the station on a trip to the Caucasus, he tried to put a letter into her hand. She asked what it was about, and gathered from his vague hints that he was inviting her to feel completely free to do whatever she wished, see whomever she wished. Bursting into tears, she thrust the letter away, crying: "I love you. I don't need anything other than you. . . ." When the train pulled out she tried to divert her thoughts by reading, in English, Jerome K. Jerome's *Three Men in a Boat*, but it fitted so ill with her mood that she laid the book aside and spent the rest of the day weeping.[22]

At Rozhdestvo in May 1969, amid springing tulips and narcissi, she rejoices in having retired from teaching. He writes, she gardens. "I love it when you are doing domestic things!" he says to her. She laughs when a chair breaks under her, and laughs again remembering it! "This is what it means to be free, to enjoy creative activity and to feel in oneself and for oneself a good love!"[23]

Again they're at Rozhdestvo in July and August. Sanya is preparing to go off on a research trip, to the north. His head, legs, back, are aching. "I hate to leave this place; I've lost my taste for travel."

Tartly she replies: "That's because you've stopped travelling with your wife. . . ." She is longing to go with him, but he explains there will be a lot of walking. Also, the superb eiderdown sleeping bag that Rostropovich has brought back for him from one of his foreign trips can only sleep one.[24]

While at the Rostropoviches', she described to Sanya how she had seen Molotov and his wife at the special store, shuffling arm in arm; the old Stalinist leaning on a walking stick. Sanya's face grew wrathful and he exclaimed: "If I had met them, I could not have restrained myself; I'd have said: Are you Molotov? I'm Solzhenitsyn. May we talk? . . . How can you live with hands dripping with blood? . . ."[25]

In August 1970, at Rozhdestvo, so loved by them both, he was in a stormy, silent mood, and they rowed. Natasha slept badly, and rose early to go for a swim in the stream. Sanya, already up, called to her to sit with him on the bench. "You and I are joined for life," she reports him as saying, "so how can there be talk of hatred between us? . . . But . . ." He fell silent, then continued: ". . . We must separate. Separate in order to meet again in the earth. You were always anxious about where you would be buried. I can see to all that in my will. Only, of course, for that you must die after me. . . ."

"But—why? . . ." she asked.

"You're always striking at me; I'm better when I'm not with you." Seeing her stricken expression he said irritatedly: "You've dragged it out of me before I've really decided. Why did you demand an explanation?"

She rushed in tears to her room. But soon they were both having breakfast with her mother, who had joined them for her eightieth birthday. The old woman, feeling the awful atmosphere, said, "Sanya, do you love Natasha?"

"Don't answer her!" Natasha cried. At that moment she knew that he did not love her, and she did not want it confirmed.[26]

Later that month she was alone in the apartment adjoining the Rostropovich house. Unexpectedly Sanya came. She burst into tears. He said, "I thought you were working well here, were in a good state of mind, but I see—you're suffering. . . ." He took her in his arms, murmuring, "I like holding you, kissing you. . . ." And suddenly started weeping too. "—You've no one to share your feelings with? No one who can advise you? Why don't you go to Suzanna [Teush], she'll advise you. . . . You must understand, in my novel I need to describe many women. I can't find heroines just by having dinner with them." They parted, both in tears.[27]

It is in her account of the night, three weeks later, when she tore up his fourteen-page letter confessing there was a woman expecting his child, that Natasha described most movingly her feelings and actions. She rushes from Veronica Stein's house into the night. Missing the last train to Zhukovka, she catches another that will take her somewhere near. Like Anna Karenina, she will end her life.

"I creep into a dark corner of the compartment. The train will leave in twenty minutes. Sitting opposite me is a young soldier. Suddenly he asks:— Why are you looking so sad?

"I didn't say I was parting from life, only: I'm just tired. . . ."

The train moves. After a few stops she gets out at a workers' village. She stumbles along the sleepers. The night is very dark. A light rain falls from time to time. Has she enough sleeping draught? No; she will take what she has, then turn on the gas. He, who has always had so little time for children or pregnant women! She can never forgive Veronica for agreeing to pass on that letter. She remembers how, during their walk in the woods at Rozhdestvo a month ago, he told her how glad he was she had given up two children for him! She veers off onto a path through a village, but a dog howls, and another, and a third. . . . It's more peaceful on the rail track, and she returns to it.

It begins to grow light; she can see the shapes of buildings. Exhausted, she sits on a bench, then rambles on and gets lost. By chance a car comes along, a taxi, and it stops. The driver scolds her for wandering alone at this time. . . . "Were you in the woods picking mushrooms? Even a tart shouldn't be out at this hour. . . ."

"Somehow the conversation with the taxi driver, and the taxi itself, brought an element of life, lessened my self-absorption; and new thoughts buzzed in my head. . . ." The first was that Veronica would never forgive herself if Natasha took her life tonight. Could she subject her to that? The second—was that before dying she wanted to know the name of the woman. . . .

She reached Zhukovka at five in the morning; drank coffee, swallowed a normal dose of the sleeping draught and, knowing Sanya would be coming in a few hours, took a sharp knife from the drawer, cut her finger, and with the blood scrawled on a white sheet the word:

I—?[28]

But it was only an early rehearsal. And when, a few weeks later, she staged her death in earnest—she failed.

With *Otlucheniye* Natasha became a genuine writer, at least on one subject, her love for Sanya. Ironically Sanya himself had scarcely been able to touch the subject of love for the past twenty years—perhaps in large measure because of that exhausting struggle with Natasha. Her passion and hysteria had been able to do what the KGB could never succeed in doing: make him frightened, and make him weep.

Alexander Isayevich spent the morning of his departure from America, 25 May 1994, writing in his denuded workroom.

Shortly after noon, in rain, the family's yellow station wagon came down the drive, followed by two blue vans. They belonged to the BBC, who had bought the rights to film the homecoming. They had interviewed the writer at his desk, and he had gleefully pointed out to them his colored pencils, a different color for different writing tasks. The procession stopped at the gates, and Sanya got out. He clasped an arm around the gatepost for a moment, and gazed back at the rain-softened birches. This, after all, was his home too. He had spent seventeen years here: the happiest and, he felt, the most productive years of his life. All departures are a kind of death. He had finished his great work. There was no time to start anything else, anything of substance. That too was a death. He could not hope to live for long back in Russia. He was going home to die.

David Remnick had asked him if he feared dying. His face lit up with pleasure. "Absolutely not! It will just be a peaceful transition. As a Christian, I believe there is a life after death, and so I understand that this is not the end of life. The soul has a continuation, the soul lives on. Death is only a stage, some would even say a liberation. In any case, I have no fear of death."[29]

To the twenty or so reporters and cameramen who clustered at the gate he said, "Good-bye. My son has answered all questions."

"Godspeed!" shouted a villager as the station wagon moved off.

"Thank you!"

The small procession of the Solzhenitsyns and representatives of the TV he hated rolled down the dirt road past the nineteenth-century cemetery, the snowmobile repair shop, took a left at Burton's Auto Repair and onto Vermont Route 131.

Joe Allen, at the general store, was left with his sign saying "No directions to the Solzhenitsyn home," a courteously inscribed copy of *The Gulag Archipelago* thanking him for guarding their privacy, and a slight grudge that the writer had not replied to his note of farewell.

From Logan International in Boston, Sanya, Alya, and Stepan, together with their media companions, flew to Anchorage, Alaska. They were to take a regular Air Alaska flight to Magadan and Vladivostok. Asked why he chose to travel to Moscow via Alaska and Siberia, he replied, "Siberia I only saw from the window of a prison convoy car." This was poetic license, for he and Natasha had traveled in Siberia. True, he had not traveled east of Lake Baikal. He thanked the people of the United States, and particularly his neighbors in Vermont, for providing him with a home. But he was stateless. "I would not take the citizenship of any other country. Now, as I return to Russia, I have a passport." He took a red passport from his khaki jacket and, smiling broadly, said, "Unfortunately it still says Union of Soviet Socialist Republics. But this is a Russian passport."

And Alaska had once been Russian territory. He was already starting to feel at home.

51

The Siberia Station

*Time to awake and to get up. Time to
arise, time for the resurrection*
—*Doctor Zhivago*

IN THE FIRST-CLASS COMPARTMENT OF AN AIR ALASKA PLANE, SANYA mingled pensiveness—pen and notebook ever in use—with a sociable animation. He signed autographs, posed for photos, and joked with Russian passengers. "You know," he told them, "I have picked out a place for my grave. It's in central Russia, and I'm inviting everyone to visit after I am gone."

The BBC camera crew filmed him solemnly adjusting the hour hands on his watch. Husband and wife glanced at each other and smiled as the pilot announced they were crossing into Russian airspace. When Stepan called across the aisle to say land was visible, his father moved with alacrity to gaze down through the broken clouds. Returning to Alya he murmured, his face radiant, "It's all changing; it's only now that everything's changing!"

The plane landed first at Magadan, in the Gulag Archipelago's most hellish circle, Kolyma. Before the doors were opened for him to alight, Sanya instructed his family not to smile, but not to look gloomy either. "Strong, thoughtful expressions . . ."

Greeted by journalists and a small band of supporters, he stooped to lay his hand on the ground, shook some welcoming hands, and gazed at the *zek*-built road winding twenty miles into the hills. He signed two of his books from the local library, and asked an official what food supplies were like; could people get tomatoes; could they make ends meet?

He said he had wanted to land here to honor the millions who had suffered and died in this region. "In the tumultuous wake of today's fast-changing political climate, these millions of victims have all too casually been forgotten—both by those whom this carnage has passed over, and needless to say, by those who perpetrated it. According to ancient tradition the soil where innocent martyrs rest becomes sacred. Let us honor it."

The family boarded the plane again for the last stage of the flight, southward a thousand miles along the coastline to Vladivostok. He thought of the cargo ships which, during months when the Sea of Okhotsk was not frozen, bore human freight, dead or alive, from Vladivostok to Kolyma: that land where the temperature sometimes fell in winter to ninety below.

Alya, exhausted from the weeks of packing, and much more by grief for her dead first child, was still anxious about Sanya's well-being. "It's going to be terrible for him, really terrible," she told an English journalist.[1] She meant, not the shock of the new Russia, but the twelfth-floor apartment in Moscow he would have to live in till their dacha was ready. He hated living in a city; when he opened a window in summer the noise of the traffic would hit him, she lamented.

Never was a writer more cared for, indeed cosseted, than Sanya by his second wife. She was the Chekhov "Darling" that he had once ordered prospective brides to read and consider: but a darling with a strong intellect and common sense, and a fiery temper—which she was later to unleash at the hordes of photographers in Vladivostok who took endless photos. "Would you like to look into our bedroom? . . . You press people are the world's second oldest profession!" she berated them, bringing uneasy chuckles.

This happened during a walk through Vladivostok's main market, on the morning after their arrival. Some two hundred cameramen and journalists made a mockery of their desire to talk with ordinary people. A crowd of about two thousand people had greeted their evening arrival; many thousands more had drifted away from the airport, for the flight was delayed and the weather was rainy and blustery. Yermolai, who had flown in from Taiwan, stepped forward to embrace his parents and brother as they descended the ramp. The damp crowd's cheers for the famous writer were respectful rather than enthusiastic. "To be frank and not to hide my soul," a former seaman remarked, "the years have passed him by." Others echoed him: "He has been away too long. I don't think there is much he can do." . . . "He is out of touch with the complexity of our lives." . . . And a single parent, surviving on seventy-five dollars a month: "He has been living for twenty years in America. I don't know what he can offer to us now." There were a few Communist demonstrators shouting that he had betrayed Russia; and a woman told a reporter he had been a traitor in the war, she had read it in the newspaper.

After receiving the traditional gift of bread and salt from two women in folk costume, the returning exile was driven, in a police car with blue lights flashing, to the waterfront, named ironically the Square of the Revolutionary Fighters. Out in the harbor, misty in the waning light of the late-May evening, lay the Russian fleet at anchor—rusting because there was scarcely enough money to launch a patrol boat. When he mounted a temporary podium, everyone could see he was dressed more like Fidel Castro than a wealthy man who had lived in America: not like his handsome sons in their casual but obviously expensive clothes.

It was here, on its eastern seaboard, that Russia had started a "small war" at the start of the century, hoping to divert the people's anger. Instead humiliation at the hands of the Japanese led to the revolutionary upheavals of 1905. Now, at another confused and angry time, Solzhenitsyn spoke for two hours. With his lank gray beard, bald dome, and flashing eyes under the vertical deep-trenched scar, he more than ever seemed an Old Testament prophet, preaching repentance. "I know I am returning to a Russia tortured, stunned, altered beyond recognition, convulsively searching for its own true identity. My heart longs for the day when my country's long-suffering people might finally find a ray of light ahead. . . ." But he doubted if he himself would live to see it. Indeed, since it had taken seventy years for Communism to wreck the country, it might take twice that to repair the damage.

No—in answer to a question—he did not believe he had come back too late. Russia had emerged from the period of trivia, and was now ready to search for an order built on her history, tradition, and spirit. Salvation would not come from the West, but from themselves. "What unifying idea will come I don't know; but the thought that comes naturally to mind is love for one's nation without servility, without false claims, with acknowledgement of sins and failings. Such patriotism could unite the Russian people."[2] And first the oppressors and executioners must repent—repent—repent.

He denounced Vladimir Zhirinovsky, a xenophobic nationalist who had gathered popular support, as a "caricature of a patriot, a clown." It was as if someone had wanted to create a purported Russian patriot so that he would be hateful to the whole world. But it was no shame to be a patriotic Russian; even the smallest nation must have its language and culture protected, since nations were the embellishment of mankind, but such a minority should not rule the Russian majority.

Demonstrating that he liked capitalism not much more than Communism, he spoke scathingly of the new class of cutthroat businessmen: "who rob the people before our very eyes, who thieve our national wealth," while others were dying of poverty. The robbers, too, must repent, and give to charity.

It was a bravura performance. All who heard him were amazed at the energy of this seventy-five-year-old man, who had been traveling for the best part of two days, and who at midnight seemed less tired than they were.

At the Intourist hotel where they were to stay, he was gratified to see a small display of his books: unaware that they had been brought from elsewhere in the city, and would be replaced after his departure by the usual stock of Stephen Kings and Jackie Collinses. Unfortunately, the new Russia needed to gorge herself on trash, and craved profits rather than prophets.

"Everyone knows his name, but no one reads his books," a brash young Moscow critic wrote. "Our Voltaire from Vermont is a spiritual monument, a hat-rack in an entrance hall. Let him stay in mothballs forever."[3] The attack drew fierce criticism, from Yevtushenko and many others, but represented a significant strand of intellectual opinion. The westward-leaning intelligentsia had no time for Solzhenitsyn's Slavophile patriotism; much more to their taste were the like-minded exiles who embraced Western democracy—and who kept their comfortable lives in the West. Rostropovich owned an apartment in Moscow, but came only for visits. Vladimir Voinovich, who had written a satirical portrait of Solzhenitsyn as a crazy nationalist riding back to Russia on a white horse (perhaps the rock on the Vermont property), visited often but kept his permanent home in Germany. Andrei Sinyavsky visited—but stayed living in France.

Few exiles from earlier emigrations had ever chosen to return wholly. But here was one man who loved Russia so much that he would stay forever: had already chosen the site for his grave.[4] Somewhere in central Russia. . . . But he hoped, before God called him, he still had a mission to fulfill. He was not sure what it was; certainly not president or any other high-ranking political post. Possibly he saw himself as the éminence grise to the political leaders, as well as inspirer and scourge of the people. He told the Vladivostok crowd that his writing was done, apart from a few short stories. "I have already written all of my books and fulfilled my literary task. Now it's time to start the hard work of rebuilding and reviving Russia."

Before a thousand-strong, rapturous audience at Vladivostok's technical university, he broke down as he described going out into the country and meeting peasants whose whole lives had been impoverished and poisoned. He had come back—when he might have remained very happily in Vermont—not because people were calling him a prophet, but because of his conscience. He could not escape his people's pain.

That came from his soul. Yet, alongside the "conscience of Russia," as one banner expressed it, was a dazzling theatrical director: Tolstoy with Eisenstein. Unique among returning exiles in choosing to land in the far east of the country, he had conceived the brilliant idea of having the BBC hire a special train for the eight-thousand-mile journey to Moscow. While he spent his days in Vladivostok speaking and looking, at the railroad station two green-painted private coaches were being stocked for a two-month trip. The train was luxuriously fitted with bars, bathrooms, and nine double-berth sleeping areas.

He explained his unusual and lengthy return journey as providing a chance to speak to the people across the whole length of the nation. And of course to see Siberia. There were mundane unspoken motives too; the fact that his Moscow dacha was not ready, and that the BBC was paying all expenses. Yet one can be sure the theatricality of the plan appealed most to the man who had once longed to be an actor. Theater vied with, yet did not corrode, sincerity. Concerned about making an effective entrance, he once insisted on four takes before he felt satisfied.

The luxury train, which had carried pampered Party leaders, drew some adverse comments. A decorator: "This is a disgrace. We thought Solzhenitsyn was a man of the people. If he really wants to meet ordinary Russians, why doesn't he ride on a normal train like the rest of us?" An elderly Matryona, who had stood on the waterfront for two hours listening to him speak: "I can't believe he is doing this. We thought he had come back to help us. Like everybody else, he is helping himself. He is actually riding in the coaches of the Communist leaders he so bitterly denounced."

Trains have played an almost mystical role in Russian history and literature. The Kaiser's Germany sent Lenin into Russia on a sealed train in order to subvert his enemy. Trotsky played a decisive part in the Civil War from an armored train. Who can forget how Anna Karenina came face-to-face with the enraptured Vronsky on a station platform and, when the journey resumed, could not read more than a few pages of her novel because she wanted to *live* life, not read about it?

One of the most magical chapters in *Doctor Zhivago* describes Yuri's train journey from Moscow to Siberia. The apparent endlessness of the journey, and the hypnotic rhythm of the engine, seemed to put him into a creative trance. It becomes a "time to wake up, time for the resurrection. . . ." "While Yuri slept his fill, the spring was heating and melting the whole of that enormous quantity of snow which had fallen all over Russia. . . . At first the snow melted quietly and secretly from inside. But by the time half the gigantic work of melting it was done, it could not be hidden any longer and the miracle became visible. . . ." The waters came rushing out, the forest stirred in its impenetrable depth, "and everything in it awoke."[5]—A metaphor suggestive of poetic creation, the Bolshevik Revolution in its brief euphoric phase, and the collapse of that brutal system, after 1989.

The synchronicities that seem to hover near great creative or destructive events, and which for that reason figure largely in Pasternak's novel, ran true to form in the disturbing weeks before August 1914. Akhmatova in a prose essay described how that summer she was returning home:

> In Moscow I got on the first mail train that came along. I was smoking on the open platform. Somewhere near an empty platform the engine slowed down and they threw on a bag of mail. Suddenly Blok appeared before my amazed eyes. I shout, "Alexander Alexandrovich!" He looks around and, since he was not only a great poet but also a master of the tactful question, he asks: "Who are you traveling with?" I managed to answer: "I'm alone." And the train pulls out.

Today, fifty-one years later, I open Blok's *Notebook* and under July

9, 1914, I read: "Mother and I went to look over the sanatorium near Podsolnechnaya.—A demon is teasing me.—Anna Akhmatova riding a mail train.[6]

Two of Russia's most exalted and refined poets, coming face-to-face among mailbags. . . . And Akhmatova increases the entranced mistiness of the experience through her reticence about what actually transpired. Then, on August 5 when the Battle of Tannenberg was raging, Blok, Akhmatova, and her husband, the poet Nikolai Gumilyov, had dinner at the Tsarskoye Selo train station. Gumilyov, later shot as a counterrevolutionary, was in uniform. When Blok left, Gumilyov said to his wife, "Can it really be that he will be sent to the front? That's the same thing as roasting nightingales."

Alexander Solzhenitsyn decided to add to the canon of momentous Russian train journeys, across its immense expanse, following the route of the Trans-Siberian Railway.

His wife, Yermolai, and Stepan were with him. The BBC documentary showed them setting out, a peaceful, happy family, and for a while—gazing at the estuary, with Manchuria on the other side—like ordinary tourists on an exceptional holiday.[7] But the pater familias was soon hunched over his black notebook, recording impressions in that cramped script developed in the Gulag. The first stop en route was Khabarovsk. There were interesting aspects of this industrial city on the Amur—not least the ships at harbor that contained nuclear waste.

Appearing before an audience at the Musical Comedy Theater, Solzhenitsyn carefully noted down all the questions and observations he received: "Is there a danger of extreme nationalism?" . . . "They don't know what is going on in Russia." . . . "If you meet Boris Yeltsin, let him know he should do more to build up Russia." . . . Visiting a collective farm, the writer noted complaints that it was impossible to get work out of the milkmaids, who were always drunk. Girls of twelve and thirteen should have better things to do than—the grumbler excused his language—make love. . . . In the days of the Pioneers children had somewhere to go, the grumbler added.

In a privately maintained cemetery commemorating a mass grave of thirteen thousand zeks, Sanya rested his forehead against a memorial stone while two priests read the Orthodox service "Eternal Memory." Deeply moved, he crossed himself continually. At the very core of his being was an absolute grief for, and solidarity with, the victims of repression. He had, in a sense, always possessed a citizenship: that of belonging to the country of Gulag. It was as important to him as his Russian citizenship. When, in the Lake Baikal region, he was greeted by a group of survivors from his own generation of zeks, his face became radiant, his smile joyful: and it was obvious there were no second, third, or fourth takes for the cameras. He spoke afterward, with the same radiant expression, of those strangers from the *Ozerlag* (lake camp) as his "true friends."

The lawlessness in Russia was now Chicago-esque rather than Stalinist. At one point early in the journey a drunk Arnold Schwarzenegger look-alike climbed on, and demanded protection money from an attendant: the train, he said, had entered his territory. After this encounter, extra security was provided.

"Nothing changes," Solzhenitsyn sighed to Alya—in sharp contrast to his joyful cry of "now everything changes!" as they had entered Russian space.

She remained with him only until Khabarovsk, when she prepared to fly off with Stepan to Moscow. It was necessary to see how the wretched building work was proceeding. In the documentary, Sanya is shown warning her not to expect long phone calls from him: she could read all their news in the newspapers. When she demurred, he chided her, half humorously and with a trace of self-irony, for preferring to waste an hour on the phone rather than read a newspaper report in five minutes. They exchanged a lingering kiss, which suggested that passion was by no means dead.

Yermolai, who remained, commented to the cameras that it would be great to spend so much time alone with his father, since they had never really had a chance to talk. The train moved on, its next stop Blagoveshchensk. A crowd of about two hundred people awaited him. "I did not expect so many," the writer said, thanking them. In fact, at some stops there were so few people interested in meeting him that worried officials had to manufacture a crowd: a frequent occurrence during the Communist decades.

But for most of those who greeted him, it was a momentous occasion. In Blagoveshchensk there was a man for whom this day was to be his crowning experience. Vladimir Shatkov presented an unforgettable appearance. Beneath a white peaked cap his gaunt, gap-toothed face had the stunned, almost angelically simple look of one who had been dragged for a time across the border of sanity. He had been imprisoned for three years, he explained, in a penal psychiatric institution—compared with which the labor camps were holiday resorts. You could be trussed up for three days, totally immobilized; you were fed drugs that made your tongue protrude from your mouth. There were people still undergoing the torture. He himself was still officially a *zek*, unrehabilitated. Solzhenitsyn, with his commandment not to live by the lie, was for him "second only to the Almighty. . . . So why would I not go to greet him? . . ."

When his Gogolesque presence appeared on the station platform, the second person of Shatkov's Trinity was signing a book for a smooth, plump, smartly suited man. Similar bland and well-dressed men were queued up behind. Shatkov came up close to warn his hero, "This man's KGB! I know him! Don't sign for him." The preoccupied writer interrupted his signature to tell the "heavies" who were dragging Shatkov away to release him. Shatkov then repeated his warning. In a slightly irritated tone Solzhenitsyn told him he could not refuse to sign a book; Russia had suffered enough from purges; there must be no show trials, but rather everyone must be given a chance to repent. The KGB man waited with a blank, unruffled expression.

Shatkov walked out of the station, his back bowed in disappointment, his hands thrust in his pants pockets. Afterward he said, "Of course I know it's difficult for him. He's been away a long time. His eyes are still bright, but"—he tapped his nose—"I think he's lost his sense of smell."

Sanya's smell was undiminished; he knew the same Communist officials and KGB men were still in charge. But as he explained later, seated in the gently chugging train with birch forests drifting past, when he was signing books he could not make moral distinctions.

The man who had said, in his Nobel speech, "One word of truth outweighs the world," and "In the struggle against lies art has always won, and always will win," was observed by Shatkov at a moment when he resembled a Western author in a bookstore, smiling distantly and scribbling his name and best wishes whether the purchaser was a hospice nurse or a serial murderer. Art not as truth but as a commodity. Shatkov was shocked, because he still lived in the world where art was pure and a great writer was—as Solzhenitsyn had said—like another government.

Yet that could never happen again—unless Russia again became a tyranny.

At Ulan Ude in the Buryat Republic, he listened expressionlessly at a banquet to a large, Mongolian-faced baritone yowling a Soviet song extolling the unity of Russians, Buryats, Georgians, and Latvians. At the end, Sanya surprisingly leapt to his feet to embrace him. At one of the customary "listen to the people" conferences, a rather impressive speaker in the packed hall spoke with irony of the "freedom" which this guest had helped to bring into being. "What freedom?... Freedom for our old people to rummage through trash cans for leftovers from the rich man's table! Go home!"

The speech stung Solzhenitsyn into a passionate reply. Yes, he had fought Communism all his adult life.... "An ideology that killed a third of our people!" His thunderous words drew enthusiastic applause. He went on to say that he had not advised Gorbachev to disrupt industry and government, nor had he advised the next administration to raise prices so steeply and suddenly. Again the applause rang.

At Irkutsk, the train was abandoned for a time in favor of a cruise on Lake Baikal on a luxury yacht. No one could begrudge the writer for taking a rich man's cruise after twenty years of uninterrupted work. And even comfortable trains can grow wearisome after a few weeks. He had already come three thousand miles. Maps give a misleading impression of Siberia; the Irkutsk region alone, of which Irkutsk city was the capital, occupies an area equivalent to Germany, Austria, Switzerland, and Italy. He had need of some days of fresh air, on the world's deepest lake.

Resuming his journey, he visited the high-powered scientific community of Akademgorodok ("Academy Town"). Founded in 1957 as the scientific center for Siberia, the town of one hundred thousand housed eighteen research institutes and a university. Now Ph.D.s, their small salaries unpaid for months, were trying to sell or barter anoraks and cheap dresses they had flown to China to buy. The market economy had arrived.

West again, to Tomsk, where he had been a transit prisoner on the way to Ekibastuz camp. In a cardiac institute, a gloomy room with two male patients who breathed with the aid of oxygen and already bore the pallor of death. "How are you? . . . I can see that; I'm sorry. . . . All the best. . . ." The camera lingered in the deathly room after his exit. One of the sick men breaks the heavy silence with a sigh and a laconic summing up: "The famous man comes and goes. The ordinary man listens, and stays behind. . . . It would have been good to speak with him, but he hasn't the time."[8]

Westward still, to Tobolsk, on the river Irtysh. "I can't imagine myself in America now. I am immersed in Russia. In years to come I shall still be assimilating what I have seen and heard on this journey." He confessed that, though he has been an optimist all his life, now he is not optimistic. He has only hope.

The little black notebook. The spidery writing, after a searching glance into the distance. The notebook will surely be at hand while he is dying. He has noted down a car drive through floodwater to a remote farm, where a babushka, Matryona in rubber boots, up to her knees in water, shrilly scolds this unknown but obviously important man for the constant flooding: "Why can't you do something about it?"

"I'm not an official," he replied; "I can't do anything."

European Russia at last: his heart leapt at the sight of melancholy brooks, meadows, and copses. At Yaroslavl, city of golden domes and spires, Alya and Ignat had arrived to meet him. We observe the three males, Sanya, Yermolai, and Ignat, as they call out to their mother to leave the washing and join them for the family conference. She comes. "*Dyevushka* [girl]!" he says. "How's the building coming on?" Not so good. "Is everything unpacked?" Of course. It's been heavy; she's wrenched her shoulder. "When can we move in?" "Do you want the truth? . . . Well, it's only twenty-five minutes' drive from the flat; I could drive you there in the morning, and fetch you at night. . . . It would be impossible to sleep there."

The Yaroslavl station, Moscow, 21 July 1994. Rain is falling. Moscow's dynamic mayor, Yury Luzhkov, is there to greet him. A crowd of some two thousand is kept back by armed riot police. The rain falls more drenchingly. "If you don't keep back," growls Luzhkov at journalists, photographers, camera crews and the *narod*, "he'll never get off the damned train!" When he does alight, beaming, waving, the clapping is warm though not ecstatic. He had met wonderful people, he shouts at the crowd: "Students, farmers, factory workers. People who live in slums, doctors and teachers who work without pay for their fellow countrymen. . . . I hope today I can start to bring their message to the ears of the leaders in Moscow. Our country is collapsing into itself. I have heard groans of anguish from every corner of Russia. The state does not meet its obligations. A snake of crime has wrapped itself round our society."

A small number of Communist demonstrators boo him, and a voice snarls: "Jew!"

Many of his genuine welcomers had been in the camps, or had had relatives there. They came to show their gratitude for the man who had told the truth.

In that murky evening light another train draws in; only it comes from the West, not the East, and it's arriving at Petrograd's Finland Station. From it steps another cleanser—Vladimir Ilyich Lenin.

Lenin and Solzhenitsyn, staring cold-eyed at each other across the corpse-filled gorge of the twentieth century.

52

The Old Believer

Be careful what you struggle for—you will probably get it.
—Russian proverb

WHEN PEOPLE IN THE STREET WERE ASKED WHETHER THEY thought Solzhenitsyn would play an important part in the country's future, there were three main responses: that he would provide moral leadership, as "the conscience of Russia"; that he had arrived too late and would have little or no influence; and "Who's he?"

There was one person living in Moscow who felt an obsessional interest in his return home. The frail, half-blind Natasha told a Western reporter she had never doubted he would come back. "I feel the same way now as when he was my husband. My feelings have not changed. Never mind how he behaved. Sometimes I feel sorry for him. I am trying to be calm. It was easier when he was far away."[1]

He had sent her money and medicines, she said, in the early 1980s, when he heard she had cancer; but there had been no personal contact. "He likes to think there is only one Natalya." She had seen him arriving at Vladivostok; from the blurred images on her television screen she judged him to be in good health. She spoke agitatedly of his accusations against her: for example that at their last meeting at the Kazan station she was leading him into a KGB trap, and that she led the KGB to a draft of *The Gulag Archipelago* in Leningrad. "My fingerprints were on the film plates!" she exclaimed indignantly. "I had made them all, risking my own freedom. I told no one. But he is the great authority, and who am I?" Still she spoke of him with reverence, reading significance into the fact that his name contained all the letters of the Russian word for sun, *solntse*.

She hoped he would visit her. Someone had to explain to him. "He left me. I did not leave him. He blames me. This is the paradox."

After the brief media frenzy over his arrival, he vanished from her screen into her memory.

. . .

Sanya settled into the twelfth-floor apartment. It was comfortable; important officials lived in the block; there were always chauffeur-driven Mercedes drawing up outside. The Troitse Lykovo dacha, still not ready, was threatening to turn into a white elephant. Alya used her old apartment, which the city authorities returned to her, as the office for the fund to aid *zeks*.

Few people begrudged him his wealth; they felt he had worked for whatever he had; it was only the robber barons they detested. But his denunciations of materialism struck the short-story writer Tatiana Tolstoya as suspect. Scanning his biography for a model of the spiritual life he advocated, she found from his American years, "Fifty acres of land . . . two houses on the lot . . . twelve volumes of collected works . . . a second wife . . . three children . . . a son at Harvard, when he could have studied at a little Vermont college . . . a son playing piano and giving concert tours when he could have stayed home and beat humbly on a toy drum. Money? The author's income is not publicized, but as early as 1974 there is mention of $2 million to $3 million. . . . What a relief! The threshold of self-limitation established by the prophet of Vermont is clearly unattainable in actual Russian life. Russians may sleep soundly."[2]

In the same acerbic article, Tolstoya compared Solzhenitsyn to the irascible and magical old man of Russian folklore, Koshei, who preferred to remain aloof from the world. He always kept a semi-magical woman "to scratch his head at night," be his wife and housekeeper, and convey his wishes pleasantly to the outside world.

To some people it seemed odd and somehow distasteful that his dacha at Troitse Lykovo, overlooking a bend of the Moscow River, was on land that once belonged to Marshal Tukhachevsky and the monstrous Stalinist mobster Lazar Kaganovich. Beria too had lived nearby. It was prime land. On Fridays the black Chaikas, bearing the people's servants, used to race straight up the "Kremlin Lane" to this luxurious preserve. But after all, Solzhenitsyn had had Kaganovich's dacha knocked down. . . . It was a symbolic gesture to have his own dacha built in its place. Besides, you could not cancel out Russia's past—that was what the Bolsheviks had done; you had to build on the foundations you had.

As for the ghost of Tukhachevsky . . . Well, there were worse Old Bolsheviks. The greatest Russian military brain of the thirties; brilliant, but with a touch of cruelty. Courageous in refusing to confess to spying at his show trial in 1937. He would be an interesting shade—if Solzhenitsyn ever moved in.

He paid a visit to Rostov, where he and Natasha had strolled as sweethearts. He recognized and hugged on the station platform a school friend, now an old woman. Another old student friend, bedridden, skeletal, was sad, and his wife angry, because Sanya could only spare fifteen minutes in their tiny home. The returning hero's guide, Sasha Kozhin, was a bearded, melancholic version of the young Solzhenitsyn. Kozhin was trying to organize a Solzhenitsyn museum, but had so far found only a few school note-books. After a few days in the living writer's company he began to see that his idol was only a man.

But the sometimes irate visitor was relaxed and genial, walking slowly like a *zek*, as he showed Alya the city. A bobbing video camera preceded him, a comet trail of journalists and old acquaintances followed. They wanted him to talk about himself; he would talk only, in a rapid-fire lecture, about old Rostov; and so they looked somewhat bored. Alya, in an elegant long skirt, was tired-looking, oppressed by the late-summer heat and sun. Though his portly stomach filled out a gleaming-white, smocklike shirt, Sanya looked cool, tireless, in rude health. When Sasha Kozhin asked him if the walking tour would be including Chekhov Lane, he said no, it wasn't important, he had only lived there for his final university year. Natasha, his companion of that year, had vanished, like an inconvenient figure from a Soviet photograph.

Alya was shown libraries, school, university, the Fedorovsky apartment, and his childhood homes or their remains. But the first and most important was still there. They passed the large KGB building into a back alley where people still sometimes came across spent shells from some back wall secret midnight execution in the late 1930s. Round the corner into a yard of sheds and hovels that hadn't changed since Sanya had lived there with his mother. Many dogs and lean half-wild cats. Bits of rusty metal. An old man who had been their neighbor in those days hobbled out of his shack. "Alexander Isayevich!" cried the old man, embracing him.

"It's good to see you! How are you?"

"The Council still won't find me somewhere else to live."

"They should, they should."[3]

Katya, his mother in law, came home to Russia. Yermolai, Ignat, and Stepan returned to Taiwan and America. Good-looking, talented, well-adjusted, and taking up well-paid professions, they could look forward to rewarding futures. Alya and Katya settled to making domestic life, twelve floors up in a metropolis, as comfortable as possible for their man: even to—according to rumor—telling him a white lie about how much a new cooker had cost. Like many older married writers, even ones not suddenly confronted with Russia's inflation, he had no idea what things cost. Another rumor suggested that Alya had ordered a $100,000 kitchen, on the grounds that they would be entertaining young writers there.

Were that rumor true, it may have disturbed her to find that some young or youngish writers were either indifferent or hostile to him. Grigori Amelin, who compared Solzhenitsyn to a hat rack in a hall, did not stop at that; delighting in the insults thronging into his brain he wrote: "put this eunuch of his own fame, this thoroughbred classic with a hernia-threatening Collected Works, a Hollywood beard and a conscience polished so unbelievably clean it glints in the sun, out to pasture. . . ." The liberal-minded novelist

Victor Yerofeyev also indulged in inflated criticism. Solzhenitsyn had become comic, a prophet not up to his role. "The humanistic pathos of Solzhenitsyn, which informs all his writings, seems no less comic, no less obsolete, than Socialist Realism as a whole. . . . A Slavophile Government Inspector has come to call on us, dragging behind him all the traditional baggage of Slavophile ideology. . . ." He was "a provincial schoolteacher who has exceeded his authority and overreached himself."[4]

Yerofeyev makes some thoughtful points in his essay, for example arguing that "a worn-out country and a worn-out population . . . dreams not about holiness, but about a normal, decent, civilized life." To westerners, Yerofeyev wrote, it might seem exotic and amusing to hear nationalists denounce every sign of Russia's Europeanization, from political pluralism to rock music, but denunciations of the West as an "evil empire" of the *spirit* were not in the people's interest. But the sneering description of the author of *The First Circle* and *The Gulag Archipelago* as a "provincial schoolteacher," a phrase he has used more than once about him, discredited Yerofeyev rather than Solzhenitsyn.

The tone of such assaults was reminiscent of those by Bolshevik writers of the 1920s on writers who belonged to the dead classes. The Futurist poet Mayakovsky, for instance, about Akhmatova and her contemporaries: "Of course, as literary milestones, as the lastborn child of a collapsing structure, they find their place on the pages of literary history; but for us, for our epoch—these are insignificant, pathetic, and laughable anachronisms."[5] Mayakovsky actually read Akhmatova's poetry every day; he was carried away partly by ideology, partly by a Russian delight in invective.

Under Communism, Yerofeyev would have been a natural ally of Solzhenitsyn. During the 1960s, the liberal intelligentsia had banded together against the common enemy; Sakharov and Solzhenitsyn had been on the same side, despite the obvious tensions and disagreements. Now the enemy had been vanquished, and the former unity was shattered.

Not only were there conflicts within their own circle, but the position of writers and intellectuals within society as a whole had dramatically altered. In the nineteenth century, writers had taken on supreme moral authority. Readers turned avidly to Turgenev, Herzen, Dostoyevsky, and Tolstoy for wisdom as well as pleasure. When the Bolsheviks took over, they molded that tradition to their own use; writers (of the right persuasion) would become "Engineers of Human Souls." The people would trust Maxim Gorky if he reported on the towering achievement of constructing the White Sea Canal. The regime set up a Writers' Union, making it extremely difficult to gain entry but like a ticket to paradise for those who did. Top writers kept a servant, chef, chauffeur, secretary, and gardener at their dacha; for the rest there were the special store, the subsidized restaurant, an exclusive hospital where the indisposed writer was met by a pretty receptionist who led you straight to the doctor's office. And after the operation, you could go to a sanatorium "where a writer could stay in a spacious room and write a novel about the working class or poetry about sunny weather while lolling on the couch . . ."[6]

On the royalties from a feeble book that no one read an author could live for two years. It was a sweet deal. The state didn't want real writing, and the feather-bedded authors obliged.

But there *were* a few real writers, writers whose work became all the stronger and more noble for the darkness around them. Tyranny makes *every* display of virtue, in whatever walk of life, stand out in sharpest relief. For writers in the Stalin era, the choice of integrity or compromise could also mean a choice between Kolyma (or death) and luxurious privilege. (Although the privileged too, of course, might perish.) To the century-old tradition of reverence for writers was added an awed gratitude to those writers who risked all in the cause of truth.

Literature has never had a more exalted standing than in the 1960s, when people wept over works by Solzhenitsyn, in particular, then spent nights without sleep feverishly typing out fresh copies, to be passed on to others. Art was the heart's blood, in Edvard Munch's graphic phrase. However, when the dissident writers went into voluntary or involuntary exile, the great majority of those who stayed learned to live more or less comfortably with Brezhnev's regime, and enjoyed getting their Moroccan oranges and Finnish cheese at half price. The prestige of the intelligentsia went into decline.

Then a paradoxical thing happened with the advent of Gorbachev's glasnost and perestroika. The intellectuals were overjoyed, became Gorbachev's praetorian guard, strove to enter parliament, and lobbied to have banned works published. In the explosion of artistic freedom, several masterpieces Doctor Zhivago, The Master and Margarita, Grossman's Life and Fate, works by Babel, Zamyatin, and Nabokov, Akhmatova, Tsvetayeva, and Mandelstam—might be jostling one another on the newly imported "best-seller" lists. These Russians! we thought—what a hunger for true literature they have!

The victors, it appeared, were Russia's great writers; not least, Solzhenitsyn. As late as 1991, writes David Remnick, he would go to readings in Moscow and hear audiences ask poets and novelists the old Tolstoyan questions: What is the meaning of life? How should we live it?[7]

Yet in this moment of triumph, there was the paradox that the intellectuals and artists were at one with the government. Two centuries of proud and courageous dissidence, on the part of the most thoughtful, was over. At that moment they lost their special moral authority, their numen. Henceforth they were just writers, with individual opinions for or against the government of the day.

They also lost their privileges. The Writers' Union was broken up into smaller competing unions, and its assets taken back by the state. Subsidies were ended, prices freed. No longer could writers get subsidized food, books, or haircuts; the specialist surgeons started charging fees. Publishers had to pay for paper and find royalties for their authors out of their own pockets. They started closing down. Dying too were the literary institutes where writers could appear for a couple of hours a day to think great thoughts over a coffee, and receive a living wage for it. Now their salaries were practically worthless, and often months in arrears.

Royalties became merely symbolic; *Novy Mir*, its sales down from two million to fifty thousand, paid fifty dollars for a hundred-thousand-word novel.[8] The best-seller list took on a Western look; the top five books in Moscow's nonfiction list for December 1994 were *How to Become a Happy Cat*, *How to Get Rid of a Tummy*, *Embracing the Universe* (eyewitness accounts of life after death), *Cleaning the Organism*, *Biorhythms and Urine Therapy*, and *Fifty Ways to Lose Weight*. The fiction list had an Arthur Hailey and a Denise Robbins at numbers two and four. Pornography flourished; native writers started to publish thrillers and romances that made Stephen King or Danielle Steel seem positively intellectual. The workman who, at Pasternak's funeral, cried out emotionally that the time would come when Russians would know *all* his works, would have been mortified to find that, when all his works were available, people would prefer to read Arthur Hailey.

Some young writers found the chaos an exhilarating challenge, just as Mayakovsky and others had done after the *last* revolution. They wanted to smash everything, and begin afresh. They were intent on explorative techniques far more daring than Solzhenitsyn's token modernist devices in *The Red Wheel*. Anarchists of the imagination, valuing style and irony, they had nothing to learn from the graybeard from Vermont, and were as likely to attack him as Stalin. He was, after all, just the reverse of the Socialist Realism coin: an upstanding hero (Solzhenitsyn) taking on a corrupt world.

Older writers who had become used to finding out what they could get away with from the censors faced another, metaphysical problem: how to handle complete freedom of expression. That freedom had not led Solzhenitsyn to write better in Vermont than he had under tyranny. Would he have written *The Gulag Archipelago* with such demonic energy if he had been writing it in Yeltsin's Moscow, with his editor calling him to ask, "How's the *Gulag* coming along, Sanya? . . . Take all the time you want . . ." rather than in a secret farmhouse in Estonia?

When his works first appeared in the Soviet Union in 1990, seven million copies were sold; but by the time he arrived in Russia the market had collapsed. In 1996 only fifteen thousand subscribers could be found for a new collected edition. *The Red Wheel* was considered unreadable by most people. The truths which the work had been going to unlock were by now "old hat" to the historians.

Sanya quarreled with his Russian agent, his son Stepan's godfather, Vadim Borisov. Borisov had been a staunch friend. Visiting Irina Shcherbak in Georgievsk in 1979, he had found her living like an animal, her mind almost gone. He had brought her to Moscow. Though he and his wife, Tanya, were barely surviving themselves as a consequence of their support for Sanya, they had looked after the old lady until her death a year later—no easy task. That service did not seem to count for much when Borisov displeased the master over the Russian publication of his books.

So far as one can establish, he expected four results from Borisov's efforts: his books should be published in large quantities; they should be cheap; they should be produced on good quality paper; and he should get a good financial return. It was extremely difficult for Borisov, negotiating with the publishers, to fulfill all these expectations. There was a distinct failure in quality, though it was not inferior to many other book productions of the time. The publishers may have been imitating the building workers at Troitse Lykovo, and Borisov, a gentle and palpably honest man, may have defended the publishers unwisely. Sanya—perhaps used to American and Svetlovan speed and efficiency—was incensed; Borisov, then editor of *Novy Mir*, fell ill. A twenty-five-year-long friendship ended. Borisov's brave, honorable life ended in 1997, when he tragically drowned in Estonia. Sanya did not attend his funeral, Alya attended, but did not speak to Tanya, once her close friend.

In terms of literary values, Solzhenitsyn arrived at his Finland Station in midwinter zero temperature. "Be careful what you struggle for—you will probably get it," says the proverb. Solzhenitsyn is "hopelessly outdated," observed Vitaly Tretyakov, editor of *Nezavisimaya Gazeta.* "Nobody believes in anything anymore." In line with that observation, the blackly comic postmodernist Dmitri Prigov could inform an interviewer that his aim was "to deconstruct the figure of Lenin and also the figure of Solzhenitsyn. They can both be responded to as pop figures.[9]

How infinitely far was that society in which a book could make Alexander Tvardovsky rise and dress, to honor the unknown author, then spend the night weeping for joy and anguish over it! . . . In which a *Novy Mir* employee could say she would gladly sacrifice her career to have *Ivan Denisovich* published. . . . In which the journal's offices became as silent and solemn as a church on the day when people crept in to buy their copies for seventy kopecks. . . .

But it must also be admitted that Solzhenitsyn was a long way from the Sanya of the fifties and early sixties: the passionate *writer*. The prophet often had wise words to say, but they were torn away by the wind. Even more than the late Tolstoy, he had turned into a polemicist. Matryona had knocked and knocked, but the writer inside was distracted by a computer's hum, and she had gone grumbling away. This was *her* house!

In October 1994, after reclusive months in which he had only ventured out to "meet the people," Solzhenitsyn accepted an invitation to address the lower house of parliament, the Duma. He thundered at them for an hour, his hands gesturing dramatically as he accused them of perpetuating the ruin of Russia. Suicides had increased, life expectancy had dropped, and the death rate was greater than the birthrate. There was no democracy, only an oligarchy. The people at the bottom, to whom he had been talking, were excluded from the system. Calling familiarly for a union of the Slavic peoples, he demanded that Russia protect her own people in the Ukraine and Kazakhstan. He feared that unless there was swift action, Kazakhstan would unite with Turkey and make Russians subjects of the Turkish empire. He also called upon the government not to privatize farmland, since that would allow "Russia itself" to be bought by the nouveaux riches.

His speech left most of the deputies unmoved. Some yawned and pretended to snore. The warmest applause came from Zhirinovsky's ultranationalist faction. *Pravda*, too, the old Communist Party newspaper, had ironically a few kind words to say: "We do not have to make an ally out of this anti-communist. But one cannot avoid being infected with his passion and desire to rebuild Russia so that workers can live honestly." A month later he had a low-key meeting with Boris Yeltsin, whose presidency he avoided attacking or endorsing.

In the fall of 1994 he became a talk-show host. The fifteen-minute program, on Channel 1 in prime time, was apparently introduced at his request. *Meetings with Solzhenitsyn* was taped in his cramped study, with Alya and a guest squashed beside him at his desk to a background of massed bookshelves. The guests, who included Svyatoslav Federov, an innovative eye surgeon, and Vladimir Lukin, former ambassador to Washington, often found it hard to get a hearing, as the host continued his assault on the moral depravity destroying Russia. The show attracted little notice from critics. One of his rival talk-show hosts, Artyom Troitsky, a rock critic with a post-midnight program called *Café Oblomov*, represented the reactions of the trivia-welcoming classes: "Why should anyone now care about *The Gulag Archipelago*? I'm afraid Solzhenitsyn is totally, totally passé." Determined not to be passé, Troitsky had turned from being a serious "rock" dissident to editing the Russian *Playboy*. Victor Yerofeyev was not slow to pass comment on Solzhenitsyn's stuffy, old-fashioned program: "It's better to have him speak than write. He writes such ugly Russian. He is once again what he always was at heart—a provincial schoolteacher."

This, and the attacks by Tatiana Tolstoya and others, a Russian historian compared to the shrieking of ravens over the still-living body of a giant.

A respectable 12 percent of Moscow viewers (as compared with 27 percent, who watched *Wild Rose*, a Mexican soap)° tuned in to the provincial schoolteacher—who claimed to receive thirty or forty letters a day, mostly from desperate older people seeking help. Eventually he decided to dispense with a guest. The program was cut back to twice a month, then in September 1995 axed altogether. Some saw a political motive in this, but it is more likely that purely commercial reasons were involved. Too many people were bored with being harangued. They preferred the new erotic program, on which the first guest was La Cicciolina, Italian parliamentarian

---

°One terminally ill man wrote to a newspaper offering his life savings to anyone who could tell him the ending of another Mexican soap, *The Rich Also Cry*.[10]

and porn queen. Not to mention *Café Oblomov*, suitably named after the Goncharov character who loved lolling in bed and settled for marriage with a plump, stupid peasant woman. On *Café Oblomov*, Troitsky and his guests sprawled on cushions and interspersed the chat with pop videos.

Sanya's first wife suffered a recurrence of cancer in 1995, and was hospitalized. Again he paid for her operation and drugs, and Alya inquired after her well-being, without direct contact. Recuperating at home in the unofficial museum, Natasha continued to express her anguish—to whoever called—over his accusations of treachery and his cold remoteness. She was touchingly proud of now possessing her own writers' union card.

One year after his return, Sanya was a neglected figure, his name rarely mentioned among the liberal intelligentsia. That would not have bothered him; he had an ingrained contempt for such people, who in his view were totally cut off from ordinary Russians, especially those unfortunate enough to be provincial. He had faithful supporters still, including Liusha Chukovskaya and Mirra Petrova, who he claimed had taught him much about women. Liusha and Mirra kept their secrets still.

Igor Shafarevich, once his fervent friend and collaborator, ceased to have contact with him, considering him too liberal. The liberal democrats were saddened by his criticisms of democracy. Yet it was Western-style parliaments—increasingly filled with "professional" politicians—that he feared. He went on laboring the case for the *zemstvos*, the rural councils set up in the nineteenth century. Indeed, he would probably have been happy with the tenth-century Kiev Rus system of the *veche*, in which the heads of households met in the town square to decide policy. In his preferred model, such local councils would have sent representatives to form a central Duma. The fact that most heads of households would be males would probably not have made him lose any sleep.

He was no one's hero anymore. As archives revealed that many Orthodox archbishops had collaborated with the Soviet power, his relations with the church were strained.

He was the ultimate dissident—alone. Partly this was a consequence of the unique way in which the right-left tendencies in the new Russia related to nationalism. "In eastern Europe, the anti-Communists were able to come forward as nationalists. In Russia, the anti-Communists came forward as Westernizers. They failed to link the struggle for democratic rights and freedoms with the restoration of the Russia the Bolsheviks destroyed. The only man who tried was the writer Alexander Solzhenitsyn, but he has been marginalised as too anti-Communist for the Zyuganovites° and too much of a Russian nationalist for the liberals."[11]

Politically he was perhaps closest to being a William Morris socialist. But in Russian terms he can best be characterized as the sole member of a modern branch of Old Believers, so admirably unwilling to compromise their faith.

°Followers of the Communist candidate in the 1996 presidential elections, Gennadi Zyuganov.

He had two short stories published in the greatly diminished *Novy Mir*, but they caused no stir. He was said to be a disappointed man, especially over the reception of *The Red Wheel;* yet the few who met him were often struck by his genial, gentle manner. He could look at his father's portrait on his desk and tell him he had lived at least two lives, to make up for his own sadly short life.

"In terms of the effect he has had on history," David Remnick has written, "Solzhenitsyn is the dominant writer of this century."[12] He is also the last writer of an extraordinary period in Russian literature in which the writer knew it was his duty to embody truth. This was why Lydia Chukovskaya was fervently loyal to him despite his political views being very different from hers; they both rejected the Western notion "that literature belongs to a sphere separate and separable from the world of human experience; both assume, on the contrary, that genuine literature is intimately linked to truth in ways that transcend aesthetic categories"; and that it can be the living memory of a nation.[13]

Lydia Chukovskaya died, in February 1996, aged eighty-nine; Sanya attended her funeral at Peredelkino. She was buried a few feet from Pasternak's grave.

It was a symbolic burial of more than an old woman. Those three writers, briefly close in Peredelkino's cemetery, belonged to another universe. Art now could forget about truth and historical memory. The performance artist Alexander Brener arrived for one of his shows wearing diaphanous panty hose, and was wildly applauded. This was, perhaps, the future.

As the second anniversary of Solzhenitsyn's return came round, there were many echoes of the past, as if Blok was correct in saying "All things repeat." Dzhuna, an attractive psychic healer with a huge television following, had a close friendship with Boris Yeltsin, just as Nicholas II and Alexandra had been intimate with Rasputin. Epidemics of cholera and typhus broke out, the plagues which had added to the carnage of the Civil War. A sudden upsurge of cannibalism occurred too. In the most flagrant case, that of Andrei Chikatilo, responsible for over fifty deaths, there was a direct link with Stalinist times; he was said to have been haunted by the memory of his brother, eaten by starving peasants in the Ukraine.

In the West, and especially America, it seemed at times as if the loss of Soviet puritanism had fueled a need to create a compensating repressiveness. There was no Gulag, but liberal people were very aware of what they were permitted to think. A copy of Goya's *Maja Nude* was removed from an American college library because it objectified women; conscientious professors were sacked for teaching texts considered sexist, or for making an off-color joke. Writers learned to self-censor their work; and since the relationship of man and woman is more fundamental than economics, there was an underswell of secret repression.

Saul Bellow, America's Nobel-winning author, took on the role of the

West's Solzhenitsyn; and his reflections, though offered in a more modest and informal way, were essentially not dissimilar. He sensed, he said, amidst a "sort of wilderness, a jungle of opinion on all questions . . . a kind of compulsive, enforced orthodoxy that I connect in my own mind with the period of Stalinism in the 1930s. It's very similar—put a toe out of line and you'll be clobbered. . . ." This was one aspect of a world he felt to be inadequate for the life of real, human people. What was on offer was not good enough, not serious enough, because the dominant scientific/consumerist ethos was simply wrong, one of the most deficient definitions of the human self that history had ever produced.

In many modern, civilized people "the core of the self" was missing, Bellow considered. They had a kind of restlessness of distraction but they did not identify themselves as human beings. Novelists, by writing novels at all, were working against this loss of self. The novel form presupposed a human self, traditionally conceived. "I think writers are in some sense bound to their tradition as writers. We are still moved by the great masterpieces we have all read. We know what Lear means when he says he is bound upon a wheel of fire."[14]

Bellow and Solzhenitsyn were both reacting, ultimately, against the Enlightenment concept of finding the most "reasonable" path to happiness. They were equally out of tune with the times.

Solzhenitsyn had long since concluded that Soviet Communism was nothing more than a laboratory for the West, in which the most extreme theory of the Enlightenment could be put to the test.

Was it also possible, now, that the single achievement of Communism was to preserve Russia, thanks to the laboratory's hygienic puritanism, from consumerist triviality? It seemed not, to judge by how much the West was flooding in: which is why Solzhenitsyn continued to thunder his warnings. Yet there were more hopeful portents. In 1931, Stalin had had Moscow's biggest cathedral, the Cathedral of Christ the Saviour, blown up. He wanted to build in its place a vast Palace of Congresses, taller than the Empire State Building, topped by a three-hundred-foot high statue of Lenin. But the marshy ground could not sustain the foundations, and it was turned into a swimming pool. Now, on the orders of Mayor Luzhkov, the great cathedral had risen again; its golden dome outshone even the Kremlin. It was said that even beggars, and the poor babushkas who with numbed fingers clutched a few flowers for sale outside the metros, put rubles in the collection boxes for the hugely unreasonable project.

In the period of the Mongol invasions, the city of Kitezh sank into a lake, to rise again when the threat was over. Akhmatova, Mandelstam, Pasternak, and Solzhenitsyn had all been sustained by a deep religious consciousness. The great Western writers had mostly lost all religious sense. Living in a world split, in his view, between two forms of scientific paganism, the Lotus Eaters of the West and the murk-enshrouded Cimmerians of the East, Solzhenitsyn had concluded that the former were the more dangerous enemy of the human spirit in the long term; though he had used them to fight the gross tyranny in his homeland. The Cimmerians—enough of them—had listened, because of their despair, and because he spoke to them with his art. When he addressed the Lotus Eaters, they were unimpressed: partly because he spoke to them with rhetoric, not art, just like a million other "opinion-makers"; but also partly because on the whole, give or take some terrible injustices, they thought their lotus-eating, tolerant way of life wasn't so bad. They could no more doubt liberal democracy than medieval Christendom could doubt the church.

Two years after the Solzhenitsyns' homecoming, it looked for a time as if the Communist Zyuganov might defeat Yeltsin in Russia's first democratic presidential elections. In Kiev and Smolensk, hungry, fearful people were digging up the public squares in order to plant vegetables. The young, it was said, were hopeful, the middle-aged apathetic, the old, angry. Solzhenitsyn, asked about his voting intentions, made a rare comment. He would vote for no one. The political parties didn't stand for anything. The answer was to strengthen local government. He was on Jesus's side, not the side of any political party. You should not mix Christ and politics.

Later in the year, through *Le Monde*, he launched a fierce attack on Yeltsin's administration, claiming that an oligarchy, some two hundred strong, consisting of former Communist leaders and nouveaux riches bandits were running Russia.[15]

But those outbursts apart, the reincarnation of the old seer of legend, Koshei, stayed behind the walls of the multifloored apartment building, of his Troitse Lykovo dacha, and of his unchanging work schedule—leaving all contact with the outside world to his semi-magical woman, Vasilisa the Beautiful—Alya.

His first wife—with whom he had lived, or was escaping from, in the decade of his greatest works—was in hospital again, seriously ill. Alya went to visit her, and took her a radio. At home again, surrounded by the mementos she could by now scarcely see, she told a visitor, "She showed care; she is a better person than her husband." Natasha had been told by the doctors there was nothing more they could do, she was slowly dying. She smiled sadly: "He has promised to take care of my funeral." When pain overcame her, she clutched a hot-water bottle to her stomach and breast, like a baby. She listens to tapes, and is trying to read a Nabokov in large print. Few people call, except a woman to help her; and the government sends groceries. Most of her friends are dead. She does not look sorry that soon she will join them.

She lives not far from Kaluga Gate, some of whose parquet floors were laid by Solzhenitsyn. Now the great curving building, through whose center runs the Leninsky Prospekt, carries over its roof an advertisement for ME-TAXA.

Following Zyuganov's defeat, the Communists changed their name to the

Popular Patriotic Union and, at their August 1996 congress, moved toward an alliance with right-wing patriotic and religious parties. "Our task is to make Russia the spiritual and cultural leader of the world," Alexander Prokhanov, one of the new leaders, told the congress. They would stand for Justice and Order, and against the cultural takeover by the West.[16] The wheel had come full circle; in his youth, Solzhenitsyn had supported the Communist Party, then moved to the opposite pole; now the Communists were—so to speak—joining Solzhenitsyn.

As weird a volte-face, on the personal level, was a discovery relating to Natasha. On being transferred from one hospital to another, she had found the new hospital needed her internal passport. She asked a female relative to fetch it for her. The woman had been staggered to find Natasha recorded on the document as being the widow of Konstantin Semyonov. Semyonov had been the journalist assigned by Novosti to edit her first memoir. It had been known that Natasha had found him courteous, cultivated, and likable; he had been a former student of her uncle, Valentin Turkin.

Veronica Stein, on hearing this news—or rumor—laughed at the absurdity of life, saying: "So she wasn't Sanya's divorced wife, she was Kostya Semyonov's widow!" Mrs. Stein believed Semyonov had been genuinely attracted to Natasha. Not even the KGB—for a Novosti editor had to be KGB—required their agents to marry their target. Natasha would have had good reason for hiding her remarriage from Sanya.[17]

But was it true? It seemed late to trouble a sad and dying woman with another ghost; but I felt she must be given a chance to rebut the rumor. I asked a woman friend to put it to her tactfully. Natasha was thunderstruck: "Is that known about? That's—my secret, my secret marriage. That means Sanya will . . . How terrible! . . . Kostya saved me after Sanya's exile; I was without a job, without everything. Marrying him allowed me to live in Moscow. He was my closest friend. . . ." He had serious heart trouble; they were married from 1974 until his death in 1981. "All that time we concealed our marriage. I was never a KGB agent, I swear it!"

She, after all—not Sanya—was the sphinx.

She—and history.

EPILOGUE

THE MONOLITH, COMMUNISM, HAS MELTED AWAY. BY THE BEGIN-
ning of Sanya's seventy-ninth year, the Soviet Union's last leader,
Mikhail Gorbachev, was touting his memoir from TV talk show to talk show
across the Western capitals, boasting that he had been given a million-dollar
advance. The man who had announced, in 1987, "We are traveling to a new
world, the world of Communism," a path from which they would never
deviate, now coyly described himself as a Social Democrat.

Boris Yeltsin was in obviously poor condition at his inauguration; exactly
one hundred years after the newly crowned last tsar, Nicholas II, had looked
"sad and depressed" following the death of fifteen hundred Muscovites,
crushed in a stampede for coronation mugs.

As the twentieth century began with a disastrous "small" war against
Japan, it was ending with a disastrous "small" war against Chechnya. The
army's humiliating retreat from Grozny had been compared by the Moscow
press to the fleet's destruction in the Straits of Tsushima in 1905. There
were rumors of trains in the Rostov sidings packed with corpses, reminiscent
of the Civil War and collectivization.

Solzhenitsyn seemed to feel that the time was demonic once more. On
New Year's Eve, 1996, he declined to join his family's celebrations for more
than fifteen minutes, saying that the Holy Spirit had abandoned Russia.[1]

"All things repeat"—in Russia anyway—and history is a timeless moment. The twentieth century has swallowed up creeds and populations, and
left behind, in Russia, Pasternak, Akhmatova, Blok, Shostakovich, Mandelstam, Tsvetayeva—and Solzhenitsyn; not, perhaps, great like the others outside of time, but great in the supreme intersection of his art and his courage
with history. They gleam like bright shells thrown up by an ocean swell;
like the orange shyly offered by a young woman to an orchestral conductor
in an icy street at night.

In Sanya's life, too, there has been a repetition of themes. The anxious
women surrounding the precious child in Kislovodsk recurred again in the
Ryazan household—Natasha, her mother, and her aunts; again in the dis-
cipleship of helpers in Moscow; and again in Cavendish, with Alya and her
mother. He liked women to be close, taking burdens from him—but not
too close.

He needed an idealized father: throughout his childhood and youth, right up into the Gulag, Lenin; then God, as Sanya returned to the religious beliefs of Aunt Irina, his grandparents, and his mother. Toward woman as helpmeet rather than helper, toward the *feminine*, he has appeared uncertain and repressive of his emotions; and it is surely no accident that the important chosen women in his life have been scientists and mathematicians. Freudian theory and intuition alike point toward his relationship with his mother for the cause of such repression. Its existence may actually have helped him to sustain the ferocious anger that makes *The Gulag Archipelago* such an overwhelming work; though later, as he lost his country and his great theme, it may have limited his art. Ironically, this was the period in which he was personally happiest, within a harmonious marriage and family life. As a man, he seems most attractive in his Kok Terek solitude, writing in secret and devoting time and love to his school pupils; and in the years of obscurity that followed, living with a wife, Natasha, who served him loyally but from whom he was able to keep a great deal of emotional space.

In that era he became almost the sole beacon of hope for those enslaved by Communism. In *Ivan Denisovich, The First Circle*, and *Cancer Ward* he was able to fuse the authenticity of personal experience with a superb unity of form. In *The Gulag Archipelago* he also showed an acute aesthetic sense, paradoxically by choosing to cast off all restraints of "moderation," allowing the work to metastasize in imitation of the camp system itself.

If the Soviet state had endured till the end of the third millennium, these works would still have judged it, and proved it monstrous.

He will not suffer the "terrible" fate of his old friend and supporter Kornei Chukovsky. When the great children's writer died in 1969, his funeral was not from his Peredelkino home, a private affair like Pasternak's, as Sanya had anticipated, but in pomp from the House of Literature in Moscow. Begging off from attending, Sanya wrote in a letter of condolence to Lydia and Liusha, "It's simply terrible to die undisgraced." Solzhenitsyn will not die disgraced, but he is ignored in Russia and somewhat derided in the West, and I am sure he will believe this to be more seemly than popularity, in an age of conformity and spiritual dearth.

Russian literature enters a new phase, moving from the rich black earth plowed up involuntarily by despotism to the uncharted Siberia of freedom—a condition in which, as Natan Sharansky has observed, it is hard to keep existential depth. The status of Russian literature, from the birth of Pushkin in 1799 to the end of Communism, has been unique and unrepeatable.

My thoughts keep reverting to Natasha. The pathos of her situation. Tolstoy refused to let his wife into the stationmaster's hut at Astapovo, where he lay dying; but that was only a few hours' banishment. Sanya has so much, and Natasha so little. Would it really be so hard to visit her just once, or even to speak to her gently on the phone? And I think of her effect on him, in that strange, terrible period when he was much more fearful of her than of the KGB. He knew he could not have betrayed her more: not only to abandon her, at fifty, but to have children being born, when she had longed for children, and had given up stepchildren whom she had loved and who had loved her. He was cruel to her one moment, then weeping with her the next. He cried a lot, according to her memoir. He must have been very close to a complete nervous breakdown. And perhaps it would have been good for him; he might have broken through to the feminine side of his consciousness. But he did not give way to the breakdown; he hardened his heart. . . . And wrote *The Red Wheel*. History.

Yet, after all, he had done enough.

I recall the ex-KGB colonel whom I met in Helsinki. Gazing over the ice-covered Gulf of Finland, he murmured, "What was it all for? Where has it all gone? . . ."

All the deaths, all the suffering: what was it for?

In May 1997, Solzhenitsyn was admitted to the cardiac intensive care unit of the Central Clinical Hospital (better known as the "Kremlin" hospital), where high government officials are treated. Characteristically, his admission was not confirmed for ten days, until just before his release; nor were any details of his illness given, though he may have suffered a mild heart attack.[2]

That same month, Olga Carlisle spoke of her feelings during her "Solzhenitsyn saga": it was "far, very far from *melancholy*. Years of great anxiety, tremendous elation, a sense of shared mission for Russia . . . and later a time of dismay when (unaccountably at first) our contributions were disavowed, but never melancholy. We had no time for it. Were I to pick one word to describe my state of mind throughout the experience it would be *feverish*."[3]

Few, if any, of all those people who, like Olga, played a part in Solzhenitsyn's decade of struggle—however "dismayed" they may have been later—do not feel honored and enriched by their involvement in that heroic, impossible, yet victorious enterprise.

In a small scruffy park behind Moscow's House of Artists, close to where Natasha sits silently in her Solzhenitsyn museum, there is a graveyard of fallen idols: statues removed from various parts of the city. Here is Stalin, lying on his side, still smirking under his mustache. And handsome Felix Dzerzhinsky, founder of the Cheka. He committed mass murder with the best of intentions, to impose his ideology on the world. Ozymandias. Not everything repeats. *He* won't rise again.

One day on his empty plinth in Lubyanka Square, will there be a man, scowling, hunched within his *zek's* quilted jacket? A young man with a trowel in one hand, a rosary in the other. It would be fitting.

Or perhaps two reddish figures like stones in a field, scarcely human, their feet trapped in clay.

NOTES

Prologue

1. Anna Akhmatova, *My Half Century*, ed. Ronald Meyer (Ann Arbor, 1992), p. 1.
2. B. Pasternak, *Essays in Autobiography* (London, 1959), p. 117.
3. Anna Akhmatova, *Selected Poems*, tr. D. M. Thomas (London, 1988), p. 117.
4. *Oak and the Calf* (London, 1980), p. 19.
5. M. Hayward, *Writers in Russia, 1917–1978* (London, 1983), p. 292.

PART I

1. Ancestral Voices

1. "*My rubicund critic, my full-bellied mocker . . .*" Lyric of 1830. *The Bronze Horseman and Other Poems*, tr. D. M. Thomas (New York, 1982).
2. *August 1914*, tr. Michael Glenny (London, 1972), ch. 4.
3. Ibid.
4. Ibid. I seem to be unusual in often preferring the version of the late Michael Glenny to that of H T Willetts, whose translation of the author's much-expanded novel came out in 1989, just as I prefer Solzhenitsyn's original text.
5. Ibid., ch. 2. For the basic information on Solzhenitsyn's ancestry I am indebted to Michael Scammell's *Solzhenitsyn* (New York, 1984) and notably an interview he conducted with Solzhenitsyn in Vermont in June 1977.
6. *Stavropol Pravda*, 26 May 1990.
7. *August 1914*, tr. Willetts, ch. 1.
8. Ibid., tr. Glenny, ch. 47.

2. Demons

1. *Polnoe sobranie sochinenii* (Moscow, 1961–65), Vol. 41, p. 376.
2. From the State Archive of Film and Photographic Documents, St. Petersburg, reproduced in Brian Moynahan, *The Russian Century* (London, 1994), pp. 22–23.
3. A realistic estimate, covering the victims of civil war, famine, collectivization, and the Gulag—but excluding the Second World War. There are also the nonexistent children who might have been born to those liquidated. It has been estimated

that Russia's population, now approximately 150 million, ought in normal demographic circumstances to be 300 million.

4. R. Orlova, *Memoirs* (Ann Arbor, 1983), p. 208.

5. Quoted in *August 1914*, tr. H. T. Willetts (London, 1989), ch. 74.

6. *Poem Without a Hero*, tr. D. M. Thomas.

7. W. Bruce Lincoln, *In War's Dark Shadow* (New York, 1983), p. 383.

8. Nathan Milstein, *From Russia to the West* (London, 1990), p. 30.

9. *Poem Without a Hero*.

3. *The Shot*

1. Bruce Lincoln, *Red Victory* (New York, 1989), p. 43.

2. Ibid., p. 46.

3. Alan Clark, *Barbarossa* (London, 1995), p. 41.

4. Lincoln, *Red Victory*, p. 79.

5. Ibid., p. 48.

6. Ibid., p. 47.

7. Ibid., p. 74.

8. V. and J. Louis, *Complete Guide to the Soviet Union* (New York, 1991), p. 235.

9. Scammell, p. 32 et seq. The account of Solzhenitsyn's relatives in 1918 is based on Scammell's 1977 interview with Solzhenitsyn.

10. Lincoln, *Red Victory*, p. 49.

11. Ibid., p. 139.

12. *45 Parallel*, 1991, no. 2, p. 21.

13. Scammell, p. 32.

14. K. Simonyan, *Hvem er Solsjenitsyn?* (Who Is Solzhenitsyn?) (Skaerbaek, 1976).

15. *August 1914*, tr. Glenny, ch. 48.

16. Scammell, p. 51 (interview with Solzhenitsyn).

4. *The Child on Tolstoy Street*

1. Lincoln, *Red Victory*, pp. 153–54.

2. Interview with N. Reshetovskaya, Nov. 1995.

3. Scammell, p. 35.

4. Prof. Dr. W. W. Krysko, "I Choose the Truth" (unpublished memoir), p. 48.

5. Scammell, pp. 35–36 (interview with Solzhenitsyn).

6. N. Zernov, *Na Perelome* (At the Breaking Point), (Paris, 1970), p. 286.

7. Memories of Solzhenitsyn's second cousin, Ludmila Glubashova. *Stavropol Pravda*, 2 Sept. 1990.

8. A. G. Shkuro, *Memoirs of a White Partisan* (Buenos Aires, 1961), p. 192.

9. Rhoda Power, *Under Cossack and Bolshevik* (London, 1919), p. 203.

10. Ibid., p. 41.

11. Interview with Reshetovskaya, Jan. 1995.

12. Ibid.

13. Gordon McVay, *Isadora and Esenin* (Ann Arbor, 1980), p. 121.

14. Memories of Solzhenitsyn's first cousin, Ksenia Vasilievna Kulikova. *Stavropol Pravda*, 26 May 1990.

15. Scammell, p. 41.

16. John Bowlby, *Separation* (London, 1973), p. 46.

17. D. Burlingham and Anna Freud, *Young Children in War-time* (London, 1942), p. 51.

18. *60 Minutes*, CBS. Interview by Mike Wallace, 24 April 1994.

19. Scammell, pp. 41–42.

20. D. W. Winnicott, *Playing and Reality* (London, 1991), p. 4.

21. Krysko, p. 67.

22. M. Muggeridge, *Chronicles of Wasted Time. Chronicle I: The Green Stick* (New York, 1973), p. 219.

23. Sigmund Freud, *Three Essays on Sexuality* (1905).

5. Rostov

1. Scammell, p. 45 (interview with Solzhenitsyn).

2. D. Volkogonov, *Lenin: Life and Legacy* (London, 1994), p. xxxvii.

3. Ibid., p. xxxviii.

4. Dmitri Panin, *The Notebooks of Sologdin* (New York, 1976), p. 11.

5. Power, p. 13.

6. Krysko, p. 71.

7. Power, p. 14.

8. Krysko, Introduction.

9. Ibid., p. 2.

10. Scammell, p. 44.

11. *August 1914*, tr. Glenny, ch. 59.

12. Richard Pipes, *Russia Under the Bolshevik Regime* (New York, 1994), p. 319.

13. Ibid., p. 316.

14. Scammell, p. 59.

15. Ibid., p. 52.

16. R. W. Clark, *Freud* (London, 1980), p. 19.

17. Interview in Rostov, Nov. 95.

18. Scammell, p. 56.

19. *Gulag* 1, I, ch. 5.

20. Interview in Rostov, Nov. 95.

21. Scammell, p. 49.

22. Interview, Jan. 1995.

23. Scammell, p. 67.

6. A Wolf to Man

1. Robert Conquest, *The Harvest of Sorrow* (New York, 1986), p. 3.

2. Vasily Grossman, *Forever Flowing* (New York, 1972), p. 70.

3. Ibid., p. 72.

4. Ilya Ehrenburg, *The Second Day* (New York, 1984).

5. Lev Kopelev, *To Be Preserved Forever* (New York, 1977), p. 12.

6. Martin Gilbert, *The Holocaust* (London, 1986), p. 615. Himmler speech of 4 October 1943.

7. Hryhory Kostiuk, *Stalinist Rule in the Ukraine* (London, 1960), p. 44.

8. Statement to the London General Press, 1932. According to the Soviet press, Shaw also said that, unlike England, the USSR had religious freedom.

9. Alex de Jonge, *Stalin* (London, 1986), p. 286.

10. Diana Trilling, *The Beginning of the Journey* (New York, 1993), pp. 196–98.

11. Conquest, p. 312.

12. D. Shostakovich, *Testimony* (London, 1979), p. 165.

13. Conquest, p. 284.

7. Crosses

1. Scammell, p. 67 (interview with Solzhenitsyn).

2. Interview with Reshetovskaya, Nov. 1995.

3. Scammell, p. 69. Solzhenitsyn's unpublished poem "The Way."

4. Ibid., p. 51 (interview with Solzhenitsyn).

5. *Encounter*, April 1976, p. 11.

6. As Natalya Reshetovskaya has argued, in an interview with the author.

7. Scammell, p. 71.

8. *First Circle*, ch. 68.

9. *Skvoz' chad*, 6th supplement to *The Oak and the Calf* (Paris, 1979), pp. 22–30.

10. Simonyan, *Who Is Solzhenitsyn?*

11. N. Reshetovskaya, *Sanya* (New York, 1975), p. 18.

12. Scammell, p. 65.

13. *Skvoz' chad*, pp. 29–30.

14. Lincoln, *Red Victory*, pp. 321–23.

15. Interview, Nov. 1995.

16. Ibid.

17. Scammell, ch. 4, and N. Reshetovskaya for the information on the school friends.

18. Victor Kravchenko, *I Chose Freedom* (London, 1951), p. 252.

8. Days of Wine and Roses

1. R. Conquest, *The Great Terror* (London, 1968), ch. 6.

2. Scammell, p. 86.

3. *Stern* interview with Irina Shcherbak, 1971.

4. Scammell, p. 99.

5. Reshetovskaya, p. 5.

6. Ibid.

7. Ibid., p. 8.

8. Reshetovskaya interview, Nov. 1995.

9. Scammell, p. 94.
10. D. Burg and G. Feifer, *Solzhenitsyn* (London, 1972), p. 30.
11. Reshetovskaya, p. 42.
12. Scammell, p. 102.
13. Ibid.
14. Ibid., p. 103.
15. "The Way," section 2.
16. Viktoria Schweitzer, *Tsvetaeva* (London, 1993), p. 150.

9. *To Be or Not to Be . . .*

1. Volkov, ed., *Testimony* (London, 1979), p. 63.
2. V. Grossman, *Forever Flowing* (London, 1986), p. 180.
3. Volkov, ed., p. 148.
4. Moynahan, *The Russian Century*, p. 176.
5. Ibid., p. 175.
6. Edvard Radzinsky, *Stalin* (London, 1996), p. 319.

10. *A Room on Chekhov Lane*

1. D. Volkogonov, *Lenin*, p. 315.
2. Scammell, p. 90.
3. Reshetovskaya, p. 12.
4. Reshetovskaya interview, Nov. 1995.
5. Reshetovskaya, p. 11.
6. Volkov, ed., p. 160.
7. Scammell, p. 109.

PART II

11. *O God of Battles*

1. A. Clark, p. 46.
2. Reshetovskaya, p. 23.
3. *Gulag* 3, V, ch. 1.
4. Reshetovskaya, p. 21.
5. A. Clark, p. 154.
6. *Daily Telegraph*, 23 March 1995.
7. A. Clark, p. 193.
8. Alexander Werth, *The Year of Stalingrad* (London, 1946), p. 137.
9. E. Klee, W. Dressen and V. Riess, eds. *Those Were the Days* (London, 1991), p. 73; and interview with Sasha Kozhin, May 1995.
10. Interview, Nov. 1995.
11. Reshetovskaya, p. 34.
12. *Poem Without a Hero*.

1 2. *Fighting for Lenin*

1. *Gulag* 1, I, ch. 4.
2. *Gulag* 3, V, ch. 1.
3. *Gulag* 2, III, ch. 9.
4. Ibid.
5. A. Clark, p. 328.
6. Ibid., p. 332.
7. Reshetovskaya, pp. 45–46.
8. *Rebuilding Russia*, p. 14.
9. Reshetovskaya, p. 49.
10. Ibid., p. 52.
11. Orlova, p. 114.
12. Reshetovskaya, p. 53.

1 3. *Everything Is Allowed*

1. Ibid., p. 55.
2. Ibid., p. 61.
3. Ibid., p. 56.
4. *Prussian Nights*, tr. Robert Conquest.
5. Ibid.
6. *Gulag* 1, I, ch. 6.
7. Ibid.
8. *August 1914*, tr. Glenny, ch. 25.
9. Kopelev, *To Be Preserved Forever*, p. 42.
10. *Prussian Nights*.
11. Reshetovskaya, p. 63.

1 4. *The Victory Spring*

1. *Gulag* 1, I, ch. 1.
2. Scammell, p. 149.
3. *First Circle*, ch. 83.
4. *Gulag* 1, I, chs. 3 and 5.
5. O. Ivinskaya, *A Captive of Time* (London, 1978), p. 110.
6. *Gulag* 1, I, ch. 3.
7. Ibid., ch. 5.
8. Reshetovskaya, p. 63.
9. *Gulag* 1, I, ch. 3.
10. Ibid., ch. 5.

1 5. *Education Sentimentale*

1. *Gulag* 1, I, ch. 5.
2. Ibid.
3. Ibid.

4. Ibid.
5. Ibid.
6. *Prisoners*, Scene 12.
7. *Gulag*, 1, I, ch. 5.
8. Ibid.
9. Vera Reck, *Boris Pilnyak* (Montreal, 1975).
10. Nina Berberova, *The Italics Are Mine* (London, 1969), p. 246.
11. Ibid., p. 412.
12. Y. Zamyatin, *We* (New York, 1993), p. 5.
13. Berberova, p. 298.
14. *Gulag* 1, I, ch. 5.

16. *New Jerusalem*

1. Reshetovskaya, pp. 92–93.
2. *First Circle*, ch. 35.
3. *Gulag* 1, II, ch. 2.
4. Reshetovskaya, pp. 78–79; and Russian ed., 66–67.
5. *Gulag* 2, III, ch. 6.
6. Ibid.
7. Ibid.
8. *Gulag* 1, II, ch. 4.
9. *Gulag* 2, III, ch. 6.

17. *Vetrov*

1. Ibid.
2. Reshetovskaya, p. 95.
3. *First Circle*, ch. 35.
4. *Gulag* 2, III, ch. 9.
5. Ibid., ch. 12.
6. Ibid.
7. Ibid.
8. Reshetovskaya, p. 100.
9. *Gulag* 2, III, ch. 9.
10. N. Mandelstam, *Hope Abandoned* (New York, 1974), p. 123.
11. N. Mandelstam, *Hope Against Hope* (New York, 1970), pp. 237–44.
12. Quoted in G. Struve, *Russian Literature under Lenin and Stalin* (Norman, Okla., 1971), p. 264.
13. *Gulag* 2, III, ch. 8.

18. *Stalin's Seminary*

1. Panin, p. 263.
2. Ibid., p. 11.
3. Ibid., p. 84.
4. Ibid., p. 259.
5. L. Kopelev, *Ease My Sorrows* (New York, 1983), p. 7.

6. Ibid., p. 26.
7. Reshetovskaya. p. 117.
8. *First Circle*, ch. 34.
9. Reshetovskaya, p. 122.
10. Ibid., p. 117.
11. Panin, p. 264.
12. John Bayley, *Pushkin* (London, 1971), p. 229.
13. Pushkin, *The Bronze Horseman and Other Poems,* tr. D. M. Thomas, p. 221.
14. Panin, p. 232.
15. Kopelev, p. 94.
16. Gordon McVay, *Esenin, a Life* (Ann Arbor, 1976), p. 119.

1 9. *Toward the House of the Dead*

1. *First Circle*, chs. 37 and 42.
2. Panin, p. 263.
3. Reshetovskaya, p. 130.
4. Ibid., p. 134.
5. Ibid., p. 136.
6. Ibid., p. 137.
7. Ibid., p. 141.
8. Ibid., p. 143.
9. Kopelev, *Ease My Sorrows*, pp. 90–91.
10. Ibid., p. 60.
11. Ibid., p. 59.
12. Ibid., p. 83.
13. Ibid., p. 129.
14. *First Circle*, ch. 6.
15. Kopelev, *Ease My Sorrows*, p. 172.
16. Ibid., p. 49.
17. Ibid., p. 90.
18. Panin, p. 292.

2 0. *The Given Field*

1. G. Kjetsaa, *Dostoievsky* (New York, 1987), pp. 86–89.
2. Christine Sutherland, *The Princess of Siberia* (New York, 1984), p. 139.
3. *Gulag* 3, V, ch. 2.
4. Colin Thubron, *Lost Heart of Asia* (London, 1994), p. 337.
5. *Gulag* 2, III, ch. 18.
6. Panin, pp. 295–96.

2 1. *Firebird*

1. Reshetovskaya, p. 154.
2. Ibid., p. 169.
3. *Feast of the Conquerors*, Act One.

4. Reshetovskaya interview, Nov. 1995.
5. *Prisoners*, Scene 1.
6. Panin, p. 312.
7. Ibid., p. 314.
8. *Gulag* 2, IV, ch. 1.
9. Reshetovskaya, p. 169.
10. Scammell, p. 311.
11. *Gulag* 3, VI, ch. 7.

PART III

2 2. *Free to Breathe*

1. Thubron, p. 312.
2. *Gulag* 3, VI, ch. 5.
3. Ibid.
4. Ibid.
5. *Stories and Prose Poems*, 1971, tr. M. Glenny.
6. *Gulag* 3, VI, ch. 6.
7. Ibid.
8. *45 Parallel*, Stavropol, Dec. 1990.
9. Reshetovskaya, p. 176.
10. *45 Parallel*, Dec. 1990.

2 3. *Shrinking the Cancer*

1. *Gulag* 3, VI, ch. 6.
2. Ibid., V, ch. 12.
3. P. Johnson, *Intellectuals* (London, 1988), p. 244.
4. *Invisible Allies* (Washington, D.C., 1995), p. 13.
5. Kopelev, *Ease My Sorrows*, p. 62.
6. Scammell, p. 346.
7. *Gulag*, 3, VI, ch. 6.
8. Ibid.

2 4. *Time to Awake*

1. Ivinskaya, p. 208.
2. Pasternak, *Doctor Zhivago*, ch. 6, section 15.
3. Ibid., ch. 7, 19.
4. Jo Durden-Smith, *Russia: A Long-Shot Romance* (New York, 1994), p. 160.
5. Y. Ginzburg, *Within the Whirlwind* (London, 1981), p. 395.
6. Robert Conquest, *The Great Terror* (London, 1968), p. 475.
7. Ginzburg, p. 407.
8. Scammell, p. 355 (interview with Solzhenitsyn).
9. *Gulag* 2, III, ch. 11.

25. *In Search of Time Past*

1. Reshetovskaya, p. 186.
2. Published, with a preface by Reshetovskaya, in the journal *Slavs*, Moscow, 1991.
3. *Gulag*, 3, VI, ch. 6.
4. Reshetovskaya, p. 188.
5. Ibid., p. 190.
6. Ibid.
7. Interview with Veronica Stein, July 1996.
8. "Matryona's House."
9. Scammell, p. 366.
10. Reshetovskaya, p. 200.
11. *August 1914*, tr. Glenny, ch. 54.

26. *Death of a Poet*

1. *Gulag* 3, VI, ch. 7.
2. Ibid.
3. *Invisible Allies*, p. 30.
4. *Gulag*, 3, VI, ch. 7.
5. Orlova, p. 147.

27. *Ryazansky*

1. *Oak and the Calf*, p. 19.
2. *Invisible Allies*, p. 35.
3. *Oak and the Calf*, p. 10.
4. Ibid., p. 14.
5. Ibid., p. 20.

28. *Launching Pads*

1. Ibid., p. 23.
2. Ibid., p. 26.
3. Scammell, p. 425.
4. Ibid., p. 398.
5. *45 Parallel*, 1991, no. 2.
6. Reshetovskaya interview, Nov. 1995.
7. *Oak and the Calf*, p. 38.
8. R. Medvedev, *Khrushchev* (London, 1983), p. 251.
9. *Oak and the Calf*, p. 46.

29. Fame

1. Roberta Reeder, *Anna Akhmatova* (New York, 1994), p. 372.
2. Ibid.
3. Ibid.
4. *Oak and the Calf*, p. 45.
5. *Panorama* (BBC 1) interview, 1 Mar. 1976.
6. L. Plyushch, *History's Carnival* (London, 1979), p. 45.
7. *Oak and the Calf*, p. 487.
8. Norman Podhoretz, "The Terrible Question of Alexander Solzhenitsyn," *Commentary*, Feb. 1985.
9. *Gulag 2*, III, ch. 6.
10. *One Day in the Life of Ivan Denisovich*, tr. Gillon Aitken (London, 1970), p. 30.
11. E. Crankshaw, *Shadow of the Winter Palace* (London, 1976), p. 229.
12. Scammell, p. 452.
13. *Invisible Allies*, p. 47.
14. O. Clément, *The Spirit of Solzhenitsyn* (London, 1976), p. 60.
15. *Oak and the Calf*, p. 486.
16. Z. Medvedev, *Ten Years after Ivan Denisovich* (London, 1973), p. 19.
17. *Oak and the Calf*, pp. 62–163.
18. *The Solzhenitsyn Files*, ed. Michael Scammell (Carol Stream, Ill., 1995), Document No. 1. Henceforth identified as *KGB Files*.
19. Ibid.
20. Scammell, p. 479.
21. Reshetovskaya, p. 242.
22. Scammell, p. 457.
23. Medvedev, pp. 22–29.

30. Love, Truths, and Microfilms

1. Reshetovskaya, pp. 263–77.
2. *August 1914*, tr. Glenny, ch. 57.
3. *Oktyabr 1916* (YMCA Press, 1984), pp. 438–69. It has not appeared in an English translation.
4. Ibid.
5. Interview, Oct. 1996.
6. Reshetovskaya, p. 256.
7. *Oak and the Calf*, pp. 73–76.
8. Ibid, p. 87.
9. Reshetovskaya, p. 247.

31. Dictating the Inferno

1. Lydia Chukovskaya, "A Process of Expulsion," in *Solzhenitsyn in Exile*, eds. J. Dunlop, R. S. Haugh, and M. Nicholson (Stanford, 1985), p. 287.
2. *First Circle*, ch. 33.

3. Ibid., ch. 6.
4. Ibid., ch. 81.
5. Reshetovskaya, p. 202.
6. *First Circle*, ch. 86.
7. Ibid., ch. 67.
8. Scammell, p. 525.
9. *Oak and the Calf*, p. 101.
10. *Invisible Allies*, p. 52.
11. *Oak and the Calf*, p. 111.
12. Ibid., p. 104.

PART IV

32. *Into Battle*

1. Scammell, p. 521.
2. *KGB Files*, No. 2.
3. Ibid., Nos. 6, 7.
4. *Invisible Allies*, p. 116.
5. Ibid., p. 53.
6. Scammell, p. 557.
7. V. Lakshin, *Solzhenitsyn, Tvardovsky, and "Novy Mir"* (Cambridge, Mass., 1980), p. 51.
8. *Oak and the Calf*, p. 144.
9. Ibid., p. 145.
10. *Invisible Allies*, p. 126.
11. Ibid., p. 141.

33. *Antiworlds*

1. O. Carlisle, *Solzhenitsyn and the Secret Circle* (London, 1978), p. 16.
2. Ibid., p. 17.
3. Ibid., pp. 42–45, and interview, Nov. 1996.
4. O. Carlisle, *Under a New Sky* (New York, 1993), p. 13.
5. *Doctor Zhivago*, ch. 6, section 8.
6. *Oak and the Calf*, p. 287.
7. *Solzhenitsyn in Exile*, p. 287.
8. *Invisible Allies*, p. 56.
9. *KGB Files*, No. 8.
10. *Oak and the Calf*, pp. 152–58.
11. Ibid., pp. 458–462.
12. Ibid.
13. *KGB Files*, No. 14.
14. *Oak and the Calf*, pp. 172–74.
15. Ibid., p. 185.

34. Life Against Death

1. *Invisible Allies*, pp. 61–62.
2. Ibid.
3. *Oak and the Calf*, p. 184.
4. Ibid., p. 180.
5. Ibid., pp. 463–80.
6. *Invisible Allies*, p. 105.
7. Carlisle, *Secret Circle*, p. 65.
8. Interview, Nov. 1996.
9. Carlisle, *Secret Circle*, p. 90.

35. Translations and Transitions

1. *Invisible Allies*, p. 119.
2. Carlisle, *Secret Circle*, p. 110.
3. *Oak and the Calf*, pp. 227 28.
4. *Invisible Allies*, p. 196.
5. A. Sakharov, *Memoirs* (New York, 1990), p. 164.
6. Scammell, p. 657.
7. *Oak and the Calf*, p. 370.
8. Sakharov, pp. 292–93.
9. Ibid., p. 293.
10. *Invisible Allies*, pp. 198–99.
11. Private interview.
12. *Oak and the Calf*, p. 225.
13. *Invisible Allies*, pp. 198–99.
14. Sakharov, p. 403.

36. Doubles

1. Z. Medvedev, p. 100.
2. Carlisle, *Secret Circle*, p. 134.
3. *Oak and the Calf*, p. 262.
4. Ibid., p. 493.
5. *KGB Files*, Nos. 23 25.
6. Ivinskaya, *A Captive of Time* (London, 1978), pp. 262–64.
7. G. Vishnevskaya, *Galina* (London, 1984), p. 388.
8. Ibid.
9. Ibid.
10. Ibid., p. 390.
11. Interview with Reshetovskaya, Aug. 1996.
12. Scammell, p. 691.
13. *Oak and the Calf*, p. 280.
14. Scammell, p. 659 (interview with Solzhenitsyn).
15. Interview with Reshetovskaya, Aug. 1996.

16. Reshetovskaya, *Otlucheniye* (Moscow, 1994), pp. 280–83; and interview with Veronica Stein, Aug. 1996.

3 7. *Sacrifice*

1. Reshetovskaya, *Otlucheniye*, p. 297.
2. Ibid., p. 295.
3. Ibid., p. 306.
4. Ibid., p. 312.
5. Interview with Veronica Stein.
6. *KGB Files*, No. 27.
7. *Oak and the Calf*, p. 307.
8. Scammell, p. 710.
9. *KGB Files*, No. 31.
10. Ibid., No. 28.
11. Reshetovskaya, *Otlucheniye*, pp. 332–34.
12. Scammell, pp. 710–11.
13. Ibid., p. 712.
14. *KGB Files*, No. 31.
15. Ibid., No. 31.
16. Ibid., No. 40.
17. Reshetovskaya, p. 347.
18. S. Volkov, *St. Petersburg, a Cultural History* (London, 1996), pp. 366–67.
19. Reshetovskaya, *Otlucheniye*, pp. 347–51.
20. Vishnevskaya, p. 405.
21. *Oak and the Calf*, p. 316.
22. Ibid., p. 317.
23. Ibid., p. 319.
24. *KGB Files*, No. 51.
25. *Invisible Allies*, p. 130.
26. Reshetovskaya, *Otlucheniye*, p. 362.

3 8. *Burnt by the Sun*

1. *KGB Files*, No. 53.
2. Ibid., No. 54.
3. Vishnevskaya, pp. 410–13.
4. *KGB Files*, No. 52.
5. Ibid.
6. *Stern* magazine, 21 Nov. 1971.
7. *Invisible Allies*, pp. 306–18, and *Sovershenno Sekretno*, 1992, no. 4.
8. Ibid.
9. P. Sudoplatov, *Special Tasks* (London, 1994), pp. 282–84.
10. Christopher Andrew and Oleg Gordievsky, *KGB, the Inside Story* (London, 1990), pp. 541–42.
11. Z. Medvedev, p. 164.
12. H. Troyat, *Pushkin* (London, 1974), p. 593.

13. Lakshin, pp. 84–85.
14. Ibid., p. 42.

39. *Encounter Battles*

1. Carlisle, *Secret Circle*, p. 140.
2. Scammell, pp. 750–51 (letter from Reshetovskaya).
3. My source is a rough copy, shown to me in Ryazan. Reshetovskaya quotes from it in her memoir—but very selectively.
4. *Oak and the Calf*, p. 512.
5. *Invisible Allies*, p. 398.
6. Vishnevskaya, p. 398.
7. *Oak and the Calf*, p. 405.
8. *Invisible Allies*, p. 130.
9. Ibid., p. 328.
10. *KGB Files*, No. 70.
11. Ibid., No. 67.
12. Ibid., No. 68.
13. *Oak and the Calf*, p. 507.
14. Ibid., p. 510.
15. *KGB Files*, Nos. 72 and 76.
16. Interview with Veronica Stein.
17. Ibid.
18. Vishnevskaya, p. 405.
19. Ibid., pp. 414–19.
20. Ibid.
21. Carlisle, *Secret Circle*, pp. 158–59.
22. *Invisible Allies*, p. 132.
23. Scammell, p. 786 (letter from Reshetovskaya).

40. *Casualties*

1. Carlisle, *Secret Circle*, p. 166.
2. Ibid., p. 172.
3. Interview with O. Carlisle.
4. *Invisible Allies*, p. 132.
5. *Oak and the Calf*, p. 341.
6. Ibid.
7. *KGB Files*, No. 77.
8. *Invisible Allies*, p. 77.
9. *Oak and the Calf*, pp. 343–44.
10. Ibid., p. 528.
11. *Invisible Allies*, p. 74.
12. *KGB Files*, No. 84.
13. *Invisible Allies*, p. 83.
14. Ibid., pp. 134–35.
15. Ibid., p. 87.

16. *Oak and the Calf*, p. 349.
17. Ibid., p. 360.
18. Ibid., p. 362.
19. Ibid., p. 366.
20. *Le Figaro*, 5 Feb. 1974.
21. *Oak and the Calf*, p. 383.
22. Ibid., p. 393.

41. *Déjà Vu*

1. "As Breathing and Consciousness Return," *From Under the Rubble*.
2. S. Koch, *Double Lives* (London, 1995) p. 15.
3. *Invisible Allies*, p. 136.
4. Ibid., p. 137.
5. Ibid., p. 189.
6. Ibid., p. 190.
7. Scammell, p. 833.
8. Ibid., p. 832.
9. *Oak and the Calf*, p. 394.
10. Private communication.
11. *Oak and the Calf*, p. 396.
12. Ibid., pp. 408–12.
13. Ibid., p. 416.
14. Ibid., p. 427.
15. Ibid., pp. 432–33.
16. Ibid., p. 438.
17. *Invisible Allies*, p. 31.
18. *Oak and the Calf*, p. 443.

PART V

42. *The West's KGB*

1. *Oak and the Calf*, p. 440.
2. *KGB Files*, No. 99.
3. Ibid., No. 120.
4. *Invisible Allies*, p. 233.
5. Heinrich Böll, "The Captive World" (1969), review of *The First Circle* by Alexander Solzhenitsyn, reprinted in Böll, *Missing Persons and Other Essays* (London, 1977), pp. 154–55, 169–70.
6. *Sunday Times*, 17 Feb. 1994.
7. Scammell, p. 895 (conversation with Panin).
8. Carlisle, *Secret Circle*, p. 183–90.
9. *New York Times*, 28 Mar. 1974.

43. *Friendly Fire*

1. Scammell, p. 856.
2. Carlisle, *Secret Circle*, p. 190.
3. *New Republic*, 29 June 1992.
4. *Lenin in Zurich*, ch. 48.
5. Carlisle, *Secret Circle*, p. 198.
6. *KGB Files*, No. 139.
7. Scammell, p. 884 (quoting an unpublished article by Alan Levy).
8. *Vestnik RKhD*, No. 137.
9. Scammell, p. 893.
10. *KGB Files*, No. 140.
11. Scammell, pp. 886–88.
12. *Invisible Allies*, p. 150.
13. Carlisle, *Under a New Sky*, p. 34; and interview, Nov. 1996.
14. Carlisle interview, Nov. 1996.
15. *Solzhenitsyn in Exile*, p. 309.
16. Ibid., p. 333.

44. *Arkhipelág Gulág*

1. *Gulag* 1, Preface.
2. Panin, p. 93.
3. *The Russian Question* (London, 1995), p. 81.
4. Sakharov, p. 406.
5. *Gulag* 3, VI, ch. 4.
6. Quoted in *Solzhenitsyn in Exile*, p. 150.
7. Ibid., p. 181.
8. *Gulag* 1, II, ch. 4.
9. Berberova, p. 523.

45. *Travels and Brawls*

1. *New Statesman*, Mar. 1976.
2. Pierre Daix, "In France after 1974," in *Solzhenitsyn in Exile*, p. 83.
3. Hilton Kramer, "The Flowers on Sartre's Grave," *Commentary*, July 1993.
4. Interview with A. Klimoff, Aug. 1996.
5. Scammell, p. 913.
6. Quoted in *Solzhenitsyn in Exile*, p. 31.
7. Interview, *Herald Tribune*, 2 Sept. 1976.
8. Scammell, p. 934.
9. Private BBC tape.
10. Clément, p. 205.
11. Lakshin, and *passim*.
12. Scammell, p. 757.
13. Simonyan.

46. The Dissident

1. *Rutland Daily Herald*, 1 Mar. 1977.
2. Ibid.
3. Private communication.
4. R. Berman, ed., *Solzhenitsyn at Harvard* (Washington, D.C., 1980), p. xi.
5. Ibid., p. 3.
6. Ibid., p. 20.
7. *New York Times*, 13 June 1978.
8. *Washington Post*, 11 June 1978.
9. *Doctor Zhivago*, ch. 15, section 15.
10. Tomas Rzhezach, *Spiral' izmeni Solzhenitsyna* (The spiral of Solzhenitsyn's treachery; Moscow, 1978), p. 73.
11. Interview with Veronica Stein, July 1996.
12. Rzhezach, p. 84.
13. Oleg Kalugin, *Spymaster* (New York, 1994), p. 144–45.

47. A Zone of Quiet

1. Barbara B. Kingsbury, *Chubb Hill Farm and Cavendish, Vermont* (Cavendish Historical Society, 1994) p. 123.
2. Ibid., p. 23.
3. "The Solzhenitsyns of Cavendish," *Vermont Life*, Fall 1983.
4. Scammell, p. 975.
5. Slayton interview, Mar. 1995.
6. Kevin Goddard, "Solzhenitsyn, a Penchant for Privacy," *Rutland Daily Herald* (Vermont), 9 June 1985.
7. *Invisible Allies*, p. 88.
8. Scammell, pp. 990–91.
9. Ibid., p. 991.
10. Ibid.
11. Ibid.
12. Private communication.
13. *Burlington Free Press*, 11 May 1983.
14. Ibid., 25 June 1985.
15. Ibid., 7 May 1983.
16. Klimoff interview, Aug. 1996.
17. Scammell, p. 976.
18. Ibid., p. 978.
19. Interview, 9 Sept. 1995.
20. Lev Tolstoy, *Diaries*, ed. Christian (London, 1985), p. 586.

48. The Relentless Wheel

1. Interview with S. Smallheer, Aug. 1996.
2. Interview in *Kultura*, Sept. 1993.
3. Ibid.

4. Interview, July 1996.
5. *Kultura*, Sept. 1993.
6. Reshetovskaya, *Otlucheniye*, p. 125.
7. *Oak and the Calf*, p. 327.
8. Ibid., p. 328.
9. *August 1914*, tr. Willetts (1989), ch. 65.
10. Ibid.
11. "War & Pieces," *New Republic*, 28 Aug. 1989.
12. *August 1914*, tr. Willetts (1989), ch. 13.
13. Ibid.
14. *Mart 1917* (Paris, 1984), chs. 8, 9, 18, 25.

49. *The Jewish Question*

1. *New Republic*, 28 Aug. 1989.
2. "Solzhenitsyn's World History," *Midstream*, June/July 1985.
3. Quoted in *New York Times*, 13 Nov. 1985.
4. Ibid.
5. Ibid.
6. *August 1914* (1989), ch. 79.
7. R. Pipes, *Russia Under the Bolshevik Regime* (London, 1994), pp. 112–13.
8. P. J. Capelotti, *Our Man in the Crimea* (South Carolina, 1991), p. 124.
9. Unpublished memoir.
10. *New York Times*, 13 Nov. 1985.
11. "Personality and National Awareness," *From Under the Rubble*, p. 199.
12. Andrew and Gordievsky, *KGB: The Hidden Story*, p. 505.
13. David Remnick, *Lenin's Tomb* (New York, 1993), p. 51.

50. *The Broken Wall*

1. Ibid., p. 50.
2. Hedrick Smith, *The New Russians* (London, 1990), p. 110.
3. *Lenin's Tomb*, pp. 265–66.
4. Carlisle, *Under a New Sky*, pp. 212–13.
5. *Rebuilding Russia*, p. 8.
6. Ibid., p. 14.
7. Remnick, "The Exile Returns," *New Yorker*, 14 Feb. 1994.
8. *Rebuilding Russia*, p. 37.
9. Ibid., p. 64.
10. Ibid., p. 67.
11. Ibid., p. 78.
12. Ibid., p. 49.
13. Remnick, "The Exile Returns."
14. Ibid.
15. *New York Times*, 27 Sept. 1993.
16. *Daily Mail* (London), 12 Nov. 1993.

17. Interview by Mike Wallace, Aug. 1996.
18. *Rutland Daily Herald*, 28 Nov. 1995.
19. Remnick, "The Exile Returns."
20. *Rutland Daily Herald*, 23 Mar. 1994.
21. Reshetovskaya, *Otlucheniye*, p. 91.
22. Ibid., pp. 119–20.
23. Ibid., p. 133.
24. Ibid., p. 148.
25. Ibid., p. 167.
26. Ibid., p. 269.
27. Ibid., p. 276.
28. Ibid., pp. 280–83.
29. Remnick, "The Exile Returns."

5 1. *The Siberia Station*

1. *Guardian* (London), 28 May 1994.
2. Ibid.
3. Grigori Amelin, *Nezavisimaya* (Independent) *Gazeta*, May 1994.
4. *Guardian*, 28 May 1994.
5. *Doctor Zhivago*, ch. 7, section 19.
6. *My Half Century*, p. 71.
7. "The Homecoming," BBC1, 10 Apr. 1995.
8. Ibid.

5 2. *The Old Believer*

1. *Independent on Sunday*, 19 June 1994.
2. *New Republic*, 18 June 1992.
3. Private tape and video.
4. V. Yerofeyev, "An Inspector Calls," *Collected Works*, III (Moscow, 1997).
5. Quoted in Reeder, *Anna Akhmatova*, p. 170.
6. Anatoly Korolyov, *Moscow Times*, 29 May 1996.
7. D. Remnick, "Exit the Saints," *New Yorker*, 1 July 1994.
8. Ibid.
9. Ibid.
10. Jo Durden-Smith, p. 311.
11. Jonathan Steele, *Guardian* Weekend, 10 Apr. 1996.
12. Remnick, "The Exile Returns."
13. A. Klimoff, Introduction to Chukovskaya's *The Deserted House* (Belmont, Mass., 1978) p. xxiii. Chukovskaya's novel was the book offered to Tvardovsky by a copy editor for his weekend reading, as an alternative to *Ivan Denisovich*. Since the journal did not dare to publish both works—it might look like a campaign—*The Deserted House* had to wait several years before it was published in the Soviet Union.
14. "Life and Saul," *Sunday Times Magazine*. Interview by Bryan Appleyard, 21 May 1995.
15. "Russia on Her Deathbed," Nov. 1996.

16. *Toronto Globe and Mail*, 8 Aug. 1996.
17. Interview with Veronica Stein, July 1996.

Epilogue

1. Private communication.
2. *The Times*, 22 May 1997.
3. Private communication.

SELECTED BIBLIOGRAPHY

WORKS BY SOLZHENITSYN

Sobraniye sochinenii (Collected works; *in Russian*). Paris: YMCA Press, 1978–   .

Fiction, History, and Plays

August 1914 (the first volume of *The Red Wheel*). Tr. Michael Glenny. London: Bodley Head; New York: Farrar, Straus & Giroux, 1972. Revised, expanded edition, tr. H. T. Willetts. London: Bodley Head; New York: Farrar, Straus & Giroux, 1989.

Cancer Ward. Tr. Nicholas Bethell and David Burg. London: Bodley Head, 1968–69; New York: Farrar, Straus & Giroux, 1969.

The First Circle. Tr. Michael Guybon. London: Collins/Harvill, 1969.

The Gulag Archipelago. Vols. I and II, tr. Thomas Whitney. New York: Harper & Row; London: Collins, 1974–75. Vol. III, tr. H. T. Willetts. New York: Harper & Row; London: Collins, 1978.

Invisible Allies. Tr. Alexis Klimoff and Michael Nicholson. Washington, D.C.: Counterpoint, 1995.

Lenin in Zurich. Tr. H. T. Willetts. London: Bodley Head; New York: Farrar, Straus & Giroux, 1976.

The Oak and the Calf. Tr. H. T. Willetts. London: Collins, 1980; New York: Harper & Row, 1979.

One Day in the Life of Ivan Denisovich. Tr. Max Hayward and Ronald Hingley. New York: Praeger, 1963. Tr. Gillon Aitken. London: Sphere, 1970. (*Not the first English edition, but a lively translation.*)

Stories and Prose Poems. Tr. Michael Glenny. London: Bodley Head; New York: Farrar, Straus & Giroux, 1971.

Victory Celebrations, Prisoners, The Love-Girl and the Innocent. The first two tr. Helen Rapp and Nancy Thomas; the third by Nicholas Bethell and David Burg. London: Faber & Faber, 1986. (*A convenient three-in-one text. The individual plays first appeared in English in 1983, 1983, and 1969, respectively.* Victory Celebrations *is also known as* A Feast of Conquerors.)

Poetry

Prussian Nights. Tr. Robert Conquest. London: Collins/Harvill; New York: Farrar, Straus & Giroux, 1977.

Political and Philosophical Works

A Lenten Letter to Pimen, Patriarch of All Russia. Tr. Keith Armes. Minneapolis: Burgess, 1972.

From Under the Rubble. Various essayists including Solzhenitsyn. Various translators. London: Collins; Boston: Little, Brown, 1975.

Letter to the Soviet Leaders. Tr. Hilary Sternberg. London, Fontana; New York, Harper & Row, 1975.

Rebuilding Russia. Tr. Alexis Klimoff. New York: Farrar, Straus & Giroux, 1991.

The Russian Question. Tr. Yermolai Solzhenitsyn. New York: Farrar, Straus & Giroux; London: Harvill Press, 1995.

BIOGRAPHICAL AND CRITICAL

Berman, Ronald, ed. *Solzhenitsyn at Harvard.* Washington, D.C.: Ethics & Public Policy Center, 1980.

Burg, David, and George Feifer. *Solzhenitsyn.* London: Hodder & Stoughton; New York: Stein & Day, 1972.

Carlisle, Olga. *Solzhenitsyn and the Secret Circle.* New York: Holt, Rinehart & Winston, 1978.

Clément, Olivier. *The Spirit of Solzhenitsyn.* London: Search Press, 1976; New York: Harper & Row, 1977.

Dunlop, John, Richard Haugh, and Alexis Klimoff, eds. *Alexander Solzhenitsyn: Critical Essays and Documentary Materials.* New York: Macmillan; London: Collier Macmillan, 1975.

Dunlop, John B., Richard S. Haugh, and Michael Nicholson, eds. *Solzhenitsyn in Exile.* Stanford: Stanford University Press, 1985.

Kopelev, Lev. *Ease My Sorrows.* Tr. by Antonina W. Bouis. New York: Random House, 1983.

Lakshin, Vladimir. *Solzhenitsyn, Tvardovsky, and "Novy Mir."* Tr. and ed. by Michael Glenny. Cambridge, Mass.: MIT Press, 1980.

Medvedev, Zhores. *Ten Years after Ivan Denisovich.* Tr. Hilary Sternberg. London: Macmillan, 1973; New York: Knopf, 1974.

Panin, Dmitri. *The Notebooks of Sologdin*. Tr. John Moore. London: Hutchinson; New York: Harcourt Brace Jovanovich, 1976.

Reshetovskaya, Natalya. *Sanya: My Life with Alexander Solzhenitsyn*. Tr. Elena Ivanoff. Indianapolis: Bobbs-Merrill, 1975; London: Hart-Davis, 1977.

———. *Otlucheniye*. Moscow: Mir Knigi, 1994.

Scammell, Michael. *Solzhenitsyn*. New York: W. W. Norton, 1984; London: Hutchinson, 1985.

Scammell, Michael, ed. *The Solzhenitsyn Files*. Carol Stream, Ill.: Edition Q Inc., 1995.

GENERAL BACKGROUND

Billington, James H. *The Icon and the Axe: An Interpretive History of Russian Culture*. New York: Vintage Books, 1970.

Carlisle, Olga Andreyev. *Under a New Sky*. New York: Ticknor & Fields, 1993.

Clark, Alan. *Barbarossa: The Russian-German Conflict 1941–45*. London: Weidenfeld & Nicolson, 1995.

Conquest, Robert. *The Great Terror*. London: Macmillan, 1968.

———. *The Harvest of Sorrow: Soviet Collectivisation and the Terror-Famine*. New York: Oxford University Press, 1986.

Crankshaw, Edward. *The Shadow of the Winter Palace: The Drift to Revolution 1825–1917*. London: Macmillan; New York: Viking, 1976.

de Mallac, Guy. *Boris Pasternak: His Life and Art*. Norman: University of Oklahoma, 1981; London: Souvenir Press, 1983.

Hayward, Max. *Writers in Russia, 1917–1978*. London: Harvill, 1983.

Lincoln, W. Bruce. *In War's Dark Shadow: The Russians before the Great War*. New York: Dial Press, 1983; Oxford: Oxford University Press, 1984.

———. *Red Victory: A History of the Russian Civil War*. New York: Simon & Schuster, 1989.

Mandelstam, Nadezhda. *Hope Against Hope*. New York: Atheneum, 1970; London: Harvill, 1971.

Medvedev, Roy. *Khrushchev*. Tr. Brian Pearce. New York: Anchor Press, 1983.

Pipes, Richard. *Russia Under the Bolshevik Regime, 1919–1924*. New York: Alfred A. Knopf; London: Harvill, 1994.

———. *Russia Under the Old Regime*. London: Weidenfeld and Nicolson, 1974.

Reeder, Roberta. *Anna Akhmatova: Poet and Prophet*. New York: St. Martin's Press, 1994.

Remnick, David. *Lenin's Tomb: The Last Days of the Soviet Empire*. New York: Random House, 1993; London: Viking, 1993.

Sakharov, Andrei. *Memoirs*. Tr. Richard Lourie. New York: Knopf; London: Hutchinson, 1990.

Shentalinsky, Vitaly. *The KGB's Literary Archive*. London: Harvill, 1995.

Shostakovich, Dmitri. *Testimony: The Memoirs of Shostakovich*. As related to and edited by Solomon Volkov. New York: Harper & Row; London: Hamish Hamilton, 1979.

Volkogonov, Dmitri. *Lenin, Life and Legacy*. Tr. Harold Shukman. London: Harper/Collins, 1994.

INDEX

isolation, 310; sense of humor, 167, 171, 182; sense of personal destiny, 48, 70–71; spirituality, 339, 430, 461–63, 500, 503; stubbornness, 39; subconscious not revealed, 484–85; teaching ability, 218–19, 226, 247; tendency toward being the best, 86–87; vituperative nature, 405–6; work habits, 317–20, 350, 443, 474, 476, 477
political beliefs: anti-imperialist views, 499; anti-liberal turn to right, 486; attack on Yeltsin in *Le Monde*, 532; awakening to horror of Stalinist Communist rule in Russia, 194; censorship letter to Congress of Writers' Union, 320–22; comparison of Soviet crimes vs. West-U.S. crimes, 70; confidence in Soviet victory in World War II, 102; crisis of mankind as spiritual not political, 455; criticism of democracies (*see* democracy); criticism of pacifism, 460–61; criticism of Soviet regime, 105, 125; criticism of West (*see* West, the); dislike of politicians, 500; early adulation of Lenin, 47, 64, 76, 103, 110, 136, 439; early advocacy of Communism, 59, 60, 61, 65, 75–76, 86–87; early commitment to "Soviet" ideal person and socialist idealism, 157, 160–61; early faith in October Revolution, 137; early political incidents at school, 66–68; early stance toward Communism, 65; early support for Lenin Revolution, 13; effect of KGB seizure of archives on, 301–2, 305; KGB memorandum on AIS opinions, 305–7; letter to Andropov about Rozhdestvo stakeout, 371–72; liberation of Soviet republics, 499; literature and politics intertwined, 110; misunderstood by modern progressives, 338–39; on pacifism, 460–61; patriotism of, 404–5; political scepticism, 63–64, 65–68, 171; politics and morals intertwined, 453; premature death of (hypothetical), effect on political power of, 378; pro-Bolshevik/anti-Bolshevik tension in, 50; public poll wanting AIS as president, 504; reaction to 1991 coup d'état, 501–2; reaction to campaign against Pasternak, 251; reaction to German attack on Soviet Union, 94–95; refusal to join Communist Party, 105, 136; remarks about Roosevelt, 150; rumors about politics of, reported by Tvardovsky, 300; scruples about prison traitors and obedience, 186–87; suspicion of Stalin, 64, 70, 86, 98, 110, 112–13, 134, 136; unawareness of Soviet Communist horrors, 75–76, 78, 80–81, 86–87, 89, 95–96; views on Marxism, 171; vision for contemporary Russia, 498–99; Western liberalism, 429–33; words to son Dmitri about political struggle for the right, 396; *zemstvos* as governing bodies, 529
political life: articles written about censored by AIS, 469–70; citizenship revocation threat, 363, 368, 385, 386, 411;

conquering of depression over KGB raid on Teush archives, 308; conspiracy charge, 140; criminal charges annulled, 244; debate on exile vs. trial of, 419–21; early school political incidents, 66–68; exile annulled, 231; fear of exile under Brezhnev, 368; first arrest of, 119–30; KGB memorandum on life of, 361–62; letter to Khrushchev, 278; loyalty pledged to *Novy Mir*, 275; meeting with Khrushchev, 274–75; meeting with Yeltsin, 528; operation "Spider" against, 377; rehabilitation of, 239; Russian citizenship restored, 501; second arrest of, 407–8; sentence to eight years in prison camp, 141; Shchelokov memorandum about, 368–70; Teush apartment archives seized by KGB, 300–302; treason charge after Paris publication of *The Gulag Archipelago*, 409; treason charge retracted, 502; wartime diaries burned, 129–30
prison camp periods: affair with Anya Breslavskaya, 162–63; asked to testify against Simonyan, 208; Butyrki, 140–41, 156, 160, 164, 185, 187; called Shurochka, by Veronica, 142; cryptology project, 187; departure from Marfino with Panin, 187–88; Ekibastuz camp, 197–203, 206–7; Kaluga Gate camp, 153–63; Krasnaya Presnya prison, 142, 143–45; Lefortovo prison arrest, 408–11; as librarian, 165; Lubyanka prison, 123–30, 132–41; Marfino *sharashka*, 165–73, 175–77; memories and sensations of camp years, 252–53; MGB Special Prison No. 1, 177–79, 181–87; mixed feelings about release from prison, 208–9; New Jerusalem, 145–53; as "nuclear physicist," 164–73; packages from Nina (NR's aunt) while in camps, 197; phonetic analysis project, 178, 181–82, 186–87, 201; playwriting at Ekibastuz, 201–3; poetry readings in Marfino, 171; prison fate, compared to Dostoyevsky's, 190–91, 192–94; Rybinsk *sharashka*, 164–65; scruples about camp pressures and politics, 158, 160–61; sense of time while in camp, 153; spiritual value of prison experience, 147–48, 206, 208–9, 213–14; transit to Ekibastuz, 190–96; Zagorsk *sharashka*, 165; Zvenigorod brick factory, 145–53
as a public figure: fame, 270, 279, 311, 392; fiftieth birthday, 340–41; mythification of, 317; Scammell's biography of, 471; "the year of Solzhenitsyn" (1990), 498
relationships with friends (*see also* Borisov, Vadim; Chukovskaya, Elena (Liusha); Ezherets, Lydia; Kopelev, Lev; Panin, Dmitri; Sakharov, Andrei; Shafarevich, Igor; Simonyan, Kirill; Teush, Veniamin; Tvardovsky, Alexander; Vitkevich, Nikolai; Zubovs): bond with male friends, 77–78, 105, 112–13; decision to stay with

ABOUT THE AUTHOR

D. M. THOMAS was born in a tin-mining village in Cornwall, England, in 1935, and grew up there, apart from a brief but influential period in Australia. He learned Russian during his national service in the army, then went to New College, Oxford, where he took First-Class Honors in English. For the next twenty years he combined writing poetry with teaching, in the English Midlands, before becoming a full-time writer. His novel *The White Hotel* (1981) became a worldwide bestseller; it won the *Los Angeles Times* Fiction Prize, a P.E.N. award, and the Cheltenham Prize, and was nominated for the Booker. It has been translated into over twenty languages. For his poetry he has received a Cholmondeley Award. Russia has been a constant inspiration in his fiction, and he has produced highly praised translations for Pushkin and Akhmatova. He now lives in his native Cornwall. He annually leads writing workshops on the island of Skyros and at Humber College, Ontario, for which he also tutors in a correspondence writing program. He has three children from two marriages.